Scarecrow Film Score Guides
Series Editor: Kate Daubney

1. *Gabriel Yared's* The English Patient: *A Film Score Guide*, by Heather Laing. 2004.
2. *Danny Elfman's* Batman: *A Film Score Guide*, by Janet K. Halfyard. 2004.
3. *Ennio Morricone's* The Good, the Bad and the Ugly: *A Film Score Guide*, by Charles Leinberger. 2004.
4. *Louis and Bebe Barron's* Forbidden Planet: *A Film Score Guide*, by James Wierzbicki. 2005.
5. *Bernard Herrmann's* The Ghost and Mrs. Muir: *A Film Score Guide*, by David Cooper. 2005.
6. *Erich Wolfgang Korngold's* The Adventures of Robin Hood: *A Film Score Guide*, by Ben Winters. 2007.
7. *Mychael Danna's* The Ice Storm: *A Film Score Guide*, by Miguel Mera. 2007.
8. *Alex North's* A Streetcar Named Desire: *A Film Score Guide*, by Annette Davison. 2009.
9. *Nino Rota's* The Godfather Trilogy: *A Film Score Guide*, by Franco Sciannameo. 2010.
10. *Miklós Rózsa's* Ben-Hur: *A Film Score Guide*, by Roger Hickman. 2011.
11. *Zbigniew Preisner's* Three Colors Trilogy: Blue, White, Red: *A Film Score Guide*, by Nicholas W. Reyland. 2012.
12. *Franz Waxman's* Rebecca: *A Film Score Guide*, by David Neumeyer and Nathan Platte. 2012.

Zbigniew Preisner by Anna Włoch.
Photo courtesy of Zbigniew Preisner.

Zbigniew Preisner's
Three Colors Trilogy:
Blue, White, Red

A Film Score Guide

Nicholas W. Reyland

Scarecrow Film Score Guides, No. 11

The Scarecrow Press, Inc.
Lanham, Maryland • Toronto • Plymouth, UK
2012

SCARECROW PRESS, INC.

Published in the United States of America
by Scarecrow Press, Inc.
A wholly owned subsidiary of
The Rowman & Littlefield Publishing Group, Inc.
4501 Forbes Boulevard, Suite 200, Lanham, Maryland 20706
www.scarecrowpress.com

Estover Road
Plymouth PL6 7PY
United Kingdom

British Library Cataloguing in Publication Information Available

Library of Congress Cataloging-in-Publication Data

Reyland, Nicholas W.
  Zbigniew Preisner's Three colors trilogy : Blue, White, Red : a film
score
guide / Nicholas W. Reyland.
     p. cm. — (Scarecrow film score guides ; No. 11)
  Includes bibliographical references and index.
  ISBN 978-0-8108-8138-9 (pbk. : alk. paper)
  1. Preisner, Zbigniew. Three colors. I. Title.
  ML410.P82R49 2012
  781.5'42092—dc23   2011030049

♾️™ The paper used in this publication meets the minimum requirements of
American National Standard for Information Sciences—Permanence of
Paper for Printed Library Materials, ANSI/NISO Z39.48-1992.
Manufactured in the United States of America.

To my parents,

Janet and Michael Reyland,

for everything.

CONTENTS

List of Illustrations   ix
Editor's Foreword *Kate Daubney*   xiii
Acknowledgments   xvii

Introduction   Against Indifference   1

Chapter 1   Preisner's Musical Background   11

Chapter 2   Preisner's Presence   47

Chapter 3   Kieślowski: Concepts and Co-workers   78

Chapter 4   The *Three Colors* Trilogy: Critical Contexts   101

Chapter 5   The Ode to *Agapē*: *Blue*   174

Chapter 6   Last Tango in Warsaw: *White*   251

Chapter 7   The Bloom of Life: *Red*   311

Notes   369
Bibliography   435
Index   449
About the Author   461

ILLUSTRATIONS

Examples

1.1	"Holy God" ("Święty Boże")	14
1.2	*Cantus firmus* from the opening of *No End*	15
1.3	"Church Song" from *To Kill a Priest*	17
1.4	Wedding song, Kurpie region	18
1.5	"Nadzieja" melody from *The Last Schoolbell*	30
2.1	Widely spaced gestures in *No End*	59
2.2	Melody on the lake from *Weather Report*	60
2.3	Melody and harmonization from *Decalogue 8*	64
2.4	Unison melody from *Véronique*'s Concerto in D Minor	64
2.5	Cellular scale fragments from *Decalogue 6*	65
2.6	Harmonic aura forming around Ula in *No End*	69
5.1	The funeral cue and its motivic structure	189
5.2	Memento theme motivic content	202
5.3	Mistakes in choral opening seen in the film	206
5.4	Tonal dislocations in the lampshade scene	208
5.5	The busker's three recorder themes	212
5.6	Links between second busker theme, bridge and *Arioso*	235
5.7	Voice-leading slotting into place for B minor	242
5.8	The memento finds its flow in the *Concert[o]*	244
5.9	Transcription of score at end of *Blue*	247
6.1	*White's rustico* (Karol's part, as heard in court)	255
6.2	The proto-*rustico*	258
6.3	*Rustico* (Dominique's half)	261
6.4	i) "To ostatnia niedziela" and ii) "Wszystko co nasze Polsce oddamy" (transcribed from Karol's busking)	265
6.5	"Ka-rol": first tango cue	275
6.6	Tango climax	282
6.7	End of the prison cue (transcribed)	303
7.1	Ai/Bolero main theme, catwalk promenade version	321

7.2   Sustaining the sonoristic smudge   331
7.3   Musical totality of cue and sound design in sunlight scene   341
7.4   "The Water-lily" (wordless version, transcribed)   347
7.5   Thematic blending in *Red*   354
7.6   Gestural and pitch continuity between *vocalise* and catwalk   360

Figures

1.1   Preisner, an axe and some sausages in *The Last Schoolbell*   12
1.2   First page of Preisner's score for *Blue*   34
1.3   Avant-garde notation in *Red*   36
2.1   "Tabs" from a page of Preisner's manuscript score for *Blue*'s *Concert[o]*   68
5.1   Preisner's manuscript score for *Blue*'s first "Van den Budenmayer" cue   186
5.2   Touching the music in *Blue*: the copyist, Julie when composing with Olivier, Julie at the end   188
5.3   Julie hears the music in *Blue*—or does she?   191
5.4   Preisner's manuscript score for the interruption's re-imagining of the funeral theme   192
5.5   i) Preisner's manuscript score for the memento theme ii) The memento from Julie's subjective point of view   200
5.6   The composing scene shot inspired by Preisner   228
5.7   Choral opening from Preisner's *Concert[o]* manuscript score   233
6.1   Preisner's first named *rustico* cue in *White*'s manuscript score   262
6.2   Karol the musician   264
6.3   "Chopin" (tango opening flourish) cue in Preisner's manuscript score   272
6.4   Preisner's Rota pastiche in the manuscript score   281
6.5   Karol composing himself in *White*   288
6.6   Subway transition cue, showing Preisner's use of quartertones and avant-garde notations   291
6.7   Manuscript score (boxes added) for apartment and prison scenes   299-302
7.1   Bolero ostinato (detail) from Preisner's first *Red* cue in manuscript score   319
7.2   Aii/First subject, angelic version, in Preisner's manuscript score (detail)   324
7.3   Bi/Second subject (the judges), from Preisner's manuscript score (detail)   326
7.4   Bii (violent variation) from Preisner's manuscript score   329
7.5   Aiii (reprise) from Preisner's manuscript score   334
7.6   Valentine composes connections to *Blue* and *White*   335

7.7   "De Waterlelie" by Frederik van Eeden   344
7.8   Valentine touches the Van den Budenmayer LP   346
7.9   i) The Van den Budenmayer lovers' triangle ii) Lyrics   348
      heard in this sequence
7.10 Kieślowskian karaoke   350

Tables

2.1   Receptional denotators used in a sample of Preisner   52
      reviews
2.2   Philip Tagg's hypothesized dualities of male-female   55
      scoring clichés
4.1   Corinthians and *Concert[o]* text comparison   128
5.1   Thematic index to the main sections of Julie's *Concert[o]*   231

EDITOR'S FOREWORD

As the Scarecrow Film Score Guides enter their second decade since the publication of the Series' first volume (for Greenwood) in 2000 on Max Steiner's score for *Now, Voyager*, this volume by Nicholas Reyland on the music of the *Three Colors* trilogy offers us an opportunity to reflect on the accomplishments of the Series thus far. Just as Dr. Reyland's volume encompasses three different films bound by unities in many musical and non-musical dimensions, so the volumes of the Series sustain unities of their own, despite the wide variety of films and scores concerned. The Series was established to promote score-focused scholarship, but that simple aim has long since been outstripped by the achievements of the Series' authors in divulging great variety in what that scholarship might consist of. There have been revisions of our understanding of some of the figureheads of film score composition and revelations concerning the logistics of their compositional practice. The impact of technology on scoring has been exposed from both its early manifestations as instrumentation to its impact on process. Some canonic score sounds that have permanently permeated the public consciousness have been deconstructed, and bewitching and complex aural textures have been explored in critical and theoretical ways that push the boundaries of music out into the wider soundscape of film. The Series' authors have unpicked and rewoven some of the fabric of the earlier "schools" of film musicology, and in doing so have become leading scholars in the discipline. So much has been illuminated in so many different ways, and yet what binds these volumes together is an essential engagement in our experience of music in film, and a fascination for the means by which we are drawn in. That original principle behind the Series has remained largely unchanged, but the disciplinary environment in which the work is undertaken has evolved, partly as a consequence of the work itself. As the editor of this Series, I am therefore delighted it has provided the environment for such fundamental contributions to our collective scholarship.

A further very recent development is the broadening of volumes from considering a single score to multiple connected scores, and while Franco Sciannameo explored the linear trilogy of *The Godfather*, Dr. Reyland's volume unpicks the complex interrelationships between the triangle of films *Blue, White* and *Red* while also forging a reading of the trilogy as a whole through Preisner's scores. While *The Godfather* films have become distilled into a popular mythology of verbal and musical quotation, so *Three Colors* have inspired their own enormous body of public and scholarly critical engagement that belies the commercial categorization of the films as "art house" and thus somehow separated from mainstream appreciation. Drawing on his own new interviews with Zbigniew Preisner, Dr. Reyland debunks some of the mythology about the composer that has sprung up in the absence of biographical clarity and definitive commentary on his works. Early in this book, Dr. Reyland observes how the Internet has facilitated the growth of speculation and rumor, and their transubstantiation into fact in matters of Preisner's development as a composer, yet he has also taken into account the valuable resources for scholars offered online, particularly when exploring and defining Preisner's "presence." This is not the forum in which to debate how the readiness of information on the Internet has evolved into a demand and an expectation that there are answers to everything available somewhere. But it does offer us an opportunity to reflect on the narrow line down which we walk as scholars, enthusiasts and fans of film music. This Series exists precisely to facilitate the interpretation of many of the smallest details of a score, some of them so precise that they are audible only on repeated and directed listening, others of them manifest only in the larger scale of the whole film and barely recognizable without that context. Whatever the level of our musical understanding, we are generating maps of our experience of the score that emerge in ever-increasing detail, and perhaps there is an implicit expectation inherent in the western musicological tradition that every note or sound in the soundscape must and can be accounted for. But Preisner's scores—and Dr. Reyland's interpretation of them— remind us that the metaphysical qualities of music, the fluid and ever-changing relationships between film score and concept, reflect each of our own unique relationships with the films as we enjoy them. One of the key features of this Series therefore is to show how readings of scores can be both definitive in their ideas but also fluid in the way those ideas continue to evolve, and thus it is hoped that this volume will appeal both to film musicologists and to those whose engagement with the scores is filtered by experience and not by scholarship.

This is the fourth volume in the Series to have had the benefit of drawing on the insights of the eponymous composer, and it is part of what makes these volumes so valuable. Mr. Preisner's willingness to be interviewed by Dr. Reyland for this volume has not only crystallized interpretative frameworks, but also enhanced the possibilities for the musicological scholarship, as we are given a privileged insight both into the process of scoring and into one of the most well-known director/composer collaborations in world cinema. I would like to thank Mr. Preisner for agreeing to be interviewed for the benefit of this volume and the Series, and to thank both him and his agent Laurence Aston for facilitating such ready access to manuscript scores and copyright permissions.

Dr. Kate Daubney
Series Editor

ACKNOWLEDGMENTS

This book has been ten years in the planning and five years in the making. I have discussed its subjects with many people, learning from them all. Anything good in what follows is indebted to those friends and colleagues; anything not so good is mine, and mine alone.

My greatest debt is to Zbigniew Preisner, for granting me access to the manuscripts of his *Three Colors* scores, meeting me in London, and for his warm hospitality and candid replies when I interviewed him in Kraków. Agata Kukułka, Mr. Preisner's assistant at that time, helped our conversations to flow; I am also grateful to Stanisław Będkowski and the Jagiellonian University's Institute of Musicology for accommodating me during my visit, and to the Research Institute for the Humanities at Keele University for supporting it financially. Laurence Aston, Mr. Preisner's manager, was instrumental in enabling our meetings to happen. His encouragement, determination and assistance have been greatly appreciated. Mr. Preisner gave me kind permission to reproduce excerpts and scans from his scores and manuscripts; further permissions were granted by his publisher, Chester Music. I am grateful to Radio Netherlands Worldwide, the Dutch International Public Broadcaster, for permission to include Frederik van Eeden's "De Waterlelie" from *A Sampling of Dutch Literature: Thirteen Excursions into the Works of Dutch Authors* (Hilversum: Radio Nederland Wereldomroep, 1962).

The Scarecrow Film Score Guides' Series Editor, Kate Daubney, has been involved in this project from the start. Her championing of the book, constant support, and tough editorial love all came into play at just the right times. I was also lucky enough to receive feedback on drafts of various chapters from perceptive colleagues and friends. My thanks go to Marie Bennett, Alice Fenner, Richard Misek and Richard Smith. I am particularly grateful to Kelly Gross for her thoughtful responses to not one but two drafts on *Blue*, and to Ben Winters for his many useful comments and suggestions.

Many other people have shared their expertise. Adrian Thomas inspired my fascination with Polish music in the first place; more recently, with Beata Bolesławska-Lewandowska, he taught me a valuable lesson about Polish scouting, while advising me on various other matters. Michał Kubicki provided several quick yet elegant translations and shared detailed recollections of nights gone by beneath the sign of the ram. Julie Brown, Geoff Chew and Barbara Kelly indicated helpful literature; Annette Davison and Nikki Dibben made a formidable tag team when discussing my work on *Blue* at a conference; Anahid Kassabian committed me to thinking about sound; Joseph Kickasola shared stimulating unpublished work; Jon Paxman dug for treasure in his attic; Gregg Redner shared his thesis chapter on *Blue*; Tobias Wollermann enabled access to his Preisner dissertation; and Martin Iddon pretty much nailed the whole damn thing in just five words.

I am also grateful to my Keele University colleagues in Music, Music Technology, MCC (Media, Communications and Culture), and Film Studies, and more widely to the School of Humanities and Research Institute for the Humanities, for their financial support and especially for granting me two periods of research leave to focus on the project. Cliff Bradbury's technical assistance has been a great help. I am also indebted to my screen music students for the passion with which they have responded, year on year, to the *Three Colors* films, consistently reminding me of why I began this task in the first place. As the book progressed, various people at Scarecrow Press became involved. My thanks go to Renee Camus, Sally Craley, Christen Karniski, Jayme Reed and Stephen Ryan. Further assistance was provided by Becky Thumpston, who helped index the book, and Steve Bird, who produced the typeset musical examples.

The *Three Colors* trilogy was completed in considerably less time than this study. The irony is not lost on me. In my defense, however, I have been co-producing a trilogy of my own since 2005. My most profound debt of thanks, therefore, is to my co-producer, Deborah Reyland. Harrison, Albert and William, in turn, have taught me more about the ideas at the heart of this book than they can yet imagine.

Dr. Nicholas Reyland

INTRODUCTION

AGAINST INDIFFERENCE

The audacious culmination of *Blue* (1993), the first film in the *Three Colors* trilogy, counterpoints Zbigniew Preisner's score for a fictitious composer's *Concert[o] for the Unification of Europe* with a cinematic hall of mirrors reflecting visions of the story's main protagonists.[1] Preisner's by turns grandiose and intimate cue, which fuses the rhetoric of neo-romantic art music with allusions to progressive rock, Polish traditional music and cabaret, is a setting of St. Paul's most famous epistle—the one about love that one tends to hear at weddings—except, of course, that the text is not about romantic love *per se* and the score does not actually set the whole of 1 Corinthians 13. What Preisner's music does articulate, however, reverberates throughout *Blue* and the trilogy's other installments, *White* and *Red* (both 1994). Made in the final decade of the twentieth century under the artistic leadership of director Krzysztof Kieślowski, and amid each film's particular concerns, the *Three Colors* address alienation and indifference in late twentieth-century Western society as represented by the trilogy's three main settings: Paris, a (then) newly democratic Warsaw, and Geneva. Preisner's score for *Blue*, I argue in this study, unveils the *Three Colors'* alternative poetics of living. Its solution is a bitter pill to swallow.

The *Concert[o]* sets an edited version of St. Paul's letter, not in Polish or French (the main languages of the films, their casts, and crews), but in ancient Greek. All direct references to Christianity are cut from the text, references to faith are excised or downplayed, and the noun stressed throughout is a particular variety of love: *agapē*. *Blue*'s climactic cue martials its considerable musical armory to assert that, without *agapē*, life is nothing, and Preisner, in one of his cleverest adaptions when setting the text, emphasizes symbolically opposed lines to make this point: "Without *agapē* I am nothing" vs. "The greatest of faith, hope, and *agapē* is *agapē*."[2] What, though, is *agapē*, and what are the side-effects of the trilogy's remedy?

It goes without saying that there are many varieties of love. Theologians and philosophers—in order to distinguish it, in part, from erotic love—tend to define *agapē* (sometimes in connection to *caritas*, the Latin term usually translated as charity) as a self-sacrificial act carried out on behalf of the other, but with no expectation of the good that may be returned to the self. C. S. Lewis, for instance, closed *The Four Loves* by contrasting "the natural loves" (affection for one's family, friendship and Eros) to charity, "first vaguely described as decency and common sense, and later revealed as goodness," which "must come to the help of . . . mere feeling if the feeling is to be kept sweet."[3] *Agapē* is a form of loving founded on acts of kindness, co-operation, philanthropy—and personal sacrifice. Terry Eagleton tallies its cost in the discussion of *agapē* which ends his recent book exploring approaches to the meaning of life, arguing "that we can only live well by buckling the self to the needs of others . . . a ceaseless dying to self [being] the source of a good life"; this doctrine may sound "unpleasantly slavish and self-denying," he adds, but only if one forgets that, "if others do this as well, the result is a form of reciprocal service which provides the context for each self to flourish."[4] An ensemble of jazz musicians provides Eagleton with the musical metaphor for a vision (probably also informed by his Marxism) of lives lived well through the practice of *agapē*. The metaphor has both obvious and more subtle links to patterns of existence, creativity and musicality represented in *Blue*, *White* and *Red*:

> A jazz group which is improvising obviously differs from a symphony orchestra, since to a large extent each member is free to express herself as she likes. But she does so with a receptive sensitivity to the self-expressive performances of the other musicians. . . . Because this flourishing is reciprocal, we can even speak, remotely and analogically, of a kind of love. One could do worse, surely, than propose such a situation as the meaning of life—both in the sense that it is what makes life meaningful, and—more controversially—in the sense that when we act in this way, we realize our natures at their finest.[5]

The key idea foregrounded by *Blue*'s climax, and at the head of the *Three Colors* trilogy, is thus diametrically opposed to activities that were more commonly promoted, at the tail end of the twentieth century, as the best route to self-expression and happiness, and which continue to be prevalent in the globally networked realms of the early twenty-first. During times when corporations, media conglomerates and governments promote (to state the obvious) individualism and personal achievement via the accrual of commodities, leisure time and wealth, the practice of *agapē* may come to seem an attractive, perhaps anarchic, alternative. After all, even Marx, who wrote that "the wealth of those societies" operating under capitalism would present itself as "'an immense accumulation of commodities,'" cannot have foreseen the specific irony of a peak manifestation of that process being British leader

Margaret Thatcher's argument that "there is no such thing as society," just "individual men and women" who "must look to themselves first."[6] Kieślowski's co-writer, Krzysztof Piesiewicz, called the trilogy's final installment, *Red*, a film against indifference—indifference to others encouraged by the isolation of the individual in late-modern Western societies—but the entire trilogy is clearly against indifference, societal dissolution and socio-economically coerced selfishness. As Janina Falkowska argues, "the films are placed firmly within the context of contemporary times, the times of spectacular technological developments, on the one hand, and of man's alienation and helplessness on the other"; through their focus on the "heart-rending" impact of this lifestyle on small groups of people, "Kieślowski makes a powerful statement critical of contemporary times."[7] Yet the trilogy also proposes an alternative. David Kehr writes similarly of isolation in the films, but also of a journey beyond it: "the trilogy charts a movement from a deep sense of solitude to an understanding and acceptance of community, to a sense of shared values and mutual interdependence . . . an epic of reconciliation, in which fragmented parts come together to make a whole, just as the three colors of the title create the French flag, and the three films in the series constitute one continuous gesture."[8]

Over the course of the three films' nearly five hours, the implication slowly builds that contemporary re-brandings of liberty, equality and fraternity—the concepts, most famously associated with the iconic motto forged during the French revolution, which sparked the idea for the trilogy—are traps to be put aside in order to recompose all three anew. The argument seeks to persuade the audio-viewer of its validity through both the stories that the trilogy tells and the ways in which they are told. Through the use of extreme, ironic and dream-like narratives—*Blue*'s psychodrama of grief, *White*'s parodic grotesque on the perils of capitalism, *Red*'s fable on fate and contingency—the trilogy sets up complementary rehearsals of its thesis. Those rehearsals are realized, in turn, by purposeful fusions of sound, music and the moving image that draw on the skill and expertise of the talented cooperative of filmmakers, including Preisner, united under Kieślowski's munificent leadership. The films propose, in their tales and their tellings, a journey one might take to live better in late-modern times: the transition from solipsistic individualism to the mutually beneficial practices of *agapē*.

The *Three Colors* trilogy, thus conceived, seems both political and didactic, its perspective uncomplicatedly of the left. Nothing so unusual there, for sure, at least in European art cinema. Yet while it is true that the trilogy mobilizes familiar cinematic concerns, they are refreshed therein through the symbolic scope of the films, the intensity of their individual stories and tellings, and the energy generated by the particular impetus, not least for the Polish crew members, of dealing with such issues at a time when countries throughout Europe were being plunged, post-communism, into radical (and hardly uncomplicated) socio-economic and political transformations. In retrospect, one might even wonder if the films form part of an East-West network of post-1980s critiques mapping a new phase of dissatisfaction with high capitalism.[9] Unlike some of their more obviously political fellow-travelers—such as television dramas *Boys from the Blackstuff* (BBC, 1982) and *The Wire* (HBO, 2002-8)—such texts do not chart the immediate societal cost of unfettered capitalism, although (like *White*) many touch on related issues. Their distinctive thematic concerns, however, include mapping the impact on individuals, communities and even nations of what Sean O'Sullivan, writing in a recent collection on Kieślowski's legacy, terms the "absent middle" depicted in recent American television dramas such as *Six Feet Under* (2001-5, HBO).[10] This absence involves a lack of certainty, security and solutions to life's major and, once upon a time, ostensibly more resolvable problems, in the wake of late modernity and high capitalism's dissolution of key social institutions and thus, to an extent, of society itself. Films in this collective of politically engaged work could be imagined to range from Mike Leigh's *Naked* (1993) and Michael Haneke's *Code inconnu: Récit incomplet de divers voyages* (2000) to Alejandro González Iñárritu's "Death" trilogy (*Amores perros*, 2000; *21 Grams*, 2003; *Babel*, 2006)—and far beyond.

Yet the trilogy does not merely diagnose a commonly noted malaise: it also prescribes a cure. Furthermore, the *Three Colors* trilogy's instructive subtext is articulated with the utmost subtlety. Its films offer not some tired old chant, but enchantment. Stanley Kubrick wrote admiringly of Kieślowski and his co-workers that "they have the very rare ability to dramatize their ideas rather than just talking about them . . . allowing the audience to *discover* what's really going on rather than being told."[11] Time and time again, the trilogy's filmmakers appear to have resisted preaching a gospel of *agapē*. Instead, they orchestrate its development between characters in order to persuade the audio-viewer of its transformative potential. Again, on the surface there is nothing new about this. Mainstream films from *Casablanca* (Curtiz, 1942) to *The Simpsons Movie* (Silverman, 2007) have pivoted on acts of heroic abnegation which seem to aid the greater good. But acts of abnegation, in popular cinema, tend to yield immediate recuperative gains for the hero, and little in the way of permanent distress.[12] The trilogy distinguishes itself by refusing to shy away from a full account of the painful cost of realizing "our natures at their finest."

"Film is often just business," Kieślowski once informed an interviewer: "But if film aspires to be part of culture, it should do the things great literature, music and art do: elevate the spirit, help us understand ourselves and the world around us and give people the feeling they are not alone."[13] The political convictions central, in my reading, to the *Three Colors* trilogy indicate that the films also constitute a contribution to a particular artistic tradition: modernism, albeit a late modernism expressed in postmodern times, and with that aesthetic tension reflecting, in turn, the personal and political tensions addressed by the trilogy. Emma Wilson has offered a nuanced critical assessment of the way in which the trilogy (and specifically *Blue*) "blurs the fine mapping of modern and postmodern," arguing that, "[i]n its cinematography and surface effects the film ironically (pre)figures a postmodernist waning of affect, within the very confines of a visual narrative which takes as its central subject the mindless solitude of the bourgeois ego."[14] She then proposes a postmodernist alternative to viewing *Blue* as "a regressive work, a latent modernist film" which "appears almost as a blueprint for what [Frederic] Jameson has described as 'the grand modernist thematics of alienation, anomie, solitude, social fragmentation, and isolation.'"[15]

Tongue in cheek, one might be tempted to respond that, if it walks like a modernist blueprint and quacks like a modernist blueprint . . . were it not for the subtlety of the reading Wilson develops from what she experiences as *Blue*'s waning of affect. Still, perhaps the present study's interpretations will thus be deemed "regressive" too. If so, they are at least honest in their regressions, in that my readings follow the dictates of the films as I have encountered and perceived them—and, most particularly, as I have been led critically to respond to them through what I *hear*, as much as what I *see*, not as a waning but a wellspring of affect, emotion and symbolism whenever I audio-view *Blue*, *White* and *Red*: i.e., the interaction of their sound designs and Preisner's music with the other key elements of their storytelling. Indeed, the readings which follow seek to make a progressive contribution to the literature on the trilogy through my concern, not with the "confines of a visual narrative," but rather with the possibilities of the audio-visual. That is not, however, to claim some form of authenticity for my readings over any other critic's. My position is postmodern, at least, in its belief in the necessity for a reciprocally illuminating plurality of coexistent readings. If this volume plays a small role in that process regarding Preisner's music and the trilogy, it will have achieved its main aim.

Regarding his decision not to name the parts of the trilogy *Liberté*, *Egalité*, and *Fraternité*, Kieślowski made the following statement:

> [I]t seems to me to be a question of the partnership with the viewer, the possibility of opening a dialogue. The moment something is named, the possibility of free interpretation is cut off. The moment you leave something unnamed, and leave the place of the name open, that place can be filled by anyone in the cinema, everyone who has bought a ticket. If *I* fill the space, it cannot be filled by the viewer. It's very simple, logical.[16]

The interpretations in this study report the findings of my personal dialogue with the *Three Colors* trilogy as it currently stands, some fifteen years into that process. Rather than closing down other avenues of interpretation, the arguments that follow, and especially my close analyses of the films' scores and sound designs, invite other film scholars, musicologists and critics, and also members of the films' large and diverse international audience, into a dialogue (or further dialogue) with *Blue*, *White*, and *Red*. While I "believe" in the readings presented below (whatever that statement might be deemed to be worth) at the time of writing, I also believe that, if these films deserve, as some strands of their reception argue, the designation "modern classics," then the "classic" in that formulation should be understood in Frank Kermode's definition thereof. The *Three Colors* trilogy "subsists in change" and is infinitely "patient of interpretation."[17]

Structure

This book has two broad phases. The first introduces framing concepts. Chapters One to Three explore Preisner's musical background, style and scoring practices, plus key themes in the Kieślowski films and their critical reception, and the nature of Preisner and Kieślowski's collaborative project. The second phase offers a series of critical readings, focused through close music analysis, of the *Three Colors* trilogy and its critical literature. Building on the study's first phase, Chapter Four surveys the literature on the films, outlining some of the trilogy's main themes, before Chapters Five to Seven advance detailed critical readings of *Blue*, *White* and *Red*. These readings draw on the existing literature while advancing new approaches to these films. The main DVDs used during analytical work for this study were the Region 1 Miramax set entitled *Krzysztof Kieślowski's "Three Colors: Blue, White, Red."* *The Exclusive Collection* (Miramax, 2003: 28658, 28656, 28655).

Chapter One, "Preisner's Musical Background," traces the composer's musical biography through the sounds of his later music, in order to paint a picture of the formative influences flowing into his work on the *Three Colors* trilogy. Sections explore the influence on Preisner of sacred and secular Polish traditional music; his autodidactic musical knowledge and the influence of rock on his development; the crucial influence of his time in "Piwnica pod Baranami," the Kraków cabaret directed by his main artistic mentor before Kieślowski, Piotr Skrzynecki, and the links between Preisner's music and other composers working for the "Cellar under the Sign of the Ram"; Skrzynecki's guidance regarding Preisner's first Kieślowski score, *No End* (1985), and in turn his influence on *Blue*; the limited inspiration Preisner has drawn from Western art music, the Polish post-war avant-garde (including Krzysztof Penderecki), and his connection to Polish neo-romanticism; and the relationship between his scoring style and other film music, both in terms of aesthetic notions Preisner has developed (regarding the "metaphysics" of film scoring, and what he terms "concept" and "climate"), and his kinship to specific composers, including Ennio Morricone and Nino Rota. The chapter concludes by connecting Preisner's style to a strand of film composition exploring possibilities between classical narrative filmmaking and avant-garde practices.

Chapter Two, "Preisner's Presence," explores the impact of his musical, artistic and philosophical influences on key traits of his mature scoring style, analyzing examples primarily drawn from scores leading up to the *Three Colors* trilogy, but ranging from his first major film score, *Weather Report* (Krauze, 1983) to his album *Silence, Night and Dreams* (2007). First, this study's theorizing of film composer "presence" is outlined, developing notions of "star presence" usually attributed to actors, in order to consider the manner in which "casting" a particular composer on a project might be expected to import a relatively stable store of widely recognized qualities into a film. The basics of Preisner's presence, as perceived by filmgoers, are then gauged through terms used in reviews of his soundtracks; that descriptive language is then critically analyzed to reveal its underlying characteristics, utilizing theories of musical expression and screen music semiotics. What emerges is the idea of an "other" presence, linked to an alternative mode of scoring practice epitomized in a range of scores (including many by the "metaphysical" composers discussed in Chapter One), in films offering different visions of life from mainstream popular cinema. Recurring traits in Preisner's style, and the manner in which they influence film narratives, are then discussed, including: his use of silence and sparseness in his cues; his characteristic approaches to melody; aspects of his harmonic language and his use of homophonic textures; the recurring presence in his films of musicians with whom he regularly collaborates; and his approach to pastiche, not least when composing as "Van den Budenmayer" for Kieślowski's films, and the critical reception of this (in Preisner's term) "semi-classical" voice.

Preisner's preferred mode of collaboration is touched on in Chapters One and Two, but becomes a focus, with specific reference to the Kieślowski films, at the end of Chapter Three, "Kieślowski: Concepts and Co-workers." To approach that topic, and to begin setting up themes explored in greater depth in phase two of this study, Chapter Three surveys key themes in Kieślowski's films and aspects of his reception. Departing from a discussion of *The Sunday Musicians* (Karabasz, 1958), a short and musical film Kieślowski cited as one of his influences, the chapter examines the double reception of Kieślowski and its construction of the director, which splits between his explicitly political contributions to the Polish Cinema of Moral Concern, and his implicitly political later productions. Topics considered include his identities as a Polish, European, and international filmmaker, and his place in these different traditions; the relationship between substance and style in different phases of his career, and, especially in the later films, the connection between thematic focus and stylistic aesthetic (including the foregrounding of Preisner's scores); the role of metaphysics in his work; and finally the production of the *Three Colors* trilogy and its "producers," i.e., the collaborators Kieślowski called his "co-workers." The shooting schedule and international financing of the trilogy are discussed, in the context of their impact on its narratives, symbolic content, and reception. The chapter then examines Kieślowski's mode of working with "co-workers," both as an example of auteurism and, in some respects, a variation thereon; his working relationship with Preisner, as it developed through their work on *No End*, *The Decalogue* (1988), *The Double Life of Véronique* (1991) and the trilogy, then provides the "co-working" case study. An issue which emerges across this chapter, which is reflected in the second phase of the book, is my reading of a continuous political engagement in Kieślowski's filmmaking, and the manifestation of key concerns—such as his later works' exploration of *agapē* and its implications—in both his films' narratives *and* their mode of filmmaking.

Phase two of the study begins with Chapter Four, "The *Three Colors* Trilogy: Critical Contexts," which carries the arguments, themes, and ideas from the first phase of the book into its close engagement with *Blue*, *White* and *Red*. First, the concepts of liberty, equality, and fraternity are examined and debated, and the trilogy is considered as an artistic project addressing these ideas in the wake of the bicentennial of the French Revolution, and thus in a spirit of creative contestation. The colors red, white and blue, and their symbolic roles in the films that bear their names, are then discussed, in order to gauge what (and how) they may be deemed to signify in the trilogy. Alternative readings of the colors as polysemous, as bearing transcultural meanings, and as having culturally specific content are examined, alongside the intrafilmic and intertextual meanings that the colors develop within Kieślowski's *oeuvre*. Existing critical overviews of the trilogy are then considered before three sections—"Kinds of *Blue*," "*White* Washes," and "Metaphysical Fiction: *Red*"—outline themes crucial, in my view, to the individual films and the trilogy, and which emerge from the critical literature on the films, but also from my own investigations of the movies and Preisner's scores; each of these sections, incidentally, begins with a synopsis of its film. Readers seeking primarily to engage with just one of the films in the series may therefore find it most useful to read the first nineteen pages of Chapter Four, which covers aspects of all three films, and then to read just the relevant section of Chapter Four on *Blue*, *White* or *Red*, before passing on to the relevant analytical chapter of the study. Given the connection of these subsections to Chapters Five, Six, and Seven, I will now outline their contents in tandem.

"Kinds of *Blue*" in Chapter Four considers the often nuanced, and sometimes problematic, attempts of academic film critics to deal with *Blue*'s music in terms of its manifold narrative and symbolic functions. Extant criticism of *Blue*'s score is analyzed, focusing on these issues: authenticity (is the score "by" *Blue*'s fictional composers really any good "as music"—and is it *meant* to be any good?); the biblical text set in the film (how St. Paul's letter is edited and transformed, how it came to be in *Blue* in the first place, and the influence of recent European conflicts on the selection of the text and Preisner's setting); authorship (the question of whether Julie is the fictional composer of the music heard in *Blue* and the issues this raises); and genre (what is the correct title of the *Concert[o]*, what generic associations does "concert" or "concerto" import into the film, and what are its relationships to other compositions and musical genres?). The section then considers aspects of *Blue* from a range of screen music perspectives: musician biopics (of real and fictional musicians, and in terms of themes of overcoming often explored in such movies); music-films (which set special critical challenges for film scholars) and the relationship between *Blue* and other films dealing with music, trauma and grief; and Kieślowski's other music-films. The latter, it is suggested, utilize music for at least two interlinked and recurring symbolic purposes: evoking the possibility of the metaphysical or underwriting profound developments in a character's inner life and personal relationships.

Chapter Five, "The Ode to *Agapē*: *Blue*," explores *Blue* and its score through the centrality of grief to its music, narrative, and symbolism. A critical consideration of the literature on grief, grief-work (the process by which humans deal with grief) and music forms a backdrop to the three-stage reading of the film presented in the chapter: "Trauma and Withdrawal," "Restoration," and what is "Lost and Found" when its central character re-engages with the traces, musical and otherwise, of her losses. In the process of analyzing Preisner's major cues in the film against this context, issues arise relating to the film's representation of femininity and, particularly, the manner in which Julie's journey from extreme liberation to a gradual re-enfoldment in society symbolizes aspects of the trilogy's main theme—*agapē*—as announced in the closing *Concert[o]*. As in the other analytical chapters of this study, while Preisner's cues are analyzed in musical detail—drawing on concepts outlined in Chapters One and especially Two—close music analysis is presented in the hopefully mutually enriching context of an overarching critical study of other aspects of the film's story, discourse and ideological agenda.

"*White* Washes" in Chapter Four begins with an analysis of the reception of the trilogy's middle film, which has often been conducted in generic terms (*White* as a black romantic comedy) and with a view to highlighting *White* as the weak or minor link in the trilogy's chain. This study's position is different: *White* remixes *Blue* and *Red*'s political concerns for an alternative, mainstream audience arguably more in need of exposure to its ideas than Kieślowski's art house enthusiasts. Key issues arising from the *White* literature—feminism, capitalism and subjugation—are then considered as reflections of the film's agenda. I argue that the primary malaise addressed by *White* is the manner in which late modernity and particularly high capitalism constrain the development of the individual's subjectivity and relationships, hence the film's (on the surface) jaundiced take on gender politics. Criticism of Preisner's score is also considered, including analyses of the role of tango and folk music in *White*, and the film's allusions to Polish cultural icons, not least the music of Chopin.

Chapter Six, "Last Tango in Warsaw: *White*," reads *White* through its score's expressive narrative: a duel between two popular styles—tango and a folk theme Preisner labels *rustico*—that is structured in relationship to a social hierarchy of musical tastes, which in turn maps the political ideology underpinning the film's social satire. The outcome of this score-wide, structural tango thus articulates *White*'s variation of the trilogy's central theme, setting its ironic and satirical sights on the accrual of cultural capital at the expense of genuine human relationships in all their power, pain and complexity. The *rustico*—a mazurka of sorts—is considered in the context of that Polish musical form's connotations; Preisner's tango (and other tangos in the film), in turn, and indeed the entire structure of *White*'s narrative, are considered through the critical literature on tango and its cultural meanings, including recent readings of tango as a spectacle of eroticized social tension. The chapter closes by considering *White* as an example of white people's representations of themselves onscreen: a living death, connected to various late-modern ills, perhaps not quite yet inescapable.

"Metaphysical Fiction: *Red*" in Chapter Four begins with an examination of the film's alleged links to Kieślowski himself, to literary sources, and to other films by the director. *Red*'s representations of magic—both in terms of its metaphysical themes and, in a sense, its impact on the audio-viewer—are then analyzed, and consideration is given to ways in which Kieślowski specialists have sought to theorize the manner in which *Red feels* magical: sound, music and image in *Red* form subtle plots, not of story but of discourse, which slowly coalesce to deliver the charge of the trilogy's finale. The score's critical reception is then analyzed, introducing issues relating to Preisner's bolero theme, the structure of certain cues, and their relationship to the film as a whole; the idea of bolero is also examined, both in terms of its Spanish origins and more recent cultural manifestations. The other central musical component in *Red*—a Van den Budenmayer song by Preisner first heard in *The Decalogue*—is also introduced here. The text of this song has never before been discussed in the literature on Kieślowski, to the best of my knowledge, yet is important to reading *Red* and its articulation of both its specific themes and those relating to the trilogy's overarching concerns. The section closes with a consideration of musical links between the three films and their scores.

Chapter Seven, "The Bloom of Life: *Red*," reads the film through a musical analysis exploring both its use of bolero and its thematic structure; as in the other analytical chapters, the film's sound design proves crucial to parts of this discussion. The analysis uses the critical analogy of sonata form to highlight key aspects of the score and film, both in order to locate essential tensions between characters and their worldviews, and more importantly their evolution over the course of the movie. A three-part structure is proposed, as is also the case in the analyses of *Blue* and *White*, but here corresponding to a sonata form's exposition, development and recapitulation; over the course of the analysis, the contribution of Preisner's score to the creation of *Red*'s narrative and experiential magic is also assessed. The chapter and study then concludes with a reflection on the trilogy's coda—*Red*'s nearly devastating ending. Existing views on *Red*'s close in the Kieślowski literature form a critical counterpoint to this study's own reading: a finale drenched in pessimism, yet bearing faint glimmers of hope.

CHAPTER ONE

PREISNER'S MUSICAL BACKGROUND

Like the placement of his cues on a soundtrack, statements by Zbigniew Preisner about his music and past are few and far between. Even when they do appear, they tend to be terse or elliptical. Given the choice, Preisner prefers not to talk about himself at all. Some journalists have consequently found Preisner "a very difficult person to interview" and the composer has candidly described himself as "not an easy guy."[1] In this regard, his uncredited early onscreen appearance as an axe-wielding butcher in *Ostatni dzwonek* ("The Last Schoolbell," Łazarkiewicz, 1989) feels fitting (see Fig. 1.1). Those who interview Preisner tend to call attention to the contrast between his height and heft, on the one hand, and on the other the music for which he is famous. One interviewer joked that Preisner "looks more like an East European contract killer than a creator of delicately harmonious symphonies"; another described "a big, burly, rumpled man . . . who looks more like a retired rugby player than the composer of film music characterized by an almost promiscuous lyricism."[2] Some aspects of Preisner's public persona may in fact be extensions into adulthood of his childhood shyness.[3] His apparent brusqueness, in turn, often stems from fierce loyalty to his friends and close collaborators.[4] For the record, on the occasions I have met him, Preisner has struck me as a polite, open, good-humored and modest man, genuinely surprised by the critical attention being paid to his music, and delighted but astonished by the enthusiasm of his many fans.[5]

Nonetheless, for the would-be Preisner biographer, his taciturn nature leads to a situation which, again, is not entirely unlike the experience of his music. Many of Preisner's cues demand that the perceiver search for the meanings of a scene: his scoring rarely delivers pre-digested explanations. With little documentary evidence to go on concerning his early life and musical experiences, one might therefore feel prompted to invent the missing links. Instead, this chapter is full of si-

Fig. 1.1: Preisner, an axe and some sausages in *The Last Schoolbell* (photo courtesy of the author)

lence and spaces where future research will help to join the dots of Preisner's past. The focus below is as much on tracing the composer's musical biography through the sounds of his later music as on elaborating his public statements. The chapter pays attention to instances where his musical voice may offer the more voluble testimony. In particular, observations can be made about Preisner's early musical experiences which suggest connections to key aspects of his later musical style, his approach to working on film scores and even, in some cases, the meaning of specific cues from the *Three Colors* trilogy. His musical origins—including his early exposure to Polish traditional and sacred musics, popular music, Polish cabaret, avant-garde Polish art music and scores by the film composers to whom he feels an aesthetic connection—contributed to the development of Preisner's distinctive approach to film composition. The hallmarks of his musical "presence"—which Chapter Two identifies as including silence and sparseness, monodic melodies, popular music-inspired approaches to harmony and homophony, the utilization of specific musicians and their characteristic sounds and a gift for knowing pastiche—relate to these origins. Preisner's early years as a composer also generated the twinned pillars of his film scoring aesthetic: his notions of "climate" and "concept."

Sacred and Secular Polish Traditional Music

Preisner was born Zbigniew Kowalski in the Silesian town of Bielsko-Biała on 20 May 1955. It is an area of starkly contrasting environments. On the one hand, the town—actually two towns that were united, four years before Preisner's birth, across the divide of the Biała River—is at the foot of the Beskid Śląski mountain range, a popular Polish holiday destination, not least for its winter skiing.[6] *The Rough Guide to Poland* describes these ranges as "an archetypal central European mountain landscape . . . a region of wooden churches, folk costumes, occasional castles and manageable hikes," yet its depiction of Bielsko-Biała is less seductive: "a place from which to catch buses . . . rather than stick around . . . it's not one of the most charming spots that Poland has to offer."[7] The town has the down-at-heel, post-industrial ambience of former textile centers across Europe, and Silesia more generally is blighted by the kind of polluting sprawl typified by nearby city Katowice.

The Bielsko-Biała area does, however, boast certain architectural delights. In particular, its places of worship—churches being a focal point of any Polish community—include the Katedra św. Mikołaja (St. Nicholas's Cathedral)—"an Escheresque vision of the Italian Renaissance"—and nearby examples of Polish wooden churches such as Mikusowice's Kościół sw. Barbary (St. Barbara's Church), "the finest example of this highly distinctive form of vernacular architecture to be found in the region."[8] Preisner was born in the midst of the partial cultural thaw that, following Stalin's death in 1953, saw Poland slipping out of the clutches of Soviet attempts to enforce hard-line Stalinism and into the greyer, but still repressive, pall of Polish communism. One continuous source of strength for Polish people coping with these different regimes was the centrality of the Roman Catholic Church to everyday life. As Preisner has commented, "Polish communism was not like it was in Russia. The priest was the most important person in the village and even the party secretary went to church."[9] Preisner's family duly attended the Catholic Church in Bielsko when he was a young child; later on, he attended church in Bobowice. It was at church, therefore, that Preisner was exposed to one of his earliest musical influences, and arguably the music that has marked the style of his later works most profoundly.

Sacred

Preisner has stated that "music was part of everyday life" when he was growing up, "so I didn't study it."[10] In Bielsko-Biała, he says, everyone became musical by singing in church.[11] Preisner's exposure to church music did not take the form of especially active participation in music-making, say as a member of the choir, although he was close to the action as an altar boy. Instead, Preisner appears to have absorbed elements of this sacred musical tradition from his place at the side of the priest. One might therefore observe characteristics of music typically heard in Polish churches and their relationship to aspects of his compositional style. One Polish hymn—"Święty Boże," arguably the country's most iconic—bears a striking resemblance to a piece of music at the heart of the present study.

Poland's most important religious songs include the supplications "Mother of God" ("Bogurodzica") and "Holy God" ("Święty Boże"; see Ex. 1.1),[12] traditional hymns Preisner remembers singing in church as a child. These are melodies whose cultural currency in Poland down the ages has symbolized more than engrained devotion in a staunchly Roman Catholic country. Poland's tumultuous socio-political topography, since the late eighteenth century alone, has seen its people bearing the effects of partition, Nazi and Soviet atrocities and occupations, and a bumpy rebirth as a nation state participating in Western capitalism. It is therefore hardly surprising, as Adrian Thomas explains, that Poland's composers, like other musicians and artists in the country, have "sometimes sought to express their national solidarity through works, and materials, which both commemorated and signified their Polishness," and, as an integral part of that national identity, "the centrality of the Roman Catholic church during periods of vicissitude."[13]

Thomas is writing here about Polish concert music (i.e., "classical" music in the Western art music tradition). Notable examples of this culturally expressive practice can be heard in Krzysztof Penderecki's *St. Luke Passion* (1966) and *Polish Requiem* (1980-84, rev. 1993).[14] In the

Ex. 1.1: "Holy God" ("Święty Boże")

St. Luke Passion, Penderecki utilizes the first four notes of "Holy God" to form a crisscrossing motif in the "Crux fidelis"; in the "Recordare" of his *Polish Requiem*, the full melody of the hymn is quoted, with the first verse of the text sung in Polish "in order to make a direct emotional and spiritual contact with a wider audience."[15] This happens, furthermore, in the context of a piece already dedicated to Polish martyrs old and more recent (the "Dies Irae," for instance, commemorates the Warsaw Uprising). Subsequently, "Holy God" forms a *cantus firmus* encoding a struggle for self-determining identity that runs throughout the movement and, more broadly, across Polish art of the twentieth century.

The "Recordare" was completed in 1983 and the *Polish Requiem* first performed in Stuttgart on 20 September 1984. During this period, Preisner composed the music for *No End*, his first collaboration with Kieślowski. The compositional *cantus firmus* in *No End* serves as a lament for a widow's dead, albeit spectrally still present, husband; it then rematerializes, virtually unchanged, in *Blue*, where it haunts Julie, *Blue*'s doubly bereaved protagonist. The music makes patterns from a five-note motif whose pitch content, Preisner confirms, consciously echoes the opening four notes of "Holy God" (see Ex. 1.2). Could one therefore argue that the searches for liberty and solidarity embodied in both films draw strength from a wider symbolic framework connected to Poland's search for identity and freedom? As a culturally engaged young artist, Preisner heard Penderecki's *Polish Requiem*. Perhaps it reminded him of the potent symbolism of a tune he had learned as a boy; alternatively, he may simply have made a parallel use of the tune in *No End*, a film similarly rich in political subtexts, thanks to its role in the devotional activities of his childhood. Whatever the origins, this use of a sacred song was entirely intentional and can hardly have bypassed Kieślowski. As the symbolic charge of the hymn is undeniable, the meanings it can be heard to import into these films, as part of a fascinating broader transit of meanings between their intimately connected narratives, requires careful consideration.[16]

Ex. 1.2 *Cantus firmus* from the opening of *No End*

More broadly speaking, from his earliest scores Preisner's music has made consistent use of recognizable characteristics of traditional Polish sacred music. These traits include: chant-like monophonic melodies; simple homophonic accompaniments; tonal and modal harmony similar to the plain-speaking devotions of Polish sacred song. This austerity of means can yield intense expressions of emotion and, in this respect, it is interesting that the idiomatic religious songs of another Polish composer, Henryk Górecki, such as his *Marian Songs (Pieśni Maryjne*, 1985) and *Church Songs (Pieśni kościelne*, 1986)—songs adapted from one of Poland's principal sources of hymns and chants, Jan Siedlecki's *Church Songbook* (compiled in 1878)—sound similar to Preisner cues ranging from the opening of the *Concert[o]* in *Blue* to the "Amore" cue from *It's All about Love* (Vinterberg, 2003). Górecki is one of the few art music composers to whose music Preisner enjoys listening. The more profound connection between their works, however, is surely a shared heritage of sacred Polish song.

That heritage would clearly have been an inspiration for the "Church Song" Preisner contributed to Agnieszka Holland's *To Kill a Priest* in 1988. Based on the murder of the Roman Catholic priest Father Jerzy Popiełuszko in October 1984, whose monthly "Mass for the Fatherland" at his North Warsaw church had made him a target for the security forces, the film features a bitter-sweet score by Georges Delerue.[17] There is, however, a captivating scene in which a probing sermon by Father "Alex" (as the Popiełuszko character is called in the film) is answered by his huge congregation singing, as one, Preisner's church song. Notably, the song is in Polish. Holland, with whom Preisner had worked on the Kieślowski films, asked her friend to provide a song similar to actual anthems sung in Father Jerzy's church. The film's language is English, but this song, like the Solidarity ("Solidarność") banners held aloft by the congregation as they sing Preisner's music, is a resolutely Polish icon in the midst of what Preisner calls a "mad" Anglophone production.[18]

Preisner's chant is reproduced in Ex. 1.3. Like the renditions of "Holy God" he heard in his youth, it is monophonic and *a capella*.[19] Unlike the *cantus firmi* in *No End* and *Blue*, however, this church song is more anthem than supplication. It is in a minor mode (connoting seriousness and the tragic) but set at a moderate tempo, powerfully doubled in octaves by the male and female voices, and sung in a rigorously accented manner (and so also connoting forthright commitment). Its most expressive detail—a plangent exploration of the $\hat{5}$-$\flat\hat{6}$-$\hat{5}$ pivot (bracketed in Ex. 1.3)—is outlined by the first three notes of the second stanza, and then resolved by the third and fourth lines of the song. The tension is grounded at the end of the final line and the melodically articulated expressive struggle overcome. This musical token of the congregation's unity with Father "Alex" could be heard to imply that the people of Poland would survive the finale to the communist era.

Crucial to Preisner's filmic presence is the way in which these and other stylistic elements permit him to evoke an atmosphere of the sacred and the spiritual. The reverberant silences which separate so many of his music's chant-like refrains, usually soaked in wet studio reverb, create cathedral-like ambiences in many of his scores and thus a sense of space not unlike those evoked when reverberant sonorities haunt the arched roofs of a fine church. Creating such spaces performs Polish variations on a recognized film music style topic that signifies the other-worldly;[20] it is also one of the most obvious ways in which Preisner's music hints at a metaphysical dimension in Kieślowski's

Ex. 1.3: "Church Song" from *To Kill a Priest*

films. Preisner's spaces and silences shape quasi-sacred spaces for re-flection within narratives encouraging perceivers to explore the idea that life has layers beyond the quotidian surface of the material world.

Secular

If everyone became musical in Preisner's home town by singing in a church, it is reasonable to suggest that he himself began to become a musician through his participation in such activities. There is, though, another equally significant Polish musical tradition to which the young Preisner was exposed as part of his everyday life: folk music. In its en-try on Polish traditional music, the *New Grove Dictionary of Music and Musicians* backs up Preisner's assertion that, at least until the mid-twentieth century, "everyone in the villages sang," and not only in church, and that incredibly talented "professional musicians, untrained in the Western sense, played for dances."[21] Preisner's father was one such musician. A chemical engineer by trade, by musical vocation he was an accordion player who performed at weddings, dances and birth-day parties.[22] As with the potential influence of church music on his own style, Preisner is wary of drawing a direct connection between Pol-ish traditional music and his own work: "I happened to grow up with folk music from which there is so much to be learned," he has stated, "but when you're composing music you're never sure where it comes from."[23] Moreover, although he recalls hearing his father play music, including compositions of his father's own creation, Preisner remem-bers "the atmosphere, but not the detail" of this performing. Yet com-paring his film scores to features of the traditional secular music he absorbed through his cultural pores as a child, both from his father's playing and from the folk music he remembers being performed in his community, suggests connections akin to those traceable from his exposure to religious music.

Some of those connections may merely demonstrate the close links between traditional sacred and secular musics in Poland. For instance, the important repertory of Polish wedding songs with which Preisner's father would have been intimately familiar includes Ex. 1.4, a tune from the north-eastern Kurpie region. The restriction of pitches (just five) and downwards slant of the melody are typical features of many Polish traditional melodies—not least "Holy God," with which this particular tune also shares its tight range of pitches. Preisner's funereal *cantus firmus* in *No End* and *Blue* is based on the same restricted palette.[24] Arguably, these cues are not merely tokens of mourning and lament specific to their narratives, but tokens of Polishness with a range of cultural resonances. Furthermore, if the *No End* and *Blue* cues are heard as being related both to a traditional Polish wedding song and "Holy God," the melody's meanings—not least as an accompaniment to the mourning of widows—becomes yet more poignant.

Given the fact that many stylistic features of Polish traditional music can be heard in dozens of other musical repertoires, it would be too bold to claim that the following features add much weight to the idea of folk music's influence on Preisner's compositions. His style is not the

Ex. 1.4: Wedding song, Kurpie region

only one, for instance, in which "monophony predominates," melodic motifs are "sharply outlined and distinct," with lines moving mainly by seconds and thirds, and forms are structured in symmetrical, strophic, verse-refrain-verse phrasings.[25] Yet even if the soaring and almost shouted male vocals or frenetic fiddle leads of much Polish folk music have no obvious analogue in his output, save perhaps for his predilection for very high vocals and treble recorder lines, his scores are hardly strangers to the following sounds, which are also typical of some Polish folk repertoires: melodies accompanied solely by a drone, or a drone and chord accompaniment, and the triple-meter time signatures of the *oberek*, *mazurek* and *polonez* dances forming, in Ewa Dahlig's words, "the image of Polishness in music" and rhythms that "reflect the specificity of the Polish language."[26] Preisner could have developed the same traits in his music independently or via other sources. Yet the circumstantial evidence tempts one to consider the possibility that Preisner, growing up proximate to the Podhale region of southern Poland and thus to the rich and oft reimagined *górale* musical culture of the region, could have reworked certain traits in distinctive music serving different functions from the original sources.[27] After all, this tradition has also enriched music ranging from Karol Szymanowski's early twentieth-century compositions to the "góralstafarianism" of reggae duo The Twinkle Brothers' collaborations with the Trebunie-Tutki Family Band. An obvious example from Preisner's film scores is the folk song-like number Preisner composed for *The Double Life of Véronique*, "Tu viendras" ("When You Come"), which is sung by Weronika's choir early in the film. With its evocations of sensuous longing, burning brows, moist lips drinking honey and quivering crops on a "torrid, sizzling day" (the "upalny, skwarny dzień" of the song's repeated refrain), the authentic twang of its erotic pastoral is deployed as an anticipation of Weronika's subsequent lovemaking with her boyfriend, although the meteorological symbolism of the lyrics is somewhat at odds with the clichéd symbolism of Kieślowski's rain-soaked mise-en-scène.[28] Yet there are also, potentially, less obvious reimaginings of folk music in Preisner's scores.

Consider the choral opening of the *Concert[o] for the Unification of Europe* in *Blue* (see Fig. 5.4 and Ex. 5.3). Its absence of anacrusis and "descendental rhythm"[29] could be heard to be tinctured with Polishness. The presence of Jacek Ostaszewski's recorder playing on many important Preisner cues (and his quite literal presence in *Blue*) might be taken as a representation of the pipe instruments, and especially the *fujarka* and *fulyrka* (flutes without and with holes respectively) of Polish traditional music. Preisner tends to develop his melodies not in the manner of classical Hollywood's late-Romantic art music archetypes—i.e., motivically integrated streams of lyrical consciousness—but rather through repetitions adorned by simple ornaments, slight pitch variations and rhythmic shifts, and en-masse transpositions of sections of a cue. The shifting pitch-centers of Karol's peasant theme in *White*—a film in which the tensions between Polishness old and new are foregrounded—forms an obvious example of these practices, and Preisner (as discussed further in Chapter Four) drew conscious inspiration from northern Polish folk music when creating this theme. The scoring of the tango in *White*'s score, on the other hand, mixes national identities by filtering the Argentinean form through a string sextet evoking the powerful string bands of the *górale* tradition.

One can clearly make a case for connections between Preisner's mature compositional voice and his exposure to folk music at home and at other public gatherings during his childhood. In this regard, the church and folk songs from *To Kill a Priest* and *Véronique* offer neat summations of the available evidence. One might even argue that the traditional musical influences on Preisner's work form an example of his country's adoption of a more positive attitude towards folk music as a resource of "forgotten and underestimated traditional values [that] may enrich present-day culture," rather than as an eminently objectionable "symbol of difficult living conditions and poverty or a tool of official policy"—a shift more widely affecting Polish music after the country reopened itself to Western Europe in 1989.[30] In the Kieślowski films, however, meditations on national identity encouraged by musical traces in Preisner's scores are both richer and more problematic: irony and distance, rather than sentimental immersion, are keystones of Preisner's evocation of these traditions. His filtering of Polish music, moreover, becomes a signifier of an "otherness" that is key to his presence, but which functions not as an indicator of Polish identity, specifically, but rather of a non-Hollywood identity and thus "different" perspective on the world from the hegemonic cinematic forms of the late twentieth century, as discussed further in Chapter Two. By the time he was a teenager, furthermore, like many other Poles of his generation, however, Preisner's secular musical experiences had come to be dominated by other popular forms, and especially those offering liberties untainted by socialist-realist "fakelore" or, for that matter, the paternalistic associations (and for Preisner doubly so) of traditional Polish musics: Anglo-American rock.

We Don't Need No (Musical) Education

Informal Training

The precise chronology of Preisner's mostly auto-didactic education in music is unclear. He told one set of interviewers that he received "private lessons in piano" at some point, "because there was no musical school" in his home town.[31] In discussion with me, he claimed never to have studied the piano and to be self-taught on the instrument, although he did take lessons in classical guitar at some point at the Bobowa Lyceum (middle school) between 1970 and 1974. The idea that the guitar is "Preisner's instrument" casts light on some of his cues and their potential significance—not least the simple guitar arpeggio with which the score of *Red* signs off, rather like a personal motto. While studying at the Lyceum, he composed his first piece of music, a setting of a Romantic Polish poet, although he cannot remember which one, for voice and guitar. Preisner then "started to learn to be a composer" between 1975 and 1978, while studying for a degree in history at the Jagiellonian Institute in Kraków.[32] He achieved his musical education by listening to recordings, learning to read scores, and using a book by the Russian composer Rimsky-Korsakov to learn about harmony and basic scoring conventions.

That book must have been Rimsky-Korsakov's *Uchebnik garmonii* ("Textbook of harmony"), first published in 1884/5, and better known under the title *Prakticheskiy uchebnik garmonii*, which emphasizes a practicality that would surely have appealed to a young musician hungry for a ready-meal of staple musical knowledge. The textbook is a methodical introduction to tonal harmony in the context of part-writing. Tchaikovsky, for one, "found his colleague's method too pedantic and resented what he saw as the spoon-feeding of students."[33] Spoon-feeding was nonetheless precisely what Preisner needed when he turned to the book as a guide. His later harmonic language implies that he may not have made it through to the more colorful later harmonies in the method; rarely does Preisner's tonal harmony progress in sophistication beyond a diminished seventh chord. Then again, Preisner's folk and rock-oriented modal harmonies offer their own alternative colors, and he was shortly to discover fresh harmonic tricks from a new wave of Polish music—shades of the spectrum beyond the Russian composer's dreams. Rimsky-Korsakov's method appears, therefore, to have provided Preisner's technique with just enough stability to permit him to progress as a composer and begin expressing himself on the manuscript page.

Preisner rightly prizes this hard-earned knowledge; he has also been dismissive of the value of institutional training in composition. "Besides technical knowledge," he has commented, "the musical schools don't have much to offer. You can be kind of stuck to certain ideas."[34] There is some truth in such statements, but there is also a defensive edge to such remarks. One might be tempted to relate this to the tension between the world to which Preisner was gaining access by developing these skills—a sphere with its roots in the elite institutions of the Western art music tradition—and his down-to-earth, familial roots in popular traditions. Many musicians steeped in vernacular musics have felt wary of exposing their lack of knowledge of the style they and many others—if recent BBC documentaries like *How to Be a Composer* and *Classic Goldie* are anything to go by[35]—continue to invest with cultural currency of unparalleled value. It is a needless anxiety: one does not dismiss the athleticism of an Olympic swimmer just because she cannot run a marathon. In film music, though, a lack of formal "classical" training has often been used as a battering ram to attack composers without an art music background.[36] Preisner's statements are pre-emptive in their defensive against such accusations. Here, however, it is vital to make a distinction between the limited means at the disposal of an essentially self-taught musician such as Preisner and the range of achievement of his cues. A limited technical palette need not mean music of limited effectiveness. There are places where Preisner's stylistic ambitions stretch his technical resources, most obviously when he seeks to mimic the Western art music tradition in the Kieślowski films. Preisner's most idiomatic scores, however, make a virtue out of these limitations, and in his collaboration with Kieślowski that virtue was intensified by the director's own inclination to render music of stark expressiveness and power.

Pink Floyd

As a teenager, Preisner's greatest musical passion was the music of Pink Floyd. Providing orchestrations for David Gilmour's album *On an Island* (2006) was thus a dream come true for Preisner. "It was unbelievable," he told me: "I was a Pink Floyd groupie—they were like God!" Work on the album led, in turn, to Preisner conducting the orchestra when Gilmour (joined by Pink Floyd keyboardist Rick Wright) played a recent gig in Poland: "Now," Preisner jokes he was thinking, "I must finish my career. Make the great music for Kieślowski, and a great concert with Richard Wright and David Gilmour in Gdańsk. It's enough!"

For many Poles growing up, like Preisner, in the 1970s and 80s, Pink Floyd's music was a near-permanent soundtrack. In his depiction of adolescence in communist Poland, Radek Sikorski offers an evocative description of being a teenage Polish fan of the band:

> We held parties at which it was the height of cool to drink genuine vermouth. Each Pink Floyd album—worth a couple of average monthly wages—was welcomed like a piece of the True Cross. We learned English by translating the texts on the jacket and thought we felt the same angst. Only later was I to discover that the anxiety of our Western contemporaries was in fact the opposite of our own: they were fed up and bored with consumerism while we craved and wallowed in its meanest manifestations. I remember my sixteenth birthday party . . . dark room, couples dancing on the parquet floor . . . to the sounds of "Dark Side of the Moon" . . . a glass of Vermouth in [my] hand, thinking to myself with self-satisfaction "How Western, how sophisticated!"[37]

As a child, Preisner had heard The Beatles, whose early hits were permitted through the censor's wall "because they are so innocent"; he also remembers doing his best to tune in to Radio Luxembourg.[38] Pink Floyd's music, however, is an acknowledged early influence on his developing musicality: they represented the first Western popular music he admits to admiring. Partly, this was down to aspects of the band's music which seemed, to Poles, to speak to their cultural situation. "Before 1989," Preisner has stated, "all you could buy in the shops was vinegar, and the Polish mentality is such that this sudden choice [in the freer markets of Poland post-1989] was very hard for people. Pink Floyd were sophisticated and smart enough to provide a metaphor for the situation with their album *The Wall*. I love albums like *Dark Side of the Moon* because it has a melancholy that is very British—very Polish, too."[39] Like Sikorski and many others, Preisner found in Pink Floyd's music a reflection of his own youthful disenfranchisement, as filtered through communism but also, as he implies here, Poland's bumpy re-entry into capitalism after 1989, a key topic of *White*. Preisner also appears to have appreciated aspects of the band's sound and well-crafted song writing, not least for their distinctiveness in the face of changing pop fashions: "They were a revolution in music and are still fresh today," Preisner claims. "They were and are the opposite to existing styles of music."

Preisner's style bears certain relations to Pink Floyd's sound on the albums the band produced from the mid-1970s, and particularly *Dark Side of the Moon*, onwards. In terms of the potential influence their music on his compositional voice, Preisner's mention of melancholy is one useful hint. Aside from its evocation of a spiritual dimension, a hardly unconnected tenet of Preisner's music is the manner in which a shadow of melancholy—cast by modal properties, slower tempos, recurring melodic gestures and his choices of instrumentation—can darken the tone of ostensibly joyful moments. Such representations, which can add nuance to a filmic narrative otherwise unrepresented by its story-telling mechanisms, are a key to the aesthetic intent and, often, success of his cues. More generally, however, the mixing of topical significations of religiosity and melancholy is a Preisner trademark in film and elsewhere. An odd couple mix of ironic pessimism and faith is a Polish character trait with a long and understandable history; not for nothing do Poles refer to Poland as the "Christ of Nations." Preisner may have found the means to articulate the musical melancholy lurking within his spiritually resonant music, though, as much through Pink Floyd's soulful progressive rock as the penitent music of his homeland.

As interviews reveal, Preisner's knowledge of the band's albums was intimate long before he worked with Gilmour. One might therefore wonder what else he inherited from his appreciation of the band.[40] There are certain parallels between Preisner's style and the precisely organized, cleanly articulated, yet at root understated and relatively simple building blocks of Pink Floyd's music: basic resources deployed to maximum expressive ends and often in the articulation of weighty narrative agendas concerning war, mental illness, loss and the fate of the self in late-modern times. Many of Preisner's films—not least the Kieślowski collaborations—deal with these topics. Preisner also aims high in terms of his solo project's philosophical themes, not least in the album *Silence, Night and Dreams* (2008), or "Life," the second part of *Requiem for My Friend* (1998), which was planned as a co-project with Kieślowski and Piesiewicz, and aimed at representing nothing less than an entire life in images, words and music. One could imagine Pink Floyd's Roger Waters attempting something similar to this meditation on the Book of Job.

More occasionally, Preisner's music seems directly connected to a specific Pink Floyd song. In *No End*, for instance, as the widow, Ula, abdicates her emotional pain through a virtual prostitution of her body, hints of "Goodbye Cruel World" from *The Wall* creep into the soundtrack. Certain aspects of Pink Floyd's sound may also have helped inspire the cathedral-like spaces evoked by Preisner's music. Pink Floyd's sense of space is evoked by temporal aspects of their work (their music rarely exceeds a laconic canter, songs tend to be long in duration, lyrical conceits extend to encompass whole albums), instrumentation (Gilmour's guitar soaring above the analogue synthesizers at the start of "Shine On You Crazy Diamond Part 1" being a paradigmatic example) and production techniques (reverb, delay and meticulous mixing combined with subtle instrumentation and texture). The soaring solo voices which roam with improvisatory freedom above the solid foundations of many Pink Floyd tracks (not only Gilmour's guitar solos but, for instance, Clare Torry's gospel-tinged vocal on "The Great Gig in the Sky" or Dick Parry's saxophone solos in the "Wish You Were Here" cycle) could have influenced the cardinal role in Preisner's music of, in particular, Ostaszewski's recorder playing and soprano Elżbieta Towarnicka's voice. Perhaps the strongest case for a link between Preisner and Pink Floyd, in this regard, can be heard in the passages from *On an Island* where Gilmour's solos soar above a bed of Preisner-scored strings.

It is tempting, finally, to connect the style of Preisner's music, and particularly his contributions to film narratives, to another alleged aspect of his early experiences of Western popular music. As well as becoming "involved in a rock group, performing songs and all of those things young people do"[41] when he was at school—Preisner sang, played guitar and wrote tracks for the band—it has been reported on the Internet that he created some of his first annotated compositions in response to LPs of popular and classical music.[42] Most intriguingly, Preisner is often said to have composed additional music to complement existing tracks. As well as indicating the development of significant aural skills, this story provokes the idea of Preisner writing cue-like fragments to complement an already, in some senses, complete artistic text: In a sense, this is precisely what film composers do. it could also encourage musings on the origins of Preisner's aesthetic of restraint. Unfortunately, the story is untrue—a space in Preisner's biography that has been filled by creative speculation. Preisner claims never to have composed short cues to go with records to which he was listening. The story therefore has more to tell one about the fate of truth in the age of "Wikiality" than it does about the evolution of Preisner's musical style.[43]

The Pope's Cabaret

Restraint is not a word one usually associates with cabaret. The pop cultural association of cabaret with glitzy Las Vegas artifice, fading superstars, vice and excess, however, ignores the mid-twentieth-century route taken by cabaret's development in Central and Eastern Europe—a path with direct links to cabaret's earlier twentieth-century peak of creativity as "a form of artistic and social activity" imbued with "the freedom of thought, experiment and expression that characterizes cabaret in its most vigorous form."[44] The cabarets of the "Chat Noir" in Paris and, in particular, Berlin's "Überbrettl" served as templates for post-war cabarets in the Eastern Bloc, due to their fusion of a safe haven for artists and free-thinkers with a stage from which to address the public and, behind the thin mask of satirical disguise, confront the authorities. Many elements of these cabarets followed in the footsteps of the interwar German cabaret musicians who appropriated, amongst other things, bitingly satirical arias from Kurt Weill's operas, most notably *Die Dreigroschenoper* (1928). They fashioned a musical genre "that was sentimental and at the same time satirical" out of songs mixing comedy and politics, and also by drawing on traditions such as folk music, popular song and operatic parody: "[A]n element of provocative artistic statement was the essence of cabaret during its heyday," smuggled onto the bill via the Trojan horse of "an atmosphere in which innovation could flourish," with clear "aspirations towards high standards" enriched by laughter, and relying in part for its impact on "the intimacy of the locale, the economy of small, often ad hoc, musical ensembles, and the directness and warmth of contact between floor and platform."[45] Such work provided a model for the tradition of witty and controversial cabaret emanating from the Satiric Theatre in the Prague Small Quarter[46] and "Piwnica pod Baranami" in Kraków ("The Cellar under the Sign of the Ram")—the venue of Preisner's first significant public forays as a musician.

Bogdan Chmura's *New Grove* entry on Preisner describes the roots of his musical style as follows:

> On the one hand Preisner continues the lyric-musical tradition of the cabaret, while, on the other [he] clearly owes much to various styles of classical music, especially neo-romanticism (as evinced by his music's monumental quality and its pathos).[47]

Given the actual pathway Preisner took towards music, and his tempered contact with Western art music, Chmura places too much weight on the classical tradition's impact on Preisner's development. He also makes the not uncommon mistake of taking the composer's more monumental cues—not least those composed for *Blue* in the name of other fictional composers—as being representative of his style; Preisner's stylistic presence and evolution are more complex. Chmura does, however, put his finger on the vital contribution of cabaret to Preisner's art and outlook, and a contribution that is every bit as much of a template for his flamboyant cues as the classical music tradition. Cabaret was a formative cultural experience for Preisner and, as with church, folk and rock music, he took from it certain musical elements and developed them in his own way. From "Piwnica pod Baranami," however, he also took an attitude—towards life, art and music's importance in both—that prepared the ground for his collaborations with Kieślowski. He also began an artistic relationship that would have a profound effect on the music at the center of the present study.

The Cellar under the Sign of the Ram

"Piwnica pod Baranami" developed the Berlin model for cabaret in a distinctly Polish context. It began in May 1956 and thus during a slight Polish thawing of cultural censure permitting a degree of artistic license that continued in cabaret long after most other art forms in Poland had fallen victim, once again, to the Party's censorial aims. The cabaret's precise origins, in this regard, are a sign of the times: the cellar was originally host to an official-sounding "Club of Artistic Youth" in the basement of the "Pałac pod Baranami," a building on the city's vast medieval market square which served as Kraków's "Palace of Culture." Yet somewhat more than beer was fermenting in this cellar. Kraków in the mid-1950s and 60s functioned as a hub of artistically mediated dissidence, just as it had fifty years earlier in the time of the "Młoda Polska" (Young Poland) artistic avant-garde. "Piwnica pod Baranami" picked up on the traditions of that movement's "Zielony Balonik" (Green Ballroom) while slotting neatly into an experimental art scene in Kraków which already included Tadeusz Kantor's Dada-inspired Cricot 2 Theatre (home to provocative and innovative productions and, later, happenings) and the then unofficial Kraków Jazz Festival. Piotr Skrzynecki, the Master of Ceremonies and creative driving force behind the cabaret, stated that its mixture of art and subversive social practice, from its very first performances in December 1956, intended to "free [its performers and audiences] from old formulas and not to accept any new ones," with the primary goal of getting "to know and understand ourselves."[48] This intoxicating motivation would not have seemed entirely out of place in San Francisco or London a decade later, albeit coming here from the leading light of a quite literally underground counterculture, the denizens of which were fuelled, furthermore, not by marijuana or hallucinogens but caffeine, cigarettes and vodka.

Packed into the cramped intimacy of "Piwnica pod Baranami" in the 1950s, 60s or early 70s, and sitting a hair's breadth away from the action on stage, what might one have seen and heard through the fug of cigarette smoke? To speak of a typical night would be oxymoronic. However, visitors recall the continuous presence of spontaneity, fun and wit, much of the atmosphere being derived from a subversion of materials paralleling the troupe's subversive message. In terms of music, one might have been lucky enough to catch the Krzysztof Komeda Sextet— Komeda being another film-composer-to-be (not least of the scores to Roman Polański's *Knife in the Water* and *Rosemary's Baby*) to pass through the cabaret.[49] Alternatively, one could have heard "Piwnica" star Ewa Demarczyk, the "Black Angel" of Polish cabaret, singing settings of Polish poetry old and more recent by composers including Zygmunt Konieczny, the key musician for many years in the cabaret— although singing is not a rich enough term to evoke Demarczyk's performance of "piosenka poetyka" (poetic songs) delivered, in her slightly harsh but passionate voice, with a guarded theatricality pitched midway between *Pierrot lunaire* and Edith Piaf.

Many of the skits making up a night's review would be musical, scored ad hoc by Konieczny and his fellow musicians under Skrzynecki's direction. The overall result was an affectionate carve up—a "mish-mash [that] must have violated all esthetic principles . . . one big mockery of all known staging, set designing, acting, musical and literary conventions," yet "not offensive, as is often the case with avant-garde projects, [because] originality of means and lack of any respect whatsoever for established canons went hand in hand with overt liking and respect for the past."[50] Texts ranging from the bible and philosophical tracts to Party communiqués and user manuals would be set to music or otherwise sent up; new poems would be performed by their creators (not least Karol Józef Wojtyła, who would later speak from a somewhat more elevated stage in Vatican City); sets would include found objects, costumes and wigs, cut up or kaleidoscopically ill-matched; bank notes and rags would be thrown from the stage; the audience might be showered with cabbage.[51] At the center of the rumpus, Polskie Radio's Michał Kubicki recalls, one would see and hear

> Skrzynecki, the master of ceremonies, never parting with a little bell whose sound accompanied his entry onto the stage, improvising his lines, with comments on the VIPs or friends who happened to be in the audience, on the current political situation, quoting from old documents discovered somewhere in Kraków archives or antiquarian bookshops, laughing and making the audience laugh.[52]

Preisner joined the cabaret troupe in 1977 as part of a wider changing of the artistic guard. Given both his desire to continue his accelerated musical education and the need to respond decisively to tight deadlines at the cabaret, it was an apt preparation for his future film scoring career. He also learned to participate in the production of musical texts in which the composer is but one of several valued creative voices. As Preisner has stated, the text matters most in a literary cabaret such as "Piwnica," just as the narrative and its subtexts matter most in a collaborative medium such as film, so one writes the music around the text to support it.[53] Preisner poured dedication into his work for "Piwnica." His output, he recalls, ranged from settings of official Party interviews about martial law (the cabaret was banned from performing during this period of the early 80s) to a song celebrating the statue of Marshall Koniev, the Red Army General who saved Kraków from Nazi destruction in 1945. It is a sign of the significant differences between Polish and Russian life under communism that such work was tolerated—so long, at least, as it was not popular enough to move the masses, as in the case of Father Popiełuszko's sermons. As Preisner has commented, not entirely in jest, "Can you imagine this in Russia? You would be on a train to Siberia the day after the concert."[54] "Piwnica" was riddled with informants, but their spying rarely seems to have caused undue alarm.

When working on his settings, Preisner would try out the first fruits of his efforts with students from the conservatoire, in order to tease out mistakes in his notation before rehearsals with the cabaret's professionals. This speaks to an admirable dedication not only to improve his basic technique as a composer and arranger, but also to continue, and in doing so respectfully uphold, the traditions and standards established by Konieczny, Skrzynecki and others. Preisner acknowledges both men as influences on his music and broader artistic outlook. It is worth briefly dwelling on the possible nature of this influence on his film career and music.

From the late 1960s, Konieczny became, like Komeda, a prominent film and television composer in Poland, to date scoring more than fifty features.[55] However, the Konieczny who influenced Preisner is the composer whose songs the young musician became immersed in after joining the cabaret.[56] One Konieczny standard, often performed by Demarcyzk, was the "Grande Valse Brilliante," which chews up the spirit of Chopin's Waltz in E flat major, Op. 18 in its setting of Tuwim's poem. The song subverts the Romantic musical rhetoric with a series of unexpected chromatic sequences, creating an aural disorientation that is wrested back, at each chorus, by a thumping re-arrival of the home key and waltz style. This play on conventions parallels the ravages of time on the protagonist's memory of a lost love, against which Tuwim's wounded hero rails. A play on musical expectations for symbolic ends goes further still in "Wiersze Baczyńskiego," which combines a wrong-footing loop of quasi-martial accompaniment, tripping up listener expectations of where phrases will end or begin, to create a dizzying minefield in and out of which the vocal line skips. The Baczyński verses come from two poems, one concerning a lung operation undergone by his wife, the other a visceral depiction of war's ravages on the body.

The spirit of both of these songs, welding together symbolic types to serve potent poetic ends, can be sensed in Preisner's first substantial film cue, the martial waltz underscoring the flight of the pensioners in *Weather Report* ("Prognoza pogody," Krauze, 1983) as they bail out of an old people's home in which, they have discovered, they will soon be permitted to freeze to death due to shortages.[57] Whether or not Preisner consciously modeled that cue on one or other of the Konieczny songs—as in the question of whether the haunting guitar theme of *Decalogue 6/A Short Film about Love* is derived from Konieczny's "Tomaszów"—is unimportant. Having breathed in the music of the cabaret with its smoke at such a formative stage in his musical career, one would expect to hear such echoes. Also, while Konieczny's harmonic daring (within the basically tonal confines of his song language) outstrips Preisner's more limited palette, his arrangements—scintillating and clear-cut textures of pure instrumental color, precisely scored for the clarity of a chamber ensemble—and wrong-footing approach to rhythm and phrasing have obvious equivalents in Preisner's scores. The elder composer's affectionate lampooning of musical traditions popular and elite (Chopin's flamboyance, for instance) have comparable moments in Preisner's film scores (such as the Chopin-like piano flourish which greets Karol's unceremonious dumping back onto Polish soil in *White*). Above all, however, there are settings which identify and amplify a key "concept" in the poems being set—the main aspect of settings at Piwnica, as discussed below, to influence Preisner's later work.[58]

For a more basic sense of the style of Preisner's cabaret work, one can turn to the film in which he appeared as a butcher, *The Last Schoolbell*, which follows the progress of a troupe of politically engaged Polish students confronting authority through their preparations to perform a *Piwnica* standard at a competition: a staging of Jacek Kaczmarski's "Lekcja historii" ("History Lecture," 1981). This multimedia extravaganza, seen and heard in the theatrical competition at the climax of the film, is integral to the story's dramatic and symbolic arcs. The piece begins with a synthesizer cluster playing over footage of the brutally suppressed 1970 riots over food prices in the Baltic ports; the strikes in 1980 in the Gdańsk shipyards; martial law's imposition in 1981. Kaczmarski's by turns propulsive and fragile song then begins. Action seeps between film and stage, and the students—dressed like ashen-faced renegades from a ghetto—are seen both on screen and "live," and crossing, for instance, between the parade in which one sees Preisner the butcher, axe in hand and wearing a garland of sausages, and the live performance. Needless to say, the troupe sweeps the boards with their performance, winning the popular vote, but angering the Party. Jacek, the singer-songwriter at the heart of the troupe's activities, is taken away by men in white coats after the show (he commits suicide); the troupe is forcibly disbanded by the authorities.

Preisner's sparse dramatic underscore in the film (there is less than ten seconds of music in the first twenty minutes, for instance) sensibly underplays its presence—a dab of romantically trembling strings here, a fierce cluster there, the latter as in his unsettling scoring of Jacek's death. This diverts attention to the musical set piece at the center of the narrative and is a tactic repeated in the Kieślowski films: the less music there is, the more the diegetically privileged musical moments stand out. There is also a blurring of diegesis and meta-diegesis (some of the action and music seem to play out in Jacek's mind) which, along with the placing of a musician at the center of the drama, makes it tempting to read Preisner's contributions to the film as anticipating his role in creating Julie in *Blue*. One might also start to wonder in what tone one might therefore take musical moments in the Kieślowski films such as the ending of *Blue* and its *Concert[o]*. As explored further below, if one encountered the *Concert[o]* on the stage of Piwnica pod Baranami, how might its sentiments—and with it, the film's meanings—diversify?

Preisner's most prominent cue in the film, however, takes the form of one of his own Piwnica songs, "Nadzieja" ("Hope"). This setting of a poem by Adam Asnyk, beseeching its addressees to find steadfast hope and courage, plays out over the final long shot of the film and the start of the end title credits. The surviving troupe members, in the back of a flatbed truck, are shot speeding through woodland and away from the brutal police intervention which broke up their gang. Shot in slightly slow motion, the youths are pictured from below, framed by sky and trees. The image has a dreamlike ambience as they speed towards an uncertain future; they are shown to bear wounds external and internal. Preisner's song, which forms an equally important voice at this moment in the film, adds to the uncanniness of the shot, and the lack of ambient sound becomes suddenly noticeable as the vocal is turned up on the soundtrack, severing this moment from the diegesis to float free as a symbol. That symbol turns the downbeat ending of the narrative towards hope. The melodic strength and optimism (the rising contour of its first three lines uses arpeggiated leaps) of Preisner's setting points towards something within the students (and, by extension, the audience) awakened by their experiences in the film. Its melody (see Ex. 1.5) is for the most part an *a cappella* rendition by female voice, shadowed in the later verses by a single line of piano harmonization in thirds and fourths, and has other typical Preisner qualities. It pivots on the flattened sixth scale degree in order to wring expressive knots from the music—a knot tied by the push into the major mode in the third line, only to be re-entangled by the descent back into a minor mode by the close of the verse. These two gestures link it to both the church song in *To Kill a Priest* and, more germane for the present study, to the Van den Budenmayer fragment Julie finds on the piano in *Blue*. The ability of Preisner's music to render affecting symbols from simple musical means, speaking of the characters but also to the audience, is one of his most impressive skills.

Ex. 1.5: "Nadzieja" melody from *The Last Schoolbell*

Skrzynecki, *No End*, and *Blue*

Skrzynecki's influence on Preisner was both philosophical and practical. Involvement with the cabaret's leader provided Preisner with an artistic father figure and formative influence which, with hindsight, molded Preisner in preparation for his personal and professional connection with Kieślowski a decade later. As personalities, the film director and Master of Ceremonies were poles apart, although they bear certain similarities. Both were lone wolves who had many friends, and each brought an outsider's perspective to the revelations of their art. One can imagine how losing Kieślowski and Skrzynecki in 1996 and 1997 respectively was a double body blow to Preisner.[59]

The Preisner-Kieślowski collaborations represent both the direct and indirect influence of Skrzynecki. As discussed above in the Introduction, and in more detail in Chapter Four, *Blue*'s pivotal *Concert[o]* sets an edited version of St. Paul's most famous letter (1 Corinthians 13) which Skrzynecki had long sought to persuade Preisner to set for the cabaret during the 1980s. More generally, however, Preisner credits Skrzynecki—who advised his troupe on how to analyze a text and reveal its inner workings—with teaching him "how to think analytically" and with philosophical conviction, and thus how "to analyze a movie and how to direct oneself musically" in that context. The scoring practice this led him to is, Preisner notes, different to contemporary scoring practices in Hollywood. From his work in the cabaret, Preisner developed a conviction that every film should have its own "concept"—a moral, symbolic or allegorical meaning beyond the telling of a captivating tale—and that everything in a film should contribute to the articulation of that concept (action, dialogue, editing, cinematography, music, etc.). As well as tutoring his colleagues in close reading, however, Skrzynecki advised a pragmatic approach to setting texts that more generally marks Preisner's scoring. Music should help the text (or rather its concept) to be revealed. When setting words this entails, most blatantly, bending phrasing, rhythm and meter to the demands of the poetry's phrasing.[60] This is one reason for the faltering rhythms and meters in Preisner's settings, which often change tack to provide more syllable-setting opportunities, but rarely use melisma. Preisner hereby developed a belief that music should not merely be illustrative of the textual surface, as those aspects of a text should be self-evident. Music, instead, should focus on revealing the concept of a text.

The connection between this approach and Preisner's aesthetic beliefs concerning how cues should contribute to film scenes—adding new information or revealing aspects not otherwise apparent in the discourse and thus aiding a film's articulation of its concept—is as obvious as it is important. It is fascinating, then, that the move from applying such ideas in the cabaret to articulating them for film seems to have been facilitated under Skrzynecki's guidance. The project in question was Kieślowski's *No End*. Preisner recalls the origins of the score: "It was my first collaboration [and] I was so ashamed. I thought this is my first and last work with this guy." Having seen the film only once at a screening in Warsaw, Preisner bought an expensive foreign tape recorder from a Pevex shop (a store in which luxury Western goods could be purchased with foreign currency).[61] Working with the screenplay, he then recorded all of the dialogue and dramatic instructions in an attempt to give him something against which to work: he was making, in other words, an audio version of the film ("She's walking. She opens the door. She closes the door. She is outside"). Preisner then tried to compose music around that guide vocal, working with a stopwatch.

That Preisner composed his first Kieślowski score in this way—not synchronized with the action, but floating somewhat independently thereof—anticipates a trademark of his scoring. Preisner's later work is typified by the degree of freedom he seeks from accentuating apparent aspects of a film's action in order to represent underlying concepts, as discussed further below. Its origins partly lay, however, in his happenstance solution to the lack of anything to go on (other than the screenplay and his memory of the film's emotional climate) when scoring *No End*. Yet the notion of "climate" is, in turn, the other foundation of Preisner's film scoring aesthetic, and it too links directly to the manner in which Skrzynecki inspired his completion of the score to *No End*. Preisner recalled for me how he felt embarrassed by his early efforts:

> I tried to convince Kieślowski that this film didn't need music. "Krzysztof, I don't feel music for this film. The silence works fantastically." He said, "Listen, I paid for you, not [just for you to] tell me that you find no music. You must find music!"

Preisner, stuck, went back to the cabaret to see his other mentor. Skrzynecki agreed to attend a new screening of the film for Preisner. Kieślowski refused to attend, fearing Skrzynecki would be very late; he was late. As Preisner tells the story:

> Piotr watched the film with me. He was sleeping . . . then he woke up. He said, "Zbigniew, it's easy. The music here must be like a Catholic ceremony and like a ghost. There is no music. . . . It has to be like a ghost."

The music in *No End* was thus designed to evoke the tradition of the open casket in the Polish home, surrounded by people singing as they mourn at the side of the body. This is the climate of *No End*: the music, like a ghost, haunts its bereaved protagonist and the audience's perceptions of her story. It was also, quite consciously, the climate Preisner and Kieślowski returned to ten years later in *Blue*, where Julie and our perceptions of her are haunted by precisely the same music: Preisner's funereal *cantus firmus*, derived from the Polish hymn "Holy God," forms an open casket in *Blue* that Julie must close before she can proceed with her grieving.

Twentieth-Century Polish Art Music

Preisner has distanced himself from the claim he has been influenced by Western art music; he told me "I have never really been inspired by classical music, but I like Górecki, Sibelius, Prokofiev." How ironic, therefore, that he has made his name, to an extent, on the back of cues aping the Romantic heritage of that tradition, and in those pieces "by" Van den Budenmayer and other fictional composers invented during the Kieślowski collaborations. The issue is further confused by the evolution of Preisner's compositional style post-Kieślowski, most notably on his solo albums, which fuse separate symbolic facets of his earlier scores into a single musical persona. In short, the degree of separation between, say, the neo-Romantic style of the "art music" in *Blue* and Preisner's more restrained "film music" cues in the same film becomes blurred in his later solo works. Because the styles of both Preisner's own voice and his "fictional" compositional personae can be considered against the backdrop of a series of Polish art music contexts, the present section examines what Preisner appears to have gleaned from the art music tradition in his homeland as he developed his musical voice.

The Polish New Wave

At one time, Preisner was publicly dismissive of the vibrant post-thaw art music scene in Poland—a scene every bit as colorful a triumph over ashen Communist dogma as the country's avant-garde cabaret and theater movements. He wrote it off with lofty proclamations like the following: "The times of dodecaphonic music of the 20th century, of the difficult music, has [sic] ended. What comes back is some kind of Romanticism."[62] Preisner may not be best placed to summarize a musical world to which he admits having relatively little sustained contact. His depiction of post-war art music, particularly in Poland, as a kind of serialist dystopia implies little knowledge of the sheer profusion of art music styles that were in existence in parallel within the tradition: for every Penderecki there is an Andrzej Panufnik, for every Witold Lutosławski an Aleksander Lasoń . Such comments are also misguided in the Polish context because serialism barely caught hold in the first place during the post-thaw years and, at any rate, was quickly subjugated as just one source of raw materials to fuel a resurgent avant-garde.

More recently, in fairness, Preisner has noted the strengths of Poland's art music culture, both in aesthetic and social terms: "In the Communist regime, music was the only thing that wasn't censored—how do you censor music? [It] can mean so many things to different people. That's why we have so much good music in Poland. I know at least thirty great composers working there."[63] And when one considers that some of the Polish art music Preisner admits to liking had emerged before he set pen to manuscript paper, the possibility of situating aspects of his film output in relation to such scores emerges. His debt to Penderecki's music, in particular, becomes more apparent.

Fig. 1.2 shows the title page of Preisner's handwritten score for *Blue*. Note the prominence given to the explanation of quartertones. One finds similar explanations at the front of countless Polish art music scores of the 1960s and thereafter. While relatively few composers in Poland explored systematically the possibilities opened up by scales made of quartertonal (or even microtonal) steps in place of the traditional (in many Western cultural communities) chromatic and modal harmonic systems, many have explored their expressive potential. A typical example of such practice would be beginning with a single "normal" pitch or harmony and then allowing, say, string instruments to

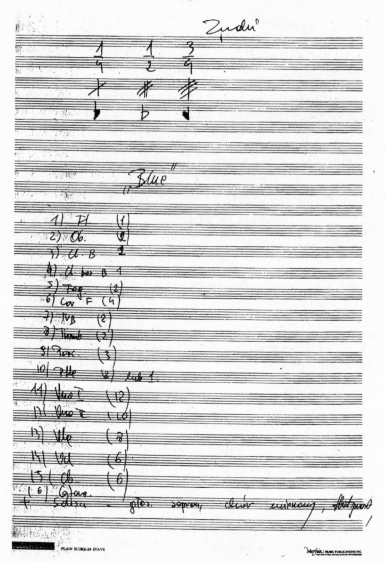

Fig. 1.2: First page of Preisner's score for *Blue*

slide to quartertones above or below those pitches, creating a shift from
focused musical sound to a pulsating band of energy exploring the
boundary between music and noise. This can sound like a cliché in
more than one musical world. Western cultures are conditioned, not
least by film music, to interpret the former as signifying "normal" and
the other as "abnormal," and it is no coincidence that this dualistic play
is familiar from countless horror and thriller scores. Furthermore, many
of those scores were composed (by, for instance, Jerry Goldsmith for
Richard Donner's 1976 film *The Omen*) under the direct influence of

experimental music by Poles including Penderecki, not least because of the use of fragments of Penderecki scores in *The Exorcist* (Friedkin, 1973) and later, much more extravagantly, in *The Shining* (Kubrick, 1980). Preisner makes use of such effects, too, and while he is a Polish composer, there is no reason to think he did not inherit these sounds just as much from Hollywood scoring practices as from sources closer to home. However, his use of these and other avant-garde techniques is arguably more sophisticated than composers who have utilized such sounds merely to sculpt shocks and experiences of suspense. Preisner had heard, first hand, their wider range of affective possibilities.

Preisner adapted his notational approach to quartertones and an allied adaptation of glissando (sliding from pitch to pitch without a break in an instrument's tone, thereby moving microtonally between pitches) from Polish scores. Proof that he did this following an inspection of certain scores comes in the layout of his cue sheets and his deployment of distinctive notational symbols. Fig. 1.3 shows a cue from *Red* in which an initial pitch is blurred by a trail of descending semitones. Sounds like these have several functions in *Red*, including (1) the denotation and connotation of tension (a stereotypical gesture, as noted above, in a wide range of scoring practices), (2) participating in a score-wide developmental process, and (3) evoking an aura of the metaphysical. The latter points suggest ways in which Preisner seeks to treat such sounds for more than just their ability to shock an audience.

Once he has scored a pitch (such as the high opening A in the first violins of the cue shown in Fig. 1.3), and rather than writing lots of other As after it and tying them back to the initial note, Preisner indicates with a line and an arrow the continuation of the pitch in the score. Once the full range of this cluster of pitches has been achieved (by the end of bar six), a thick line of solid black marker pen forms a meta-arrow indicating the continuation not of individual pitches but the entire block of sound. Note also how the second and third violin parts, which enter at bar seven, are not notated until they begin to play their angular melody. Finally, observe how the time signature, $\frac{6}{8}$, and expressive indications (placid, mysterious, without vibrato) are provided just once, above the system of staves at the start of the cue, rather than on each stave of music; the doubling of the second violins' high melody an octave below by the third violins is also indicated by an arrow and verbal instructions, rather than being fully notated, with the dynamics for both the second and third violins being indicated just once at the bottom of the entire system.

One might imagine how this economical approach to score writing would have appealed to Preisner's mindset. Through a mixture of his education, personality and aesthetic temperament, he seems to have been calibrated for maximum efficiency. Many film composers, furthermore, have developed forms of shorthand: the time-pressures of the job demand it.[64] In Poland, however, the conventions Preisner adopted originate in the scores of a composer with a similar interest in orderly

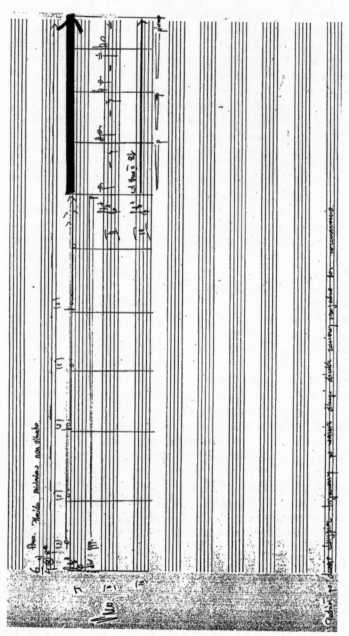

Fig. 1.3: Avant-garde notation in *Red*

restraint: Andrzej Panufnik (1914-91). As Thomas writes, "Panufnik was responsible for inventing the now universally acknowledged score layout where pages are left blank of all but the active playing parts,"[65] with scores arranged in this way dating back to his wartime *Tragic Overture* (premiered in 1948). The spread of this approach in Poland was due to its adoption, for economical and aesthetic reasons, as the in-house style of Polish state music publisher, Polskie Wydawnictwo Muzyczne (PWM). Preisner could have come across such conventions in many of the contemporary Polish scores he encountered in the 1970s and 80s. Penderecki's scores are nonetheless the most likely source for these devices.

For a time, Preisner was intensely interested in Penderecki's music. The men became friends, Preisner enjoying dinners at Penderecki's house outside Kraków with the composer and—rather crucially from the perspective of *Blue*'s inception, as explained later—his wife. Of Penderecki's earlier, more experimental scores, Preisner particularly admired the *St. Luke Passion* and *Utrenja* ("The Entombment," 1970). As well as adopting certain techniques and notional devices from these scores (including, alongside the glissandi, quartertones and cluster nota-tions, an upward-pointing arrowhead instructing performers to play the highest note possible), he sought to emulate the powerful orchestrations and tension generated by Penderecki's music. To Preisner's ears, these elements are interlinked: the music had a tension generated by the dia-logue between groups of musicians—much of the *St. Luke Passion* plays out as a bruising exchange between elements of its massed ranks—and also between stylistic elements, as avant-garde and older musical styles confront each other in the scores. Preisner seeks to inten-sify such effects when scoring by carefully recording his cues in a stu-dio, exploring opportunities for dialogue and instrumental coloring through the resources of stereo multi-channel mixing, as discussed be-low, for instance, in relation to certain cues in *Blue*.

In his Kieślowski scores, these elements take their place in his mu-sic's broader stylistic palette. Some of Preisner's earlier scores, how-ever, made attempts blatantly to mimic the Polish avant-garde. His first cue for *Weather Report* may begin in a style reminiscent of Koniec-zny's songs, yet it concludes with an extraordinary shift in style, which in turn shapes an important narrative symbol, as the music metamor-phoses into a wondrous sonority. As the sun rises and the motley band of escaping pensioners taste freedom, Preisner's cue is emancipated from traditional approaches to become a tingling, sonoristic heat haze. His score to *Lubie nietoperze* ("I Like Bats," Warchoł, 1986), in turn, orchestrates a symbolic opposition of sound-worlds. The extended techniques accompanying the vampiress's bat fancying, and other noc-turnal predilections, forms a stark contrast to the Konieczny-style chamber music whose plainly diatonic respectability satirically parallels the heroine's search for sanity in the sanatorium to which she retreats in an effort to be cured of the "belief" she is a vampire. (Spoiler alert: she really is a vampire.) Preisner's genre-bending score to this odd contribution to the vampire canon—an art-horror film also blending sexploitation and political allegory—provides an early example of his attempt to use such sonorities not merely for localized dramatic effects, but to represent narrative information otherwise unrepresented by the filmmakers. If neither sound-world entirely convinces in *Lubie nietoperze* —Preisner's avant-gardism lacks fluidity, his more conventional music lacks grace—his attempt to enrich the narrative through the design of his score remains admirable.

Neo-romanticism

The experimental side of Preisner's scores was gradually curtailed by his development as a composer; as he found his voice, these sounds found their place as a significant but specialist tool in his armory. Such a journey is hardly without parallel in the country's art music scene. Indeed, given his professed admiration of some contemporary Polish music, and especially Górecki, it is interesting to consider the possibility that Preisner is a borderline example of a broader trend: the Polish composers who found a way back to tradition in the 1970s and 80s, not least through an engagement with traditional Polish music, in the aftermath of a more experimental phase. Górecki's delicate and haunting *Three Pieces in Old Style* for strings (1963), for example, are all based around a traditional Polish hymn or anthem and couched in a modal language a far cry from the bulk of his work at the time, which was as avowedly experimental as any of his peers. They were an early indicator, though, of where he and others were heading: reconnecting, ears refreshed by experimentalism, to a once tainted musical past now ripe for revisiting. And Poland's folk music past was not the only tradition to which composers now returned:

> The terms "new tonality" and "new romanticism" were much bandied about at the time. Although not exclusive to Poland, of course, the epithets and associated trends arose as a delayed reaction against the complexities of total serialism imported from Darmstadt [site of a new music summer school and a major artistic and ideological centre for avant-garde music and thought in post-war Europe] and, more immediately, as a riposte to sonorism.[66]

The wave of Polish art music to which Preisner's scores might thus be linked, connected to and yet distinct from the return to folk music, is neo-romanticism.

Neo-romantic is a term, Jann Pasler writes, "used to refer to the return to emotional expression associated with 19th-century Romanticism," and since the 1970s it "has become synonymous with neoconservative post-modernism, especially in Germany, Austria and the USA," and thus music aiming for direct emotional appeal and a continuation of an earlier tradition (albeit sometimes with an apparent failure of awareness of the profound aesthetic questions raised by such anachronism), that has nonetheless, "[b]y pleasing the ear, using standard orchestral forces and writing operas and symphonies embodying this aesthetic . . . succeeded in attracting large audiences."[67] Penderecki is the archetypal Polish example of a composer who did not so much fashion a nuanced rapprochement between avant-gardism and earlier traditions as perform a breathtaking back flip into a late nineteenth-century idiom. By the time Stanley Kubrick used Penderecki to amplify the most abject moments in *The Shining*, the composer was, ironically, already rewriting his musical identity in the manner that has since permitted him to become a doyenne of conservative factions of the classical musical establishment at home and abroad. Most notable, in this regard, are his sequence of symphonies and oratorios such as *Seven Gates of Jerusalem* (1996) and *Credo* (1998). Another Polish neo-romantic is Eugeniusz Knapik, whose extraordinary *Up into the Silence* (1996-2000), a seventy-minute song cycle, is notable as much for its "embrace of a post-romantic idiom with which . . . [his Polish precursors] Karłowicz and Szymanowski would have identified" as its epic scale and expressive luxuriance (Thomas, 292-3). Within this neo-romantic stream, a succession of pieces including Wojciech Kilar's *Requiem for Father Kolbe* (1996) and Penderecki's *Credo* have developed, dealing with spiritual and sacred issues in an eminently approachable, if not forthrightly commercial, musical medium. Noting the dates of these pieces of the 1990s, one can envisage Preisner's *Requiem for My Friend* as a contribution to this canon.[68]

The most obvious Polish neo-romantic parallel to Preisner can be drawn with the concert music of the other prominent Polish film composer of the late twentieth century: Kilar (1932-), and not merely because Kilar scored Kieślowski's *Blind Chance* (1981). Kilar has sought to maintain an art music career alongside his work as a film composer, and in his art music a more conscious appropriation of vernacular music—compared, at least, to Preisner's absorption by cultural osmosis of traditional musics—was sparked by a desire to break away from modernist tenets.[69] Such appropriations can be heard in Kilar's film music, exemplified in efficient pastiches such as his restrained klezmer cues for *The Pianist* (Polański, 2002). He has also sought to engage with secular and sacred Polish musics in his concert works. This has led to a degree of controversy.

One critic has accused Kilar's neo-romantic turn of "cocking a proto-postmodern snoop at avant-garde conventions while creating a whole new set of his own . . . [including] regular rhythms, pulsating percussion, textural build-ups, dynamic contrasts, steady tempos, simplified gestural and harmonic language and easily assimilable motivic content."[70] This description of Kilar's neo-romantic grandiosity could not apply to most of Preisner's underscoring. Strikingly, however, this depiction of Kilar could be mapped almost directly onto Preisner's fictional musical personae. The possibility that the inspiration for Preisner's neo-romantic fictional personae came from closer to home than the Austro-Germanic canon is intriguing. That such music is typified by the style of recent Penderecki—a style Preisner vehemently dislikes—raises, in turn, further questions about the manner in which music like *Blue's Concert[o]* should be interpreted. To what degree do Preisner's neo-romantic avatars satirize a tradition he disdains?

Music in the Bloodstream of a Film

In magazine polls and interviews, Preisner usually lists his favorite film composers and scores as including Ennio Morricone for *The Mission* (Joffé, 1986), Vangelis for *Chariots of Fire* (Hudson, 1981), Michel Legrande for *Un homme et une femme* (Lelouch, 1966) and Nino Rota for the first two *Godfather* films (Coppola 1972/74); when asked to choose an absolute favorite, he has opted for Rota's *Godfather* scores. While it has proved difficult to get Preisner to divulge specific details concerning his sense of kinship with these works, when I asked him directly to name the best thing about these scores, he provided the following reply:

> They all seem to be born from the same source. Their music is in the bloodstream of the films they score. It is creative, metaphysical, narrative.

It is unclear whether the older scores listed above had a formative influence on Preisner's scoring practices or whether he has since felt a connection between his work and these composers. Certainly, there are superficial similarities. In the case of Morricone, for example, his prominent use of the recorder and female *vocalise* suggests a potential influence on Preisner's style (although the soaring melodies of Polish folk music and David Gilmour's guitar solos are equally plausible inspirations). As the above statement also connects to a body of comments Preisner has made about his intentions as a film composer, however, and link to central concerns in his scores for the Kieślowski films—the evocation of climates and concepts not entirely represented, and perhaps unable to be fully represented, by other parameters of a film's story-telling apparatus—those intentions are examined here. Consideration is then given to whether the above composers' music expresses similar aesthetic approaches to Preisner's conception of scoring, in order to situate Preisner's approach within a wider body of practice.

Metaphysics, Concept, Climate

Two representative Preisner statements concerning what he terms the metaphysics of film music read as follows:

For me, soundtrack music is absolute metaphysics. It is like blood rushing through the veins. You can hear it, you can feel it, but you just cannot see it directly. Ideal soundtrack music adds something which is not shown in the film but which is left to be guessed. It is some kind of complement.

To make music for a film is very easy. The question is why should we use music at all. The connection between the film and the music is completely metaphysical because you never see the music; you only feel it. . . . Most American films use a composer like John Williams, where there is music all the time to tell you what to think and how to feel. A bit of danger: some scary horns. A love scene: romantic strings. But the French writer Baudelaire was right when he said that the matter for the artist is not to describe what he sees, but what he feels. [71]

The topic of metaphysics is a recurring theme of Kieślowski studies and one to which this book returns below. It relates to the oeuvre's exploration of the possibility that, in Kieślowski's own words, the world "is not only bright lights, this hectic pace, the Coca-Cola with a straw, the new car. . . . Another truth exists. . . . Good or bad, I don't know, but something else."[72] As already hinted, Preisner's music often plays a vital, and sometimes primary, role in articulating moments where Kieślowski's films suggest something else touching the surface of reality. In the above comments, however, Preisner seems primarily to be working towards a definition of film music function. What Preisner says film music should and should not do to be "creative, metaphysical, narrative," and in order to deal with "feelings" in a certain way, is thus of particular interest.

Rather than arriving at the tail-end of a film project, Preisner prefers to score films where he has become involved early in the preproduction process, thereby having time to understand the "concept" in the film and to give his score a chance to "grow-up" (his term) in that context. While he does work with a copyist, partly to iron out any residual technical chinks in his technique from his auto-didactic training,[73] he prefers not to use the orchestrators offered to him in Hollywood. This is partly because, he says, "If you are cooking in the kitchen, you decide how many, what proportions, etc., or you ruin the soup." The soup, for Preisner, is the concept. From the perspective he developed with the guidance of Skrzynecki and then Kieślowski, every element of the filmic apparatus should connect logically to the conception of the director. If the director has a concept, an intellectual or symbolic idea that the movie is "composing out," the composer's task is to tune into that concept and channel it musically.

This study concerns three films in which that process contributed to a trilogy's critical and commercial success. One can understand it just as well, however, by considering a failed Preisner project. Parts of *Requiem for My Friend* originated in music Preisner had scored for *The Island of Dr. Moreau* (Frankenheimer, 1996). When he came onto the project, Preisner connected to original director Richard Stanley's concept for the film. Stanley wanted Preisner to add music that would make a sophisticated intellectual contribution to the storytelling. The music had to be about the birth of a contemporary God: a man who wants to create a new kind of humanity, like a fertility doctor, but also like a Hitler. What results in the story, Preisner thought, is a new religion—and that religion has to fall, because playing God always ends in disaster. The music needed to articulate this rise while foreshadowing its fall. Preisner thereby began to set the text of the apocalypse from the Bible, particularly the passages describing people metamorphosing into animals.

The real apocalypse, however, occurred in the production. While Preisner was on a mammoth plane journey to Australia to meet up with Stanley, the director was replaced by John Frankenheimer.[74] Preisner duly told him the idea for the score. Frankenheimer had a different vision for the film and another composer in mind (Gary Chang, who did eventually score the film), but they initially agreed to try working together. Preisner had just returned to America to finish the film score when he had a dream in which the recently deceased Kieślowski accompanied him to a screening of the finished movie. In the dream, Kieślowski stood up, midway through the film, and started to leave the theater. Preisner asked him why he was leaving. "This is a terrible film," Kieślowski told him: "Why are you composing music for this bullshit?" The next morning, Preisner contacted his agent and exercised the clause in his contract that permitted him to walk away from the project in the event of a change of director.[75] The already completed music was reimagined in the "Lacrimosa" of the *Requiem*. The experience of the abandoned project and Preisner's involvement in the early 1990s with other films lacking a concept (or in which producers and studio executives intervened to rewrite a director's vision) tapered Preisner's engagement with Hollywood.[76]

An aesthetic touchstone for Preisner is Charles Baudelaire's *Curiosités esthétiques* (1868). In particular, Preisner likes to quote from a long letter Baudelaire wrote to the editor of *La revue française* in 1859, in which he refuses a commission inviting him to write about the meaning of certain paintings. Preisner calls this fifty-page rejection letter a bible for all artists, thanks in part to its statement that "the art that is not noble is not necessary." Concepts must be present and, moreover, in Preisner's view, politically appropriate if he becomes involved in a film. Music should additively complement, rather than emptily complimenting, the other elements of a film. A score should not, therefore, tell the audience what to feel, but rather form an independent response to the story: an articulation of the composer's (and/or filmmaking team's) conception of a film or, if relevant, their emotional responses to a situation. Such notions of style and function speak to the artistic and institutional contexts in which Preisner developed as a cabaret and then film score composer—contexts which indicate reasons he has not fitted into the Hollywood system. On the other hand, whatever the innovative aspects of Preisner's scoring, his cues can scarcely be said to confront the audio-viewer in the manner of, say, Jean-Luc Godard's confrontational soundtracks.[77] Preisner's statements bring to mind what film theorists, following Eisenstein et al. (1928) in their pioneering statement on sound, describe as, at one extreme, Hollywood-style parallelism in which music accents that which is already represented, and an avant-garde alternative of counterpointing image and sound in which music represents something not already illustrated or, more profoundly, sparks new information through the stark disjunction of its significations with those of the remainder of a film. Preisner says:

> I hate stupid music. When the music only is telling the audience what is already visible, there is no use listening to it.[78]

Preisner is talking specifically here about "mickey-mousing" and music that closely (but rarely exactly) syncs to the action, e.g., scary horns for an already scary scene. "Parallel" scoring practices, in this view, add nothing to the film's equation of meaning, although they can of course intensify or otherwise amplify a sequence's affective qualities. In the alternative "contrapuntal" practice, at its most profound, the scoring's rip in the fabric of the discourse tears open an insight for the perceiver, confronting one with the torn halves of a broken reality, and provoking one somehow to piece them back together. Preisner's most ambitious scores are both less obvious and less radical, respectively, than either Hollywood parallelism or avant-garde counterpoint, and arguably attempt something more subtle and difficult to pull off: the formation of a somewhat independent narrating voice in a film.

A simple example of a Preisner score forming a novel contribution to a narrative can be heard in *Decalogue 5* and its extended version, *A Short Film about Killing*. "I wanted to underline the drama," Preisner has said of this film, which concerns an apparently motiveless young murderer, his actions and eventual execution, but "I wanted to focus [more] on this kid's dreams, in a psychological way."[79] To do this, Preisner responded, through a number of peculiarly sentimental piano cues in his score, to an aspect of the film that, in collaboration with Kieślowski, he had decided to emphasize in the narrative. Importantly, the score begins doing so before ideas explored later by other aspects of the film (which reveal, for instance, that the killer experienced a tragic loss that perverted his morality) clarify what the music has foreshadowed. Disturbingly, the film confronts the perceiver with the possibility of sympathy for an apparently motiveless killer long before his clinical execution draws more obvious pangs of compassion. Preisner's score therefore plays a vital role in structuring the film's polemic against any taking of life. The effectiveness of that polemic may be measured, in part, against the film's alleged role in the abolishment of the death penalty in Poland.[80]

Film Music Composers

Preisner's approach to *Decalogue 5* begins to suggest why Preisner appreciates, say, the athletes running in slow motion through the water's edge at the start of *Chariots of Fire*. They progress to the sound of Vangelis's main title theme, its slow-motion patter of electronic percussion evoking their footfalls, its piano theme their grace, beauty, the timelessness of memory and thus, simultaneously, the pain of life's fleeting moments of transcendence. It also begins to suggest why there may be a kinship between his work and, say, Rota's introduction of Michael's theme in *The Godfather*, first intoned at the climax of the murders he commits in Louis's restaurant—the ominous pallor of the brass proclamation and falling sequences foreshadowing everything one needs to know about the destination of the youngest Corleone. It is a truism that no reading of a film scene including music is complete without consideration of the score's distinctive contribution; some readings, though, will be more incomplete than others. These cues were created by composers whose music has a degree of independence permitted to them through a close collaborative relationship to a director. Their concomitant musical remit includes doing something other than closely synching score to narrative action.

Preisner's favored film composers also compose music that—to a degree because of its independence and prominence in a film—becomes individually memorable. This is partly due to the music's self-contained quality, partly to the fact that these cues stem from popular as much as art music traditions. The music Preisner most admires speaks plainly, which is not to say simplistically, in order to communicate information within a narrative, and also with an individual sense of musical style which helps to create an instantly recognizable "climate" for productions in which their music works with other parameters to articulate key "concepts." They are composers who have established a unique voice in this manner, who can (as Chapter Two explores further) be imported as a star-like presence into the films that they score, bringing with them a baggage of intertextually mediated associations of mood and meaning, and who have often played a significant creative role throughout the production of films on which they are engaged, rather than being drafted in to perform the last-minute heroics of composers scoring many Hollywood films. They are also primarily contributors to serious, but not elitist or extravagantly confrontational, works of film art, the institutions, financing of and audience for which permits this alternative model of scoring practice to flourish.

These scores also form part of a continuing scoring tradition, with important forebears ranging from the gramophones accompanying *Un chien andalou* (Buñuel, 1929), through Terrence Malick's compilation score for *Badlands* (1973), numerous Kubrick films and John Carpenter's self-composed score to *Halloween* (1978), and on to more recent examples such as *Das Leben der Anderen* (Henckel von Donnersmarck,

2006), scored by Gabriel Yared, *Children of Men* (Cuarón, 2006), with its original music by John Tavener and a compilation score of additional tracks including Penderecki's *Threnody for the Victims of Hiroshima*, and even passages of the Pixar animations *Finding Nemo* and *WALL-E* (Stanton, 2003 and 2008), both scored by Thomas Newman. Claiming a specifically European tradition of metaphysical scoring would thus be simplistic. The influence, however, of European art cinema on scoring practices that, in opposition to more traditional Hollywood models, seem (in Miguel Mera and David Burnand's words) "not so much about the representation of character or emotion, but about epitomizing a way of life or delineating an alternative fantasy vision for society"[81] may be a productive line of inquiry when dealing with music in the strand of non-Hollywood cinema (such as the late Kieślowski films) that, by exploring creative tensions between classical narrative filmmaking and avant-garde practices, seeks to intensify film's symbolic and storytelling potential, amplifying affect and symbolic impact.

One notable exploration of such scoring in this under-theorized area of film music is Richard Dyer's analysis of the work of Preisner's favorite film composer, Rota. Following Rota's own description of his attempt to write music "that keeps itself apart . . . that runs alongside the film and doesn't submit itself to it," thus expressing "above all the spirit of the film rather than the materiality of a succession of images" (a statement close to Preisner's aesthetic credo), Dyer identifies how Rota's music "carries on alongside the narrative, broadly in tune with it but not underscoring every minute action, gesture or shift in emotion à la [Max] Steiner."[82] This leads to music which "offers a perspective on [the narrative]" and "a kind of irony, but one that encourages attachment rather than detachment": music forming an affecting narrative adjunct, as it were, rather than disruption.[83] On the one hand, Dyer's identification of Rota's "side by side," non-Hollywood but also not avant-garde, approach to scoring feels immediately applicable to large quantities of art cinema scores as yet ill-served by theories addressing Hollywood and/or radically non-Hollywood practices. There is a great wealth of films, including Preisner's work for Kieślowski, in which scores float like oil on water, structuring a kaleidoscopic multiplicity of interacting agencies to generate meaning.

One could argue that "metaphysical" or "side-by-side" scoring forms a truly contrapuntal tradition of composing for film, albeit not in the disjunctive, montage-inspired sense of the Russian Formalists, but rather in the more musical sense of an independent voice contributing uniquely to a collective polyphonic texture. Such scoring may sometimes go "unheard" within the texture, as it accentuates more prominent voices and contributes to the collective harmonic effort; sometimes it might leap into the foreground, strike up the band and lead the dialogic discourse. Such scores do not challenge the vestiges of narrative cinema by tearing apart its illusions of reality; nor, though, are they a mere sop to more conventional approaches. They seek actively to enrich the nuanced layering of a film's narrative and symbolic information, and the affective impact of its delivery system. This is not to devalue alternative scoring practices, nor indeed critical readings thereof (which can of course locate representative connotations within ostensibly accentual practices). As Lawrence Kramer and others write in their foreword to a recent collection on film music, "the notion of music as representation includes the notion of music as accent because representation itself has accentual capabilities; representations can be forceful or subtle, restrained or exaggerated, involved or detached, and so on ad infinitum," arising "from the fluctuating interplay of narrative, image, and music in any and all combinations, including those in which narrative or image merely accent a musical statement."[84] At the climax of *Blue* this reversal is precisely what happens: images accent Preisner's music in the service of narrative, symbolism, affect, climate and concept. By the time of his Kieślowski collaborations, then, the influence of the traditions and experiences through which Preisner's musical development can be traced had led him to a point at which he could practice one of the most interesting forms of scoring to have emerged in recent cinema, thereby making his significant contribution to some of the finest films of the late twentieth century.[85]

CHAPTER TWO

PREISNER'S PRESENCE

In *Three Colors: Blue*, Zbigniew Preisner gives voice to a trio of fictional composers inspired by a fourth, the tersely expressive Van den Budenmayer. In the novel *Exit Ghost* (2007), Philip Roth gives voice to Nathan Zuckerman and further fictional authors impressed by another imaginary writer, E. I. Lonoff.[1] By almost Kieślowskian coincidence, Roth/Zuckerman's depiction of Lonoff's style describes prose with qualities similar to aspects of Preisner's finest music:

> [T]he narrow range of Lonoff's prose and the restricted scope of his interests and the unyielding restraint he employed, rather than collapsing inward a story's implications and diminishing its impact, produced instead the enigmatic reverberations of a gong, reverberations that left one marveling at how so much gravity and so much levity could be joined, in so small a space.[2]

Substitute "Preisner's music" for "Lonoff's prose" and one virtually has a thumbnail sketch of the composer's aesthetic and an evocation of how, within the context of a film's multi-authored texts, his contribution fashions "enigmatic reverberations" that leave one wondering how so little music can suggest so much.

In Chapter One, a number of musical points of origin for Preisner's style were identified, alongside influences on the formation of his aesthetic of restraint and his focus on creating scores capable of evoking, in the composer's terms, a "climate" and contribution to a film's articulation of its "concept." The functions performed by a composer's film music are intimately tied to its means of expression; the reverse, obviously, is also true. The present chapter therefore outlines the key stylistic features of Preisner's "narrow range" and "restricted scope," as expressed in the scores leading up to and including the *Three Colors* trilogy; a section is also devoted to the neo-romantic style of his fictional musical personae, including Van den Budenmayer.

Texts surveyed below are mostly limited to the period leading up to the *Trilogy* for the following reason. After the *Three Colors* films, which can be thought of as the peak of the first stylistic period in Preisner's output (his years of apprenticeship and early maturity), his fictional and personal voices have mingled more freely in his film scores, and especially in his solo works. It is still anticipated that the following guide to Preisner's style will be useful to readers seeking better to understand his music since 1994, including the albums *Requiem for My Friend* (1999) and *Silence, Night and Dreams* (2007), and also his more recent film scores. In these works, however, aside from the fluidity of interaction between his musical personae, there has also been an increase in his creative use of electronic instruments and the recording studio's resources; hear, for example, *It's All about Love* (Vinterberg, 2003) and *A Beautiful Country* (Moland, 2004). This may suggest the transition to a new style period. The present chapter's function is to set the scene for the ensuing analyses of the *Three Colors* scores and thus the first pinnacle in a scoring career that now spans twenty-five years and about fifty films. These are the works in which Preisner's compositional voice blossomed for the first time—they are the films and creative collaborations, indeed, which permitted that blossoming to occur—and, while Preisner's style has continued to evolve, these scores reveal the reliably constant features of his voice by the time he came to score the trilogy. What emerges, I hope, is an image of Preisner's presence.

Presence

John Ellis argues that the casting of star actors in a movie "provide[s] a foreknowledge of the fiction" to come; for Richard Dyer, a "star's presence in a film is a promise."[3] Actors can accrue, in the perception of filmgoers, a stable set of associations by consistently playing certain kinds of roles (think of Isabelle Huppert), by having a recurring on-screen persona (Jack Nicholson "doing Jack") or by becoming known for extra-filmic deeds that play into one's reading of the films they inhabit (such as Christian Bale's arrest for alleged assault in the week of *The Dark Knight*'s [Nolan, 2008] European premiere). Associations filter interpretations of a performer's films as part of a reception process beginning long before perceivers have experienced the latest text.

In the *Three Colors* trilogy, an obvious example of "presence" contributing to the films is Juliette Binoche's casting as Julie in *Blue*. Ginette Vincendeau has contrasted Binoche's filmic image to Beatrice Dalle and Sandrine Bonnaire, two other French actresses who emerged as stars in the 1980s. In doing so, Vincendeau incisively describes Binoche's presence:

> In comparison to Dalle's pop sexual persona (a throwback to [her role in *Betty Blue*]) and Bonnaire's earthy naturalism, Binoche's image is

cooler, more cerebral, more anguished. At the same time, her distinguishing characteristic is her ability to evoke, alongside the cool exterior, the intensity of passion. One key to her success is this play on surface and depth, which has turned her into an icon of neoromanticism. Another is her ability to shift between two feminine archetypes which seem to require French names: the *gamine* and the *femme fatale.*[4]

Cool, cerebral, anguished, playful, fatal, her surface repose masking darkness and passion: it reads like a summary of Julie. As Ellis leads one to note, however, one's knowledge of Binoche's presence inevitably colors one's reading of her individual performances. *Blue* is thus rendered cool, cerebral and anguished, for some audio-viewers, by the mere fact of Binoche's presence; her immaculate performance in *Blue*, in turn, further contributes to the formation of her onscreen persona.

Could the same be true of "star" composers? Can composers be heard to have a presence? A commercial imperative underpins such constructions. Casting a star like Binoche, who turned down *Jurassic Park* (Spielberg, 1993) to work on *Blue*, anchors not only audience expectations of content, but also studio expectations of revenue.[5] Whether or not the same is true of composers—and outside filmgoers with a specific interest in film music, it seems unlikely that many people choose to see a film merely because it features a score by a musician they admire[6]—composers are obviously "cast" by directors, producers, music supervisors and studios because their contribution can be expected to bring widely recognized qualities to a picture. One can easily think of examples where an actual star musician's presence lends a film a specific ambience: Sting's songs for Mike Figgis's *Leaving Las Vegas* (1995), for instance, or Miles Davis's contributions to Louis Malle's *Ascenseur pour l'échafaud* (1958). It could also be argued that the cultural cachet of certain directors (and even actors) has been amplified by the recurring presence in their films of music by a preferred collaborator: think of Alfred Hitchcock and Bernard Herrmann, Tim Burton (and Johnny Depp) and Danny Elfman, and, of course, Kieślowski and Preisner. How many traits commonly prized in Kieślowski's films, one might wonder, and considered benchmarks of his auteurist identity, are mediated—even generated—by the presence of Preisner's music?

If a composer can have a presence, gauging the most notable features of its impact on audiences is made easier, in the early twenty-first century, by the "instant reception history"[7] provided by online reviewers, fansite authors and bloggers. When a composer is contracted for a score, musical characteristics are anticipated that will fit well with other components of the filmmakers' vision for a production. Those characteristics will inflect the narrative for its audiences and provide, if not foreknowledge of its content (especially as a film's original score rarely features in its trailers), then at least a cue to the film's style, themes and content. Directors, producers and audience members—including many of the film music writers one reads on the Internet—do not tend to have an expert knowledge of film music theory to call upon when making such distinctions. Nor, on the whole, do they have a stock of what Philip Tagg calls "constructional competence" in general music theory to utilize, i.e., what pedagogues term, somewhat pejoratively to those without such knowledge, "musical literacy." Tagg's term relates to the minority of people who have been educated to a high enough level, usually in a Western art music context, to describe musical sounds and their theoretical functions within that art form's specialist terminology. Such a listener is capable of hearing a diminished seventh chord and observing that (a) this is a diminished seventh and (b) the next harmony heard will probably move towards a cadential resolution. Most of the time, however, listeners (including, actually, those who are "musically literate") primarily rely not on the abstract theoretical reflections permitted by "constructional competence" but on "receptional competence" to interpret, with "quick and dirty" immediacy,[8] the expressive connotations of music.

All listeners develop a "receptional" cultural knowledge concerning music's ability to signify, for instance, non-musical ideas (like varieties of emotion, nationalities or locations). In the case of a diminished seventh chord, especially when scored as a trembling sonority to provide a further layer of signification, listeners steeped in film know that this sound signifies moments of tension, just as in many other musical repertoires—such knowledge is intertextual and draws on the breadth of one's musical life. Further layers of expressive connotation will also be obvious to these listeners, as the musical style and gestures rendering individual realizations of such figures will, in turn, figure other kinds of affect and signification.

Tracking the "receptional denotators" used by Internet writers on film music—i.e., the visual and verbal associations their writing contains to evoke both the nature of musical sounds *or* their affects and connotations—offers a novel way to approximate the cut of a composer's presence and with it any contribution to the formation (in Michael Long's term) of one or more "expressive registers,"[9] as perceived by a wider community of filmgoers. In the context of the present study, analyzing terms used to describe Preisner's music within online discussions of his music provided intriguing results. On the one hand, the terms indicate manifest aspects of his musical presence, in terms of its most common emotional cues and other significations. On the other, if subjected to even a small amount of critical pressure, the terms reveal latent associations that listeners tend to make concerning his scoring—associations that, in turn, offer insights into perceptions of Kieślowski's cinema and the trilogy. Most intriguingly, Preisner's scores, and thus the Kieślowski's films in which they occur, are revealed to be saturated with commonly accepted semiotic and expressive marks of tenderness, sadness, expressivity, tragedy, the supernatural, otherness and—above all—the feminine.

Table 2.1 shows "receptional denotators" writers used to evoke affects and qualities of Preisner's music in a sample of online reviews.[10] Merely noting the recurring terms provides a rough sketch of Preisner's presence. His music *chills*, *enchants* and *touches* his listeners; they find it *attractive*, *beautiful*, *delicate*, *elegant*, *gentle*, *hesitant*, *interesting*, *intricate*, *minimalist*, *pastoral*, *romantic*, *sad*, *sensitive*, *somber* and *unusual*. Preisner, of course, rarely scores light-hearted movies: his preference for serious dramas dealing with major themes means that, where cast, his presence reflexively intensifies perceptions of such qualities in a film and its composer's scoring. Two theoretical approaches can nonetheless help to clarify the functionality of the "meta-climate" of Preisner's presence in a film: Patrick Juslin's studies of the signification of emotion in music and Tagg's work on the manifest purposes of screen music's signifying systems and their latent ideological functions. The former indicates Preisner's ability immediately to invoke certain kinds of emotional climate, the latter his skill at taking recognized scoring clichés and utilizing, or sometimes subverting, them to aid a film in its articulation of its concept.

Like a person's facial expressions and body language, music wordlessly communicates information indicating different emotional states. Juslin has demonstrated experimentally how "expressive cues" (his terminology, tantalizingly, parallels a key term in film scoring)[11] including "tempo, sound level, timing, intonation, articulation, timbre, vibrato, tone attacks, tone decays, and pauses" can be manipulated to signify the expression of strong emotions including tenderness (i.e., expressions of love), sadness, happiness, fear and anger:

> For example, sadness expressions are associated with slow tempo, low sound level, legato articulation, small articulation variability, slow tone attacks, and dull timbre, whereas happiness expressions are associated with fast tempo, high sound level, staccato articulation, large articulation variability, fast tone attacks, and bright timbre[.][12]

Surveying the receptional denotators used to describe Preisner's music, his scores appear to be dominated by sadness and tenderness expressions, rather than those for anger, fear or happiness. In turn, there are more similarities than differences between tragic and tender forms of expression, according to Juslin, including slow mean tempo, slow tone attacks, low sound levels, legato articulation, large timing variations, soft duration contrasts, slow tone attacks, and a final *ritardando* at the end of a phrase. Tenderness and sadness are differentiated, in turn, by sound level variability (small for tender, low for sadness), timbre (soft for tenderness, dull for sadness), and use of vibrato (a slow vibrato for sadness). Such fluctuations are subtle and one could imagine how film scores exploring a continuum between tenderness and sadness would

Atmospheric	Eloquent	Introspective	Romantic
Attractive	Enchanting	Introverted	Romantic
Attractive	Enchanting	Lovely	Romantics
Attractive	Enchanting	Minimal	(one
Balance(d)	Enjoyable	Minimalistic	for the)
Beautiful	Enjoyable	Minimalistic	Sad
Beautiful	Enthralling	Moody	Sad
Beautiful	Ethereal	Morose	Sadness
Beautiful	Far from	Moving	Sensitive
Beautiful	dreary	Mysterious	Sensitive
Captivating	Gentle	intrigue	Short
Charm	Gentle	(feeling of)	Simple
Chilling	Ghostly	Never run-of-	Slow
Chilling	Gorgeously	the-mill	Slow
Complex	recorded	Otherworldly	Somber
Complexity	Graceful	minimalism	Somber
Complicated	Haunting	Pared-down	Somberness
Crystal clear	Heart-	Particular	Sparse
Curious	warming	Pastoral	Spectral
Darker de-	Hesitant	Pastoral	Touching
spair	Hesitant	Perceptive	Touching
Dislocated	Highly dis-	Perfection	Tuneful
Eclectic	tinctive	(arranged to)	Understated
(wildly)	Highly memo-	Powerful	Unusual
Deep	rable	Precision	Unusual
Delicate	Imaginative	(utter)	Waves
Delicate	Immaculate	Pristine	(feels like)
Delicate	Interesting	Pure	
Delicate	Interesting	Refinement	
Depth	Intricate	Restful	
Elegant	Intricate	Rippling	
Elegant	Intricate		
Elegant	Intriguing		

Table 2.1: Receptional denotators used in sample of Preisner reviews

anchor its precise emotional connotations with narrative specificity in relation to its full audio-visual context—although, as Juslin notes, children as young as four are able to manipulate expressive cues musically to signify alternative emotions. Together, though, these different sets of expressive cues unite in an overarching emotional bracket.

Juslin states that the "single cue combination that was most expressive according to listeners had the following characteristics (cues in order of predictive strength): legato articulation, soft spectrum, slow tempo, high sound level, and slow tone attacks," so that "the most expressive cue combination was highly similar to the cue combination that expressed sadness and tenderness best."[13] By typically expressing sadness and tenderness, Preisner's style therefore signifies expressivity itself. Juslin observes that "the so-called 'separation calls' associated with social loss"—the cries that infants (and others) make when separated from their mothers (or other loved ones and objects) by factors ranging from a lost line of sight to actual bereavement—elicit "strong sympathetic responses in listeners,"[14] and he suggests that this may be why "listeners find performances with a sad expression particularly expressive."[15] Perhaps the fusion of tenderness and sadness cues, evocative of the loss of someone or something that is loved, gives such expressions their particular intensity. Many of the films Preisner has scored deal with the loss of those to whom a character feels especially tender, such as parents, children and partners. The majority of the protagonists who suffer such losses in his films are, in turn, women and children.

Some of these expressive cues have a basis in forms of vocal expression that appear to be cross-culturally wired into human behavior through evolutionary adaptations. Other cues are governed, Juslin notes, by cultural influences; cross-cultural expressive cues are also "modulated" through social experience.[16] Along this continuum of modification lies the shift from music's statistical cueing of strong basic emotions (expressive cueing) to its syntactical evocations of more complex emotions and other non-musical ideas (which one might term cultural cueing). Statistical changes, to oversimplify, alter the manner in which a melody, harmony or musical figure is presented, while syntactical alterations change the content of a melody, harmony or figure. Music's syntactical parameters (its cultural cues) are like a rudimentary sign language; its statistical elements (expressive cues) are more like body language. Tagg's work on screen music semiotics provides a productive framework for understanding the cultural cueing of generic musical figures within a given repertoire.

Grouping the terms from Table 2.1 into subsets suggests further nuances of Preisner's presence. For example:

Atmospheric, Chilling, Curious, Darker, Deep, Ethereal, Ghostly, Haunting, Intriguing, Moody, Morose, Mysterious intrigue, Otherworldly, Sad, Sadness, Somber, Spectral, Unusual

These words bear connotations of the occult, metaphysical, spiritual and supernatural, and also of the tragic—concepts that go hand in hand in many cultures, where death and its inevitability, obviously, lead many to speculate on the possibility of death's transcendence through magic, religion and the occult. They invoke the possibility of a metaphysical dimension above and beyond concrete reality. The role of such themes within films scored by Preisner, not least in the Kieślowski collaborations, hardly requires emphasis here: metaphysical possibilities are among the key concerns in *No End*, *The Decalogue*, *Véronique* and the *Three Colors* trilogy. Musical figures typical of Preisner's style that evoke such cueing are identified below.

Another grouping of the "receptional denotators" used by the online reviewers reveals the kinds of terms Tagg has revealed to be stereotypically, and somewhat problematically, regarded as musical markers of the feminine. For example:

> *Attractive, Beautiful, Captivating, Charm, Delicate, Elegant, Eloquent, Introspective, Intricate, Introverted, Graceful, Lovely, Pastoral, Romantic, Sad, Sensitive, Sparse*

Through a long process of social sedimentation, such terms have come to be associated with musical figures ("style topics") heard, typically, in association with non-musical significations of the feminine. As Tagg argues, "music—even without words or accompanying visuals—is capable of creating and communicating semantic fields of considerable ideological potential . . . manag[ing] to influence our attitudes towards such phenomena as male, female, nature, Native Americans, etc."[17] These musical codes do not simply work as a narrative short-hand in audio-visual texts, permitting culturally conditioned listeners access to crucial information that might otherwise take considerable filmic exposition. When musical sounds gain cultural currency as clichéd significations of, for instance, what women ideally are/should aspire to be— feminine equals attractive, beautiful and charming, say, or pastoral, romantic and sensitive—their deployment can be argued to shape and support systems of ideology that seek to subjugate women into prefabricated models of subjectivity which benefit, primarily, the male beneficiaries of sexist societal hegemonies. As Tagg has proven, there is also a link between musical qualities evoking the adjectives discussed above, such as the mournful and metaphysical denotators, and those evoking the stereotypes of the second subset: together they form a meta-signifier for "female subjectivity."

Tagg's well-known analytical comparisons of perceptions of television main title themes demonstrated how, according to the world of screen music semiotics,

> women are twice as likely as men to be associated with the outdoors;
> women are 7 times more likely than men to be related to seasons or the weather;
> women are 12 times more rural than men;
> women are 13 times more likely than men to be associated with quiet and calm;
> women are 25% more likely than men to be associated with love;
> women are never asocial and never carry weapons;
> women may often be sad, melancholic or nostalgic.[18]

Much of this is patently untrue; the rest is highly debatable. Many of the denotators used to describe Preisner's music, however, demonstrate how his music evokes similar ideas and draws on the traditions of screen music signification contributing to this situation. Tagg's experiment asked listeners to decide whether the theme tunes concerned either a male or female character, and then subjected to statistical analysis the receptional denotators test subjects invented to describe the contrasting musics. "Female" tunes were thus revealed, for instance, to be slower, more legato, more static and softer in timbre than their "male" counterparts; considering their musical characteristics alongside the visual and verbal associations made by listeners led Tagg, in turn, to hypothesize polarities of gender as expressed by mainstream screen scoring practices:

male	female	male	female	male	female
fast	slow	sudden	gradual	active	passive
dynamic	static	upwards	downwards	outwards	inwards
hard	soft	jagged	smooth	sharp	rounded
urban	rural	modern	old times	strong	weak

Table 2.2: Philip Tagg's hypothesized dualities of male-female scoring clichés

To observe that Preisner's music shares many of the qualities and associations Tagg found to be stereotypically representative of the feminine, however, is not to say that Preisner or his collaborators are sexist. Far from it. The key critical question concerns the specific uses to which Preisner and Kieślowski put such ideas. In particular, closely analyzing the ends to which Preisner's scoring articulates such significations—and more broadly the way he deploys his presence's "meta-climate" of femininity, expressivity, tenderness and sadness—leads me to suggest that such connotations have more typically been utilized, in his work, to advance an alternative, more progressive, political agenda.

Such thematic and symbolic concerns point to another (or an Other) realm of meaning in Kieślowski's films—concerns explored in contrary motion to those of mainstream narrative cinema. Films in the classical Hollywood tradition, for instance, teach perceivers to experience the realm of magic, feelings, emotions, intimations of mortality and the innocence of childhood, and so on, as being the concerns of a particular department of the human race. From *Sunrise* (Murnau, 1927) and *Now, Voyager!* (Rapper, 1942) to *The Witches of Eastwick* (Miller, 1987) and *Bridget Jones's Diary* (Maguire, 2001), these matters have been branded, by music and many other filmic devices, as "women's issues." Could the Preisner-Kieślowski films, by dealing with such concerns outside of their usual "box"—and, furthermore, saturating their narratives with further audio-visual intimations thereof, such as, alongside Preisner's music, the extravagant color-coding of the art design in the trilogy and its protagonists' lack of clear teleological goals—be argued to be an attempt to reclaim consideration of such matters for a different or more diverse audience, and for purposes other than the maintenance of a cultural status quo?

As Paul Coates has suggested, while one could read the predominantly female protagonists of the late Kieślowski films as imprinting "a
world whose negativity increasingly 'feminizes'—disempowers—us all
. . . it may also be deemed positive, with virtues culturally coded as
'feminine' . . . the right nostrum for many modern ills."[19] Alicja Helman goes further, arguing that the telos of Kieślowski's career can be
considered a move from the cool rationality of men to the sensitivity,
compassion and openness of women, with Valentine in *Red* the culmination of that process, "embodying ideal femininity":

> Kieślowski continually raises his estimate of the feminine dimension
> in nature and culture. The feminine is not viewed as a necessary or
> even valuable supplement to the masculine, but as an alternative to it.
> The world as women see and feel is a different one, with values that
> can also reveal themselves to a man, if only he divest himself of
> prejudices and admit new perceptions. In his last films, Kieślowski
> unequivocally shows women as those who "see" better, feel more
> deeply, and understand more fully, because they are better "equipped"
> to do so. They have a greater range of sensitivity, capacity for com-
> passion and ability to open themselves to others.[20]

One might feel Helman's take on male and female minds is too rigid,
but the points she and Coates make are revealing. Kieślowski's cinema
was increasingly "feminized," particularly during the late Preisner collaborations, and his "feminine turn," moreover, gathered momentum as
music became an increasingly prominent feature of the films. Preisner's
presence therefore provides both a prompt and support to this transition
in Kieślowski's cinema, and thus, moving beyond gendered readings,
towards the polemical thrust of his trilogy: the moral imperative to
be—in the face of everything in late modern society that compels one
to desire to be otherwise—sensitive, compassionate, kind to others, and
responsive to human needs beyond those of the selfish consumer.

Do a wider range of films and scores trope superficially sexist filmic conventions to challenge broader cinematic and societal conventions, utilizing the musical cues as a trigger announcing a shift into this
alternative "expressive register"? Films one might suggest in this context include Mike Leigh productions with Andrew Dickson's sparse
scoring for harps and strings, such as *Naked* (1993), with its depiction
of masculinity in crisis; the introspective and mournful music of Gustavo Santaolalla in Alejandro González Iñárritu's films or Ang Lee's
Brokeback Mountain (2005); the fragile heart of *Million Dollar Baby*
(2004) evoked by Clint Eastwood's cues for acoustic guitar; the delicate
piano tracery of Thomas Newman's themes for the nuanced identities
of the male protagonists of *The Shawshank Redemption* (Darabont,
1994) and *American Beauty* (Mendes, 1999). These sounds, like many
of Preisner's Kieślowski cues, could be argued to demarcate fictive
spaces for contestation. They subvert stereotypical musical signifiers to
assert a universality of concern with "othered" realms of experience,
opening them to people of diverse ages, nationalities, genders and sexu-

alities in the service of non-mainstream visions of humanity. This is one way in which European art cinema scoring sometimes tries to epitomize a different way of life, delineating fantasy, but not fantastical, visions of society by adopting an alternative approach to Hollywood scoring. That so much of Preisner's presence is derived stylistically, as charted in Chapter One, from his absorption of Polish musical influences only intensifies its potential to express difference and otherness; that so much of his presence can in turn be associated with "love" (through its expressive cueing of tenderness) renders it potently apt in films, such as the *Three Colors* trilogy or *It's All about Love*, reexamining aspects of that multifaceted concept.

Preisner's scores fulfill such functions, in part, through his presence's announcement of their intention to do so. Clichés are troped, opening a realm of expectations within which the same clichés are then examined and rewritten through the telling of stories about characters removed from mainstream cinematic conventions. This is not to say that the Kieślowski collaborations are, say, barn-storming feminist or anti-capitalist tracts. Indeed, the musical moments which can at first seem most subversive—such as Julie seizing control of the *Concert[o]* score and thus soundtrack in *Blue*—may ultimately yield to a more problematic and pessimistic perspective. But the scores and films do attempt to address the concerns of subjectivities more usually constrained, in film and in life, by cultural cliché. When they succeed, they become potentially transformative experiences for the audiences experiencing their alternative perspectives.

What musical parameters, then, are manipulated by Preisner to intimate his presence? The following sections explore the "constructional" foundations of the "receptional" architecture outlined above, noting ways in which Preisner's musical background filters into the most typical gestures of his music, in part by considering specific cues composed in the run-up to, but also within, the *Three Colors* trilogy. While not seeking exhaustively to pin down every "receptional denotator" associated with Preisner's style, what follows seeks to support the argument that Preisner's music has a presence created by his career's triangulation of musical background, scoring approach and choice of collaborations.

Silence and Sparseness

Preisner's absence, paradoxically, is a signifier of his presence. At a macrorhythmic level, his individual cues tend to be widely spaced across a film's narrative. While he says "I don't measure the music, it's only the function that's important," so that "[s]ometimes the score is 50 minutes, and in the next film, maybe 10,"[21] one would never expect a Preisner-scored film to have a nearly continuous soundtrack. This partly relates to the institutional contexts in which he tends to work: in place of the hyperexplicity of Hollywood films with continuous dramatic underscoring, one encounters a sparseness of music marking the film "Not-by-Hollywood" and thus flagging up its potentially alternative agenda, not least as art first, commerce later. But it is also an issue of personal aesthetics and compositional ability, and the novel poetics of film music that can develop in collaborations open to the unconventional. In this regard, Preisner's comments on Kieślowski's main demand for a film score is revealing: "Krzysztof always told me, 'I'm not a musician but I want music which I can breathe after,' so I tried to write music which has this sense of ease."[22] So central is this notion to Preisner's aesthetic that he has since co-opted these words as his own: "I like it when the music is breathing, and that is the most characteristic quality of my music."[23] This stylistic tenet has also been reflected in critical writing on the composer, as in Jon Paxman's discussion of how the timbre of the acoustic guitar central to *Red*'s score—strings plucked or strummed, and then reverberating while fading into silence—leads to "music that breathes, pauses, and encourages us to feel a depth of sensitivity and reflection that does not exist simply within the visual context."[24]

Not suffocating a film beneath a wall-to-wall carpet of underscoring is one way to let it breathe. Preisner extends his approach, however, to the structuring of individual cues: rests and pauses introduce breathing spaces at the microrhythmic level; he orchestrates cues in a manner creating "vertical" spaces within their sonorities; his use of reverb, delay and other studio effects creates a sense of a huge space within which his music's sounds are heard.[25] Rests breaking up the linear continuity of his cues, careful orchestrations creating an inner sparseness to his sound, and reverb adding depth of musical field are further elements shaping the spaciousness of Preisner's music. His approach to orchestration and use of reverb are discussed in later sections. The following discussion examines ways in which Preisner uses sparseness, rests and silences to inflect a film's meanings.

Examples of Preisner's wide spacing of cues are easy to find. *Decalogue* is rich in examples. For instance, after the opening cue of *1* (discussed in more detail below), more than fifteen minutes pass before music is heard again; in *2*, almost fifteen minutes pass before music is heard at all. It is notable, though, that his two earliest films, *Weather Report* and *No End*—films that became source books for Preisner in terms of key aesthetic and stylistic elements, but also, in *No End*'s case, of raw materials to be reused in later scores—already contain this trait. *No End* contains a fascinating example of sparseness and the manner in which music that "breathes" can encourage one to feel and reflect upon things not otherwise implied by a film's discourse. As Ula frantically searches her home for photographic hints of her dead husband's increasingly enigmatic past dealings, a pair of fast, high and rising notes in the violins ring out (see Ex. 2.1).

Ex. 2.1: Widely spaced gestures in *No End*

The first two notes most obviously connote Ula's inner panic, as her presumed knowledge of Antek and thus of herself fragments. The strong emotion is signified through expressive cueing (cues for fear include staccato articulation, large sound variability, fast mean tempo, large timing variations and fast, shallow or irregular vibrato) and also through the cultural cueing of style topics (think of the shower scene in *Psycho*). They also create an uncanny effect thanks to their sheer isolation. No further music occurs—until, that is, the gesture repeats about sixteen second later. An ostinato in the cellos then begins, marking time more conventionally, and a thematic development unfolds. Up until that point, the juxtaposition of a sudden burst of frightening music and a pronounced lack thereof has created an unsettling experience: like Ula, perceivers may experience a pang of panic at music's prolonged absence, as one expects continuation. Emotional responses are triggered, music theorists and psychologists concur, when something expected fails to happen or is delayed. As Leonard Meyer explained it, "[a]ffect or emotion-felt is aroused when an expectation—a tendency to respond—activated by the musical stimulus situation, is temporarily inhibited or permanently blocked."[26] Within Preisner's tense silences, however, one can also reflect on what has occurred. In turn, this may intensify the emotional experience. One might invest *No End*'s spaces, for instance, with anxieties for Ula, or *Blue*'s blackouts and ellipses with empathy for Julie. An experiential conduit is thereby formed, the perceivers' immediate and more reflective emotional experiences becoming proximate to the experiences of a protagonist.[27]

The cue from *No End* blurs the border between widely spaced yet separate cues and the other type of musical breathing Preisner introduces, both between and within the phrases of his scoring, by means of rests and pauses. The spaces within *Weather Report*'s most striking cue make the music sound, retrospectively, entirely Preisner-like; arguably, this was the cue in which he found his voice on film. Yet they also make a key contribution to the film's most poetic and moving sequence. There are pauses between phrases during which, again, the audio-viewer has time to feel suspense and reflect on the meanings of the scene. The escaping OAPs, some high on heroin following an encounter with a hippie commune, are floating in boats on a mist-shrouded river. The symbolism of these images is enticing. Aside from the obvious association of a Styx-like passage to the afterlife, the stoic grace and beauty of their weathered faces is a thing to behold. Preisner's cue consists of two elements: a high mist of string harmonics, looping like a Mellotron chord, and beneath it, scored for what sounds like a plucked violin and a dulcimer (a combination heard in Polish traditional music), a bewitching melody. Plaintive and faltering, it develops by transposition and subtle changes to the patterns formed by the interlocking melodies of its instrumentation.

Spaces are evoked in at least four ways. First, there is the registral space between the high string harmonics and the melody, the latter scored in mid-register; second, there is an evocative friction between the A♭ triad in the harmonics and the exploration of a melody rooted in C minor, with the sustaining Gs in the melody, in particular, rubbing up against the A♭s (Preisner's favorite intervallic tension, 5̂-♭6̂); third, the melody's pitches, once struck or plucked, resonate then fade; fourth, there are extended pauses between the already rhythmically faltering melodic phrases (see Ex. 2.2). Most compositionally intriguing is the close of the cue, where the rests within the melodic phrases themselves start to expand and the tune becomes atomized. One or two pitches at a time, fret work and figuration embellish the melody, but simultaneously the melodic phrases float apart, like a boat slipping its mooring. The increasing spaces heighten tension; they also permit the audio-viewer to attend to other aspects of the scene (such as the close-ups). The score evokes a sense of magic, fragility and sadness; more strongly interpreted, one might hear the increasing musical spaces as a symbol of freedoms being attained by the ageing fugitives.

Ex. 2.2: Melody on the lake from *Weather Report*

Antek's opening monologue in *No End* ("I died four days ago") is sculpted by Preisner's cue to sound like a recitative. Developing out of the initial statement of the "Holy God" *cantus firmus* during the film's opening, the somber continuation of the cue for low brass makes space for his speech registrally, literally scoring under his tenor, and through Preisner's use of long rests. The composer's faltering melody—limping along with a ratio of two parts music, one part silence that *Blue* will revisit—accommodates, and thus accentuates, the dead man's monologue. This is a personal version of a solution many composers for film have developed: making space for voices in the manner of a recitative and by not blending, say, male voices with mid-register instruments where the frequencies of their pitches might mask one another. The style of the cue also reminds one, however, that this kind of monodic unison, sung in octaves and separated by reverberant rests, is similar to the religious songs Preisner heard in the churches of his youth.

When the same melody returns in *Blue* as that film's funeral march, the gaps resonate with loss in other ways, not least when visually amplified by Julie's blackouts—visuals that pause with the music in an extreme intensification of this practice. *White* and *Red* contain other examples, however, such as Karol's peasant theme (see Ex. 6.1), the rests within which remind one that, alongside popular devotional music from Poland, its secular folk musicians also play on meter in unpredictable ways. Similarly, *Red*'s return to the Van den Budenmayer song first heard in *Decalogue 9* contains extra beats of rest at the end of each bar (see Ex. 7.4), subtly disrupting the metrical flow into a jagged edge mirroring the shards of broken glass on which the camera alights, encouraging one to consider their combined intimations of fragmentation and loss.

When asked by journalists why he includes so many silences in his music, Preisner likes to joke that he uses them to call his agents and check his accounts. Speaking to me in more serious vein, he explained his debt to Christian mystic and philosopher Simone Weil, who wrote that "[t]he central point of music is the silence which separates a rising from a falling movement," a combination leading to a "spiritual rising" and "the paradise for which every soul yearns."[28] Elsewhere she writes as follows: "The cry of the Christ and the silence of the Father together make the supreme harmony, that harmony of which all music is but an imitation. . . . The whole universe . . . is only the vibration of that harmony."[29] A key inspiration of her musings, in Preisner's reading thereof, was the notion that silence can be powerful but must be carefully prepared and then succeeded. It is also a matter of the proportion between musical elements, and then between music and other aspects of a filmic discourse. If every moment is scored, there can be no sense of foreground and background: no perspective. Intriguingly, given Weil's motivations for her interest in silence, reflections on the meanings of Preisner's silences in the literature also take a religious turn.[30]

Discussing the prominence of reverb in Preisner's music, Paxman suggests that, in *Red*, "the pervasive reverb . . . suggests the resonances associated with religious buildings, such as churches and temples, and it consequently helps assert the mysterious, metaphysical undertones of both the musical themes and the subject matter itself."[31] For Srajan

Ebaen, "[a] certain minimalism and precision of expression" in his
scores "[turns] feelings inward into deeper, emptier realms of perception where one encounters the presence of holiness, spirit and seren-
ity."[32] Ebaen then compares Preisner's sound to the spiritual and musical spaces shaped within Jan Garbarek and the Hilliard Ensemble's
fusion of plainsong and jazz improvisation on the album *Officium*
(ECM, 1994). Most intriguingly, Audrey Ekdahl Davidson links Preisner's control of time in his music to Messiaen, Górecki, Pärt, Tavener
and other composers since 1900 who have manipulated music's temporal dimension to explore spiritual and religious themes. The result is
music, as she puts it, which rejects "the modern pressure of time . . . in
a way returning to an essentially medieval sense of the temporal, which
held that time is contained within eternity and is dependent on God at
every moment." Her analysis of Messiaen's striving to "create a music
that takes the listener into a realm of the imagination beyond the usual
considerations of time as he or she encounters them in the workaday
world" seems particularly apposite when considering Preisner in the
context of his metaphysically inclined collaborations with Kieślowski.[33]
The spaces formed between and within the cues of a Preisner score may
not have pretences to the eternal, but they do fashion, in a sense, the
sonic architecture of chapel-like spaces within a narrative. Preisner is
continuously building moments within which the perceiver might take
refuge and reflect on what one has seen and heard, rather than rushing
headlong into the next haze of meaning. The experience of hearing music reverberating in the sacred spaces of his youth leaves an imprint on
film scores that open the possibility of a similar experience of reflection, mystery and perhaps even enlightenment for the audio-viewer. In
turn, this contributes musically to one of the most intriguing Kieślowski
projects: his construction of a site for serious spiritual reflection in the
cinema.

Melody and Monody

One leaves the cinema after experiencing a film scored by Preisner,
according to Tobias Wollermann, "with a melody by Preisner on one's
lips."[34] For John Walters, his melodies are "as insinuating as nursery
rhymes" yet "performed with the dignity of ancient anthems."[35] These
qualities stem from the way in which the melodies are spun, like the
threads of a spider's web, from a single material. Preisner unfurls his
melodies as developing variations on an initial motif, with each phrase
subtly reformulating the basic materials of its predecessor. This means
that a melody's meme-like motifs become imprinted on one's memory,
like a pop song's hooks, without becoming redundantly repetitive. An
example is the *cantus firmus* in *No End*, which turns the basic pitch
content of "Holy God" into an incrementally evolving melodic puzzle.

While the "digestibility of Preisner's music has obviously helped it sell in large numbers all over the world,"[36] the memorability of his tunes also lends them a precious quality in film narratives. His basic musical ideas quickly lodge in one's mind, so that when they recur in new variations thereafter, they can inform the listener of changing situations by encouraging one to read the latest passage of a film in the context of another. This is an obvious and conventional thematic function of film music, but it is to Preisner's credit that he seldom uses his melodies "stupidly," as he would term it—i.e., merely to indicate, in the manner of a classical Hollywood leitmotif, that Julie is onscreen, or that someone is thinking about Karol.[37] An exception that proves the rule is his family theme for *When a Man Loves a Woman* (Mandoki, 1994), which remains constant in the midst of a drama in which everything else fragments around a mother's alcoholism, thereby constantly reiterating the core of the film: the family's all-transcendent belief in itself. That recurring leitmotif, as such, expresses Preisner's evocation of the concept of the film: their center, in spite of everything, will continue to hold. More typically, however, Preisner's themes take on a wealth of symbolic information beyond referring to people, places or events "in a manner analogous to proper names in language."[38] Their independent developments and interactions with other filmic elements also signify layers of novel connotation and denotation in a film.

A number of recurring melodic traits may be deduced by surveying a range of Preisner's melodies. In a film, they may take on a unique symbolic significance; outside of a specific narrative's significations, they indicate further ways in which his style and presence translate traces of his musical background. One thread, running from *No End* to *Blue* via the church song in *To Kill a Priest*, and beyond that to the "Amore" cue in *It's All about Love* and even "To Know" from *Silence, Night and Dreams*, is the evocation of plainsong and the monodic hymns of Polish popular traditions. Religious chants can repeat a note many times, with pitches above and below the axial note functioning as expressive ornamentation; such melodies are often unaccompanied and sung in unison by many voices. Preisner cues are often melodies "hinging" on a single pitch. The constant stress of the repeated notes connotes insistence and a longing for release brokered by subsequent cadences. It also evokes religious songs via the sound's style topical associations, bringing some of the spiritual resonance of Preisner's presence into being. This can be the case whether melodies are instrumental or sung. The main theme of *Decalogue 8* begins as a solo violin melody; it is then harmonized simply, at the distance of a third, by a second violin. Both versions sound like a church song (see Ex. 2.3).

The religious heritage sounds even more clearly when human voices sing Preisner's melodies. Sometimes he consciously plays on this effect, for instance in *Blue* and *Véronique*, where cues need to evoke the experience of congregational singing and to shape, for the audience, an enveloping collectivity of experience intensifying, in each

Ex. 2.3: Melody and harmonization from *Decalogue 8*

case, aspects of the narrative and its symbolism. This can be heard and seen in its purest form in *To Kill a Priest*, but is evoked in Weronika's fatal performance, and also at *Blue*'s climax. Ex. 2.4 shows the melody from *Véronique*'s Van den Budenmayer Concerto in D Minor, which is scored for soprano and strings (piano and mixed choir pad out the background harmonies), in a monody quintupled across five octaves. That one knows this tune already—it has been heard in various guises before coming to fruition here as part of Van den Budenmayer's oratorio-like Concerto—means that, as the lines sway in unison, one feels compelled to join in, syncing oneself to the fateful momentum of the story. This emulates the metaphysical charge of these moments in the film: audience linked to film, voices linked to voices, Weronika's soul departing and Véronique feeling its departure, bonds being forged. In a film about doublings and connections, this particular instance of "unisonance" (a concept discussed more fully in the *Blue* analysis below) has a remarkably apposite quality. Experientially, it is also a glimpse of what Weronika and Véronique share: a connection.

Ex. 2.4: Unison melody from *Véronique*'s Concerto in D Minor

The opening of the *Véronique* Concerto includes another recurring trait of Preisner's tunes: proceeding from one note to the next by step or small intervallic leaps. Examples abound, but *Decalogue 6*'s theme is a particularly rich example of this kind of scale-like construction and the manner in which Preisner's melodies evolve by cellular variation (Ex.

2.5). The restlessness of the melody is amplified by the faltering five-bar, three- and four-bar phrasing, and by the harmonic settings through which the pattern is refracted (F♯ minor, then B minor, later D major, etc.): if the music is symbolic of some kind of love, it is one in which any sense of grounding is constantly undermined, evoking both romantic love's giddiness but also the sense in which, in *Decalogue 6*, different views of that love's reality depose one another by the end of the story. Within the tune's phrases, many of the rising and falling patterns explore a span of a minor third. The prototypical Preisner melodic gesture here is the descent through the lowest three notes of a minor scale—a fixture from the opening of *Weather Report*'s march-waltz, via *Blue*'s funeral march, through to "To Know" in *Silence, Night and Dreams*. Contrasting the emotional connotations of such tunes to alternatives like the bolero in *Red*—where, less typically, wider leaps abound and the melody has a less predictable pattern—is informative: one set is imbued with solemnity, the other ebullient hope. The contrast is sometimes evoked by Preisner within one piece. In "To Know," the dialectic between the penitent choir and Teresa Salguiero's rhapsodic solo spans the melodic range of Preisner's style.

Ex. 2.5: Cellular scale fragments from *Decalogue 6*

Injecting anguish into many of Preisner's melodies, another recurring characteristic is a fluctuation between the flattened sixth degree of a minor scale and the fifth. The *locus classicus* of this sound is *Decalogue 1*'s recorder melody, where the anguish is further intensified by qualities of Jacek Ostaszewski's recorder playing discussed further below. *Decalogue 1* explores the fragility of boundaries between stark oppositions: ice and water, good decisions and bad, fate and will, faith and reason, and ultimately life and death. These are dramatized in Kieślowski's heartrending story (a boy drowns in a pond after skating on ice that his father's calculations have "proven" safe) and symbolized visually throughout the film (as when ink blots seep into white paper, or a computer cursor blinks against the darkness of a screen). Nowhere, however, is the concept more affectingly evoked than in Preisner's repetitive exploration of this plangent intervallic pivot. The soundtrack to *Weiser* repeats the trick, rescoring the gesture for muted trumpet; indeed, once one knows it is a Preisner trademark, one hears it every-where in his music. Sometimes, however, the turning point functions as an expressive target for a melody—a crux through which a melody must pass, as in the "Church Song" from *To Kill a Priest* and the Van den Budenmayer memento theme in *Blue*. On such occasions, the music's passage beyond the turn can bear narrative significance.

These melodic gestures all occur within the scale Wollermann labels the "gypsy minor scale" in Preisner's music and calls the "epitome of Slavic music."[39] Putting aside this rather sweeping gloss on the complexities of modal practice in Central European and Eastern European musics, it is debatable if, outside of a few examples such as Karol's peasant theme, this minor scale is more central to Preisner's practice than two other modes: the Phrygian and the Aeolian. A number of Preisner tunes explore the initial chromatic semitone of the Phrygian mode, most notably the bolero in *Red*. There, however, the harmony combines with the generic setting of the dance form to suggest Spanishness, not via a reference to actual traditional Spanish music, but rather to other musical evocations of Spain as an exotic realm (as in *Carmen*, Ravel's *Bolero*, etc.). This signification of otherness further invokes realms of the feminine, erotic, mysteriousness and magical that are key to *Red*'s narrative concerns, but every bit as interesting, compositionally, is the manner in which Preisner's score teases out the semitonal twist in his theme. It gradually releases a nexus of darkness that gathers, like *Red*'s climactic storm clouds, around the discourse of the film.

The fact that these scales form the melodic-harmonic bedrock of Preisner's musical language—alongside, of course, the Aeolian mode, the minor mode for a vast range of Western popular music in which the leading note is distinctively flattened—can perhaps be linked back to his studies of Rimsky-Korsakov's *Practical Manual of Harmony*. Section 1.9 of the manual considers just two minor modes as the correct ways of constructing minor key music: the "natural minor mode" (Aeolian) and "harmonic minor mode" (Wollermann's "Slavic" mode). More basically, the sheer amount of time Preisner's scores spend in minor keys—save for the sunnier moments in *Red*'s bolero, every single cue in the *Three Colors* trilogy is in a minor mode—implies the core contribution to his presence of this basic musical evocation of the tragic. His music is encouraged to stay in the minor modes by the subject matters of the films he scores; the way he scores those films encourages his employment to score other tragic films. Through such Catch-22s is a film composer's presence formed.

Harmony and Homophony

When harmony occurs in Preisner's music, it usually articulates the minor modes mentioned above. The musical textures doing that articulating, in turn, are mostly homophonic. Homophony takes two forms: textures dividing clearly into melody and accompaniment, and "homorhythmic" textures in which each voice moves in the same rhythm. Simple examples include the tango from *White* (melody plus accompaniment) and the start of the *Concert[o]* in *Blue* (homorhythmic texture in two parts), although it is worth noting that Preisner's melody-plus-accompaniment homophonies are often tripartite in conception: melody, harmonic filler and bass. This suggests a further relationship between his scoring style and musical background. Preisner's immersion in popular traditions, as opposed to art music, means that his harmonic lingua franca is homophonic rather than polyphonic. The ostensible simplicity of homophony, as opposed to polyphony, is also a way in which Preisner maintains the sparseness of his presence: his attempts to write music that breathes are rarely contrapuntal.

There is another way in which Preisner's control of harmony and texture evokes repose. In tonal polyphonic music, the aggregate harmonies and individual lines move forwards by conventions which lend pieces, for listeners used to the tradition, an inexorable momentum. In homophonic music, harmony can seem more static and cyclical. In rock songs, for instance, the rhythm section or vocal/instrumental melodies propel the music. Preisner's original score for the *Concert[o]* cue in *Blue* demonstrates this essentially pop-oriented aspect of his harmonic practice. The chords indicated in writing across the top of the score (see Fig. 2.1) read like tabs on a cheat sheet, put there by Preisner as an aide-memoire, perhaps, when he orchestrated the chords he had conceived to accompany this passage. It makes sense for a musician who began composing for voice and guitar to think in this way—albeit, ironically, as he plays the role of "art music composer."

This harmonic thinking nonetheless lends a peculiar quality to Preisner cues aping the tonal art music tradition. The driving force of that tradition, a contrapuntal-harmonic structuring of musical form and content fusing thematic and harmonic materials to structure and expression, is absent from his music. His neo-romantic cues might therefore seem to lack credibility, if assessed merely as failed facsimiles of that tradition. Their harmony does not ring true. It may be more interesting, though, to consider ways in which that falseness might play a role in a narrative's symbolism (as discussed in Chapters Four and Five regarding *Blue*). Musical falseness may add salient truths to a narrative. It may also help cues to function both as just-about-passable artificial art music *and* dramatic underscoring, as in *Véronique*'s Concerto performance, contributing aptly to key narrative moments without demanding the kind of attention that a more contrapuntally sophisticated score might require. Some critics have criticized Preisner for not being Mahler; the more subtle point may be that, at most junctures in the films he has scored, Mahler really would not do. The presence of art music would overload the film, drowning out one sea of significations with another.[40]

Fig. 2.1: "Tabs" from a page of Preisner's manuscript score for
Blue's *Concert[o]*

Typical of music with its roots in popular traditions, propulsion is created through a rhythmic articulation of a static underlying harmony (think of the start of Bob Dylan's "Hey Mr. Tambourine Man," for instance, a plain major chord enlivened through Dylan's strumming patterns), although there are of course plentiful examples from art music (Wagner's extraordinary E♭ major prolongation at the beginning of *Das Rheingold*, for instance). Examples from the *Three Colors* trilogy can be heard in *Blue* in the second section of the *Concert[o]*, where the throbbing rhythm lends appropriate ardency to the visuals; in *White*, at the start of the tango cues where a solo violin melody is accompanied by a homorhythmic chordal texture; and in *Red*, throughout most of the bolero cues. The technique can also be traced back to Preisner's earliest films. In the escape cue from *Weather Report*, the oom-pah-pah of the militaristic waltz is the backdrop to the striving, occasionally faltering, melodic line.

The *Weather Report* cue is an example of another Preisner trait: harmony which repeats unchangingly while a melody moves more freely. An archetypal example would be the first cue of *Decalogue 1*, where the strings hold a single minor chord, the solemn environment against which the recorder's lament is sounded. That lament, as already noted, moves between the fifth and sixth scale degrees of its minor scale; the first and last note of each gesture is part of the string chord, but its expressive peak, the piquant flattened sixth, is not. This demonstrates one typical way in which Preisner evokes a sense of space and tension in his music. Because the harmonic layer acts as a pedal tone, it evokes an aura of unchanging stillness. When the melody then plays notes dissonant to the pedal, a degree of harmonic dissonance and thus tension results; such tension only intensifies when such textures continue unabated, heightening expectations of release.

Pedal point notes and sonorities, of course, are stock-in-trade for film scoring: for lurking menace and building tension, reach for the sustained bass and cello tones; for bated breath and incipient horror, score the same gesture for high violins. Preisner is by no means above such uses, as his very first film cue—a high string cluster accompanying the opening shots of newly arrived coffins in *Weather Report*—demonstrated.[41] A cue like this is less Polish avant-gardism, more Hollywood horror. However, Preisner's pedals are sometimes more subtly accomplished, employing an attention to musical texture and restraint that does credit to the Polish traditions they evoke. As Ula masturbates in *No End*—she is seeking to summon Antek's presence through an erotic ritual and, sonically, by incanting his name—Preisner's cue gradually sustains pitches culled from G Dorian (see Ex. 2.6), scored for strings and brass. An icon of sadness (it sounds at first as if G minor will materialize), bound to the funereal "Holy God" *cantus firmus* by mood and mode, is gradually transformed (the E♮ is unexpected).

Ex. 2.6: Harmonic aura forming around Ula in *No End*

The accrual of suspensions and mild dissonance could be read as a crude parallel to her building excitement. This reductive reading, however, does little justice to a scene infusing the erotic with a sense of the metaphysical, and in which Ula almost seems to take control of the soundtrack, turning it into an instrument of shamanistic intent—nor to its musical and visual richness. Preisner creates a massing of harmonic expectation but withholds the crucial leading note of the mode, just as Ula's orgasm and desired vision of Antek come close, but are not achieved; the spell is broken by her son crying out in the night, and when she arrives to comfort him, he is initially shot framed against a poster of brass instruments—the masculine family her mother was just underscored by as she sought to summon his father. Such richness, including hints of the mystical, is something Preisner's scores achieve again and again with suspended, gradually expanding clouds of pitches, and not least in *Red*. The finale of the trilogy is filled with scenes which could easily, if scored less subtly, have seemed like New Age hokum. Instead, his control of harmony and texture connotes the proximity of metaphysical possibility.

An alternative means for evoking momentum and tension in a static harmonic environment is an ostinato: a repeating accompaniment pattern, often in a bass register, providing an insistent background pulse behind more varied foreground materials. In *Decalogue 7*, Preisner scores the theft, flight, search for, and second theft of a little girl with an ostinato figure adding a hint of gumshoe noir to the proceedings; the chiming electric guitar intoning its repetitions also suggests the modern crime genre. Evoking the strung-out emotions of the girl's mother and grandparents, the ostinato forms a strikingly adult juxtaposition to the fairy-tale perspective of the infant, who relishes her journey into a realm of magical plays, fairgrounds, and houses in the woods filled with bears. The score focalizes the action, often seen from the perspective of the child, through the emotions of her relatives. Similarly, in *At Play in the Fields of the Lord*, the lengthy journey of the missionaries through the jungle by river is underpinned by a Preisner ostinato transposing, through a simple harmonic formula, in order to suggest both the movement and repetition of their journey. The harmony is traveling counterclockwise through the circle of fifths, furtively slipping into subdominants rather than assertively leaping into dominant realms. When asked about his tendency sometimes abruptly to transpose rather than modulate, Preisner stresses that more sudden shifts can connote a break of some kind. This can signify time passing or, as in the courtroom scene in *White* (analyzed in Chapter Six), changing points of view.

Like a change of key in the middle eight or final chorus of a pop song, Preisner moves his harmonies *en masse*. In the courtroom cue from *White*, musical breathing smooths the harmonic divide. Elsewhere, it is the equivalent of a purposefully jarring montage, splicing together separate keys for startling effects. Nowhere is this more apparent than in the Concerto cue from *Véronique*, in which an upward rush of sudden modulations both parallels and anticipates aspects of the narrative (Weronika's increasingly racing heart, the upward tilt of the shot as she exhales, the flight of her soul to Véronique, the gaze up from her coffin's-eye-view) while ramping up tension and expectations of arrival as the singer approaches her fate.

Preisner's Voices

In a reflection of the troupe mentality of "Piwnica pod Baranami" and Kieślowski's approach to collaboration, there are times when Preisner's musical presence is notably mediated through other voices. Whenever one hears Ostaszewski's recorder playing or the laser beam of Elżbieta Towarnicka's soprano, one knows instantly that this is a Preisner score, so closely are their voices associated with his sound. Preisner himself links his use of distinctive collaborating musicians to the casting of a film:

> As a composer it's important to find musicians with strong personalities. It's like the casting process for a film director. My leading actors are the musicians . . . and without doubt they convey the character of the music.[42]

And elsewhere:

> I use the orchestra very much in the same way as a director uses his actors. I have lead roles, and then we have those who are a little more in the background. So sometimes the orchestra has a supportive role, and sometimes there are different lead roles—it can be the piano, a guitar or a solo voice.[43]

What do these "strong personalities" contribute to Preisner's soundtracks?

The decision to bring individualism to the fore suggests an alternative practice to classical Hollywood scoring, where permitting a strong and recurring solo voice to surface in a film might risk rupturing the transparency of the medium: strong musical casting calls perceiver attention to the presence of a score. Such practices, however, can function productively in films where the audio-viewer needs to be rendered more active, not least by noticing the soundtrack and considering its implications, in Hollywood films and elsewhere. Like the reuse of earlier scores in the *Three Colors* trilogy and the mentions of Van den Budenmayer, or a hit song dropping on the soundtrack of a rom-com,[44] Preisner's performers prompt one to question where one has heard that music before and thus more actively to engage with the music. They also, of course, brand the music "by Preisner" in the same way Preisner's presence helps to create "brand Kieślowski," therefore fulfilling a function of art cinema style: a unique stylistic fingerprint, distinguishing the authors from other authors *and* the anonymity of some mainstream directors and composers. What, however, do the voices add to the presence of Preisner's scoring style?

Like many other aspects of Preisner's music, his collaborators' voices are markers of femininity, otherness and heightened expressivity, and thus indicative of an alternative range of concerns articulated by his films. This is obvious when the solo voice is literally feminine, as in Towarnicka's performances. As Tagg has demonstrated, however, woodwind sounds such as Ostaszewski's recorder, the clarinet in *White*, the sax on *Mouvements de désir*, or even, arguably, the muted trumpet on *Weiser* can signify the feminine or Other in Western cultures. The delicate piano playing of Konrad Mastyło and later Leszek Możdżer, the glass harmonica in *The Last September*, the harp and acoustic guitar in *Blue* and *Red* also evoke the feminine, especially when combined with Preisner's propensity for tragic and tender expressive and cultural cueing. These significations are often intensified through Preisner's soloists' deployment of vibrato. There is also the sense in which a soloist's lines in a score—most strikingly in Ostaszewski's recorder playing, his woodwind instrument sounding precisely like musicalized breaths—become a voice addressing the listener. Perhaps Preisner's presence is especially sensitive to voices that sound as if they are alone in a sparse landscape; as Tagg pointed out, according to the semiotics of screen music, women are more likely to be alone than men. Combined with the penetrating directness of Towarnicka or Ostaszewski's timbres, the effect of such scoring can be extraordinary: the audio-viewer is compelled to attend to personae demanding one's attention.

Other critics have discussed aspects of Preisner's instrumentation in terms that may be argued to evoke aspects of his presence. Paxman has noted his desire to link a solo instrument to the "soul" of a story; in this context, he notes the "occasional . . . often instrumentally exposed . . . *piano* or *pianissimo*" guitar cues in *Red*, which manifest "a sense of isolation: a theme relevant to all three main characters in this film."[45] Charles Eidsvik, discussing the scoring of *Decalogue 6*, links the guitar to Tomek and the piano to Magda, arguing that Preisner's "music celebrates loneliness and longing" and "conspires to romanticize" the narrative.[46] This reading also brings to mind the flute and clarinet duet at the close of *White*, accompanied by sparse gestures on the harp and piano, which underpins its closing revelation of the rekindled, but also newly problematized, romance of Karol and Dominique.

Van den Budenmayer and Pastiche

How does Preisner's sensitive presence square with the rhetoric of his grander cues, the strength and striving of which more stereotypically evokes blustering masculinity and narratives of teleological achievement, not least when composed "by" Van den Budenmayer? In a subtle observation, Mark Russell and James Young point out that, because Preisner likes the "intimacy" of music scored for just a few instruments as much as a full orchestral sound, "despite the size of the instrumental forces . . . it still retains a characteristic starkness, often due to widely spaced unison voicings."[47] Thus "economy" remains a watchword: "he uses what is required and nothing more."[48] Preisner himself links this facet of his style to Kieślowski's requirements for a score:

Kieślowski liked simple music, although played by a huge orchestra. That is why in order to stress the emotions and to achieve a strong effect I wrote in unison and in widely spaced octaves. It gives the impression that the sound is very expansive and monumental.[49]

The music's links to strong effects and monumental forces nonetheless calls attention to another strand of aesthetics within cues by Preisner's neo-romantic avatars.

Preisner's grandest cues in the Kieślowski collaborations give voice to fictional composers including (in *Blue* alone) Julie, Patrice, Olivier and, most famously, Van den Budenmayer. Stylistic differences between Preisner's restrained dramatic underscoring and more grandiose diegetic personae are outlined below, in the context of a discussion of his wider engagement with pastiche. First, the origins of his most famous fictive voice are traced, in the hope of clearing up some of the confusion surrounding this figure. Preisner has had fun playing with perceptions of his fictive and personal compositional voices. Probed knowingly by Mikael Carlsson and Peter Holm, he explained that Van den Budenmayer "lives in France," is a French composer, and is certainly not his alter ego; he merely uses his music because "I like it! It's much more beautiful than my own." He doesn't use Bach or Mozart, he continues, because "Van den Budenmayer isn't that popular, and I like to discover something new." This tall tale, though, has a sorrowful conclusion: Van den Budenmayer died in March 1996 (just like Kieślowski, the interviewers note). In the same interview, Preisner flatly denies that he composed the Concerto in E minor from *Véronique*.[50]

Clarity on the matter is not helped, in turn, by the fact that some of the composer's more honest accounts of Van den Budenmayer's genesis contain errors. In the Russell and Young interview it is noted, regarding Van den Budenmayer's genesis, that in *Decalogue 9* "the main character, Dorota, has a moment of revelation in her flat and she puts a record on."[51] For starters, this actually occurs in *Decalogue 2*. More to the point, the composer of the diegetic music in *Decalogue 2* is never revealed; Dorota is an orchestral musician and, while she is shown performing in this bleak Mahlerian adagio, the identity of its composer remains a mystery. Van den Budenmayer does, however, crop up in both musical and titular guise in *Decalogue 9*. In this interview, Preisner continues: "We thought about using a classical record of some kind but we decided that it was better that I would write a piece of music."[52] The intention was to use a pre-recorded composition, but the license proved too expensive, hence the decision to invent an alternative. "That was how Van den Budenmayer came into being," Preisner persists, "it was a red herring. But then the idea developed—that Van den Budenmayer could crop up in each of the films. In fact there are references to him in *The Double Life of Véronique* (he is credited with the 'Concerto in E minor') right through to *Three Colors: Blue* where Julie (Juliette Binoche) listens to some of his vocal music in a record shop booth. He became an alter-ego."[53] It is, of course, in *Three Colors: Red* that Valentine, and not Julie in *Blue*, listens to this CD—and a track reprising the Van den Budenmayer song first heard in *Decalogue 9*.

Jonathan Broxton and James Southall winkled the most detailed explanation out of Preisner:

> When Kieślowski shot [*Decalogue*], he originally wanted to use some of Mahler's music, but this proved too expensive to license. He asked me to compose something original in Mahler's style, and we were looking for the name of a composer—something different, something to be taken seriously as "proper" music. Both Kieślowski and I liked Holland, and the name Van den Budenmayer looks as if it comes out of Holland, so we chose that. Afterwards, we got thousands of questions about Van den Budenmayer. We gave him a birth date but 200 years earlier and he even started appearing in music encyclopedias![54] At one point, someone wanted to take me to court accusing me of stealing his music! Nowadays, if I write bad music, I accredit it to him![55]

The possibility of Mahler being in Van den Budenmayer's aesthetic DNA originates in the *Decalogue* screenplays where, as Annette Insdorf notes, rather than Van den Budenmayer, "Ola refers merely to Bach and Mahler when Roman asks her what she sings."[56] Preisner recalled, when I asked him about this, that Kieślowski initially planned to use Mahler either in *Decalogue 2* or *9*, or perhaps both (Preisner himself has forgotten), to imitate the practice of his friend, Krzysztof Zanussi, a director and classical music enthusiast. If this was intended for *Decalogue 2*, one might wonder whether Symphony No. 2 "Resurrection" (1888-94) was the planned composition, given the episode's theme of resurrection and the fact that its forces are certainly prohibitively large for a small budget; if intended for *Decalogue 9*, Symphony No. 4 (1899-1901), the finale of which incorporates a soprano singing about a child's perspective on the afterlife, might have corresponded better to Ola's bright character, youthfulness and potentially tragic end. Unfortunately, Preisner has forgotten which piece by Mahler the director originally wanted.

Preisner informed Kieślowski that it was impossible to record Mahler on the *Decalogue*'s tiny music budget, due to the forces required, and suggested instead licensing the rights to use an existing recording. The only possibility, apparently, was a Deutsche Grammophon recording, and this proved too expensive—there was no suitable Polish recording available, so no way of avoiding a fee. Preisner therefore offered to try composing something classical or, in his term, "semiclassical" to fill the hole—a crucial moment in his career. By the time they shot *Decalogue 9*, director and composer had discovered Frederik Willem van Eeden, the Dutch poet set for its song (and the music recurring in *Red*). Consequently, and because both men liked Holland so much, they christened their new fictional composer Van den Budenmayer, his name and nominal birthplace making it plausible that he could have set van Eeden's words.[57]

Bach and Mahler are useful pointers towards Van den Budenmayer's style, and by extension those of Preisner's other fictional
voices, in that this development of his presence combined aspects of
Baroque formality and Romantic expressivity. Yet Van den Budenmayer's voice is not merely an amplification of Preisner's aesthetic of
restraint: it is also a sanitization. Preisner's neo-romantic cues jettison
much that comes naturally to him in order to achieve his "semi-
classical" sound, and most notably the popular and traditional musical
coloring of his harmonies and melodic writing. When writing in character, Preisner sticks pretty plainly to the first few chapters of Rimsky-
Korsakov's textbook on harmony, jettisoning his music's modal tinges
and rock changes in favor of a conservative diatonic palette. As a post
on the rec.music.movies list by "Vance Maverick" noted regarding *Blue*
around the time of the trilogy's release, these limitations lead, on the
surface, to the most "crippling absurdity in the story":

> A world-famous composer's death is universally mourned. (Plausibil-
> ity problems already!) The film's music is his music; and while I
> thought it worked beautifully in the film, it made no sense as concert
> music, and certainly not as the kind . . . which emanates from the
> Conservatoire in Paris. Real simple stuff, with harmony out of Schu-
> mann and faintly modern halting rhythm.[58]

While it is an error to identify all of *Blue*'s music as Patrice's, the description of harmonic limitations is fair, and the old-meets-new conservatism characterized by the post is not a million miles from the composer's own assessment of Van den Budenmayer's style: "His style is
close to Neo-Romanticism, with its mixture of Classical Romanticism
and the compositional techniques of contemporary music."[59] The post's
key point, however, is to note that the scores work perfectly plausibly in
the films, but not really as concert music.[60] Classical, semi- or otherwise, is not Preisner's lingua franca; it is a second language in which
the composer's creative chutzpah and expressive élan overcome problems of grammar and syntax. Yet even if it does not fully convince as
concert music, is it not simplistic to believe that, in films as sophisticated as the Kieślowski collaborations, its very artifice might not also
be a carrier of meaning? As self-confessed music critic "Rooprecht"
asked on the IMDb discussion board—when comparing *Blue*'s *Concert[o]* ("bland, unimaginative and amateur . . . no more than a kinder-
gartener's attempt to play through the 'confutatis maledictum' passage
of Mozart's Requiem") to *Red* ("much more imaginative")—"do you
think they purposely made the music sound lifeless and uninspired? . . .
If so, I'm impressed."[61] Given the composition's connection to "Piwnica pod Baranami" and Preisner's apprenticeship there in satirical
pastiche, readings of *Blue* must consider this possibility.

Aside from his changing approach to harmony, other aspects of
Preisner's presence metamorphose when he dons his neo-romantic
masks. Irena Paulus observes that the fictional composer's "work is

characterized by great leaping intervals," their "acrobatic" nature being "exceptionally melodic," and by the orchestration of themes for high voices and, specifically, Towarnicka.[62] As noted above, Preisner's melodies tend to move by step or small intervals. As Van den Budenmayer, perhaps because he is creating horizontal material out of staid tonal harmonies, the arpeggios compose-out the underlying chords as heraldic rhapsodies. Such pattern-making, rather obvious in comparison to Preisner's more personal approach to melodic writing, undoubtedly packs an expressive punch. Other traits of Preisner's style, however, can become cumbersome when amplified. The pauses and faltering rhythms, for instance, sometimes clunk like a bad gear change when scored loudly for a mass of voices and instruments rather than a soloist permitted to extract expressive nuances from a line to help the music flow. Even on the rare occasions, however, when the gaps in Preisner's training show through the enthusiasm of his semi-classical concoctions, it is useful to bear in mind the multiple roles such cues are performing in their audio-visual context. They are never there merely to be listened to as concert music, but instead to be experienced as part of a multifaceted narrative discourse.

Preisner went through a musical apprenticeship in which pastiche for an immediate symbolic purpose, rather than refinements with an eye on a place in the Western art music canon, were the order of the day. Working in the cabaret, Preisner developed the chops and the nerve to imitate Mahler and Penderecki for Kieślowski. It is also where he developed the ability to mimic other musical idioms, if only just well enough for theatrical and, later, cinematic purposes. In the trilogy, this ability can be heard in relation to the Chopin pastiche and the tango in *White*, and the bolero in *Red*. These are no more authentic than the *Concert[o]*'s portrayal of Western art music, and Preisner has been upfront about the ironic purpose of some of these cues. In *White*, for instance, he claims "the music score is completely ironic," as in the use of a cue aping Chopin as Karol arrives "home at last" and is thrown onto a rubbish tip: "The music becomes very like Chopin, a Polish cultural icon," Preisner explains. "At that time Poland was one huge garbage dump. The juxtaposition with the Chopin piano music was to emphasize this."[63] If the musical gag seems obvious in isolation, one must again consider its multifaceted audio-visual context: the Chopin allusion, as analyzed later in this study, is just one of the icons of Polish identity being dumped along with Karol.

Preisner's personae and pastiches are considered compositional and filmic devices that reveal, on close analysis, layers of symbolism not dissimilar to those achieved by the cues scored in the style of his more personal presence. One could never answer satisfactorily the questions of quality posed by his film scores' most committed critics, primarily because their criteria for criticism are misplaced, as discussed further in Chapter Four.[64] As the many awards that his film scores have won from panels of his peers suggest, however, by creating "semi-" musics alongside the cues in his more individual voice—and with the intention, above all else, of exemplifying the climate and concept of a film—this self-taught musician has composed, time and again, scoring the quality (and sometimes *lack* of quality) of which deserves recognition for its musical and narrative sophistication.

CHAPTER THREE

KIEŚLOWSKI: CONCEPTS AND CO-WORKERS

In 1994 the French film magazine *Positif* asked a panel of filmmakers to contribute short articles about an actor, film or director which for them held a special significance.[1] Kieślowski contributed a list of ten films and chose to write in depth about "the one you don't know, which for me is as important as all the others": *The Sunday Musicians* ("Muzykanci," 1958), a ten-minute documentary by one of Kieślowski's teachers at the Łódź Film School, Kazimierz Karabasz.[2] In this short film, twenty to thirty workmen, "their thick hands and fingers indelibly stained by labor," gather in a dimly lit, "medium-sized industrial unit." They unpack an ensemble of "[h]orns, trumpets, trombones, mandolins, guitars, accordions" (there are no strings or pianos, Kieślowski notes, all of the instruments being "rather crude"). The players place their music on "rickety stands"; some don spectacles held together by Elastoplast. The rehearsal begins. Kieślowski writes:

> The men start playing. They play clumsily and, even though the music is as simple as their instruments, it's rather difficult to make out a melody. The conductor quickly interrupts them. . . . It isn't the first time they've rehearsed this piece, and he's annoyed that the musicians seem to have forgotten everything they learnt at earlier rehearsals. He loses his temper. . . . They rehearse again and again. Gradually, and after many interruptions—during which the conductor takes various musicians to task and, humming, shows them how and when to play—the melody starts to appeal. By the sixth or seventh minute the music becomes recognizable.

Karabasz then instigates the conceit that makes his documentary filmic: a montage juxtaposing the men performing their music ("their hands, their faces, . . . their fluid, uninterrupted playing") with the eerily still machinery of the tram depot where, earlier in the film, they had been shot performing on quite different instruments. Hammers and soldering irons are silenced as "the sound of the music mixes with the sounds of the depot"—or, rather, transcends it.

The short's significance to Kieślowski is hinted at in *The Double Life of Véronique*, which pays an affectionate homage to *The Sunday Musicians* in the scene where Véronique rehearses a scratch orchestra of young children trying to play a melody in unison.[3] One can imagine, in both cases, his sympathy for the travails of an artistic director seeking to lead a troupe of performers into meaningful production. Yet Kieślowski's loving description of *The Sunday Musicians* also suggests other connections between this, for him, influential short film and traits now prized in his own documentary and fiction films:

- the focus on a telling detail within the quotidian flux (Elastoplast, not Sellotape, holds together the spectacles, situating the film historically and socio-culturally);
- ordinary people perform an extraordinary task (the performance of ordinary tasks, in turn, reveals beauty in everyday life);
- a transcendent moment, mediated through artistic production, occurs amid the daily grind;
- an admiration for simple, melodic, even crude and naïve music (and for the people who produce it);
- an attempt to represent the unfilmable (art transcending life) through the filmable details of the material world;
- an affecting but unsentimental humanism.

Many of these traits, as ensuing chapters discuss, are articulated within the *Three Colors* trilogy.

Kieślowski's own interpretation of what is special about this film—written from the perspective of a man in the process of completing a trilogy marking the zenith of his output and simultaneously preparing to announce his retirement—is also significant:

> It's rare for a short film to express so much, in such a beautiful and simple manner, about the fundamental human need to create. Because, apart from satisfying our elementary needs—survival, breakfast, lunch, supper, sleep—we all aspire to something more, something that can give meaning to life and elevate it. The more difficult this is to achieve, the greater the joy when one succeeds.

Kieślowski's description of creative activity as a fundamental human need reads like a commentary on his immersive work on the trilogy. The films, in turn, echo this view of creativity as central to a well-lived life. His creative method, though, was distinguished by the stress he placed on the input and opinions of the people he termed his "coworkers." The *Three Colors* trilogy was shaped through a mode of filmmaking that performatively practices what it preaches: a community of collaboration in which each individual was free to make an individually significant contribution. This is particularly exemplified by

Preisner's working relationship with the director, which is examined below. Like the trilogy itself, the practice espouses the virtues of a life (and career) lived through *agapē*.

Kieślowski's statement on *The Sunday Musicians* could also be read, however, as a not so thinly veiled justification of his art. By his death in 1996, the value of his films had begun to be challenged as vigorously, in some quarters, as they were being feted elsewhere, both in Kieślowski's native Poland and internationally, in the context of his emergence as a figurehead of European cinema. The following section of this chapter discusses this "double" reception, identifying key themes in his work and recurring criticisms in the reception of his films—some of which the present study challenges.

The Double Reception of Krzysztof

For a thinker of Slavoj Žižek's caliber to state that the very mention of Kieślowski "triggers an immense aesthetico-ideological controversy," and then to write a book on the topic seeking ways in which his films might thus be "redeemed,"[4] indicates that there must indeed be a problematic division in the director's critical reception. As the ultimate destination of Kieślowski's turn from documentary to fiction filmmaking, the *Three Colors* trilogy is the crucible for these debates, although the tipping point is generally agreed to be *No End*, in which the film's contribution to the so-called Polish Cinema of Moral Concern, its Solidarity-related subplot, recedes into the background of its story about a widow unable to bear the loss of her husband. For some, Kieślowski's shift from documenting the unseen lives of real people living under Polish communism to an evocation of the inner lives of trans-European ciphers was a journey away from films motivated by ideological necessity and into fables loquacious with whimsy.[5] This was paralleled, the same critics tend to argue, by a shift in style from beautiful starkness to superfluous beauty.

Such a journey, as Vincent Amiel has noted, was scarcely unique to Kieślowski amongst leading European filmmakers during the second half of the twentieth century. "The journey of Kieślowski," he observed, "is of the same nature of a Fellini or of a Resnais throughout their filmography: from realism to artifice, of the will to testify to the affirmation of an arbitrary subjectivity."[6] For Kieślowski's creative path to have provoked, in some quarters, such controversy therefore hints at broader ideological currents shifting beneath the surface of his reception. That discourse outlines, in turn, conceptions of Polish and European art cinema from Polish and other perspectives. Tracking its arguments permits one to touch on key markers of Kieślowski's late style, to adumbrate recurring tropes of the Kieślowski literature and to identify flashpoints in his work's reception concerning politics, nationalism, style, subjectivity, metaphysics and the ultimate substance of his films.

Constructing Kieślowski

Geoff Andrew's BFI guide to the *Three Colors* trilogy dutifully notes the awards with which the films were showered and provides apposite examples of the "for the most part, enthusiastic reviews" of its constituent parts in the mainstream press: one reads of *Blue*'s "genius" (*The Financial Times*), *White*'s "black, scathing East European comedy . . . abrasive yet humane" (*The [London] Times*), and *Red*'s "deft, deeply affecting variation" of key Kieślowski themes (*Variety*). He then examines the reservations expressed by other critics, which "tended to fall into two camps: claims that the trilogy was too 'arty' and lacked the edge of his earlier, more political Polish films; and complaints that the director's elliptical story-telling style had taken a turn for the worse."[7] Derek Malcolm's view, "opined" in the *Guardian*, states that *Blue* and *Red* (set in Paris and Geneva respectively) were "headily stylish" and thus less authentic than the more earthy (and thus authentically Polish) *White* (which moves between Paris and Warsaw); Geoff Brown similarly complains in *The Times* that *Blue* featured not so much characters as "impenetrable ciphers" and a narrative one remains outside of, "looking in, admiring the artistry, feeling nothing."[8] For many audio-viewers, the idea that one could "feel nothing" in response to either the tale or the telling of *Blue* must seem equally impenetrable, but the tone of these reviews is not exceptional.

Marek Haltof's study of Kieślowski offers a detailed account of his reception, productively encompassing Polish views of the trilogy which further delineate the fault lines. Geoffrey Macnab's *Sight and Sound* review of *Blue* is quoted by Haltof because its sentiments parallel the harsher Polish perspectives. For Macnab, *Blue* encapsulated Kieślowski's late style's "blithe abandonment of social issues and retreat into a remote, metaphysical realm where personal experience is all that matters"; *Blue* is emblematic of this descent, its "swirling classical music, sumptuous production values and *la belle* Binoche" all contributing to "moments when the movie seems like an upmarket brandy commercial."[9] Not all Polish critics agreed with such sentiments. Tadeusz Sobolewski lauds Kieślowski as a "tale-maker," creating stories inspired by real life but with an ulterior motive ("whether allegorical, instructive or philosophical"); in this respect, "through his bald attempt at a spiritual search, [Kieślowski's late works] constitute his crowning cinematic achievements."[10] Filmmaker Antoni Krauze, in turn, finds the release from Polish topics and the documentary aesthetic in the late films to be artistically inspiring, arguing that, while many "Polish films suffer under the weight of this Polish culture and history," Kieślowski's later cinema was liberated enough to engage alternative, but equally pressing, cinematic and moral concerns.[11]

Many Polish reviews, though, were more negative. For some, the problems are superficial or, more precisely, superficiality. Haltof quotes Mariola Jankun-Dopartowa, who accuses the trilogy of kitsch sentimentality and telling tales patronizingly familiar from soap operas and "magazines for thinking women."[12] For others, the superficiality is symptomatic of a deeper malaise in his oeuvre. Haltof himself accuses Kieślowski's final films as being "colourful postcards from Kraków, Paris and Geneva [which] replace the portrayal of the unrefined Polish reality," as witnessed by his (Haltof's tone makes clear) both more poetically and ideologically satisfying documentaries and early fiction features.[13] Thus caricatured, the form and content of the trilogy are precisely what one would expect of films pre-packaged for distribution on the art cinema circuit and, indeed, for exhibition in close succession at three major European festivals.

This strand of Kieślowski criticism parallels a broader rejection of much art cinema as "posh tosh," in filmmaker and polemicist Alex Cox's memorable phrase, designed to play well with the self-obsessed bourgeoisie rather than to reveal harsher aspects of reality. Cox's critique of such cinema focuses on films adopting conventions of the "well-made play." His diatribe against Bergman's *Fanny and Alexander* (1982) contemptuously states that "every image—even a shot of a dead dog—is a thing of beauty."[14] Such objections—think of the play of light and shade in the shot of dead animals at the start of *A Short Film about Killing*—have also been laid at Kieślowski's door, as in director Pedro Almadóvar's criticism that the cinematography in "*Blue* is very beautiful but it is too self-conscious, there are too many filters, too many personal touches by the director of photography."[15] The underlying charge to such criticism, identified by Brian Henderson in his writings on Godard, is that highly prized aspects of art cinema such as cinematographic signatures or composition in depth (so beautiful, so mysterious, so bourgeois) deserve to be flattened like the strata of society to which such cinema panders.[16] These threads are united, regarding Kieślowski, in Jonathan Romney's *New Statesmen* review of *Red*. Having set the film up for a fall by reporting that, on viewing it in the cinema, it seemed so magical as to undermine "all my misgivings about *Blue* and *White*," he reports that, after viewing *Red* for a second time on video, he was left wondering "whether I'd simply let myself be conned by the film's considerable art, and whether all its apparent depth was purely illusionist's sham."[17]

To begin to counter the notion that these films are merely well-made tosh for posh, or at least middle-class, audiences, one can argue that the themes and style of the later Kieślowski films can be read as part and parcel of an attempt to reconstitute the representational potential of cinema. They stylistically recalibrate the medium, not least through a foregrounding of music and sound, to push at the boundaries of film's ability to denote and connote the inner life. This permits an examination of issues just as politically and philosophically valid as the type of social realism Kieślowski is so often discredited for abandoning. The *Three Colors* trilogy are films that know humankind cannot live on bread alone, or even on bread and freedom.[18] These views are expanded in Chapters Four to Seven. It is also valuable to consider, however, the wider ideological and institutional context of the oppositions articulated above, which do not only represent arguments about Kieślowski but operate within broader agendas.

In her essay on nationality and authenticity in the *Three Colors* trilogy, Julia Dobson examines the motivations behind representations, for good or ill, of the trilogy as "the apogee of 1990s European arthouse cinema."[19] Noting how its multiple locations, languages and stars' nationalities posed challenges to simplistic notions of national cinema, she suggests that this sounded a threat to the critical gatekeepers of such traditions. Dobson observes (following Homi Bhabha) that "a national cinema clearly serves complex ideological purposes in both its reflection of, and contribution to, shifting concepts of national (cultural) identity."[20] Such formulations require an "other" to calibrate themselves against. Her reception history of the trilogy finds Kieślowski and his films being alternatively positioned, by French and Polish critics, to assert difference arising from "a confused anxiety over the transgression of boundaries of national cinemas, enacted by the phenomena of international co-production which the trilogy represents."[21] Intriguingly, something like the "almost hysterical desire to reinforce traditional boundaries"[22] that Dobson diagnoses in French reviews of the trilogy (primarily those in *Cahiers du cinéma*) can be located in Polish rejections of the films. Highlighting what the trilogy does in place of social realism is to highlight what Kieślowski did instead of "evoking the Romantic tradition of the artist in Polish culture as an individual who defends both the population and the perceived national culture under the rule of oppressive regimes."[23] This, in turn, reinforces a view of Polish filmmaking, or at least of "good" Polish filmmaking from this critical perspective, that fails to reflect certain realities of the Polish situation post-1989 and does not exactly form a cohesive historical narrative for events before that date. The emerging definition of Polish cinema is every bit as "constructed"[24] as the view of Central European cinema formed by some French writers and, for that matter, Anglophone critics who called *White* a welcome return to form because it foregrounded Poland's economic and political flux post-1989—i.e., a proper or authentic subject for a Polish director, paralleling cherished strands of social realism in British cinema—as opposed to all of that tendentious meaning of life stuff, which is better left, such criticism comes close to implying, to stuffed shirts like the French.

There are multiple ironies here. Some French and Anglophone critics favorable to *White*, for instance, overlooked the fact that Kieślowski's émigré status arguably "precludes him from authentic representation of contemporary Poland"—the very criticism they leveled against his take on Paris in *Blue* and which was indeed held against *White* by some Polish critics.[25] Such ironies highlight, however, how the ideological points being scored by criticism of the trilogy need to be set aside when analyzing the films anew, in order better to extricate the artifacts and consider them from alternative perspectives. Dobson incisively notes how the nationalist discourses surrounding the trilogy run counter to Kieślowski's aims for the project and particularly his "interest in the complex interface between the ethics of the individual and the moral, legal, and financial codes of contemporary society"—issues which "explicitly transcend all notions of national specificity."[26] Hence the trilogy's oblique relationship to the French tricolor and revolutionary motto, she suggests, and thus to icons which "might have suggested a national specificity" but, in these films, act "solely as a springboard for their existentialist explanations of the human condition in a concrete contemporary setting."[27] Kieślowski had evolved into an artist concerned with the most superficially simple, but ultimately intractably complex, problems of existence. In doing so, he moved out of sync with simplistic national and international narratives of what a Polish filmmaker should do. Yet moving out of step in this manner—demonstrating through actions, as much as representing through art, what it means to be liberated—was arguably the more patriotic gesture.

Substance and Style

Kieślowski's ostensible shift in focus from the political to the personal was received by some critics as a betrayal of the Polish viewer, with Kieślowski ending his career, according to Paul Coates, "in breach of the long-standing unwritten contract between [Poles] and artists unofficially commissioned to speak of public affairs, *res publica*, not their own personal ones."[28] This dismissal of Kieślowski's later films as apolitical, as the Introduction to the present study has already suggested, can be challenged directly. To treat issues of subjectivity seriously in late-modern times, for instance, can be interpreted as a politically engaged response to cultural narcissism as represented in cinema, for instance, by the postmodern substitution of irony, remake, pastiche or collage for the interrogation of substantive issues (*Red*, it will be recalled, lost the Palme D'Or at Cannes to Tarantino's *Pulp Fiction*). As Terry Eagleton argues, "meaning-of-life queries, when launched on a grand scale" (like the *Three Colors* trilogy), "tend to arise at times when taken-for-granted roles, beliefs, and conventions are plunged into crisis":

> Maybe all men and women ponder the meaning of life; but some, for good historical reasons, are driven to ponder it more urgently than others.[29]

In a Polish context, with democracy and capitalism resurgent post-communism, the trilogy's critique of the late-modern human condition assumed a particular urgency. Its critique was hardly irrelevant, furthermore, to the citizens of more established democracies.

Dina Iordanova has argued for the need to bear in mind, when assessing Polish and other non-Western European cinemas, a Central European mindset which transcends, yet is intimately connected to, communism's cultural aftermath. Even when assessing post-communist films migrating into the European art cinema mainstream, output from these regions still tends to demonstrate, she claims, "idiosyncratic tendencies."[30] One tendency is to focus on lives crushed by circumstance beyond an individual's control. "It is so difficult to find a film in Poland, the Czech Republic, Slovakia or Hungary," Hungarian director István Szabó has remarked, "which is not about lives crippled by politics and history, about victims and losers."[31] Damaged lives are a continuous theme linking Kieślowski's later films to his earlier works. Yet unlike pre-democracy Ula in *No End* or the characters of the *Decalogue*, whose political environments strangle hope for subjective development, the post-democracy protagonists of *Véronique* and the *Three Colors* trilogy seek ways out of their traps and, crucially, begin to find a way forwards. Julie, like Ula, may be "plagued by irreversible memories of bygone events, tainted with original sin, haunted by feelings of guilt and remorse,"[32] as she passes through a "crucible of suffering" (to borrow Christopher Garbowski's term) similar to *No End*'s heroine.[33] But Julie attains liberation from that pain, to a degree, as do all of the protagonists in the trilogy. Ula kills herself; Julie sacrifices aspects of her life to live again. The shift is hardly as simplistic as a move from tragedy to transcendence, but the trilogy at least admits the possibility of hope. That admission is the crucial shift in tone.

Kieślowski's later protagonists' journeys therefore continue to stress a key political theme in his earlier work, but under new sociocultural circumstances: how one lives with, and beyond, painful events in a particular cultural context. Discussing the *Decalogue*, Kieślowski stated that he didn't "want local conditions to veil the broader horizons of human existence":

> I do not want, because of never ending queues in front of our stores, to avoid identifying key moments of human Fate.[34]

He also suggested the continuity of his engagement with such themes in the documentary *I'm So-So*. Under communism, he said, cinema's "descriptive tools had been used for propagandistic purposes" and yet, outside Poland, people "don't know what it means to live in a world without representation,"[35] but rather with forms of cinematic repression. Western cinemas have other ways of repressing audiences, of course, and the director's concern with the self may indicate why his films were enthusiastically received by audiences beyond Poland who have arguably always lived with cinematic representation—but not always with liberating representations.

Kieślowski's later films redrawing of the stylistic boundaries of this medium, in order to address sidelined concerns about the inner life of his subjects, is inextricably connected to Polish and broader cultural contexts. Critical objections to Kieślowski's later style, including the prominence of Preisner's cues in these films, must be reconsidered in this context. Haltof, for instance, views the late films' style as being linked to a dilution of substance that is part and parcel of Kieślowski's abdication of the nationalistic role Polish artists are meant to adopt. Two problems thus fuse into one:

> The camera does not reveal, as in his early films, but intrudes, and calls attention to itself through the symbolic, "unnatural" use of colours, camera angles and lighting. The same can be said of Zbigniew Preisner's music which sometimes takes over the films. Kieślowski's change of direction can be described as follows: from functional to "expressionistic" photography, from unobtrusive soundtrack to overwhelming musical score, from ordinary characters in everyday situations to literary characters set in a designer's world, from the particular to the general, from outer to inner reality and from realism to "artiness." A director of detailed observations became a director of metaphysical experiences.[36]

To highlight, as emblematic, the musical aspect of this critique: a shift from unobtrusive underscoring to overwhelming cues in films focusing expressly on subjectivity and the self is precisely what one might expect of a cinema seeking to heighten evocations of the inner life. Music's main function, in mainstream and other narrative cinemas, has been to signify the unfilmables of emotion and thought. The forwardness of Preisner's music in the later films, and especially of the neo-romantic confections "by" Van den Budenmayer and similar personae, reflect stylistically this commitment to the exploration of subjectivity. Music and sound are notably incisive tools in the armory of films seeking to immerse their audience in a protagonist's subjective travails.

Subjectivity

Kieślowski's later concerns were never only going to be of interest to a Polish minority in the mid-1990s. Žižek notes the danger of "hasty historicizing" when discussing Kieślowski's output: "It is easy to identify his 'roots' in the unique moment of Polish socialism in decay; it is much more difficult to explain the universal appeal of his work, the way his films touch the nerves of people who have no idea whatsoever about the specific circumstances of Poland."[37] Iordanova, in turn, notes a "transcendental and philosophical stance" in Kieślowski—what Malcolm calls his "push inwards towards the metaphysical"[38]—that has influenced the direction of European cinema in the 1990s and beyond, most obviously in the realization of planned Kieślowski-Piesiewicz projects such as *Heaven* and *Hell*, but echoed in recent texts as ostensibly different from Kieślowski as the TV series *Lost* and *Six Feet Under*.[39] Such texts suggest, for Iordanova, "a continuing general interest in [his] universal ethical existential line in film-making."[40]

Yet does Kieślowski address these issues with profundity? A related line of attack to objections to the style and substance of Kieślowski's later work is to suggest the naivety of what Tadeusz Szyma called Kieślowski's "pseudo-metaphysics."[41] Regarding *Decalogue 1*'s questions about the existence of God and why people have to die, Sobolewski relates how "[o]ne of Kieślowski's students at the Katowice film school once remarked contemptuously: '[H]e's asking the questions of an eight-year-old!'"; Sobolewski rejoined, "Yes, they are the questions of an eight-year-old—and those of a philosopher."[42] Reading interviews with Kieślowski, one is often struck by the shrewdness of his philosophical mind. Yet many remain unconvinced of the validity of its investigations as mapped onto film, most especially when it turns to probe issues of the supernatural, religious and spiritual.

Aspects of Kieślowski's later works explore the margins of reality, fictions of subjectivity, and metaphysical possibility. This slices against the grain of modernist criticism's Marxist-materialist, and usually atheist, perspectives on reality and must have made it difficult for some critics to espouse Kieślowski. They may also have been aware that these were issues being articulated less delicately in more commercial texts, with said commerciality tainting the Kieślowski canon by association; for more postmodern critics, in turn, it may have been a case of right ballpark, wrong ballgame. An *X-Files* episode entitled "Born Again" (1994), for instance, utilized the steely aesthetic and sardonic tone typical of the series (underpinned by Mark Frost's quasi-serial underscoring for synthesized strings) to offset its dollop of sentimental hokum: the tale of someone born with the heart of another. The story tropes, surprisingly precisely, the reincarnation/doppelgänger archetype explored in both *Véronique* and the *X-Files* episode's exact Kieślowski contemporary, *Red*. Was Kieślowski merely reproducing the same kind of hokum, tarted up in art house clichés for a (superficially) more discerning audience? As discussed below, *Blue* bears a striking resemblance to *Truly, Madly, Deeply* (Minghella, 1990), a British melodrama pitched at an upmarket, middlebrow audience, and the similarities linking *White* to a number of Polish productions satirizing, for those excluded from the benefits thereof, the surreal side-effects of Poland's burgeoning economy post-1989. Is all that one gets in Kieślowski a socially distinguishing shift in tone, rather than an intensified level of cinematic argument revealing new perspectives on material reality?

Annette Insdorf defends Kieślowski's exploration of such issues directly, becoming almost Fox Mulder-like in her defense of extreme possibilities. She cites Brian Greene's *The Elegant Universe* (1999) to defend the plots of *Véronique* and *Red*:

> [O]ur universe may merely be part of a multiverse, a vast structure that contains many similar, but alternate universes. Why shouldn't this include areas where "twins" of ourselves live out completely different lives based on different choices . . . [becoming] bound up in a "branching" universe, one in which each major decision leads the universe to branch off into a new reality[?][43]

There are regional contexts, too, through which one might seek to defend similar concerns. For Janina Falkowska, Kieślowski's output is located within a rise, from the 1970s, of a metaphysical cinema in Central Europe. Such films, at first, dealt generally (because specifics were not permitted by the censor) with religious issues and evoking "religious feelings in the sense of general spiritual longings or the awareness of the supernatural."[44] She quotes Bohdan Pociej, who sees in such films a search for God ("the Great Unseen" through "the seen and in the seen") articulated by stories, the composition of a frame, uses of music, and so on. Examples run from Zanussi's *The Structure of Crystal* (1969) to Łukaszewicz's *Faustyna* (1994), with Kieślowski's output ranged in between.[45]

Again, however, a localized impetus can have transnational implications (not least as later Polish filmmakers began to achieve fame beyond their country's increasingly permeable borders). For Haltof, *Véronique*'s "slow paced enigma, beautifully crafted and governed by a sense of mystery, appears to be almost the essence of "European Art Cinema," due to its personal character, sensuality, and self-referentiality and to the fact that it is saturated with art film clichés"; of the latter he lists its episodic and elliptical narrative, unexplained occurrences, use of magnification, doubling, symbolism and mirrors to heighten the theme of duality.[46] For Coates, too, such cinema pushed the right buttons in a wider Western audience. Kieślowski's "quizzical, sometimes pained and always thoughtful probings of coincidence and mystery resonated with West Europeans disenchanted both with institutional religion and the contrasting capitalist and Marxist economic gospels."[47]

The disenchantment noted by Coates, and the particular angle a Polish "outsider" perspective might offer, connects to the late-modern condition evoked by Eagleton and suggests a potentially productive context for reevaluating Kieślowski's engagement with the outer limits of material reality. By blurring the boundaries of the real, and in turn rendering reality more opaque, personal acts (not least of faith) are foregrounded: in the absence of history and facts, all one has to go on is perception and narrative. Both can only be subjective. The thematic focus of Kieślowski's output sought "to describe what really dwells within my hero[es]"[48]—subjective states and unique experiences of reality—although he could list but a handful of filmmakers who had achieved "that miracle": Welles, Tarkovsky, Bergman a few times, Fellini and Loach. Might one therefore argue that he was interested in "[t]he realm of superstition, fortune-telling, presentiments, intuition, dreams," not because of some misplaced New Age sentimentality, but rather because they form vibrant representations of "the inner life of a human being . . . [and thus] the hardest thing to film"?[49] Extreme narrative possibilities thematicize subjectivity.

Joseph Kickasola's synthesizing list of themes in the later films explores this crossing-over of key concerns: "The issues of ultimate good, evil, the existence of the soul, predestination, the existence of God, spiritual search, temptation, and salvation/redemption are consistently present . . . forming the basis for an overall metaphysical context."[50] Connected to these issues, Sobolewski offers a key to theorizing the link between style and substance (including the prominence of Preisner's music) in late Kieślowski. He abandoned true documentary "for something in a way of 'inner documentary' attempting to render unexpressible, agnostic states concerning not just one character, but interpersonal, intersubjective states, through the aid of abstract form."[51] Kieślowski recalibrated cinema's stylistic compass to chart complex inner territories.

Other critics have been led by a close engagement with films in the *Three Colors* trilogy to similar conclusions. Andrew argues against the negative reception of the films by seeking to understand how, if they were obscure and beyond interpretation, they achieved their critical success and attracted "large, very appreciative audiences;" he asserts that, "[c]learly, they *did* make sense, *did* mean something to the vast majority of those who saw them."[52] But what, and how? Andrew argues that the achievement was possible because, "though his later films deal with the 'irrational' subject matter of emotional and spiritual lives, they do so . . . in a thoroughly rational manner." More specifically and regarding, in this case, *Blue*:

> Without resorting to the near-continuous use of explicit dialogue or voice-over narration generally favoured by even the most sophisticated contemporary American cinema for the exploration of inner emotions (e.g., the films of Woody Allen, Terrence Malick, John Sayles or Martin Scorsese), or . . . clumsy, contrived "subjective camera" . . . Kieślowski focuses so closely and precisely on Julie . . . that we are continually aware, without her needing to verbalise her feelings, of her intensely private responses to the world around her.[53]

Such techniques, he continues, are not deployed self-consciously. This cinema never promotes "style for style's sake," but instead explores the medium's possibilities in search of sound and image newly "resonant with meaning."[54] Richard Rushton makes a similar comment. When Kieślowski films seek to "open the ground of new cinematic vistas" these are not "playthings, or distractions, trivialities or seductions. . . . [T]hey represent a striving towards new discoveries (of the cinema, of humanity), as strategies of destabilization that are unnerving to the same degree as they are beautiful."[55] One may also recall André Bazin's words on reality and cinematography: "the image is evaluated not according to what it adds to reality but what it reveals of it."[56] This feels like a credo for Kieślowski's late films, especially if this conception of "image" can be expanded to encompass audio-visual collusions of sight and sound.

Metaphysics

The existential and experiential aspects of the "realities" explored by Kieślowski are usually explained, or brushed under the carpet, via reference to metaphysics. Metaphysics, Peter Van Inwagen explains, "is

the study of ultimate reality"[57]—but what is reality, how can it be ultimate, and how does one access that reality in order to render it discuss-
able? A more fundamental issue to philosophers of metaphysics is the
idea of realities and appearances, and the notion that "it is sometimes
possible to 'get behind' the appearances the world presents us with and
to discover how things really are: we have discovered that the earth is
really rotating, despite the fact that it is *apparently* stationary."[58] Inwagen therefore defines metaphysics as a field of inquiry which seeks
answers to three questions: "What is the world like?," "Why does that
particular world exist?," and "What is our place in the world?" These
are Kieślowskian questions.

The typical objections of logical positivists to metaphysics, in turn,
provide a final context for the objections of some critics to Kieślowski's
later works on the grounds of his turn from "reality":

> In saying that metaphysical questions and statements were meaning-
> less, the logical positivists were not saying that these questions and
> statements were pointless or that they were divorced from the real
> concerns of human life. They were advancing a much more radical
> thesis. They were saying that these "statements" and "questions" were
> not really statements and questions at all, but merely sequences of
> words that had the superficial appearance of statements and questions.
> Thus, for a logical positivist, a metaphysical question like "Why is
> there a World?" is a mere piece of articulate noise that, because it has
> the grammatical form of a question, has been mistaken for a ques-
> tion.[59]

This sounds remarkably similar to certain complaints about Kieślowski:
not merely that his questions are childish, but that they are not important questions at all but merely the appearance thereof: all style, no substance. Yet to deflate the logical positivist position (having pointed out
that their view of reality is also a dream, or rather just another phe-
nomenologically actualized picture that human minds have read into
shadows cast on the wall of life's caves), Inwagen argues that metaphy-
sicians take capacities "designed for purposes quite unrelated to questions about ultimate reality and [push] these capacities to their limits."[60]

Inwagen is talking here about intellectual capacity, not film technique. Yet similar imaginative leaps can take place in terms of the language of film. Kieślowski's later films push the parameters of film style
to do things those parameters did not evolve to do and (rather like
Kant's argument about the limitations of the human mind) probably
cannot ultimately do because of their internal restrictions. Kieślowski
himself recognized such limitations; he also allowed himself to be
called a metaphysician.[61] What his later films seek to do is, logically,
impossible: to provide access to the experience of another subjectivity's
thinking and feeling, mediated through a mode of cinematic discourse
harrying the limits of the medium. For many, however, it is equally
impossible not to value the attempt.

Productions and Producers

Andrew's assertion that "there was little that was extraordinary" about the *Three Colors* production and that "it is what the films 'say' and how they 'say' it" that make them interesting is true in the sense that, compared to some famously troubled shoots (such as *The Island of Dr. Moreau*), the period was relatively lacking in incident.[62] It overlooks, however, the speed at which the co-workers completed their trilogy in less than three years and the manner in which the mode of collaboration on the project enacted concepts central to the trilogy's thematic concerns.

Shooting and Financing

All three films were shot between September 1992 and May 1993. In September 1993 *Blue* was premiered at the Venice film festival; *White* and *Red* followed swiftly onto the festival circuit. The schedule exhausted the director, who announced his retirement at the press conference accompanying *Red*'s premiere in Cannes; some believe it contributed to his death. Often, he would shoot one film by day, review dailies or edit another film in the evening, then write or rewrite scenes for yet another film at night.[63] As Andrew reports,

> shooting took about nine weeks for each film, with breaks between filming kept to a minimum; indeed, the day after filming for *Blue* was completed, Kieślowski began shooting the Parisian scenes for *White*. The production process was speeded up even further by Kieślowski's habit of shooting one film at the same time as he was editing its predecessor. In this way, he was able to achieve the remarkable feat of premièring the three films at major festivals within a few months of each other: *Blue* in September 1993 at Venice; *White* in February 1994 at Berlin and, finally, *Red* in May 1994 at Cannes.[64]

This was not, however, a particularly novel approach for Kieślowski and his co-workers. All ten installments of the *Decalogue* were shot and edited within twelve months. Insdorf explains that the production crew "would occasionally shoot parts of one film in the morning, of a second at another location in the afternoon, and of a third in the evening," partly in response to "ludicrously short rehearsal time and limited film stock."[65] While the financial limitations on the internationally funded trilogy were not as strict as those challenging the Polish and German television funded *Decalogue*, working on the different sections of the trilogy simultaneously did not merely permit a tightly budgeted production to roll out on time. The method permitted a symphonic richness to develop within the tripartite production. Kieślowski and other co-workers, including Preisner, dovetailed patterns linking part to whole *in media res*, directing the project towards the articulation of its overarching concepts. The trilogy is richer for having been made in this fashion.

The trilogy is also a product of when it was made in the historical development of the Polish film industry. As Haltof notes, as much as 73% of the Polish cinematic repertoire by 1992 consisted of Hollywood films. Alongside this intensified competition at the cinemas for Polish productions, changes were occurring, post-communism, to the funding structure of the Polish film industry. These shifts, Haltof suggests, led some filmmakers to look outwards to more universal themes and thus, potentially, to other funding bodies and audiences:

> The end of a fully subsidised and centralised Polish film industry controlled through state censorship and the emergence of a new audience, for whom not only communism but Solidarity were history, brought some inevitable changes to film production and distribution, as well as to film thematics and stylistics. Co-productions, multinational enterprises, competition with Hollywood and a plurality of styles and genres changed the film landscape in Poland at the beginning of the 1990s.[66]

Not for the first time in Poland's recent history, artists found themselves entertaining a crisis of identity, yearning simultaneously to "catch up with Europe" through "new post-totalitarian art that, while addressing some universal issues would reflect national uniqueness."[67] The motivation, however, was not merely aesthetic, and permitted a taking advantage of new streams of funding, distribution and, ultimately, remuneration and cultural capital for individual artists and their national institutions.[68] For instance, Poland signed up to the Eurimages Foundation in 1992 to secure further sponsorship for its films. The Polish-Swiss-French *Three Colors* trilogy was supported by the foundation, like *Véronique* before it; it also had a French producer (Marin Karmitz), a multilingual cast and production team, and distribution through globally positioned players Miramax and Artificial Eye. The contrast to the communist-era *Decalogue* is obvious: the series was a Polish/German co-production, co-funded by TOR and its Eastern Blok ally Sender Freies Berlin for broadcast on each country's state TV channel.

The institutional and political changes lightly shade the thematic content of the films. The sense of the trilogy taking place in a broader geo-political context (i.e., the possibility of European unification, a big idea post-Maastricht Treaty in the early 1990s) provides a backdrop for many events in the films: the commission for Patrice's *Concert[o]* in *Blue* comes from the European Commission; Poland is depicted, for better and worse, as part of a unified Europe in *White*; plot points in *Red* hinge on newly flexible international travel, the spread of modern problems (e.g., cross-border drug trafficking) and enhanced telecommunications. The casting of three female stars also reflects the broader production context, and Coates even suggests that the "serial aesthetic" embraced by Kieślowski for the *Decalogue* and the trilogy, and planned for future productions *Heaven*, *Hell* and *Purgatory*, was one part aesthetics, one part hard-headed economics.[69] A serial entices viewers to return to the cinema for each new installment, increasing ticket sales, while amplifying the series' projection of its concepts as ideas unfold both more gradually and in counterpoint.

Co-workers

The interactions of Kieślowski and his co-workers are the primary source of *Blue*, *White* and *Red*'s achievements. In some ways, their cinematic practice follows a distinguished lineage of auteurism. As Nick James has argued regarding the first part of the trilogy, *"Blue* is very much an auteurist film in the old-fashioned sense in that it represents the work of six craftspeople at the top of their form, many of whom had worked together before": Kieślowski, Piesiewicz, Preisner, cinematographer Sławomir Idziak, sound man Jean-Claude Laureux and Juliette Binoche.[70] To this list one can add editor Jacques Witta, sound mixer William Flageollet, producer Marin Karmitz, and the "script consultants"—an informal circle of filmmaker friends including Agniesza Holland and Krzysztof Zanussi who read scripts and responded to early cuts of the films.[71] The ensuing discussion of how the trilogy's team operated provides the backdrop for a specific case study of this process: Preisner's working relationship with Kieślowski. It also begins to outline the manner in which the team's mode of collaboration can be read as an embodiment of the trilogy's key concepts.

Co-worker reflections on Kieślowski's mode of collaboration are reminiscent of the relationship between the conductor and musicians in *The Sunday Musicians*. Witta has even used a musical metaphor when commenting on the manner in which Kieślowski sought out his collaborators: he wanted to work with people he could tune up like musical instruments, making them all sound together to produce a harmonious result.[72] This was the case from the inception of a film. According to Karmitz, he read a twenty-page treatment Kieślowski had written for *Blue* in Cannes on the night of *Véronique*'s premiere;[73] following the producer's enthusiastic response, Kieślowski produced similar treatments for *White* and *Red*, and the pair then worked together on them for some time. Kieślowski then proceeded to write a draft script for each film with Piesiewicz.[74]

At this stage of script development, the director involved not only the "screenplay consultants" and mooted cinematographers, but also other key creative figures, including Preisner. What distinguishes the Kieślowski productions from other auteur-driven projects, perhaps, may be the subsequent selflessness of the director's steering of the ship; being non-selfish yet also a great artist, Holland wryly observes, is unusual for a man *and* an artist.[75] This was not merely a case of casting the right team to realize a personal vision. Time and time again one reads testimony to Kieślowski's active seeking of alternative ideas and perspectives to enrich the films. As Witta comments, this relates, in part, to Kieślowski's training at the film school in Łódz, and to a mode of collaborative practice, overseen but not dominated by a director, which typifies work emanating from this center.[76]

Witta recalls that, when working with Kieślowski, he was asked more often than by any other director "what do you think?" This seems especially noteworthy in Witta's case, due to Kieślowski's love of the editing process. Whether it is true that there was never any tension or quarrelling, as Witta has claimed, it is clear that the director led his ensemble of collaborators, like the leader of a jazz band, to bring out their finest flights of invention within the context of a project the trajectory of which he was shaping. A small example is provided by Julie Delpy. Asked by Kieślowski how she pictured Dominique's character in the scene where, enraged by Karol's physical and psychological impotence, she sets fire to their Paris hair salon, Delpy said she was reminded of a cat she had owned as a child: always in heat and a monster to boot. He told her to go with this image when playing the scene, as it helped to define her character's outer monstrousness and inner needs. Delpy's playing of Dominique subsequently developed a brutally cool exterior masking a desire for warmth. This led, in part, to the director's reimagining of the ending and the reshoots on *White* before the final cut.[77]

On *Blue*, Binoche's impact on the film, beyond her performance as Julie, ranged across the board. She advised on dialogue (the Polish to French translation of the screenplay, she felt, was sometimes awkward) and used her own clothes for her costumes (primarily so she could forget she was wearing them and thus achieve a greater intimacy in her performance). Full-frontal nudity was cut from the film following a frank discussion with Kieślowski about the effects it would have on perceptions of her performance, and the final enigmatic smile in the film was included at her request.[78] It was not merely the film's stars, however, who influenced the films significantly. At Idziak's suggestion, the screenplay's idea that Julie would be a jogger was replaced with swimming, bringing into play one of the film's signature locations, its swimming pool, and from Idziak's perspective enriching *Blue*'s symbolism: the surface of the water, for him, evoked a liminal zone between surface and depth, life and death, and so on. In the editing suite, Witta and Kieślowski together struck upon the idea of the blackouts which occur when Julie is interrupted by music. They were not premeditated, but rather an improvisatory response to the developing narrative when they began to cut the film to Preisner's music.[79] Finally, Kieślowski's goal of cutting each film down to one hour and thirty-five minutes was achieved, in part, with Karmitz's assistance. The producer claims he had a significant role in assisting the director in deciding which anecdotal and superfluous material would be cut.

Preisner's memories of working with the director, discussed below, provide similar examples of respectful and creative interactions. As the analyses in this study explain, a close comparison of Preisner's notated cues and the trilogy's soundtracks reveals how, in a sense, Kieślowski also became a composer at times, treating Preisner's cues like daily footage he could edit for narrative essentials. This even appears to have been true of his work alongside Preisner in the recording sessions for the films. Cues were sometimes re-orchestrated mid-recording session, through a process of mostly harmonious interaction between composer and director. Preisner was not being isolated for special treatment by a director who would literally consider the merits of having an oboe or clarinet lead a cue, or an ensemble of seven versus nine instruments. "At scoring sessions," Preisner reported, "Krzysztof very often reacted to my music by trying to bring out and highlight the most important thing for him."[80] Similarly, Delpy notes the distinctive farewell she waves to Karol at the Paris courthouse after their divorce hearing—a curiously controlled hooking inwards of fingers clothed in a black satin glove. Kieślowski wanted a gesture distinct enough to register when it was reused, in a literal and metaphorical reversal of context, later on in *White*, when she locks hands with Karol in her Warsaw hotel bedroom and draws him into bed.[81]

Where Kieślowski finally took control was in the construction of a film's final cut. Up until that point, he often deferred to the expertise of others: "I try to get as much out of everyone as I can," he once stated: "I'm always expecting people to tell me something simply because I think that they often know better than I do. I expect it from actors, cameramen, soundmen, editors, electricians, assistants, everyone."[82] He certainly expected it from Preisner. Few people, however, could teach him anything about editing. As Falkowska notes, "the final shape of the films belongs to Kieślowski himself," because he "spent long hours at the editing table, polishing and mastering the ideal version of the films."[83] Editing, not directing, was Kieślowski's passion. When he announced his retirement, he stated, perhaps not dishonestly, that "[a]ll I'll miss is the editing table."[84] Stok says he was "ruthless" as an editor: "He would throw scenes away if they didn't ring true with the main thrust of the film."[85] Hence the working through of thirteen versions of *White* with that film's editor, Urszula Lesiak, the last cut barely resembling the shooting script.

Is it true that Kieślowski made movies "just so I can edit them"?[86] The director "kept cutting for dramatic compression, retaining only the essential scenes, characters, and images,"[87] but also because it was the site of his own creative endeavor and, arguably, his most impressive creative decisions. The trilogy's screenplays, for instance, were in no way shooting scripts. They were "blueprints," Insdorf notes, from which "literal details" were juxtaposed with "suggestive images" to be fleshed out during the transition from script to screen, discovering as much as amplifying their affective and allegorical resonances.[88] According to Witta, "For *Blue* we made thirty versions with different constructions. The film kept transforming and progressing," an observation to which Insdorf adds that *Blue* "certainly grew shorter, replacing exposition with economical ellipsis." Insdorf continues:

It was indeed during the editing stage that Kieślowski became a true "composer"—arranging and rearranging the strips of celluloid like the musical notes that he said "all exist, waiting for someone to order them."[89]

Cutting and pasting, juxtaposing, layering and cross-fading his palette of materials, Kieślowski revealed in the trilogy a comprehensible, telling whole.

Preisner and Kieślowski

Miguel Mera and David Burnand praise the *Three Colors* trilogy as "a benchmark for collaborative purpose between director and composer that is rarely achieved, either in mainstream or art-house movies."[90] While similar testimony could be paid to the collaborations between the director and his other key co-workers, his need for such teamwork was acute in the case of music. "I don't know anything about music," he told Danusia Stok, but "Zbyszek Preisner is somebody I can work together with, rather than just ask him to come up with a given effect."[91] Kieślowski gave a basic example of how this process worked:

> I often want to put music in where he says it would sound absurd, and there are scenes where I don't imagine having music but which he thinks should have music, so we put the music in. . . . [H]is thinking is more modern, full of surprises. That is, it surprises me where he wants music.[92]

Yet once they had spotted where music might exist in a film, it is clear that the pair worked together on what it should seek to accent or represent, and indeed on how those significations might best be articulated through music. Preisner also disputes Kieślowski's claims about a lack of musical understanding, while being modest about his own contribution to their partnership. "For a film director," he stated in an interview, "the important thing is to know what he wants from the music, if he has a conception of its function. And Krzysztof knew this. I followed what he wanted, nothing more. . . . Sometimes he inspired me; sometimes I inspired him."[93]

Occasionally, they disagreed strongly. In *Véronique*, when the father is seen making his models, everyone involved in editing the production was against Preisner's cue for the scene. Kieślowski told the composer that his music was "cheap and banal." Preisner argued his case. He did not like the father, a man stuck in his childhood. The cue was banal, Preisner claimed, because the *man* is banal. When the film was finally screened with the music, the co-workers were swayed by the nuance the cue added. At other times, Preisner fought against a request to score music for a scene. Again in *Véronique*, when the puppeteer shows Véronique how the puppets dance, Kieślowski wanted some kind of dance music. Preisner rejected the suggestion as naïve. The only sounds heard, he suggested, should be that of the puppets, like bones clicking together. On the other hand, in the scene where Véronique is awoken by music which stops when she enters the kitchen, the idea for mysterious music being the awakening factor (intriguingly anticipating uses of music in *Blue*) was Preisner's. The composer, however, does not recall any discussion as intense regarding music for the trilogy. By that stage, the director trusted his musical director's decisions. Developing that trust had taken ten years and fourteen productions.

Preisner's longest account of how he and Kieślowski came to meet and work together reads as follows:[94]

> It all started in 1982. Poland is the sort of country where you just bump into people, and this is how I met Kieślowski. I was involved in writing a score for another film, and he was in the studio at the same time. We ended up going to a restaurant together—a very bad restaurant which served nothing but vodka and herrings. So we ate herrings, drank vodka, and he said to me "It's my first film and I'd be grateful if you'd write good music." He went rambling on like this for an hour, and I went away and did completely my own thing. He never had to ask me to write good music again.[95]

Preisner's "audition" with Kieślowski—a wide-ranging conversation fuelled by food, drink and, no doubt, the director's chain smoking—has something in common with the way in which Kieślowski selected lead actors and other co-workers. Screen tests and a philosophical *viva voce*, designed to discover if the candidate could be "tuned up," were parallel considerations. Preisner clearly enjoyed the social aspect of their relationship, as inaugurated by this memorable dinner: the pair and their families became close, sharing holidays together as well as meals and other social activities, both on and off productions. Off-set, Preisner recalled during our conversations, they rarely discussed film, music or the arts: skiing, cars, women and, occasionally, the meaning of life were more common topics of discussion. They would never have gone beyond their first film together, however, if their creative relationship had not immediately produced distinctive results.

Of their seventeen films together, for Preisner *No End* was the most important educational experience; it was also the foundation of Kieślowski's collaboration with Piesiewicz and other key co-workers. Regarding music's potential, however, to enhance a film's story and subtexts, *No End* was also a formative experience for the director. "That film," Preisner told Carlsson and Holm, "had something that has been with me ever since," so much so that "the music came back to me after [Kieślowski's] death"—the funeral march from *No End* and *Blue*.[96] The manner in which Preisner—an inexperienced composer at the time, working with a leading figure in his nation's cinema—was permitted to shape aspects of the film would soon become typical of Kieślowski's projects:

To start with, Krzysztof didn't really know what he wanted from the music. . . . He used it because it was the way that you used music, and somebody had to write it. . . . I knew from the beginning that I wanted to do something different with film music. I wanted to create some additional elements. With *No End*, I had the idea that the orchestra musicians should sing [the funeral march]. I wanted the effect of people in a church singing, so I told the orchestra, you play the pizzicato on the strings and sing at the same time. They mutinied against me. They said, "Why don't you get a choir? We can't sing at the same time. We'll be out of tune." I told them I wanted something natural. And that music, in the way it went together with the film, showed Kieślowski that music is not only something played by an orchestra, but it also has some kind of philosophy—and the philosophy can have many sources.[97]

While asking musicians in an orchestra to sing while they played had long been a staple of Polish avant-garde compositional practice, it may be true that Preisner encountered resistance from his session musicians. The revealing aspects of this anecdote, however, are that the idea that (1) the music should sound unlike conventional film music and more "natural," like a congregation chanting at a funeral, (2) that this should give the music a distinctive presence in the film, partly by (3) blurring the border between tale and telling, diegesis and nondiegetic realms, and (4) by drawing attention to the score's "side-by-side" perspective on a narrative's proceedings. One example occurs when Ula's son begins to play Preisner's adaptation of the "Holy God" chant on the family piano at the end of the film, and just before her suicide. Crossings between narrative levels are a staple of film scoring practices, but often occur in Kieślowski's films in marked ways. Here, the music's crossing between afterlife and life, nondiegetic score and diegesis, anticipates the border crossing Ula will undertake, as she moves beyond the diegesis and into the uncertain realm of the final shots, which show her reunited with her husband. Similar ideas are revisited and enriched in *Blue*.

Working on the *Decalogue* television series in 1989 and the two "short" (actually elongated) feature films that emerged from it was, after *No End*'s audition, a further learning opportunity for Preisner: twelve stepping stones towards artistic maturity. It was also a twelve-step program for Kieślowski to work through in terms of music's potential contributions to his films. Preisner's ambition was "to write completely different music for each film" and "to prove my ability to write music in various styles."[98] Again, however, the moments in those films where music accrues significance beyond accenting the action stood out, in retrospect, for the composer as typical of their collaborative intentions. Preisner describes this music as existing "on a borderline," not classical music, but demanding a certain level of conscious attention that meant that "at the same time it wasn't film music" (i.e., "unheard" dramatic underscoring) either.[99] In *Decalogue 2* and *9*, music became an integral part of the narrative of the films, picking up on the more integrated aspects of music in *No End* and providing further examples of "music . . . considered as part of the initial concept."[100] Such considerations became central in *The Double Life of Véronique* (1991) and the trilogy. As Preisner reports, "Krzysztof wanted [music] to have the strength to be an element of the film's narrative":

> This started to happen with *Dekalog* but was really explored with *Véronique* and the *Three Colors* series, which allowed the music . . . to become part of the story. Sometimes there was no need for words and dialogue when he used my music.[101]

Preisner's statement is borne out by the integrality of Preisner's pre-production involvement in the films. A draft script for *Véronique* read, the composer recounts, as follows for the scene where Weronika dies mid-performance: "Weronika sings: beautiful song."

> I said: "OK, Krzysztof, but what?" He said: "I don't know: find something." So I looked and I found the words from Dante's *Divine Comedy*. He said: "OK, that makes sense."[102]

The richness of the resulting scene reflects, in part, the composer's close pre-production involvement. As Kieślowski put it:

> Everything was very carefully written down in the [*Véronique*] screenplay. Where the music would go, what the music would be like, the nature of it and so on . . . but the fact that it was described didn't really change anything because a composer has to come along, in the end, and make something of what's been written in a literary language. How can you describe music? . . . You can write all this down but the composer's got to come along and find the notes. Then the musicians have to come along and play these notes. And all this, in the end, has to remind you of what was written down in literary language. And Zbigniew Preisner simply did it wonderfully.[103]

Idziak has noted the importance, for the full production team, of having access to so much of Preisner's music before shooting commenced on the trilogy's films, not merely to set the right mood but also to influence creative decisions affecting other aspects of the production.[104] While this was obviously fundamentally important to *Blue* and *Véronique*, its impact on other less obviously musical films, such as *Red*, should not be underestimated. Preisner also took an active role in working with the actors playing musicians in the films, for instance uniting Irène Jacob and Elżbieta Towarnicka at his home in Kraków to sing along with the playback to *Véronique*. Preisner wanted Jacob to study how to breathe in the same way as the soprano, so that "the audience . . . [would] be absolutely convinced that it was Irène singing in Polish."[105] For *Blue*, in turn, Binoche observed Preisner at a scoring session, in order to help her think her way into how her character approaches composing in *Blue*:

Juliette Binoche was with me during the recording of the music for the
concert before the shooting started, a good and very useful experience
for us both. She was able to observe the working method of an orchestra and the techniques of composition and I was able to explain to her
how an orchestra is recorded.[106]

While not literally learning how to compose (just as Jacob did not learn
how to be a concert soprano), Binoche studied how a creative musician
might behave by watching Preisner. The composer's commitment to the
projects throughout its production strongly affected what one sees and
what one hears.

Preisner and Kieślowski's accounts of their collaborative process
sang from the same hymn sheet. As Preisner explained:

[We] worked together very closely [from the first version of the
script] right up to the final stages of the film, the mixing, which is a
crucial moment when we worked out the proportions of the music to
everything else. At the stage of the final mix we took decisions about
the music and the effects and sometimes I'd add music. . . . For *Véronique* I recorded about 80 percent of the music before the film was
shot and for *Blue* I recorded almost all the music before the shooting.[107]

Kieślowski, in turn, highlighted the degree of interaction from script to
screen as exceptional, "in that he's interested in working on a film right
from the beginning and not just seeing the finished version and then
thinking about how to illustrate with music," thus permitting considerations of "the way [music] should say something that's not there in the
picture . . . [and] describe something which perhaps isn't there on the
actual screen but which, together with the music, starts to exist."[108] This
is not really so exceptional: Gabriel Yared's work with Anthony Minghella, as documented by Heather Laing concerning *The English Patient*
(1996), offers just one contemporary parallel to the *Three Colors* films.
The number of such partnerships are nonetheless dwarfed by the slew
of films in which scoring, in spite of its centrality to perceptions of a
film, is an afterthought. All films remain mutual creations and, as Giorgio Biancorosso has argued, once a film is perceived by audiences, it
will always be read as a "collaborative endeavour" in which "it is often
hard to credit an individual for a specific choice or effect," the most
prominently "credited names" (Kieślowski, Godard, Burton, Spielberg,
etc.) being "no more than publicly recognizable figureheads for work
that is fundamentally done by teams of people."[109] Some film collaborations, however, are surely more genuinely collaborative than others, as
in the case of the Kieślowski co-workers' efforts to intensify music's
potential to articulate the trilogy's narratives, concepts and ideals.

CHAPTER FOUR

THE *THREE COLORS* TRILOGY: CRITICAL CONTEXTS

Three Concepts

Liberty, equality, fraternity: "Is any motto better known?" asks Pierre Nora, "[o]r triter, appearing as it does on the façade of every town hall in France"?[1] In film as in life, from the police headquarters in *Casablanca* to the words emblazoned on the courthouses in *Blue* and *White*,[2] the motto that rose to prominence during the French Revolution (along with its colorful emblem, anthem and national holiday) and accompanied the definitive establishment of the French Republic in 1880, has become so well-worn as to feel like a cliché: modernity's fetish words.[3] One might therefore wonder, with Mona Ozouf, "[D]o we really see, can we actually still hear, these three words that so haunt our public life?," or have they become more like a logo than an emblem attuned "to the freight of the meaning they carry?"[4]

For the motto to be a *lieu de mémoire* rather than a banal transnational slogan, Ozouf argues, there must be acts of reimagining and recontextualization. The *Three Colors* trilogy is one such act. That the films are not merely synergistic appropriations of a master brand's pseudo-profundity reflects their creators' engagement with the inconclusive and questioning spirit of the motto itself, the mood of which "is indicative more than imperative."[5] Liberty, equality and fraternity are concepts to be contested. The motto, to adopt terms Kieślowski used regarding *Red*, is written in the conditional mood: what *could* be, not absolutes that already are. The *Three Colors* trilogy, an artistic statement arising in the aftermath of the bicentennial of the French revolution in 1989, lives up to Ozouf's requirement that such work should be "a symbol of the impossible rather than . . . a mirror of reality . . . something other than a chant of three tired old words."[6]

The orientation of Kieślowski's own discussion of the need to re-imagine the motto—to forge some kind of Liberty-Equality-Fraternity Redux—is noteworthy in this regard:

> Debates and mediations about what these words actually mean seem appropriate to me, for we often use words whose meanings we have forgotten. They become merely symbols of certain events and so become detached from reality, life, the concrete. . . . We have to reflect not only on where we find ourselves, but also on the meaning of these words that have shaped us throughout history, through eras, years, wars, revolutions and generations. These things are where we come from—the first, second and tenth commandments, but also "liberty, equality and brotherhood."[7]

The director's stress here is on the need for reflection by individuals, not just political bodies and public institutions. From Kieślowski's perspective, the key to actualizing the motto's meanings is to project them onto a personal, and thereby political, plane. It had been Krzysztof Piesiewicz's idea to base a trilogy around the motto's concepts and to dramatize a consideration of their meanings to contemporary society, but Kieślowski shrewdly focused that inquiry inwards, on what those words might mean to individual subjects in the context of their relationship to other people and contemporary societies. "The West has implemented these three concepts on a political or social plane," he told Stok, "but it's an entirely different matter on the personal plane."[8] The films investigate lives and societies constructed, but also crumbling, in the shadow of these concepts.

One might be tempted to ponder what the Kieślowski of, say, *Blind Chance* would have done with the trilogy. Some may rue—as another signifier of Kieślowski's alleged abdication of political responsibility—a missed opportunity in *Blue*, *White* and *Red* to consider the motto's potential to highlight, say, the blatant inequalities of late-modern capitalist societies.[9] As Ozouf notes, commentators at the time of the bicentennial noted the fraudulence of placing "the word *liberty* on the facades of prisons, to speak of *equality* when some went hungry, and to extol *fraternity* when immigrants were mistreated in urban slums"; such paradoxes help keep the motto's memory "as fresh as an open wound" in French society.[10] Recent Francophone cinema, not least under the unflinching direction of Michael Haneke in *Code Inconnu* and *Caché* (2000 and 2005), has dissected such issues (both films, incidentally, starred Binoche). In *Blue*, by contrast, the political and socio-economic paradoxes raised by Binoche's rich widow and her interaction with obviously disenfranchised characters, including a busking beggar and a sex worker, are not the film's focus. Instead, the political zoom of the trilogy is focused on the grain of the human condition and, specifically, the behavior of individuals at a time when once hallowed ideals have been hollowed out by the mechanisms of late modernity and high capitalism. *Blue*, *White* and *Red*'s explorations of liberty, equality and fraternity seek ways of refilling that void.

Liberty

Within political-philosophical debates on the meaning of "liberty"—from founding texts such as John Stuart Mill's *On Liberty* (1859) to Isaiah Berlin's *Two Concepts of Liberty* (1958) and beyond—a recurring pair of interlinked notions, "negative" and "positive" liberty, recur in different guises interlinked by the ideas of liberty as being *free from* and liberty as being *free to*. American philosopher Gerald MacCallum's meta-critical theory of "Negative and Positive Liberty" (1967),[11] however, diagnoses the duality as a false dichotomy and, instead, posits a tripartite conception:

> MacCallum defines the basic concept of freedom—the concept on which everyone agrees—as follows: a subject, or agent, is free from certain constraints, or preventing conditions, to do or become certain things. Freedom is therefore a triadic relation—that is, a relation between *three things*: an agent, certain preventing conditions, and certain doings or becomings of the agent. Any statement about freedom or unfreedom can be translated into a statement of the above form by specifying *what* is free or unfree, *from* what it is free or unfree, and what it is free or unfree *to do or become*.[12]

One might therefore summarize liberty as follows: X is free/unfree from Y to do or become/not to do or become Z. This formula provides a useful tool when considering Kieślowski's statements about liberty and *Blue*, not least as a means of identifying the film's specific contribution to this debate.

In discussion with Stok, having noted that the concepts of liberty, equality and fraternity are inextricably linked, Kieślowski claimed *Blue* is about "the imperfections of human liberty"[13] and the question of how far people are ever really free. The initial inspiration for the film is usually ascribed to Piesiewicz:

> One night, I saw a Polish composer being interviewed on television. He was with his wife. I said to myself that this woman must have an important role in his life.[14]

This may, however, have been an artful deception on the part of the filmmaking team, concocted in order to hide the actual inspiration for Julie's character and situation. Flying to Paris with Kieślowski, Preisner told me that he bumped into Elżbieta Penderecka, Krzysztof Penderecki's wife, on a plane. Preisner introduced Kieślowski to her and afterwards joked with the director, "Krzysztof, I believe that, for example, this lady, if something happened with Penderecki, . . . could finish his score." That, according to Preisner, was the origin for the idea of *Blue*. Preisner was impressed by the Pendereckis' close relationship and its productive contribution to the business side of the composer's career, and while the director and his co-writer apparently loathed Penderecki's music (in spite of Preisner's enthusiastic recommendations of various CDs), the idea of exploring a composer's relationship with his wife began to develop.[15] This is also one reason why, in *Blue*, the living composers' styles bear a passing resemblance to Penderecki's neo-romantic compositions ("it's his music, of course," Preisner informed me). The film's twist, however, was to deal with what happens to a composer's life and creative partner when those roles are suddenly erased. Julie—like so many other people in the West in the time of late modernity—finds her traditional roles erased and a vacuum in their place.

On the surface, as Kieślowski noted, it would seem Julie is perversely free after the accident and experiencing a "luxurious" situation:

> She's completely free at the beginning because her husband and daughter die, she loses her family and all her obligations. She is perfectly provided for, has masses of money and no responsibilities. And here the question arises: is a person in such a situation really free?[16]

Julie even seeks to intensify that state of "freedom" by further severing her ties to her past:

> In this sort of film there ought to be many scenes with her visiting the cemetery or looking at old photographs and so on. There aren't any shots like this at all. There's no past. She's decided to cross it out.[17]

And yet her past does not stay silent:

> If the past comes back it does so only in the music. But it appears that you can't free yourself entirely from everything that's been. You can't, because at a certain moment something like simple fear arises, or a feeling of loneliness or, for example, as Julie experiences at a certain moment, the feeling of having been deceived. This feeling changes Julie so much that she realizes she can't live the way she wanted to.[18]

The musical flashbacks in *Blue* are both harbingers of later experiences that call Julie's newfound liberty into question and, more potently, excruciating reminders of the things she has buried in order to shape her illusion of freedom: her grief and her musicality. Returning to the +/- liberty formula, Julie feels freed by her bereavements and loss of spousal and parental responsibilities to do anything—or rather, as she says in the film, to have and do nothing instead of something. However, her liberty is a crumbling façade. Julie is not yet free of her grief—it is buried in a shallow psychological grave—nor of her creative urges, which stem from the same buried past and break through, like a zombie's hand through the soil, confronting her with the falsity of her ostensible liberation. In turn, emotional revelations about her past intensify this nexus of dissatisfaction, forcing her to confront the fact that she is not free to do, become or, ultimately, be anything (or even nothing) as of yet. She must *act* to free herself anew.

Kieślowski framed his discussion of Julie's situation in socioeconomic terms by stressing her financial situation and then offering exemplifying parallels relating to, for instance, owning a car or a satellite TV. This is, in part, fairly typical of the director's discursive conversational style. In this context, however, Julie is revealed as a metaphor for broader currents of the late modern condition, as emotional attachments become comparable to the ownership of malfunctioning commodities:

> Is the cult of television a prison or is it freedom? Theoretically it's freedom because, if you've got a satellite, you can watch channels from all over the world. But in fact you immediately have to buy all sorts of gadgets to go with the television. And if it breaks down you have to take it to be repaired or get an engineer to come and do it for you. You get pissed off with what's being said or shown on television. In other words, while theoretically giving yourself the freedom of watching various things you're also falling into a trap with this gadget. . . .
> Well, that's freedom and the lack of freedom as regards objects. The same applies to emotions. To love is a beautiful emotion but in loving someone you immediately make yourself dependent on the person you love. You do what he likes, although you might not like it yourself, because you want to make him happy. So, while having these beautiful feelings of love and having a person you love, you start doing a lot of things that go against your own grain. That's how we've understood freedom in these three films. On the personal level.[19]

Such a view of freedom could be imagined to symbolize a nuanced consideration of capitalism after Polish communism (one can buy a new TV, but will it ultimately make one a happier person?), democracy over dictatorship (one has the vote, but does one have people and parties worth voting for?), or anything "good" one might attain in one's life (to remain free from doing anything, one must continue to do something else). Liberty thus emerges as a conceptual Catch-22, manifested in *Blue* in relation to Julie's "prison . . . created by both emotions and memory":

> There comes a moment when [Julie] starts to feel fine. She starts to function normally, smile, go for walks. So it is possible to forget. Or at least to try to forget. But suddenly there's jealousy and she can't get rid of it. . . . She tries to fight it off and she does so in an absurd way. She suddenly becomes so good that she's too good. But she can't get out of the trap. She puts it quite clearly at a certain moment in the film, that all this is a trap: love, pity, friendship.[20]

To forget, Kieślowski reminds one, takes an act of will that has within it the seeds of the selective amnesiac's destruction: one must remember what one is forgetting in order to forget it. Yet everyday life skews matters further still. Julie's life reminds her of what she seeks to forget, just as a satellite television can malfunction, robbing her of even an illusion of freedom from those buried memories and impulses. To be free, one must act; more profoundly, one must realize that freedom is literally unobtainable, and that the nearest one might come to it is continuously to seek to achieve it. Liberty is attainable only within a framework restricting one's liberty. *Blue* therefore recalibrates Mac-Callum's formulation into an endless feedback loop: x is free/unfree from y to do or become/not to do or become z, which in turn breeds the fresh impingement y^1; so x frees herself from y^1 to do or become/not to do or become z^1, which now breeds impingement y^2; and so on. Liberty—from the past, from one's music, from one's grief—can only be achieved through a certain lack of liberty, which in *Blue* requires Julie to sacrifice tangible aspects of the freedom that initially, after her bereavement, seem within her grasp. Richly, this conception of liberty is filtered through the film's meditation on grieving, gender politics, creative endeavor and interpersonal relationships, and often primarily through the contribution of Preisner's score and its pointed deployment throughout *Blue*.

Equality

Ozouf's discussion of equality suggests that, even though *White* is expressly about that concept, like the other trilogy installments its themes must inevitably shade into the motto's other components:

> Were liberty and equality then twins, peacefully [and] religiously harmonious . . . [o]r were they enemies? Twins to be sure, in the sense that only individual rights can be universalized, and yet also enemies, because liberty is indeterminate, whereas equality requires determination (equal to whom? equal to what?), thus giving rise to the modern woe, the need to compare oneself to others.[21]

This late-modern side-effect of our apparent equality—the need to keep up with or, more honestly, to exceed the achievements of the Joneses—lies at the heart of *White*'s treatise. Just as Kieślowski realized freedom cannot exist without constraints, *White* cuts through lofty notions of equality by considering the way people actually behave towards each other when notionally free enough to feel equal:

> *White* is about equality understood as a contradiction. We understand the concept of "equality," that we all want to be equal. But I think this is absolutely not true. I don't think anybody really wants to be equal. Everybody wants to be more equal. There's a saying in Polish: There are those who are equal and those who are more

equal. That's what used to be said during Communism and I think it's still being said. That's what the film's about.[22]

Echoing George Orwell's famous line in *Animal Farm* (1945)—"All animals are *equal*, but some animals are *more equal than others*"— Kieślowski stresses how such phrases continue to hold value in post-communist economies: the system changes, pigs become men, but so much else really stays the same. In capitalist societies, moreover, everyone is ideologically coerced into becoming a pig at the trough. *White*'s Karol will become such an animal and veer perilously close to losing the kinder face of his humanity.

Karol's humiliation by his wife Dominique, and his subsequent revenge, plays out in a manner which satirizes early 1990s Polish capitalism, with playful and earthy humor to offset its less palatable ironies. It is not merely that *White* highlights the idiocies of new Polish capitalism as the background to a romantic farce of role reversal and lovers reunited. Rather, Karol's trajectory becomes an ironic allegory of life under capitalism with resonances well beyond the wild frontier of Poland's freed markets, legal and black, around 1993. *White* highlights key dilemmas of late-modern life, and not least the clash between objects and emotions in a world fetishizing satellite TVs and foreign cars in the place of time-worn mottos and beliefs. Kieślowski stated:

> Everything [Karol] ever had is taken away from him and his love is rejected. Consequently, he wants to show that not just is he not as low as he's fallen, not just is he on a level with everybody else, but that he's higher, that he's better.[23]

Karol does this by seeking to establish himself as a capitalist success, which in turn enables him elaborately to extract revenge on the person who has wronged him:

> [H]e does everything he can to prove to himself and to the woman who, to put it mildly, has spurned him, that he's better than she thinks. And he does. Therefore he becomes more equal. Except that, while becoming more equal, he falls into the trap which he's set his wife because it turns out that he [still] loves her—something he didn't know.[24]

At the end of *White*, Karol and Dominique thus discover that equality only comes at the loss of certain freedoms and commodities which, throughout the film, each had cherished as a marker of what makes them more than equal. To be equal, in *White*, is to have less. Like the freedoms Julie sacrifices in *Blue* to reintegrate with her community, in *White* the pair must set aside belongings and, indeed, freedoms to obtain something richer.

Fraternity

Kieślowski's description of the concept of fraternity as it pertains in *Red* emerged from his discussion of *White*:

> I've got an increasingly strong feeling that all we really care about is ourselves. Even when we notice other people we're still thinking of ourselves. That's one of the subjects of the third film, *Red*—fraternity.[25]

Again, a trilogy installment's take on one of the motto's concepts evokes a kind of antithesis and, in this case, the gulf between notions of brotherhood and their manifestations in a society privileging individuality and self-indulgence through consumption and narcissism. Even Valentine, the most apparently selfless of *Red*'s characters, is depicted by Kieślowski as acting, at least in part, in order to please herself:

> Now the question arises: even when we give of ourselves, aren't we doing so because we want to have a better opinion of ourselves? . . . There's something beautiful in the fact that we can give something of ourselves. But if it turns out that while giving of ourselves we are doing so in order to have a better opinion of ourselves then immediately there's a blemish on this beauty. Is this beauty pure?[26]

Red therefore examines the contrast between notions of virtue borne, in reality, of self-centered moralizing, and the possibility of a more genuinely fraternal mode of philanthropy and relationship. It seeks to articulate how fraternity, like liberty and equality, might be reimagined in late-modern times—or reengineered through the concept of *agapē*.

On the surface, there might seem to be little relationship between reimagining fraternity and the topic Kieślowski subsequently claimed that *Red* "is really about": the question of whether "people aren't, by some chance, sometimes born at the wrong time."[27] Yet his identification of "the essential question" asked by *Red* hints at the manner in which the film may be read as an allegorical reflection on deliberations about fraternity. Valentine and the old judge, Joseph Kern, should have been born at the same time, Kieślowski asserts; at the end of *Red*, Valentine appears united with a younger judge whose life parallels the old judge's past. One is led to believe that this may right a historical wrong. The narrative, as it were, philanthropically heals the wound at the heart of its fiction, putting right fate's wrong turn. But do the filmmakers do so to offer a gift to their audience, such as a gesture of hope at the close of the trilogy's potentially bleak coda, or for selfish reasons, such as winning critical plaudits or making money at the box office? Like freedom and equality, acts of fraternal affection may only be achievable in the presence of their shadow: selfish desire.

Ozouf notes how fraternity has come to be held as a right, not a duty, through its merging with the concept of "solidarity"—a term freighted with obvious revolutionary significance in recent Polish history[28]—and she argues for an understanding of the concept that begins to shade *Red*'s concerns back into *Blue*'s meditation on liberty and *White*'s on equality. Fraternity is "that which compels us to come to one another's aid," an "instinctive sympathy," a realm of "concerns and feelings, hopes and strivings." She also quotes an attempt to explain to school children why the three words must thus remain together:

> If you take away one of the three, the remaining two no longer make any sense. Without liberty, equality can be the most abominable form of slavery, for under a tyrant everyone is equal. Without fraternity, liberty leads to selfishness.[29]

And selfishness paves the way, to return to Terry Eagleton's jazz band metaphor, for a society of people playing solos, heedless of the other members of their ensemble, fighting to be heard in isolation, and thus making a din of indignation. Considered together like the interdependent motto terms, *Blue*, *White* and *Red* structure a subtle counterargument to late-modern capitalism's politics of the will, and its effects on the experience of subjectivities embroiled in the traffic between the plusses and minuses of democracies old and new. The *Three Colors* trilogy offers no pat answers to the dilemma of how to live better in such societies, yet each film hints at a hope that the three concepts can be redeemed for any one person at any given moment. Throughout the trilogy, small acts of abnegation, sacrifice, reciprocation, generosity and basic human kindness pave the way for renewed experiences of liberty, equality and fraternity. The timeworn motto is reborn in the spirit of *agapē*.

Three Color Schemes

As Andrew points out, while the trilogy's French-Polish-Swiss coproductions were officially titled *Trois couleurs: Bleu*, *Trois couleurs: Blanc* and *Trois couleurs: Rouge*, "they were also widely known, even at their festival premieres, by their English titles"; for brevity's sake, it became common to refer to them as *Blue*, *White* and *Red*.[30] Those words also highlight one of the most arresting features of the trilogy: the chromatic play of its art direction, lighting and camera filters, which reflects its titular blue, white and red. What do these colors signify in the trilogy—and how?

The choice of blue for liberty, white for equality and red for fraternity does not reflect a stable relationship, in post-revolutionary France or anywhere else, between the colors of the tricolor and the motto's three terms; any such relationship is arbitrary. True, the tricolor emblem was, Ozouf reports, "born on a precise date, July 17, 1789," when Louis XVI pinned red and blue ribbons alongside a white cockade already affixed to his hat; red and blue were the colors of the city of Paris, white the royal shade. Also, the words were sometimes emblazoned across the flag, partly as a gesture of appeasement to demonstrators who had wanted the whole flag a bloody revolutionary red as a symbol of the new Republic. But if the flag and its colors stand for any one aspect of the motto at all, it is probably liberty. For the Third Republic, Raoul Girardet writes, the flag "stood for adherence to the 'liberties' of 1789 . . . and at the same time for equilibrium and continuity in the face of ever-present subversive threats."[31]

One might therefore argue that the colors attached to the films carry no specifically French, let alone transnational, symbolic significance, and that this lack of specificity may have appealed to Kieślowski. Certainly, the director stated that he titled the films *Blue, White* and *Red*, rather than *Liberty, Equality* and *Fraternity*, because colors as titles are more semantically ambivalent, and even contradictory, thereby encouraging a more interpretative dialogue between film and viewer.[32] He even suggested (perhaps not entirely playfully) that, if funding for the trilogy had come principally from Germany, he would have colored the trilogy differently:

> Actually, freedom ought to be in red . . . it would be revolution, blood, and so on. But I term it "blue" for the simple reason that on the French flag—and the film's finances came from France—blue is the first color. If a different country had provided the finance—Germany, for instance—and I had made it as a German film, then yellow would have taken the place of blue and one would have had "yellow, red, and black." It really is not important. However, the very fact that it has this name means that it is open to possible interpretations . . . [and] that "blue" need not mean "freedom" at all, but actually be its complete opposite; and that it can be freedom too—for why shouldn't it?[33]

While indicating the director's desire not to permit the films' meanings to be corralled into a chromatic cul-de-sac, Kieślowski's statement that the three colors are "really . . . not important" is neither a perceptual nor a cultural reality. People situated in different cultural communities flood the colors with meanings according to their societies' dictates. The following reading, for instance, will make sense to some Western Europeans and Americans:

> Watched in order of their release, the films progress through a literal warming, a triumphal emergence from isolation into community, from the numb, bloodless chill of "Blue" through the pale fire of "White" to the blushing, blossoming heat of "Red."[34]

The reading of red as "blushing" and "blossoming" may relate, in this case, to the notion of romance connoted by that color in a culture which views red through the dozen rose-tinted spectacles of commercial bonanzas like St. Valentine's Day. As Kieślowski pointed out, however, colors take on different meanings in different places, even within the

West: "I've met numerous people from various parts of the world—and even from our cultural sphere—who have explained that there are vastly different relations between these colours."[35] Coates sensibly argues that the "'meanings' of blue, white or red are cloudy connotations, 'outrunning' any cloth they might decorate . . . [and] invit[ing] the viewer to a dialogue that may well lack a clear ending."[36] Kickasola too argues for the semantic ambivalence of color, arguing that the "chromatic dialogue" in the trilogy structures "visual motifs of a polysemous nature" and thus "screens to receive our projected feelings."[37]

Some critics are still tempted to argue for transcultural symbolism in relation to the colors' meanings. This is an easy game to play. They could be related, simplistically, to the hue skin goes when people die, the color of daylight, the tone of skin flushing when aroused. Irina Paulus makes a more sophisticated argument along these lines, quoting Johannes Itten's *The Art of Colour* and linking color to musical atmosphere, and tragedy, in *Blue*:

> Blue is always cold, red warm. Blue works in an introverted way, as if it were withdrawn into itself. . . . Blue is like a muffled power that is possessed by nature in winter, when all germination, all growth, rest in darkness and quiet. Blue is always shadowy, and in its strongest shades leans towards the dark. It is the intangible nothing, and yet it is present, as the transparent atmosphere is also present.[38]

Yet rather than clutching at essentialist straws concerning the colors' significances, it may be most productive to read, intrafilmically, for their significance within the world of the trilogy. A web of associative meanings connects occurrences of red, white and blue in the films. Furthermore, Kieślowski and his co-workers intertextually branded those colors, like mottos on a flag, over the course of his entire oeuvre, with blue, white and red symbolically deployed in Kieślowski's films from at least *No End* onwards.[39] The occurrence of the colors in recurring contexts, in turn, channels their significance into consistent semantic zones.

Blue

Given that one can speak of feeling blue, but not white or red, it is perhaps unsurprising that the color coding of the first film has inspired the greatest amount of discussion in the Kieślowski literature. Some writers have sought intertextual meanings,[40] others meanings developed by *Blue* itself.

Andrew argues that, "Throughout [*Blue*], blue will be used not as a sign of 'freedom,' but to create moods of melancholy and coldness, and to draw attention to the resonant emotional associations conjured up by objects and places in Julie's mind."[41] A blue lampshade, blue pitches on manuscript paper, a blue sweet wrapper, a blue folder of notes and photos: all are objects causing Julie's most disturbing paroxysms of grief and acts of repression. The color thereby conditions the audience via structured associations. Falkowska develops such an idea, noting how the color blue takes on precise meanings in *Blue* without the need to refer to clichés of melancholy, coldness or "the blues." The blue candy wrapper, for instance, having become freighted in the opening sequence (where it is played with by the daughter, who dangles it out of the window of the family's speeding car) with "connotations of melancholy[,] . . . changes into the colour of mourning when we learn from the subsequent sequence that Julie's husband and daughter have died in the accident."[42] Certainly, if one's knowledge of blue's symbolism came only from watching Kieślowski films, or even just from *Blue* itself, one might draw similar conclusions to those seeking familiar external reference points for the color's meaning.

However, would blue's association with melancholy, sacrifice, mourning, maternal tears, trauma, loss, withdrawal, coldness and separation be the only thing one learns from *Blue* about the color? Coates quotes Kandinsky on dark blue's intimation of "the deep seriousness of things where there is no end"[43] and adds that, "As the cinematic colour of 'day for night' . . . it signifies the proximity of darkness and dream, those traditional domains of the metaphysical manifestations of such interest to 'late Kieślowski.'"[44] Paulus quotes another shade of blue emerging from Itten's study of color, the blue that "fills the spirit with flutterings of faith" while suggesting "the abyss of terror, superstition, spiritual unease and loss," and yet also "signifies the kingdom of the supernatural and the transcendental."[45] There is more to blue than "the blues," just as there is much more to *Blue* than grief. Julie, in a sense, moves through various shades of blue *en route* to another color entirely: after briefly surfacing in *White*, she finally reappears in *Red*.

In this respect, the trajectory of blue's significations in *Blue* may be significant. For Žižek, drawing on "standard colour psychology, blue stands for autistic separation, for the coldness of introversion, of the withdrawal-into-self."[46] Julie in *Blue* can thus be related to the color's prominence in *Decalogue 3*, a film about a spurned former mistress that, "In its tonality and mood . . . announces *Blue*: not only is *Blue* its predominant colour, but its universe is cold and distanced," and one never feels able to breach that distance between audio-viewer and protagonist, even when one learns of Ewa's suffering.[47] The cuckolded husband in *Decalogue 9* also suffers in a film saturated with blues. However, for Emma Wilson, developing ideas from Julia Kristeva, "all colours, *but blue in particular* as the first colour perceived by the child's retina, take the adult back to the stage before the identification of objects and individuation," thereby shaping what Kristeva calls blue's "noncentred or decentring effect."[48] This diametrically opposes the view of blue as an alienated withdraw into self, positing blue instead as the world before one can comprehend individuation and experience alienation, because one believes everything and everyone to be connected, or to be as one. Both readings, though, may be apposite to *Blue*.

Julie, after she has been bereaved, is dragged slowly out of her time of withdrawal and back into connections to the world.

White

Critics have played all kinds of games with the meanings of the "blanc" in *White*'s French title. Insdorf connects it both to Karol's assisting of Mikołaj's suicide attempt and his impotence. "[H]ow pungent," she writes, "that *tirer à blanc* means firing a blank," and that "'firing a blank' can also mean sterile."[49] Wilson connects the title, and the film's flashbacks to Karol and Dominique's white wedding, to the term *mariage en blanc*'s near homonym *mariage blanc*, or "unconsummated marriage."[50] She also cites Richard Dyer's study of white people's cultural representations of whiteness, particularly the link between whiteness and death, and his view of white as blankness or annihilation. She quotes: "Death may in some traditions be a vivid experience, but within much of the white tradition it is a blank that may be immateriality (pure spirit) or else just nothing at all."[51] Dyer, as considered in detail in Chapter Six, links this blankness to "a sense of the dead end of whiteness" surfacing in a range of recent films made by white people and featuring prominent uses of the color,[52] many of which, like *White*, center around examinations of masculinity in late-modern crisis. Insdorf and Wilson's "failures"—to shoot a gun, to be fertile, to be potent—all fail to satisfy stereotypical markers of success for straight white men. To this whitewash, one may add the term "bieła tango" ("white tango"), a Polish dance tradition which Preisner says is familiar in local halls across the country, and in which women, not men, instigate the dancing. *White* features a tango where Karol is seeking to regain the upper hand.

Kieślowski himself hinted that the emptiness of white is a key to the film's whiteness. He stated in an interview that white is not freighted with symbolism to the degree of blue and red because it is so hard to capture on film: it is an *absence* of color, as he describes it,[53] echoing Dyer. For Kickasola, this permits white in *White* to function, even more so than blue and red in the other two films, as "an emotional canvas onto which we will project various meanings derived from our interaction with the narrative."[54] Reading Falkowska's strong interpretation of white as symbolizing not only "the starkness of Karol's life, but also the cruelty" of his wife's indifference—she sees the color, like Dominique, as ironical, cold, insensitive—one might feel that Kickasola has a useful point to make about the limits of productive interpretation, although both critics agree that the whiteout, when Karol finally sexually satisfies Dominique, is a blast of equality.[55]

White as a color can thus go at least two ways: on the one hand, it can symbolize purity, goodness, transcendence; on the other, a blankness, the void, even death—a disturbing dualism of the kind one finds reflected in many Kieślowski films. Intriguingly, Andrew links this dualism to *White*'s score: "*White* proffers an account of love as an emotion which may be either blind, cruel, possessive and immature," he argues, "or warm, curative, transforming and mutually advantageous," just as "the color white has a double-edged resonance in the film, evocative of purity and filth, both physical and moral."[56] In his reading, Preisner's score similarly contrasts ironic but positive flourishes of tango and piano virtuosity to the "plaintive, lonely-sounding melody for oboe or clarinet" that alerts the audience to the film's "more serious undertones."[57] Like the actors in *White*, he suggests, Preisner achieves "a careful balance between meticulous comic timing and emotional veracity."[58] While opening the possibility that the films have differently "colored" scores, it must be noted that one of the film's most critical cues is heard as the other prominent color in *White* occurs—a fourth shade that also occurs at key moments in *Blue* and *Red*. At the end of *White*, when Karol gazes up at Dominique in her high prison window and, finally, the pair experience a kinder form of love, "cruel and indifferent white gives way to the warm tones of gold and orange which promise the presence of feelings, however unfulfilled they may be"[59]— a promise Kehr reads back into the very blankness of white as a "void that might be filled."[60] The final shot of the film, however, is of Karol's pale face.

Red

Rather than focusing one's experiences from the perspective of a single protagonist or notion, *Red*'s reds direct one to the intrafilmic connections between its characters, animals, objects and occurrences, and thus to the manifold fraternities of the film's story, discourse and subtext. Jon Paxman's analysis of this process is telling: "the colour . . . is developed as a metonymical construct to signify destiny, suggesting as it does a mysterious, portentous connection," not least between Valentine and the young judge, Auguste.[61] Like the *mise-en-shot* linking the two in the opening sequence of the film, the many reds in their apartments serve "as an additional corroborating channel to deeper, mystical connections."[62] In this sense, the use of color in *Red* makes it part of the trilogy in which color and music play the most similar roles. Preisner's score forms the other key ingredient of the metaphysical glue binding the young judge and Valentine together.

A number of critics have nonetheless pursued extra-filmic color symbolism in their interpretation of red in the trilogy. For Kehr, red is "the color of blood, danger, embarrassment, violence, and love"; for Irène Jacob, who plays Valentine, her character and the old Judge "blush inside themselves, red for rage, shame and confusion."[63] Insdorf expands on this sentiment, suggesting that red evokes "the pulsating of blood in the body—not necessarily violent or sexual . . . but a rhythm like that of telephone wires that physically transport the human spirit."[64] Like the insistence of Preisner's bolero and its ostinato rhythm, red thrums throughout the film, evoking "danger, blood, warmth, passion and, perhaps most importantly here, the life force."[65]

As Kickasola points out, while "it is [diegetically] plausible that red would be present in the frame" whenever the color occurs, "it is clear from the film as a whole that the look is stylized" and that the color is there to evoke notions of "blood and love, trauma and tenderness,"[66] but also to play a wider role. One is leitmotivic: it relates a set of characters in the manner that a score's variations on a basic musical motif might link together members of a family. In *Red*, however, the color also functions more obliquely, by gradually impinging on one's consciousness and forming an enigmatic penumbra at the edge of one's attention: why is that color here, and what does it mean? The resolution of that enigma, in the closing frames of the film, is one of the means by which *Red* ends the trilogy so affectingly.

As with "unheard" music, color often passes "unseen" in film, although some films use color ambitiously and most films tinker with mood through both stereotypical color connotations and the affective impact of contrast. Colors, like music, can be deployed in ways that make their emotional cues and cultural representations more experientially resonant. The orgasmic whiteout in *White*, for instance, dazzles like the sun, especially in the dark of a cinema, just as explosions of sound in *Blue* make one jump. Other uses of color recall the deployment of style topics by film composers. Are there such things as color *topoi*? Borrowing Raymond Monelle's distinction, one could differentiate, in Kieślowski's films, between *indexical* color topics to which audiences in a cultural community have been reliably conditioned intertextually to respond by their culture's standard representations thereof, and *iconic* ones, with which only perceivers knowledgeable of a particular artist's work will be familiar.[67] All films, consciously or otherwise, deploy such devices; in Kieślowski's cinema, however, these devices are made to work harder than usual, not least in their iconic roles and contribution to a narrative's symbolic representations.

Insdorf's honest observation, concerning *Red*, that most audioviewers do not notice the sheer amount of red the first time around, but later come to notice "how the very color red has connected characters, scenes, and perhaps temporal dimensions,"[68] stands for the impact of the signature colors in the other episodes of the trilogy. Yet once one notices them, one sees them everywhere, although the use of color throughout the trilogy is more balletic than a cold list of appearances and contexts can begin to suggest. A moment of grief in Julie's blue lagoon of solitude is shattered, for instance, by a deluge of children diving into her neighborhood swimming pool wearing white bathing suits and red armbands, as if to remind her and the perceiver, via the trilogy's metonymic color symbolism, of everything else she lost (parity, community) along with her child and husband. Such recurrences create a sense of unity across the trilogy, making the films parts of its universe. The presence of Preisner's music provides one narratorial frame that unites the trilogy stylistically—given the distinctive changes to cinematographer between films, for instance—but the film's diegetic contents are marked for wholeness by the conceit of their palette. Like Preisner's scores, however, the color design of the films becomes so apparent that it renders opaque the transparency of the films, drawing attention instead to their art and artifice, and thus rendering the perceiver more active—although not merely active, surely, in order to notice that one is being beaten over the head by a colorful stick painted "Example of Art Cinema as a Mode of Film Practice." Perceivers gradually note the colors and cues, and then question their purpose, the accrual of awareness demanding critical acts linking both to the trilogy's concepts.

Overviews of the *Three Colors* Trilogy

The key divisions in Kieślowski reception outlined in Chapter Three are represented in critics' attempts to read the trilogy as a whole, not least in terms of responses to the trilogy's focus: its take on the motto's terms and on aspects of love. Andrew quotes Kieślowski as saying that, "If you were to speak to, say, Bosnians or Croatians about their idea of political freedom, they'd contradict each other, whereas they'd probably have the same idea of personal freedom, or of love. There are so many things that separate people around the world today that one ought perhaps to look for factors that unite people . . . just to state that such things exist."[69] Haltof, in turn, calls the films "not so much a trilogy about liberty, equality and fraternity but, as Tony Rayns has said, 'a trilogy about love in the 1990s.'"[70] More precisely, one might argue that the trilogy concerns the *absence* of certain types of love by the mid-1990s and the suffering thus caused, not least as people seek to experience liberty, equality and fraternity.

Kickasola offers a historically contextualized rebuttal to views of the films as superficial. He argues that the trilogy is dealing with concepts applicable to "any democratic society," in terms of the "inherent tensions" those ideas generate when they clash with "an all too imperfect universe" and its emotionally messy inhabitants. This, in turn, is precisely the project one might expect to issue from a director in a newly democratic country seeking to "transcend local politics."[71] Hence the films' focus on "individuals who can't quite find their bearings, who don't quite know how to live . . . and are desperately looking," because they have lost faith in something bigger—the fairness of life (*Blue*), love (*White*) or the decency of other human beings (*Red*)—and the need to revisit aspects of existence symbolized by the motto to forge a "*modus vivendi* [and] to regain some sense of equilibrium, happiness and shared humanity."[72] That *modus vivendi*, Kieślowski subsequently clarifies, is revealed anew through the trilogy's particular take on love. The relationship that develops between the Judge and Valentine, for Kickasola, "interrogate[s] the very definition of love (the bedrock beneath 'fraternity')," and he develops this idea to state (especially persuasively if one tweaks the "love" in what follows to *agapē*) that "the entire trilogy has been built upon this concept":

> The liberty of *Blue* is posited to be the fruit of love, as demonstrated by the final sequence. The inverted approach to equality in *White* is shown to be the product of love's absence and its surprising reappearance the hope for the film's redemption. *Red*'s fraternity is revealed to be a path to a more far-reaching love, stretching beyond ordinary temporal friendship into the vast expanse of cosmological possibility.[73]

Žižek provides a parallel reading of the trilogy as a whole before discussing the role of music in the trilogy:

> Insofar as *Decalogue* relates to the Old Testament Commandments, one is tempted to read the *Colours* trilogy as implicitly referring to the three New Testament virtues: Faith, Hope, Charity (Love); the triad of Liberty-Equality-Fraternity can only function in an authentic way if supported by the *other* triad, Faith-Hope-Charity.[74]

Liberty, in this view, becomes a true form of freedom only if sustained by *agapē*; hence, in *Blue*, Julie takes the path from cold, abstract freedom to the fuzzier liberties of a spirit granted life by partly subjugating herself to others. Similarly, he reads *White* as ending with a sign of hope, and *Red* as an argument for the manner in which faith, i.e., trust in others, permits the Judge to reenter society. He then connects the end of the trilogy to the one proposed as the climax of the *Decalogue* although never filmed. The *Decalogue* was to have ended with an explosion destroying the tower blocks ("a pun on the last judgement"); in the *Three Colors*, disaster ensues when the ferry sinks, killing over a thousand people, save for the trilogy's main protagonists, who "miraculously survive the catastrophe" because, having embraced these virtues, they have pleased a kinder, New Testament God.[75]

Within this context, Preisner's scoring is "a musical constant," making possible "a familiar and yet at the same time individual experience for the spectator"; Preisner "redeems completely," Žižek states, the idea of the trilogy on the musical level.[76] The music is a discursive constant in the telling of the tales, and a narratorial presence and perspective is maintained throughout by Preisner's presence. It is clearly the case that, in terms of the telling of the stories, with cinematography and editing, for instance, being undertaken by three people, music and sound (a team that also remained constant) bears much of the weight of consistency. Preisner actually makes very few musical links between the films in the form of, for instance, leitmotivic relationships. Yet the consistency of musical voice engenders a sense of a continuous and politically alternative perspective, even as the specific styles and materials of the music are devised to suit each particular narrative.

Other writers have sought metaphors from the arts and sometimes music to symbolize the trilogy as a whole. For Kehr, the trilogy "fol-

lows the traditional pattern of the three-act play: an opening statement
of themes and images (*Blue*), a reversal of those themes (*White*), and
finally a synthesis and resolution (*Red*) that moves the themes to a different level," thus forming an "epic of reconciliation, in which fragmented parts come together to make a whole" constituting "one continuous gesture."[77] Andrew, in turn, attempts a bold musical metaphor
for the trilogy. Alongside "contributing directly to the story of *Blue*, and
play[ing] a significant role in enhancing all three of the trilogy's films'
moods and meanings . . . the overall structure of the trilogy itself" can
be considered "in terms of rhythm, tone and range, not so very unlike
that of a symphony."[78] This idea develops from his description of *White*
as a lighter middle movement, a lull before the final storm, and a
chance to draw breath between the draining first and last "movements"
of the action:

> if one views the trilogy in symphonic terms, [*White*'s] often jaunty
> mood and fast-paced narrative suggest that it may be seen as a delight-
> ful *scherzo allegretto*, wisely sandwiched between the sombre *mode-
> rato* of *Blue* and the magisterially expansive *allegro non troppo* of
> *Red*.[79]

This neat conceit could be further refined. Symphonies can also form
epics of reconciliation. A piece can begin by tearing open a breach between key materials, and then proceed by seeking to bridge that divide,
generating dramatic conflict and, if reconciliation is achieved, permitting a sense of wholeness and fulfillment to succeed tension and fragmentation. One might even argue that there is a way in which the trilogy feels even more symphonic: the structure of the whole
(fragmentation overcome by the reconciliation of parts) is nested within
the structure's opening movement (i.e., *Blue*), like a motif whose enigmatic implications are unpacked over the course of an entire symphony.

Given the three "movements" of the work, however, and its sharply
etched "soloists," i.e., its main protagonists, each voiced by a virtuoso
performer, one might prefer to consider the trilogy as being like a concerto grosso, and thus a piece in which a group of protagonists interact
with each other *and* with an orchestra or "society," their collective odyssey a search for a *modus vivendi*. For Joseph Kerman, concertos offer
allegorical "relationship stories," as roles and relationships between
individuals and groups change over time, musical forms thus becoming
"a mnemonic field with markers rather than a preset matrix for narrative" that permits individual perceivers to find personalized readings of
the patterns, relating a piece, for instance, to social and political issues.[80] The relationships between the protagonists and their environments in the trilogy, as between the soloists and orchestra in a concerto,
are the imprecise signifiers of a multiplicity of individual yet intercon-
nected readings. And just as following a soloist's journey in a concerto
may prompt musings on the stuff of life, following the films from a

musical perspective invites one to consider afresh its meditations on liberty, equality, fraternity, and the unifying conceptual motif of *agapē*.

Kinds of *Blue*

Three Colors: Blue is a study in bereavements literal and symbolic, personal and societal. Its protagonist, Julie, seeks liberation from a galling double loss. In the film's brutally clinical opening, a car accident kills Julie's composer husband, Patrice, and her young daughter, Anna. In an instant, chance abducts both Julie's family and her defining roles as a mother and wife. After an unsuccessful suicide attempt and a period of convalescence in hospital, Julie tries to free herself from her pain. First, she seeks liberty through repression and avoidance, entering a period of ostensibly splendid isolation by cutting personal and material ties to her past. Second, she is pressed, against her conscious will, into a nexus of relationships with new people and elements of her former life, primarily via her connection to music, and particularly to her husband's unfinished final composition—a *Concert[o] for the Unification of Europe* commissioned to be performed throughout the continent on the night of this fictional event. Julie therefore slips into a dialectically opposite activity: painful confrontations with the traces, musical or otherwise, of Anna, Patrice and her past, not least by tracking down her husband's mistress, who is carrying his child, and by completing the unfinished *Concert[o]*. Throughout *Blue*, Julie is haunted, terrified and, occasionally, beguiled by music from the *Concert[o]* and elsewhere. When she finally re-engages purposefully with music, she locates a path leading beyond the worst of her grief, as represented by the closing ten minutes of the film: an audacious montage of the film's main characters synchronized to her version of the *Concert[o]*.

In 2002 Nick James, editor of *Sight and Sound*, nominated *Blue* as a recent film to stand shoulder to shoulder with works in the journal's ten-yearly critics' poll of the greatest films yet made and topped in 2002 by *Citizen Kane*, *Vertigo* and *La règle du jeu*.[81] James's nomination confronted the notion that great films are no longer being created, but also criticisms leveled against *Blue*, specifically, and later Kieślowski more generally as representing the dead end of art house chic.[82] "[F]ar from an enraptured hymn to graceful looks and elegant posturing," he argued, "savage irony and remarkable austerity . . . hold sway":

> [Y]ou might say *Blue* is too small a film and that its historical impact was slight. But if cinema as an art is still alive, it will be in a large part due to film-makers like Kieślowski who know the whole history of their craft and yet revivified their means and methods constantly, however modest the scale.[83]

Coming from the editor of a British Film Institute journal dedicated to examining, but also to promoting, art house filmmaking, such praise may form part of a broader mission. James's key critical point, however—that while *Blue*'s means may be modest, its aesthetic or moral achievement feel disproportionately significant—is a provocation to which this section, in preparation for Chapter Five's close analysis of *Blue*, seeks to attend by considering the complex of critical issues generated by this small but substantial film.

(Mis)hearing *Blue*

The Kieślowski literature's thumbnail sketches of *Blue* strike notes of somber affirmation while highlighting themes in its critical reception. "Shot, scored, scripted and performed with great sensitivity," Andrew writes, "*Blue* is an admirably tough, penetrating study of loss, grief and loneliness; even the deeply affirmative tone of its coda is free of maudlin sentimentality"[84]; Kehr picks up on *Blue*'s focus on a self in crisis, labeling it "a film of intense subjectivity" and "psychological drama"[85]; Insdorf depicts an "emotionally dark, visually haunting, and musically ravishing" experience.[86] Kickasola offers particularly strong testimony which unintentionally highlights an absence in *Blue*'s critical reception: sustained, well-informed or detailed discussion of Preisner's score.

> This film is an incarnation of grief: its unwieldiness, lulls, rhythms, frightening unpredictability, bursts of aggression, nebulous sense of time, and utter emptiness. The film is a requiem composed in images. . . . It is a masterwork of phenomenological articulation. Kieślowski excels most when he speaks the language of *experience*, not words. The images are insightful, even devastating poetry, illuminating the many nuances of bereavement.[87]

In spite of his metaphorical evocation of a musical genre (the requiem mass), Kickasola's summary exhibits a form of scopophilia common in screen studies and pitilessly exposed in criticism of films as sonically rich as *Blue*.[88]

Yet even when critics place music at the core of the film's successes, problems can occur. Insdorf offers a balanced view of the carriers of *Blue*'s significance, noting how it is "intricately structured, aurally as well as visually" right from the start.[89] By placing music and cinematography alongside plot within the film's tripartite center of gravity, she also highlights Preisner for praise alongside Idziak, whose use of filters, experimental techniques and camera-on-shoulder work in *Blue* earned him the credit "Screenplay Collaborator":

> Preisner composed the entire score before shooting began: the music is thus a "pre-text," its melodies, textures and rhythms engendering action. Because the main characters are indeed composers, the score is part of the plot, and its authorship part of the film's mystery.[90]

Her subsequent analysis of the film must be praised for taking music so seriously. Its details, however, are sometimes flawed, as in the following statement concerning the scene in which Julie is interrupted by music emanating from an uncertain source while recovering from the accident on her hospital room's private veranda. "[N]otes from the *Concerto*," Insdorf writes, "engender [Julie's] fearful stare at the camera, which tracks away from her, and then back toward her, as blue enters the frame."[91] The music in the scene is not from the *Concert[o] for the Unification of Europe*: it is a variation of the music from Patrice and Anna's funeral, as heard in the film's preceding scene. Insdorf is not alone in this mishearing. Andrew too writes of Julie being "visited . . . by a funereal fragment of a concerto he (she?) was composing to commemorate the Unification of Europe."[92] The problem with these mistakes is that the question of *which* music is occurring *where* in *Blue* is often a matter of plot. To mishear the themes is to misunderstand components of *Blue*'s basic story; this problematizes, in turn, the resultant critical interpretations.

Alongside literal mishearings of *Blue* in the literature, one might note a different, more interesting strand of what one might term creative (mis)hearings of the film: notably strong interpretations of its audio and musical content bending the facts of the soundtrack to a critically engaged agenda. One such reading is provided by Emma Wilson in her book on Kieślowski, although it would be more accurate to describe this as a creative unhearing.[93] In a reflection of her visually focused consideration of "image itself—its capacities and properties" as "the prime concern of Kieślowski's filmmaking"[94]—she identifies as "profoundly a cinema of regret and loss," but also of trauma and survival[95]—Wilson reads the blackout scene as an anti-flashback in which the sudden absence of anything at all signifies aspects of Julie's trauma:

> Kieślowski . . . refuses flashback or "images-souvenir" in *Bleu*. Instead he makes his viewers share Julie's trauma by denying vision altogether and placing the very "trous de mémoire" we assume the protagonist experiences in the structure of the film. . . . The viewer shares the protagonist's lapses of memory as Kieślowski attempts to rethink the cinematic representation of trauma.[96]

If one were merely a "viewer" of these moments in *Blue* as opposed to an audio-viewer—if, say, the blackout was silent as well as dark—one might eagerly agree with Wilson's reading: the blackouts are a (de)selective act of memory by a widow and bereaved mother repressing memories of her trauma's cause (the accident). But this is *not* a silent scene.[97] While the images lapse, sound, and more particularly music, floods the cinema. Wilson's reading still works if one takes the music as "unheard" emotional accentuation, underscoring Julie's distress, and by denying audio—and specifically music—the power of acting as a musical souvenir and manifestation of potentially traumatic

recall. Yet life, cinema and, for that matter, Preisner suggest it has precisely that potential.[98] In my experience of screening *Blue* for audiences, this is also an atypical reading of the scene and similar interruptions in the film: even when unprompted, students tend to hear Julie
consciously experiencing music of tragic significance. It is one of
Blue's attractions, of course, that such scenes confirm no single reading
of the music's location or role. Their ambiguities, in turn, permit readings like Wilson's—provocative criticism requiring detailed consideration alongside closer hearings of the film.

An obvious obligation of the analysis of *Blue* in the present study is
to provide a basic guide to the score's themes and structure, clearing up
misapprehensions in the literature; my analyses of *White* and *Red* also
seek to provide such guides. The analyses, in addition, extend the few
existing studies in the musicological literature by addressing film-wide
strategies in Preisner's scores and their symbolic significance in the
films. In my view those are not, however, reason enough to write detailed and sustained, musically centered analyses of the films in the
Three Colors trilogy, and so Chapter Five, for instance, seeks also to
make an independently useful contribution to film criticism on *Blue*
through a reading of the film, focalized through analysis of the music,
as a meditation on grief, liberty, love and life in late-modern Western
societies.

For *Blue*'s music is Julie's climate; often, it is also the prime mover
of the film's plot. It therefore cloaks every aspect of the film. Climate,
as Chapter One explained, is one of two key scoring principles Preisner
developed when working on his first Kieślowski film, *No End*. Following Piotr Skrzynecki's suggestion that the score to *No End* should be
"like a ghost" haunting the film, Preisner created a "side-by-side" scoring practice, distanced from both diegesis and narration, in order to
form an atmosphere permeating, yet also floating somewhat free of, the
tale and the telling of a film. It is often impossible to say with confidence whether Preisner's scoring is diegetic, non-diegetic, meta-
diegetic or even para-diegetic: the music partakes of all these putative
realms, explores vectors of movement between them, yields to none.
When I asked Preisner where the music in *Blue* is located, not least in
the blackout scenes, Preisner echoed his *Piwnica* mentor's suggestions
for *No End*:

> Sometimes the music is like your feeling . . . like a dream or a mem-
> ory, perhaps a bad memory. . . . If you lost somebody, sometimes you
> remember his face or eyes . . . or a funny moment in life. Sometimes
> music, by accident, when I am listening to the radio, reminds me of
> the situation when first I was listening to the music. My memories
> come back to the situation by accident. We tried to create, with
> [*Blue*'s] music, her life with her husband. . . . This is the climate
> [Julie] was living in.

Describing a later blackout in one of *Blue*'s swimming pool scenes, Preisner said the music is "like a ghost: she is afraid, you know." In such moments, sound design, visual effects and Preisner's music merge into a macro-climate similar to Philip Brophy's notion of the "sonic": an audio environment encapsulating the film and its experience, or climate as a cinematic snow globe.[99]

The concept of climate is also useful to a discussion of *Blue* because it need not be a static metaphor: like the weather, a film's climate can change. When the film begins, Julie's snow globe is pristinely still; suddenly shaken by the accident, a blizzard commences, obliterating all; gradually, the pieces align in new constellations. The combination of chance, choice and fate in such a metaphor may appeal through its connection to symbolic tropes within the Kieślowski oeuvre, but more immediately obvious is the manner in which *Blue*'s musical and sonic climate maps a process of change for its bereaved main protagonist. In part, this centers the film's meditation on grief. The arc also structures an allegory on the question of "what it means to mean"[100]: i.e., how one should live at the turn of the twenty-first century.

Climate thereby merges into Preisner's other key creative principle: that a film's score should articulate its concept. At the start of *Blue*, Kehr notes, "liberty becomes a tragic notion."[101] Liberty equals alienation, as reflected visually when Idziak's lens can "barely hold a single, small object in clear view" and aurally by a sound mix that often "renders the dialogue almost inaudible, with only the sudden, sharp passages of music . . . cutting through the perceptual fog."[102] Fragmentations in *Blue*'s scoring, audio and other aspects of its narration diagnose the wreckage of Julie's bereaved subjectivity, itself a token of other wreckers of late-modern life. Their subsequent evolution, alongside her diegetic re-engagement with music and community, provides both a palliative for her pain and a signpost to recovery, again with broader symbolism concerning a potential answer to the "absent middle."[103] At the film's close, music and image collude to fashion symbols of reintegration and continuity, opposing the events and style of *Blue*'s earlier, more fragmentary and cinematically avant-garde passages, as Julie liberates herself from the worst of her grief by accepting the conventions and constraints of a less isolated existence. This far from simplistically happy ending, underscored by the *Concert[o]*, inaugurates the trilogy's poetics of *agapē*.

Criticism of *Blue*'s Score: Authenticity, Text, Authorship, Genre

Aside from commentaries on individual cues, discussed in context in Chapter Five, the Kieślowski literature's response to *Blue*'s music has homed in on two issues: quality and authorship. Many readings of the *Concerto[o]*, in particular, have focused not on its narrative and symbolic functions, but rather on its authenticity as a putative example of

Western art music; as a sidebar to this, the question of the identity of *Blue*'s fictional music's composer has arisen. Such considerations also raise issues concerning the *Concert[o]*'s text and musical genre.

Authenticity and Text

Positive responses to the quality of the music in *Blue* have been over-shadowed by the weight of negative judgment on Preisner's score and, especially, the *Concert[o]*. These range from passing snipes to broader critiques, although even the latter fail precisely to analyze the music or its text. But is the music *meant* to be any good? Coates asked the director outright: "How are we to take the symphony [sic]—as a master-piece, or ironically?"[104] Mark Asch voices a similar ambivalence: "Un-fortunately, [Julie's] reconciliation [with the vestiges of her past] comes partly through her completion of her composer husband's final piece, an (intentionally?) turgid concerto for the unification of Europe."[105] John Orr notes (rather redundantly) that "Preisner is not Mahler" and then argues that the power of the music to save Julie "is itself 'saved' by its sacred text."[106] The music, in other words, could not bear the symbolic burden alone: St. Paul does the heavy lifting. For Sobolewski, following a familiar critical path, the music is a symptom of the "suspiciously artful" manner in which the "nihilistic rebellion" of Kieślowski's earlier cinema evaporates at the end of *Blue*, as Julie's epitome of the meta-physical rebel is "dissolved in a *schmaltzy* finale . . . a highly sentimen-tal and banal musical score which accompanies the words of the *First Epistle to the Corinthians* about love, which sound almost ironic, as there is no such love of which Saint Paul speaks, in the heroine."[107] Such readings gloss too many details to be taken fully seriously. In par-ticular, one can argue that the variety love of which the score speaks— *agapē*—is precisely the focus of Julie's closing epiphany, *Blue* and much of the remainder of the trilogy.

Žižek's complaint is more developed. For him, "the index of what is false about the film is its musical score":

> This hymn, devoid of any ironic distance . . . is composed in the New Age style of Gorecki's [sic] third symphony, inclusive of a funny ref-erence to the non-existent seventeenth-century Dutch composer Budenmeyer [sic].[108] What if this apparent lapse in quality signals a structural flaw in the very foundation of Kieślowski's artistic uni-verse?[109]

So thanks to its score, in this view, *Blue* veers close to becoming a film for "the Brussels European Union *nomenklatura*—it is the ideal film to satisfy the needs of a Brussels [sic] bureaucrat who returns home in the evening after a day full of complex negotiations on tariff regula-tions."[110] This witty statement is hamstrung by its musical generaliza-tions. The depiction of Górecki's Symphony No. 3 (1976) as "New Age," for instance, confuses aspects of the piece's recent commercialization with its musical and textual content, and misses the more obvious Polish comparison: Penderecki's neo-Romantic Symphony No. 2 (1979-80), which, like the *Concert[o]*, comes complete with interpolated quotations ("Silent Night") and helped to inaugurate Penderecki's ensuing swathe of bureaucrat-friendly tomes.[111] It is also unclear whether Žižek is referring to the *Concert[o]* or the entirety of the score. Most surprisingly, however, given his persuasive focus elsewhere on the ambivalence of key moments in Kieślowski's work, Žižek does not follow through on his fascinating suggestion that the score, and thus the ending of the film, might be purposefully marked as inauthentic, or more complexly as simultaneously true and false, and that this might be a creative strategy, not a failing. If Julie is reinserting herself into the conventions of society at this point, for instance, and if this is not an entirely happy event but a compromise entailing a substantial new loss, might one not expect to hear music that rings untrue—or whose "side-by-side" distancing permits it concurrently to ring true and untrue?

The most tedious subtext to criticism of the *Concert[o]* is a damning of the music as if it were being offered as a piece of actual Western art music, as opposed to a fictionalized representation thereof performing unique symbolic functions in the context of a narrative film. The *Concert[o]* is not designed to shape its meanings through the syntax and codes of Western art music; Preisner's skill at pastiche does not extend that far, as he would be the first to admit. It is designed to "fake" the look and sound of such music well enough that (a) it does not cause a distraction by sounding utterly inappropriate (although clearly it distracts a small number of audio-viewers) while (b) carrying its full weight of narrative meaning concerning both the foreground drama and the subtexts of the film. Judging it as a failure of art music ("not Mahler") is misplaced. It should be judged as music in a narrative film pitched at an art cinema audience, not at a place in the Western art music canon.[112]

Refreshingly, Andrew seeks to identify what kind of composer Patrice appears to have been in the fictional reception contexts offered by *Blue*.[113] The *Concert[o]* "cast[s] light on Patrice's real status as a 'serious' composer; if he is acclaimed, in death, as a great artist both by patriotic funeral orators and, presumably, by the Eurocrats who commissioned the work, that suggests merely that he was known for popular, accessible anthems rather than original, adventurous compositions."[114] Kieślowski's own view on the artistic value of the *Concert[o]* was also poised: "I think that symphony [sic] might have sounded worthy [of the title masterpiece], if only . . . " he told Coates in answer to that question on the seriousness of the *Concert[o]*.[115] Kieślowski goes on to explain how the script was written in 1990, so against the backdrop of "Europe 1992" and the Treaty of Maastricht. If unification ever happened on a grand geo-political scale, Kieślowski suggests, "all sorts of elevated tones and exceptionally weighty words—to put it positively—or bombast—to put it negatively—would sound and be in accord with the ceremony of European unification," but because "Europe did not unite . . . [the piece] clearly has to be taken ironically as a pro-gramme."[116]

One might also note that Julie never suggests any particular love or admiration for the *Concert[o]*. If anything, her brutal edits suggest a certain disdain for the versions by her husband and, later, her lover Olivier. Casting the score into the back of a garbage truck at a certain point in the film is layered with significance, but on one level this action structures a rebuttal of her copyist's view that the music is too beautiful to be destroyed. For Julie, finishing her own version of the score seems more like a cathartic expulsion of poisonous matter than the creation of a to-be-treasured artifact. Nonetheless, her *Concert[o]*, fused to the closing images, transcends its intentionally emptier rhetoric to reflect the ambiguities of *Blue*'s closing situation.

Remembering that this anthem is the creation of the Piwnica sati-rist—and in fact was first mooted as a Piwnica number—may also aid those concerned for its "lack" of artistic sophistication. Preisner shares the late director's ironic skepticism about grand European projects, real or fictitious, a trait ingrained within many Poles' identities, given the country's subjugation by fellow Europeans throughout much of the past 150 years. The co-workers' first conception for the close of *Blue* was, at one level, the embodiment of pan-European hubris. "The original idea for the *Concert[o] for the Unification of Europe*," Preisner told me, "which explains why the music is so pompous, was to have twelve cit-ies, twelve orchestras, twelve screens; a choir in London would start, then the orchestra in Berlin, then in France, etc." A thousand musicians, all playing together, out of which, gradually, a unity would form, with different instruments coming from different capitals, "and everyone playing the funeral march at the end—an image of unification" or per-haps, ironically, failing to play together in the pre-digital age of satellite time lags.

Alongside his striking description of the music's pomposity, Preis-ner's use of the term "funeral march" to describe the unison melody after the climax of the *Concert[o]* is noteworthy. This is not the funeral music which interrupts Julie on the balcony, but it shares certain of that theme's traits (which could excuse misidentifications of either melody by some writers). This permits the end of the *Concert[o]* to hint at the co-workers' belief that such a project was doomed to collapse, while underscoring the irony of Julie's unification with her new society, which is far from triumphant. Such dualism is reflected throughout the trilogy, especially at the films' endings, and also in Kieślowski's more positive spin on the *Concert[o]* when responding to Coates's question about quality: "[t]hese words about love continue to be just as valid," Kieślowski argued, but in a different context than a once-mooted Euro-pean unification. Julie's existential journey is that context, and through it the film's inquisition into living well in a late-modern society.

With appropriate bathos, the original conception of *Blue*'s ending proved too expensive to shoot. "It was calculated that the staging of this would cost as much as the three movies in total, so they didn't do it,"

Preisner chuckled when I asked him to recall the decision-making process. Plan B, to shoot a live concert in an opera house in Paris, also proved too costly. Kieślowski and Karmitz needed a cost-effective solution, and the director credited Preisner with Plan C—the closing montage—which the composer calls the ending's "retrospective." As so often in film, brute practicality therefore lent a hand in decisions one might otherwise attribute solely to the "genius" of one or other creative figure.

Orbiting these nuances is a further, strikingly specific historical context for the score. At the time *Blue* was being written and its fictional composers were imagined to be composing their piece for the unification of Europe, Preisner recalled during our conversations, "a couple hundred kilometers away, in [former] Yugoslavia, people were at war and killing each other." A key concern for Preisner when writing the *Concert[o]* was how to compose a work for the unification of Europe, fictional or otherwise, against the backdrop of a contemporary European war, with all the bleak ironies thus entailed. The post-communist dimension to the Yugoslav Wars (1991-95) and their atrocities resonated strongly, for obvious reasons, with many Poles, and Preisner wanted to compose a piece that would not do a grave disservice to those embroiled in that conflict or to its victims.

His solution was partly musical, partly textual.[117] The main decision Preisner made was to use Skrzynecki's edit of St. Paul's letter in 1 Corinthians 13—"the only words that can be set," he believed, in such a complex situation. Kieślowski had long trusted Preisner to come up with texts for their collaborations, thanks to his time under Skrzynecki's literary guidance in the cabaret, but initially baulked at the concept of a setting from the New Testament. "Krzysztof was absolutely against using anything that had any relationship to religion," Preisner recalls: "He didn't want to be associated with Catholicism or any other religion." When Preisner gave him Skrzynecki's original letter containing the edited text, Kieślowski pantomimed a fit of rejection. The composer then pointed out that the edited version had no religious sentiments at all: Skrzynecki had excised "every single specific reference to religion." What remained, Kieślowski came to agree with Preisner, was a well-spring of humanist sentiment. "Here is the big war in Yugoslavia," Preisner told Kieślowski, and "here is the *Song for the Unification of Europe*. What we must tell people is that this is impossible, existing like this." Neither the cuts to the text nor the emphases of Preisner's text-setting have been accurately discussed in the Kieślowski literature to date.[118] Table 4.1 reproduces an English translation of the full text of 1 Corinthians 13 and, alongside it, a translation of the text heard in the film.[119] As analyzed more fully in Chapter Five, the *Concert[o]* omits or overshadows direct allusions to Christian faith, encouraging a generally humanist reading, rather than a specifically Christian one.

1 Corinthians 13

13:1 If I speak in the tongues of men and of angels, but I do not have *agapē*, I am a noisy gong or a clanging cymbal.

13:2 And if I have prophecy, and know all mysteries and all knowledge, and if I have all faith so that I can remove mountains, but do not have *agapē*, I am nothing.

13:3 If I give away everything I own, and if I give over my body in order to boast, but do not have *agapē*, I receive no benefit.

13:4 *agapē* is patient, *agapē* is kind, it is not envious. *agapē* does not brag, it is not puffed up.

13:5 It is not rude, it is not self-serving, it is not easily angered or resentful.

13:6 It is not glad about injustice, but rejoices in the truth.

13:7 It bears all things, believes all things, hopes all things, endures all things.

13:8 *agapē* never ends. But if there are prophecies, they will be set aside; if there are tongues, they will cease; if there is knowledge, it will be set aside.

13:9 For we know in part, and we prophesy in part,

13:10 but when what is perfect comes, the partial will be set aside.

13:11 When I was a child, I talked like a child, I thought like a child, I reasoned like a child. But when I became an adult, I set aside childish ways.

13:12 For now we see in a mirror indirectly, but then we will see face to face. Now I know in part, but then I will know fully, just as I have been fully known.

13:13 And now these three remain: faith, hope, and *agapē*. But the greatest of these is *agapē*.

Concert[o]

13:1 If I speak in the tongues of men and of angels, but I do not have *agapē*, I am a noisy gong or a clanging cymbal.

13:2 And if I have prophecy, and know all mysteries ~~and all knowledge, and if I have all faith~~ so that I can remove mountains, but do not have *agapē*, I am nothing, I am nothing, I am nothing.

~~13:3 If I give away everything I own, and if I give over my body in order to boast, but do not have agapē, I receive no benefit.~~

13:4 *agapē* is patient, *agapē* is kind, it is not envious. *agapē* does not brag, it is not puffed up.

~~13:5 It is not rude, it is not self-serving, it is not easily angered or resentful.~~

~~13:6 It is not glad about injustice, but rejoices in the truth.~~

13:7 It bears all things, believes all things, hopes all things, endures all things.

13:8 *agapē* never ends. But if there are prophecies, they will be set aside; if there are tongues, they will cease; if there is knowledge, it will be set aside.

~~13:9 For we know in part, and we prophesy in part,~~

~~13:10 but when what is perfect comes, the partial will be set aside.~~

~~13:11 When I was a child, I talked like a child, I thought like a child, I reasoned like a child. But when I became an adult, I set aside childish ways.~~

~~13:12 For now we see in a mirror indirectly, but then we will see face to face. Now I know in part, but then I will know fully, just as I have been fully known.~~

13:13 And now these three remain: faith, hope, and *agapē*. But the greatest of these is *agapē* (x 4).

Table 4.1: Corinthians and *Concert[o]* text comparison

Readings of *Blue* seeking to recuperate the film or its director as Christian propaganda thus have their work cut out. Carla Rabinowitz claims the *Concert[o]* as a Christian message, pure and simple, because 1 Corinthians 13 is "is a bedrock statement of Christian theology":

> Human beings, the Apostle is saying, cannot save themselves. Goodness won't get you into Heaven; neither will wisdom, self-sacrifice, or even holiness. What is necessary is grace; in St. Paul's sense, the absolute and unmerited love of God, and the willingness of the human soul to open itself to and return that love. . . . [T]his is what he says . . . and so does Kieślowski.[120]

The precise text and setting hole this type of reading beneath the waterline; such views also contradict many aspects of the narrative (self-sacrifice is clearly germane) and the composer and director's publicly stated intentions for the setting. While Kieślowski's explanations of the choice of text were not entirely forthcoming about its origins or edits, the general thrust of such statements seems tricky to misread. As recorded by Andrew:

> Kieślowski was adamant that the text from Corinthians should not be interpreted in a purely Christian sense: "It was consciously chosen as the only text in the Bible which doesn't speak of God; it says that love is more important than faith. We could have chosen other songs or poems about love, but this fragment showed that people have always thought this way, even 2,000 years ago; if I live without love, I am nothing."[121]

Yet other critics besides Rabinowitz have sought to argue for a Christian, and more specifically Catholic, reading of *Blue* (and its director) through misapprehensions of the *Concert[o]*'s text.[122]

As in the *Decalogue*, the meditations on morality of which were consciously continued in the *Three Colors* trilogy, it seems more appropriate to claim that a specific religion's ideas are being used in *Blue* as a spiritual scalpel, in order incisively to cut to the heart of more universal human concerns. The text's edits—roughly half of the text is struck through—remove many direct references to Christian tenets, suggesting that the "faith" expressed in *Blue*, as Coates memorably puts it regarding the director's religiousness as a whole, is "unchurched."[123] Like Kieślowski the editor, Kieślowski the faithful seemed keen to slice away needless exposition to get to his version of truth. The first cut to the text removes a clear reference to Christian "faith"; the central cut excises rejoicing in Christian "truth"; the third deletes the complex passage on prophecy, in a sharp contrast to the reference allowed to remain in line two, where prophecy is deemed a mere prop, reduced to "nothing" in the absence of the more important *agapē*.[124]

Blue's religious text was filleted by Skrzynecki and then filtered by Preisner's setting and Kieślowski's audio-visual realization to reveal a lyric suitable to a pan-European hymn of togetherness but also, more importantly, to further illustrate the plight of its protagonist and, in turn, what her journey through grief has to say about wider contemporary concerns. The final message is conflicted: every silver lining in *Blue*, as elsewhere in the trilogy, has a cloud. Arguably, however, this is the significance of St. Paul's letter and, certainly, of *Blue*'s cost-benefit analysis of living through acts of *agapē*.

Authorship

The authorship of *Blue*'s fictional compositions is the other recurring musical concern in the film's critical reception. First and foremost, this is an issue of story. When the journalist confronts Julie on her hospital veranda with a flashbulb and the question of her husband's music's authorship—she asks outright if Julie composed his music for him; Julie offers no response—it becomes a plot enigma. For James, the occurrence of the musical blackout in this scene thus "relates to the question the journalist shouts after Julie as she walks off and which is our key for the rest of the film: 'Did you write your husband's music?' Immediately we're wondering if that sudden orchestral passage was from Julie's memory or if it was some kind of new composition."[125] Issues of authorship also arise from the busker's music Julie encounters during her period of isolation. In the scene when Olivier tracks her down, the characters hear the busker performing tunes which, one is led to infer, may be connected to Patrice's unfinished score. At no point are these enigmas closed. One could take this as evidence of the film's exemplification of art cinema practices, i.e., ambiguity and open-endedness in the place of the teleology of mainstream narrative cinema's drive towards clarity and resolution. The issue of authorship in *Blue*, however, is more than just a branding exercise.

The fictional music in *Blue* is all "by" composers voiced by Preisner, and one of the notable achievements of Preisner's score is his differentiation of Patrice, Olivier, Julie and Van den Budenmayer's voices. Even when one hears their individual versions of the same piece, there are telling divergences which illuminate aspects of the plot. One sees but does not hear Patrice's score, save for when it is unfurled by the copyist for Julie and when Olivier plays its opening at the piano; parts of Olivier's attempted completion of Patrice's work are heard and, later, edited under Julie's firm guidance; Julie completes her own version of the piece, having apparently had a hand in editing Patrice's score already, and her version *is* heard in full at the end of the film. So Julie has an input into all of the creations, but they too mark hers: "her" music becomes part of an interrelated community of scores, just as she is drawn back into a wider society over the course of the film. There is also music by Van den Budenmayer, by the busker (a role played by Preisner and Kieślowski's regular recorder player, Jacek Ostaszewski), and there are a handful of cues most likely to be heard, at least on first audio-viewing, as dramatic underscoring and thus the film's and Preisner's "own" music.

Stating that Julie "apparently" had a hand in Patrice's score, however, and the frequent trickiness of differentiating between the fictional music and nondiegetic underscoring in *Blue*, highlights the nuanced issues to which critics respond when debating over who wrote what. Even without engaging in the post-structuralist critical thickets through which Kelly Gross has ably scythed[126]—thickets that become more tangled still when one considers the hitherto unrevealed authorial hands stirring the textual pot (such as Skrzynecki)—one might question the certainty of Roger Hickman's assertion that Julie's completion of the work reveals "that she was the true creative force behind [Patrice's] fame."[127] Similarly, Paulus seems too bold in declaring that the authorship issue is resolved by the scene in which a musical memento Julie finds on her husband's piano "by" Van den Budenmayer continues to be heard after the notes on the manuscript paper run dry (the scene is shot subjectively from her score-reading point of view).[128] Julie may well, in some sense, be "composing" the continuation of this melody, but it makes too big a leap to suggest that she is therefore *the* composer in *Blue*. Kehr is more balanced and musically insightful, arguing that Julie may or may not "be the actual author of her husband's music . . . but she is certainly his most gifted interpreter, bringing the dead score back to life after Olivier nearly buries it with a trite orchestration."[129] It looks most likely, on the evidence of the film, that Patrice was not a complete charlatan. He may have needed substantial editorial corrections from his wife, Julie, to complete his scores, but the evidence of two hands on the manuscripts, the latter similar to the one in which one sees Julie scoring at the close of the film in her signature blue ink, supports the reading that she collaborated on his music's finalization, but not necessarily on its inception.

Bearing in mind Kieślowski's statement about Julie's creative role in the music, which supports this conclusion, it is tempting to read the communal authorship of music in *Blue* as a comment on collaborative creative practice *per se*, and more specifically on the role of an artistic director, such as Kieślowski, when supervising co-workers:

> Maybe she's one of those people who aren't able to write a single sheet of music but is wonderful at correcting a sheet which has already been written? She sees everything, has an excellent analytical mind and has a great talent for improving things. . . . But it's not all that important whether she's the author or co-author, whether she corrects or creates. Even if she only does the corrections she's still the author or co-author because what has been corrected is better than it was before. The music is cited all through the film and then at the end we hear it in its entirety, solemn and grand. So we're led to think that she's played a part in its creation.[130]

By completing her own version of the *Concert[o]*, Julie individuates within a community of creativity. Julie has engaged with her musical climate, controlling it and, in a sense, enabling the peak of her second phase of grieving, as explored in Chapter Five. She has also become

embroiled in a collective endeavor. By the end of *Blue*, then, the authorship issue transcends its status as plot enigma to foreground other
concepts, such as the question of how to author one's self. As Insdorf
has noted, "human beings need to live" just as "a score that has been
composed needs to be performed."[131] Scores like the *Concert[o]*, one
might add, can only be performed with the help of a large ensemble.
Julie has chosen to become a soloing collaborator in *Blue*'s *agapē* ensemble, to recall again Eagleton's jazz band. The manner in which she
shapes her solo passages, in turn, narrates her journey through the enforced (but perhaps not entirely negative) liberation of her grief and
back into a complex set of relationships to her world. To read this narrative of grieving and its associated symbolism more clearly and to as-
sess the manner in which it relates to a series of film and score-wide
strategies, Chapter Five analyzes this aspect of *Blue* in the context of its
exploration of the dynamics of grieving.

Genre

There is no contemporary genre of musical piece called the concert—
the name, alongside concerto, by which the *Concert[o] for the Unification of Europe* is referred to during *Blue*, hence this study's use of *Concert[o]*.[132] There are concertos and symphonies, oratorios and overtures,
songs and sonatas, and many more genres besides, and pieces composed in those genres might well be heard at a concert—which is, to
state the obvious, a performance event at which music is presented to an
audience. Nonetheless, William Weber's *New Grove* entry on the
"Concert" suggests etymological links to "Concerto" and, notably,
meanings associated with both terms that may be connected to music's
conceptual function in *Blue*:

> The word's origins are uncertain, but like "concerto" it may derive
> from the Latin *concertare* ("contend, dispute") and *consortium* ("soci-
> ety, participation"), although it may also be linked with the primary
> Italian meaning of *concertare* ("to arrange, agree, get together") and
> the English "consort."[133]

Society, participation, agreement, getting together: these are key themes
in *Blue* and relate to the symbolic roles of Julie's composition of a *Concert[o]*.

A recent discussion of the term "concerto" by Michael Long, in
turn, indicates further reasons, readily accessible to those with a receptional knowledge of Western art music constructed in part through the
experience of film and other popular cultural forms, why *Blue*'s central
composition is cast in a particularly apposite form. Unlike a symphony,
that "red-blooded American cultural icon," Long posits that the word
"concerto" acts as a trigger in Anglophone imaginations, thanks to an
"imaginative construction" of the idea of "concerto" in musical multimedia denoting ideas of "the exotic or the foreign."[134] The verbal trig-

ger's "otherness," in turn, contrasts with a musical trigger for "concerto" Long identifies in the same sources: the "pianistic 'power-chords'" (such as the opening of *The Warsaw Concerto* in *Dangerous Moonlight*, 1941, or The Toys' "A Lover's Concerto," 1965), establishing the "rhetorical zone" within which music thus demarcated as "concerto" operates.[135] Rather than the term's intimations of the "exotic" or "foreign," such sounds conjure up notions of "maleness, whiteness, and sophistication," and thus a "potential threat" to any "other" conjured up by the word "concerto" when they occur within the same textual frame.[136]

The *Warsaw Concerto* offers an intriguing contrast to *Blue* in this regard. Like Julie's *Concert[o]*, which has enjoyed a life outside of its film, *The Warsaw Concerto* is "a sort of liminal classic residing . . . on the borderline between the popular imagination and 'authentic' concert hall consumption."[137] *Dangerous Moonlight* concerns pilots fighting for the Allies during World War II, including the Polish pianist-aviator whose performances of the concerto locate the piece within the diegesis. Heroism and masculinity, and in this case non-Polish constructions of Polish heroism and masculinity, entwine here with the notion of "concerto." In *Blue*, though, Julie's grieving and interlinked actions as a composer-editor challenge traditional gender stereotyping, as analyzed in detail in Chapter Five. She deconstructs the masculine clichés of Patrice and Olivier's versions of *Blue*'s *Concert[o]*, not least by striking out a series of piano powerchords in its introduction, and reconstructs a more stereotypically "feminine" version of the piece. *Blue*'s *Concert[o]* thus brings into symbolic play the conflict Long identifies between musical and textual triggers for "concerto," in the context of the film's meditation on grief and broader consideration of how to live a better life. It is a marker of the richness of *Blue*'s argument that the potentially positive aspects of Julie's deconstructive challenge—the emancipations Julie embraces at certain points in the film—are in turn problematized by the clichés of Julie's musical reconstruction, which counterpoints her return, after a period of empowered isolation, to a more traditional female role in her cultural community. The *Concert[o]*, as such, also "contends" and "disputes."

There is another musical genre often heard at major public events—and furthermore one particular piece of music pressed into service at such gatherings—which provides an intertextual context for the *Concert[o]*: national or international anthems, and the finale of Beethoven's Symphony No. 9, its choral "Ode to Joy" setting words by Friedrich von Schiller. A small pocket of literature has touched on *Blue*'s *Concert[o]* in these contexts. These readings are interesting for the wider world to which they relate *Blue*, and in turn for the manner in which that world informs finer points of interpretation concerning the film. The pan-European nature of Kieślowski's later films, not least in terms of their funding, locations and casting, was discussed in Chapter Three. Philip Bohlman considers the *Concert[o]* in a geo-political context well-suited to internationalized filmmaking. "Forging international

anthems," he notes, "has become a preoccupation of many attempting
to create policies of regional and global unification at the turn of our
own century."[138] Such preoccupations may be related, at least metaphorically, to Kieślowski's turn from specifically Polish political issues
and instead to films exploring ties that bind individuals across dividing
lines like nationality, class and so on. Bohlman, however, reads the
Concert[o] as a fictional extension of the tales Eurocrats spin about
attempts to create a European anthem in the early 1990s. *Blue* can be
heard to capitalize on such myths and the surrounding pan-nationalist
hoopla:

> It is the composition—actually the completion—of a *Concerto for the
> Unification of Europe*, for example, that provided the central narrative
> for Krzysztof Kieślowski's film, *Bleu*, for which Zbigniew Preisner
> composed a score that turns the anthem inside-out, then reconstructs it
> so that the grand European chorus at the end can sing forth its biblical
> text.[139]

In what manner, though, is the *Concert[o]* anthemic?

Bohlman's discussion (elsewhere in the same study) of Benedict
Anderson's concept of "unisonance," and its role as the "echoed physical realization" of an "imagined community," is informative here, especially if one bears in mind *Blue*'s performance of *agapē* when reading
Anderson's description of the experience of unisonance: "How selfless
this unisonance feels!"[140] Unisonance is "the sonic moment that occurs
when people from throughout the nation gather in a shared performance
of music"; although "each singer may not fully be aware of the extent to
which she or he is joining with others throughout the nation," a "unisonant moment . . . allows 'each' person to sing the music of the
'whole' nation with 'all' other citizens."[141] This begins to suggest ways
in which the *Concert[o]* fulfils various symbolic roles in *Blue*. National
anthems blur the boundaries between the individuals making up a conceptual entity such as a nation; moments of unisonance occur when
individuals enact, through song, the blurring of self into collective.
This, in a sense, is what occurs to Julie at the end of *Blue*: a shift back
from alienation and individuation, albeit imposed in the harshest possible terms, to "society" and "participation." What was intended to provide a moment of unisonance for the fictionalized citizens of a united
Europe functions here as an anthem for Julie to compose and, in her
mind's ear, to perform as she reintegrates into society. This is clarified
by the visuals, which show a "unisonant moment" as, while music
plays, Julie's connections to her community are revealed by the closing
montage. It also becomes a moment of musical unisonance for the
film's audience, who may link to the music, and thus also to Julie and
her experiences, through a desire to "join in" with or mimetically mimic
the wordless mass of voices. Throughout *Blue* the film's apparatus
strains to position the audio-viewer within experiences proximate to
Julie's evolving and audio-visually embodied subjectivity. Here the

unisonant music, with its move from text to wordless murmuring, takes the leading role in a shift from specifically Christian sentiment to the articulation of a unisonant, more universal, hypothesis.

As Bohlman notes, by "mythical consensus," Beethoven's Ninth Symphony's setting of "Schiller's Enlightenment paean to universal brotherhood"[142] has become the touchstone for any such musical endeavor. Links between *Blue* and Beethoven have been considered by Roger Hillman in an article on cultural memory and film soundtracks. *Blue*'s music, read by Hillman as "crowning the new unity of the EU member states," seeks to perform a task that ultimately proves as impossible for Preisner and/or the fictional composers in the story as "the comparably foregrounded 'Prize Song' in Wagner's *Meistersinger*."[143] In *Blue*, the precise difficulty of the musical challenge is to deal with the shadow of the *Concert[o]*'s "profilmic cultural event, the 'Ode to Joy.'" Hillman contrasts that piece's appropriation by the Nazis to its cooption by the European Community less than fifty years "on from its territorialization of national [Austro-German] treasure"—a rich European context indeed against which to consider the *Concert[o]*'s "transcending of standard borders of relationships and nationhood." Julie's gift of her family home to her husband's mistress, for Hillman, therefore echoes, like the *Concert[o]*, "the unforeseen alliances possible in a Europe emerging from a postwar state of numbed grieving," and in which replacements for the tarnished Beethoven were felt to be needed by some. In this vein, Hillman goes on to explain the efficacy of Preisner's specific style to the achievement of such a piece of music. Observing—unusually for the literature, and usefully—that his musical presence is rooted in vernacular traditions as opposed to art music, in the *Concert[o]*, "accessibility prevails":

> [T]his vision of a new Europe music is intended as a binding force, releasing spiritual energy beyond the political. Beethoven's Ninth, the shadow model, has shown in its reception history how invasive the political can be. The Greek text of Preisner's music, on the other hand, seeks out the roots of European civilization, rather than attempting to reflect its current stage resulting from a changed political constellation.[144]

Preisner's score thus becomes part of the "accretions of history," in Nicholas Cook's words, which have settled like snowflakes over Beethoven's final symphony: a "babble of commentary," creative and critical, through which "a thousand Ninth Symphonies came into existence."[145] One of these Beethoven's Ninths is the music of "infinite sublimity and dramatic power" and expressing "that sympathy with humanity which makes it the most wonderful musical revelation that could be desired, or that is ever likely to be devised" heard by F. J. Crowest in 1899.[146] This is the "impossible height" to which the music of the *Concert[o]* might have leapt. And yet, as Cook notes, Beethoven's symphony is no simple celebration of universal brotherhood:

"Beethoven's last symphony proclaims the ideals of universal brother-hood and joy; that is unmistakable. But at the same time, and just as unmistakeably, it casts doubt upon them. It sends out incompatible messages"—not least in its transformation of the "bad taste," in Charles Grove's words, of some of Schiller's poetry into musical terms.[147] Perhaps its neatest parallel to the Ninth, then, is that the Concert[o], while on the one hand helping to heal Julie's wounds—traumas, if one pleases, symbolic of Polish and other geo-political stigmata—on the other it also articulates the dark side of her choices. The Concert[o]'s "Ode to agapē," like Beethoven's "Ode to Joy," has a productively mixed set of messages that parallel the film's depiction of Julie's emergence from grief. In this respect, at least, the two pieces seem comparable.[148]

Musician Biopics, Music-films, Kieślowski's Music-films

There are at least three categories of film in which music plays a prominent role that offer contexts within which to consider Blue: films about musicians, music-films, and Kieślowski's music-films.

Musician Biopics

The obvious distinction between Blue and musician biopics, whether "slice-of-life" or entire life stories, is whether the film concerns a real or fictional musician. That Blue is about a fictional composer might raise doubts about its relationship to such films. John C. Tibbetts, however, questions viewing real musicians' biopics as "authentic," as there is "no use trying to reconcile story with history" in such features.[149] Blue, like other films about fictional musicians, may thus be argued to draw on staples of the musician biopic genre as part of the symbolic strategy of deploying a musician at the heart of its story.

John Patterson caricatures the narrative trajectory of musician biopics as follows:

> A poor musician struggles out of the direst poverty, suffers the tor-ments of the damned, transforms his or her field of endeavour, and is redeemed by the power of love. The narrative trajectory always moves inexorably upward toward salvation and self-knowledge, like a par-able or an AA confession.[150]

Alongside the presence of cinematic clichés depicting musical creativ-ity in action—manifestations of which range from the extravagances of *Lisztomania* (Russell, 1975) to the relative restraint of *Amadeus*'s meta-diegetic moments (Forman, 1984)—one might read aspects of Blue in light of certain of these stock in trades. In particular, Blue shares with many musician biopics what Gross has identified, from a perspective developed through disability studies, as a parable of overcoming known as the normalcy narrative. Sometimes the adversity overcome relates to a disability, sometimes to the circumstances of a protagonist's birth, and sometimes to both, as in the Ray Charles biopic *Ray* (Hackford, 2004). Gross's view of *Blue*'s seeking "to rehabilitate and repair deviance or to obliterate difference [i.e., Julie's trauma] through cure" thus strikes a chord with other musician biopics.[151] There are, for instance, films which seek to rehabilitate or repair aspects of the lives of their composers, such as Chopin's overt masculinization in *A Song to Remember* (Vidor, 1945). The problematic nature of the ideology uncovered by Gross's reading, however, can be clarified by paralleling it with more spectacular manifestations of the parable in horror films, where "normalizing a monstrous deviance of some kind"[152]—a deviance which, like all disability, is not medical but culturally constructed— means slaying or exiling the beast. One such example is an intensely musical film.

In *Unheard Melodies*, Claudia Gorbman examined *Hangover Square* (John Brahm, scored by Bernard Herrmann, 1944), a film in the classical Hollywood style and connected to "countless lives-of-composers and -songsters films" which foregrounded music to "play out themes and variations on the human psyche."[153] In such films, Gorbman argues, music diegetically marked as the product of a character's imagination can serve "double duty in a film score," providing "semiotically rich 'keys' to delineate character—all the more so owing to music's ideological status as gaining access to emotional 'truth' (especially Romantic music)"—alongside "the usual illustrative functions of the film score, namely, providing emotional and rhythmic accompaniment."[154] In *Blue*, Preisner's avatars deploy a musical language like some Romantic and neo-Romantic styles, but also like classical Hollywood scoring practices derived stylistically and aesthetically from Romantic music, and thus steeped in traditions symbolizing unmediated access to subjectivity.

Gorbman's analysis of *Hangover Square* calls attention to a deviant character whose responses to music are uncannily similar to Julie's in *Blue*, further demonstrating the cinematic tradition fusing representations of musicality and difference. The film concerns George Harvey Bone, a "well-mannered (read repressed) composer" who has psychotic episodes triggered by music: during blackouts set off by "discordant sounds," he metamorphoses into a "murderous, bug-eyed aggressor, a strangler and a pyromaniac" called the Fulham Road murderer.[155] His mental illness (Gorbman wittily diagnoses Hollywood schizophrenia) "is expressed via music—the discordant music that triggers his psychosis" and crucially, from the perspective of *Blue*, is depicted as sounding within his musical mind. Julie's psyche wants her to heal by confronting that which she has buried. By completing a *Concert[o]*, she works through aspects of her grief. Bone's psychosis seems hell-bent on liberating him through destructive acts, before he is burnt at the metaphorical and musical stake when flames engulf him while performing his piano concerto.

A further similarity, less obvious but just as interesting, relates to the way in which Bone, like Julie, has music beyond his control rupturing his conscious perceptions and apparently seeking to make him act differently. George is besieged by his music, with snippets of the piano concerto "turn[ing] up unaccountably on the street, at nightclubs, at public festivals, and nondiegetically on the soundtrack"—just as music bursts into Julie's consciousness, the busker in *Blue* seems to know passages from the *Concert[o]*, and she sees and hears significant music on the television (including, coincidentally, in a scene set in a night club). Gorbman's conclusion about this musical invasiveness is suggestive: "The viewer starts to hear music from all sources . . . interpenetrating in the most disturbing manner. Concurrently with the progressive blending of musical types and levels of narration, the distinction between George and his murderous alter ego begins to break down."[156] In *Blue*, music breaches barriers between Julie and buried aspects of her grief, and then her surrounding community. Like *Hangover Square, Blue* remains faithful to classical narrative filmmaking principles as theorized by Gorbman: the music does not break the rules of transparency and continuity editing, but rather bends them substantially to heighten the intensity of the narrative and its symbolism. Julie is not slain, of course, but some of her responses to her loss—including different ways of grieving as a woman in her society—are eventually set aside to permit her normalization.

Music-films

Invented in an attempt to capture the unusualness of *Fantasia*'s genre (Algar et al., 1940), Nicholas Cook coined the term "music film," by analogy to the term "music video," to describe films in which music and sound are notably prominent but function "not as the projection through ancillary media of an originary meaning, but [in] the construction of a fundamentally new experience."[157] Cook argues that there needs to be a strong degree of conformance between music and other filmic elements if a movie is truly to be a music-film. Many films prominently using music fail to fit this criterion. Jean-Luc Godard's "Armide" sequence from *Aria* (1987) is one example, Cook argues, because in spite of a certain alignment between the meaning-making strategies of text, music and pictures, what emerges is "an instance of irreducible contest between media"[158]—the type of contest Annette Davison uses to define the innovations of Godard's "non-Hollywood" scoring practices.[159] Kieślowski and Preisner's music-films, by contrast, operate (like *Hangover Square*) in a region between modernist and classical practice. Innovative or avant-garde techniques are utilized to intensify the conformance of music and the sum of a film's narrative and symbolic apparatus. It is therefore more productive to think of *Blue* within a stratum of European music-films that Julie Brown has identified, while, usefully, hyphenating the term to make it more distinctive on the page. Within these productions, pointed uses of music intensify the provocations of a film's story and subtexts, rather than disrupting the telling thereof in the manner of a film "made politically."[160]

Taking the view that these music-films "take music as their subject" and thereby raise "special questions about [music's] role in cinematic representation,"[161] Brown lists examples from Renoir to Visconti and notes more recent exponents including Malle, Truffaut and Haneke; she does not mention Kieślowski, but he could easily be added to such a list, alongside directors including Bergman, Minghella and Tarr. She also calls attention to Royal S. Brown's observation of a wider trend since the 1960s in which music takes on a "privileged status as ideal image," becoming an intellectual focus in films such as Bergman's *Through a Glass Darkly* (1961) and Kubrick's *2001: A Space Odyssey* (1968), and therefore demanding attentive criticism if a film's content is to be more fully engaged.[162] Music-films call for the development of a film criticism practiced from a multiplicity of perspectives including musicology. Julie Brown's reading of *Un coeur en hiver* (Sautet, 1992) exemplifies this form of critical practice: an interdisciplinary account of the manner in which music and other systems of signification parallel and counterpoint one another in the production of the film's layered meanings. She examines, in particular, the role of Ravel's Piano Trio (1914) in the film, arguing that it articulates aspects of its characters' search for self-knowledge and a means of emotional expression—but also the film's reflections on musical subjectivity and Ravel's biography. *Blue* and, to an extent, *White* and *Red* demand similarly pluralist attention, and Robynn J. Stilwell's analysis of another music-film—one with which *Blue* shares many superficial similarities—offers another productive model for such endeavors.

Like *Blue*, Minghella's *Truly, Madly, Deeply*, produced in 1990 with a score by Barrington Pheloung and featuring prominent diegetic music by J. S. Bach, concerns the grieving female partner of a deceased musician. As Stilwell argues, "Few films have relied so heavily on music for storytelling as *Truly, Madly, Deeply*," let alone a film that "explores grief and mourning"[163]—*Blue* being the obvious, and near contemporary, exception. In *Truly*, amateur pianist Nina (played by Juliet Stevenson) is devastated by the sudden loss of Jamie (Alan Rickman), her lover and a professional cellist. Music's role in their lives obviously foregrounds the topic, but it is the fluid interaction of different musics and their symbolic freight that makes *Truly* truly a music-film:

> The use of music in the film transcends the boundaries of classical film scoring and gives psychological depth. The traditional functions of a non-diegetic score are to provide emotional inflection within a scene and continuity between scenes while doing its work unnoticed, but the underscore of *Truly, Madly, Deeply* interacts with other cinematic elements and with other musics in the film to an unprecedented degree, generating a level of purely musical symbolism.[164]

In particular, "the musical numbers actively construct the relationship between the characters."[165] For instance, Jamie and Nina sing duets such as Joni Mitchell's "A Case of You," where Jamie's good sense of tuning, Stilwell keenly notes, steadies his partner's wayward pitch. Stilwell argues that these moments of seemingly positive occurrence simultaneously bring home to the audience "the gap in Nina's life" created by her bereavement. Most relevant to *Blue*, however, is *Truly*'s careful use of the "Adagio" from J. S. Bach's Cello Sonata No. 3.

In *Truly*, Bach's movement attains the slippery quality Gorbman notes of the music in *Hangover Square*, sliding between the diegesis and nondiegetic underscoring "or remaining ambiguously suspended between the two."[166] Jamie returns as a ghost to help Nina overcome grief rendered with excruciatingly snotty immediacy by Stevenson: like the Bach, Jamie slips between realms. The use of the "Adagio," however, is more than a symbolic foil for his journeys between life, death and limbo. One first encounters Nina playing the piano part to the piece and singing Jamie's absent cello line. Later, in a magical scene transcending the film's sometimes maudlin sentimentality, Nina, finding herself unable to play on in an enactment of this ritual, is suddenly prompted by a cello note, as Jamie apparently manifests to perform the cello line and, more generally, to help her move forward in her grief.[167] When Nina does start to leave the worst of her grief behind, reengaging with the world around her, Jamie is shown singing his part alone and without her accompaniment. Finally, she buys a new piece of Bach to learn, having met a new boyfriend. As in *Blue*, the film creates a structural fusion of music and drama: the changing content, presentation and relationship between musical and dramatic elements reveals aspects of Nina's grief as she moves from immersive lament to forms of forgetting and renewal.[168] Also as in *Blue*, a musical film-wide strategy is central to *Truly*'s affecting narrative, and to its articulation of how women should behave in the face of bereavement in Western society. Unlike *Blue*, *Truly* offers a more upbeat assessment of these conventions and of grief's potential cleanly to be overcome.[169]

Kieślowski's Music-films

A detailed discussion of Kieślowski's music-films deserves a study in its own right. In summary, however, from *Personnel* (1975) to *The Double Life of Véronique*, via *Blind Chance*, *Camera Buff* (1979), *No End* and *Decalogue* parts *2*, *9* and *10*, especially prominent musical moments in Kieślowski's films serve at least two recurring functions: articulating moments in which the possibility of the metaphysical is evoked and/or profound developments in a character's life or personal relationships.[170] This is exemplified by the most fascinating musical moment in *Personnel*, which follows life backstage for tailors in a Polish theater staging Verdi's *Aida*.

The operatic backdrop to Kieślowski's first feature-length fiction film indicates ways in which, even in a film from the preliminary stages of his fiction-making career, Kieślowski sought to use music to nuance both a story and its symbolism. As Tadeusz Lubelski writes, for the small opera company in *Personnel* to be staging the lavish *Aida* is "the acme of artificiality and misconceived inspiration"; protagonist Romek's brushes with the opera's music consequently chart a disintegration from "the naïve youthful belief that contact with real Art will yield some intimation into higher things" to the realization that the truth is "inferior to, uglier and worse than [his] idealised image."[171] High art, *Personnel* suggests, is to be handled and approached with care—a sentiment worth bearing in mind when weighing up the quality vs. satire argument concerning the "authenticity" of *Blue*'s *Concert[o]*.

"Does such [i.e., 'good'] art exist?," Romek asks a fellow costume-maker. His answer comes not through the opera but through a chance meeting backstage with a musician. In a tiny scene charged with possibility, Romek chances upon a violinist rehearsing. He strikes a few quiet notes on the nearest percussion instrument in response to the violinist's invitation to participate in music-making. For Kickasola, from this "spontaneous and hopeful duet" a "moment of grace emerges," stopping the film from sliding entirely into "a despondent picture of the possibility of art and meaning."[172] A personal relationship is orchestrated through music, hinting in turn at dimensions of meaning beyond the material realm—a potential of music developed much more fully in Preisner collaborations including *Decalogue 2* and, as discussed below, *Red*. "Good" art may indeed exist, *Personnel* argues, but it may also be found in the nooks of less obvious locations. *Blue* is an example of the former; its *Concert[o]* exemplifies the latter.

Blue and its pivotal composition are also emblematic of a further characteristic of the Kieślowski music-films, and especially the works created with Preisner as a compositional co-worker: these are films with music "in the bloodstream" and, at times, the films' concepts are articulated primarily through the contribution of the composer's cues. This is hardly unique to the Kieślowski-Preisner collaborations, of course, and to an extent *any* music in *any* film can be read, more or less strongly, as performing such a role. More unusually, however, Preisner's music for the Kieślowski films is often the sole driver of plot. Sometimes, in other words, the score does not merely help a film to tell its story: the score *is* the story. As well as accenting and representing in parallel or counterpoint to other components in the production's story-telling system—sometimes puppeteering "unheard" in the background, sometimes leaping into the foreground of the discursive interplay—Preisner's music frequently bears the brunt of the storytelling. The preeminent example of these practices is *Blue*.

White Washes

Three Colors: White is a comedy of blackly serious intent. In *White*, Karol Karol (played by Zbigniew Zamachowski), a Polish émigré and hairdresser working in Paris and married to salon-owner Dominique (Julie Delpy), is humiliated when his wife divorces him on the grounds that their marriage is unconsummated: Karol the artisan is impotent. Simulating an arson attack by Karol on their salon, she then hounds him out of Paris, stripping him of his money and belongings, before further disgracing him by allowing him to hear her, over the telephone, making love with a more functional lover. This humiliation is overseen and overheard by Mikołaj (Janusz Gajos), a fellow Pole Karol meets on the Metro, where he has been reduced to busking on his hairdresser's comb to make money (the pair bond over their shared knowledge of Polish songs). Mikołaj smuggles Karol back into Warsaw in a coffin-like suitcase, which is then stolen at the airport by thieves who, on discovering that their cargo is the literally and metaphorically worthless Karol, beat him up and tip him onto a rubbish tip on the outskirts of the city. He then returns to the Warsaw hairdressing salon he established with his brother, Jurek (Jerzy Stuhr), and hatches a plot to take revenge on Dominique. Amassing a small fortune on the wild frontiers of Polish capitalism—and by almost killing the, for a period, suicidal Mikołaj in return for a lump sum—Karol wills his money to his ex-wife and fakes his own death to bring her to Warsaw. The subterfuge is achieved, in part, through the black market purchase of a Russian corpse—as Karol's henchman remarks, you can buy anything in this postcommunist Poland. When Karol sees Dominique crying at his "funeral," he experiences pangs of doubt about his plan; these heighten when he appears to her in her hotel room after the funeral and they make love, with mutually satisfying results: Karol the capitalist is a potent success. Yet he follows through on his plot, creeping out of her room as she sleeps; she is awoken by the police and arrested for Karol's murder. Symmetry of maltreatment is thereby achieved, but Karol gets more than he bargained for in victory. When he visits Dominique in prison at the end of the film, she signals to Karol that she still loves him and wishes to remarry. Karol cries.

White has received short shrift in the Kieślowski literature, with many critics treating its story and storytelling to a less rigorous theorizing than *Blue* and *Red* due to its comedic content and ostensibly more straightforward, generically dictated mode of filmic discourse. Haltof concisely surveys the Western reception of its story:

> The majority of critics discuss *White* as, to use Geoff Andrew's description, "a droll black comedy, complete with such generic staples as missing corpses, cunning schemes and sexual humiliation." Western critics in particular also see the second part of the trilogy . . . as commenting on the ties between Poland and the West. Coates, for instance, states that *White* "dramatizes Polish fears of exclusion from Europe," and "Karol's impotence may be that of the Pole confronting locked European doors."[173]

Noting that Karol is impotent only when abroad, Haltof agrees that the political interpretations "seem to be valid" and describes the film as "a bleak vision of the post-1989 state of affairs."[174] Such views of *White*—as a black comedy in which politics provide superficial grist to the farce's mill—are fairly typical. They are also unfair. *White* is a gem. Haltof notes that *White* received a similar reception from some Polish critics. Certain Polish reviewers were even less engaged than their foreign counterparts, reading *White* merely as a "comic interlude" in the trilogy, "a disappointing film devoid of serious examination of Polish reality and filled with suspicious art-house clichés," or a "sketchy picture of the new 'capitalist' Polish reality" filled with "simplifications"; Haltof quotes self-explanatory review titles including "Downwards," "Cold," "The Colored Emptiness" and "Without Color."[175] Other reviewers argued that the film failed on its ostensible genre's own terms. Sobolewski, for instance, felt that *White* does not work fluently as comedy ("a comedy with a lump in one's throat") and in turn argued that it lacked both the acutely accurate depiction of Polish reality of Kieślowski's earlier *Camera Buff* or of interior mental reality in *Blue*.[176] Contrastingly, Paul Coates wonders if Mirosław Przylipiak's observation is correct: "Polish critics contrasting a Kieślowski accepted abroad with one rejected at home partly reflect[s] a domestic inferiority complex *vis-à-vis* the West—a hypothesis surely corroborated by the widespread negative Polish reaction to the one Kieślowski film to thematicize that complex, *Trois couleurs: Blanc*."[177] Some Poles felt it was a bit rich for an internationally celebrated émigré to return to his country and satirize its current state. Coates notes, however, that, in spite of the negative reception in some quarters, the rejection level of *White* was only 38 percent in Polish reviews. Perhaps many other Poles recognized, with Kieślowski, that, "If something is your own, you're entitled to have a critical opinion of it, more so of things that aren't yours. . . . Of the people we love, we demand and expect more; it's the same with places. . . . It's awful, but it's mine!"[178]

What, specifically, demanded this critique in Poland, post-1989? Several critics hint that *White* has greater portent than the above reviews indicate. Andrew calls *White* "a deft black comedy with genuine thematic substance,"[179] succeeding as a black comedy while providing, in the context of the trilogy, an appropriately weighted change of tone and lull before the final storm (*White* is the middle movement of Andrew's "symphony"); Insdorf contends that the film is "one of Kieślowski's deceptively simplest films, a cinematic poem . . . [of] layered richness"[180]; Wollermann argues that the film is a tragicomedy in which the comic elements actually deepen the effectiveness of the tragedy.[181] The last view chimes with Kieślowski's own description of *White*, not as a comedy to make people laugh, but as a sad ("smutna") or lyrical comedy designed to make one think.[182] In this vein, Andrew notes that *White* revisits many themes from earlier Kieślowski films, such as "the painful impossibility of equality in love" (*Decalogue 6*), "impotence, insecurity and infidelity" (*Decalogue 9*), "a man awaiting the release of his love from prison" (*Blind Chance*), "a criminally materialistic Poland where everything can be bought" (*Decalogue 10*), and actors, most notably Stuhr (*The Scar* [1976], *The Calm* [1976], *Camera Buff*) and Zamachowski, who starred alongside Stuhr, also as his brother, in *Decalogue 10*.[183]

These elements, Andrew argues, constitute aspects of Kieślowski's "worldview,"[184] a perspective still present in *White*. Andrew also observes, acutely, that many of *Blue*'s themes are varied in *White*: our relationship to the past, the interplay of freedom of choice, chance and fate, lives haunted by the dead or the absent, objects invested with an emotional resonance, "and the sense that love, in all its many, often perverse manifestations, is the prime motivator behind human action."[185] At the end of *White*, he notes, love achieves the healing force it attained at the end of *Blue*, as the couple put away childish things (as St. Paul declared to the Corinthians that one must) and realize that their farcically amplified, pettily vindictive acts were, in a sense, "declarations of love."[186] One might also argue that, by the end of the film, each has sacrificed much—Karol his "life," Dominique her freedom—to achieve this epiphany,[187] just as Julie had to sacrifice one kind of liberty in *Blue* to move forward.

Andrew's overall judgment of the relationship between the romantic themes in *White* and its socio-political content, however, is an oversimplification: "though the film derives much humour from its sardonic depiction of the dog-eat-dog mores of contemporary, capitalist Poland," he writes, "social comment [as in *Blue*] is included first and foremost as a contextualising reflection of the emotional conflict between its two protagonists."[188] Yet it is plausible to invert this relationship, i.e., to claim that the emotional conflict is actually the foreground to a political background not merely addressing the dog-eat-dog mores of the new Polish capitalism, but darker undercurrents of high capitalist societies the world over. Moreover, its lighter tone and style can be read as a functional variation on the serious themes addressed in the trilogy's outer panels, rather than a thematic digression, in a movie pitched to address a quite different, and potentially much wider, audience than the art house denizens who saw *Blue* or would see *Red*.[189] *White* is a sardonic Trojan horse, constructed to smuggle graver subtexts.

Just as the symbolic subtleties of the story are played down in the literature, its mode of discourse is similarly disregarded as merely functional. There is a tendency to argue that "the formalist aesthetic exists in subdued form" in *White*, due to generic considerations (satiric comedy rather than reflective drama,[190] and to thus view the film as a stylistic departure for the late Kieślowski films—but not, intriguingly, thus as a positive return to the more direct manner of his earlier films connected to the Cinema of Moral Concern.[191] As such, the storytelling is judged a partial failure against the standards of the other late films—even by critics, ironically, who believe those stylizations were themselves a failure. Haltof, for instance, describes *White* as "not as refined," featuring "functional photography . . . at the service of the story"[192]; Andrew also suggests the film is "less ornate, less expressionistic and generally more conventionally naturalistic" than *Blue*, although he notes its Kieślowskian "precision."[193] There is truth to these views, but they are too sweeping.

Kehr offers a more nuanced perspective. He encapsulates *White*'s realism by contrasting its fusion of medium and message to *Blue*, noting the role of the cinematographer in sculpting the preceding film's interior landscape and, above all, *White*'s political connotations:

> Julie lives in a subjective, inwardly focused, visually oriented environment, Karol in an objective, aggressive, action-oriented world. *White* was photographed by Edward Kłosiński, a cameraman who worked previously with Kieślowski only on the second episode of *The Decalogue*, but who has done extensive work for Andrzej Wajda (including *Man of Marble* and *Man of Iron*). And *White* does have the visual sweep and social orientation of a Wajda film—wide framing, eye-level camera placement, a number of characters interacting in a shot, in a way that creates a subtle sense of theater. *White* is the most public of the three films, the most overtly political, the most readily accessible.[194]

Kehr's parallel between *White* and Wajda is telling. The idea of *White* as a latter-day contribution to a cinema of post-1989 moral concerns cuts against the general tone of its reception as an incidental affair, but tallies with this study's argument for Kieślowski's later films' political orientations. It also forms a counterpoint to the most critically developed strand of the film's scholarly reception—feminist engagements with the text's representation of women—and to the tone of discussions of the film's take on the Polish capitalism. These issues are considered below, in the context of my view that *White* does indeed have serious political intentions and that its accessibility of style is part of its rhetorical armory. By making its story and telling more accessible, its ideological content is rendered more direct, effectively to convey its message, one imagines, to those who Kieślowski felt needed to hear it most urgently in the mid-1990s: his compatriots on the front line of Poland's engagement with high capitalism. Yet one can also argue that its surface political themes interweave with its representations of an embattled romance, coiling therein to form a knotty social satire with something to tell audiences in Wests old and new. Preisner's music—less prominent, ostensibly blunter, on analysis surprisingly subtle—plays a central role in the telling and selling of *White*'s comedy and its polemic.

Feminism, Capitalism, Subjugation

Far from being intentionally prejudiced in his representations of women, Kieślowski made a conscious attempt to focus on women in his later films, albeit in the context of a broader balance of the sexes. As he put it, simply, regarding the trilogy: "The first film is about a woman, the second about a man, and the third about a man and a woman."[195] Insdorf, in turn, argues that *White*'s voyeurism is "benign" (at various points in the movie Karol spies on Dominique) and its cinematographic gaze sympathetic; she also suggests that, far from being a mere object, there is a lot going on behind Dominique's porcelain features.[196] For Alicja Helman, however, there is nothing benign at all about *White*'s gaze. Taking a reflection theorist's stance that phallocentric cultures offer distorted reflections of women, in turn compelling men in the real world to treat women according to the dictates of such fictions, her views on *White* trope classic formulations of mainstream cinema's male gaze—indeed, its white, Western, straight, lower middle-class, socially conservative, masculine gaze—constructing woman as image/man as bearer of the look, with women thus primarily defined by their "to-be-looked-at-ness."[197] Women who enjoy such cultural productions are masochists; men enjoying them are sadists; those making them are unspeakable.

For Helman, therefore, *White*'s "view of women . . . is absolutely traditional and of the kind that provokes the most determined feminist attacks."[198] One can see why one might think this in response to "the story of the fall and rise of Karol, who—having suffered painful humiliation by his wife—eventually finds a way to subdue her."[199] Her character sketch of Dominique, in this context, is suitably damning:

> Dominique . . . is the French wife of a Polish émigré, a beautiful, sensual blonde whom the authors and camera treat as a sexual object, the goal of male desire. Sexuality completely determines Dominique's existence, and sex alone motivates her behaviour. Dominique looks and behaves like the embodiment of male dreams.[200]

Furthermore, Dominique submits to Karol "unhesitatingly" and indeed rather ludicrously (she should surely be livid at finding him alive!) at the first hint of his renewed potency, demonstrating "woman's function as sexual object point-blank."[201] And then there is the ending of the film, with Dominique seen in the distance high up in her prison tower, a shot in which Žižek finds echoes of "a courtly model of the cruel lady admired in her inaccessibility,"[202] and Helman something worse:

> Feminist theory postulates that patriarchal culture "imprisons" women by denying them the status of subjects, and reducing them to their allotted roles of mother, sexual object and sign of social exchange among men. Erased from history and culture, woman appears "eternal" and unchanging, constructed by the discourses that imprison her. In *White*, Dominique is simply locked up in prison, thanks to which Karol will be able to regain both her and her affections. The starkness of this solution suggests a metaphor for patriarchal culture, which tells us that only a woman in chains can be possessed.[203]

Worst of all, one might add, Dominique seems happy to be imprisoned, and only wants release so that she can return to her master's side, like

an abused but loyal pet.[204] Following this view, Dominique is a distillation of Kieślowski's discourse on women up to *Véronique* and a "set-
tling of his accounts" with an image of femininity that had haunted his
earlier work. Helman describes Irena in *Camera Buff*, Witek's doctor
wife in *Blind Chance* and Ula in *No End* as "'homebodies,' women
whose feelings, actions and desires revolve around family life."[205] Concerning the female characters in the *Decalogue*, she argues that "women
in Kieślowski's [earlier] films seem to exist exclusively in terms of
their biological role. They are wives, lovers, mothers or daughters: what
they are as human beings seems of little significance."[206] She therefore
concludes that Kieślowski's "viewer sees [women] first and foremost as
the 'eternal Eve,' not as historically conditioned women inhabiting a
contemporary Poland, who could—and do—do a thousand things over
and above contracting associations with men."[207]

The problem with this reading is not its basic feminist intent, with
which one could hardly take issue, but rather its literalness in the face
of a cinema so obviously concerned with explorations of moral opacity.
It is also a sweeping caricature of Dominique's motivations. In one
moment, she fits the bill, behaving—as Delpy described her character
setting fire to the salon in front of Karol—like a cat driven mad by being permanently in heat; in the next, she is telling him that he doesn't
understand her, that she loves him and needs him, even while hating
him, too. There is more to her motivations, in other words, than sex.
Yet even if she is primarily motivated by desire, given that there is no
hint here that she is anything other than fully in control of her needs and
wishing merely to have them more fully fulfilled, one could also view
her as empowered, driving a man out of her life in the hope that he will
return transformed properly to satisfy her. More generally, however,
one might challenge the stance that sees Kieślowski's female protagonists "first and foremost" as homebodies, plus the general impugning of
Kieślowski's attitude to women.[208] To address *White* specifically, reading the imprisonment of Dominique as a straight-faced troping of "patriarchal culture 'imprison[ing]' women by denying them the status of
subjects" seems forced, not least in the context of Helman's own persuasive argument that the films from *Véronique* onwards are revisions
of his earlier takes on the feminine.

Helman sees the other late films as representing "a new and infinitely more fascinating, subtle and complex" image of femininity.
Could it not therefore be the case that there is more to Dominique than
meets the gaze? It is not all good news in the later films, of course:
women are still viewed as "other than men" and the camera, if anything, seems even more in love with their bodies than before. Žižek
identifies a contrast between the last four films and Kieślowski's earlier
output in which beauty was "devalued"; there are many beautiful
women, but they are not dressed or shot as such. "Compare this," he
suggests, "with Irène Jacob, Julie Delpy and Juliette Binoche, who are
not only intrinsically beautiful, but *also treated as such* by the camera
which lovingly traverses their bodies."[209] He also argues, contra Hel-

man, that, while *Blue* and *Red* are told from a female perspective, worship of women for their "pre-rational intuition"[210] could in fact be perceived as an even more degrading act: in these films, a "woman is good insofar as she retains her pre-rational, intuitive, passive attitude, renouncing any aggressive drive herself."[211] Yet Žižek's argument about *White* hints at a more nuanced reading of Dominique's subjugation. Both Karol and Dominique are products of a world that constructs, and constricts, their actions and subjectivities. Noting how possession is a recurring theme in Kieślowski's work, Žižek argues that, in *White*,

> this topic is directly translated into the terms of the exchange economy of the market: becoming rich, buying, and then "getting even." In a stroke of genius, Kieślowski links this commodity possession (in the conditions of a return to capitalism in post-Communist Poland) to sexual possession/impotence.[212]

On a parallel path, Kickasola reads the end of the film as signifying that Dominique "has always loved" Karol, but, as a "product of the West, . . . also needed a man with power"[213]; similarly, Coates suggests that the feminine viewpoints of the later films purposefully disempowered *all* Western perceivers as a reflection of our position in modern capitalist societies[214]—and how intriguing it is to consider the role of Preisner's "feminine" presence in constructing the environment for such reflections. Wilson, in a careful reading of feminist issues arising from *White*, destabilizes simplistic descriptions of the power relationship between subject and object in *White*'s gazing, seeing aspects of the film not as cinematic voyeurism *per se* "since the relationship between voyeur and exhibitionist appears most properly Kieślowski's subject."[215] This argument—that *White* is not sexist but rather a kind of meta-bigotry, utilizing an obviously sexist plot as a symbolic symptom of a darker malaise—is taken up below in the present study, not least regarding the film's music. Preisner's scoring often plays on conventional musical representations of femininity and the power divide in clichéd constructions of heterosexual male-female relationships, most obviously—but also, it turns out, most subtly—in *White*'s alternation of a tango with a quite different dance.

The primary malaise addressed by *White* is the constraining effects of late modernity and particularly high capitalism on the development of an individual's subjectivity and interpersonal relationships. In Chapter Six I propose a reading of the film in which the machinations of Dominique and Karol's relationship are a parable on the pitfalls of life under capitalisms both new (as in Warsaw and Poland post-1989, i.e., the New, now Western, formerly Eastern Europe) and more established (as in Paris and France, i.e., the Old, more established, Western Europe), and thus a trenchant, beautifully pitched contribution to the trilogy's overarching discourse on how to live a better life near the turn of the new millennium. That the film addresses itself to a more diverse audience of cinemagoers, rather than merely to intellectuals in the art house more conscious of their surrounding cultural conditions, may make its polemical intent seem quite impressive.

Kieślowski himself implied the need to center readings of the film on this topic. "I'm not against Polish entrepreneurialism," he once stated, "but people now care for nothing but money. I don't know what happened to us."[216] Describing the post-communist "picturesque and photogenic muddle" of Poland, he suggested, without too much exaggeration and anticipating a key line in *White*, that it is "possible to buy anything in Warsaw today: a tank, a kilo of uranium, houses whose owners have disappeared, forged passports, stolen cars, a birth certificate, a real or fake university diploma"; in Warsaw, he added—stating that this was the subject of *White*—an impatience, a drive to become rich, to acquire material goods, had overtaken all other concerns.[217] What is lost when people become subjects of capitalism? What slips off of life's shopping list? This is *White*'s inner theme.

Kieślowski was not the only Polish filmmaker reflecting on the tough and cynical world of the new capitalism immediately after 1989. For Haltof, the "references to wild Polish capitalism along with its sarcastic humour" mean that *White* should be viewed alongside other Polish films of the early 1990s, such as Władysław Pasikowski's *Kroll* (1991) and *Psy* ("The Pigs," 1992, starring *Blind Chance*'s Bogusław Linda): action films dealing with the underworld and representing the post-Solidarity generation's "nihilism and disillusionment with the new reality."[218] Haltof also considers *White*'s similarity to *Lepiej piękną bogatą* ("It's Better to Be Beautiful and Rich") by Filip Bajon, a rags to riches "fairy tale" in which a weaver inherits a factory and becomes a modern-day capitalist princess;[219] her transformation parallels Karol's from barber to mob boss. Karol, though, is an everyman and, moreover, a comic staple in at least two ways implying humbleness and satirical content to Polish audiences. Karol (Charlie) is "a name 'reserved' in Polish cinema for comedies such as *Och, Karol*" ("Oh, Charles!," 1985, Roman Załuski) and in Zamachowski, *White* stars a Polish actor whose film persona imports a presence of "ordinary characters struggling under the pressure of politics."[220]

Whether or not one reads engagement with such topics, for Kieślowski, as a return "to the theme of social-orientation"[221] explored in *Blind Chance* and *Camera Buff* and thus the Cinema of Moral Concern—and I would argue that *White* is a political film of moral convictions whose concerns are addressed not solely to a Polish audience—it seems dubious to put aside this aspect of the film. It is more productive, perhaps, to consider its implications for reading other aspects of *White*. Kickasola sensibly counsels against interpreting *White* "as a realistic mimetic narrative"; rather it is a "cartoonish satire on contemporary materialism and the loss of traditional values."[222] The film's critique of money, power and materialism make the Kieślowski of *White* "a smiling version of Aleksandr Solzhenitsyn (on this issue): critical of totalitarianism, but pessimistic about the negative effects of materialism inherent in contemporary capitalism."[223] The overt satire is apparent in

the grotesque human being that "a primitive market economy as grotesquely speeded up as the action in a Keystone short" enables Karol to
metamorphose into, amassing wealth just to frame his wife for murder,
break her heart and leave her doubting her sanity. The satire is as obvious as the gaudy neon sign outside Karol's Warsaw salon, which
Kickasola reads as "synecdochic for the whole of European identity"[224]
in the time of late capitalism. One could go a step further and call it a
synecdoche for the late-modern West.

Kieślowski suggested that Karol's profession is symbolic in this
regard. Hairdressers, he stated, at least in Poland, aspire to class mobility; not part of the intelligentsia, they nonetheless want something more
than their lot in life.[225] Whatever the truth of this view of Polish hairdressing, Karol is clearly intended as a symbol of the new Poland, exaggerating deeper traits. Yet when he succeeds on its wild frontier,
Kickasola notes, he seems more ridiculous than at any point when he
was being humiliated by Dominique, becoming "a caricature of new
capitalism: quick ascension with quick profits based on the beck and
call of others"[226] in a "critique of soulless capitalism [that] hits its apex
in the purchase of the corpse" and a life literally commoditized.[227] One
might also be reminded of the father's death in *Decalogue 10*, and its
initial meaning for the brothers played by Zamachowski and Stuhr: a
get-rich-quick scheme in which the profundity of death is swept aside.
The lyrics sung by Artur's punk band in *10*, the aptly named "City
Death," seem just as apt to a discussion of *White*'s satirical intent as to
10's subversion of the Commandments:

> Kill, kill, kill
> Screw who you will
> Lust and crave
> Pervert and deprave
> Every day of the week
> Every day of the week
> On Sunday hit mother
> Hit father, hit brother
> Hit sister, hit weakest
> And steal from the meekest
> 'Cos everything's yours
> Yeah, everything's yours.[228]

It is over this type of anti-*agapē* that the heroes of *White* and the
trilogy seek, but fail fully, to triumph. One glimpses the possibility in
Mikołaj and Jurek, an odd-couple of paternal and maternal substitutes—one existentialist businessman, the other a homebody—and
emasculated men to rival any of Helman's subjugated women.[229] As
Andrew notes, though, even Karol's relationships with this pair are mediated by capital as much as by affection: "In *White* every relationship,
however close, is at least partly predicated on some sort of economic
exchange, involving love as currency,"[230] such as Jurek's bartering over
how many heads of hair Karol should cut per week to pay rent. Yet

they, too, like Karol, are not bad people. Karol is just "pragmatic," re-inventing himself "according to the rules of the game the world around him is playing."[231] Like the dancers in a tango, Karol's moves are somewhat predetermined, in articulations of the living death so keenly diagnosed by Dyer as whiteness's symbolic role in contemporary cinema. Under such circumstances, only a supreme act of will—of self-sacrificial, philanthropic *agapē*, the polar opposite to capitalist one-upmanship—can permit lives of equality to be glimpsed.

Criticism on *White*'s Music

Kieślowski and Piesiewicz decided early on that Karol would play part of "The Last Sunday"[232] on his busker's comb in *White*, thereby attracting Mikołaj's attention. This old Polish tango, in which a suicidal spurned lover begs for one last Sunday together with his departing lover, was referred to by Kieślowski as "The Last Sunday, tomorrow we'll part," in a quote from the lyrics which begins to indicate its links to the narrative (separation and suicide). In the same discussion, he anticipated that Preisner's music in *White* would "have a certain simplicity characteristic of music written for silent films, but it won't be played on a piano":

> It'll be a bit more complicated musically. I suspect that it'll be inspired, to a certain extent, by Polish folk music such as the mazurka, for example, music which is a bit coarse yet at the same time romantic.[233]

Wollermann quotes press notes from Preisner indicating this same crucial mixture of coarseness and romance in their intentions for *White*'s score.[234]

Preisner gave me a colorful account of the origins of the film's main themes. Flying with Kieślowski from Warsaw to Paris to work on *White* on a "very bad" Russian plane—they were seated right at the back, due to Kieślowski's theory that, should the plane crash, this gave him the best possible chance of escape—director and composer began eavesdropping on the increasingly animated, vodka-fuelled conversation of two Poles seated in front of them. The conversation ran like this: "Why are you flying? *Going to Paris.* Job? *No job; I know a good place, the Polish church.* Do you know how to find it? *No.* My daughter pick me up; she is cleaning the Polish embassy; I will have driver from embassy pick me up!" One hour and many shots of vodka later, the pair were firm friends: "*Can you help me?* Yes, of course, my daughter will help you get job too!" Overhearing this cocktail of nationalism, sentimentality, optimism and exaggeration, Preisner turned to his equally amused colleague and proclaimed: "Listen—this is music for the film! This guy is the tango!" At this point, Preisner reports, he sang the first melodic phrase of *White*'s tango to the director: "The world is for us. Let's go!"

White's tango dominates the film's musical climate during Karol's immersion in capitalist fantasy. It is, however, punctuated with visions of alternative realities. Those punctuations, initially, are visions of Poland as experienced by homesick Poles abroad, Preisner says, and music in its own way equally warped by sentiment and nostalgia. Even while Karol is in Paris, however, the other strand of the score acts as a beacon drawing him towards an appreciation of "home." The *rustico* theme in the film—the folk-like cue accompanying many of Karol's more melancholy moments—is a vision of traditional music from the north of Poland (the Kurpia and Mazovia regions specifically) and therefore music with which Preisner had become familiar through his father's folk repertory. Connections can be made between the *rustico* theme and a variety of mazurka, although for Preisner, because the *rustico* is in $\frac{3}{4}$, not $\frac{2}{4}$, it is better heard as "an allegory of mazurka," the genre's typically clear dance rhythms obscured by Karol's soft-focus fantasies. The scoring of *rustico* melodies on the clarinet is also important. As Preisner recounts, with comic exaggeration, "everybody played clarinet" in the Poland of his youth; they were cheaply available and relatively easy to learn. The clarinet is therefore, in a Polish context, a marker of Karol's humble origins. It is also a signifier of his idiocy. Poles, Preisner notes, call someone a clarinet—a "klarnet"—as a term of abuse indicating stupidity and commonness.[235]

Such visions are subjugated by the tango when Karol's nostalgia for home and Dominique cedes, on his return to Poland, to his plot of revenge. Behavior marked musically as stupid and humble is thus supplanted by music marked, in a Polish cultural context, as upwardly mobile. Yet the folk music continues to return during this phase of the film. It cannot now be heard as the nostalgia of a Pole abroad; it is the siren's call of a different "home"—Kieślowski's overtaken concerns—heard by a character who, if he stopped to think about it, would find himself a stranger in his homeland. This transformation of the *rustico*'s symbolic purpose in *White*—from music lamenting an absent homeland to music lamenting the absence of something more profound—is an example of Preisner's ability to shape longer-range musical symbolism as part of a score's contribution to a film's articulation of its concept. Why does this Poland not feel like Poland to Karol, prompting such melancholy themes? The answer to that question cuts to the core of the film's dilemma.

Preisner has stated elsewhere, regarding *White*, that the tango "is a musical form that has become very characteristic for the modern Poland, and since the film is about the new situation there, the tango suited [it] well,"[236] because the genre is both popular in, and symbolic of, aspects of contemporary Polish life. Preisner also asserted that, in *White*, "the music score is completely ironic,"[237] demonstrating awareness of the economic situation's implications for life in Poland post-1989: "Tango in Poland is the dance for common people, ironic and primitive," he notes, "yet at the same time it has real forward momentum."[238]

There is clearly more to Preisner's tango in *White*, therefore, than a celebration of Polish free enterprise. Its politics are not merely sexual. *White*'s tangos have been commented on in the literature. Haltof notes the performance of "The Last Sunday," although his assertion that it "reappears later in the film incorporated into Preisner's score"[239] is not backed up with musical analysis and is difficult to prove, given the absence of obvious motivic links between it and Preisner's own tango. Haltof is nevertheless correct to note a sustaining, through Preisner's invention, of generic notions implied by "The Last Sunday," which "clearly comments on the action" with its "suicidal lyrics . . . refer[ring] to Karol's state of affairs with Dominique as well as Mikołaj's personal problems."[240] Haltof also reads Preisner's tango as stressing Karol's need for revenge: "like a male dancer in a tango, Karol is clearly in charge . . . after his return to Poland."[241] Insdorf pays closer attention still to Preisner's tango, perceptively describing his score as "narrative rather than ornamental":

> This Argentine musical form is appropriate to Kieślowski's pattern: the tango is simultaneously lyrical, playful, and deliberate—like Karol's scheme. The tango music begins after Karol has returned to Poland, and it accompanies his intricate planning. As anyone who has ever essayed an Argentine tango knows, the man is in control: even if the high-heeled, swirling skirted woman is the one who does the flashy steps, she can move only to the extent that the man's hand— quietly but insistently controlling the bottom center of her back— allows her to. As Karol becomes increasingly self-confident via his wealth, he manipulates Dominique in an elaborate—if long-distance— dance. And, like *White*, the tango expresses romantic longing through formal constraints.[242]

Much of this is spot on, although, as discussed in Chapter Six, female tango dancers are not always so helpless, the form representing complex cultural nuances, especially in Poland, that intensify its "narrative rather than ornamental" contribution to the film. Moreover, the tango sometimes sounds beneath scenes of a different significance, such as Mikołaj and Karol's drunken ice dance—the tango here, Falkowska asserts, carrying "connotations of the Poles' love for the grandiose and the emotional excess that this music evokes."[243]

On the topic of longing, Insdorf also mentions the "yearning" signified "in a recurring solo, whether on oboe or clarinet," although she takes her analysis of the score's other theme, the mazurka-tinged *rustico*, no further.[244] Discussion of Polish music in *White* instead centers on the "Home at last" cue heard when Karol is tipped onto the rubbish dump, and thus a piano flourish with a dual purpose: while signaling the impending commencement of Preisner's grand tango, the cue also calls to mind Poland's preeminent Romantic musical hero. As Preisner notes, "The music becomes very like Chopin, a Polish cultural icon," but the use is, again, "ironic because Poland was one huge garbage dump."[245] Counterpointing an allusion to nationalistic pride in Chopin's music with the image of a Pole quite literally down in the dumps is in line with the humor elsewhere in the film: as musical puns go, it is coarse but effective in execution as well as in symbolism. Yet in fact this is a double pun, the sequence also trampling on memories of another Polish cultural hero and the ending of Wajda's *Ashes and Diamonds* (1958). Falkowska therefore calls the music at the dump "a humorous polonaise underlin[ing] the irony of the whole situation," with Kieślowski transforming "patriotic iconography into a powerful grotesque reminiscent of the writings of Sławomir Mrożek or Witold Gombrowicz."[246] There is more, though, to this moment than a pun on the less than illustrious realities of new Polish capitalism. Hallowed ideals are trounced in *White* in the rush to material gain, just as the film's ironic intertextuality tramples on sacred cultural texts. This symbol, like so much else in *White*, is simultaneously bitter, funny and sad.

Haltof connects the less prominent role of Preisner's music, compared at least with *Blue*, to the less flamboyant tone of the filmmaking in *White*, and adds that the film is "deprived of the usual references to Van den Budenmayer," which helps the music to be "less overpowering."[247] Music is subtly foregrounded in the film by Karol's comb playing and later his duet with Mikołaj. It is admittedly not as obvious, however, as the screenplay's intended inclusion of Van den Budenmayer, which would have occurred at Karol's fake funeral in the form of organ music and, later, a performance at his graveside.[248] Most obviously, the planned use of Van den Budenmayer related to art music's potential to signify a certain kind of taste and thus social class. The film's scoring takes Karol, in effect, on a journey from rustic mazurka to cosmopolitan tango and, if Van den Budenmayer had stayed in the final cut, onward into enlightened attainment and the ranks of the bourgeoisie.[249] The orchestra at the graveside would, of course, have meant a show off's funeral, along with the American cars he books in the screenplay just because they are more expensive than their Polish equivalents. Taste, class and their relation to *White*'s music and concepts are analyzed further in Chapter Six.

One Polish popular song heard in *White* from Karol's comb goes unidentified in the literature. Like a further song mentioned in the screenplay, that performance has interesting, though quite different, socio-political resonances. In a musical interlude cut from the final film, Karol's henchman Bronek is caught pinching a computer from the office; Karol makes him sing as a punishment. The henchman chooses a Communist mass song and thus a chunk of socialist-realist propaganda half-remembered from his youth. "To the barricades, you nation of workers, lift high the banners red," he begins, but he ends up humming it, unable to remember the anthem's words; "Nice song," Karol says sarcastically. The loss of words from the communist anthem seems apposite here, in a time when the country was singing a quite different economic and political song. This idea is articulated in *White* by the other piece of music Karol performs for Mikołaj in the Metro, hence the ultimate redundancy of the cut scene.

In summary, *White* has received the least musical attention of the trilogy's constituent scores. Wollermann offers some useful observations in his analytical overview, and these are discussed in context in the analysis to follow; most critics touch on one or other tango; a few mention the allusion to Chopin; no one allots sustained discussion to the *rustico*. Consequently, the structuring of the score—its alternation of *rustico* and tango—and the symbolic significance of this musically articulated progression has also been largely ignored. It might seem, even, that there is little need here for a detailed musical analysis: the music in *White*, as opposed to, say, *Blue*, is surely the most coincidental in all Kieślowski's late films. Yet it is simply not the case that less prominent music—particularly in a film where subtext is everything—has less interesting things to signify. Music is subtly foregrounded in the narrative by Karol's amateur musicianship: this should be enough to set critical apparatuses tingling, for music never merely accents the image or narrative of a film, even when it is not as integral to the plot as in the case of a music-film like *Blue*. Music in film always accents and represents a diversity of codependent and independent meanings in the audio-visual text. When music is present, whether subtle or ostensibly simple, "cinematic content . . . arises from the fluctuating interplay of narrative, image, and music in any and all combinations, including those in which narrative or image merely accent a musical statement."[250] In turn,

> music becomes thickly textured, in the sense of demanding thick description; it resonates with an intertextual polyphony that can no longer go unheard or unexamined. Like all representations, it exceeds its immediate purpose.[251]

Just as, for Wilson, the image of Brigitte Bardot on the poster for Godard's *Le mépris* by Dominique's apartment window in Paris (where Karol sees her greet her lover before phoning her and being aurally emasculated) opens a rich vein of criticism, paying careful attention to the details of music and sound in *White* opens opportunities to read subtexts as yet underplayed in the literature. To take a musical moment in *White* apparently unnoticed by other Kieślowski scholars as one example: in a passage of great subtlety (crafted by William Flageollet's sound design from, in part, Preisner's music) fragments of *Blue*'s *Concert[o]* are heard. Immediately, *Blue*'s musically mediated message bleeds into *White*, intensifying its symbolism. Furthermore, the specific verse of the *Concert[o]* heard in *White* comments on the blackness at the heart of the film and, at that particular stage in its story, of Karol. Like the rest of the music in *White*—and most particularly the more audible and obviously symbolic vacillation between tango and *rustico*—such representations deserve a more intensive analysis.

Metaphysical Fiction: *Red*

Three Colors: Red is a metaphysical thriller. Valentine (Irène Jacob), a lonely student and part-time model living in Geneva and apart from her possessive boyfriend, accidentally runs over a German Shepherd called Rita. She finds the owner—Joseph Kern (Jean-Louis Trintignant), a retired judge—who disturbs her in his indifference to his pet's fate. She takes the dog to the vet and discovers it is pregnant; it then runs away from her, back to the Judge's house. Valentine and the old Judge exchange views on the value of humankind and whether people act for the greater good or selfish reasons. Each learns from the other, but the fundamental change is to the Judge's outlook. He has been eavesdropping on his neighbors' telephone calls; Valentine persuades him to admit his guilt to his neighbors and the authorities. He does so and goes to court; he is reprimanded and his ability to eavesdrop curtailed. As their relationship deepens, it becomes apparent that the events leading to the Judge's bitterness and isolation—he was cuckolded by the only true love of his life—are paralleled by events affecting Valentine's neighbor, a young judge called Auguste (Jean-Pierre Lorit), whom she does not yet know, and who is dating one of the old Judge's neighbors. Auguste is also being cuckolded by his lover, and once he discovers it, he plans to pursue her across the ocean to England on a ferry, humiliating himself as the old Judge once did. Valentine also plans to board the ferry to meet her boyfriend. The dog gives birth; the ferry sinks. A terrible storm, the beginnings of which interrupt Valentine and the Judge's final conversation in a theater, overwhelms the ship. The judge learns of this on the TV she has lent to him. Over 1,400 people are feared dead; two others (Auguste's cheating girlfriend and her other lover) are missing on a yacht. Seven survivors, however, have been pulled from the water: Julie and Olivier from *Blue*, Karol and Dominique from *White*, Valentine and Auguste, and a barman. The film ends with shots of the Judge and Valentine. He looks out of a broken window, enigmatic but shedding a tear; she is seen in a close-up and freeze-frame extracted from the news footage, standing next to Auguste and thus meeting her potentially perfect match for the first time. The camera zooms in to frame her against a vivid red backdrop. A strikingly similar image has been seen throughout the film on a billboard advertisement starring Valentine. As the credits roll, the final version of Preisner's main theme for *Red*, a bolero, closes the *Three Colors* trilogy.

A synopsis of *Red*'s action has virtually nothing to say about the impact on the audio-viewer of Kieślowski's final film. As Kickasola has noted, "it is difficult to do the film justice on the printed page."[252] Nor can a synopsis do more than touch on the complexity of its paean to the redemptive power of friendship in the face of the economic, cultural and technological isolations of late-modern times. One might begin to compensate for the banality of description, however, by noting that Kieślowski, according to *Red*'s editor, Jacques Witta, emerged from screenings of *Red* in tears. The taciturn director was undone by his final film. Compared to what Witta calls "the lyrical, more glamorous . . . stylistic exercise" of *Blue*, *Red*, it seems, was personal: a "much deeper" reflection on life, on the gulf of experience and optimism that occurs between old age and youth, and on the need to bridge the things that divide people in search of salvation.[253] Many critics have therefore engaged the film as if it is a reflection of the director's personality, life and career, not least in terms of his relationship to the oppositional figures of the Judge and Valentine: notably, the trilogy's meditation on fraternity concerns not one but two main characters. Considerations of that relationship, the film's evocation of metaphysical suspense, and a survey of critical responses to *Red*'s soundtrack follow below, identifying themes taken further in Chapter Seven's analysis of *Red*.

Despite the scandal (felt, at least, by many connected to the production) of the film losing out in the Palm D'Or competition to *Pulp Fiction* at Cannes in 1994,[254] *Red* has received a laudatory reception of "heightened language"[255]—not least from Tarantino, who called the film a masterpiece and, Marin Karmitz implies, acknowledged that the wrong film had won.[256] In the director's adopted homeland of France, Insdorf notes, "*Red* sealed Kieślowski's reputation as what Agnes Perk called 'the most important European filmmaker.'"[257] Even in the context of his restrained response to the director's late films, and a survey of Poland's lukewarm reception of the trilogy, Haltof calls it "probably the most sophisticated and widely praised part of the trilogy."[258] For Kickasola, *Red* "demonstrates an extraordinary balance of Kieślowski's approach to form, the image, and metaphysical issues."[259] To Falkowska, *Red* is "a poem on love . . . and, like *Blue*, . . . a thesis on the nature of moral dilemmas, brotherhood and friendship": *Red* is "a miracle fable."[260] It is also a film which benefits from the presence of Preisner's most dramatically replete scoring in the trilogy and, arguably, his finest film score yet.

A Conditional Sonata

Kieślowski called *Red* a film "in the conditional mood" which questions, partly by hinting that Auguste and the Judge may not exist individually but in fact be the same soul in versions born forty years apart, "whether people aren't—by chance—sometimes born at the wrong time":

> The theme of "Red" is in the conditional mood . . . what would have happened if the Judge had been born forty years later. It would be lovely if we could go back to the age of twenty. How many better, wiser things we could have done! But it's impossible. That's why I made this film—that maybe life can be lived better than we do.[261]

Identifying the demons exorcised by Kieślowski in *Red* is a job for biographical detectives. One acknowledged artistic inspiration, though, was Kierkegaard's novella *Repetition* (1843), and its expression of the idea that "Maybe you can repeat something, but better" to rectify past mistakes.[262] *Red* imagines life lived with the benefit of hindsight and so drives harder than ever, for Kickasola, at "the very core [metaphysical] issue: the brokenness of reality and [the] desire for redemption."[263] Rather than living a life full of regret, *Red*—like *Blue* and *White* before it—explores the possibility of enjoying it the first and, in material reality, only time around.

Red, therefore, is not really about reincarnation or transmigrating souls, unless one wishes to read it with stultifying literalism, although critics have understandably pondered the significance of its metaphysical mysteries.[264] As Žižek observes, the notion of the double life, as seen most obviously in *Blind Chance* and *Véronique*, "clearly resonates not only in *Red*, but also in *Blue* and *White*" with Julie and Karol's symbolic rebirths; it comes to a head in *Red*, however, where "Auguste and the Judge are thus not two persons, but versions of one and the same person existing simultaneously."[265] Yet just as Žižek notes, regarding *Véronique*'s second life, that "there are things more important than singing . . . like the simple human goodness radiated by Véronique,"[266] it seems feasible that the second lives in the trilogy exist not as mystical enigmas *per se*, but rather as a pretext for more richly textured symbolism. *Red* demonstrates, via metaphysical fictions, something one might seek to do in the material world: live better, and with rather than merely beside people, through the practice of *agapē*.

Kieślowski likened the Judge to "a [film] director" or "a chess-player who foresees the movements of the game" and in a sense allows "the trilogy to begin,"[267] but it is simplistic to conclude that the Judge is thus "Kieślowski's rather obvious self-portrait."[268] The self-portrait emerges from the dialectical tension between Valentine and the Judge. Kieślowski aligned himself with the Judge ("[T]o a great extent, he reflects my worldview") but he also felt close to Valentine ("There is also this naïve look that Valentine casts on people and things. You could say that their opposing positions are mine").[269] Irène Jacob, who plays Valentine, suggested that this opposition highlights an interior moral struggle within the director and crucial to the theme of the film. "The confrontation between these two characters," she says, "surely corresponds to an interior questioning for Krzysztof: how can the hopes of youth coexist with the experience of maturity."[270] This confrontation and the need to overcome it are not merely articulated by *Red*'s story.

Given the Kieślowski collaborations' purposeful fusions of form and content, one would expect that, if the director puts aspects of himself under the microscope in *Red* to examine universal issues, that argument should be imprinted on the telling as much as the tale. Thinking in this vein, some critics have noted the role of framing in the exchanges between Valentine and the Judge. Andrew observes "a series of scenes of sustained psychological symbiosis" in which "electric, claustrophobic intimacy" is evoked, in part, by the "alternation of medium shots, two-shots and very occasional close-ups."[271] Kehr, in turn, observes a change of technique in *Red* from *White* and *Blue*. Because "shared knowledge creates a powerful bond between Valentine and the Judge," he argues, "Kieślowski films them in densely composed, space-collapsing two-shots that seem to press them together, in a clutter of doorways and window frames, into some special, private dimension": this evokes a "shared isolation" within which "something important passes between them—a sense of fraternity."[272] Like the montage of icons ending *Blue*, such techniques accrue signs of *agapē*.

The different parts of Preisner's bolero theme also reflect the film's central dialectic and—in a longer-range parallel to the shot sequences described above—articulate over the course of the narrative a process of intertwining. Indeed, one idea eventually synthesizes the other into its realm, achieving a subtle victory. The first relates to Valentine, the other to the judges, and the primarily thematic dialogue forms a commentary on, as well as an engine within, the telling of what Kickasola calls the film's "search for truth and its terrible pitfalls":

> One needs a sort of faith to weather the agnostic storm. Valentine, symbolizing love via her namesake saint,[273] suggests that faith is also a matter of action—a reaching out amid the meaninglessness. The Judge's face, behind the glass of his window as he watches Valentine . . . suggests a type of imprisonment, a self-induced isolation that allows him to see and hear all, but touch no one. That glass will be proverbially and literally shattered.[274]

Preisner's bolero, Chapter Seven argues, functions alongside other discursive elements in the film to articulate and intensify *Red*'s surface narrative and conceptual undertow, structuring a sonata-form-like opposition of, and ultimately reconciliation between, two initially opposed symbolic orders searching for reciprocation. If *Red*'s main characters are a portrait of Kieślowski, Preisner's score highlights the complexity of his collaborator, with the ultimate emphasis on hope.

It's a Kind of Magic

Red has a power that was capable of reducing its director to tears and seasoned commentators to nervous wrecks.[275] Emerging from seeing the film for the first time in a shabby Surrey cinema in 1995, I remember feeling exhilarated but perplexed, as if I had just experienced alleged proof of the existence of the supernatural realm, but could not quite figure out how the trick had been performed. In the theater discussion near the end of *Red*, Valentine confides in the Judge that she feels something important is happening all around her. *Red*'s cinematic magic is to induce in the audio-viewer sensations proximate to Valentine's wonderment, just as *Blue* exposes one to uncomfortable sensations proximate to Julie's grief. To experience *Red* is to be immersed in an experience of the cinematic uncanny. Yet the film is not magic: it is smoke and mirrors moving at twenty-four frames per second. How does the film achieve its enchantment and what is the role of Preisner's music in casting that spell?

This study proposes two linked methods. One relates to the moods evoked during isolated moments in the film—moments which gradually link together, with increasing pervasiveness, as a metaphysical penumbra at the edge of one's conscious experience. The other relates to the manner in which the film articulates an intensified experience of classical narrative teleology through its high saturation of enigmas in the story and (less usually) the discourse of the film, thereby invoking within the perceiver a feeling of "something important" happening and, more importantly, building—like *Red*'s gathering storm—towards a moment of cinematic epiphany.

Magic Moments

The reason why doing justice to *Red* through words is so hard, Kickasola persuasively argues, is because "[s]o much of its import—indeed, its essence—lies in the phenomenological realm. [D]escription can reveal something of the semiotic power of the image, but little of the experience Kieślowski crafted through his abstraction of time and space."[276] Kieślowski's finest interpreters have nonetheless tackled this impossible task. Kehr, for instance, called the trilogy "an epic of reconciliation," observing how "Kieślowski makes it seem as if the entire work is pointing toward a single point of convergence, toward one grand climax" before evocatively describing its effect (in the Kieślowski literature's most memorable turn of phrase) as "the narrative equivalent of a planetary alignment."[277] He also implies that such cosmic effects are achieved as much through the film's mode of telling as its story, rendering it genuinely cinematic. Notably, he highlights the role of synthesis:

> With *Red*, Kieślowski takes a step toward a thematic abstraction, and a concentration on entirely cinematic means of expression, that occurs no place else in his work. To find anything like it, it's necessary to go back to [D. W.] Griffith's *Intolerance*, with its grand vision of historical synthesis, played out in the pure and beautiful mechanics of montage.[278]

It is Kickasola, however, who has done most to pin down the mechanisms by which Kieślowski's films evoke an aura of metaphysical possibility. Music critics will feel a certain sympathy with the problem he notes with describing verbally the non-material workings of film, a difficulty Kickasola likens to "the theological paradox of Divine Transcendence and Immanence" and highlights because, in his view of Kieślowski, this traffic between immanent means and transcendent effects is precisely the point:

[T]he tensions between realism and formalism, so common in cinema since its inception, take on a metaphysical telos in the works of Kieślowski. By creating a metaphysical [narrative] context and utilizing abstract techniques to offset an everyday attitude in the viewer, Kieślowski harnesses the powers of abstraction and steers them toward transcendence, encouraging us to join in his search.[279]

Signposts to transcendence identified by Kickasola include the films' manipulations of time and space; extreme close-ups; time-lapse filming; reflections and distortions; unconventional lighting and editing; manipulations of point-of-view shots; and close-ups abstracting the ordinary to an oneric opacity.

A signature effect is a close-up of a human hand: think of Julie, Karol and Valentine's fingertips tracing music/maps in the trilogy, or Valentine and the Judge pressing hands through the car window at the end of *Red*. The close-ups are framed to remove any reference to the hand's owner, establishing it as potentially universal or even, by proxy, as the perceiver's own. Valentine's hand pressing through the window against the Judge's has an obvious narrative context in *Red*; in terms of the film's subtext, the sight of human hands pressed together also links to its concept, and all the more potently by invoking the audience's embodied knowledge of tactile contact, in a reversal of the wincing induced by the parallel shot in *Blue* of Julie scraping her fist against the wall. But such shots, Kickasola argues, also render the familiar strange: are these hands or something else entirely? When one first experiences such images, the thrill of aesthetic pleasure is shorn, momentarily, of concrete meaning. The moments demand not semantic audio-viewing but what Michel Chion calls *reduced perception* (the term is adapted from Pierre Schaeffer's concept of "reduced listening"): *observing* the audio-visual traits of something becomes the point of perception, rather than a consequent search for value and meaning.[280] Through such manipulations, Kickasola contends, "Kieślowski predisposes the audience, through style and subversion of its preconceived patterns of viewing, toward an expanded metaphysical view of the film. The Transcendent possibility resonates in the wonder of both the plot elements . . . and the dynamics of the images themselves."[281] The trilogy's stories, and especially the ways in which they are presented, predispose perceivers to wonderment.

Preisner's music in the trilogy sometimes performs functions analogous to these visual "dynamics," as do elements of the films' sound designs. The universalizing close-up of the hand, for instance, finds its musical rhyme in passages of Preisner's choral cues which switch from a distinctive, vocal soloist to a unison, wordless chorus. This is precisely the effect at the climaxes of both *Véronique*'s Concerto and the *Concert[o]* in *Blue*. As discussed above, moments of vocal "unisonance" have a heightened phenomenological impact on the audio-viewer, but on a straightforward semiotic level, the shift from a single, distinctively embodied voice singing actual words to a united

group singing wordlessly, as occurs in both compositions, is a universalizing gesture akin to the tightly framed hand. The fact that one might
sing along, literally or mimetically, and "feel" at one with the voices
only intensifies such feelings. In the trilogy, such gestures symbolize
the shift from individual to communal, and from alienated soloing to
the fraternity of an ensemble.

There are also moments in Preisner's scores where music—usually
because it starts suddenly or has been fragmented into units separated
by elongated rests and pauses—is momentarily abstracted to exist in a
limbo between music and what Michel Chion elsewhere terms "mute
music"[282]: sounds one may not claim for sure as music, because no
source in a film names them as such, and to which one may thus respond, not semantically, but through broader affective and metaphorical
channels.[283] At its grandest, this includes moments in *Blue* such as Julie
being interrupted by her first musical visitation in hospital. The ambiguities of this scene are addressed in Chapter Five, but among them one
could argue the case that the interrupting music is not music at all, but
rather a form of sonic address from an other (or pair of others): this
"mute music," an outburst of her repressed grief, might sound, before
one thinks "funeral march" or "previous scene," like the deathly howl
of a visiting specter.

The uncanny effect of the moment is rendered cinematically
prominent through loud music and a blackout, but Preisner uses flecks
of such effects throughout the trilogy—tiny isolated sounds that, until
the music continues after the elongated pause, impinge on one's consciousness but do not hang around long enough for the perceiver to be
sure she has heard them in the first place. A kind of reduced listening is
thereby enforced. In *White*, for instance, cues regularly begin with an
isolated, high oboe tone; a full cue always follows, but for a moment
one is confronted with the abstract signature of a sound that speaks but
does not tell. It feels like a breakthrough of cinematic will. In *Red*, the
final cue of the entire trilogy, save for the end title bolero, consists of
just three notes plucked on a guitar. There are many meanings one can
read into this cue, but one might feel, more immediately, a sense of
fracture at this moment, as if strands of a metaphysical web are being
snapped, liberating characters but also the co-workers: three notes, three
films, 3-2-1, cut. Preisner's faltering style enriches filmmaking seeking
to abstract the familiar and evoke the unreal, harnessing the potential
for musical abstraction—a state from which one might momentarily
wrest music, with one's words "gleaning the unsaid off the palpable,"[284]
but to which it will always return—to invoke an effect of transcendence.

Moments in *Red* analyzed for such effects by Kickasola include the
absolutely extraordinary scene in which sunlight floods the Judge's
living room. At the same moment, as the action and sun are becalmed—
perhaps, the film hints, at the Judge's command—a cue begins and
sounds stir on his surveillance equipment. This masterclass in audio-
visual collusion accrues an excess of significations, as analyzed in

Chapter Seven, as the concrete exceeds the material. Kickasola's study and reading of such moments demonstrates critical sensitivity to color, movement, shape and speed in such passages—to the visual—but he rarely touches on the contribution of music or sound to the manner in which the films articulate such effects, and even when, as here, there is a vital musical component to a scene. He offers a telling analysis, for example, of the sequence when Valentine, her moral compass spinning in response to the force of the Judge's polar opposite of a worldview, drives away from his house in tears. Valentine is patently confused and Kickasola notes of the cinematography that "opposite motions (all moving quickly and abstractly) suggest an eternal space (at a moment of spiritual crisis in the plot)."[285] He does not say anything, though, about Preisner's cue for this sequence—even though, as argued below, it is clearly an example of, in his own words, "[m]usic [that] amplifies the abstract nature of Kieślowski's images, particularly in his later films" by cutting against the emotional grain of the scene.[286] Examining Preisner's musical contribution to such moments is a theme of the analysis to follow.

In his analysis of *Red*, Andrew places a particular responsibility on sound for subliminally suggesting "the workings of something which may justifiably be called destiny,"[287] in a sonic parallel to the accruing significance of certain images that point towards the revelation at *Red*'s close—a teleological process for which there are accompanying musical forces. Kickasola's main sonic focus, though, argues that "Kieślowski's approach to sound follows his liminal aesthetic" (his focus on the tipping point between immanence and transcendent possibility) through "spatiotemporal experimentation and musico-rhythmic influence."[288] The latter term is explored in Chapter Five's analysis of the rhythm articulated by sound design before the car crash in *Blue*; the former is unpacked here.

As an example of spaciotemporal experimentation, Kickasola discusses the audiotape Véronique listens to on headphones, and in turn what the audience hears: the audio-viewer experiences both what Véronique listens to on the tape (an electroacoustic collage with elements of *musique concrète*) and the mundane sounds she makes while wandering around her apartment. For Kickasola, this structures "a bicameral world that is at once marvellous and disconcerting," thus serving "as an amplification of the central duality theme that has run throughout the film: the idea that two worlds could exist," with the tape like "a transmission from another coexistent world."[289] He utilizes Chion's theories to pinpoint the workings of this strange effect. In place of "syncresis" (cause and effect linkage of sound and vision, with or without concrete audio-visual evidence to support it) or "spatial magnetization" (the suggestion that sounds come from within the frame or just off camera), this is an instance of what Chion terms the "superfield" and exemplifies through his discussions of the "phantom audio-visual" in Tarkovsky's films.

Kickasola quotes Chion on *Sacrifice* (1986) and argues that one might also apply such notions to Kieślowski:

> [O]ne can hear sounds that already seem to come from the other side,
> as if they're heard by an immaterial ear, liberated from the hurly-burly
> of our human world. . . . [I]t calls to another dimension, it has gone
> elsewhere, disengaged from the present. It can also murmur like the
> drone of the world, at once close and disquieting.[290]

By analogy, Kickasola examines the helicopter haunting *Red*'s sound
design. It is not obviously "there" in the diegesis until, at the very end
of the film, "we look [or rather listen] back and see [or rather hear] that
it functioned as a harbinger."[291] There are plenty of similarly "bicameral" moments in *Blue* and *White*, as when Julie appears to be listening
to the busker, who may or may not actually be present in the diegesis,
or Karol is surrounded by a cloud of sonic pigeons whose material reality remains debatable. More sweepingly, one could apply the notion of
the spacio-temporal superfield to almost all of *Blue*'s score—so much
of that film is concerned with articulating a bicameral interpenetration
of realms, i.e., Julie's unconscious of repressed memories and their musical breakthroughs into her conscious world—but also to passages in
Red where the music slips its conventional narrative moorings to float
freer within the "fantastical gap" between diegetic and non-diegetic.[292]
Such enigmas open up the possibility of hermeneutic readings, especially if one traces the trajectory of the slippage for broader structural
gestures, such as the shift from fragmentation to coalescence during
Blue. Following Kickasola's broader argument, however, one might
claim that the Kieślowskian superfield shapes an ambiguity and thus a
transcendent "excess" of semiotic slipperiness that invokes awe, demands interpretation and ultimately resists definition, thereby evoking
the liminal aesthetic that intensifies these particular experiences of
cinematic wonderment.

I Put a Spell on You

Kieślowski was hardly the first European art film director to pepper his
films with sounds and images transcending the material. From Tarkovsky's shot of swaying water weeds at the start of *Solaris* (1972) to
Ken Loach's hawk on the wing in *Kes* (1969), merely to pick examples
from directors Kieślowski particularly admired, the art film demarcates
itself as other than the mainstream partly through the prominence of
such images. One might nonetheless argue that the magical aspects of
experiencing *Red* are intensified by more mainstream cinematic methods, the director having learned as many important lessons from his
time as a documentary maker, and also from Shakespeare and ancient
Greek drama, as from the art film tradition. Kieślowski and his storytelling team could do the mundanely material in narrative filmmaking,
and primarily the business of plot, so well that a narrative's working-
through of its situation can also feel like sleight of hand. In *Red*, however, they extend the intensity of plotting to the film's means of presentation. The film is saturated with enigmas and plotlines, not just in

terms of the story being told but also the terms of its telling. Mysterious images and sounds are introduced, repeated, echoed and rhymed throughout the film, as *Red* begins hypnotically to suggest the proximity of an immaterial realm; many of these elements also gravitate towards the ending's "planetary alignment." The entire film is a long, slow plot twist, and *Red*'s sound and music—including its suitably circuitous bolero—help to spellbind the audio-viewer.

Kieślowski himself called attention to one small example of how *Red* seeks to make its audiences intuitively aware of its enigma-saturated discourse. When Valentine peers after the runaway dog into the darkness of a church's doorway, she steps into the backdrop of a much earlier shot—the moment on the ballet school steps where she guzzles a bottle of water during *Red*'s opening sequence. I confess that, while I had noticed a different detail about this scene that made me feel suitably smug, this connection had passed me by until I viewed the relevant DVD featurette.[293] Yet the point of such repetitions—other examples of which include shots of a particular locale always filmed from the same camera position, as when Valentine's car ascends or descends the road to the Judge's house—was not that they should be noted consciously. Rather, they were intended to pile up subconsciously until one might suddenly intuit the governing rule: something is happening all around one in this film—the irrational planned with extreme precision, in Kieślowski's words—to shape one's expectation of revelation.

Red is therefore, in a sense, a study in prolepsis. Its iconic image, the closing shot of Valentine against a field of red, is regularly foreshadowed, most obviously on the billboard advertisement featuring Valentine, during earlier scenes. Cinematographer Piotr Sobociński explained that the idea of the audio-visual enigmas in the film originated when he was viewing footage of what became *Red*'s final freeze frame, the trilogy's ending having been shot months before principal shooting began. The idea of evoking audio-visually the sensation that the old Judge, fate or some other force is sculpting events came into being and the film was then planned to hint at this possibility in every conceivable way, rather like a novelist who writes the final chapter of a story,[294] and then directs every event in a book inexorably towards that conclusion:

> It was like a game of billiards: we already knew the final configuration of balls on the table, and we had to work out the patterns that would get them there. When you see the billboard poster recreated in the stop-frame at the end of the film, you have the impression that nothing happened accidentally.[295]

Kieślowski, according to Insdorf, described the experience of *Red*'s plotting and shooting as a process of "retroactive reasoning," and she too quotes Sobociński to explain this:

There was no storyboard, of course, just associations whose meanings must be hidden rather than disclosed. Having then defined a network of subtle associations, we reversed the usual cinematic logic. Instead of omens forewarning of some future happening, we designed later scenes to show that some earlier, apparently casual events, were important to the story.[296]

The retroactive reasoning, however, was not merely visual.

Andrew notes some of the sonic manifestations of this technique, such as the aforementioned helicopters whirling over the first shots of Valentine and Auguste. The foghorn heard as the photographer tells her to "look sad," Valentine prefiguring her pose in the final frame and "suggesting that, in imagining something sad, she has some premonition of what will befall her," connects to the air horns heard at the end of the film, and points, "by way of a small omen she herself doesn't even notice, to the mysterious, hidden forces that [the film implies may] determine our fate."[297] Kickasola calls such moments examples of "the bracket, encouraging emotional perception before identification," and he too notes the helicopters and the foghorn, sounds which evoke "the impression that the cosmos accompanies this drama and steers it."[298] What makes these clues accrue their uncanny suspense, however, is that, unlike in a conventional thriller, one has little or no idea of the *significance* of the things accruing before one's ears and eyes, or even if they *are* significant. There has not been a murder, for example, so one does not know that the clues are leading to the discovery of, say, the identity of a killer. One might only intuit, because the film gradually forms a web of connections, that there must be some revelation to which all of these junctures are leading; on repeated audio-viewings— and *Red* is tailor-made for repeat audio-viewings—the wealth of these strategies becomes clearer. Consequently, when the moment of plot predication arrives and all of the sequences are closed, if the effect affects one, it is because the film connects and resolves so many enigmas all at once. Alongside the image of the closing "bracket" of Valentine and a red background rhyming with the advertisement, foghorns and helicopter engines are heard, and Valentine and Auguste are united at last, in the trilogy's final revelation of fraternity: all of its main protagonists, having learned to experience *agapē*, are saved from the waters. Everything entwines and the threads are tied together in an ostensibly satisfying knot—although satisfaction then loses some ground to disconcerting ambivalence.

How does *Red*'s score contribute to this process? Unlike *Blue*, there is no "reveal" of a full score at the end of the film after foreshadowing hints: in fact, the final scenes play out in musical silence. *Red*'s sense of a subtly gathering momentum is nonetheless shaped in significant ways by Preisner cues. Obviously, music can generate momentum in a single cue through sensuous means (an ever more propulsive rhythm, gradually increasing volume, etc.), and there are certain basic ways in which the musical elements of Preisner's bolero develop a sense of perpetual motion whenever it occurs in the film. *Red*'s main theme accelerates one's sense of narrative momentum towards destinations yet unrevealed, like piped background music on a magical mystery tour. The choice of a bolero also presents repetitions suggestive of a cyclical or mechanically premeditated process. Rhythm, thematic structure, harmonic movement and form coalesce in a spiral of connection.

There are also small musical figures in *Red*'s score that are returned to again and again. Sometimes they are treated to abstracting developments; at other times they simply recur, contributing musically to the film's layered accrual of connections. One such detail, as noted above, finds its predication in the final cue of the film: a rising arpeggio of guitar pitches linking back not only to earlier cues in *Red* but also to *White* and *Blue*'s scores; another is a quartertonal fluctuation in the bolero's ostinato, telescopically isolated and then expanded in later cues. Yet there are also moments in *Red* where Preisner's cues do something uniquely calibrated to a scene in question. The scene where light miraculously appears, or rather appears to be miraculous, in the Judge's house is a case in point: the "miracle" is in the audio-visual fusion, as crafted by Preisner and the other co-workers to achieve a breathtaking cinematic moment.

Critics on *Red*'s Music

Red is Preisner's favorite score in the trilogy. In contradistinction to *Blue* (where the music, he feels, is "too presentative, too prominent") and *White* (where the function of the music was often bluntly ironic, and thus too blunt to appeal to his personal tastes), *Red*'s combination of subtlety and depth is an attempt at Preisner's preferred style of scoring. His primary idea for the score was to evoke a very specific cultural climate; this climate can be read to stand as a metaphor for what this study reads as the trilogy's main concept. *Red*'s musical climate evokes, for its composer, Switzerland, a country admired by both Kieślowski and Preisner.[299] "I am living in Switzerland now," he told me, "and [*Red*'s] music is very close to Switzerland. It's a rich country of lonely people, dark, and at the same time, not depressing in the French part." The tension between surface prosperity and underlying spiritual anxiety is articulated, most obviously, by the bolero's contrasting subjects—the first dripping significations of beauty, wealth and elegance, the second evoking more disturbing concepts and relying, throughout *Red*, on extended string techniques adapted from Penderecki. Preisner attempted to make a score intimating "this culture, . . . this aloneness, richness, life, people," evoking the "climate of how [the protagonists] lived in that country"; in turn, he also articulates a perspective on the late-modern West. The bolero's circular themes and ostinatos are deployed in *Red* to evoke, the composer says, related senses of ennui and entrapment: the boredom, but also frustration, that comes from being trapped in a gold-plated hamster's wheel, its repetitions dominating one's temporal experience, rather than progression or transcendence.

Preisner has previously only partially explained the symbolic connotations of *Red*'s bolero. "In *Red*," he told Carlsson and Holm, "I chose a bolero to describe the circular movement, which is the theme of the film."[300] He has also recalled that it was composed before filming began.[301] The full story of the cue's origins is intriguing. The theme was able to "have [the] strength to be an element of the film's narrative"[302] by being included amongst the thoughts of Preisner's co-workers— Sobociński's retrospective description of *Red*, for instance, is as a "bolero-film"[303]—because Preisner had composed the cue for another film from which it was rejected. Given the theme's seemingly perfect fit to manifold aspects of *Red*, it comes as a surprise to discover he had composed it some months earlier for *At Play in the Fields of the Lord* (Babenco, 1991), where it was to have accompanied—of all things—the bombing raid on the Amazonians (talk about late-modern ruination). In *At Play*, the repetitions of the ostinato were designed to evoke the hum of the plane's engine and to sculpt the building tension of the bombing run. The film's Hollywood producers rejected it as sounding, Preisner says, "too smart," but the composer had become enchanted with the idea of using a bolero as film music, not least because it could so easily be made to stop and start, grow and subside. The theme was therefore prominent in his own thinking by the time he came to score *Red*. This helps to explain *Red*'s taut thematic developments.

Through discussions with Kieślowski and his colleagues, Preisner identified what his bolero needed to achieve: an *idée fixe* within *Red*. He stated:

> We wanted to stress the recurrence of situations and events in our lives. Bolero is a musical form based on the repetition of the theme, with increased expression after each repetition. It was supposed to be the music about the will to fight, the will to live, the unexpectedness of events and the willingness to discover more about people.[304]

Few critics have picked up on the questions raised by Preisner's notion that the music articulates a will to fight, discover and live—a side to the bolero that evokes, for this music analyst, the dramatic potential of its thematic oppositions and, potentially, the score's sonata-like working through of their interrelationship as a parallel to Valentine and the Judge's dramatic exchanges.

Teleology is replaced by circles in many accounts. Insdorf argues that, because *Red* is "[l]ess a linear construction than an intricate play of reflections . . . Preisner's 'bolero' is a brilliant aural complement: the lyrical melodic theme is developed and then repeated, its very structure expressing the cumulative resonance characteristic of *Red*."[305] Wollermann suggests that the dramaturgy of the film is, in a sense, a circular conception ("Kreisformig"): at its center lies the relationship of Valentine and the Judge about which events cycle. He claims that this gives the film a sense of propulsion via a dramaturgic "perpetuum mobile" akin to the bolero rhythm, noting Sobociński's telling use of "bolero-film" and expanding on it to suggest that, as in Ravel's *Bolero*, the repetitive elements, enriched from scene to scene, accrue a sense of forward momentum.[306] He also describes the theme as kaleidoscopic. Like Ravel's bi-partite *Bolero* theme—an obvious model for Preisner's cue—while there is little motivic variation of the base components of Preisner's melody, sonority, harmony and dynamics do change, as if refracting. Paxman also focuses on the bolero's repetitions. Because the judges double each other's lives, he claims, *Red*'s bolero "stands as a metaphysical signifier that parallels the recurrent events within the narrative through its own repetitions"; for Paxman, the theme's "application is therefore leitmotivic."[307] He expands upon this concept, which connects to Preisner's notion of an *idée fixe*:

So we hear a repeated event—the bolero—itself containing repeated events in the form of motivic repetitions, contextualized within a mystically and metaphysically infused thematic dialogue . . . a symbolic musical structure that both prefigures and parallels the film's narrative discourse.[308]

A shadow creeps into Andrew's hearing of the score, in response to the bolero's more dissonant, Pendereckian variations. "Preisner's sometimes ominous, purposeful bolero," he writes, serves "to illuminate the tensions and the emotional inevitability of the blossoming friendship between the misanthropic recluse and his redemptive saviour."[309] He also states, tellingly, that the film engineers its aura of mystery and suspense through meticulous filmmaking processes within which music plays a key role:

A level of taut suspense is also present throughout, due to the unresolved moods of Preisner's music, to Kieślowski's imaginative use of sound (the conversation in the theatre is interrupted by shocking bangs, one from a window blown open by the wind, one from a bucket dropped by an unseen cleaning lady for whom, in an echo of Kern's story, a janitor keeps searching), and to the many questions we inevitably ask ourselves about the film's outcome.[310]

The "unresolved moods" are the score's connection to the Polish new wave. Kiefer, too, notes a twist in tone within "a swirling bolero, which modulates into a minor key to raise the neck hairs just as certain scenes take on a supernatural charge."[311] The analytical detail is wrong, but the intuition is right: there are two distinct parts to the bolero, each with a contrasting "mood," and Preisner deploys them to sketch characters, to connote and denote plot points, to participate in the "magical" effects discussed above, and to structure the teleological momentum generated by the film's dialectics of being.

No critic has considered the generic heritage of Preisner's bolero, just as few did more than touch upon the fact that *White*'s tango is a dance form with a rich history, in Poland and elsewhere, on which that film inexorably draws. This may be because the bolero is less prominent as a cultural (and indeed cinematic) symbol than the tango, at least in Central Europe—which is not to say aspects of the film and score do not resonate productively with the form's intertextual associations beyond Ravel. Willi Kahl and Israel J. Katz call attention to the human subjects of the bolero, its *boleros* and *boleras*,[312] reminding one that the dance has a symbolism of its own which *Red*'s use, consciously or otherwise, imports into the film. In purely musical terms, Preisner's bolero has a relatively distant relationship to the Spanish dance and its Latin-American forms. It takes certain key rhythms, as discussed in Chapter Seven, but its meter is in $\frac{4}{4}$, not a triple time,[313] and its thematic structure, while appropriately oppositional, is also formally rather different. Like *White*'s "mazurka," *Red*'s main musical theme is a "memory" of bolero, not an attempt at authenticity.[314] *Red*'s memory of bolero tradition can be thought of in at least three different ways.

First, in the early nineteenth century, an evolution of the bolero tradition in Seville's theaters gave rise to the so-called Bolero school. The dance was said to have required much grace and elegance—like Valentine on the catwalk and Preisner's first theme, it represented "elevated" tastes and a disciplining of the earthy origins of its sexually charged, low-rent exoticism.[315] One might extend considerations of the other values being disciplined, therefore, within the score's "bolero sonata" to include the range of "others" represented as spectacle in Seville's theaters during the 1800s: an exotic alternative, sexually flagrant and "uncivilized," sanitized for bourgeois entertainment. In *Red*, this otherness could be related to Valentine's perception of the old Judge. Second, theatrical versions of the bolero were executed by groups of couples. Comprised of equal sections, each dance began with a promenade; Valentine's catwalk performance, accompanying the exposition of *Red*'s bolero music, is thus appropriate. Middle sections then contained more complex and energetic movements, and also more solo dancing, but always the couples come back together in the end. In *Red* there are several crossing couples: Valentine with the Judge, his dog, Auguste, her boyfriend, her brother, her mother and her photographer; Auguste with Karin, his dog and eventually Valentine; Karin with Auguste and her other lover; the old Judge, Valentine and the memory of his cuckolding partner. One could thus regard *Red*'s story as a staging of the dance's theatrical form in which romantic permutations are worked through until, finally, the fruit machine of fate hits the three-cherry jackpot and the right couple (or metaphysically extended trio) ends up together; the film's characters become *boleros* and *boleras*. Third, when the darker side of Preisner's bolero underscores, for instance, Auguste's discovery of his lover's infidelity, another bolero tradition is evoked. José Quiroga, writing on bolero song performances by Olga Guillot, identifies "the bolero of despair and eros, the song that produces the erotic charge of steamy sex under a red lightbulb, or the one sung by the woman after the man has left her panting, and she hides a knife under the pillow on a creaking bed where the sheets are wet."[316] The most important dance in *Red*, however, is between Valentine and the Judge's value systems. In this sense, the structural distinctions of the theme connect to bolero tradition while reinforcing the sonata-form-like opposition asserted in the analysis of Chapter Seven.

Red's atmosphere, for Haltof, owes something to the other main element of Preisner's score. Although he dismisses the bolero's role as "primarily . . . romantic" in the film, he notes that the Van den Buden-mayer song in *Red* forms an important link between Valentine, Joseph and Auguste.[317] Insdorf calls the reappearance of Van den Budenmayer "eye-winking,"[318] following the director's line that such references were primarily included to flatter attentive *cinéastes*. There is surely more to it than that. Why is this song from *Decalogue 9* being reused, for instance, and what do its specific lyrics and symbolism add to *Red*'s narrative? Another melancholy tune could have been composed and, in a more synergetically inclined sector of the film industry, Preisner's song "Love at First Sight," which can be heard on *Red*'s soundtrack album, could have been a contender.[319] Andrew, however, recognizes the "poignant" song as *Decalogue 9*'s and notes that "the doctor [the protagonist in the earlier film], like Kern and Auguste, was to suffer the painful indignity of witnessing his beloved's infidelity"; he also calls attention to the song's *Decalogue*-inspired title on the soundtrack CD for *Red*, "Do Not Take Another Man's Wife"[320]—although this is not Preisner's title from the score, which bears the name "Nymph." In turn, "Nymph" is not the name of the poem Preisner sets in the song. The intertextual web is finer still.

The composer is clear on the primary reason for the song's reuse in *Red*. "It is an aloneness song," he told me, and its significations of soli-tude complemented the climate Kieślowski wanted to structure in *Red*. The director persuaded Preisner to allow the reuse of the song, just as he had persuaded him to reuse music from *No End* in *Blue*; in both cases Preisner would have preferred to compose original music. In part, Kieślowski argued, this would bring music "lost" in the earlier films to the attention of a wider audience. Preisner, however, feels that there may have been another motivation. He suspects it marked the sense of an ending for the director, not just of the trilogy, but also of his career. On being given the poem to set for "Love at First Sight" by Kieślowski, which Preisner composed to be performed (by Zamachowski) directly after *Red*'s ending at its Warsaw premiere, the composer recognized that the director was marking the end of an era with an unusually theat-rical gesture. Similarly, reusing cues from the earlier scores created a sense of recapitulation which Preisner now considers the action of a director who had decided to stop making films.

Wollermann calls the cue the "Song between the Worlds" and, while he too observes that it was used in *Decalogue 9* in connection to a man betrayed by his partner, he argues that its use in *Red* evokes a

range of further meanings: its musical symbols of loneliness and melancholy transfer to both the Judge and Valentine, and at a certain point
also to Auguste.[321] Wollermann also suggests, intriguingly, that the
song evokes an angelic presence influencing the Judge for the better. It
symbolizes a mechanism of release from the Judge's "glass prison,"[322]
for instance when it is heard accompanying his confessional letter writing, as if Towarnicka's voice is powerful enough to shatter his home's
prison walls, like a stage trick in which a soprano breaks a glass. This
view forms an interesting counterpoint to Kickasola's interpretation of
the song's function in *Decalogue 9*:

> [Ola, the soprano in the film] functions in two primary ways: a sexu-
> ally alluring, bitter reminder of Roman's loss of prowess and a spiritu-
> ally wise counterweight to the youthful immaturity of Mariusz. This
> duality is skillfully expressed in a close-up of Ola's moving hands
> conducting the music of Van Budenmayer and the subsequent tilt
> down to her knees, revealed by a suggestively short robe. She is un-
> questionably beautiful, the sort of woman Roman might have slept
> with in his decorated sexual past. Yet it is the same Ola who inspires
> him with music and the general beauty of the world, who urges him to
> think.[323]

Ola is a "nymph" to Roman: a symbol of erotic desire, but also of purity. Similarly, there are moments in *Red* where the Judge seems primed
to demand more of Valentine than platonic friendship. Yet ultimately it
is her purity that rewrites his world.

No critic has hitherto uncovered the poem set in the song, discussed in Chapter Seven, and its ramifications for readings of *Red* or
Decalogue 9. The trilogy's final score is fortunate and unusual, however, in having received two sustained and substantial discussions from
musicologists. Paxman and Wollermann's detailed analytical comments
are discussed later, but it is useful to introduce a few of their framing
observations here. Like *White*, Wollermann notes, *Red*'s score has just
two themes.[324] The major difference, he suggests, is that *Red's* music
adapts itself to different narrative situations through the composer's
kaleidoscopic retunings of its engine, the bolero.[325] This is true: Preisner achieves his most supple—and in a sense most conventionally filmic, because it is so carefully calibrated to other components of the
discourse—Kieślowski score in *Red*. Wollermann also considers the
musical connection to *White*: its tango is heard in the musical din of the
record shop where Auguste and Valentine separately seek to purchase
CDs of the Van den Budenmayer song.

One can identify tenuous musical connections, in the form of such
repetitions, between *Blue* and *White* and then *White* and *Red*; *Blue* and
Red, in turn, are linked by the appearance of Van den Budenmayer's
music. Alongside one or two subtle further touches, there are no other
substantial attempts to unify the trilogy's music: no network of leitmotivic complexity interconnects *Blue*, *White* and *Red*. The unifying force
is Preisner's presence. The obvious musical links that do exist are fur-

thermore prescribed by the screenplays (e.g., the allusions to Van den Budenmayer), and were shaped as much by the director and sound designer as by the composer. Illusions of unity, whether linked to the aesthetic concerns of strands of Western art music aesthetics or to the scoring practices of classical Hollywood—a practice connected, in higgledy-piggledy fashion, back to the same art music concerns[326]—are not among Preisner's intentions, although at times his scores reveal developmental intricacies. His scores seek primarily, however, to contribute intimately to the narratives and their symbolic concerns, rather than to layer motivic mock-profundity onto a film through its score.

Paxman analyzes the first musical sequence in *Red* and, from it, extracts the essence of Preisner's contribution to that scene and, in many ways, to the trilogy as a whole and his other Kieślowski collaborations. Paxman, too, is concerned with the way music participates in making "the film [progress] with mystical purpose,"[327] and he links this to the thematic content of the bolero and an "unresolved dialectical tension, manifested through music and image alone, lend[ing] a certain directional quality to the film by the creation of expectation."[328] He also hears this tension as sonata-form-like, although such considerations are understandably curtailed by the limited purview of his essay, which solely focuses on the film's first cue. His primary concern, however, is to explore the delicate interplay of music and everything else in this section of the film. Instead of "mutual implication"[329] or "hyperexplicity"[330]—Hollywood practices unsuitable, Paxman argues, for "weighty, complex subject matter"[331]—the film accrues layer upon layer of connotation rather than denotation. He usefully quotes Kieślowski in this regard, while reminding one of views on music and meaning in film (and elsewhere) from music scholars ranging from Chion to Lawrence Kramer: "You can describe something which . . . doesn't exist in the picture alone or the music alone. Combining the two, a certain meaning, a certain value, something which determines a certain atmosphere, suddenly begins to exist."[332] More accurately, the film's audio-visual fusions create the conditions within which meanings, values and atmospheres might be actualized by individual perceivers.

As part of that alchemy, Paxman notes, Preisner's scoring had to be highly flexible, contributing a "remarkable variety of technical, narrative and sub-narrative roles" as well as to "methods of filmic development through music-image synergy and dialectical tension."[333] In this regard, Paxman argues, *Red* offers a "beautiful model of understatement, allusion and communicative subtlety."[334] The first musical sequence alone, Paxman notes, could serve as a master-class for students and filmmakers, connoting so much and yet explicitly stating so little, not least through the absence of expository dialogue. The sequence does contain, however, a full statement of Preisner's bolero and the inauguration of a dialectical opposition, the enigmas of which, alongside other aspects of *Red*'s story and discourse, encourage the audience to parse *Red* for answers, not least regarding the meanings of its intimate and imaginative score.

CHAPTER FIVE

THE ODE TO *AGAPĒ*: *BLUE*

Three Colors: Blue is a tragic concerto that cedes, at its close, to a glimmer of hope. The tragic register is established by the film's opening. A reluctant soloist, Julie, is torn from the security of her familial ensemble by a car crash that kills her husband and daughter. After her traumatized initial responses to the event, she withdraws into the film's central movement, isolating herself through the performance of a series of bathetic cadenzas. Voices from society's orchestra then entreat her to enter into dialogue, banging on her door like fateful timpani in the middle of the night or beguiling her with plaintive melodies; at times, her own unconscious becomes one of these antagonists, its musical phantoms inviting her to contact buried aspects of her self. Finally, dramatic gestures from within and without force her to take action. Julie quells her antagonists with demands of her own, on the surface to isolate herself further, but eventually realizing that liberated solitude is not her ideal state. Julie is no soloist; she needs the security of the rank and file. The concerto therefore ends with a musical vision of the state engendered by her reconstituted network of relationships: life lived, but also constrained, through expressions of *agapē*.

Grief is central to *Blue*'s story and, for many audio-viewers, the film's exploration on this universal facet of human experience is the conduit through which they have come to feel strongly connected to the film.[1] Making bereavement the hook for an interrogation of liberty in *Blue* (as the filmmakers did), however, or reading Julie's subsequent journey as an allegory on broader issues (as this study proposes), need not be taken as diminishing the film's power as an essay on loss. If anything, these dimensions make its perspective on grief yet more resonant. As D. J. Enright concludes in *The Oxford Book of Death*:

> Life helps us shape our thoughts about death, and often serves as our metaphor, the known invoked to adumbrate the as yet unexperi-

enced. Hence to talk at all interestingly about death is inevitably to talk about life.[2]

The broader themes *Blue* broaches intensify its engagement with death; that engagement, in turn, enables it to speak with frank intensity on life. Julie's bereavement is horrific and her initial responses concomitantly severe. James describes an "extreme grief expressed in a need to clear the entire past out of her mind"[3]; for Juliette Binoche, "That was the film": the silences and repressions, with which she replaced her intuitive desire to act emotions, so central to her immaculately controlled performance as Julie.[4] Such is the depth of Julie's silencing of self that, for Žižek, *Blue* is not "about mourning, but about creating the conditions for mourning," with the trajectory of the film mapping Julie's journey from traumatized withdrawal to the point (which Žižek identifies as the very last shot, when she allows herself to cry openly for the first time) at which "Julie can *start* the work of mourning."[5] This reading feels more in tune with the film than interpretations of *Blue*'s conclusion as a rosy new dawn. Falkowska, for instance, sees Julie emerging from "her state of lethargy" and becoming "a new person . . . full of compassion, forgiveness and love."[6] It is hardly so simple. Yet even the passage from withdrawal to engagement with one's grief is a progression bearing the potential for a narrative arc and symbolic resonance. *Blue*'s narrative, its symbolic resonance, and music's role in the articulation of both can therefore be productively contextualized through a discussion of studies of mourning.

Grief Works

Far from depicting mourning as an aberrant experience, John Archer's *The Nature of Grief*—a study of its intertwining evolutionary and cultural mechanisms—understands grief "as a natural human reaction, since it is a universal feature of human existence irrespective of culture, although the form and intensity its expression takes varies considerably."[7] Grief may seem like an odd adaptation, given the psychological burden of its suffering, but Archer locates it as an evolutionary trade-off: grief is the flip-side of the pair and parental bonding vital to the success of our species, or "the price we pay for being able to love in the way we do."[8] Archer's subsequent description of grief, in this context, brings to mind specifics of Julie's grief and its manifestations in *Blue*. "[G]rief," he writes, "involves a rich array of feelings and thoughts, which go beyond the separation reactions occurring in animals" and include "higher-order mental processes, such as intrusive thoughts, hallucinations, feelings of a change of identity, and defences against the distressing aspects of grief."[9] Crucially, grief assaults one's sense of an integral self through losses "intimately tied up with those aspects of our life which are most important to us, such as close personal relationships, family, home, job, and cherished possessions . . . emotionally charged and resistant to change, and . . . central to our self-esteem."[10]

That identity and sense of stability were illusions in the first place—
"One phone call or a few seconds on the motorway is enough to change
someone's life,"[11] Archer writes, inadvertently summarizing Kieślowski's entire oeuvre—but they are powerful illusions. Re-
constituting or replacing them is a key purpose of grieving.

The grieving process rewires connections between interior and exterior, subjective and objective, as bereaved people recompose their
narratives of self within a dramatically altered society:

> The process of changing the ideas we hold about our identity so that
> they match changes in the outside world is highly emotional and
> painful, and may take a long time to complete. It is this process
> which forms the essence of grief. . . . The crucial feature in all this
> is that the person has lost an essential part of what has become, in
> terms of inner experience, part of his or her self.[12]

This process is the essence of Julie's story in *Blue*. Her identities as a
mother, wife and musical collaborator are shattered at the start of the
film. The resulting narrative offers an original perspective on the post-
bereavement reconstitution of subjectivity and its wider symbolism.

Julie's journey, created by a team of predominantly male filmmakers, does not follow the pathways of stereotypical female responses to
grief in late-modern Western societies. Instead, her grief initially follows what tend to be deemed more appropriate responses for a man.
They then veer, as "normality" also returns to other aspects of the film,
into modes of grieving that are, stereotypically, understood as more
appropriate for women.

In his novel *The Naked and the Dead* (1948), Norman Mailer
writes of a soldier, Gallagher, and his numbness in the face of terrible
news from home:

> In the days that followed the news of Mary's death, he worked furi-
> ously on the road, shoveling without pause in the drainage ditches,
> and chopping down tree after tree whenever they had to lay a cordu-
> roy. He would rarely halt in the breaks they were given every hour,
> and at night he would eat his supper alone and curl into his blan-
> kets. . . . Gallagher showed no signs of his grief except that he be-
> came leaner and his eyes and eyelids were swollen as if he had been
> on a long drinking bout or had played poker for forty-eight hours at
> a stretch.[13]

Gallagher exhibits a stereotypically masculine approach to grieving. He
works desperately, avoiding all chances to think, seeking isolation from
reminders of his situation and refusing to exhibit signs of grief: if he is
crying, he is doing so in private, his swollen eyes hint. The protagonist
of Paul Auster's *The Book of Illusions* (2002), academic David Zimmer,
also throws himself into work after a period of traumatized withdrawal
following the deaths of his wife and infant sons in a plane crash. He
researches and writes a book about an obscure (and fictitious) silent

film comedian, traveling the world's film archives to avoid returning to his now empty home. Julie initially grieves similarly to Gallagher and Zimmer: she works tirelessly at doing nothing of significance (smoking, swimming, eating ice cream, potting plants), and she does so in isolation, occupying herself with trifles rather than facing up to things she has chosen to avoid. Such grieving recalls Freudian notions of "withdrawal" when a limit to the pain one can cope with has been reached, Archer argues, but withdrawal needs eventually to be reconciled with the "way in which people neutralize painful stimuli and thoughts associated with the loss [in] a series of interactions or confrontations."[14]

The dual-process model of grief therapy proposed by Margaret Stroebe and Henk Schut incorporates "this tension between approach and avoidance as its basic dimension."[15] Reading Julie's story through this model, her period of withdrawal can be identified as "restoration-oriented": she does new things, seeks distraction from her grief, denies its existence. Her new life is superficially free from pain, but nothing is healing beneath the surface because, the theory argues, she is not oscillating between the two states of grief-work and acknowledging the full extent of her suffering. There is no "loss-oriented" work, but oscillation is the key:

> Both coping styles are likely to have different sorts of costs, confrontation being physically and mentally exhausting and suppression requiring mental effort and perhaps also having consequences for health. . . . Oscillation between the two may enable the person to obtain the benefits of each and to minimize the costs of maintaining one strategy for too long. The process is portrayed as time-related, being biased towards loss-orientation early in the grief process and restoration later on . . . .[16]

This temporal description of the process begins to indicate how the representation of Julie's grieving is tied to film-wide strategies in *Blue*'s scoring and other aspects of the narrative discourse. When music bursts through in *Blue*, for instance, it can be read as the sound of "loss-oriented" grief-work calling to Julie and fragmenting her "restoration" work in order to encourage more passionate forms of lament, and thus the forms of grieving deemed appropriate to females in Julie's late-modern, Western cultural community.

Every individual responds differently to every instance of grief within a framework of basic adaptations, but there are influential culturally mediated trends, especially in terms of sex differences. In particular, women are "more inclined towards emotion-focused coping and men towards problem-focused coping"; studies have proved that "widows benefited more (in terms of showing a greater decline in distress) from a problem-centred therapy whereas widowers benefited more from an emotion-focused one."[17] Men, in other words, tend to need help to let grief intrude more fully and to deal with its emotional impact; women tend to benefit more from approaches designed to stop the intrusions from happening and, instead, to deal confidently with practicalities.[18] Taken out of context, it may seem dangerously essentialist for Archer to state that, when coping with grief, "Men are likely to be less expressive and more concerned with maintaining other aspects of their lives . . . [while] women tend to concentrate more on their feelings."[19] One must, though, take into account the cultural constructions of gender and emotion at play in, for example, facts like Israeli males weeping less often than their British counterparts.[20] There can be no evolved reason for distinctions like this: the differences are determined by culture.

The gendering of grief as a subset of emotional expression carries cultural baggage dating back at least as far as Euripides. In *The Bacchae*—"a play by a man, about men, for men," as theater director David Greig describes it—"Euripides shows that the [Apollonian] values associated with masculinity—rationality, logic, control and articulacy—do not cancel out the 'female' Dionysian forces of emotion, instinct and physicality. As Pentheus—the play's man's man, all cleverness, nonwise, because not in touch with his Dionysian side—is warned by the chorus, 'Intellect must always submit to the power of the scream.'"[21] Julie, *Blue* suggests, not least through its musical interruptions, must also submit to the power of the scream. In *Death's Door: Modern Dying and the Ways We Grieve*, Sandra Gilbert writes, too, of the gendered dynamics of grief and of stereotypical masculine Western behaviors which prioritize the diffusion of grief through ceremonial elegies—an Apollonian system of checks and balances, inherent in the rhetoric of grand oratory, which holds grief at a safer distance.[22] Women's historical social role, and not merely in the West, has often been to wail in Dionysian frenzy at the grave side: to lose control in response to the funeral elegy, rather than to compose the elegy and thus, perhaps, recompose oneself.

What fascinates about *Blue*, in this context, is that initially its female protagonist bucks cultural stereotypes of emotional expression and grieving. At first, Julie grieves like a man. (Why are you crying?, she asks her ageing housekeeper after the accident; because you are not, comes the reply.) Eventually, however, she is forced—by friends, by neighbors, by chance—to shift from "masculine" modes of restorative repression and avoidance to a rapprochement with a more "feminine" engagement with emotions and loss. Her grieving becomes more stereotypically female and, while the act of composing suggests the mediating rhetoric of the funeral elegy, the music she creates as part of her "loss-oriented" grief-work becomes saturated with signifiers of femininity. The very fact that she begins engaging with music, rather than rejecting it, may imply her embrace of a more conventional femininity, bearing in mind, as Richard Leppert reminds one, that music has "long played the role of the eternal feminine in European consciousness."[23] As her grieving, music and other elements of the film become more conventional, so too does her social position. In freeing herself from her grief, Julie begins to lose certain freedoms created by her bereavement. By the end of *Blue*, for instance, she is shown quite literally crushed in a relationship featuring a man on top. Her tears at the film's close therefore suggest a mourner embracing a fuller spectrum of pain, past *and* present, and not merely in relation to her bereavement. The power of *Blue*'s representation of these processes emanates from its plot events and discourse. As music is central to both, it is informative briefly to consider a study of music and mourning with parallels to the above arguments.

In "Music, Mourning, and Consolation,"[24] psychoanalyst Alexander Stein posits a "biphasic relationship of loss and consolation" with similarities to the loss- and restoration-oriented model of grieving, arguing that both find "outward expression in distinct yet related musical forms, one of grief, one of solace."[25] He charts several uses of, or responses to, music with directly comparable episodes in *Blue*. Musical intrusions into the life of the bereaved, such as Julie's musical blackouts—her repressed grief and loss-oriented grief-work calling—and other interruptions, are diagnosed as "a compromise formation, a condensed symbolic transformation of unconscious mental functioning . . . which may appear or sound absurd, chaotic, unreal, or incapable of being contextualized, but ultimately its associative significance can be deciphered."[26] Such deciphering is part of the analytical work undertaken below, which considers the symbolic significance of the music and sounds which compromise Julie's withdrawal. Directly related to these intrusions, in turn, are Julie's attempts to distance herself from music by jettisoning its material traces from her life, as when she throws Patrice's *Concert[o]* score into the back of a garbage truck. Stein discusses times when "a particular piece of music, precisely by being so intimately linked to the lost object, can be too searing and too real a reminder of the loss . . . pierc[ing] the protective mechanisms on which the bereaved rely."[27] In *Blue*, both the musical intrusions and expulsions register Julie's responses to the agony of her bereavement.

When Julie engages anew with composition and completes her version of the *Concert[o]* towards the end of *Blue*, her loss-oriented engagement with music relates to what Stein calls the fundamental function of "auditory symbolism" through music, i.e., expressing "feelings associated with grief and bereavement" by means of "aesthetic representations in response to a traumatic event."[28] Music, for creators, performers and listeners alike, can become a means "effectively to represent experiences and affects too intense or overwhelming to express directly."[29] However, before Julie can engage with her loss and reconstitute aspects of her self through aesthetic symbolism, she must console herself through forms of restoration-oriented activity which are differently musical. Julie regains a healing sense of "flow," it is argued below, through activities including listening to *Blue*'s busker and the rhythmic repetitions of swimming.

Stein contrasts the way in which "apprehension of time, both conceptual and sensory, is frequently distorted when there is a traumatic breach" with the ways in which music—rather like counting slowly to

ten when frustrated, rocking back and forth, and other "lulling mechanisms"—can be made or listened to in order "to quell anger or fear" and
"for self-soothing during traumatic or painful events."[30] When music
interrupts Julie, it tears her sense of time apart *and* ruptures cinematic
time: depictions of these events and their aftermath fracture *Blue*'s
mode of representation. After the accident, *Blue* is cut in a series of
jarring confrontations between scenes, the montage echoing the devastating crash. Yet as Julie begins to rediscover flow—through repetitive
activities, listening to lyrical melodies, by beginning to compose—both
Julie *and* the film's style begin to "heal," i.e., to rediscover forms of
temporal regularity, as *Blue*'s editing and deployment of music becomes more conventional. This culminates, following the film's ultimate representation of "flow" regained—Julie's creative immersion in
completing the *Concert[o]*—with a gesture so conventional it occupies
a diametrically opposed position to the more avant-garde fragmentations of the earlier passages: a musical montage. *Blue* thereby shifts
slowly from an innovative style, evoking fragmentation and alienation
both personal and societal, into a more conventional mode of representation evoking continuity and communion.

For Stein, music's most powerful consoling function is achieved
when it facilitates "a restitutive transformation of internal experience
and affect," making one feel "held, understood, consoled."[31] There are
moments in *Blue*—when Julie hears the busker, when she works with
her would be lover Olivier—when music seems to be creating such
feelings for her. Intriguingly, Stein's hypothesis on consolation understands it as "closely related to the capacity for empathy and . . . perhaps
even predominantly derivative of it,"[32] i.e., "the inner experience of
sharing in and comprehending the momentary state of another person"[33]—a moment in which one shares the experience of the other "not
like our own but *as* our own."[34] Empathy, thus defined, feels aligned to
the alienation-breaching practice of *agapē* espoused by the *Three Colors* trilogy as a whole: its argument that, whatever the concomitant
losses and social impediments it may generate in late-modern capitalist
societies structured to privilege isolated and selfish selves, people must
still strive to connect. This is exemplified in many of *Blue*'s musical
scenes, but most extravagantly in the gesture of unisonance through
which the *Concert[o]*'s wordless climax extends Julie's ultimate act of
consolation to the film's perceivers, as if to heal the world.

One of Stein's descriptions of musical consolation—"music con-
soles . . . by temporarily relieving or diminishing feelings of pain by
providing an illusory response ensconced in rhythm and sound to the
dominant wish of the bereaved [i.e.,] reunion with the lost object"[35]—
therefore reads like a summary of the broader framework that forms, in
my view, the conceptual heart of *Blue* and the *Three Colors* trilogy.
Something that is lost is found—or at least the possibility of finding it
is briefly experienced cinematically. Kieślowski stated, regarding
Blue's artistic motivations, that he had "an increasingly strong feeling,"
while planning the film and the trilogy, "that all we really care about is

ourselves."[36] By the end of the film, as *Blue*'s reclusive concerto soloist is synthesized into the orchestral masses, Julie is collaborating anew on a communal life within her society, primarily via the completion of her musical ode to *agapē*—a map of her relationships, past and present, tracing her journey through grief. Giving little ground to sentiment, and without shying away from depicting the sacrifices her choices entail, this powerful music-film challenges Julie, and through Julie its audiences, to carry on caring about something other than one's self—whatever the cost. It also challenges one to concentrate wholeheartedly on the contributions to the film's narrative of sound design and, especially, Preisner's music.[37]

Part I: Trauma and Withdrawal

Hell

Blue begins with the controlled intensity of a sequence that astounds, not least in light of the gap between script and finished film. The screenplay's opening reads as follows: "A crowded motorway. Eight lanes of cars speeding in both directions. The rumble of lorries, roar of engines, drone of motorbikes as they weave their way among the cars. Hell."[38] None of what is telling about the start of *Blue* is contained within these words, most of which are pared down, Insdorf notes, "to one tire speeding on a highway."[39] Elegance, economy and nuance replace clumsy exposition. The result is a ruinous poetry.

The film emerges from a keening rush of sound. A gathering wind sculpts tension, strapping the audio-viewer into the film like a seatbelt; *Blue*'s sound design will ensure that one crashes, with Julie, into its broken heart. Because of the shock of the action that follows, however, one might easily overlook a significant detail about the opening: one hears before one sees in *Blue*. The film hints, from the outset, that Julie and the audience alike will need to listen carefully. The opening prefigures a recurring experience in *Blue*—a blackout flooded with sound—before beats of bassy rhythm seem to warp the blackness of the screen, calling tinges of blue into the frame's periphery. Sound is thereby marked, from the off, with the potential to override image.

The shot gradually reveals itself as the wheel of a speeding car. Other vehicles speed past; horns sound; all is velocity, danger, the possibility of death; one braces for impact. Kickasola captures the sequence's urgency with a description of what he calls the musical rhythm of the introduction. "No music is played," he writes, "but the genius of the sound design is its marvelous rhythm," which he likens to "the 'fate' rhythms that characterize funeral dirges"; thus, when the accident occurs, "[t]he sudden halt in the fate rhythm is terrifying."[40] Posts rushing past at the side of the road initiate this pulse; later in the sequence other "instruments" take over. The angular juxtaposition of cross-rhythms in the sequence, their irregular accents another source of unease, casts doubt on the possibility that this "funeral dirge" can be heard as a sonic prolepsis of the funeral march to be heard a few scenes hence: this is not so much a stately lament as a chaotic rush to the scaffold. The larger-scale sonic gesture Kickasola identifies, however, is clear: a continuum of sound established and then brutally interrupted. This severing gesture will recur, audio-visually, throughout almost all of *Blue*.

Aside from the interruption motif a number of other key ideas are presented by *Blue*'s opening. After a close-up beneath the car reveals something leaking out—brake fluid, the loss of which is emphasized by post-production drips, which pick up the sequence's rhythm and accelerate its pulse—Julie's voice (one hears her before one sees her) calls out to Anna. The car has been parked at the roadside so that Anna can pee. The camera, having panned right to follow Anna into the bushes, now swings back to the car and her parents. This relatively languid move, clearly marked for attention in the context of the opening's otherwise terse and documentary-like montage, is a cinematographic motif in the *Three Colors* trilogy which evokes the connections existing, or yet to be forged, between characters.[41] Here it represents a bond about to be broken.

A further motif is heard, not seen, in the immediate aftermath of the crash.[42] The introduction's final crescendo begins as the car sweeps past a young hitcher, failing to pick him up in an act of selfish indifference for which fate exacts the highest price. Like the boy, one hears before one sees the crash—the point at which, for Insdorf, the soundtrack is rendered "dramatically potent,"[43] demanding to be heard. Responding to that potency, one might note an unnerving sound as the boy turns and runs towards the car. The noise, ostensibly a post-production wind effect, is the culmination of the howl with which *Blue* began. It will return later to haunt Julie as a reminder of the origins of her grief.

The Faltering Funeral March

The next scene begins with a soothing breeze: Julie's breathing, with a blurry pillow feather swaying in its wake. The sensuous gentleness is an effective narrative feint, softening the perceiver up for a forthcoming blow. Shot as a reflection in the black pit of Julie's pupil—*Blue*'s celebrated close-up of Julie's eye was filmed by Idziak using a 200mm lens—a hospital doctor confirms that her husband and daughter are dead. The action and shots establish what Orr calls *Blue*'s "mind-screen"—the sensory, emotional and intellectual point of view from which the action of the film is henceforth focalized—as Julie's perspective. As Orr writes, "The extreme magnification of the lens also evokes the illusion of seeing through the eye into the soul. What we see and hear for the rest of the film is her soul."[44] *Blue* is now immersed in Julie's climate.

Having been told of the accident's outcome, Julie considers suicide. Her attempt begins with a crash (Julie smashes a window) and the first startle effect in the film—one of many sonic shocks in *Blue* which both echo the car crash and keep the perceiver in a condition of anxiety proximate to Julie's condition. While Julie makes her clumsy bid (she cannot bring herself to swallow the pills), an electronic alarm bell dings quietly in the background. Bells will be heard again shortly in *Blue*, and this alarm bell sounds a B natural—a pitch-class to be prominent in Preisner's score. B is the pitch-center of a musical memento Julie will retain in relation to her husband, and B minor is the key of the *Concert[o]*; that memento, in turn, will sound in the context of the *Concert[o]* as another window, this one intact, frames the final shot of the film. The choice of pitch-class seems as careful as the telephone ringing in A at the start of *Red*, a film in which A major is the main key. By instinct or design, Laureux and Flageollet's sound design in the trilogy is sometimes literally musical.

Blue's close, though, is as distant from Julie here as the skydivers glimpsed experiencing hedonistic forms of liberty on the tiny portable television Olivier places before her at the start of the next scene. The set has been purchased so that Julie can bear witness to the televising of Anna and Patrice's funeral. While Julie asks Olivier if the funeral is today, one hears a baby's crying mixed low in the sound design. This is not the last time that a child's cries will haunt the periphery of Julie's climate, and it is typical of *Blue*'s meticulous sound design to play both on innate human responses to a sound (a baby crying is one of the most powerfully affecting)[45] and its potential for symbolism (here obvious, Julie having just lost her child). The sequence is shot subjectively from Julie's point of view. Olivier remains out of focus—the camera/Julie refuses to focus on another person—but his voice is more pronounced than his image. She does not want to look at him, but cannot ignore his sound.

Further sound effects counterpoint Julie's attempt to control her emotions while watching the funeral. Two involve a door: a hinge whining, a door slamming shut. Both could be interpreted symbolically in the context of the funeral—a scream of pain, a gesture of finality—but again, the sounds also yield uncomfortable affects. Another sound, possibly Foley, possibly the springs of her hospital mattress being inadvertently captured alongside Binoche's breathing by Laureux's close miking, could be heard as an example of what Chion identifies, with reference to a remarkably similar sound and narrative context in Andrei Tarkovsky's *Solaris* (1972), as "free counterpoint" yielding "a phenomenal effect" of greater symbolic ambiguity.[46] In *Solaris*, when cosmonaut Chris's wife, who committed suicide, is brought back to "life" by the planet Solaris, the sound dubbed over the action is identified by Chion as breaking glass. Although the sound has no obvious diegetic purpose, Chion argues that one does not hear it as "wrong." Rather, it suggests "that [Chris's wife] is constituted of shards of ice; in a troubling, even terrifying way, they render both the creature's fragility and artificiality, and a sense of the precariousness of bodies."[47] The taut metallic clicks in this scene from *Blue* are similarly prominent while lacking diegetic purpose, yet they intensify one's sense of Julie's fragility, or even her fracturing, as she seeks to control tears she is unwilling to cry.

That Julie experiences her family's funeral mediated through a television set is a fact understandably commented on at length in the literature on *Blue*, which has sought to understand how that medium inflects the message of this scene. Kickasola notes a similarity to the snowy television images at the opening and close of *Decalogue 1*—an image of another of Kieślowski's lost children—and it could be argued that *Blue*'s reuse of this device enhances the scene's power by playing on the intertextual resonance.[48] Like the aunt viewing Pawel's frozen image in *Decalogue 1*, Julie is distanced twice over from her child, with "what is lost in transmission," according to Kickasola, "stand[ing] as a vacancy in Julie's life."[49] Alternately, Wilson notes the disintegration of the television sound and image at the end of the sequence and reads it as a foreshadowing of the blackouts Julie will begin to experience in the next scene. They are not switched off but "disappear as the screen goes out of focus and the scene is disrupted by interference [as] her mind blanks out"; for Wilson, this is the first evidence of Julie's retreat into denial.[50] That the haze of static also creates an audio-visual barrier between music and Julie—the broadcast of the funeral contains *Blue*'s first cue—also seems significant. In the published screenplay, Julie herself detunes the signal, creating the barrier between herself, her dead family and this music. Her barrier will soon be spectacularly breached.[51]

It is thus through a fuzz of television static that one begins to experience Preisner's first cue in the film. From the start, then, music's location in *Blue* is mediated and, here quite literally, side-by-side with the main action. This "on-the-air" sound will shortly enjoy "the freedom of crossing boundaries in cinematic space."[52] Even here, however, the music's link to diegetic reality sounds questionable. Instead of the tinny sound of a tiny television's speaker, one hears the music and subsequent eulogy in unrealistically warm tones. The need to listen carefully has already been implied by *Blue*'s discursive apparatus, but this rhetorically privileged moment—the first appearance of music in any film, as Paulus notes, is a tool for "giving deliberate accent to the scene"[53]—is permitted an unrealistically full and resonant sound. This draws one in, inviting interpretation.

The film does not explain the identity of the fictional composer of this faltering funeral march, but two para-filmic texts reveal that it was not originally conceived as music by Patrice or by Julie. It was created as a funeral march "by" Van den Budenmayer. In the screenplay, a TV voiceover states that this is "a march by the deceased's favourite composer, Van den Budenmayer . . . played by students from the Academy of Music who bid their professor farewell."[54] That Preisner scored the cue with the fictional Dutchman in mind is proven by the cue sheet itself (see Fig. 5.1); it states, across the top of the page, the identity of its "real" composer. The omission of any mention of Van den Budenmayer at this juncture in *Blue* has created confusion. Had the voiceover remained, it seems less likely that Insdorf and Andrew, for instance, would have misidentified the music as part of the *Concert[o]*.[55] This funeral march is not part of the *Concert[o]*.[56] That work, and in particular the different Van den Budenmayer theme Julie weaves into it—which this study will call the memento—will relate primarily to the consolations of Julie's later, loss-oriented grief-work. The faltering funeral march, first heard as Patrice and Anna's coffins are displayed on the television screen, is a signifier of the trauma of her loss. Overcoming this music—the faltering funeral march repeatedly returns as a reminder of her repressed grief—becomes vital to Julie's grief-work. Ultimately, she must supplant one Van den Budenmayer theme with another in order to progress. Not to hear this musical exchange is to miss something crucial in *Blue*'s plot.

The faltering funeral march is in G minor, has the mood indication *Lacrimoso* (*Marciale*), moves at the stately pace of 54 beats per minute and is scored for a brass and wind septet mixing instruments found together in military-style wind bands; the full ensemble (clarinet, bass clarinet, trumpet, two horns, trombone and tuba) is briefly visible over the coffins as the first television image emerges.[57] On the one hand, the music establishes a funereal register by matching many of the traits Stein identifies as typical in mourning music, i.e., "reverentially hushed tones, steady, restrained and measured tempi, a relatively uncomplicated and stable metric surface, and a straightforward, even spare thematic motif."[58] On the other hand, the lament's militaristic scoring indicates the deceased composer's importance to the bourgeois establishment within *Blue*'s fictionalization of French culture. That this is styled as a state funeral signals Patrice's status within that establishment and, in turn, the not-so-fictional patriarchal superstructure within which he participated. The corollary of this is that his wife is defined *in absentia* as precisely that: a wife and a mother to his child, and thus a woman whose public identity was confined by her sex and supporting roles. One impact of Patrice and Anna's deaths will be to release Julie to test a more liberated form of identity. Initially, however, *Blue* shows Julie being forced towards crying, in a stereotypically appropriate Dionysian manner, in response to an Apollonian funeral rite designed by men, amongst other things, to make women cry. Significantly, at the end of this scene, Julie halts her crying.

Of the small band of musicians, a tuba player and trombonist (played by young men), and then a clarinetist (a young woman), are shot in close-up. The sexes of the performers are significant. As discussed in Chapter Two, the brass are stereotypically deemed a masculine instrumental family by screen scoring practices, the woodwind more feminine. The musician-actors in the scene were probably cast merely for what they could play, although that they are thus divided

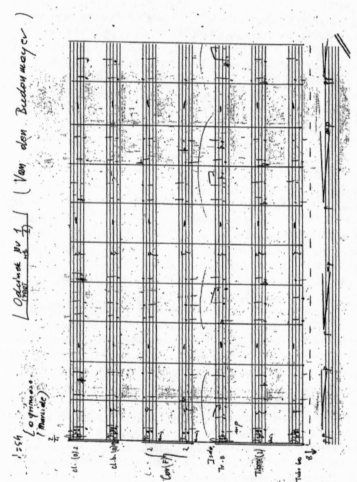

Fig. 5.1: Preisner's manuscript score for *Blue*'s first "Van den Budenmayer" cue

asserts the point that boys tend to learn brass, girls tend to play wood-wind, because that is what societal conventions point them towards. By picking out these groupings, however, *Blue* suggests an ulterior motive. In terms of its immediate plot trajectory, the next cue could be heard to use similar instrumental means to signify, in the absence of unambiguous visual signs, the presence (or indeed absence) of a male and a female when Julie experiences her first musical interruption and blackout. In this respect, one might note that, while the brass close-up frames two men, the close-up of the clarinetist ties the sound of a woodwind instrument to an image of youthful femininity. The latter musician is also shot following Julie's attempt to "touch" the smaller coffin.

A close-up of Anna's coffin plaque reveals her name. Again Julie "touches" the casket, but more shakily this time, in one of the most affecting moments in the film. Aside from signifying her precarious psychological state, Julie's touch—of the coffin, but also of the broadcast of the music—relates to later moments in the narrative. When the copyist touches a score of the unfinished *Concert[o]*—her finger framed in close-up like Julie's here—Julie reacts with barely controlled horror. The copyist's touch ignites the sound of the opening chorus of the *Concert[o]*, just as Julie's touch of the same page of music, again shot in close-up, will inaugurate the *Concert[o]* montage at the end of the film (see Fig. 5.2). What does the copyist's touch disturb, for Julie, and why is Julie able to touch the music herself only at the end of the film? *Blue* is establishing a connection between music, tactility and the people in Julie's life who can no longer be caressed.

Preisner's cue layers further meanings within this already rich scene. The most distinctive feature of his funeral march is its rhythmic limp. As noted in Chapter Two, silences are a stylistic fingerprint in Preisner's scores and have recurring functions. While evoking some of them here—e.g., the sacred, melancholy, pensiveness, dignity—the faltering gesture could be heard to fulfill a more specific function. This funeral march consists of three pairs of three-bar phrases, separated by silences. Two bars of each phrase are filled with music (like the coffins); the third is empty (like Julie). The pattern may be heard to symbolize Julie's separation from her family—but that is not all.

Preisner's cue is actually considerably longer than the music one hears in the film. No doubt he supplied enough music to accommodate however much footage the director eventually chose to use. It is typical of music in the trilogy, though, and especially of *Blue*, that the cue has been chopped down in post-production (see Ex. 5.1).[59] Elsewhere in *Blue*, the cuts are purposefully brutal—music suddenly stops mid-phrase or even mid-note, in an echo of the opening car crash. This precise piece of musical surgery—achieved with the help of the composer during the editing process—retains a sense of the original cue's ternary form. All but the first phrase of Preisner's lyrical central section is removed, the music cutting instead to the last two bars of the *da capo* repeat; the third pair of phrases sounds, in this edited version, like a

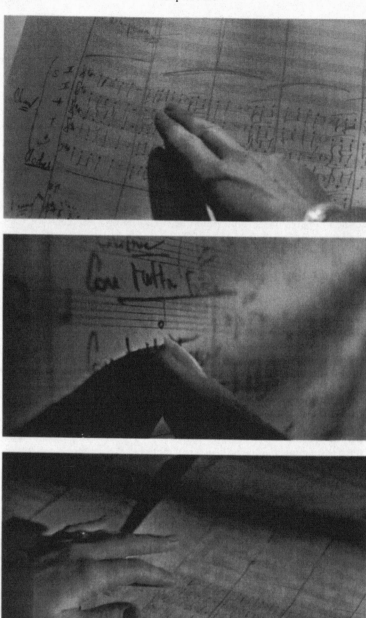

Fig. 5.2: Touching the music in *Blue*: the copyist, Julie when composing with Olivier, Julie at the end (photos courtesy of the author)

summary of the first two pairs. Having just three pairs of three-bar phrases interrupts a more familiar hypermetrical pattern: music proceeding in groupings of four. One expects, when the cue ends, to hear more. It falters at this macro-rhythmic level, leaving one wanting more and feeling cheated by its finality. It is a musical bereavement.

Ex. 5.1: The funeral cue and its motivic structure

Work in the cutting room seems to have enabled Preisner to yield something semantically richer than the composer can originally have intended, in keeping with Kieślowski's desire to help his co-workers attain their finest forms of expression—coincidentally or otherwise, the precise working relationship Kieślowski deemed Julie to have with her late husband's music. Explaining this richness requires a little more analysis. The melody of the march is dominated by a descending three-note motif. As the bracketed x motifs and boxed progression in Ex. 5.1 show, this can be heard locally in the melody and also nested within the music's middle-range voice-leading (and indeed as its background contrapuntal-harmonic structure). Descending gestures in minor modes are culturally encoded as emotionally negative gestures; think of Chopin or Liszt's funeral marches, for instance, and the many descending phrases that intensify their pervasive gloom. The 3̂-2̂-1̂ gesture, however, allied with i-V-i harmonic progressions, is one of the most basic, yet potent, ways in which tonal Western art music signifies something (a phrase, a movement, an entire composition) coming to an end: it is a contrapuntal-harmonic pincer movement.[60] By permeating the march with this gesture, Preisner encoded a cue that is intensely closural; the rests and editing, in turn, create a hypermetrical disruption that makes the cue sound simultaneously incomplete.[61] The result is a poignant dualism. Everything has ended for Julie; everything is unfinished.

As the scene closes and the television broadcast decays into static, Julie presses her lips together. Attention is drawn to this gesture by close-up, close-miking, cutting and music, the film marking as significant Julie's turn towards closing off her pain and rewriting her self. Further gestures of closure will follow before the end of her period of withdrawal.

Interruption No.1/Ellipsis No. 1

The published screenplay's description of music's role in one of the most extensively analyzed scenes in *Blue* provides an object lesson in the chasm between script and screen, and especially in films where music is permitted to take a leading role in the storytelling:

> INT./EXT. HOSPITAL. DAY.
> Julie is lying on the terrace in a comfortable deckchair. . . . The terrace is quite large, partitioned by high balustrades made of blue glass. . . . A ray of sunshine pierces the blue glass and falls on her face. She closes her eyes. At that moment, loud music resounds. It seems to last only seconds. When she opens her eyes, sensing somebody else's eyes on her, the music stops.[62]

What occurs in *Blue* is more complex and mysterious: a bi-partite scene of interruption (music suddenly heard) and ellipsis (music heard as the image fades to black) that has generated some of the most sophisticated readings in the film's reception. Both scene and reception require careful analysis.

Interruption No. 1

As Julie dozes off on her hospital room's veranda, a delicate peal of church bells sounds as if in the distance. The immediate sonic purpose of these (presumably) post-production bells is to establish a sense of the outdoor environment of the hospital gardens overlooked by Julie's room. Much of the effectiveness of what follows rests on a stark sonic contrast. The initial sound design, like the establishing shots, evokes a sense of a wide-open space and Julie's isolation within it. What follows evokes interiority. The bells also prepare a harmonic contrast: their major modal halo is interrupted by music lurching into a minor mode. Finally, they remind one that this scene comes in the aftermath of a funeral at which bells may also have tolled, although the present changes, with ghastly irony, sound more like the kind rung at marriages or a christening.

Julie dozes off in the sunlight—look closely and one sees her hand fall from the book to her lap. Her fragile moment of relaxation, however, is about to be shattered. When Julie's neck snaps to attention, music blares out and blue light flares across the screen; a self-reflexive example of the startle reflex is triggered (see Fig. 5.3). Whether or not one really leaps, one experiences a sensation binding one to Julie's fight or flight response. Indeed, this sequence as a whole could be considered a boundary-pushing experiment in intensified cinematic empathy. When the second part of the scene then bends a fundamental convention of sound cinema (the image track ruptures, plunging the cinema into darkness), what one experiences—what one is *forced* to experience—is music alone. Through a surprising reversal of audio-visual convention, one sees and hears what Julie does, but also *as* she does.[63] Thanks in large part to Preisner's robust scoring, this is an unnerving moment.

Fig. 5.3: Julie hears the music in *Blue*—or does she? (Photo courtesy of the author)

Preisner's cue reimagines the previous scene's faltering funeral march (see Fig. 5.4). In that reimagining one hears the distance he had traveled, as a composer, between the caution of *No End* and confidence of *Blue*. The theme was intensified into what Preisner terms "scary ghost music" at the director's behest. Preisner would have preferred subtler, less demonstrative scoring akin to the more restrained interruption music heard later in the swimming pool, but agreed to carry out his director's bidding in order to achieve the desired effect. So the funeral's small wind ensemble, reminiscent of *No End*'s restrained scoring of its *cantus firmus*, is replaced, for the initial blast of the cue, by a full orchestral quota of strings and brass (four horns, two trumpets, trombone and tuba). That the composer, recalling his discussions with Kieślowski, uses paranormal terminology to describe the startle effect is intriguing; elsewhere, it will be recalled, he stated that Julie experiences the interruptions as if she has witnessed a ghost.

After the blackout in the second part of the scene, the journalist, quizzing Julie on the whereabouts of her husband's final composition,

Fig. 5.4: Preisner's manuscript score for the interruption's re-imagining of the funeral theme

voices the question that Julie—and the audio-viewer—have been forced to consider by Preisner's strident cue: where, or *what*, is this music? Answering that question, indeed analyzing *Blue*'s entire score, could easily degenerate into a stultifying discussion of whether the music, at any given moment, is diegetic, non-diegetic or meta-diegetic. Each position is plausible in this scene. In order to be meta-diegetic, in the conventional understanding of that term, a cue must be heard as if the narrative has granted one access, quasi-telepathically, to music occurring in the mind of a character. The excess of reverb in this cue, obvious in the moments following its shocking first phrase, could be heard to signify this kind of interiority. Meta-diegetic music could also represent a repressed memory or hallucination on the part of a physically and emotionally traumatized survivor (one of Stein's "compromise formations"); Julie is experiencing, after all, a variation of the funeral music she last heard in the broadcast of her family's burial. If one likes this interpretation, one might also consider this to be the sound of Julie's compositional imagination breaking through for the first time in *Blue*, albeit perversely, to play with the tones of the funeral march. If the music is meta-diegetic it is being composed by her, in some sense, albeit unconsciously and probably undesirably. A more interesting question is thus suggested: What are the details of her rescoring and what might her creative unconscious be trying to tell her through these changes (discussed below)?

Instead, the music could also be heard as non-diegetic. Perhaps the blue light flaring through the painted window is all that awakens Julie and shocks her, with Preisner merely underscoring her startle and disorientation. Alternately, it could also be interpreted as diegetic music, streaming from a subjective point of view embodied by the camera Julie stares into, as if heard from a zone of audition somewhere between the startled composer and the music's "actual" origin in front of Julie. Chion notes that, due to the omni-directional nature of sound, spatial point of audition (more or less capturing a character's aural perspective) is a *zone* of audition rather than a precise point. For the same reason, film cannot easily evoke the equivalent of a subjective point-of-view shot through sound (in order to give the impression of hearing literally what the character experiences). To achieve that, cinematic convention dictates an analogue: "the *visual* representation of a character in closeup that, in simultaneous association with the hearing of sound, identifies this sound as being heard by the character shown."[64] Julie is not shown in close-up (nor is anyone or anything else), although her look to the camera could be taken to indicate a teasing of this convention to signify that she is probably, if not definitely, hearing the music. The evidence, however, seems purposefully ambiguous.

One consequence of this ambiguity is a plethora of competing readings in the literature, regarding both the music and the streaming blue light, which could come from the blue-tinted windows, yet seems uncannily vivid and animate. For Andrew, examining the images, "physically, there is no explanation" for the blue flashes, nor for the "washes and/or fade outs" later in the scene and film.[65] Innovatively, however, he suggests such images play a symbolic role for the audience akin to dramatic underscoring: they are non-diegetic visuals, giving connotative subtext to a scene by symbolizing forces forming obstacles in her quest for freedom, and in an instance when the more typical cinematic vehicle for such functions, music, is otherwise engaged. For Insdorf, "[t]he splashes of blue, combined with music, express the return of the repressed—that which Julie must sooner or later confront—whether it is grief or the need for another human being."[66] This amounts to an early example of "Julie's 'sight,' especially inner, [being] expressed by Preisner's score"[67]—a productive reading, if one accepts the possibility that some of the interruptions may in fact be *self*-interruptions by a fertile compositional mind seeking to heal itself through the act of composing and, in the process, to pass important messages to other aspects of that mind's consciousness. The movement of the camera and Julie's fixed gaze, in turn, "suggest a presence" to Kickasola, "though no presence can be accounted for."[68] Like intuitions in earlier films, such as *Véronique*'s vision of Weronika singing, the sequence is less "suggestive of a real spiritual presence" than "the more shocking, relentless, and unpredictable intrusion of memory and loss."[69] Insdorf supports an apparitional reading and echoes Preisner, arguing that, starting with this scene, "[m]usic has a ghostly presence in *Blue*," with "notes from the *Concerto* engender[ing] her fearful stare at the camera. . . . She looks as if she has seen a ghost."[70]

The most intriguing reading of the relationship between what one sees and hears in this sequence is Georgina Evans's reading of Julie as someone who, as a result of the head trauma of her accident, is experiencing acute synaesthesia, a condition the most common form of which involves "colored hearing," i.e., an unbidden visualization of colors and shapes in response to certain sounds:

> The fact that Julie appears to us with a sutured eye, after the blurred vision of Olivier [when he delivers the mini-TV], strongly hints that her distorted vision may not simply be a filmic symptom of her introspection, but the result of real physical injury. The most overpowering "blue" sound, coinciding with the loud burst of concerto, which wakes Julie in hospital, appears to surprise her greatly, suggesting that the experience is new to her. The fact that Julie's synaesthesia seems to subside throughout the recuperation process of *Bleu*, never again achieving the startling intensity it had on the hospital terrace, hints that it is a symptom of the damage that she is slowly recovering from, a manifestation of the disease of grief and its associated art.[71]

As Evans notes, "the experience [of colored hearing] is frequently projected outside the individual, rather than being an image in the mind's eye."[72] Following this logic, one could conclude that, while the music may be resounding in Julie's mind, it might make her simultaneously "see" the flaring blue light. Such music manifests as both audio and vision to the synaesthetic, and is both inner and outer, meta-diegetic and diegetic—or side by side itself.

   Pinning down where and when the music or its visual corollary occurs in the film, however, may not be as significant as paying close
attention to its signifying details or the manner in which such experiences evolve for Julie, and for *Blue*'s perceivers, over the course of the
narrative. Evans notes how, "as time goes on, the world [for Julie] becomes less strange, and blue reappears with less vigor . . . her perceptions becoming increasingly 'normal.'"[73] Does a similar process of
"normalization" occur in the film's deployment of its score? In her recent re-theorizing of the diegetic/non-diegetic binary in film music
studies, Stilwell seeks to shift attention away from noting where isolated instances of music occur and towards the overall trajectory of musical occurrences exploring these zones. In place of the "failure of
metaphor" of the diegetic/non-diegetic binary (failure in the sense that
they are often taught and conceived as separate filmic realms), Stilwell
argues for a focus on moments when "the boundary between diegetic
and non-diegetic is traversed," because such an act "does always
mean."[74] When music moves through what she terms the "fantastical
gap," analysts must move from feature spotting to longer-range observations of the transitions articulated. Where, though, in light of the ambiguity of its location in this and many other scenes, might one say the
music begins in *Blue*—and where does it end up?
   Stilwell's essay also significantly expands the notion of meta-
diegetic, moving well beyond the familiar notion of sound or music
within the mind of a character, in a way which seems more aptly to
capture the role of Preisner's score in *Blue* as a manifestation, at times,
of Julie's musical thoughts and climate:

> [W]e might refine the concept of the meta-diegetic as a kind of rep-
> resented subjectivity, music clearly (through framing, dialogue, act-
> ing, lighting, sound design, or other cinematic process) situated in a
> character who forms a particular strong point of identifica-
> tion/location for the audience. The character becomes the bridging
> mechanism between the audience and the diegesis as we enter into
> his or her subjectivity. This is a space beyond empathy; its location
> with regard to the diegesis does, however, reach out and engage us
> in a way that starts to tear at the fabric of the usual conception of
> diegetic/non-diegetic—or, it acknowledges a relationship between
> audience and film that diegetic/non-diegetic has displaced by con-
> centrating on the construction of the text within its own bounda-
> ries.[75]

It is vital to note, however, that while *Blue*'s music spends most of its
duration seeking to bridge the empathic space between the audience and
Julie's climate, there is a significant shift towards the end of the film,
and particularly when her version of the *Concert[o]* is finally heard in
full. At that moment, the score moves into a normative function: accompanying a montage. Even the more radical re-theorizing of
diegetic/non-diegetic recently proposed by Ben Winters, who seeks to
reclassify almost all film music as diegetic, allows that music "that

functions to unify a montage sequence might well be understood as 'narrating' from an external perspective the events we are witnessing, passing in a compressed time-frame, and [be capable of being] labeled 'non-diegetic.'"[76] At the end of *Blue*, music's journey through the fantastical gap, having been cast adrift by the funeral sequence and then blown further from familiar shores by the balcony scene, gradually returns to a more conventional mooring, precisely as convention returns to Julie's life and other aspects of the film—such as the role of blue light, reduced in the film's final frames to an unthreatening, perhaps even optimistic, reflection of sky on a window pane. The shift along the axis from meta-diegetic (as theorized by Stilwell) to non-diegetic (as still accepted by Winters) is a shift from ambiguity and innovation to convention that contributes tellingly to the film's symbolization of what is lost alongside Julie's closing gains.

Ellipsis No. 1

After the journalist says hello, the screen fades to black and, according to Kieślowski's explanation, time stands still for Julie as she hears the music continue:

> The idea is to convey an extremely subjective point of view. That is, that time really does pass but for Julie, at a certain moment, it stands still. A journalist . . . says "Hello" and Julie replies "Hello." . . . Two seconds go by between one "hello" and the other. What I want to show is that for Julie time has stopped. Not only does the music come back to her but time stands still for a moment.[77]

This evocation of lost time evokes the kind of traumatic breach of temporality during mourning discussed by Stein. The shift from sound and vision to music alone, in turn, creates a semiotic rift for the audio-viewer, the uncanniness of which parallels the warping temporality of the protagonist's experience. One is therefore invited to focus on the music by this striking reinvention of a cinematic commonplace.

Fading to black usually denotes that a significant period of time has passed between successive scenes in a film's telling of its story. Here, the shift from close-up to blackout and back again forms an experimental extension of cinema's "key shot," in Julie Brown's term, "for establishing character subjectivity": the "close-up character shot with added underscore . . . [at] the moment when the subjective content of character and music merge."[78] By focusing attention on the rescoring of the funeral march, the blackout also encourages consideration of the ways in which the cue might be seeking to tutor Julie. The blackout invites one—as Adorno and Eisler once argued musical interludes in films should attempt to do more often[79]—to pay attention to the passages being juxtaposed in this development of what was, previously, a uniformly orchestrated cue, and to what those developments might imply.

Preisner's first ellipsis and blackout cue, and its audio-visual setting in the narrative, amplify aspects of the faltering funeral march's scoring and symbolism. The rests become more obvious, for instance, when there is nothing, i.e., no visual action, to experience during the blackout's periods of musical absence. The faltering is also exaggerated, at a higher rhythmic level than the rests, by changes in tempo between phrases, which switch from *agitato* in the brass and string assertions to the slower *placido* of the oboe's lament. Like Julie, the music loses time or, at least, slows down. Considering the way in which the music is demarcated by the exaggerated faltering, one might also hear two musical personae being created. One sounds strong, its confidence robustly scored in octaves—a scoring, Preisner asserts, that was Kieślowski's call—for brass and strings. The other voice is the solo oboe, "lonely and abandoned by the rest of the orchestra."[80] One could hear in these changes a musical unpacking of the gender symbolism accrued by the funeral sequence's images. A masculine, dominating phrase (Patrice) and its feminine, fragile consequent (Anna) are separated from each other by the rests and also, of course, from another persona whose isolation is represented, on screen, by the nothingness of darkness and, in sound, by reverberant chasms (Julie). The cue represents all that Julie has lost and demands that she countenance her bereavement. More prosaically, the oboe's lament, being separated in texture and forces from the community of the ensemble, sounds as bereft as Julie should feel, at this moment, while symbolizing a solo voice shorn from a society. Either way, Preisner's development reinforces aspects of Julie's situation and entreats her to confront her reality.

Or, indeed, her Real. For Žižek, the interruptions and ellipses are instances of the Real shattering Julie's conscious realm. Jacques Lacan and his followers, including his most prominent contemporary exponent, Žižek, "view human subjectivity as a mobile intersection of the three registers" called the Imaginary, the Symbolic and the Real:

> The imaginary designates a stage where the infant perceives its own identity as continuous with that of its mother and the surrounding environment; it refers, therefore, to a plenitude that becomes suppressed on entry into the symbolic, the stage at which the child participates in language and establishes a separate identity. This suppression is marked by a sense of loss because the imaginary can now be accessed only by the symbolic.[81]

Later in the film, Julie indulges in the healing powers of a symbolic language—the busker's music—which speaks to her need to reshape herself at that stage of her grief; the *Concert[o]* montage, in turn, can be characterized as an escape into the Symbolic and various other forms of necessary untruth. Such moments contrast sharply with the interruptions and ellipses, which could instead be read to symbolize the Real bursting in. Note that this is not the reality of everyday life, i.e., the world "of pensions or income tax,"[82] as Alastair Williams puts it: it is the incom-

prehensible mass of everything prior to the filtering of the symbolic
order through which one learns to process experiences of the world.
The Real can be terrifying, not least because, minus the shield of the
Symbolic, the things one has repressed or avoided thinking about can
break through and call for attention. In Julie's case, the music is a
scream of unmediated grief.[83]

At the journalist's "Bonjour," Julie looks around, notably unsee-
ingly. Who is this other voice, she may be thinking: is *she* a real presence (or a Real one)? Unfortunately, the voice is horribly concrete, in
the form of an investigative journalist. The interrupter asks Julie about
the state of Patrice's *Concert[o]*. Julie says it does not exist—a partial
lie and, given the existential issues at stake, a lie laden with symbolism.
Given what she has just experienced, acting as if this music, or indeed
any music relating to her previous life, does not exist seems like a psychologically important stand. Music must not exist. It is her husband
and daughter, her past and her loss. It is everything she needs to suppress.

The Memento

Aside from the sounds of instrumentalists and singers practicing as
Olivier leafs through documents in Patrice's office desk—files including, he discovers, photos of the dead composer with his mistress—
music briefly recedes into the background of *Blue* when Julie visits her
family home. It returns during the scene that begins with Julie leafing,
slightly frantically, through folders of large pages of handwritten orchestral score. As she does so, a single line of piano melody—a new
theme—sings out, just before a black grand piano comes into view at
the foot of the stairs of this exceedingly well-appointed, split-level music studio.

Julie's rush down the stairs—as if in response to a question posed
by the first phrase of the cue—indicates one manner in which a typical
Preisner gesture, faltering, can inflect a narrative with something oth-
erwise absent (see Fig. 5.5[i]). In bars of $\frac{5}{4}$, rather than the $\frac{4}{4}$ suggested
by the melody's basic phrasing, the "extra" beat teases out the tension
between the moments of discovery in the scene; in the spaces, the piano's sustain pedal keeps pitches ringing, like a musical bating of the
breath. The melody's style and faltering are reminiscent, and with good
reason, of the faltering funeral march. Julie is searching to the accompaniment of a theme that will, in a sense, become the symbolic shield in
her battle with the grief symbolized by the earlier cues. The new
theme—the Van den Budenmayer memento—will literally and figura-
tively oppose its musical animus, the Van den Budenmayer faltering
funeral march, in several scenes to come. Ultimately it will triumph in
the *Concert[o]*, but without entirely shaking its own funereal associations, thus rendering the victory ambiguous.

The pauses and phrasing also initially suggest an external musical agency guiding Julie's actions. The tune's opening, rising phrase and subsequent pause create the sense of an antecedent question demanding some kind of consequent answer, such as her descent of the stairs. The second phrase's consequent, in turn, might be imagined to be Julie's search of the lower part of the room; the third is answered by her discovery of the memento manuscript. The montage cuts from a long shot at the top of the stairs, which had been following her search, to the medium close-up of Julie nodding as she picks up and reads a small fragment of manuscript paper retrieved from the piano. Up until this point, the music could be non-diegetic. As she descended the stairs and the piano came into view, one might be tempted briefly to hear the music as diegetic and emanating, in some sense, from the instrument or even the scrap of manuscript itself. Julie's actions then suggest that the music is meta-diegetic: a musical thought within her mind as she searches for the scrap of music to match it. Floating free of a precise location, the trajectory of Preisner's music through this fantastical gap fashions a slow metaphysical zoom.

As Julie folds the manuscript scrap in half, the cue suddenly fades. Her silencing may remind one of other film characters who, as in Janet Halfyard's analysis of the Joker's manipulation of Danny Elfman's score in *Batman* (Burton, 1989), demonstrate the force of their agency by taking control of a soundtrack. The sudden fade as she folds the paper suggests, however, that she is not so much seeking to control the music as silence it. Once the music has been calmed, a sound from outside the room (the maid crying because Julie is not crying) distracts Julie. I remember everything, how can I forget? Marie asks her, voicing a question Julie could well be asking herself: How can I forget this music and all that it portends? The fate of the scrap of music in her hand relates to Julie's plans for forgetting.[84] Later, having dealt with a visit from Olivier and her solicitor, Julie returns to the music room and reconsiders the scrap of manuscript. Thus begins one of the most striking fusions of sound, music and action in the trilogy. Initially, one sees and hears—disorientatingly—only music: the scrap of manuscript's line of B minor melody, scored in the treble clef. Ceasing to see and hear music in the scene, again at Julie's command, will be significant.

That the music one sees and hears (see Fig. 5.5[ii]) is presented from Julie's subjective point of view and zone of audition is established in at least three ways. First, Chion's rule for the signification of subjective point of audition clearly applies: one sees Julie in closeup both reading and apparently "hearing" (in her mind's ear) the music, the sight of the music providing a visual confirmation of the sonically signified concept. To amplify this further, a tracking extreme close-up, similar to the one of her eye in the hospital,[85] is used to trace, note by note and basically in time with the soundtrack, the line of melody. Second, a simple shot/reverse shot sequence is constructed, showing the music, then Julie reading the music, then the music again. Notably, the

Fig. 5.5(i): Preisner's manuscript score for the memento theme

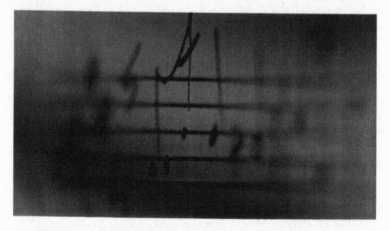

Fig. 5.5(ii): The memento from Julie's subjective point of view (photo courtesy of the author)

most obvious use of this common editorial device yet in *Blue* involves not Julie and another character but Julie and a fragment of music. In his study of *The Decalogue*, Christopher Garbowski identifies the special role of shot/reverse shot sequences in Kieślowski's films and the very special role therein of POV shots. This setup "confronts the protagonist with the *other*," he writes, and in doing so provides "a powerful stimulus for self-transcendence."[86] In *Blue*, Julie's other is the interrupting music, and whether one deems that it comes from Julie's unconscious or an external source, it eventually proves to be a powerful stimulus for change. Garbowski notes Frankl's dictum that "man is a responsible creature and must actualize the meaning of his life."[87] Although she is in no state to do so yet, Julie must become responsible anew for her life, in large part in response to the music that will haunt her, but also shepherd her, towards that moment of actualization. A changing relationship to music is the key to Julie's self-transcendence of grief.[88] Third, shots are screened through a blue filter when one sees the music from Julie's perspective; when one sees Julie herself in the frame, the manuscript paper looks notably whiter. This will not be the last occasion one "sees" Julie's perception of music as "blue," and however the blueness is understood here—as an effect of synaesthesia, say, or a non-diegetic connotation—it may be more important to note the connection of such shots to later ones, and especially moments when Julie sees differently colored music.

The melody one hears is a repetition of the piano theme heard in the previous scene (in fact, a double repetition, the second attenuated). The memento is also funereal, yet it seems to signify stoicism and grace in the face of melancholy. This may relate to the gestural language of the cue, which contrasts "mimetic motifs . . . that call to mind sighs or other vocalisations allied with sadness"[89]—the sole component of the faltering funeral march's restricted pattern-making—to more rhapsodic expressions of sorrow. Cast in B minor, a tonal region distant from the funeral march's G minor, the cue feels as if the action is picking up from where Julie was interrupted. The cue is marked *placido*, the expressive marking of the plaintive oboe phrases during the first interruption and ellipsis. This connection to that feminine sound may lend weight to the idea, developed by some critics, that the Van den Budenmayer memento can be considered Julie's theme. Preisner rarely consciously assigns a leitmotivic function to his themes. Rather, he prefers to align a nexus of characters and narrative events with certain themes in order to associate them with aspects of a film's climate and concept. A case could be made, however, that part of the memento theme's functioning is not so much acting as a musical intertitle flashing up to say "Here's Julie!" whenever it appears, but rather, as Paulus puts it, to map musical transformations which parallel "the transformations the young woman passes through as she struggles with pain, memory and a new life."[90] Certainly, in this scene the memento becomes fused to *Blue*'s representation of Julie's subjectivity by means of its audio-visual presentation. It is also "played very expressively," thus "nourishing her subjectivity,"[91] and bears interiority-signifying reverb.

The memento melody is more intervalically liberated than the mono-motivic faltering funeral march, so it bears more hallmarks of Van den Budenmayer's style, thanks to its arpeggio-like leaps and descents. Its rhapsodic nature relates to its ambitus and harmony: it scales an octave through its initial arpeggiation and centers itself, at the brief peak of this process, around B minor's relative major, D major. As it does so, a three-note descending figure, F#-E-D (motif y on Ex. 5.2)—hints at an opposition of major and minor scale fragments, and thus of their different cultural encodings of happy and sad or, more precisely, not-tragic and tragic, by contrast to the descending motif and minor-scale fragment which dominated the faltering funeral march. At the end of the memento melody, however, motif x closes the theme; it is just as prevalent in the memento's voice-leading.

The genetic heritage of the two themes—their "Budenmayeran quality"—is therefore clear. They are similar in many ways: minor keys, similar tempos, aspects of phrasing and rhythm. They also share, as noted above, a faltering rhythmic structure, have an underlying motivic core and clearly evoke the register or topical field of "funereal." Yet there is a crucial difference. This theme has a yearning quality. Bitter-sweetly, it encapsulates an attempt to pull away from motive x and B minor and towards the major modal colorings of motif y and D major.[92] In direct but poignant musical terms, Preisner patterns a musical journey similar to the one Julie plays out across the film as a whole: a move from the tragic into an ostensibly more positive alternative, and then back into the tragic again, but fortified by the journey. Here, though, Julie cuts the music dead at the moment it alights, for the second time, on the more positive implications of D major and motif y. Her life is still a long way from anything so upbeat.

Ex. 5.2: Memento theme motivic content

As the melody loops and the written music runs out, empty staves are all one is shown. What one sees is thus an absence. That is not, however, what one hears.[93] The music should, by the logic of meta-diegetic convention, stop at this moment, but instead it continues looping as Julie's attention, the camerawork implies, drifts to disturbing the piano lid's supporting arm. The obvious suggestion here is that the music is looping inside Julie's head. A more subtle argument would be that she is authoring a continuation of the music, rather than merely reading it.[94] Admittedly, there is no development of the tune here, just repetition, but the simplest way to extend a composition is to repeat an existing component. Julie, one might argue, is taking a step towards creative musicianship. If so, it is repugnant to her. Far from being the healing activity it will become by her time of loss-oriented activity, during her time of withdrawal the music's invasion of her subjectivity makes her skin crawl. She therefore acts decisively, cutting it dead.

Julie makes the piano's lid slam shut, creating a shock great enough to silence the music and the past it recalls. That connection back is further recalled by a telling element of the sound design. While the melody has been looping, tension has been building as the scene evolves from melancholy to something more anxious. The music stays the same, the camera work is consistent, but the scene's *mise-en-bande* changes decisively. Kickasola notes the strange "hollow, whistling wind" in this scene, which crescendos as Julie teases the arm of the piano and induces the lid to fall.[95] For Kickasola, crashing "the lid tragically confirms to Julie that the world remains cruel and relentless."[96] Where the looping melody suggests relentlessness through repetition, the noise reminds one of why the world now seems so harsh to Julie: the sound is strikingly similar to the wind effect heard in the aftermath of the car crash. Then the slamming keyboard lid, unleashing an explosion of jangling dissonance from the strings inside the piano—the instrument's body shocked out of melodiousness—on the one hand invokes another gesture of closing and control, and on the other an echo of the car crash's severance.[97] Illuminated as if she is murderously enraged, the blue of the outside swimming pool's water beamed onto her face by the now-slammed lid, Binoche adds a haunting sonic gesture of her own. As nerves and strings jangle, she shuts her eyes (another gesture of control) and loudly sucks in her breath (another breeze), before closing her mouth and holding it shut, just as she did after watching the funeral. It looks and sounds as if she is ingesting the music's spirit, in order to internalize and suppress it.[98]

The Copyist and the Lampshade

Further moments of withdrawal—of Julie closing herself off from the world and her past—are articulated musically before the end of the first part of the film.

The Copyist

At the start of the scene in the copyist's apartment, Julie is glimpsed through piles of rolled up music. It is a telling shot: the iris-like framing rhymes with close-ups of eyes and music elsewhere in the film, as if the cinematography is hinting to the perceiver that, if one is truly to see Julie, one must perceive her, here quite literally, through music. An incomplete draft of the *Concert[o]* is then found by the copyist and unrolled.

Lots of corrections, she says, noting the blue penmanship crossing through and embellishing the black bulk of the notation; no more than usual, Julie replies. The exchange denotes Julie's familiarity with her husband's working practices. Noting that the corrections are in blue ink, and apparently in a different hand (it is Julie's, the film later reveals), the nature of their working relationship becomes more apparent. The score depicted tallies with Kieślowski's answer to the question of who, in *Blue*'s fiction, composed Patrice's music: the husband, but Julie improved it. By the end of *Blue*, Julie will have taken creative ownership of her own version of the *Concert[o]*. Even in this scene, however, Julie behaves proprietarily regarding the manuscript and what it symbolizes. Bowled over by the music's beauty, the copyist cannot resist touching the score. Swooning about how much she loves one of the choruses, her fingers alight on the *Concert[o]*'s choral opening. Instantaneously one hears the music begin. Hitting this sync point with music so prominent in the mix, the editing calls attention to the scene's musical content, the significance in *Blue* of touching music (especially this part of the *Concert[o]*), and the audio-visual phrasing of the scene.[99]

What one hears, sung in ancient Greek, is Preisner's setting of the opening lines of St. Paul's best-known letter to the Corinthians, 1 Corinthians 13:

> If I speak in the tongues of men and of angels, but I do not have
> love [*agapē*], I am a noisy gong or a clanging cymbal.[100]

The cue is choral, the words obscure, at least to most perceivers the first time around. Julie, though, knows what the words mean and appears to be disturbed by the intimacy with which the copyist has handled the music. She grabs it, rolling the score up and so hiding the tones and words, and takes it away. Downstairs she catches up with a garbage truck glimpsed at the start of the scene and throws the score into its jaws. Patrice's draft *Concert[o] for the Unification of Europe* is crushed with the city's detritus.

One can begin to fathom Julie's surprising reaction by listening carefully to the sounds in the background just before the copyist's touch ignites the cue. One hears a young child, probably a girl, calling out in the breaks in the dialogue. The child's voice resounds; the copyist says of the music, but also connotatively of the child, that it is very beautiful; the music begins. The infant's voice is perhaps an example of what Chion calls "phantom audio-vision": the presence of the sound effect evokes Anna's absence.[101] The music then obliterates the child's presence, its song of men and angels a token of Julie's loss. This chorus will recur twice more in the film—once beginning with Julie's touch, once in another tactile context symbolizing the maternal. Notably, Julie does not change the words or sounds of this passage in her version of the *Concert[o]*. In the copyist's flat, however, just as she cannot permit the young woman to touch the music, she can barely stand to touch it herself. Up until this moment, music has been silenced by the power of Julie's grief when the TV mysteriously lost its signal, folding up the memento and slamming the piano lid. The bundling and then destruction of the score marks an escalation in the urgency of Julie's actions to free herself of music.

As the score is consumed by the garbage truck a macabre effect is created by the music and sound. The final bar of the choral introduction to the *Concert[o]* is only just audible in the film, subsumed in the mix beneath the effects for the jaws of the truck, which close with a melancholy groan. What one hears, thanks to the interference between voices and sound, is a cluster of voices glissandoing down. The effect was achieved in post-production, according to Preisner, by manually slowing the analogue tape of the music: hence the two choral swoops, the second synced to Julie's sinking shoulders, as if she is breathing out the last breath of the chorus. A metallic whine, heard with the chorus, meshes with the music. It sounds as if the *Concert[o]* has been eaten alive.

One musical detail in the cue has implications for the tonal design of the *Concert[o]* and *Blue*'s score as a whole. When Julie let the piano lid slam, the memento melody was hovering around D major. Here, the cue picks up with the pitches outlined by the outer notes of motif y: F♯ and D. There is thus a sense of continuity between the scenes, although without the third pitch of the D major triad (an A) there is modal ambiguity. Will this music ascend, like an ode to joy, into D major or sink into the doldrums of B minor—and how, in turn, will its harmonic turn speak to Julie's fate and the film's broader symbolism? The final dyad in this cue, C♯-E, could go either way as part of F♯^{7} (the dominant of B minor) or an A major triad (the dominant of D). Here it is blurred, in the opposite of an answer, as the tape is slowed and the jaws close.

It is slightly disappointing to note, in the midst of *Blue*'s musical subtlety, some sloppiness about the score seen in this scene—sloppiness that leads one to question Paulus's blanket assertion, concerning the precision of visual representations of music in *Blue*, that "not a single detail is left to chance."[102] Preisner's is not the musical calligraphy one sees on *Blue*'s diegetic score pages. Kieślowski had asked to use his actual manuscript, but Preisner knew that his musical hand was too small to shoot well. The composer instructed the director to have the production team find, somewhere in Paris, a copyist with a more flamboyant hand. The copyist, Preisner recalls, had worked for the Palais Garnier, and was asked to embellish the music with mistakes and amendments, the latter to appear as if they had then been corrected by a second hand. Unfortunately, the copyist seems to have been a little too liberal with the mistakes. A comparison of page to sound reveals the problem. The music onscreen is somewhat nonsensical: not even the melody line precisely matches the melody heard (compare Fig. 5.2, upper image, and Ex. 5.3—the mistakes are indicated with asterisks). There are indeed lots of "corrections" in the blue hand, but it is hard to believe Julie would have let this draft be passed to a copyist without making considerably more.[103]

Ex. 5.3: Mistakes in choral opening seen in the film

The Lampshade

The scene in which Julie dupes Olivier into sleeping with her—a perverse act of anti-*agapē* which, rather than intensifying their relationship, is intended to reveal to him that she is flawed and thus not to be idolized but instead left alone—contains one of *Blue*'s rare candidates for relatively clear-cut non-diegetic underscoring.[104] A second occurs in the final scene of the film's charting of Julie's process of withdrawal, although as in earlier cues, the contribution of the music to the evocation of Julie's climate overrides considerations of precise narrative location, and the cues could still be subsumed within Stilwell's broadened notion of the meta-diegetic.

At the end of the scene in which Julie moves into her new Paris flat and hangs up her daughter's lampshade, a blackout occurs. Unlike the interruption ellipsis, this is a standard cinematic usage, signifying the passage of time (ensuing events occur an unspecified number of months later) and formally closing the first act of the film. In any film with music, underscoring such a structurally significant scene calls on a composer to deploy appropriate devices. Music can use its medium's own semiotic resources to imply a sense of closure, although not, at this juncture in a film, finality: the story is not yet over, even though a chapter is ending. Certain rhetorical gestures can function across many scoring styles—an ascent in register, a build up in texture and volume, a firm tonal cadence—but in the context of any given film, the precise musical materials used by the composer (the themes, harmonies, orchestrations, rhythms, motifs, topics and so on) carry the potential for further connotations. Preisner's cue for this scene transcends the generic functions of such cue making. Partly, this is because the materials used have already accrued nuanced connotations; partly, it is because Preisner brings structural inventiveness and delicacy to the scene, which is one of the finest musical passages in the trilogy. The cue is all the more remarkable, however, for having been sculpted in post-production to help the scene find its most eloquent expression.[105]

The action of the scene is simple and moving, its symbolism complex and even disturbing. Julie has arrived in Paris and rented an apartment in a block with no children, as she specifies to an estate agent; she has also returned to her maiden name. In this sequence she enters it for the first time. The contrast to her country mansion is obvious. She looks around—the *mise-en-scène* a ruin of emptiness and detritus—locates the brightest room and hangs her daughter's blue light shade, the sole memento (apart from the musical memento) she has saved from the house. She walks around the lampshade, reaches out to touch it and then bows her head into it, bringing her quivering fist and most recent physical wound to her mouth to prevent a descent into tears. Unpacking the contribution of Preisner's cue benefits from a shot-by-shot analysis, as this scene is one of the film's most penetrating analyses of Julie's inner state, with its musical, sonic and temporal ruptures evoking a climate of disjunction and separation that, while intensifying the action to hand, creates a symbolically functional contrast to the musical sequence which closes the film: the *Concert[o]* montage. That grandiose sequence epitomizes continuity and community. The present scene is a quietly harrowing study of fragmentation, entropy and alienation.

Shot 1 (30:26) When Julie enters the flat, the camera looks down on her in a medium shot which then pans to follow her as she walks into the next room. For the remainder of the scene, shots hover more or less at head height, except for a moment when the camera pans up to, and then back away from, the ceiling to follow her pinning up the lamp shade. Two important ideas are thus signified. First, the opening shot suggests the symbolic destination of the scene, i.e., attaching the lampshade to the ceiling; second, it begins to evoke the distance between Julie, on whose perspective the camera focuses for most of the scene, and another location or perspective above or otherwise detached from her. The brief flamboyance of the pan up and down recalls the roadside shot in the opening sequence, which connected the family's members. Here it connotes the absence of two of the family's elements. The music and sound design accent these visual connotations while representing novel ideas of their own.

Certain sounds continue at a low level throughout the scene, establishing a carefully produced *mise-en-bande* to rival the *mise-en-scène*'s desolate mess. Once the door opens—a mundane but effective audio-visual flourish marking the opening of the scene—Julie's footsteps and movements create one stratum of noise. The more symbolic stratum, however, is the muffled background chatter and shuffling which suggests occupied spaces surrounding Julie in her new environment. While hinting at the society outside her walls that will, in the next act, come knocking at her door, the sounds of family life continuing all around Julie, and yet distanced, bring her isolation and its form into focus.[106]

A quiet pedal note, scored low on the clarinet, now emerges. The clarinet pedal establishes both an emotional register—the clarinet often has wistful or sad connotations in Preisner's scores—and a musical register for the scene. This benchmark is important: the music is set to depart through intertwined changes of mood and register.[107] A guitar follows, etching the first phrase of the memento's melody. In a significant departure, this is the first time that this theme has been stated in a key other than B minor. Here it is played in G minor, the key of the faltering funeral march, and thus the tonal region most obviously connected to Julie's loss and past. The guitar and clarinet are interesting scoring choices in this regard. The woodwind instrument was pictured at the funeral, being performed by a young woman, and juxtaposed with shots of Anna's coffin and Julie's stricken response. The guitar's most obvious topical significations, not only in screen scoring cliché, include the angelic or child-like, and pastoral settings stereotypically associated with "feminine" instruments like harps. The cue's opening phrase therefore evokes Julie's perspective but also the presence of Anna in her memory, anticipating the act Julie will shortly carry out: hanging up her memento of her daughter. It is also a notably delicate climate: this passage treats *Blue*'s shattered protagonist with tenderness and respect.

Shot 2 (30:57) The notes of the guitar's first phrase, like the sustained piano notes in previous statements of the theme, hang on in the elongated rests, fading slowly. As so often in Preisner's music, this creates a sense of suspended time and a space for reflection. The vanishing points also articulate a broader division between the cue's musical gestures: the pauses between phrases in this cue make the melody falter more exaggeratedly than any music yet heard in the film. The phrase also ceases, usefully, before the discrete but significant cut to the scene's second shot, which initially frames Julie in a medium-long shot entering her bathroom (diegetic time is disjointed, if perhaps only by a few seconds, from the previous shot) and turning on a light. There is then a contrast in velocity (camera pan speed and Julie's actions) as she suddenly rushes to pick up the cardboard box she was carrying when she entered the flat. The urgency of the gesture contrasts with the more deliberate pacing of the musical flow underpinning this flourish: a slow audio-visual zoom into Julie's state of mind. The two further changes of shot in the scene occur less obtrusively and are smoothed over by music that continues across them. The temporal cut is nonetheless significant. When Julie regards the lampshade's baubles a few seconds later, a further cut will suggest another traumatized fragmentation of her sense of temporality, and thus of the film's.

The next musical phrase continues the statement of the memento on the harp. The continuation of the theme is, however, the least interesting thing about it. Strikingly, the cue has been transposed into a new key (A minor) with no harmonic preparation whatsoever, and while the drama of Preisner's transposition is muted by the pause between the phrases, the key change, in tandem with the faltering silences, intensifies the scene's fragmentation. The mix of the score places the first gui-

Ex. 5.4: Tonal dislocations in the lampshade scene

tar phrase in the left channel, then the second harp phrase to the right, in a manipulation of the stereo image further reflecting the scene's many dislocations (see Ex. 5.4). The music is being atomized, like the lampshade's strands of baubles, and like Julie's dissolving sense of self.

Shot 3 (31:22) The third shot's cut to a medium close-up of Julie calls little attention to itself, the music and action continuing across the edit point. The second phrase of Preisner's cue is also positioned in the edit to cease just as Julie inaugurates the second prominent sonic motif in the scene, which begins when she lifts the blue bauble lampshade out of the cardboard box and then attaches it to the ceiling light. The cue makes space for an important new audio event, accentuating its presence through absence.[108]

The lampshade's sounds are as beguiling as the trinket's multifaceted appearance. The clicks and clacks of its dangling molecules captivate one's attention, drawing one towards their source. Like Julie, one yearns to touch them, which in turn may remind one of what she can no longer touch: Anna, the lampshade's previous owner, but also music. As she hangs it up, clattering frequencies fill a spectrum of sonorities from around the lowest pedal note in the scene to heights of register not yet touched by the music. Once she has hung them, their clattering gradually stills and the band of sound attenuates in an upwardly arcing gesture, until only the higher frequencies remain; the sounds map a journey between low and higher realms. As Julie begins to circle the lampshade, its sounds and beads dissolve one's sense of her presence—the blue circles, in particular, fragment the view of her face—as if she is becoming impermanent. At this precise moment, the final part of Preisner's broken-backed cue begins, a reciprocal sonic space having been created for the score.

The third and fourth phrases of the cue are again transposed a tone upwards, taking the memento theme back to its home key of B minor. The harmonic gesture feels formally satisfying if heard as a précis of musical events thus far in *Blue* occurring at a rhetorically appropriate point. Furthermore, it points towards the music's ultimate destination: the film's final cue, the *Concert[o]*, is steadfastly scored in B minor. The progression from G to B in the first act is thus nested within the film's broader tonal progression to B minor. By attaining the new "height" of B minor, however, the fragments of the harmonic progression have also created a ladder-like structure appropriate to the scene at hand, while furthermore symbolizing a fractured whole: a family of thematic phrases, divided into three, and pulling apart from one another. The scoring of the theme has also shifted from harp back to the similar, but more warmly intimate, sound of the acoustic guitar. Such sonorities will mark other significant points in the structure of the trilogy.

Shot 4 (32:04-22) Guitar notes and bead sounds sustain over the final change of shot, which cuts to a close-up of Julie's face, taken from her right-hand side—the half that falls in darkness. Again, the cut breaches a strictly linear temporal succession. On repeated viewings, one begins to wonder just how long she has been standing next to the lampshade, trying to muster the courage to touch it. The room, for instance, now seems darker: has she been standing there all day? Where the beads once fragmented one's view of Julie, blue reflections now form specters on her face. She seems on the brink of dissolution—of turning into light, or even music. The cut also brings the potentially rhapsodic nature of the cue—the arch of the memento melody, accentuated by the cue's transpositions—back down to earth. The memento melody's final phrase closes with the resignation of motif x; here, this seems mimetically to anticipate a bow to come from Julie, as her actions merge with the scene's sonorous content.[109]

First, Julie reaches out to touch the crystalline tears of the lampshade, their more occasional clicking recalling the sounds in her hospital room as she watched the funeral on television and tried not to cry. She touches a strand, but only barely. Close-ups of hands are a recurring symbol in Kieślowski's films and tend to have special significance. One recalls, when one sees Julie's hand here, her horrific act of self-harm in a prior scene; one may also recall the touch of the copyist on the opening of the *Concert[o]*, or her daughter's hand holding a sweet wrapper. Julie's touch in this scene of such an iconic item—her memento of Anna, underscored with her musical memento of Patrice—continues an association between the physical touching of *Blue*'s music and shards of her grief. Here, the tactility of the moment is emphasized by the clarinet's highest pedal note, which seems to be called into existence by her action; its registral transfer, moving octaves higher than the first two clarinet pitches, also completes the scene's gesture of ascent. Julie takes her hand away and makes a shivering fist; she brings the fist to her lips and then bows her head, sinking it into the beads.

Blue has fully exposed Julie's shattered subjectivity. She stands alone with her grief, in a dark and empty flat, and with only two small mementos of her past to remind her of her former life and identity. When Julie's fist comes up to her lips, it seems designed to stifle a wider convulsion of the body; instead, the clicking of the beads cries for her, like the old servant back at the mansion. Again, Binoche plays Julie as struggling both to control and close down the possibility of catharsis. Her forehead bowing into the beads, in turn, creates a subtle audio flourish: a symmetrical bookend to the opening door at the start of the scene, here merging with the close of Preisner's cue. At this moment, Kickasola notes, "one feels Julie has hit some emotional seafloor after floating aimlessly for some time."[110] This is not merely an affect of the story. Image, sound and music have merged, bringing the film to a halt. Julie's bow parallels the descent of motif x and the cue's arrival on the tonic, which (in spite of the modulations) evokes the sense of something coming to rest, although not (because of the modulations) reaching a point of closure. Julie has reached the nadir of her bereavement. When light returns after the fadeout at the end of the scene, the film begins to document the next phase of her grief.

Part II: Restoration

Interludes with a Busker

The next door to open in *Blue* is the entrance to a café in Julie's new neighborhood. One is led to surmise (the waiter knows her usual) that she has become a regular. The fade out and dialogue denote that time has passed. Quite some time, one later learns—at least three months. Like the fade out, Julie has been passing time in a new period of isolation. On the day the film catches up with her, however, something changes. She hears music again.

Žižek argues that *Blue* is a "double-life" film, with Julie creating an alternative life after the accident—a canny observation, not least because it echoes the structural similarities between *Blue* and *Véronique* (each begins with a section about half the length of the bulk of the film to follow).[111] However, the story told here is perhaps more like Witek's in *Blind Chance* than Weronika's second chance in *Véronique*, as Julie's tale has a three-part structure: Julie's withdrawal, her period of restorative isolation, and then a period of re-engagement with her community and loss, although the division between the second and third section is a subtle boundary. The reappearance of music in her life, in the form of a busker's soprano recorder melodies, participates in her restoration and sets in motion events that will lead from her self-enforced quarantine to re-engagement.

There are three scenes in the second part of the film during which Julie hears the busker's music; she interacts with him further on a fourth occasion. These scenes have various narrative, symbolic and musical themes to present, the most important being the contribution of music to Julie's rebuilding inner strength during her grief's dormant period. One sees several representations, in the busker scenes, of Julie undergoing ad hoc music therapy. Most importantly, her fragmented life begins to regain a sense of "flow" as she experiences his melodies.

Coffee, Ice Cream, and Syrup

As Julie pours coffee onto her ice cream and begins to eat, she hears the busker's music for the first time.[112] The busker, playing a white soprano recorder, is performing on the street outside. An annotation of the music (see Ex. 5.5[i]) does little to evoke its most captivating qualities: a piercing sonority and significations of intense expressivity. The recorder's timbre is somewhat arresting. The lines of the soprano recorder, played here (as both musician and actor) with grace by Ostaszewski, become arrows penetrating Julie's inner sanctuary. The instrument's color, white, may signify equality. This sound will connect deeply to Julie. In a sense, she will become it.

Ex. 5.5 (i-iii): The busker's three recorder themes

As Julie becomes entranced by her Pied Piper, the sounds of the café and street outside fade out on the soundtrack; simultaneously the recording of the busker becomes wet with studio reverb.[113] Again, one experiences her subjective zone of audition, and while she does not black out, a peculiar lighting effect further suggests her subjective perspective. Shadows disappear and reappear around her coffee cup, as if the sun is passing, in time-lapsed motion, behind a cloud. While rhyming with the temporal shifts of the interrupting ellipses, and other grief-related fragmentations of both Julie and the film's experience of time, this is not the same kind of experience for Julie or, for that matter, *Blue*'s audio-viewers. It is smoother, less disruptive, more beguiling.

Unlike all of the music thus far in *Blue*, the busker's tune flows and does not falter. The melody's rhythm and phrasing are regular, with each phrase rolled out in a single breath and series of slurred *legato* lines. Neither in terms of meter or phrasing, in other words, does this music suggest fragmentation. Quite the opposite: it is music which, for the first time in *Blue*, offers to heal the ruptures of the discourse and soundtrack. Note how Julie nods her head, unselfconsciously, to the stream of melody. Julie is allowing her sense of self-control to wane and her subjectivity to seep into the materiality of the music; in later scenes in the screenplay removed from the film, she practically dances to the busker's playing.[114] She is starting to "flow."

Achieving a sense of "flow"—a stream-like rhythm to one's everyday activities related to one's immersion therein—has been proposed as essential to an individual's sense of well-being. Psychologist Mihály Csíkszentmihályi first described "flow" in the 1970s, in relation to his observation of work by a group of artists. He sought to theorize what the artists found so satisfactory about immersing themselves so intensely in the completion of canvases which, once finished, they had no expectation of selling or particular affection towards. Rejecting sublimation or the achievement of extrinsic goals as the artists' motivation, Csíkszentmihályi theorized some kind of intrinsic incentive: the activity of painting must itself be rewarding *qua* activity.[115]

It is striking to compare Julie's periods of musical immersion in *Blue* to factors Csíkszentmihályi has theorized as marking the experience of flow: concentration, a loss of self-consciousness, awareness narrowing down to the activity itself, distortion to one's subjective experience of time, a lack of awareness of bodily needs, effortlessness. Across the different rhythmic levels of Julie's life at this stage of her grieving—such as the macrorhythm of repeatedly visiting the same café for coffee and ice cream, where she hears the microrhythms of the busker's music—she can be seen and heard listening to music to experience the healing sensations of continuity, immersion and control associated with "flow." Listening, period, may be challenging enough at this moment. By the end of *Blue*, however, she will be editing and composing but still represented as if experiencing "flow," and thus undergoing musical experiences in marked contrast to the invasions of her self that mark her grief's more violent intrusions and its rupturing of her sense of time. Regarding Julie's musical destination, one might also note that this busker melody has obvious links with tunes already heard in *Blue* and soon to be heard again. Most obviously, it contains multiple versions of motifs x and y. One could almost consider it an improvisatory variation on the film's Van den Budenmayer themes—the kind of link between the busker's music and Julie's wider musical climate that she will recognize in a subsequent scene.[116]

The music is unabashedly sentimental and almost syrupy in its pouring forth of markers of expressivity. Pejoratively to dismiss its musical content for this reason, however, would be to miss its point. The busker's music *has* to be a cliché of heightened Romantic expressivity at this stage in *Blue*, and thus of that period's heights of display, emotionality and virtuosity—and, above all, self-aware individualism—as this is music that has to signify music entangling with, and refilling, Julie's hollowed-out subjectivity. Yet the cliché of such music in turn "taking one outside of oneself" may be even more significant. The music engineers changes to Julie's self, but it is permitted to do so precisely because, for Julie, it offers a means of transcendence.

The recorder and material that the busker performs are, in these senses, apt choices. First, there is the penetrating sound. A soprano recorder gets inside one's head, quite literally, making the resonant skull cavities hum in sympathy. This is aided in *Blue* by the mix: the overdubbed recorder is artificially prominent in the mix, as if to suggest Julie's concentration on its sound. Second, it is one of the most voice-like of all musical instruments, its tone production rising and falling with the breath of the player. The result is a vibrato-laden sonority. Vibrato is a signifier of intensified emotion usually excised by Preisner from performances under his supervision, but not here. The melody sounds like a poignant ballad, its lilting § connoting the rustic or pastoral and so a feminine topic, matching the obvious connotations of the soprano recorder's high and "weak" woodwind timbre. The screenplay calls for its sound to be produced "thinly."

The film is wrenched out of this idyll by a hard cut from the café's muted browns and yellows to a long shot of Julie diving into a deep blue swimming pool—the first glimpse of the film's most memorable visual symbol—and by the slash of Julie's elegant dive. The color contrast is notable: the café is shot with the warmer, orangey tones held back in the trilogy for moments of transcendence, joy and revelation. The wrench of the cut to the film's more familiar blue-toned palette is not quite as jarring as some other cuts. Here, although it cuts across the 8-bar hypermeter of the cue's phrasing and interrupts an expected fourth phrase, Julie's arcing dive almost feels like the next phrase of the busker's melody, so elegant is the timing of the cut. In the scene where Julie begins to experience healing "flow," the rhythm of the editing also becomes more lyrical.[117]

Bliss

Responding to a scene in *Véronique* where Weronika's double comes to rest in a sliver of sunlight, Kickasola suggests that "[m]oments like these are critical in Kieślowski's films because they function without words but exude an extraordinary phenomenological impact: we *feel* the warmth and sympathize with her inner state and need for respite."[118] The Kieślowski music-films, as noted already in the present analysis, contain pivotal moments in which Preisner's music or the sound design are deployed to push audio-viewers into the experiential realm. In *Blue*, many of these moments are startling shocks. When Julie, echoing the scene in *Véronique*, experiences a moment of blissed-out plenitude as she listens to the busker while basking in a sunny park, the phenomenological counterbalancing of *Blue*'s more anguished moments entices one to relax with her and enjoy this brief but telling liberation.

In addition to the sunshine, Julie basks in musical warmth. The moment of bliss occurs as, ostensibly, she listens to the busker. The scene's representation of the mesmerizing effect of music on Julie as she begins to "flow" evokes a statement by Henri Bergson: "A melody to which we listen with our eyes closed, heeding it alone, comes very close to coinciding with this time which is the very fluidity of our inner life."[119] In turn, this may remind one of Kieślowski: "It's a saying as old as the world—freedom lies within. It's true."[120] If Julie has been healing internally through her repetitively rhythmic regime of simple pleasures—coffee and ice cream, swimming (another kind of "flow"), listening—then her moment in the sun marks the pinnacle of the restorative period of her grieving; as her doctor tells her in a nearby scene, she is clearly in good "spirits." But is she only *listening* to this music?

Most critical responses to this scene fixate on the old lady and the bottle bank, reading Julie's ignorance of that struggle—a recurring motif in all three films, each time eliciting a revealing response from the central protagonist—as a sign of self-absorption.[121] In what, however, is Julie so immersed that she does not notice the struggling old lady? One could argue the case that she is not listening to the busker but *composing* the music one hears, and that she is enraptured by her own musical thoughts. Any creative musician knows this kind of "flow": one's mind and inner ear become so engaged with "hearing" a new musical idea that one fails to hear what someone real is saying. The busker is not seen during this scene: one only hears what one at first assumes to be his diegetic music-making. He could indeed be "present," outside of the frame. Yet given music's "side-by-side" liberty in the film, Julie could also be imagining—and thus composing—the music that she hears. If she *is* creating the music, this scene is an indication of the role that making music will play in her final phase of grief-work: re-engaging with the traces, musical and otherwise, of her loss.[122]

The screenplay is revealing here. Julie is in a trance, it says, and does not notice the old lady. That much one also learns from the film. However, the screenplay states that, "Perhaps she wants to hear the music which sometimes resounds in her thoughts, but this time there is complete silence."[123] Obviously a decision was made during the filmmaking *not* to have silence and instead to overdub the busker onto the soundtrack. One could still choose to hear this as non-diegetic music, as Paulus seems to ("now it is in the background and not diegetic music")[124] or imagine the busker to be "off" but diegetic. The idea that the music is *inside* Julie, though, is the more intriguing possibility and the careful treatment of sound in the mix may support this reading. While the noises in the park, including children playing, are treated naturalistically, the busker's music is treated with the same reverb as the effect signifying its shift from "natural" diegetic sound to Julie's subjective zone-of-audition during the previous busking scene.

That Julie's state of mind in this scene is different from its grief-stricken status during the musical blackouts is signaled by the dazzling whiteouts which form bridges within the montage juxtaposing shots of Julie and the old lady. This image could be explained, prosaically, as diegetic light flaring from the bottle bank or another reflective surface, or more intriguingly as a non-diegetic symbol of Julie's blindness to the fate of others, but one might also consider its structural implications as the diametric opposite to Julie's blackouts. In the dark ellipses, music rips into Julie's mind, violating her sanctuary with the return of the repressed. In the whiteouts, if one accepts that she may be the source of the music one hears, the music is at her beck and call, expressing emotions of which she needs to speak, and perhaps performing delicate psychological surgery.[125]

In this respect, it is useful to consider the detail of the music. The cue seems to start in mid-phrase (see Ex. 5.5[ii]), as if one is catching up with Julie mid-thought, but crucially it reaches a point of closure. As Julie basks and heals, the music—unusually for *Blue*—is permitted to reach a point of cadence, and thus to form a neat parallel to her restful state of mind. The cue is melancholy and scored in the memento's key of B minor, and it carries most of the previous busking scene's expressive markers into this new theme. However, it has a piquant chromatic twist suggesting a lighter-hearted mood: Preisner's favored $\hat{5}$-$\flat\hat{6}$-$\hat{5}$ turn (see motif z as marked in Ex. 5.2).[126] There is also a moment of harmonic arrival in D (via motif y) and, while the melody does not settle there and eventually cadences in B minor, there is a brief sense of transcendence.

Julie has far to travel. The golden light is the trilogy's color coding of positive occurrences, but it also makes visible the fading scar on her left eye—a subtle piece of makeup highlighted by the warm tones, and reminding one that, while she may be engaging in flowing and restorative grief-work, Julie is nowhere near fully recovered physically, let alone psychologically. Like the old lady's bottle, wedged half in and half out of the bottle-bank, or the modal mix of the melody, Julie is in between states. Now she needs to oscillate.

Meeting the Busker, Avoiding Olivier

In the third busker scene, Julie expresses concern when she comes across him lying unconscious on the sidewalk. "Are you sick?" she asks, sliding his recorder case towards him. He embraces it and rests his head upon it, muttering that everyone has got to hold on to something. The fortune-cookie wisdom seems to suggest a way Julie could move forward in her grief. That he is literally holding on to a musical source could, in turn, be read to imply that she too must hold on to music, and in doing so retain contact with aspects of her past.[127] That past is about to contact her in the fourth and final interlude.

Olivier has tracked Julie down. He discovers her in the café, staring at her own reflection in the back of a metronomically ticking spoon; the camera shows her face mirrored in its flowing beat. She does her best to appear displeased, perhaps hiding a smile behind her glass. An arrival outside the café breaks the tension: the busker is dropped off and kissed on the cheek by a woman in a chauffeur-driven car.[128] When he then begins to play, the barrier between Julie and Olivier, once so carefully patrolled by Julie, is bridged by a musical matter. Do you hear what he's playing? she asks Olivier. It sounds like . . ., he replies. She concurs. The melody may remind one of the Van den Budenmayer memento[129]; Julie and Olivier recognize the allusion (see Ex. 5.5[iii]).[130] What Olivier could not recognize, though, at least at this moment in the story, is that the memento is destined to be part of the *Concert[o]*. Only Julie knows about this. Furthermore, it is important to recognize that the busker is not playing the memento, nor part of the *Concert[o]*: this is a new theme. In time, Julie will absorb this busker melody into her version of the *Concert[o]*.

Recognizing the lack of a precise relationship between the busker's tune and other elements of the score matters because of a relatively offhand comment by Kieślowski which has been the cause of some controversy in the literature.[131] "Music notes exist, waiting for someone to order them," stated Kieślowski regarding this scene: "That two individuals in different places can think of the same music is an example of what unites people."[132] It can, of course, be true that more than one person can come up with strikingly similar ideas at the same time. An assistant on *Véronique* was convinced, for instance, that its Concerto was based on Carl Orff's *Carmina Burana*; at the time, Preisner had never heard of Orff's score. No person could come up with precisely the same symphony as another, but an overlap of melodic motif is more than a mere possibility: it is common. The key to grasping the significance of this scene in *Blue*, however, may be the final part of Kieślowski's statement, i.e., "what unites people." The musical similarity, like Julie's eventual borrowing of the busker's tune, is a gesture of communion heard at the point in the film where her self-imposed isolation has been decisively breached. Events now in motion will force her proactive reengagement with music and society.

Julie interrupts the busker to ask him how he knows the music. I invent lots of things, he tells her: I like to play. Within the world of *Blue*'s side-by-side scoring, of course, it makes perfect sense that a busker on the street has access to the musical climate of the film.[133] That the music heard in the scene might be lodged in the fantastical gap between literal diegesis and Julie's metaphysical climate is suggested by a nuance in the sequence. The cue plays continuously as, presumably, Olivier exits and Julie, famously, holds the corner of a sugar cube to the surface of her coffee; the white of the cube is contaminated by the black drink.[134] The continuity of the music, however, does not entirely mask a disruption in the action, which cuts between Julie dunking the cube and dropping to her knees to ask her question. As the sequence cuts from her conversation with Olivier to the sugar cube, and then again to her interrogation of the busker, the melody begins, dry of reverb, then accrues it, and then becomes dry again. Its status is in flux. Perhaps what really irks Julie, then, is that the busker has invaded, and stolen from, the film's climatic representation of her inner musical life.

Interruptions and Ellipses

Moments in *Blue* where Julie exerts control over music gradually exceed moments when music controls her. Pushing her into this loss-oriented grief-work are two more interruptions and three more ellipses. Her reactions to these "compromise formations" chart her progress towards her re-engagement with her loss, which is achieved, in part, by deciphering the "associative significance" of *Blue*'s musical disturbances.

Interruption No. 2: Dreaming of Music

Blue's second interruption consists of two sonic events. One is a brutal incursion, the other a playful reverie. Julie is awakened by sounds of violence. A man is being assaulted on the street and flees into her apartment building's stairwell to escape his assailants. Clattering up Julie's stairs, ringing doorbells, hammering on doors, the man is the sound of society's orchestra calling for a soloist's attention. As the percussive blows get louder, Julie becomes visibly terrified; her face, bathed in blue light reflected from the lampshade, reminds one that her terror is not merely of the unfurling event. When the man finally hammers on Julie's door, the soundtrack splinters—the sound seems purposefully distorted—as the barrier between Julie's sanctuary and the exterior world disintegrates. Orr argues "[t]his is mindscreen as soundscreen," with the "ear-splitting" noise of the hammering "evoking the paradox of an unbearable closeness to the immediacy of things."[135] Julie's response—she refuses him entry, condemning him to a beating or worse—therefore represents more than self-preservation. To let him in would be to let it *all* back in. The severity of her mental state is symbolized by the sin of her inaction.

The suspense continues as Julie creeps out into the stairwell, asks if anyone is there, and gets locked out of her apartment. A light timer clicking off, a window banging, and her front door slamming in the draft create diminishing aftershocks, before Julie sits on her stairs, at first observing the comings and goings on the landing below, as her neighbor Lucille receives a furtive male visitor. Julie then nods off to sleep. As she drifts off, music and blue lights seem to nudge Julie awake; eventually she settles and appears to be dreaming of music. A doorway has been opened after all.

What one hears is the memento theme, now scored for pizzicato strings and a wordlessly murmuring chorus—alto, tenor and basses, so a somewhat masculine timbre—performing the melody in unison octaves. Perhaps, as in her previous life, Julie is taking a fragment of Patrice's music and elaborating it. What is fascinating here is that she appears to be doing this literally unconsciously. Is this merely an irrepressible urge to create returning to its former strength as she experiences her gradual restoration? The music's symbol of a unisonant community—people performing the same tune in unison—beckons playfully. It is an enticement from an ensemble to a soloist: come out and play. Julie's consciousness, as she stirs and tries to catch the fading melody, cannot quite join in the game. Tellingly, however, this precise music will appear at a pivotal moment in her version of the *Concert[o]*. Julie is dreaming of music she will commit to paper at the climax of her grief-work.

The link between the music and Julie's need to reconnect to her loss is connoted visually by the play of blue flecks of light. Previously, similar flecks have reflected off her daughter's lampshade; here, the lights dancing across her face, as the music sounds, have no obvious diegetic source. Like the music, however, the lights disappear when she opens her eyes, returning as she drifts off again. Following Evans, one might see and hear these uncanny additions as evidence of injury-induced synaesthesia—now less extreme, as Julie recovers, than its occurrence in the first interruption. The precise nature of the music and light, however, are key. These are not just any manifestations, but symbols of her husband and daughter, expressed in a community of lights and voices. A stinging doorbell and dropped flowerpot, at the startling cut to the next scene, then interrupt the interruption, echoing the car crash as if to remind one of the distance Julie must still travel.

Ellipsis No. 2 and Interruption No. 3: The Hitcher and the Pool

The second ellipsis and third interruption occur in consecutive scenes. Because the interruption is a response to the events that trigger the preceding blackout, it is productive to consider them together.

Ellipsis No. 2 occurs in the scene when the hitchhiker, Antoine, returns Julie's crucifix necklace; he explains that he witnessed the aftermath of the crash and offers to tell her what he saw. No, she says, definitively, just before the screen blacks out and the robust string and brass version of the faltering funeral march, last heard during the first ellipsis and interruption, invades again. Temporality warps once more for Julie, and for audio-viewers cinematic time bends, as the motif of the blackout provides a cinematic flashback to the first ellipsis. Has the action gone back to square one? Julie is stronger here, however, and only the first two phrases of the invasion cue are heard—the masculine blast and, after a reverb-soaked pause, the feminine lament. Julie seems able to call time on this invasion.

This is a slightly different take of the cue.[136] The more significant sonic evolution, however, is that within the void of the blackout—a space previously evacuated of all sight *and* non-musical sound—something other than music is heard. A haunting wind effect, similar to the one noted in the build up to the slamming piano lid, has been present in the background of Antoine and Julie's conversation, chilling perceptions of the scene with a wintry *mise-en-bande* to match the dark *mise-en-scène*, as if Antoine has brought the weather of that terrible day with him to the restaurant. That it continues during the ellipsis, however, calls one's attention to it, not least by its contrast to the previous ellipsis. The vast space evoked sonically recalls the desolate farmland of the crash site, now haunted by the funeral march—a hell repressed within Julie, filled with ghosts she does not wish to confront, even as events beyond her control conspire to lead her towards a confrontation. After the blackout, as Julie laughs heartily at the memory of the joke Patrice was telling just before the crash, she seems successfully to have repressed these symbols of her loss by exercising control over her sonic climate and cutting the ellipsis short. The film then cuts to Julie in her sanctuary: the extraordinarily blue swimming pool in which she bathes, usually at night and, with one startling exception, entirely on her own. That sanctuary, though, is about to be invaded by music, the content of which suggests that, while her control over music is growing stronger, she is as yet far from dominant.

Blue's pool is an extraordinary space and symbol, especially as lit and shot here.[137] The pool was Idziak's idea. In another example of the co-working ethos, the original idea (that Julie would jog) was changed to furnish the film with a symbol of life's thin borderline with death, and thus the dead, whenever Julie swims across its membrane. Kickasola notes that, when Julie hovers under water in a fetal position at the end of the interruption scene, looking both animate and inanimate as her black hair forms wraiths around her still and pale body, Julie "hovers in this liminal state between life and death"[138]; for Kehr, similarly, it is a "tomblike" space into which Julie dives "to wear herself out and neutralize her senses."[139] Hundreds of mostly blue doors on the levels of the swimming baths above the pool (presumably changing rooms) suggest burial chambers or doors in her mind that she wishes to keep closed, as yet, to maintain her increasingly fragile sense of isolation. Is *Blue* referencing Bluebeard?[140] Interrupting music is about to unlock another door in Julie's mind.

The "flow" of Julie's swim—undertaken, perhaps, to soothe memories stirred by Antoine and the ellipsis—is broken when, as she begins to lift herself out of the pool, Preisner's most complex cue thus far in the score begins. At the start of this processional variation on the Van den Budenmayer themes, the faltering funeral march interrupts Julie again. Immediately, however, that theme itself is interrupted by the opening phrase of the memento theme and thus by the closest thing the score has to a projection of Julie's will. The cue is in B minor, the tonality of most of the second part of the film, and here absorbing the G minor funeral march into the memento's home key. By interrupting the funeral march in this way, Julie's unconscious could be heard to be wresting control of this icon of suffering through an act of compositional development. Indeed, this cue is the first piece of clear musical development in the entire score. Up until now, development has been limited to re-orchestrations and—perhaps—motivic variations on the Van den Budenmayer themes performed by the busker. Here, however, two separate and, in both symbolic and musical senses, opposed themes are brought into conflict. The themes have obvious connections—both, of course, are funereal—but it is their differences here which create the force of the moment and suggest the more intriguing ramifications.

First, if one accepts that Julie's mind is the source of this music, here is a sign that she is a composer capable of producing innovations of her own, rather than just clearing up someone else's mistakes. The cue is orchestrated with a wind and brass section vying against the strings, the lushness of the latter orchestration a contrast to brittle reminders of the funeral. Second, while one only hears one- or two-bar snatches of the faltering funeral march, entire phrases of the memento are sounded. That these memento phrases are in $\frac{4}{4}$, not $\frac{2}{4}$, means that this theme—music with a future in her life, unlike the token of her past—dominate the moment. Third, the memento theme is no longer faltering on the extra beat of its $\frac{5}{4}$ origins: it is achieving its own sense of flow and becoming stronger, i.e., more directed, than its opposite. Fourth, the faltering in the funeral march—spaces where its rhetorical interrogation of Julie hitherto remained unanswered, except by the wind—are now filled in, expanded even, by the answer of the memento material. In many ways, the cue suggests a subtle shift in the balance of musical power.[141]

Ellipsis No. 3: The Concert[o] and the Mice

Julie has again been swimming vigorously in the pool when she experiences the film's third ellipsis. This is her daytime swim—a notable shift, as she is clearly more at risk of meeting other people—but a necessary one. Julie's need to restore "flow" to her life is especially strong here, due to the terrifying discovery of mice living in her flat. This sounds faintly ridiculous on the page, but it not at all foolish in the film, given the symbolic resonance of the mice and Julie's brutal response to their presence, the symbolism of which is revealed by music's deployment in the sequence's deft montage.

Julie has discovered a female mouse and its litter in her larder.[142] So disturbed is Julie by this discovery that she initially plans to leave the flat entirely—leaving it to the mice, in effect, in a gift foreshadowing the family home she will shortly offer to her husband's mistress and her offspring. Remembering a neighbor's take-no-prisoners ginger tomcat, however, she decides to set it loose on the rodents. At the swimming pool, she swims to distract herself from the complicated guilt generated by this undertaking. The mice, of course, are another invasion of her isolation, but one that is freighted with further significance: a mother who has lost her infant is confronted with a mother blessed with many.[143] The invading mice represent everything Julie is trying to forget, or at least hold at a safe distance, in her new life. Like the copyist's score, the blue lollipop, the mansion and Olivier, the mice must therefore be purged.

That the mice are reminders of Julie's daughter and lost motherhood is implied by Preisner's cue and its relationship to other moments in the film. The mouse-killing sequence is juxtaposed in a montage with

Olivier taking delivery of a copy of the *Concert[o]* score.[144] He carries
it to the piano (like the mouse moving its offspring) and plays the opening chorus—the cue heard previously, in its full choral version, when
the copyist touched the score. First he plays just the upper voice; at the
second phrase he also adds a harmonizing line. What one hears is considerably changed from Preisner's original cue for this scene. The
changes, in part, speed up the sequence: the rests between phrases are
shortened and the final phrase is cut. The cut and Olivier beginning
only with the upper line removes some of the modal ambiguity of the
chorus, accentuating its shades of D major. The gentle playing, stripped
of the cue's strength by withholding the harmonization and omitting the
octave doublings, then contributes to the delicacy of the music when it
switches, at the cut, to accompanying the maternal mouse, lit blue and
scurrying around her brood.

The disturbing meaning, for Julie, of the copyist's touch—of this
music, about this subject, composed at that particular time in Julie,
Patrice and Anna's lives—now becomes clearer. As the music continues, the female mouse touches her babies; she is picking up her litter,
one by one, and transferring them, futilely, to a safer hiding place. As
the ambience of Olivier's room cuts to the cramped space of the larder,
post-production squeaks emulating the mother and her litter are heard.
When the copyist touched the score, with the sound of a child playing
in the background, it must have felt to Julie like a double defilement.
This music about angels, stained in Julie's love for Anna, brings home
the desperation of her actions.

In the swimming pool, therefore, when Lucille—who has seen
Julie frantically running down the street and followed her—asks if she
is crying, Julie is unsurprisingly plunged into another ellipsis (the same
two phrases as Ellipsis No. 2). Julie is crying, but her tears are hidden
by the water. Lucille, a stand-in daughter of sorts for Julie,[145] is not
fooled, especially on seeing Julie's look of bewildered angst when the
disruption ends. The perceiver should not be fooled either. Not only is
Julie sobbing falteringly as Lucille hugs her, the music has almost answered Lucille's question. The returning funeral march informs one that
Julie had to kill the mice because their life was linked, in her mind, to
the absence of her own offspring. In a simple act demonstrating reciprocity and thus *agapē*,[146] Lucille offers to clean up the mess before Julie
goes home.

Ellipsis No. 4: The Sex Club

The setup for the final ellipsis involves Julie's visit to Lucille's place of
work: a sex club. Having cleared up "the mess" after the mice, she calls
on Julie to return the favor. Lucille's father is in the audience at the club
with Lucille due on stage (talk about the return of the repressed). He
leaves just before she is due to perform, but she is understandably
shaken. When Julie enters the club, she enters a realm of loud music,
carnal moaning, and the contrast of darkness and neon. The music for

this scene, Preisner felt, required a different voice from the climate of the film thus far, so his assistant on the film, Philippe Cohen Solal (later of Gotan Project), created a pair of cues suggesting a DJ set. The first piece structures one's immediate perceptions of this cavernous hell, thanks to its distortion and thudding reverberation. Everything else about the music seems tainted, style topically, with markers of down-at-heel sexual objectification: the cheesy organ, hard electronic beats, gruff male vocal samples, and slapping bass.[147] The seediness of the scene runs deep, however, relating not merely to Lucille's father and the club's other customers, but also to Patrice.

In the midst of the seediness an important, and positive, visual event occurs: a pan back and forth between the two women in medium close-up. The move evokes the shot at the start of the film linking Anna to Julie and her father. In the club, the move reinforces the film's connotations that Lucille—who has an almost infantile fascination with bodily functions and the realm of the senses—is becoming a surrogate daughter to Julie. The camera motif is a sign of relationships in the trilogy, its visual grammar alluding to something metaphysical that cannot be shown, i.e., an interpersonal bond. In this place of dismal penetrations, Julie's isolation is breached for the better. In a neat parallel, the pan ends by uniting Lucille and Julie within the frame, with two further women glimpsed performing on stage between their faces. The sex performers' act of feigned intimacy contrasts sharply with the revelation of Lucille and Julie's connection—a connection forged through their reciprocal acts of *agapē*.

At this moment, the diegetic music changes because the performance on stage finishes. A less ominous piece of electronica begins. The B major of the initial porno-style music is replaced by F♯ major. A new tonal realm—although, as the dominant key of B, hardly a leap away—is thus opened for the film as Julie enters a phase of revelation. This music still upholsters the club's domain of sexist masculine fantasy. A seedy sax oozes clichés, a string pad intimates an entry into the realm of the fantastical,[148] but the music is also more melodic and, overall, less fierce. The Hammond organ, for example, now carries melodic fragments rather than just stabbing chords. This may reflect the shift in focus to Lucille and Julie's relationship; it also articulates the film's shift in focus to Julie's story.

As the music changes Lucille points out to Julie that she is on TV.[149] If you pay you get to peep, Lucille said earlier; now Julie gets to peep into her husband's seedy past as her world and identity threaten to fragment anew. The program shows Olivier examining sketches for the *Concert[o]* with the investigative reporter who harangued Julie earlier in the film; stills of Julie are glimpsed, including the exploitative photo taken in the hospital after the first ellipsis. The broadcast's discussion reveals that the *Concert[o]* was to be played just once, and simultaneously, in twelve European cities on the night of European Unification. Incidentally, the Concert/Concerto confusion in *Blue*'s literature appears to emanate from this scene, for which the screenplay specified no dialogue and which the co-workers presumably developed together at a later stage in production. Olivier calls the piece a concerto, not a concert, twice.[150]

In swift succession, Julie is then dealt two severe blows. One, a copy of the *Concert[o]* exists and Olivier is going to complete it; the threat of another person literally getting their hands on this music will by now be obvious. Two, she sees pictures of Patrice and his mistress slipping from a blue folder she once refused to take from Olivier. At a stroke, her mental mementos of Patrice begin to rewrite themselves, suggesting an alternative narrative of which she was hitherto unaware. As the voiceover lauds a great man, the pictures reveal a liar and a cheat. The camera zooms in, as Julie peeps closer and the ambient sounds of the sex club fade back up in the mix. The sax unleashes an ejaculatory climax: an ironic parallel to Julie's moment of recognition, in the grimly fitting surroundings of a sex club, regarding her husband's sexual infidelity.

After eliciting a confession from the copyist—you should not destroy something so beautiful, the copyist chides the widow—Julie tracks Olivier down. Olivier, in turn, lures her back to his flat: If only I could play it to you, he suggests, his pianist's fingers caressing his imagining of the music. He wants her to listen to what he has done thus far with the *Concert[o]* (a sequence discussed below),[151] but quickly professes that his primary reason for offering to finish the piece was to make Julie do something in response. Conversation turns to the photos of the mistress and Julie discovers how to find her. What are you going to do, asks Olivier off-camera, the shot fixed on Julie in medium close-up. Thus begins the oddest of the four ellipses. The blackout briefly immerses Julie in the funeral march and its symbols of her grief. Unlike the previous ellipses, however, when the image track fades in again after just one phrase of music—Julie stopping it even quicker than before—she is smiling. The past, it appears, no longer exercises a hold on her: it has changed shape, after all, and in a sense liberated her further from its ties. The brevity of the ellipsis and smile indicate, above all, that she is stronger.[152] Her period of consolation and restoration has been profitable.

The ellipsis at Olivier's apartment is the last one hears in *Blue* of the faltering funeral march. From this moment on, the memento theme and B minor are in the ascendancy. Julie's re-engagement with the world and her past will be mediated through musical activity exploring those tonal and musical realms, as her creativity blooms, uninhibited for the very first time, and her grieving enters its loss-orientated phase. This is therefore also the last time one hears Preisner's allusion to "Holy God" in *Blue*. Kieślowski's love-hate relationship with his homeland took an interesting turn towards the end of his career, as documented in Chapter Three. The director wanted increasingly to make films that were not weighed down by an iconography of Polish history and symbols. Is this musical point of abandonment a small symbol of that shift, akin to the fun the co-workers had with other Polish icons in

White? Or does the disappearance of "Holy God" instead clarify their position on organized religion? Alongside a text scrupulously edited to remove specific references to Christian iconography, the *Concert[o]* is dominated by the secular Van den Budenmayer memento, as opposed to a Van den Budenmayer theme draped in Polish religious and cultural iconography (including its connection to *No End*). Most significantly, however, the thematic substitution parallels Julie's progression. Memento supplants funeral march; an active engagement with memory, however painful, replaces repression of grief. As Julie enters a wider community of past and present reference points, the soundtrack abandons its most distinctive musical link to Poland, instead embracing a theme forming part of a fictional European anthem. Isolation segues to community. Yet as positive as this may seem for Julie, the memento remains a funeral march. One song of mourning replaces another. As she liberates herself from the worst of her grief, the loss of alternative freedoms must be mourned.

Part III: Lost and Found

The Composing Scene

Three versions of Olivier's take on the *Concert[o]* are heard in *Blue*. Julie's reactions to the music—shifting from indifference to action and finally immersion—chart the pendulum of her grieving as it swings decisively into loss-oriented work and, with it, away from the liberties of her time of restoration and back towards social convention. Julie's first visit to Olivier's flat, during which she interrogates him about the mistress and experiences the final ellipsis, begins with the opening notes of his sketch for the completion of Patrice's *Concert[o]*, Brussels having hired him to finish the job.[153] The same cue is heard, with a telling difference marking its style of performance, when Julie looks in on her ailing mother in a nursing home.[154] The third version is the centerpiece of one of the trilogy's most memorable scenes: Julie edits Olivier's score, recomposing his music as she recomposes her self.

Julie's reinsertion into the society from which she was catapulted by the crash is symbolized by the editorial work she carries out on Olivier's orchestrated sketch for the *Concert[o]*. In this remarkable cinematic depiction of composition—remarkable for dramatizing the act of composition in a manner interwoven with story and subtext—Julie feminizes Olivier's score. The decision to score her in notably masculine terms immediately prior to these actions thereby structures a revealing juxtaposition.[155] Gross argues that, by "'softening' Olivier's aggressive, percussion-driven version of the *Song*, it may be argued that Julie 'feminizes' the music . . . [t]he potential political ramifications of this act . . . play[ing] on stereotypes of 'feminine' and 'masculine'-type musical sounds in Western art music."[156] As Julie remakes Olivier's *Concert[o]*, it comes to reflect the role she is choosing to adopt, with the music's signifiers of masculinity being replaced by clichés of femininity. Julie is leaving behind the assertive, alternative and emancipated femininity of her first phase of grief, which subverted clichés of masculinity and permitted her to enjoy atypical freedoms, not least as a grieving woman. This happens as Julie oscillates into, again, more stereotypically feminine and loss-oriented grief-work. The soloist is returning to the rank and file of societal convention.

The sequence is an incisive concoction of action and editing that permits one, instantaneously, to understand its sounds and images as music "in the conditional tense,"[157] i.e., music in the process of becoming something else.[158] The music transfers into an impossible auditorium formed of Julie and Olivier's coupled imagination. The editing she commits with Olivier is also an experience of purest "flow." The communality and reciprocity of the action—for Olivier and Julie, but also for perceivers of the film, who once again become intimate with Julie's audio-visual perspective through *Blue*'s subtly innovative grammar—forms a poignant gesture of inclusion as Julie reenters her society. Yet the music also signifies the concomitant cost.

On Julie's arrival at Olivier's apartment, the dialogue establishes that it may be for the best that she knows about Patrice's infidelity. Now she is liberated in a quite different way to rebuild her life. Exercising that liberty by taking interest in another man's music, Julie asks Olivier to show her his work on the *Concert[o]*. Three shots ensue, merging into a continuous whole: one virtuosic, one mysterious, one an oasis of plenitude. The more telling cuts to the scene are in its audio. As the music is shaped like sonic putty by Julie and Olivier,[159] one hears music that *might* be, rather than music that was or yet is—music of potentiality, experienced as Julie opens up to be rewritten.

To reverse the more typical analytical paradigm, one can ask what the visuals in the sequence add to the music, sound and dialogue; what is seen, in a sense, underscores what is heard, a trait taken further in the finale. The first shot shows one of Julie's neatly manicured fingernails tracing a seemingly endless line of blue-toned manuscript paper—the image is filtered to enhance that color, suggesting, as elsewhere in the film, a subjective shot from her perspective (see Fig. 5.2). Are these the violins? Julie asks, touching the score. The violas, Olivier corrects her. Throughout *Blue*, physical contact with parts of the *Concert[o]* has been a source of anxiety, even pain, for Julie. She caresses the manuscript here, indicating a changing relationship to the things that it symbolizes.[160] The score to be heard is Olivier's sketch for a completion of the *Concert[o]*. Music and image swiftly part company, however, as the visuals move into a fantastical gap of their own.

As Julie's finger traces the music, its manicured nail obviously an index of her femininity, one hears brazenly masculine sounds. Olivier's version of the *Concert[o]*, with its thundering drums and blaring trumpets, is all brawn and little brain. "And now . . ." he says, heightening the tension in the moments before the soundtrack spews his full scoring of the previously heard piano fragment.[161] Above the stave one sees a peculiar expressive instruction blending Italian and English. *Con tutta force* is not an indication found in Preisner's cue sheet for this music. That the word "force" was implanted in the film's visual score, however, connotes the masculine quality of the music. With power then comes speed, in another cliché of screen masculinity: at the word *force*, the music begins to race across the screen, the image speeding ahead of the sounds one actually hears.[162] One could imagine that Julie, a well-trained musician, is reading ahead in the score and "joining" together separate pages of manuscript in her mind's eye, hence its "impossible" width of page; it is not uncommon for proficient score-readers to be some bars ahead of the music they are "hearing." The gradual blurring, however, forms a segue into the next shot, as the visual reality of the diegesis dissolves, along with Julie's perception of the material world, and she escapes into musical thought. The transition also subtly immerses the perceiver, in a symbolically pertinent contrast to the unsubtle ellipses, inside a cinematic experience proximate to Julie's own.

Julie brings Olivier's sonic juggernaut to a halt by ordering the removal of the percussion, and the image cuts to a long shot framing Julie and Olivier working together on the music.[163] She sits on the sofa, listening to his playing and imagining the full orchestration, then moves elsewhere to make a correction to the manuscript; he remains seated at the piano. This image is gradually blurred until an abstract visual is formed: a skin-tone surround with a whiter central circle, itself host to a central point of color (see Fig. 5.6). This slow loss of focus, which was Preisner's suggestion, masks a technical issue with the scene. Kieślowski wanted to shoot the action without the shots becoming reductively didactic regarding the activities depicted. Preisner, describing his solution to me, stood up to demonstrate the origins of the shot, which mimics how he sometimes concentrates while composing (his hand gradually covered his eyes as he portrayed himself entering a realm of musical thought by blocking out visual stimuli). Perhaps he made the same gesture when discussing the scene with Kieślowski and Idziak.

The shot encouraged by Preisner's description, as well as solving the immediate problem, permitted the co-workers to remind audiences of images elsewhere in *Blue*. First of all, there is the sense that one is seeing an eye: the image rhymes with the shot of Julie's eye in the hospital (reflecting the doctor) and also anticipates the shot of Olivier's eye at the end of the film (reflecting Julie). Second, the loss of focus takes the image to a point—a gray area, so to speak—midway between the musical blackouts and white-outs Julie has experienced at different points in her journey. From a Lacanian perspective, one might imagine that the white-outs immersed her in the plenitude of a false Imaginary as she listened to or, better still, imagined the busker's tunes; the blackouts symbolized the invasion of the Real, in the form of musical symbols thereof, and what she has repressed. In this scene, as she takes

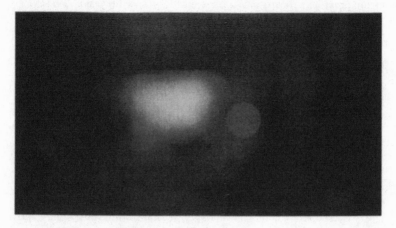

Fig. 5.6: The composing scene shot inspired by Preisner (photo courtesy of the author)

control of symbols sonic and visual, she fully embraces the Symbolic. Julie is reinserting herself into the fictions that will permit her more normally to exist.

Without percussion, Julie orders Olivier—and her own imagination—as the picture begins to blur. The recording of their voices in the mix shifts slightly at this point: suddenly they feel closer to the perceiver. This is clearly the point at which the film cuts from live action sound, recorded during shooting, to a sequence made in pre- or post-production. Removing the percussion cuts some of the cue's bluster, but the bulk of the brass has to go too if the music is to begin to sound feminine. The section repeats, at first without the percussion, then with just one trumpet instead of the full battalion; yet any trumpet, signifying stereotypically male preserves like the military and hunt, is a marker of masculinity, so it too must be cut. The sequence is heard first with solo trumpet, then without. The excision reveals flute lines, a "feminine" adornment to Olivier's cue that Julie foregrounds by switching attention to the woodwind. Like the shot, the music's gender is blurring.

The music skips ahead to the next section, which was glimpsed when the score rushed ahead under Julie's finger, but has yet to be sounded. "*Piano, piano, sul, sul tasto*" she whispers, suggesting a newly delicate dynamic and expressive marking—be quiet, be gentle—and a particular technique of string sound production. "Sul tasto" is an instruction to bow or sometimes pluck near or over the fingerboard of a stringed instrument; it translates as "on the fingerboard" and in French as "sur la touche," terms which call to mind the intimate act of touching music for Julie and what such contact—physical or imagined—has signified. The *sul tasto* indication is also sometimes related, in Italian, to *flautando*. The effect creates a sound in which certain harmonic partials in an instrument's timbre are reduced, creating an ethereal effect that sounds more flute or recorder-like. The *New Grove* describes *flautando* thus:

> An instruction to produce a soft flute-like tone. It requires string players to draw the bow lightly and fairly rapidly across the string with a point of contact near to or over the fingerboard. A more precise term for such an effect is *sul tasto* . . . as in Paganini's *Caprice* no. 9 which contains the direction *sulla tastiera imitando il flauto* ("over the fingerboard imitating the flute").[164]

The call for a "soft flute-like tone" brings to mind the recorder-playing busker and his role in Julie's rehabilitation, which Julie is about to recall more vividly.

Julie suggests another improvement with which Olivier agrees: instead of the piano, a flute. What one hears is not a flute, of course, but the soprano recorder—the instrument of the busker, as both Olivier and Julie clearly recognize. The music thus appropriates and rewrites a sign taken from Julie's restorative phase of grieving, as she engages with materials from her past and, by reshaping them, structures a normative feminine identity for her self. Two female critics note these shades of *Blue*. Gross locates the upside to Julie's use of "her compositional ability as a tool with which she can now protect herself from the onslaught of music from the past," shaping and editing the music and "telling it what to do for her own pleasure."[165] Paulus finds the downside. While "Julie has liberated her inner ego" through music, she has "at the same time stepped into the cage of the quotidian, of love, obligations and monotony."[166] The final orchestration continues to the end of the cue, when the camera cuts to the third image of the sequence: Julie, in medium shot, infused with the *Concert[o]*, "flow" and possibility.

Details of the music being re-orchestrated here assist in the scene's balancing of positive and negative connotations. Gesturally and topically it remains fairly maudlin: as well as moving through various minor chords, the recorder's melody pivots around a wrought chromatic turn reminiscent of the tune Julie "heard" in the park. This section of Olivier's score, however, also features a rising harmonic sequence. His *Concert[o]*, again, relies on sequences to spin out its ideas, but here he counterbalances the descending sequence of the first section of his score, i.e., the sequence from B minor down to A minor then to G minor, by reversing the harmonic process. The cue's second section starts in G major, which cadences onto C minor; then A major prepares D minor; finally B major leads to E minor. The progression through the dominant springboards G, A and B reverses the original descent through those chords, while turning their minor coloring major, which marks them as non-tragic, although they cadence, of course, onto a rising sequence of minor chords (C, D and E respectively). Plentiful falling x motifs in the recorder offer further signs of resignation.

Is that it? Julie asks Olivier as the music stops. Significantly, she wants to hear more music, rather than to cut music dead. Olivier does not know where to go next with his score, but Julie has a clue: the Van den Budenmayer memento, which she alludes to as a "counterpoint" that was meant to come back at the end of the piece. Was the memento theme intended to become the counterpoint to another melodic line in the *Concert[o]*? There is no evidence for this in Preisner's score. As a symbolic gesture, however, the reference to counterpoint is fitting. Counterpoint joins individual voices in a polyphonic unity of lines encoding co-dependent meanings. As a metaphor, this could be offered as an alternative to Eagleton's vision of a jazz band's enactment of *agapē*, although a contrapuntal close to the *Concert[o]* would also have made sense in the original conception of the piece as an anthemic celebration of European unity: a unisonant plurality of voices, each individual, yet united in celebratory polyphony. In *Blue*, it will be images that counterpoint the finished score. Try weaving it back in, Julie tells Olivier. Julie will do the same, weaving the memento and other significant souvenirs into her version of the *Concert[o]*, as she counterpoints elements of her past life with the texture of her present.[167]

Julie's *Concert[o]*

> [I]f this film has a conclusion and a core at all, then one finds it in the music. (Kieślowski)[168]

Not only does *Blue*'s closing montage—Julie's own version of the *Concert[o]* on the soundtrack, a succession of people to whom she is now connected on screen—present an "acoustic psychogram" and "deep view" of Julie's subjectivity as the story ends: the montage extracts the film's double-edged thesis on liberty and love.[169] "If there ever was an attempt to render the experience of epiphany in cinema," Žižek claims, "this is it."[170] That epiphany relates to the concept of "Paulinian *agape* . . . given its ultimate cinematic expression"[171]—an expression that was "shot," according to Kieślowski, "as an illustration of the music."[172] The following analysis, divided into sections that parallel not cuts in the image track but divisions in Preisner's score—Table 5.1 provides a thematic index of the melodies starting these sections—seeks to provide an appropriately close audio-visual reading of one of the most audacious musical sequences in recent European cinema.

Introduction

> If I speak in the tongues of men and of angels,
> but I do not have *agapē*,
> I am a noisy gong or a clanging cymbal.

As the montage begins, Julie is shown composing in her flat. The blue lampshade, her souvenir of Anna, hovers above her as she weaves Patrice's memento into her version of the *Concert[o]*. The camera cuts

Section	Theme

Table 5.1: Thematic index to the main sections of Julie's *Concert[o]*

close to what she is writing. Julie is crossing out part of the scoring of the *Concert[o]*'s ending and indicating that it should be re-orchestrated for *flute sol.*, i.e., the busker's recorder. This tune, when heard, turns out to be one of the busker's melodies. Its interpolation into Julie's *Concert[o]* is thus a further souvenir: a musical memory of the restorative stage of her grief-work, integrated into the aesthetic product of the loss-oriented phase of that process. As she completes her immersive work, her "flow" stops with a click of her pen lid and she telephones Olivier (twice). Their brief conversations confirm that, while she may not be willing to claim co-authorship of the *Concert[o]* he is completing for Brussels, she is willing to accept his love and to reciprocate. After she hangs up, she turns back to the music, one of her eyes wet with unspent tears. She reaches out and touches the music. Finally, *Blue* begins to flow.

Julie's touch ignites the *Concert[o]* in her full and finished version. Her fingers alight on the opening chorus of the music which, at the copyist's apartment, provoked her destruction of a copy of Patrice's score.[173] Here the manuscript is no longer shot through a filter staining it blue: she "sees" this particular music, and its connotations, differently now. The manuscript has become something more than the horror of repressed trauma, its recomposition having become a means by which she has faced her bereavement. Where blackouts and unbidden musical intrusions once reigned, her score now stands (to recall Stein's words) for "experiences and affects too intense or overwhelming to express directly."[174]

Where does the music resound? The montage is an audio-visual realization of Julie's climate, images uniting with music in a collusive sounding out of her transforming subjectivity. The style of the editing is a contrast to earlier passages in the film, suggesting connection rather than isolation. *Blue*'s splintered editing, its cuts echoing like aftershocks from the opening crash, also seems healed by her touch. Music now flows over fades to black and back in again, rewriting the significance of ellipsis in the film. The score even continues flowing, in a strikingly conventional gesture in this film's context, over the end title credits. A trajectory is thus completed, arcing through the fantastical gap of *Blue*'s musical climate, as the score moves, broadly speaking, from diegetic to "meta-diegetic as a kind of represented subjectivity"[175] and then, for the end title sequence, into the non-diegetic realm. As it closes, *Blue*'s editing, scoring and soundtrack thus embrace the conventions of continuity. The film's stylistic wounds have been healed and, with it, *Blue* has become more traditional. This also reflects Julie's fate.

The sync point as the music drops in response to Julie's touch is electrifying. The impact of the opening of the *Concert[o]* (see Fig. 5.7) relates, in part, to the theme's familiarity: *Blue* has tutored one to expect this musical arrival. Its power also relates, more directly, to its volume (again very prominent in the mix), its scoring for a mass of human voices, and its bittersweet combination of textural starkness and warm intervals (thirds and sixths). The ambiguity of the harmony is also pertinent. In spite of the number of voices at Preisner's disposal (SATB, with the sopranos further divided into two parts), the third pitch-class required for an unambiguous harmonic triad (indicating either D major or B minor) remains absent. If one catches one's breath at the bravado of the opening gesture, one holds it in anticipation of har-

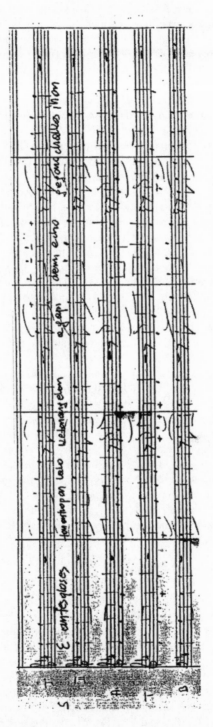

Fig. 5.7: Choral opening from Preisner's *Concer[o]* manuscript score

monic resolution. The first lines of 1 Corinthians 13 contrast the gifts of a prophet, which St. Paul makes sound almost artistic, with the need to belong. Creativity cannot equal, it seems, the fruits of *agapē*. The harmony and the presence of melodic motifs x and y, with their alternative connotations, parallel the text's ambivalence and, in doing so, aspects of Julie's position at this moment in *Blue*. By reinserting herself into the world, she is gaining and losing in equal measure.

Visually, the opening of the score is counterpointed by images of closure. Once the music begins, Julie rolls up the score, but this time not to destroy it. Conceivably, it will be a gift to Olivier, selflessly offered to help him finish his version for performance. She exits the flat, slamming the door shut on the blue lampshade—which she had hung, it will be remembered, after entering that same door at the start of the highly fragmented scene that closed the first part of the film. The lampshade partially masks her exit, staining her blue like the ink glimpsed moments earlier on her fingers, and complementing the color of her ring and clothes. At one stage, Julie consumed everything blue, as if to hide it; now she permits herself to be colored by its stain, the indelible ink of her past now part of her present. The slamming door, the last notable sound effect in the film, is a final gesture of closure and synched to the music so that it sounds, like an emphatic bass drum, on the beat between the first two phrases of the chorus. Julie's actions are in consort with her music, just as she once swayed to the busker. She is flowing.

The camera floats to the right and into darkness, searching for the montage's next image. When that shot enters from the right, sliding across until it fills the screen, one can think back, through the ellipsis, to the pan across the flat, emplotting the two gestures as a single long move from left to right. This motif—which will be extended compositionally, as if in developing variation, by the flow of the camera throughout the closing montage—has been seen before in *Blue*. It was the move linking Anna to her parents; it united Julie and Lucille in the sex club. Here it is extended within the audio-visual fantasia of *Blue*'s closing montage, as music and image immerse the perceiver in an experience of continuity and community, and an analysis of the costs and benefits of *agapē*.

Agitato (Instrumental Transition)

Julie's *Concert[o]* sustains the tension generated by its introduction through harmonic and rhythmic means. Rather than immediately confirming the expected arrival on the tonic B minor, the direction in which the final gestures of the introduction were heading, the bridge forms a dominant prolongation intensifying expectations of that arrival. Preisner engineers this through simple chordal pattern-making. The dominant seventh of B minor, F♯ major, alternates with a diminished seventh rooted on E, and thus including two pitches from the faltering funeral march's G minor triad, G and B♭. This favorite Preisner harmony stokes up the "dissonance" requiring resolution, alludes to Julie's darkest times, and permits the music to anticipate the next phase of the *Concert[o]*. The movement between F♯ and G in the melody (see Ex. 5.6), Preisner's plangent interval of choice (5̂ to ♭6̂), gracefully foreshadows the solo soprano's melody and, in particular, its chant-like movement by semitones above and below F♯. One has heard this ornamentation before, originally in the memento (see motif z as marked in Ex. 5.2). It was also part of the pivotal turn in the busker's second melody, or in Julie's imagining thereof, during her moment of sun-warmed plenitude in the park (see Ex. 5.5[ii]). The turn and its anticipation connect that brief glimpse of healing and, possibly, composition to the *Concert[o]*. The connection will shortly be rendered explicit.

Ex. 5.6: Links between second busker theme, bridge and *Arioso*

The image arriving on screen is anticipated by the bridge's stylistic allusions. After the ardent string gesture that plunges into the transition, the rhythmic kick in the melody, syncopated to the throbbing lower strings, recalls the tango-like cue to which Olivier stripped before his desultory sex with Julie back at her old house.[176] It also anticipates the tangos that will underscore the battle of the sexes/sex-related battles in *White*, and bolero-like moments, musical and dance-like, in *Red*. The image in the montage depicts sexual intercourse as a struggle or fight. Julie and Olivier are shown making love, at first somewhat abstractly (a hand gripping a neck), before the couple are revealed, Julie apparently pressed up against the glass of a fish tank. Given the importance of shots of hands elsewhere in Kieślowski's films, one might ponder who is being throttled here, and by what. Crudely put—and Preisner's music encourages crudeness, its tango-connotations tincturing one's perception of the shot just as much as the sickly green waters of the tank—a man is back on top in Julie's life and she is shown here to be not just subjugated but suffocating in her new position. The music to come, however, embellishes the shot's connotations in a switchback from profane to sacred. Julie will shortly be shown and scored earning something from the sacrifice of her body.

Arioso

> And if I have prophecy,
> and know all mysteries so that I can remove mountains,
> but do not have *agapē*,
> I am nothing,
> I am nothing,
> I am nothing.

Rather than a climax, the sound one hears after the silence at the end of the bridge is a chaste, thirdless sonority scored for solo soprano, female chorus and a bassoon—its reedy voice sounding like an organ and amplifying this section's spiritual connotations. This, finally, is an arrival on the tonic B minor, but one which, with its open fifth signifying the spiritual and pure in place of the earthy and sexual, turns the music in a new direction. When the bassoon's second note does supply the third of the chord midway through the first bar, the mood has already been set by the initial harmony and, more obviously, the heavenly host of the chorus, which taps into significations of the angelic stretching back from the opening of Elfman's *The Simpsons* main title theme at least as far as compositions by the twelfth-century Notre Dame polyphonists. Most striking of all, in this context, is Towarnicka's voice. The solo soprano's tone is not angelic—or rather, it is not equivalent to the romanticized cherubs of tacky Christmas cards or the mellow monks on Gregorian chill-out CDs. Its pure, vibrato-less laser, penetratingly sustained even in her highest registers, sounds genuinely uncanny and perhaps even frightening: this is the sound of a Sublime (in Edmund Burke's sense) and even supernatural voice addressing humankind and filling those who hear it with awe. Her voice, above all, commands attention. What she says cannot be ignored.[177]

Is she addressing Julie? One might imagine Towarnicka's voice to be coming *out of* Julie, like the music she breathed out while dreaming on the stairs outside her apartment, but here leaking in a quasi-religious ecstasy as she gasps in Olivier's clutches. More obviously, the female voice promotes itself as a marker of her subjectivity and encourages one to consider what it says in relation to her motivations. The core message of the text is that, without practicing *agapē*, Julie, like anyone else, has and is nothing. Erotic ecstasy, like the ability to smite mountains, is a parlor trick in the presence of *agapē*. One can but wonder at the contrast between the love depicted and the love of which the voice sings. Like Dominique and Valentine to come, Julie's life seems here to have been rendered meaningful, in large part, through the love of a man and all this entails regarding her position in society. Yet this sacrifice and sex have another role to play. By accepting the burdens of her new position, Julie loosens the bonds of her grief.

The ambivalence of the moment has been commented on by other critics. For Orr, "the entwined bodies . . . seem framed as a romantic trope to trigger the union of the grand finale," yet "a closer look suggests . . . [an] underwater consummation where the motions could be read as a desire to escape in the final convulsion of drowning."[178] Wilson, similarly, sees the lovemaking as "asphyxiating" and working "to identify *Bleu* as a film of oblivion, of the drowning of memory," but also "of resurfacing and rebirth."[179] For Žižek, that rebirth is happening in Julie's imagination, with the ending staged, from this moment on, as Julie's "solitary fantasy, a dream-like event not really involving contact with another person . . . [but] as if the woman experiences it alone in a dream."[180] Yet that fantasy, for Žižek, is not entirely negative: it sets the stage for Julie's "Paulinian epiphany." Julie drowns within one dream of freedom to fantasize the birth of another.

Julie's apparent passivity is not only signified visually. In contrast to the driving throb of the instrumental transition, here there is almost a complete absence of rhythmic momentum: the tempo also drops slightly and the first two beats of the *Arioso* are suspended in a pulseless void. New purpose only gradually emerge in the score. The harmony rocks gently between tonic and dominant before moving, once again, to a diminished seventh on G, its G and B♭ still, perhaps, recalling the anguish of G minor and the funeral theme. Extra instrumental voices swell the texture and a slight peak in tension is achieved before the section's open-ended i-V cadence. Combined with the lyrics, this strengthens the rhetoric of the passage's question: without *agapē*, what can one achieve in the face of life's suffering? The swell occurs on the line referring to the smiting of mountains and draws attention—in a favorite trick Preisner will repeat several times in the *Concert[o]*—by augmenting the richness of the music just before stripping the texture to its bare essentials. The soprano sings "Without *agapē* . . ."? The answer, set thrice to drive the message home via one of Preisner's cleverest emphases, then resounds: " . . . I am nothing," times three. By the third annunciation, however, there is an injection of anxiety. Preisner extends the clangorous final sonority (the harmony is the diminished seventh again) by two extra beats, signifying a potentially endless "nothing" but also raising expectations of "something" to supplant the void.

Earlier in the film, on several occasions, Julie stated that nothing was precisely what she wanted: no love, no family, no money, no past, no future—no traps. Now the *Concert[o]* and images argue—as the camera slips into another transitional ellipsis—that she is abandoning nihilism to embrace the something of *agapē*. Closing this circle, the first "I am nothing" is sung to a reminiscence of the busker's third melody, which in turn anticipates the full return of that theme at the end of the *Concert[o]* (see Ex. 5.9). That melody originally performed a vital role for Julie, i.e., assisting in her reestablishment of "flow," but the new context turns it inside out to reveal the limitations of her first period of grieving and, perhaps, of late modernity's encouragement of solipsistic solitude. When the melody returns in full at the end of Julie's *Concert[o]*, though, it will have been redeemed by its journey through *agapē*.

Espressivo; Placido, Cantabile

> *Agapē* is patient, *agapē* is kind, it is not envious.
> *Agapē* does not brag, it is not puffed up.

The knowing bathos of Preisner's "I am nothing" is matched in the next section of music by the ironic pathos of the choir's declamations on the subject of what *agapē* is or is not. This is puffed up musical bragging of the highest order. The launch pad for the pyrotechnic display is the diminished seventh chord at the end of the *Arioso* and the fuzz of timbral dissonance Preisner scores to enhance its intensity: a rolled cymbal and piercing woodwind chord form an alarm bell calling time on nihilism. The sound contributes an interesting audio-visual effect to the start of the next shot, which depicts the hitcher, Antoine, silencing his alarm clock—one does not hear an alarm sound effect but may nonetheless imagine hearing one thanks to Preisner's scoring—and then sits up to ponder Julie's crucifix, which she allowed him to keep after he tried to return it to her. Antoine's thoughtful stillness, as he considers the motivations of Julie's relinquishing of the necklace, is in stark contrast to the music.

The musical setting demonstrates precisely what its words decry, in a kind of anempathic word-painting. In doing so, it introduces an uncommon (at least for Preisner) textural complexity. Six voices formed of the divided choir sing three superimposed fragments of text: the subdivided sopranos and altos sing "*agapē* is patient, *agapē* is kind" in an energetic mixture of dotted rhythms and semiquavers, while the tenors and basses intone, in regular crotchets, "*agapē*" and "kind" respectively. The counterpoint puffs up the music as the words become unclear; a simple truth blurs as artifice is introduced. During these moments, the harmony moves into B minor's relative major, D major. The major mode, obviously, tends musically to figure positive, or at least non-tragic, experiences. Yet this moment of modal overcoming is short-lived, contributing to the irony of the passage when the harmony convulses onto another G-rooted diminished seventh chord, and then back into B minor. Is there a suggestion of critique of the protagonist here from Julie's choir? Like the chorus of an ancient Greek tragedy, they seem to be cutting her earlier efforts at liberty down to size, as if her splendid isolation was egocentric, late-modern solipsism and so, in a sense, too "puffed up" to discharge in full the duties of her grieving.

> It bears all things, believes all things,
> hopes all things, endures all things.

Like an internal monologue in which Julie runs through a check-list of better ways to live, the solo soprano continues to adumbrate what *agapē* is and is not as the music evolves into a passage marked *placido cantabile*. The music and images demonstrate, initially, the humbleness of *agapē*. A blackout underwrites the solo soprano; in turn, she is ac-

companied by music simple enough to have been scored merely for a
Piwnica singer and piano. The communication, rather than blurring, of
these words—bearing and enduring seem of particular resonance at this
stage of Julie's grief—is permitted by the clarity of the music. However, this is also the start of the first of the *Concert[o]*'s longer-breathed
passages, which create a sense of development and growth, breaking
free of sequence and more predictable forms of pattern-making. This
begins by developing the harmonic progression and melody of the "I
am nothing" passage, changing direction at what one would expect to
be another diminished seventh chord. The music, instead, is about to
present its alternative.

Does the musical growth of this passage about accepting pain and
hope mirror Julie's growing acceptance of her present reality? The developmental nature of the imagery may add weight to such a reading.
As the music mirrors yet develops a previous idea, so too do the images. The camera floats right to reveal Julie's mother, reflected in a
curved surface reminiscent of her daughter's face when it was shot in
reflection on the back of a spoon in the café. That earlier image was an
icon of Julie's isolation; here it reminds one of the similarities of her
position, at that stage of the story, to her mother's isolation; in turn, this
highlights the choice Julie has made to move beyond an alienated life.
Her mother will remain trapped, the images suggest. The initial reflection, presumably in a TV screen now dead of daredevil pensioners, is in
turn revealed to be part of a prison of mirrors, entrapping her within a
maze of self.[181] She then closes her eyes and bows her head; a nurse
arrives to check on her well-being. Is she dead? There is no reason to
believe something so melodramatic, but the music and words clarify
that she has suffered a metaphorical death. *Agapē* "never ends," the
soprano sings, the chorus swelling affirmatively behind her, but everything else must die, like the prophecies, language and knowledge one
must set aside—a sharp parallel to the mother's mental and physical
decline.

As the camera slips away from Julie's mother and into darkness,
the music reaches an unsatisfactorily pre-emptive declaration of closure. Preisner's score reveals that he had originally intended for a second soprano to double the first at the point when the images of the
mother are revealed, to accentuate the mirroring in the visuals. What
one does hear, as the development gathers pace, is the chorus answering
the soloist and mirroring her lines (they sing "set aside," then "If there
are tongues . . .") before their forces join her for the declamatory peak
of the passage (declaring that knowledge ceases in the face of *agapē*).
This is fist-shaking rhetoric and as preachy as the *Concert[o]* and *Blue*
get. Ironically, however, this sermonizing stresses the need to set aside
organized religion—e.g., prophecies, speaking in tongues—in order to
embrace more significant forms of knowing.

In this regard, one might note that the musical syntax ironically undercuts the sensuous apotheosis. A lack of closure is signaled metri-
cally, melodically and harmonically: religion, the music suggests, is not

the answer. The extra beat in the first "half" of the $\frac{5}{4}$ bar (on knowledge ceasing) throws a spanner into the works, permitting all of the syllables of the ancient Greek to be fitted in to the bar, but derailing its rhythmic momentum. That clunky gear change, in turn, is exacerbated by the harmonic changes, which return from D major to B minor, not via a conventionally smooth harmonic progression, but instead through a jarring G-rooted diminished 7th chord. Finally, the harmonic changes mean that the melodic motif one hears at this undermined climax is F♯-G-F♯. By this point in the film, one would predict only one melodic line as a closural gesture: a descent through motif x, coordinating harmonic, melodic and contrapuntal closure. The F♯-G-F♯ motif's prolongation of $\hat{5}$ signifies no such resolution. The *subito tacet* that follows—a full pause of the forces, the abrupt final chord careening into a reverberant void—feels sudden and lacking indeed.

Ad libitum

The bleakness of the ensuing silence is scarcely consoled by the solitary violin line that breaks it. Its connotation of being bereft—a jagged, falling tritone fragmenting its gesture of lament—means that the *Concert[o]* again implies what *agapē* is by representing what it is not. The loneliness Julie has rejected—loneliness now represented by her mother—is extended by this passage to the loneliness of Julie's surrogate daughter, Lucille. As the camera continues its journey along the filaments of Julie's metaphysical web, it comes to rest on the sex worker's face: two of her colleagues perform behind her, but she is separated from them by a mesh. In spite of her bullish proclamations to the contrary concerning her job and lifestyle, Lucille's life has a banal but affecting irony at its core: for all her couplings, she is lonely. Her family is lost to her and her only true friend is a woman she as yet barely knows. Like the violin, she is in solitary confinement; the mesh even brings a hint of the confessional. Her pensive face nonetheless suggests an insight into her situation, gleaned perhaps from the bond to Julie that the camera's movement recalls, its panning reflecting the visual *agapē* motif last seen when Julie came to save her at the club. The next audio-visual gesture suggests, in turn, redemption.

Placido

> And now these three remain: faith, hope, and *agapē*,
> But the greatest of these is *agapē*.
> But the greatest of these is *agapē*,
> But the greatest of these is *agapē*,
> But the greatest of these is *agapē*.

Blue rises from the hell of Lucille's club on angel's wings. In a moment that epitomizes the integration of sound and image in the film, the camera seems to mickey-mouse Preisner's music. A rising, broken chord is strummed on the harp; in response, the camera lifts rapidly, a gesture of ebullience and hope—if such a camera move, like the uplift of a rising melody, can kinesthetically evoke such connotations. A heavily pregnant belly being scanned by ultrasound comes into view; the camera then rises further to zoom in on the ultrasound image. It shows Patrice's son, and Anna's half-brother, safe and alive in his own enclosed space: his mother's womb. The solo soprano, backed by the harp and a hum of a vibraphone, states that of faith, hope and *agapē*, the greatest of these is the last. In a sense, one hardly needs reminding of this. The heavenly music and sights on the screen, especially when one sees Sandrine's smile as she looks at her son on the monitor, tells one everything one needs to know about this kind of connection. More affectingly, however, the shot calls Julie to mind: another mother, earlier in the film, looking at her child enclosed in womb-like darkness (a coffin) on a different monitor (the tiny TV).

The chorus join the soprano to repeat the incantation "the greatest of these is *agapē*" three times, the music gradually accelerating towards climax. Preisner's three repetitions thus recall and redeem the three settings of "I am nothing." *Agapē*, the repetitions clarify, is the opposite of the existence Julie lived beforehand. Impetus builds as the soloist and female chorus are joined, on the last statement, by male voices; the rhythmic propulsion of the string accompaniment also intensifies, lower strings recalling their propulsive role in the instrumental bridge. The final chord, a diminished seventh on G, is reinforced with another woodwind and percussion "alarm." The climactic moment is reminiscent of the climax of Weronika's performance in *Véronique* and the diminished seventh chord that strikes her dead. Here, however, the diminished seventh will be answered by the breath of life.[182]

Tutti murmurando (memento)

As the metallic haze of the diminished seventh sonority fades away, the image of an eye emerges from the blackness, rather than being discovered by the moving camera. The change to the montage's visual grammar is significant. The eye is green; close inspection of earlier frames in the film suggests that it is one of Olivier's eyes. He is watching Julie: the image of her naked back is reflected in his eye. The shot reminds one of Julie's pupil reflecting the doctor at the start of the film, and of the abstract image forming around their musical merger during the composition scene. Now, though, she is reflected in the eye of another. Whether or not this marks a point of exit from her mindscreen to a more universal perspective—and the shift in grammar from *panning through* darkness to *emerging from* darkness may suggest as much—one realizes that she is being looked at and, thus, looked out for. The music, too, signifies the embrace of a society.

The Van den Budenmayer memento theme begins to play as Julie's image comes into focus. This is the most significant moment in the entire score—its big reveal—as the theme one has been tutored to expect to hear in the *Concert[o]* finally arrives. Perhaps the formal satisfaction of this long-delayed arrival creates, for the perceiver, a sense of pleni-tude proximate to Julie's in her newfound connections to the world; the extreme close-up of Olivier's eye has also shaped a point of symmetry. It is the arrival of the memento theme, however, that truly permits the film, and Julie's story, to close with a sense of completeness. Once it has sounded, the *Concert[o]*, the film—and Julie's grief—can begin to end.

The rhetoric of closure is strengthened by other musical means. The opening of the melody, which outlines B minor's dominant, F♯ major, and then the tonic, resolves the dissonance of the G diminished seventh chord, as the progression's voice-leading slots into place like the mechanisms of a clock preparing to chime (see Ex. 5.7). This per-mits the *Concert[o]* and film, finally, to cadence in B minor with a sense of security. It also concludes the shift of musical gravity away from the film's initial tonal center, G minor—its ghost in the *Con-cert[o]* having been the diminished seventh chords—and the faltering funeral march. Julie has selected a key and melody that render the cli-max of her score *in memoriam*, but not enslavement, to her grief. The melody ends with motif x's descent—a gesture notably avoided by Preisner up until this point in the *Concert[o]*, in which lines have tended to hover around B minor's fifth and sixth scale degrees, F# and G, thus prolonging $\hat{5}$ and building anticipation of this eventual descent and arrival.

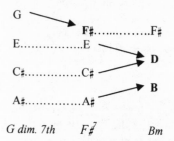

Ex. 5.7: Voice-leading slotting into place for B minor

What one hears is therefore wordless yet wondrous. Very quietly, the solo soprano and string orchestra hum and pluck the memento theme in octaves and in unison. In musical terms, this is a symbol of utmost unity, reminding one of the sung prayers Preisner heard as a child around coffins and in the church, as people enacted moments of unisonance to celebrate and commemorate. The voices' mouths are closed, the sound emitted barely a hum, as if to recall Julie's firmly shut mouth at various earlier points in the film and, with it, the repressive motivation of such gestures. Here, though, the "mmm" shapes a timbral contrast to the singing in the next passage of the music: as the final shot of Julie's face weeping incontrovertible tears is revealed, the voices shift to an open-mouthed "aaa." The choir mouths a transition from repression to release. One also hears the solo soprano resurfacing amid the choir, Julie's thematic and sonic icons revealing the individual embraced by the communal. Music conceived, in *Blue*'s fiction, to unite the masses in the end comes to symbolize one self's journey into a relationship with other people and itself. It is an icon of Julie's self-transcendence.

This is a far cry from what the screenplay envisaged for the *Concert[o]*. Its ending tells that "the joyous hymn about love which—according to Patrice—could be the salvation of Europe and of the world . . . becomes serious, announces something dark, dangerous" just before we see Julie "her face in her hands . . . crying helplessly."[183] This "dark, dangerous" vision is a reminder that interpretations of the end of the film must balance hope with ambivalence. Liberty from something permits liberty to do something else, but that something inevitably breeds new constraints. The end of the film was conceived to symbolize, amongst other things, the complexity of a 1990s Europe in which some enjoyed freedom while others perished in war. In the end, it also signifies Julie's second loss: her empowered femininity in the middle of the film, which she sacrifices in order to return to society. While it permits closure and suggests community, the Van den Budenmayer memento, as the composer has noted, is still a funeral march. Liberty, throughout *Blue*, is accompanied by death.

Yet the music does not end here. It develops beyond the funeral march to suggest, for Julie at least, a small hope. This is anticipated visually. Just before the images cut to the end title after the shot of Julie weeping, she looks down and then back up, a hint of a smile tweaking one corner of her mouth. Insdorf comments illuminatingly on this shot, linking Julie's face behind the window's glass to other closing images in Kieślowski's films. In the final shots through a window at the end of *No End*, *Véronique*, *Blue*, *White* and *Red*, the aperture becomes "a charged frame through which characters emerge into a new state of lucidity and/or connection."[184] The connection of *Blue* to the endings of the other films in the trilogy is of particular interest. For Insdorf, the "last shots of all three films present the hard-won victories of the characters over isolation and despair," with tears on their faces that reveal "a person capable of finally crying"; consequently, "[b]efore Kieślowski rescues all these characters from the ferry accident [at the end of *Red*], they essentially save themselves."[185] However, there is a key difference between *Blue*'s window and those in the other two films. The barred prison window in *White* and the broken judge's window in *Red* are partially open; Julie's is intact and firmly closed. Noting elsewhere the shot of Majka behind solid glass at the passport office in *Decalogue 7*, Insdorf suggests that such a shot "suggests separation."[186] By extension, Julie's window implies that her reconnection to society is only partial and thus partially happy—not least because, however reconciled she becomes to her bereavement, she will forever be separated from her husband and daughter.

As the first statement of the memento closes—the soprano's voice, perhaps serendipitously, surfacing briefly just after Julie's face appears—a small brass group enters, marked *marciale*, to perform a brief introduction to the ensuing repeat of the theme. This plodding sound (not made any more graceful by the insecure tuning of the performance) reminds one of the funeral band earlier in *Blue*, as if heard here from an ironic distance. Could the masculine connotations connote Julie's increasing strength? The performance dynamic certainly strengthens, from *pianissimo* to a *piano* reinforced by the entry of the choral tenors, the altos and basses singing "aaa" sounds, plus selected woodwind instruments; all parts are then instructed to crescendo *poco a poco*, shaping expectation of arrival at a climactic chorus. The more sophisticated change, however, is a carefully engineered shift from ⁵⁄₄—the faltering pulse of the memento in most of its former incarnations—to ¼ (see Ex. 5.8). The music ceases to limp as the choir swells and their voices release their open-mouthed aaa(*gapē*)s, and the theme, in a sense, is healed, gaining strength and beginning to flow more assuredly forwards. During the central passage of the film, on several occasions, Julie synchronized her body to the fluidity of the busker's music and other regular pulses; she also swam in a metronomic rhythm. All signified her search for "flow." Now, as a composer, she heals the memento of its limp in her version of the *Concert[o]*: composer, heal thyself.

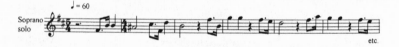

Ex. 5.8: The memento finds its flow in the *Concert[o]*

Just before the shot of Julie fades to black, the music erupts into the loudest and most elaborate statement of the memento in the film, broadening out as if in response to her almost-a-smile. The first thing one notes, as the full orchestra enters, is the sound of the soprano recorder. Partly, this is because it is harmonizing the melody, rather than playing it in unison: the final statement of the memento is a three-part harmonization, with the bass voices and recorder embellishing the other voices' octaves. The recorder's note also cuts through due to timbre and register. One's attention is thereby called to the fact that one has yet to hear the recorder in Julie's *Concert[o]*, in spite of the prominent role she found for it when editing Olivier's version. Shortly, one will hear this instrument—a memento of her time of isolation—playing solo as her ending of the *Concert[o]* escapes the bluster at the start of the end credits.

A crucial effect of the scoring throughout *Blue* being quasi-classical and primarily instrumental, beyond establishing the upper middle-class social *milieu* within which its characters circulate, now comes into focus. Discussing the ambiguities promoted by art music in film, Mike Cormack investigates the hermeneutic possibilities of non-vocal music's lack of semantic fixity: classical music, he writes, "can add complexity and ambiguity to film scores, rather than simply limiting the range of meaning."[187] On the one hand, *Blue*'s closing *Concert[o]* of unifications personal and political seems destined, not least through its allusions to (neo-)Romantic music, to import what Caryl Flinn describes, regarding uses of pre-modernist art music in film, as "an impression of perfection and integrity in an otherwise imperfect, unintegrated world."[188] Yet on the other hand, Preisner's scoring utilizes music's ability to mean more than one thing at a time. So, while paralleling the uplifting "unification" aspects of the narrative and music's role in Julie's grieving, *Blue*'s score—through the gesture, say, provided by the funereality of the semantic register of the memento theme—at the same time parallels darker tones within the story.

As Dean Duncan suggests, by extending an argument about the semantic polyvalence of programmatic music to uses of art music in film, readings thus encouraged must move beyond the binary positions of parallelism or counterpoint.[189] Throughout *Blue*, Preisner's scoring has been working towards the moments, as the film begins to close, when it must parallel more than one position simultaneously, in order to evoke the dualism of *Blue*'s late-modern core. The ironic distance provided by Preisner's "side-by-side" presence, of course, aids this process. One might even claim, following Royal S. Brown, that the pseudo-classical nature of the soundtrack strengthens its hand: classical cues on the soundtrack of non-mainstream films of the 1960s and thereafter, Brown argues, "no longer function purely as backing for key emotional situations, but rather exist as a kind of parallel emotional/aesthetic universe."[190] Preisner's achievements in *Blue* include moments that underscore and undermine in equal measure.

The *Concert[o]*'s anthemic pomp has already been somewhat undercut by its funereal character and other factors. The climatic passage, for instance, is slightly ungainly: the swing of the offbeat triplets in the accompaniment jars against the martial dotted rhythms of the melody. The climax's grandiosity (note the orchestration's tubular bells and timpani) seems appropriate to the context of the piece's official purpose, but these "flaws," and the fact Julie cuts it dead just as it seems ready to self-immolate, subvert it to express the more nuanced context of Julie's return to society—and the filmmakers' seasoned views on grand European projects at the time *Blue* was made. Most obviously, the *Concert[o]*'s climax is not permitted a full and unequivocal moment of closure. The repeat of the memento ends abruptly, before a final x motif and cadence in B minor can sound. Instead, a *fortissimo* E minor chord hangs in the air, connoting uncertainty. Julie has something else to say.

End Credits

Preisner's manuscript score for the *Concert[o]* indicates that, after the general pause, the recorder should perform a closing statement, in faltering $\frac{5}{4}$, of the memento theme. This is the correction Julie is shown making just before the montage begins.[191] An alternative ending to the film could conceivably have had this brief melody—which does close in B minor with a descending x motif—playing out over a field of blue, such as the Yves Klein blue backing the actual end titles; the blue could then have faded to black before the end credits rolled in silence.

What one actually hears is rather different (see Ex. 5.9). Preisner recalls that he produced this extra music to cover the longer than expected end titles without breaking the mood of the *Concert[o]*. Being a music-film, however, it feels appropriate that *Blue*'s music, and therefore the narrative, should continue to evolve during the end titles. When one experiences the film, the music flows seamlessly on, encouraging one to hear the extra cue as the conclusion of the *Concert[o]*. The tune is the third of the busker's melodies—the one Olivier thought sounded familiar because it has motivic connections to various Van den Budenmayer themes. Heard as Julie's intended ending to the *Concert[o]*, she can be imagined to have chosen to introduce the theme here, and then developed it in a particular direction, for musical and symbolic reasons relating to her loss-oriented grief-work. On the one hand, it picks up on the anticipations of its melodic content earlier in the score. On the other, it suggests four ways in which Julie has taken ownership of her grief.

First, this melody is entirely her creation—or rather, her memento. Patrice could not have envisaged it and so its inclusion represents Julie's own creative will. She is no longer merely editing or rearranging the *Concert[o]*: she is making it her own. Through the act of borrowing, Julie is finally authoring her music and, by extension, her life. Second, the melody is a symbol of her grieving, as opposed to the *causes* of her grief. Coming from her time of isolation, it is a memento of her period of restoration revisited in the time of her loss-oriented grief-work. That she is able to keep this memory alive in her *Concert[o]* could be taken as a positive sign of remembrance rather than repression. Third, as the recorder repeats the melody, it is harmonized by two further instruments, which sound like a clarinet and, later, a violin doubling the clarinet an octave higher. The clarinet's link to Anna—recall the clarinetist at the funeral—might suggest that Julie's *Concert[o]* closes with an instrumental carrier of Julie's subjectivity, the solo recorder, united with symbolic voices representing her daughter, but also, recalling the violin solo in the *Ad libitum*, representing her surrogate daughter, Lucille. Past and present thus unite. Finally, the closing section of the piece reveals music of a grace and subtlety rarely heard elsewhere in the film; the lampshade hanging cue is the closest point of comparison. Recalling that earlier cue's sound-world at the close of *Blue* has a formal function: the musical sound of the end of the first act returns to end the second, just as images recalling that scene were glimpsed at the opening of the montage. Is this Julie's own voice, though, or Preisner's, peeping out from behind the mask of his avatar?

Ex. 5.9: Transcription of score at end of *Blue*

At such moments, Julie's voice seems closest, amid *Blue*'s fictitious
creators, to an evocation of Preisner's presence, and it seems apt, at the
close of the film, that a fourth and final musical communion—Julie-
Preisner—should be intimated by their ode to *agapē*. Significantly, perhaps, Julie's borrowed recorder melody begins as Preisner's name appears in the credits.

 Yet even this is not quite the end. In the midst of the trio, and then
once again to provide the closing notes of the film, a harp marks time
with tolling F♯s. This may also remind one of the lampshade scene: the
guitar's last plucked contribution began on F♯. Suspended, unresolved,
perhaps irresolvable, here the F♯s form an ambiguous point of aperture

rather than closure, the film ending not with the finality of B minor but the question of its dominant.[192] Julie was last seen behind a pane of glass, in an image Kieślowski's films encourage one to read as a sign that she still has some distance to travel before her journey back from grief could be considered complete. The close of her *Concert[o]*, a couple of minutes later, underscores that intimation. Julie's story, like the trilogy itself, is not yet over, as one discovers at the end of *Red*. Preisner's final musical touch in *Blue* leaves one hopeful, but uncertain, that a positive resolution will occur.

Concert[o] Conversations

Some critics interpret the end of *Blue* optimistically;[193] others find darker shadows.[194] These contradictions pay testimony to the ambivalence of *Blue*'s ending. Its musical and textual content, however, deserve to be taken more fully into account in assessments of the film's "core." The *Concert[o]*'s conservatism, gendered clichés and hamstrung grand oratory have already been considered in the context of what Julie loses alongside her closing gains; the film's return to conventions of continuity editing—epitomized by the device of a closing montage with, arguably, non-diegetic music—has also been noted. What remains is to be considered is its foregrounding of the trilogy's key idea.

With reference to *Blue*'s book-ending close-ups of Julie and Olivier's eyes, Žižek argues that the kind of grieving Julie is finally depicted as undergoing—her stereotypically feminine outpouring of tears—can only occur at the end of *Blue* thanks to a new loss. The two shots stage, he suggests, "opposed aspects of *freedom*, the 'abstract' freedom of pure, self-relating negativity, withdrawal-into-self, cutting the links with reality, and the 'concrete' freedom of the loving acceptance of others, of experiencing oneself as free and finding full realisation in relation to others"; so when Julie openly cries, the loss-oriented stage of her mourning has moved into gear, signifying that "she is reconciled with the universe."[195] With (but slightly amending) Žižek, one might argue that these are not *only* tears "of sadness and pain, but the tears of *agape* [sic], of a Yes! to life in its mysterious synchronic multitude."[196]

Insdorf's consideration of Kieślowski's intentions for *Blue* connects to the same duality: "Having tried to live in 'liberty'—without memory, desire, work, or commitment—[Julie] is ironically returning to love, which Kieślowski acknowledged to be contradictory with freedom."[197] For Insdorf, this "reflects the refusal of pessimism" in *Blue*, her faith in the optimism of the ending bending the film's ambiguity, and countering the director's professed ambivalence about its close, to amplify her own critical interpretation. Rushton, on the other hand, echoes Žižek, embracing *Blue*'s ambiguities in a discussion of the relationship between freedom and love articulated by St. Paul's letter and, thus, Julie's *Concert[o]*:

These words assert that in one's quest for freedom—"absolute freedom"—one may try to cut all the ties that bind the self to anything or
anyone else so as to absorb all the knowledge that the universe can offer, to steadily progress towards the super-human. But if one has all of
these things, and noone [sic] with whom to share them, then the bits
and pieces of one's existence amount to nothing. And is this not
Julie's story?[198]

Without *agapē*, *Blue* concludes, I am/she is/we are nothing. But *agapē*
comes at a price.

At the end of *The Meaning of Life*, Eagleton outlines an answer to
familiar existential dilemmas that accords with, and amplifies, aspects
of *Blue*'s conclusion. Most strikingly, he posits *agapē*'s centrality to a
well-lived life, going on to illustrate his understanding of the concept
through his jazz band metaphor. As Eagleton points out in contextualiz-
ing this image, the lineage of thought to which Julie succumbs by the
end of *Blue* has a longer heritage than St. Paul's famous letter. "For
Aristotle," for instance, "happiness is bound up with the practice of
virtue," and "for his great Christian successor Thomas Aquinas," this
sign of well-being "would be an example of love."[199] However, Eagleton notes the tragedy encoded in the virtuous and charitable love espoused by Aquinas, Aristotle and St. Paul's notions of *caritas* and
agapē. St. Paul, after all, wrote that "we die every moment"—a comment Eagleton relates to "the fact that we can only live well by buckling
the self to the needs of others, in a kind of little death, or *petit mort*. . . .
In this way, death in the sense of a ceaseless dying to self is the source
of a good life," a doctrine which may sound "unpleasantly slavish and
self-denying" if one forgets that, "if others do this as well"—uniting in
their performances of *agapē*, so to speak—"the result is a form of reciprocal service which provides the context for each self to flourish."[200] He
continues:

> This kind of activity is known as *agapē*, or love, and has nothing to
> do with erotic or even affectionate feelings. The command to love is
> purely impersonal: the prototype of it is loving strangers, not those
> you desire or admire. It is a practice or way of life, not a state of
> mind. It has no connection with warm glow or personal intimacies.
> Is love, then, the meaning of life? It has certainly been the favourite
> candidate of a number of astute observers, not least of artists.[201]

Kieślowski was one such artist, and he gave much (and ultimately,
some would argue, all) of himself so that his co-workers might achieve,
with him, creative fulfillment. Julie, his most compelling fictional creator, can be read as achieving a "happiness" which means she must suffer, too, at least some of the time. Like equations of liberty, *agapē*'s
plusses and minuses form an inextricable dualism of profit and loss.

By the end of *Blue*, Julie has experienced individuation and community both creatively through her musical ensemble (composers collaborating on individual yet connected compositions) and through her

new society of personal relationships with Lucille, with Olivier, with Patrice's mistress Sandrine—a virtual stranger to whom she gifts, as if to epitomize *agapē*, the home she had once shared with her husband and her daughter. Julie has therefore moved decisively into the loss-oriented stage of her grief-work by engaging in the virtuous, charitable, self-sacrificial form of love that is "a taxing, dispiriting affair, shot through with struggle and frustration": a love that may even "bring you to your death."[202] No wonder Preisner's score for *Blue* ends with a funeral march yielding but a glimmer of hope. Such is *agapē*.

CHAPTER SIX

LAST TANGO IN WARSAW: *WHITE*

White is a tango of stories and subtexts. There are many dueling parties: Karol and Dominique, East and West, Paris and Warsaw, Europe old and new, economic systems, life and death, light and dark *mise-en-scène*. Even Karol's hair styles—fluffily unthreatening at first, later oozing oily self-confidence—seem dialectically opposed for symbolic purposes. It is apt, then, that a tango resides at the center of *White*'s score. Two tangos, in fact: "The Last Sunday" and one of Preisner's own invention. Yet there is more to these tangos than an obvious representation of ritualized dueling and/or courtship. Structurally, the score itself forms a semiotic tango in which one musical dance is contained by another with quite different cultural connotations. Preisner's score structures an opposition of music alluding to Polish folk song and tango, the latter ultimately subordinated within a thematic structure alternating a pastoral *rustico*, as Preisner labels his folk theme in the score, with the more cosmopolitan genre. Over the course of the film, the implications of these themes and their shifting emphases entangle with the remainder of the narrative. The structure of the score, in turn, emphasizes *White*'s underlying concept.

White's score might thus be heard as a filmic example of what Robert Hatten, writing on Beethoven, has called "expressive genre." Analyses of expressive genres consider broad transformations in a work's intimations of mood, style, and style's associated social status, and note the changing expressive states evoked by music's culturally encoded significations. There are several archetypal expressive genres. Some movements or works explore just one state (pastoral, heroic, comic, etc.), while others involve a change. For example, Hatten reads the slow movement of Beethoven's "Hammerklavier" sonata (1817-18) as an example of a "change-of-state" expressive genre that he calls "tragic-to-transcendent." His reading rests on the movement's modulation into G major, which is accompanied by a hymn-like texture that,

Hatten explains, marks a religious or spiritual topic associated with a higher societal sphere, and thus "a vision of grace in the midst of tragic grief."[1] The movement may therefore be heard to symbolize the possibility of transcendence through abnegation and the "positively resigned acceptance"[2] of one who has sacrificed much to gain something greater.

A consideration of the concept of expressive genre, and particularly change-of-state narratives, holds potential for film music analysis, drawing as it does on a store of literature already dealing with narrative and music, albeit in a different repertoire.[3] First, it involves not a search for frozen architectural unity in a film's score (e.g., the potentially stultifying search for leitmotivic coherence) but rather for a succession of events embodying a transformation: the teleological essence of most story arcs. Second, such work could permit the extension of an already widely used body of theory on screen music—Tagg's work on semiotics—through a process of comparison and contrast to Hatten's research, itself a development of Leonard Ratner's work on style topics in the Classical period.[4] In essence, Hatten's work empowers one to develop the type of music-analytical cultural critique presented by Tagg's groundbreaking analysis of the *Kojak* TV theme, and later studies, over longer spans. Style topical connotations of mood and social register do more than trigger Pavlovian cognitions and emotions at specific but isolated points in a film. They also participate in longer-range strategies devised to affect an audio-viewer and, in turn, to sculpt aspects of their perception of a narrative's story and subtext. This is not the place for theoretical exegesis,[5] but my reading of *White* seeks to indicate the potential value of such an approach by providing a musically mediated analysis of *White*'s expressive genre and its crucial role in delivering the film's polemical content. *White* is a double change-of-state, tragic-to-triumph-to-transcendent expressive narrative in which the protagonists, like the persona Hatten invites one to read into Beethoven's *Hammerklavier*, achieve victory not through personal gain, but through individual acts of abnegation.[6] In the context of the trilogy, such acts recall Julie's sacrifice of personal liberty in *Blue*, Kern's admission of guilt in *Red*, and more generally the trilogy's engagement with the concept of living one's life through *agapē*.

White generates this symbolic charge by playing on social distinctions of musical taste, as identified by Pierre Bourdieu in his classic study and represented here by the cultural connotations of Preisner's *rustico* and the tango in Western societies. Bourdieu's *Distinction: A Social Critique of the Judgement of Taste* models "the relationships between the universe of economic and social conditions and the universe of life-styles" in the consumption of cultural commodities from food and sports through to paintings and music.[7] To cite just the very basics of his critique, objects of culture consumed by an individual are defined, above all, by the individual's social origins and level of education, the former being the strongest form of influence. "To the socially recognized hierarchy of the arts," he writes, "and within them, of genres, schools or periods, corresponds a social hierarchy of the consumers.

This predisposes tastes to function as markers of 'class.'"[8] His study of musical tastes proved "a strong opposition between the dominant class on the one hand and the working classes" on the other; the pattern was sometimes disrupted, however, by social climbers accruing extra "cultural capital" through means other than their education or background, and who thus become associated with alternative musical tastes to those of their origins "through social trajectory."[9] Karol is one such social climber and *White*'s shift from *rustico* to tango, and then back again, marks aspects of his socio-economic journey.

Bourdieu identifies three levels of musical taste roughly commensurate to upper, middle and working class: legitimate taste, middlebrow taste and popular taste. Argentine tango, in Polish society, may initially have impinged on legitimate tastes as music in the process of being legitimated by a white, Western elite; more likely, however, tango is akin to "the major works of the minor arts" adopted by middle-class consumers to demarcate their societal position from those down below. Tango was originally, of course, a popular art form created by a working class, or even an underclass, and reflecting its specific socio-economic conditions. In *White*, however, the tango—just as it rose from the slums of Buenos Aires to become an internationalized commodity for middlebrow entertainment—accompanies Karol's rising trajectory as he eschews his lowly roots. His newfound societal clout, attained via capital earned on the wild frontier of Polish capitalism, is accompanied on the soundtrack by music of greater social distinction than the folk-inspired music accompanying his earlier appearances. It therefore comes as no surprise to hear Preisner's *rustico* echoing not the sophistication of Chopin's "legitimating" approach to the mazurka or polonaise, say, but rather a plainer processing of the traditional musics Preisner absorbed as a child. It also seems unsurprising that, ultimately, the *rustico* theme transforms from being an icon of nostalgia and homesickness to a signifier of authenticity and self-transcendence. It is a short cut, typical of many films' uses of world or folk musics in their scores, to the signification of "primitive" authenticity and moral authority, as opposed to "civilized" sophistication.[10]

White is a film that sets itself against the accrual of cultural capital and its consumerist accoutrements. It argues instead for the greater value of the things that money cannot buy, and of which money can easily make one lose sight. *White*'s moral, in a sense, is a direct contradiction of the film's signature line: the film argues, simply but forcefully, that no, one cannot buy just anything nowadays. This is a variation on the trilogy's political and philosophical leitmotif: the notion that sacrifice, philanthropy and selfless love trump everything, and not least the self-interest, financial gain and accumulation of consumer goods depicted by *White*'s caricature of early Polish capitalism. *White* seeks to communicate these notions to a potentially wide audience by tweaking the late Kieślowski style, putting its argument in terms accessible to the Karols of the world, as much as to the Julies or Valentines—i.e., those less likely to encounter a *Blue*, and still less a *Red*, but open to the charms of a somewhat generic comedy in which low humor sweetens a polemical pill made easier to swallow, in part, by the wit and panache of Preisner's music. There are barely twenty minutes of Preisner in *White*: nine for the tango, eleven for the *rustico*; the disparity hints at the greater symbolic weight of the *rustico*, in spite of the literature's focus to date on the significance of the tango. Yet typically, a little of his music says a great deal, in this case in the context of a film that is both obviously and more covertly political.

The *Rustico* Mazurka

The first theme that one hears in *White* is the *rustico*, Preisner's impressionistic allusion to his country's traditional music. This theme is one of the clearest examples in Preisner's output of the direct influence of folk music on his scoring style. It is a remembrance of the mazurka. The *mazur* is a folk dance from the Mazovia region, although by the seventeenth century its popularity had spread throughout Poland. There are three main forms, of differing speeds. Preisner's is closest in pace to the *kujawiak*, a dance of moderate tempo with elongated phrase lengths. Like the tango, the mazurka is a dance for couples (indeed for a community of couples who dance in a circle); unlike the tango, crucially, it is a representation of union and equality rather than subordination.

The stylistic markers of mazurka in Preisner's theme are obvious. The theme (see Ex. 6.1) is scored in a triple meter with a displacement of accent to the second of each pair of bars, in an example of music that might be said to "reflect the specificity" of Polish language through its paroxytonic accents.[11] Preisner's *rustico*—his name for it in the score is evocative, obviously, of the genre's pastoral origins—further reflects the rhythmic qualities of traditional mazurkas in several ways. Its three main rhythmic groupings (a, b and c in Ex. 6.1 i) are among the most common mazurka rhythms; the second and third phrases utilize a descendental rhythm. Paroxytonic and descendental characteristics are present in individual bars or operating across two-bar phrases (see Ex. 6.1 ii and iii). The melodic AABB phrase structure is also typical to those identified as schematic by early compilers of mazurkas[12] and Preisner's often simple scoring of the tune could be related to traditional renderings in which *dudy* or *gajdy* (Polish bagpipes) or a *fujarka* (shepherd's pipe) play the tune, accompanied merely by a drone. These reedy sounds and sustained accompaniments are evoked by Preisner's woodwind melodies and pedal-points.

The theme is clearly marked, therefore, as rustic by its folk music derivation. However, Preisner's *rustico* differs from tradition in significant ways. As noted above in Chapter Four, it is in ⅜ rather than ⅔. Furthermore, on the one hand it falters rhythmically on its bars of rest, like the faltering funeral march in *Blue*. One could read this as an exaggera-

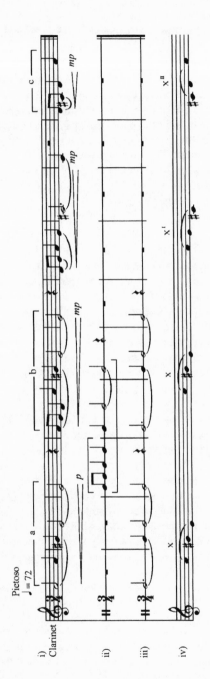

Ex. 6.1: *White's rustico* **(Karol's part, as heard in court)**

tion of the music's descendental character while noting that, as in *Blue*, when heard in audio-visual contexts, the pauses accentuate moments of longing, pain, separation and loneliness. On the other hand—and as distinct from Chopin's fifty-plus mazurkas, say, with which Preisner's shares but superficial similarities[13]—Preisner's *rustico* does not "consistently exploit bold contrasts between joyous vigour and Polish *żal* (profound melancholy)."[14] This mazurka is decidedly down in the dumps. Yet the score as a whole can be considered to exploit just such a contrast, between the *rustico*'s *żal* and the tango's vigor. As Wollermann has noted, Preisner has explained that his music for *White* drew on the folk music of his country by being both melancholy and wild.[15] He achieves this through the *rustico*'s juxtaposition with its musical animus, the tango—a reminder that its symbolism must be interpreted in a pugilistic context.

The Suitcase and Karol

The *rustico* theme is not initially stated outright by the score. Rather, it buds, opens and then finally blooms, extending its thematic tendrils over widening intervallic spans until it has reached its full musical and symbolic height. The full ladder of pitches is heard first when Karol is seen spying on Dominique's apartment, and later when he looks up at her Rapunzel-like prison cell. She does not let down her hair to be rescued but, while the unfurling of the *rustico* maps out the distance between them, it also connects them by symbolizing what is pure at the heart of their, for the bulk of the film, poisoned relationship.

More immediately in *White*, the music and sound design of the opening montage sculpt an audio-visual character sketch of Karol Karol. Every bit as artificial as any of the sonic confections in *Blue*, William Flageollet's creation forms a "sonic," to use Philip Brophy's term, into which the action of the film, and thus one's perceptions of Karol, are inserted.[16] The opening "sonic" and cue combine tellingly in a sequence that cuts between a suitcase on an airport conveyor belt and Karol arriving at the courthouse for his divorce hearing. They collude to lay bare, before one has any truly salient information about his predicament, much that one needs to know about Karol's plight and persona. Like so much else in this apparently simple film, what seems unassuming and plainly made reveals, on inspection, deliberate and intriguing filmmaking.

The film begins with a series of thudding blows as a heavy object—its weight sounds as dead as a corpse—hits an airport conveyor belt. This series of blows is being rained in on Karol. He is the content, one later discovers, of the suitcase, and here is receiving a physical assault to parallel the psychological bruising he will receive at the Paris court. However, by starting, like *Blind Chance*, with a flash-forward, *White* shapes an enigma that immediately captures the perceiver's attention—what is this suitcase and what does it mean?—while loosening the narrative's sense of temporality and of its protagonist's subjectivity. Like Karol's life in these moments, the film's timeline is fractured. As Insdorf notes, the juxtapositions also suggest that Karol, "like the trunk, is being pulled along a predetermined path."[17] There is a contrast, in other words, between teleology and fragmentation; one could in fact argue the toss over whether the suitcase is a flash-forward or the diegetic present, with everything that follows until one sees the suitcase again as an elongated flashback. Either way, it is notable that, at the moment Karol takes control of his destiny by loading himself into the suitcase, the discourse returns to a predictably unfolding present, rather than the opening's suggestion of a man at the mercy of greater diegetic and narratorial forces.

Aside from the wince-inducing thumps received by the suitcase—experienced more sharply, and thus as black comedy, once one is aware of its content on the shot's reprise later in the film—the experiential discomfort for the perceiver is heightened through a fusion of music and sound. The first pitched noise heard is a high sustained B, most likely emanating from the conveyor belt's machinery and captured in situ by Jean-Claude Laureux. Karol's clarinet then enters on middle C, so a major seventh below the B—a chromatic interval that Western ears are entrained to hear as dissonant, uncomfortable and in need of resolution. So when one sees Karol, one is already prepared to feel that he, too, must be uncomfortable: a fish out of water in Paris. Indeed, he is in "Hell," as the screenplay puts it in a direct echo of *Blue*'s opening ("A terrible noise, vendors shouting, street organs grinding, children crying").[18] Also like *Blue*, the scripted hell at the opening of *White* is pared back visually but enhanced by subtle audio.

Consequently *White*'s opening may also remind one of the fate of *Blue*'s traveling vehicle and its occupants, implying a bad omen for this suitcase/man on screen—not least because the two (man and cue) are so seamlessly connected by the discourse. When the montage cuts to Karol arriving at the courthouse, there is a surprising lack of disruption due to the smooth sonic transition shaped from conveyor belt to street. The end of the second phrase on Preisner's solo clarinet cue also hangs over into the street scene, the motion of the conveyor belt and cue being taken up by the motion of the camera tracking Karol's feet moving along the pavement. This links man and suitcase: they are, as the film later proves, one and the same. There are no organ grinders in this 1990s hell, but the audio-viewer is assaulted by traffic noise, sirens, a pneumatic drill, and air brakes that sound a gasp of horror as Karol turns away from a couple kissing passionately, and thereby reminding him of what he has been unable to do with Dominique.[19] All attack the ears, evoking Karol's discomfort and anxiety both on the conveyor belt and as he arrives at court for his hearing.

Scuffed shoes and cheap clothes aside, Karol's pathetic quality is further evoked by Preisner's *calando* clarinet writing, in an example of Preisner assigning a specific timbre to a character for symbolic purposes—or, rather, to a character at certain points in the film: Karol will later be scored by a string sextet, with quite different connotations. While non-Polish audiences might never pick up on the depiction here of a "klarnet," there is a timbral blandness to the clarinet's initial meandering around its middle registers. Further aspects of the score also imply Karol's weakness. As noted above, screen scoring clichés associate woodwind instruments with the feminine. Karol—by not being scored boldly, say, like Olivier's trumpets and drums in *Blue*—is being musically emasculated; the pastoral and tragic connotations of his music also participate in this semiotic othering. In a few short seconds the score portrays him as weak, adrift and helpless, as uncertain of his direction in life as the fragmented phrases of the clarinet's lines—a suggestion further exaggerated by the fact the cue is broken into three parts to accompany the three separated shots of the suitcase.

The cue's harmony also drifts. The melody is not obviously minor or major, but rather a chromatic collection in which tritones and semitones dominate, and in which, while both C and E♭ may be heard to function briefly as reference pitches and perhaps to anticipate the C minor of the tango, neither attains a sense of tonal centricity. The harmony, like the character, is unmoored. Partly as a result, the melodic ideas do not sound clear-cut, although small phrases contain the seeds of more distinctive music to come. Two gestures—the descending semitone and a three-pitch descent from a small falling interval (semitones) to a larger one (marked "x" on Ex. 6.2)[20]—hold, in miniature, the motivic universe of Preisner's entire score, and clearly of the *rustico* melody (see x in Ex. 6.1 iv). Also, the start and end pitch-classes of the first phrase of the cue—C and A—will be the two main pitch-centers in the score. The three-note motif, heard in the two shots as the suitcase disappears for the time being, is both a summary of what has already been heard and a gesture that, slightly altered, will form the basis of the *rustico* theme proper. Preisner is no formalist and the unity shaped between the materials of his score is not the source of its value in *White*, although some may find such details pleasing. It does suggest, however, a link between his crafting of precise musical materials and his considered approach to a score's unfolding over the course of a narrative.

Ex. 6.2: The proto-*rustico*

There is another sound in the opening of the film that takes on a motivic function: pigeons. When Karol first encounters the birds on the courthouse steps, he watches a pigeon in flight in a moment of metaphysical awe. His awe is repaid with ordure. This slap in the face (well, on the shoulder) summarizes all that has been connoted thus far about Karol: he is the kind of person who, if he dares to dream above his station, will always be cut down to size. Associating Karol with the pigeons, moreover, literally links him to vermin: the pigeon as winged rat, the *klarnet* of the bird family. In terms of Kieślowski's oeuvre, the symbolism is yet grimmer. When a pigeon alights on the doomed child's windowsill in *Decalogue 1*, it is a harbinger of death; later, the pigeon returns to haunt the bereaved father. Is Karol being marked for some form of death, too? Yet pigeons, notably common birds, are also born survivors. As the two words of the courthouse legend over Karol's shoulder indicate—sardonically framed as he wipes away the droppings—the pigeons have liberty (they can fly and do whatever they want) and also equality (they flock). Highlighting what Karol does not have, they hint at what he could attain.[21]

Hearing a Plea: The *Rustico*

Sonically and dramatically, the film cuts to the eye of Karol's personal storm when it moves into the courtroom where the divorce proceedings are being heard. The sound design is appropriately less busy as the focus shifts to actors and dialogue, although the reverberant acoustic connotes a sacred, church-like space—one in which to break, not make, a marriage. At a crucial point during the court hearing, however, music and sound collaborate to shape a symbolically resonant moment, as Karol begins his plea to the court and, subsequently, the film flashes back to his marriage ceremony. This sequence begins with the question "What about equality?" and coincides with Julie from *Blue* gatecrashing the courtroom as she searches for Patrice's mistress. Temporally, this situates *White* as overlapping with the close of *Blue* and unites the diegetic arc of the trilogy's first two narratives. However, Julie's interruption may also be read to bring *Blue*'s key idea into play within *White*. Equality, Julie's presence hints, can only be achieved through the liberations of *agapē* and thus a self-sacrificial love far removed from the bitter recriminations on display here. Eventually, Karol and Dominique will recognize this to be true. At this stage, they are deaf to the possibility. Karol speaks, but Julie leaves unheard.

The need for perceivers to attend closely to Karol's speech is signaled by the piercingly high oboe G# that begins Preisner's second cue. Marked *pietoso* and *cantabile*, and played at a lyrical 72 beats per minute, the *rustico* melody now unfolds in two statements. The first accompanies Karol's speech; the second, differentiated by transposition and a change in instrumentation, coincides with the shift into flashback and, arguably, a change in point of view. Scored for Karol's clarinet, the first statement (see Ex. 6.1 above) fuses with Karol's speech in Polish, the court translator's French and, for some viewers, the subtitles, forming a tripartite potency as Karol explains that he still feels hope and wants to save the marriage. Wollermann suggests that the melody imitates a series of searching rhetorical questions, as if the music is paraphrasing Karol.[22] A sense of questioning is typical of Preisner's faltering melodies and here the trait is used to good effect.

The melody is first heard in A major, but with a flattened 6th. It swiftly confirms its major modality, but at first the tune seems destined to fall into D minor with a rustic raised 4th (its G♯). The monologue's musical accompaniment thereby begins by continuing to evoke the melancholy pastoralism already associated with Karol, while preparing a modal contrast that, when the tune settles into A major, sounds a hint of hope to parallel Dominique's flicker of a smile as she listens to him. The G♯'s emphasizing of the *rustico*'s rusticity (Wollermann calls this mode the "gypsy minor scale"), alongside its remembrance of the mazurka, roots Karol in a symbol of Polishness and the pastoral to indicate his low social standing in the civilized surroundings of the Parisian court. However, the folk music style of the cue also carries clichéd connotations of authenticity, as if Karol's words speak a truth transcending his current predicament. The music suggests that his love is true. It may even say that love is *the* truth.

The final phrase of the first melodic statement stops a bar short, having been interrupted by Preisner to leave a question mark hanging in the air. This has the immediate function of creating anticipation of an answer to the judge's question (was the marriage consummated?), bumping up intensity for the audio-viewer. Indeed, such an expectation has been building throughout the speech, thanks to the faltering phrases (an unfinished melody is unconsummated, too). But it also leaves a door open to the possibility of an alternative response to Karol's softly spoken "nie" and its translation, "non." As those words sound the image cuts to something notably other: a vision of Dominique leaving the church after a marriage ceremony, and exiting a tunnel of darkness into a blaze of white light to be confronted, at first, by scuttling pigeons, their wings beating applause for the happy couple, and then by a flock of human well-wishers. She turns, looking radiantly happy, to smile at the person whose subjective point of view the camera represents and, in turn, the audience, who also bask in the glow of her gaze. The screenplay confirms that the point of view is most straightforwardly read here as being Karol's, but one might wonder whether the flashback is his or, rather, his alone. The action, while shot from his perspective, may be focalized from that of another character.

Focusing on sound and music, one might argue that this metadiegetic moment is occurring within Dominique's imagination, as time stops for her within the court and she daydreams of when she, too, felt love and hope. After the vision, she snaps her head up to answer an apparently unheard question from the judge—a moment that reminds one of Julie being called back to reality and time by the journalist's interruption in *Blue*, after her first musical vision. *White*'s flashback melody then stops a further phrase earlier than the first statement of the *rustico* melody, adding to the sense of interruption. Shifts in key and timbre also suggest the break from Karol's perspective to another person's. In the flashback one hears her footsteps (walking away from

Karol's point of view as, in the "reality" of the courthouse, he waits to say the no that will doom their marriage to divorce), plus the rustling of her dress, alongside a cor anglais playing the tune (an alternative feminine timbre to Karol's clarinet), as the melody is transposed up a minor third to C (see Ex. 6.3).[23] The cue was wet with reverb during its first statement, but the insistent tone of the cor anglais marks this still more obviously, the sense of space highlighting that this is a moment of subjective introspection for one or more of the characters. Reading these moments as Dominique's flashback and an articulation of her happy memory of their marriage renders her more sympathetic, or at least more complexly motivated, than some depictions of her character have suggested. She knows the truth of their love, the rising contour of her second phrase perhaps suggesting this inner strength, but she also knows that she needs Karol to take the long road to fulfill its promise.

Ex. 6.3: *Rustico* (Dominique's half)

If this is Dominique's flashback, then this is also partly her theme, and one could hear the bipartite structure of the *rustico* suggesting two parts for two people. The theme thus becomes a memory of the hope buried in the rubble of their relationship. As love duets go, this is no simplistic throb of longing. By being redolent of a courtship dance from Polish folk music, the music marks his speech and her flashback as the authentic moral center of the film. It implies something Karol and Dominique cherish but do not want to acknowledge, led astray by alternative agendas, and not least a desire for selfish gain. It also hints that they will discover the truth, through the establishment in each half of the theme of a major mode—but not yet. As revealed by the slash of a smile on Karol's face when he later watches an old man struggling to put a bottle into a recycling bank, this humiliation unleashes a devil: he is "revitalized," according to the screenplay. Things slotting into place are a motif in the trilogy and here, putting aside the obvious phallic pun of the bottle wedged neither in nor out of an opening, the moment suggests the beginning of a twist to Karol's character. And this Karol will sing a different tune.

(Not) Making Love

Much that was originally intended for the salon burning scene, both in the script and Preisner's score, is cut from the finished film. The screenplay describes explicit sex and contains descriptions of Dominique "freeing her breasts" that tally with the ungainly gaze of the flash

Fig. 6.1: Preisner's first named *rustico* cue in *White*'s manuscript score

of stocking it calls for in the courtroom. Such objectifications were cut from the film, and with them go aspects of Preisner's cue including tension-building pedal points and trilling presumably designed to intimate the stirrings of desire. With the sex toned down, romance is emphasized by the characters' gentler gestures—relaxed smiles, the playfulness as Karol tickles Dominique's nose with her hair—and by Preisner's score, in which the melody of the *rustico*, here named as such in the score for the first time (see Fig. 6.1), now speaks uninterruptedly, completing its statement.

The *rustico* is again heard in C, but now scored for an oboe joined, towards the cue's end, by a flute which mainly doubles the oboe at a consonant third. This sweetens the music harmonically, and the fact that the two lines move in easy consonance has obvious symbolism: like the couple, these lines briefly move in consort. With the cue being allowed to complete its melodic statement, unlike the version in the court cut short when the judge interrupted Dominique's reverie, this is also the first clear establishment of C as a pitch-center, making good on the promise of the film's first note and, in doing so, perhaps shaping a sense of formal arrival and, even, structural fulfillment. If so, this is a wry pun, as Karol's performance ends not in fulfillment but failure, sparking Dominique's fury. The melody stops at the moment sexual content begins and potential energy yields to spent reality. The irony of their ensuing argument—you do not understand me, she claims, but clearly she does not understand him either in certain respects—is underlined by the absence of Preisner's delicate music, which argued otherwise. The musical environment reveals the tragedy of the characters' inflamed predicament: they are still in love.

Next Pigeon, *Last Sunday*, First Tango

A clatter of pigeon wings calls Karol's attention, the sound design implies, to a bust in a shop window. The bust does not look that much like Dominique, but its frilly cap forms a similar shape to the curls with which Karol framed her face in the salon; her flawless alabaster glaze also evokes Delpy's pale makeup. Whether the pigeon exists diegetically, though, is an interesting question: one does not see it, any more than one sees the recorder player while Julie basks in sunlight in *Blue*, or the helicopters and planes that hover over various meetings between Valentine and the old judge in *Red*. Perhaps the sound is triggered in Karol's unconscious by the sight of the bust. Later on, pigeons are diegetically established as sticking close to Karol with some kind of Kieślowskian metaphysical glue. Here their presence is purely sonic.

A second clap of wings is heard as Karol stands, transfixed by the statue and just before music is heard. This new tune, the next cut reveals, is being played by Karol on his comb. The prize-winning hairdresser has been reduced to using the tool of his trade, and thus a source of his sense of integrity and self, to busk for spare coins on the Metro (see Fig. 6.2). In a direct contrast to Julie's well-funded busker, Karol is not busking just because he likes to play: it is an additional humiliation. That Karol busks on a comb is thus ingenious. It forces him to create a primitive reed instrument, thus intensifying his association with wood-wind-like timbres culturally encoded as unsophisticated, not masculine, and thus pastoral and feminine, and by clichéd extension more plaintive and weak. Because it is played, quite literally, by his own breath, emasculated music and man start to merge. Yet Karol is a failure even at busking. After the first two phrases, more or less pitched in E minor, the performance warps sharp, rendering him both literally and metaphorically hard to look at/listen to. His second attempt at the refrain of the song then provides a laugh-out-loud moment, so utterly wretched seem performance and performer.[24]

Fig. 6.2: Karol the musician (photo courtesy of the author)

The tune is "The Last Sunday," a song also known in Poland as the "Suicide Tango" or "Death Tango" (see Ex. 6.4, which transcribes this performance). Karol is delving into the songs of his childhood for his busker's repertoire, the screenplay reveals, hence the old Polish popular song. The lyrics "editorialize," to borrow Rick Altman's term, by playing on song's ability to perform narrative functions beyond the range of original dramatic underscoring:

> More complex, and in the long run more interesting, are the many feature film attempts to take advantage of popular song's ability to perform certain operations better than "classical" music. [For instance, w]hile "classical" music is particularly able to provide routine commentary and to evoke generalized emotional reactions, popular song is often capable of serving a more specific narrational purpose. . . . From *High Noon* to *Miller's Crossing*, nondiegetic popular song lyrics provide a unique opportunity to editorialize and to focus audience attention.[25]

i)

ii)

Ex. 6.4: i) "To ostatnia niedziela" and ii) "Wszystko co nasze Polsce oddamy" (transcribed from Karol's busking)

This song's lyrical and intertextual associations connect both to Karol's story and the story of the fellow Pole who recognizes the tune: the suicidal, bridge-playing existentialist Mikołaj.

Composed by Jerzy Petersburski in 1935 with words by Zenon Friedwald, and most famously performed, in various recordings, by Mieczysław Fogg, "To ostatnia niedziela" ("This is the/The Last Sunday") was an immensely popular mid-1930s Polish tango. It describes the final meeting of the song's persona—who has been usurped in his idol's affections by a "second, richer, better" one—and his beloved, as he begs her for one last Sunday together before a future spent apart. That future, later verses imply, will be suicidally curtailed for the singer. (What is to be done with me? Who knows? he muses morosely; later he speaks of only one solution, one way out.)[26] In *White*, as well as reflecting Karol's rejection and Mikołaj's suicidal intentions, the song's first verse also indicates the story's obsession with doublings: the second, richer, better one who comes along and steals away the beloved, in Karol's life, will ultimately be *himself*, reborn on his return to Poland as he schemes to reverse the polarity of the song and place Dominique in the position of begging for one last time together, and for her freedom, if not quite for her life.

The song has a still darker relationship to death. In a detailed online overview of Petersburski's career, Grzegorz Musial relates this horrifying story:

> In the sadistic Nazi concentration camps, "The Last Sunday" was often played by a small brass orchestra while Jewish prisoners were led to the gas chambers and ovens to be executed. . . . It was also played in the Treblinka concentration camp by a Jewish orchestra and a choir . . . while other Jewish prisoners were marching to the gas chambers. Each musician was dressed in a clown-like shining blue frock and an enormous bow-tie.[27]

White's ruminations on death, real and symbolic, are enriched by its inclusion of "The Last Sunday." The score's second tango, Preisner's

own invention, will dominate later phases of the film. It will be an alto-
gether different proposition, yet even with its socio-economic aspiration
related content, which flows through some of the more straightforwardly comical moments in the film, it cannot escape being heard in the
context of "The Last Sunday." A thread of tango-related despair is
thereby sustained throughout *White*'s most enjoyable moments.

The song's melodic and style topical melancholia—and for perceivers unaware of the tango's titles, lyrics and connotations, the significations of its keening lilt and the melodramatic realm of the tango
may be all there is to be gleaned—introduces us to Mikołaj and the
tragedy lurking beneath his exterior's crumpled benevolence. The white
letters and arrow on the red sign in the background as Mikołaj appear
also point, with bleak irony, towards an exit point with the word
"Quick," just as he notices Karol and a man desperate enough to help
him with his final departure. Mikołaj interrupts the soliloquy with a
bathetic "Your fly is open," spoken in Polish; Karol's embarrassed little
raspberry of a note after this interruption by a fellow countryman is
amusing. Mikołaj knows Karol will understand Polish because of the
song and, in a flash, the tango and a shared heritage of Polish popular
culture establishes their connection as Poles in Paris, and furthermore as
people with potentially similar tastes. This is someone, the song tells
Mikołaj, with whom he might do business.

Equally important in this regard is Mikołaj's distaste for the
busker's next offering. The major key—E major to the suicide tango's
E minor—martial rhythms and pathological optimism of the second
Metro tune (which Mikołaj cuts dead with a curt "I don't like it") would
be enough to suggest to most non-Polish viewers, and Poles too young
to know the melody, that this song has militaristic and thus, potentially,
Communist associations (see Ex. 6.4ii). The song is called "All that we
have we give to Poland" ("Wszystko co nasze Polsce oddamy") and is
the anthem of the Polish Scouting Association, with whom it has been
associated since 1918. Like "The Last Sunday," it is part of a collective
Polish subconscious of popular culture relating to life before World
War II. Its lyrics are patriotic platitudes—a sort of "Everything I do, I
do it for Poland"—penned by Ignacy Kozielewski, although the melody
has a different origin, the First World War song "Na barykady" ("At the
barricades"). Karol's performance thus suggests that he was once a boy
scout. This chimes with his earnest, somewhat gullible qualities. That
Mikołaj does not like it, and that Karol does not continue the tune, indicates something else about their characters. One would hardly expect a
jaded lover and an existential nihilist to feel much affinity for the dated
patriotism of this song, with its air of fortitude and relentlessly perky
arpeggiation. Just as significantly, however, post-war Polish scouts often performed ceremonial duties at schools and in civic celebrations
marking major Communist anniversaries. Scouting movements
throughout the Eastern Bloc were created or co-opted to recruit new
Party members and to spread propaganda, and the Polish Scouting anthem helped render the movement ripe for propaganda uses. Karol can

instantly gauge, from his dislike of the song, that Mikołaj was not thick with the Party: they know they can trust one another. A new friendship, born of music, is then cemented over slugs of Glenfiddich, although it is the pigeon that alights on Mikołaj a little later on that really seals the metaphysical deal. The tango, anthem, alcohol and bird mark the friends' fates as shared and, potentially, equally tragic. A primary joy of the film is that both of those fates will be averted.

"Today a second, richer, better one than me came"

In response to Mikołaj's job offer—his new friend does not reveal that the assisted-suicide seeking client is himself—Karol soliloquizes about Dominique's beauty, how much he loves her, and the fact that, because of this, he could never do such a thing, even in his current predicament. Preisner's *rustico* cue for this scene has a two-part form and can be considered a parodic variation on the salon cue serving two main purposes. The first is to indicate that Karol is now idealizing Dominique, as also demonstrated by the stolen bust: he is permitting nostalgia to get the better of him and projecting her onto a higher plane. The second part harmonically contaminates the love duet by reinstating a hint of chromaticism last heard in the opening of the film, and it is played as the threat of the words of "The Last Sunday" are made flesh and Dominique is glimpsed (through net curtains) and then heard (down Kieślowski's most corrosive technology, the phone) taking a notably "better" lover.

Preisner's music achieves these complex symbolic effects, and a host of further narrative functions, with disarming simplicity. This *rustico cantabile* is scored for an accompanied flute, the highest and most nymph-like of the "feminine" woodwind instruments thus voicing Karol's idealization of his wife. The melody, in turn, is accompanied by strumming harps and guitar, summoning associations of the angelic. Dominique may be many things, but she is clearly an angel only in Karol's imagination. The music is also elaborated. Melodically, the flute adds arabesques, feminizing the tune further with obviously "pretty" ornaments; a fifth and extra phrase is added, too, varying the final refrain and thus performing a higher level of ornamentation.

Rhythmically, instead of being separated by two bars, the melody's two-bar phrases are separated by rests in which the chords of the harp ring on and time is marked by the chime of a bell-like acoustic guitar. Initially, this faltering follows the rhythm of Mikołaj and Karol's speech, making space for their beats of understated recognition between phrases of discourse; the fifth phrase, in turn, extends to fit the action. But the spaces also evoke emptiness and Karol's loss: one is reminded of the pauses in the faltering funeral march in *Blue*, where bars of rest became resonant with Julie's pain.

A tiny guitar gesture, reminiscent of the close of the end title in *Blue* and foreshadowing, not least because it begins on an A, the guitar cue closing *Red*, directs the audio-viewer's gaze upwards—harmonics exaggerating the rising end point of an already ascending perfect fifth—with Karol's pointing up to and then across from the Bardot poster to Dominique's bedroom window.[28] Wilson argues for a continuing thread in Kieślowski's cinema dealing with voyeurism and gender, discussing moments in *White* alongside *A Short Film about Love*. She argues, regarding the earlier film, that what the voyeur sees is whatever he or she wants to see: it is their fantasy, not a sexist director's. As such, when Magda (impossibly, except as meta-diegetic fantasy) sees herself through Tomek's telescope, "Kieślowski draws voyeurism into question, making us think further, in particular about power, fantasy and wish-fulfillment."[29] She also argues for nuances in the relationship between voyeur and exhibitionist in *White*. Dominique may be seen to be "blonde, polished, impervious"[30] and linked by the camera to the image of Bardot on the poster ("a stellar icon of blonde, visible femininity"),[31] but the gaze at Dominique is not cinematic voyeurism per se, "since the relationship between voyeur and exhibitionist appears most properly Kieślowski's subject."[32] Most notably, Dominique engages directly with her voyeur when phoned, confronting Karol with her ecstasy and unbounded subjectivity. Consequently, in *White*, "the distance between voyeur and object of desire is maintained, but the fixity of the power relations enacted is by no means certain."[33] Like the musical genre, the tangos *White* portrays need not follow a clichéd narrative path.

Before the action betrays that Dominique is not alone, a passing siren (linking back to the film's first shots) and oboe melody hint at events to come. The second part of the cue begins by falling through a B♭ minor triad to a sustained A, creating tension by unmooring any sense of tonal centricity established by the first part of the cue, and also by jarring against expectations of modulation shaped by the theme's previous airings. Rather than going on to assert the expected major modality, B♭ minor is established, thanks to the sudden arrival of a pedal B♭ (also signifying the ominous). The passage's discomfort is heightened by its dissonant clash with elements within the sound design. Shades of the hell of the opening return as vehicle brakes sound a cluster of metallic tones around the harp and woodwind voices.

This corrupted version of the *rustico* theme also has a raised fourth and raised sixth, the modal alterations evoking the category of the exotic: these are the not "Western" tones of Ionian or Aeolian modes, or even the familiarity, within *White*, of the "gypsy minor scale." By tying the feminine to the musically exotic and images of an obviously sexually active woman, the music and image make Dominique seem doubly different from Karol's idealizing image.[34] The melody ends not with an affirmation of the major mode and its positive emotional connotations, but rather with a melody and accompaniment poised ambiguously between B♭ minor and a B♭ diminished seventh chord—a pregnant pause already heard in *Blue* at several junctures. The last version of the *rustico* ended warmly, the harmonic fulfillment of C major mirroring the bulge in Karol's trousers; this cue ends with a parody of that moment, as another man takes his wife and place.

With surprise and horror, Karol hears the sound of Dominique's building orgasm when he phones her; Karol is so pathetic at this stage of *White* that he even fails at *coitus interruptus*. This is represented comically, but disturbingly, for the audio-viewer by the fact that, even when he takes the receiver away from his ear—usually the moment at which, by cinematic convention, meta-diegetic access to a character's inner ear is relinquished—her intensifying moans continue to sound at the same volume. If it seems distasteful for the film to link female sexual pleasure to horror, this need not lead to a simplistic reading. The mazurka's gradual corruption over the course of the first phase of *White* suggests that one's distaste should be directed at Karol, the man from whose perspective the drama is being related: his character is beginning to see Dominique in a corrupted light, as his fantasy bifurcates into angelic idealization and a misogynist's whore.

Karol's internalization of this angel/whore persona will permit his meaner side to intensify. Visually, this is implied by the blood-red taint to his face—which could be a blush of naivety, arousal or murderous bloodlust—as he listens to her, the glass of the phone booth giving him a demonic appearance, as if he had descended into the similarly red interior of the sex club in *Blue* and seen Dominique performing therein. Like Lucille's father in the sex club's audience, one might suppose, he is simultaneously repulsed yet attracted, subjectively entangled but driven to objectification. Initially, this rage is channeled into his confrontation with the kiosk attendant when he demands his two Francs back; it will manifest again, clearly directed at Dominique, later in the film. This aspect of Karol is unpleasant, and the unpleasantness is intensified by Preisner's manipulation of his initially plainly sweet and uncorrupted *rustico* theme, as the score perverts its pastoral. Yet this cue, like Karol and his love for Dominique, will ultimately be redeemed. Preisner's cue will return, notably altered, to underscore the final scene of the film (see Fig. 6.7 and Ex. 6.7).

Departure

For the final cue in France, and the last cue in the first act of the film, Preisner provides a downbeat variation of the accompaniment to Karol's speech in court, returning to A major, the key of that moment. This emphasizes the difference that has evolved between his and Dominique's portions of their theme. Over the course of the first thirty minutes of the film, Preisner's development of the bipartite *rustico* has mapped the increasing distance between Karol and Dominique. Dominique's half of the theme has evolved motivically and harmonically, moving away from Karol's stagnant portion. The pitch and timbre of her cues have risen away from him, too, thanks to the changes in key, register and scoring: cor anglais, oboe then flute sound increasingly distant from the middle registers of Karol's clarinet.

Preisner's intended cue for this scene is more elaborate than what one hears in *White*. The manuscript score is a two-part variation of the previous scene's distorted love duet. Harp and piano, and then a guitar, support a wind quintet of two clarinets, bassoon, oboe and flute.[35] In the film, as the suitcase is seen for the second time winding along the conveyor belt and then being loaded onto the plane—again its occupant being carried forwards by events, although now they are slightly more within his own control as he opts to leave Paris by any means—all one hears are two clarinets performing the first part of the cue. Instrumentally, Karol is thus depicted as doubly melancholy and weak by the doubling of his instrument, and one might wonder if the score hints at two Karols: the one who has died, in a sense, in France, and the one who will be reborn in Poland. Like the box containing Schrödinger's cat, the suitcase holds more than one possibility. The melody also returns to its minor-sounding inflection, the narrative context of the falling minor third making the music seem gesturally crestfallen. Karol's theme is even mixed deeper into the background than previous cues, the music's status on the soundtrack castigated alongside its referent. At least the sound effects are sympathetic. The hum of the conveyor belt's B natural now sounds consonantly with the pitches of the melody; the second clarinet's low B doubles this tone at the octave.

To the sounds of jet engines at full throttle, the suitcase is loaded onto the plane that will transport Karol, in more than one sense. The black hole in the side of the plane is like a grave into which the case plummets, but Karol will soon be reborn, in a field of white, after this symbolic death; the screenplay describes him lying inside it in a "fetal position." Falkowska evokes the double-edged Polish resonances of the suitcase and this scene. The suitcase is "a symbol of survival which refers to the endless emigrations of Poles who were often forced to live out of a suitcase for years," representing "a means of escape from the world of humiliation and inequality."[36] On the one hand, it is hard not to hear the raging jets as the sonic embodiment of the late-modern hell imagined by the opening of the screenplay: it is the single harshest mechanized sound in the trilogy, a blaze of white noise. Karol's gentle, rustic theme has been blown away by technology, commerce and modernity; the airplane, so symbolic of wealth and entitlement, epitomizes the Western world out of which he has been ejected. In a sense, however, its sound is also his baptismal fire. Karol will emerge from this sonic bath like a bug from a cocoon, swiftly evolving to embrace capitalism, greed and his darker half in order to take revenge on Dominique. He will continue to be inserted into a "sonic" of such sounds in the second part of *White*, their symbolism finding a musical match in the cues bearing Preisner's tango.

The Upwardly Mobile Tango

Home at Last

"It's alive!" exclaims the chief baggage thief, having stolen Karol's coffin-sized suitcase from Warsaw's (then) new airport on the presumption its 165lbs would add up to something more rewarding than just some "bloke." "Jesus—home at last," Karol exclaims; "Jesus, Karol," exclaims his brother Jurek, when Karol arrives back at their Warsaw home and salon. The symbolism is hardly opaque: Karol has risen again, although like Christ he too will only walk the earth for a short period, second time around. The moment is wryly blasphemous, and to Poles, potentially triply so. Karol's arrival back home carries out three profane acts. Jesus emerging from the tomb aside, the image of Karol on the rubbish tip puns on the image of Maciek at the end of *Ashes and Diamonds*. And as if that were not sacrilegious enough towards icons of Polish identity, Karol is also accompanied by a flourish of piano virtuosity that plays on the association of Chopin's music and Polishness.

As the thieves' car pulls up and the cases are unloaded, a church bell chimes a series of As in the distance. The bell proclaims Karol's arrival too, creating a tonal continuum linking back to the "home" key of the *rustico* melody, A major, and the tonal center for the trilogy's moral center to come, which Preisner's score establishes around Valentine in *Red*. The bell also contributes to the symbolic rebirth's religious aura. The white snow on the ground, in turn, suggests a blank slate, even if it is achieved here in surroundings of abject squalor: a rubbish tip surrounded not by metaphysical pigeons but a plague of squawking gulls. Karol has sunk as low as he can go; he is literally down in the dumps. Indeed, as Haltof notes, the scene is "an apt illustration of the Polish idiomatic expression of 'being at home' (literally, 'on one's own junk'")." [37] The only way is up.

The grandiosity of the Chopin allusion, in contrast to the surroundings, contributes to the humor of the scene while signposting the rising social trajectory of Karol's subsequent journey. The irony of flamboyant piano music—connoting the salons of Paris, national pomp and Polish pride—counterpointing the image of a tip and human refuse is delicious. One only really hears the music as Chopin-like, though, because of the story's return to Poland, in an instance of film's ability to change the way one hears a piece of music; usually critics focus on the reverse. Virtuosic (at least by Preisner's standards) piano writing, juxtaposing dramatic chords and tinkling descents, at this particular moment and in this particular film, could *only* signify Chopin, even though the music, in truth, bears but a passing resemblance to Chopin's music. Preisner's dense chords hardly replicate Chopin's gift for voicing, the runs are scarcely filigree, and there is no sense of the fluidity of Chopin's technique or phrasing. What panache there is, in fact, Preisner's cue leaves

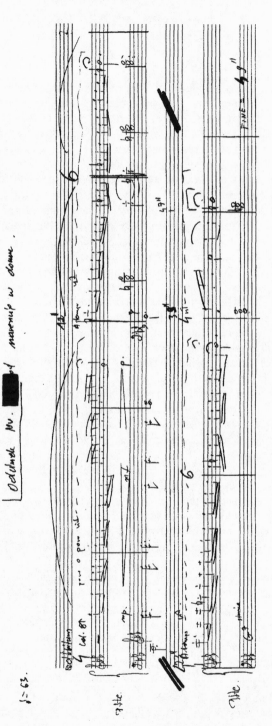

Fig. 6.3: "Chopin" (tango opening flourish) cue in Preisner's manuscript score

the pianist to provide, as what one hears in the film contains doublings and rhythms not present in Preisner's manuscript score (reproduced in Fig. 6.3). Preisner provided a sketch of Chopin-like music to be fleshed out by the pianist and then more fully realized within the audio-viewer's imagination.

This indication of Preisner's inventiveness when confronted with his technical limitations as a composer will fail to impress those who found his *Concert[o]* from *Blue* similarly inauthentic as an approximation of Western art music. Yet it is also an example of a moment where Preisner permits, through scoring practice, his soloists to bring their voices into the soundtrack, in an instance of creative co-working ranging beyond the restrictions many musicians at film sessions experience. As with the unconvincing art music at the end of *Blue*, moreover, the very inauthenticity of the Chopin allusion can be heard as fully intentional. Karol will be faking it from hereon in, donning a mask of sophistication in order to carry out a scheme that cuts against his interior truth. Music by Preisner that is somewhat like Chopin, but actually a knowingly rum pastiche, fits perfectly the image of kitschy middlebrow taste one might associate with a wannabe member of the *nouveau riche* struggling for social distinction.

The lack of a more precise allusion to Chopin also means that the piano flourish can function as the grandiose opening of Preisner's tango—a stylistic context in which the cue, arguably, works even better. Being in C minor, the tango is scored as the dark side to the C major renditions of the *rustico* marking the happiest moments so far in the film. In place of pastoral romance, the chords summon up images of ritualistic posturing at the start of a dance or duel. It also harmonically centers the music like nothing thus far in the score, which has rarely settled in any key for too long and sometimes tended towards chromatic opacity. The i-V^7-iv-V harmonic progression leading to the C minor chord at the start of the string sextet's tango theme, coupled with the grand rhetoric, places a robust cadence in C minor as well as Polish soil beneath Karol's feet. His arrival home is therefore emphasized by the score's first strong harmonic arrival, the leaden voicing of Preisner's chords enhancing the sensation of centering. Finally, the piano introduction sculpts a wonderful moment when Jurek recognizes and mouths the name of his brother. The question is a swathe of dominant preparation, accrued by the piano; the answer is Jurek's wondrous "Karol," falling in the rest between the end of the piano's dominant preparation and arrival of the tonic with the start of the first violin's melody.

The stress in *White*'s second phase on basic diatonic structures of tension and release, expectation and closure, create an aura of attainment and goal-directedness around its reborn hero, underscoring a character previously portrayed as impotent and emasculated in a manner that makes him seem more potent and heroic thanks to the cultural associations generated by tonality's drive towards closure, as famously formulated, from a feminist perspective, by Susan McClary.[38] Furthermore, while it may share with the *rustico* a recurring downwards melodic contour, the tango's most striking melodic characteristic is the series of ascents in the violin melody breaking free of those negative droops to form miniature erections of joy. This is not an entirely facile point: heroic themes encoded as masculine from Strauss's *Don Juan* to John Williams's *Indiana Jones* are full of similarly priapic gestures emphasizing a protagonist's alpha-male qualities and sexual potency. The Karol of the *rustico* was impotent; his tango is musical Viagra. The flourish and theme announce a man who will achieve the things Western society stereotypically equates to masculine prowess: power, wealth, a fancy car, and the sexual domination of a beautiful woman.[39]

Another signal that the new Karol will be no push-over is provided by the instrumentation. Wollermann argues that the string sextet and modality of the theme suggest a Slavic quality, with the instrumentation suggesting a Polish string band. The tango's musical image of Karol, however, is pitched midway between barnyard and a different kind of salon, as his thematic underpinning switches from rural authenticity to urbane sophistication, shifting to a genre of higher social distinction and adopting instruments that symbolize bourgeois success—the strings— thanks to their association with the orchestra, chamber recitals, and other socially elite forms of musical entertainment. (Preisner titles the cue "Tango" in the manuscript score.) This fusing of Karol to the music is accented audio-visually. In this example of transscansion, the two syllables of "Ka-rol" seem to speak for the first two notes of melody (see Ex. 6.5), at least for an audience primed by Jurek's astonished but silent utterance, and then the delightful cut to the establishing shot of the Karol Karol Salon, its neon sign winking the name Karol almost in time to the music. The red and white neon sign is a signifier of modernity and wealth, or at least of the aspiration to both.[40] Karol notices it and Jurek tells him that the embellishment is only to be expected because "we're in Europe now." This is not the Poland of pastoral idyll or Communist industry, it would seem, but an upstart liberal Western democracy keen to establish its capitalist credentials. The last time neon featured in the trilogy, it was in Lucille's sex club. The salon's sign is as vulgar as Preisner's cod-Chopin, and every bit as pungently ironic.

More obviously, by being a tango, the cue positions Karol as a man in control of the feminine other, and thus of his personal destiny. Like the lead dancer in a tango, with his hand in the small of his partner's back, Karol will lead the dance. He will be the puppeteer, the music suggests, pulling Dominique's strings, positioning her at his mercy and then vanquishing her. Preisner's music is not the only thing that sells Karol's transformation from Chaplinesque tramp to a would-be Michael Corleone: hair styling, sharper suits and Zamachowski's brilliant physical transformation have much to do with this, too. But the Karol tango plants the character on an entirely different footing from his previous manifestation: underscored by a tango like this, one could get away with murder. Yet tangos are not merely triumphant tales of one-upmanship. They are often tragic texts, as "The Last Sunday" has al-

Ex. 6.5: "Ka-rol": first tango cue

ready insinuated, with complex socio-political resonances. Karol's plans, in fact, will gradually go awry. A brief explanation of the origins and exporting of tango helps to clarify why underscoring that plot twist, and its political subtexts, with a tango was an even more intelligent decision than Preisner and Kieślowski may have realized.

Tango and Entanglement

Tango is a Latin American song and dance musical genre. Today it is primarily associated, Gerard Béhague reports, with "the most popular Argentine urban dance of the 20th century . . . develop[ing] in the *arrabal* or *orillas* (poor slum areas) on the outskirts of Buenos Aires" from musical traditions which "often referred to current events and frequently voiced social protest."[41] For Marta E. Savigliano, tango's "dance, music, and lyrics share a stubborn fatalistic quality rooted in tragic sociohistorical episodes."[42] Preisner's Karol tango can be likened to the *tango-milonga*, instrumental music with strong rhythmic characteristics. In films roughly contemporaneous to *White*, obvious examples of such a tango can be heard in the form of "Por una cabeza," heard in both *Scent of a Woman* (Brest, 1992) and *Schindler's List* (Spielberg, 1993).[43] "The Last Sunday," however, is a Polish example of a *tango-canción*, a vocal work with instrumental accompaniment and a strongly sentimental character, the lyrics of which expressed "views of love and life in highly pessimistic, fatalistic and often pathologically dramatic terms."[44] How appropriate, therefore, that tango should be used in *White* to symbolize Karol's urban exploits in Warsaw, forming a direct contrast to the rustic mazurka against which Preisner's score sets the tango in dialectical tension, and in doing so musically accentuating the film's enactment of socio-political critique.

The Polish popularity of these two types of tango—vigorous dance and pessimistic tragedy—is not hard to divine when one considers that the same attributes sit side-by-side in strands of the country's own traditional dance music, such as the mazurka's alternation of joy and *żal*. The tango came to interwar Poland, and particularly to Warsaw, as part of its internationalization during the first decades of the twentieth century, when it enjoyed fashionable status in Paris and London, and then widespread European accord, thanks to the emergence of early gramophone stars such as Carlos Gardel (who famously recorded "Por una cabeza" in 1935), the Argentine folk hero whose mythology came to symbolize "the fulfillment of dreams of the poor."[45] Early interest in tango was also stirred by the visits to Europe of the sons and daughters of wealthy Argentine families, who introduced "their 'scandalous' Tango to their European friends," particularly in Paris.[46]

The tango enjoyed a spell of intense interwar popularity in Poland, as it flourished in a newly independent country—rather as in *White*, but here sixty years earlier—where, as economic progress filtered out into an increasing urban populace, musical materials, dances and mediating technologies from tea dances to gramophones and wireless sets (at least after Polish Radio began broadcasting in 1926) were consumed in order to establish the cultural distinctiveness of this more cosmopolitan class. As elsewhere in Europe, tango in Poland became associated with the aspirations of the urban middle class. Sheet music was published (such as Aime Lachaume's "Regina Tango," 1913, Warsaw), cabarets such as The Black Cat in Warsaw resounded to visions of life "Under the blue sky of Argentina," and Polish artists recorded cover versions of international tango classics (such as Stanisław Ratold's "Tango z rewji" [1922], a cover of Edouard Malderen's "Tango du rêve"). By the mid-twenties, tango had surpassed popular dance forms such as the shimmy, foxtrot and waltz, a commercial turning point being the composition and success of an original Polish tango, Zygmunt Wiehler's "Nie dziś to jutro" ("If not today, tomorrow will do") for cabaret star Hanka Ordonówna. After this, Jerzy Płaczkiewicz explains, "tangos in Poland, as a home production, were coming down in streams."[47] Leading musicians and literary figures including composer Witold Lutosławski and poet Julian Tuwim contributed settings and lyrics to the tango craze, making easier money than they could through their primary artistic endeavors.[48] The cultural significance of the Polish tango was so great that, by the end of 1937, it was a concern of the Nazi propaganda minister. On 14 December 1937, one week before Pola Negri, star of Polish stage and screen, would be heard singing the title song of *Tango Notturno* in Polish cinemas, Joseph Goebbels wrote in his diary that "Pola Negri swallows too much money."[49] The Nazi invasion on 1 September 1939 fractured the Polish tango craze, however, just as it stamped out so much else in contemporary Polish life and culture.

Tango was consumed, first and foremost, as a recorded product in Poland, rather than as a tradition brought to the country by live performance. As Płaczkiewicz argues,

> it should be noted that Warsaw, [as opposed] to Paris, Madrid or Berlin was not the aim of traveling groups of Argentine musicians and singers. Tango came to Poland through gramophone records, newspapers, rumors and radio. Poland was . . . well prepared to welcome it, as there had always been a sort of hunger for exotic novelties.[50]

As with the Parisian fetishization of oriental cultures at the turn of the twentieth century—also partly driven by an Orientalist desire to obtain, contain and consume the exotic of another culture through capitalist commercial mechanisms—Poles hankering after the blue skies of Buenos Aires were doing more than merely participating in the latest musical fad. Tango in Poland was a cultural complex of aesthetic and commercial imperatives, and "no other country in Europe became such an object of tango-fever."[51] For Savigliano, such adaptations mark a shift from authenticity into the romanticization of the genre. When the tango was watered down in the course of its national and international successes, the confessions of the typical tango persona—a humble ruffian—rendered him a Romantic hero, Savigliano maintains, "justifying all of his abuses, mistreatments, and excesses through love." And indeed, also as a commercial success, as in cases where local heroes like Gardel became international recording successes and, "no longer a ruffian, attained social mobility."[52] Karol in Warsaw is one such success story: a social climber, not a pining Romantic for whom love forms the ultimate excuse. Savigliano notes:

> Vengeance and resentment were transformed into melodrama and nostalgia, and the ruffianesque characters blended into romantic heroes. Tango, in its lyrics and choreography, became more polished, and the musical time slowed down and turned sentimental.[53]

Pimps thereby ended up "dressed in coat tails, drinking champagne" in the cabarets of Warsaw, the ruffians "sentimentalized and exoticized" just as in London and Paris, and the dance "persisted on the stage as an erotic proof of the promise of Civilization."[54]

The fit of such contexts to Karol's tale, especially in terms of the film's commentary on another newly minted democratic and capitalist

Poland, is striking. *White*'s dark fable of early 1990s Polish capitalism looks back, through its nostalgia for tango, to the peak of another Polish free market, and it can be argued that it utilizes that period's most prominent popular musical form to layer nuance into its satirical view of later Polish capitalism. The symbolism of the tango most obviously apparent in *White*, however, relates to its famous choreography. Like the music, the dance has its roots in *arrabel* culture, "in that dance figures, postures and gestures reflect some of the mannerisms and style of the *compadrito*, a popular hero similar to Don Juan, and a pimp in the early Buenos Aires *barrios* (districts)."[55] Its movements and postures have been associated with the posture of the *compadrito* (stiff upper body), knife duels (smooth footwork) and period footwear (forward tilt of spine relating to high-heeled shoes), but the "major theme of the tango as a dance for embracing couples is the obvious domination of the male over the female, in a series of steps and a very close embrace highly suggestive of the sexual act" and highlighting "the contrast between the very active male and the apparently passive female."[56] The significance, again, of the music and dance's symbolism in a film foregrounding a battle of the sexes, and literally revolving around sex itself, is obvious, as is its ostensible support for straightforward feminist objections to the film's purported sexism.

The personae at the heart of the tango ritual are iconic:

> One a pimp/gigoló, the other a prostitute/entrepreneur . . . [their] relationship entails a double masquerade in which each edge of the male-female compound is exploited and recombined, eclectically: he performs a dependent sentimental ruffian, she a self-made treacherous broad. They are locked in yet another parody: that of heterosexual bourgeois mores.[57]

The dance forms an assertion of *machismo*, confidence and sexual opportunism. Yet such assertions need not be sexist, and perhaps open the possibility that Preisner's tango traces Karol's regeneration as a (hu)man, following his initial humiliation, in positive terms. Other critics, in turn, have offered an alterative analysis of the tango's engendering capabilities and the manner in which they structure a subversive semiotic core to tango music and dance.

Savigliano argues for "the patriarchal, moralizing gaze" of tangos overwhelmingly written and/or performed by men.[58] It is certainly tempting to read tangos as "male confessions that talk overwhelmingly about women"[59] and thus, in terms of cinematic theory—not least in a structural tango like *White*'s expressive genre—as film, music and dance reducing women to the status of spoken objects on the lips of speaking subjects.[60] The view of tangos in which "man is the creator of the tango dance because he conceives it on the woman's body,"[61] and furthermore a dance in which "female eroticism helps to draw attention away from male intimacy and simultaneously elicits complicity amongst men"—low cut dresses slit to the hip, moves revealing the secrets of a plunging neckline—also chime with the manner in which, for some critics, Dominique's portrayal in *White* is unadulterated heterosexual male fantasy. Yet vitally, the dominated woman in a tango is not powerless to affect the moment-to-moment power play of the dance, even if the surface outcome is usually secure both choreographically and ideologically.

As Savigliano writes, "There is no doubt that he leads and she follows, but she can foresee his next move even before he thinks of it."[62] From this tension—a manipulation or subversion—springs the dance's true drama. Tango lyrics often tell of prostitutes escaping into the arms of rich clientele from their pimp lovers, through class transgressions initially set up through erotic services including the dancing of tangos. In the danced tango, a woman can influence her partner's directing of the dance by nuance or force, subtly increasing the distance between bodies, at one extreme, stamping on his feet at another. In ruffian tangos, the tearful confessions of the male *compadritos* relate the loss of their beloved *milonguitas* to richer men of a higher social rank, as in "The Last Sunday." Through such tales, ambiguities of gender identity were "set in motion" while "class alliances were destabilized" and "class inequity was questioned."[63]

Even when a tango is present in *White*, therefore, all may not be as it seems. The ostensible paean to capitalism, social mobility and masculine hegemony that Preisner's tango seems destined to assert can be read as a foil for more subversive intents. This phase of *White*'s narrative, on the surface, plays on tango's more straightforward associations to distinguish between Karols old and new. Yet tangos make cultural representations containing the seeds of their own self-destruction.

Dominating Dominique

When Karol stands on the banks of the Wisła at night, preparing to jettison his symbolic two franc coin into the black river, he seems on the brink of letting go of the past and accepting defeat. The coin, however, sticks uncannily to his hand—with Insdorf's "metaphysical glue"—and he appears to have an idea.[64] Lights coming from the old town and business district across the river spark a light in his eyes as his fist clenches; the muffled passing of a train overhead modulates into a brighter haze of passing car engines as Karol's moment of illumination intensifies. Music then marks his epiphany.

The signification of impetuousness in this version of the tango comes not from a significantly increased tempo (both cues are at 120 bpm) but an intensified sense of surface velocity sculpted by a busier accompaniment. In screen music, fast tempos and faster rhythmic surfaces, as Tagg demonstrated, stereotypically symbolize masculine attributes such as strength, dynamism, the urban and activity. Here, they intensify the tango's existing contrast to the $\frac{3}{4}$ *rustico* by heightening the stridency of its goal-oriented four beats to a bar. Pertinently, this begins to occur as the image of Karol blacks out and, in Wilson's terms, one is granted access to his inner cinema, a collision that "disturb[s] the divide between psychical and material reality,"[65] and also disturbs the audio-viewer with its insight into Karol's inner world.

At first one might imagine that the blackout marks the end of the first act of the film and the passage of time. It becomes clear, however, that Karol is imagining a voyeuristic vision of a cowed Dominique. It is an unsettling moment in terms of story (for what it reveals of Karol) and discourse (for the break in continuity) that parallels Julie's musical blackouts. Over a shot of Dominique returning alone to an as yet unidentified room, and enclosed by its darkness, one hears two things: the tango and the sound of Karol's heavy breathing. One might imagine this as a voyeur's visual and aural point of view: a peeping tom's intuition. The panting breath, a guttural male consequent to Dominique's antecedent gasps down the phone in Paris, and the tango smother Dominique like the darkness, rendering her audio-visually as a "spoken object." This leaves one in no doubt that what Karol is about to do is designed to permit this image to occur as part of his revenge. After this, every laugh induced by his actions in *White* must end with a shudder.

On a more prosaic level, here and throughout the scenes revealing the machinations of Karol's revenge plot, the tango's driving rhythms and harmony propel the action with intimations of pace and fluidity belying Kieślowski's struggle to edit this portion of *White*. As it stands, an entire subplot is cut and, with it, at least one cutely knowing Preisner cue: a Nino Rota homage (entitled "Don Karol" on the soundtrack CD) which plays on the *Godfather* theme, and adds further incredulity to Karol's criminality subplot (see Fig. 6.4), while linking back to the second busker cue in *Blue*. Kieślowski made the cuts because this satirical funny business, in the end, was not as amusing as the team had hoped and detracted attention from the revenge plot. So after the fantasy, the tango continues under shots of Karol at work in the salon and earning money, and then his arrival at an interview for a second job. This secures the connection between *White*'s intratextual theme of financial accrual and the tango's upmarket intertextual connotations. The tango also moves into the second part of its structure and, with it, a symbol of Karol's ascendancy into a cliché of masculinity.

The build-up of the bridge passage in Preisner's tango (see Ex. 6.6) forms a textural accrual of increasing density and strength, rising higher and timbrally hardening, with the thrusts of the bows increasing in volume and rhythmic intensity as the penultimate bar shifts to double time. The similarity to a man thrusting sexually, impotently or otherwise, is there if one chooses to hear it, as elsewhere in other musical repertoires.[66] The crucial point here, perhaps, is that climactic release does arrive, in the form of a chorus articulating a unison melody, powerfully scored in parallel octaves for the three violins, viola and cello, while the

Fig. 6.4: Preisner's Rota pastiche in the manuscript score

bass hammers out a pedal C. The strength with which this unison takes hold of the ensemble suggests Karol will be successful in his efforts to attain victory by force. Karol is thus musically potent long before he is financially and sexually successful, and simultaneously attains a higher musical class ahead of his social trajectory.

Overdubbing *Agapē*

The most subtle collusion of music and sound in the trilogy occurs when Karol practices French conjugations in his room and then kisses his idolized bust on the lips. Sonically, there are two obviously telling components to the scene; a third is much more subtle. One is the sound

Ex. 6.6: Tango climax

of pigeons. Linking back to the vision of the wedding day—but also to Karol's divorce hearing, his first sight of the bust, his meeting with Mikołaj and discovery that Dominique has taken a "better" lover—the sonic motif could be heard as diegetic noise distracting him from his lesson and sending him into the reverie that leads to him kissing the bust. The pigeon, again, is a heard but unseen presence; its position in the diegesis is plausible, but unconfirmed. Like music breaking into Julie's conscious mind, the pigeons could be heard as Karol's unconscious interrupting his foreground thoughts. Are the flapping wings telling him to embrace love, not revenge?

The second obvious sonic element, the voices recorded on the language tape, add further instructions and oblique editorializing. As the tape switches to a male voice, the verb *dormir* ("to sleep") is conjugated and Karol begins to daydream; as the voice then runs through different versions of *dormir* its similarity, sonically, to "Dominique" becomes apparent. Next, as Karol approaches his idol, the verb "to leave" is adumbrated, leading to "would that you had left" being heard as he approaches to kiss it; if only you had left for Poland with me, Karol may be thinking, you would have been spared. Finally, the past subjunctive of the verb "to please" is heard, beginning with "Would that I had pleased" and thus a pun on Karol's situation: if only he had pleased Dominique in the past, none of this would be necessary.[67] Throughout the sequence, the sound design's purpose seems like a read-out of Karol's thoughts, and thus a fulfillment of a purpose more usually left in narrative film to underscoring. There is also, however, music in this scene.

Karol's new occupation as a security guard involves working near a flea market; his language tapes may thus be pirate copies. Certainly, when he switches on the tape, one hears more than just the French words, as if the tape is an overdubbing onto a different original. Very faintly, but unmistakably thanks to Towarnicka's vocal timbre, one hears a fragment of the *Concert[o]* from *Blue*. A section of the *Concert[o]* has been dubbed low in the mix. The usage is important. The music is the *Arioso* from Julie's setting of 1 Corinthians 13:

> And if I have prophecy,
> and know all mysteries so that I can remove mountains,
> but do not have *agapē*,
> I am nothing,
> I am nothing,
> I am nothing.

Text, voice and interfilmic link provide an editorializing commentary on Karol's situation. In *Blue*, the music is heard as Julie and Olivier are seen in their underwater embrace, making love but shot in such a way as to appear in a struggle of some kind. As noted in Chapter Five, the musical and visual content add up to an ambivalence undercutting the romanticism of the shot with troubling sexual politics. Julie is embracing Olivier and thus *agapē*, but she is allowing herself to be subjugated to do so, and thereby losing an aspect of her liberty to benefit the greater good. Subjugation, of course, is precisely what Karol intends to do to Dominique, and by force. One sees him kissing his porcelain idol, a quite literal sex object unable to resist his embrace; longer-term, he will also have his way with the real Dominique before removing her liberty. That the feminine purity of the soprano vocals is dubbed over on the tape by a man's voice (i.e., the French lesson) may add to the sense of female agency being suppressed by masculine force.[68]

Yet the words of the song and their setting admonish Karol for his actions and plans. He may well be on the cusp of becoming a man who can move mountains, or at least masonry,[69] through his accrual of wealth and power; he might even believe that he is doing so out of love of one kind or another. But without *agapē*—without self-sacrificial love that is not puffed up, does not brag, is not envious, is kind—he will be, as Preisner's setting of Julie's music reminds the listener, "nothing." Tapes have been messengers in Kieślowski's output before; there is an important musical message in *Véronique*. This subtle moment adds further testimony to the alchemy of the creative relationship forged by Kieślowski and his sonic co-workers. *Agapē* and equality were obviously at the forefront of the production of this scene in *White*.

The Deal

As Karol exchanges his nest egg for US dollars, buys vodka and then embarks on a meeting with the smallholder from whom he will buy land, thus beginning the makings of his fortune, the third, lighter and less ardent section of Preisner's tango is cued. Marked *cantabile* and *leggiero*, the middle eight of the tango modulates to its relative major of E♭ and then, before returning to C minor for its close, briefly moves through C major—a brightening of mode connoting attainment and a change for the better. Karol's plan, the music hints, is starting well. The tango's association with pecuniary success in the film also intensifies here, first as we see Karol's Złoty being counted, second as he purchases a notably expensive bottle of vodka and puts it into the businessman's briefcase now accompanying him in place of his coffin-like suitcase. The clash of the tango with a rural *mise-en-scène* is also sharp enough to provoke comment. This scene should be scored with anything other than a tango. Karol is bringing his new ideology of commercial and emotional one-upmanship to the land, however, and in doing so polluting the pastoral idyll with his new musical coding. The idyll, in turn, critiques his motivation.

This cue also binds together a montage of events in a conventional example of one of music's main rhetorical functions in narrative film: covering elisions and creating pace or directedness in the face of editing fragmentations. This is one way in which the style of *White* goes musically against the grain of the more radical discursive effects achieved by *Blue*'s initial bending of conventions. Indeed, as the film moves further into the business of Karol's plan of revenge, the most conventional filmmaking thus far in the trilogy takes hold. This is not the time, however, for the critical audio-viewer to go with the narrative flow. Through such conventions, Claudia Gorbman has argued, music aids "the process of turning enunciation into fiction, lessening awareness of the technological nature of film discourse" and increasing "the spectator's susceptibility to suggestion."[70] In doing so, it "greases the wheels of the cinematic pleasure machine . . . easing the spectator's passage into subjectivity,"[71] and, in particular, into pre-fabricated ideological positions with which one might disagree, were the storytelling more obvious, less rhetorically persuasive or sensuously all-encompassing.

As *White*'s film-making language becomes more conventional, it sweeps one, like many mainstream films, towards the realization of Karol's goal: revenge on Dominique—an event one is encouraged to begin to anticipate and, most problematically, to root for. Just as Julie's more radical confrontation with gendered expectation was matched by *Blue*'s more avant-garde techniques, *White*'s submission to the will of its male hero's conquest becomes more traditional in its methods. Like other films centered on a man demanding satisfaction, *White* uses audio-visual editing techniques as teleologically oriented as the harmony of Preisner's tango. Yet is this merely a case of stylistic means matching subtextual ends? In the context of a trilogy in which ostensible convention rarely holds up under scrutiny, the more compelling possibility is that, by using cinematic conventions often utilized to render one sympathetic to an avenging male hero, Kieślowski is hijacking traditional filmic storytelling techniques to suture the audio-viewer into a position of sympathy for Karol, and thus a lack of sympathy for his intended female victim. This potentially makes one feel like Karol's accomplice in his quest and in doing so—crucially—*White* opens one up to the impact of the revelation that Karol experiences at the end of the film, as the nature of the storytelling becomes more innovative, and conventions of story and discourse yield to something less conclusive but richer.

Recurrences of Preisner's tango throughout the rest of the film—with a notable exception discussed below—continue to pursue a dual role as a conventional continuity device and quest music eliding the temporally separate developments in Karol's business/revenge plot. The repetition of the music in interrelated narrative contexts also accrues an intrafilmic significance that permits the music to denote very specific story information at key later instances of the film, and where no other discursive mechanism would be able to make that contribution. In terms of its dual role, when Karol, a year on from Mikołaj's aborted execution in the underground and thus into his money-making scheme, arrives with slicked back mobster hair to offer Mikołaj a job—it is a year later, the film denotes, because it is Christmas once again—the tango underscores Mikołaj's recognition that Karol has risen high enough in the world to have a chauffeur-driven burgundy Volvo: a foreign car and thus a status symbol. This is clearly now a "second, richer, better" Karol than the busker Mikołaj first encountered on the Metro. Wryly but tellingly, the transscansion experienced initially with the tango, associating its melody's first two notes with Jurek's wordlessly mouthed "Ka-rol," here shifts to "Vol-vo," as if the music itself has become part of a TV advertisement emphasizing a brand name. While nearly turning the film itself into the commercial enterprise of product placement, the transscansion also links "Ka-rol" to "Vol-vo": his commonplace and comic name is re-branded, synergistically, with a degree of quality, wealth and even foreign "otherness." The other notable variation of this instance of the tango is the cue's ending, which extends the repeated accompanimental rhythm beneath Karol's observation of a coffin and its mourners leaving a house for a funeral. Sonically, attention is called to the moment by the sound of prayer bells near the coffin and church bells tolling in the distance, recalling Karol's arrival in Poland. Tango, commerce and the hatching of the revenge plot synchronize at this point, as Karol intuits precisely how to use his wealth and power to destroy Dominique by faking his death and holding a mock funeral.

The film then cuts to the offices where Karol's import-export business will run: a tower block of capitalist prowess standing proud across from its ideological opposite, Stalin's Palace of Culture, a towering, neo-Gothic birthday cake with nested minarets to emphasize its phallic dominance of Warsaw's skyline.[72] Against this backdrop, the new business partners enjoy a brief duet: they hum (Mikołaj) and play (Karol on his comb) a reminiscence of "The Last Sunday." While obviously mapping how far both characters have traveled since the music was last heard—events have included Mikołaj's thwarted suicide attempt, which is analyzed below—here the song's associations with death take on a fresh meaning. The rendition, furthermore, is immersed in a sonic environment presumably intended to capture and replicate the traffic and wind noise from the streets below, but which could also be heard as a

return to the jet noise from earlier in the film. Either way, it places the
song and the friends in sonic hell: a soulless, technological, capitalist,
commercial and personal danger zone counterpointing the moment's
musical sense of achievement.

Aside from a further rendition of the tango to connote Karol's patina of business acumen, heard immediately after the second airing of
"The Last Sunday," two other telling occurrences of the tango mark the
latter stages of the film. The first helps Kieślowski out of a problem of
plausibility and narrative clarity through the tango's accrued association
with Karol's newfound deviance and power. In the screenplay, the end
of the film is more comprehensible. After making love to Dominique in
the hotel, Karol decides to abort the plot and a planned escape to Hong
Kong; he dilly-dallies, however, buying flowers for his ex-wife before
making the all-important phone call; this leads to her arrest; he then has
a revelatory meeting with Mikołaj at which it is acknowledged, more
explicitly than in the final film, that Dominique and Karol truly love
each other. The morning-after scene in the final cut of the film, in
which Karol picks up the hotel room phone, seems to think better of
doing so, and then creeps out to leave her to her fate, would thus originally have played in a context that would have made Karol seem more
sympathetic. The reason he does not phone Mikołaj to call off the plot,
in the screenplay, is because he has spotted a florist out of the window
and thinks he has time to pop out to buy Dominique flowers before
placing the call.[73]

Having cut this somewhat tiresome business, the same material was
used instead explicitly to suggest Karol leaving Dominique to be
framed for murder, with no hint that he might come back to save her.
Specifically, the audience needs to read the moment he puts the phone
back in its cradle as the moment he decides to follow through with the
plot. Clear-cut cruelty is nowhere inherent in the actor's behavior; it is
suggested by editing and, above all, music. Instead, Preisner's tango
enters, connecting the moment when Karol replaces the receiver to
every step thus far in his rise to power and revenge. Second thoughts
cast aside, the theme connotes, he is still going to put Dominique to the
sword and complete the film's reversal of humiliation, as suggested all
along by the tango's intimations of power play. A neat sonic detail adds
nuance: the dial tone on the phone is an A, the pitch-center of "home"
in the trilogy and, in *White*, of Karol's half of the *rustico*. He hangs up
on it here, as if he is hanging up once and for all on his connection to
the old Karol. The C minor tango takes its place, triumphantly assuming
the dominant position.

The final use of the Preisner tango occurs over the closing credits.
This could merely be heard as a conventional recapitulation of a key
theme at the end of the film, and is actually the first time that the entire
tango is heard from start to finish, rather than cut into segments and
fitted to the action. This is entirely conventional: soundtracks often play
out to a suite of key musical moments from a film, giving the composer
a chance to shine while acting as a synergistic advertisement to obey

the last instruction of the End Title sequence (i.e., "Now go out and buy the soundtrack"). However, given the centrality of music to the trilogy, and the importance of *Blue*'s end title sequence, further meanings of the last tango in *White* deserve to be considered. First, one could simply be hearing the whole of the tango because the plan has reached fruition: a complete rendition of the music signifies, in this reading, completion of the plan and closure of the narrative. Yet the ending of *White*'s action does not imply closure, but rather a moment of aperture and ambiguity: one expects the couple's story to take a new twist, as it will in the coda of *Red*. How Karol and Dominique come to be on the ferry in *Red* is not explained. The tango at the close of *White*, though, by reminding perceivers of Karol's newfound power, connections and wealth, indicates that such a man could continue to buy anything in Poland post-1989: his ex-wife's freedom, for instance, and her new life with a "dead" husband. An entirely new plot could thus be imagined to have been hatched by this final tango: a plan to reunite the now equalized lovers, rather than further divide them.

A Short Cue about Killing and *Agapē*

From time to time, as the second part of *White* progresses, the score feints like a dueling tango dancer and the *rustico* returns to hint at things to come. There is, however, one montage which pits *rustico* and tango directly against one another, structuring a sequence of formal complexity, affective charge and resonant symbolism.

The morning after purchasing his first plot of land, Karol awakens, quite literally, as a different class of man: he is now an owner of property. After washing his face with cold water, he restyles his hair, looking at his reflection in the glass pane of a picture of the Virgin and Child. The film then cuts to Karol's finger tracing a path across a map—just as Julie's finger traced Olivier's music in *Blue* before rewriting it, and thus aspects of herself. He colors in his plot of land on the map with a red felt tip pen (see Fig. 6.5), his actions echoing Julie's score annotating in *Blue*. Finally, the sequence cuts to Karol entering a phone booth to begin his search for Mikołaj and the means of earning money to buy more land: he agrees to assist the unnamed suicidal man.

The sequence is scored by Karol's portion of the *rustico*. Announced by a high oboe tone then followed by the solo clarinet, the cue is precisely the same as the version in the courtroom during his speech, save for including the theme's final note and therefore being a complete statement of his portion of the love theme. While appropriately solemn, it seems a peculiarly obvious moment in the context of so many ironic tangos. Wollermann, too, wonders about the use of the melancholy melody here, and suggests that the image of Dominique-like beauty in the religious painting might be key—the picture acts as a reminder of why Karol is acting and informs the audience of his thinking.[74] Alternately,

Fig. 6.5: Karol composing himself in *White*

it could be heard as a musical flashback to Karol's state of mind at the
time of the divorce, reminding the perceiver of his humiliation and thus
motivation for his present undertaking. A longer-range analysis of the
cue's context in this section of the film reveals a further layer of potential meaning. It is typical of Preisner's film music that it can sometimes
be heard simultaneously to advance the narration on parallel fronts.
This is one such example, with the cue having a local function, while
preparing a longer-range process in which it provides but the first musical installment.

Ten seconds of oboe G♯ are all Preisner needs to imbue the shot of
Karol combing his hair, in reflection, with a metaphysical aura, although strange electronic disturbances to the sound design—metallic
warpings with no apparent explanation—intensify the moment's uncanniness. The hard and focused oboe tone accompanies Karol's experimental combing of his hair into the Michael Corleone look he will sport
in later scenes; the tone ends as he stops to consider his efforts. There is
an obvious sculpting of tension and release in these ten seconds of tone
and two seconds of silence. At the moment Karol stops, the sequence
encourages the audio-viewer to focus, like him, on the new Karol gazing iconically back at himself, and also out at the audience. Like the
warping on the sound design, he is bent out of shape.

One also sees Karol's face overwriting a female icon, like the voice
overriding the *Concert[o]* on the language tape, at a time when his plan
to dominate Dominique is gathering momentum, but also when he is
preparing to carry out an entirely unchristian sin to accelerate his
scheme: helping another mother's son to commit suicide for money.
Karol is concerned here only with his own reflection and certainly not
with the religious. Indeed, religion throughout *White* is treated as a
joke: the church is something to leave money to in order to thwart
crooks, or a place where Polish chancers in Paris hang out selling
forged passports.[75] However, just as in *Blue*, where specific Christian

texts were overwritten to articulate broader concerns, in *White* similar translations from Christian dogma to broader humanist sentiment occur. In a bleakly ironic variation on *agapē*, when Karol offers to execute Mikołaj, as Kickasola notes, he inverts Jesus' maxim "Greater love hath no man than this, that a man may lay down his life for a friend."[76] Karol seems to be laying down his friend, not for friendship, but for money; the *agapē* of the moment, though, is that the first bullet is a blank, offering Mikołaj the second chance he needs.

To backtrack slightly: after the silence when the images cut away from Karol's newly slick look, the clarinet's melody unfurls over Karol's finger tracing the route to his plot of land. Given the connection to Julie tracing music in *Blue*, it is hard not to imagine that the map performs a similar role to her musical recomposition of her subjectivity. The map could almost be imagined, in fact, as music: the lines on the map remind one of staves on the manuscript paper seen in *Blue* and, most particularly, as the clarinet's mournful tune continues, of the melodies heard in response to Julie's gaze and touch. This notation, however, sings a song of Karol in response to his tactile ministrations. The cue continues as he is depicted, hair back to its fluffily inoffensive style, entering a phone booth where he finds an address for Mikołaj's bridge club. The clarinet imbues the entirety of the sequence with regret, cutting against the grain of the tango with a reminder of the tragedy surrounding Karol's course of action.

Preisner scored a full version of the *rustico* for the sequence, complete with its second "Dominique" section in C major, but the music is put on pause at the end of Karol's part, articulating incompleteness. Karol's portion ends on E and thus the dominant tone one would expect to resolve to the tonic of A. But it does not do this, nor segue into Dominique's half, rendering the music doubly unfinished. Consequently, when the music begins again a few minutes later, with Dominique's part of the theme, there is a sense of completion structured by the recommencement of Preisner's cue.

At the start of this second sequence in the passage, Karol spins his lucky two-franc coin; he then kills its progress by banging it flat on the table. He is allowing chance, in a recurring Kieślowski trope, to dictate his fate as a would-be executioner; fateful coins also spin in *Blind Chance* and *Red*. The music that follows provides no sense of relief and makes it clear that he will carry out the act, with developments to the cue moving the *rustico* back in the direction of the corrupted chromaticism experienced before Karol's return to Warsaw. A high harp trill between B and C provides an unnerving stridulation effect,[77] intensifying the drama of the moment in which one waits to discover the outcome of the coin spin. The trill also takes up, in a delayed mickey-mousing, the motion of the coin that Karol has stilled with an executioner's decisiveness: the coin still spins for the audio-viewer awaiting Karol's call. Mournfulness and tension then combine in a bassoon melody outlining a rising fifth from F to C, before falling back, chromatically, to B, as Karol sighs and then glares into his inner cinema and at the person on whom he is laying the blame for his course of action.

The nature of this private showing is first revealed musically by the arrival of Dominique's half of the *rustico*. One then sees a second flash-forward to Dominique's arrival in the still secret hotel room, which will turn out to be her lodgings in Warsaw after the funeral, and to take place a few seconds before Karol reveals himself as still alive. When one does not know that this will happen, though, the scene is apparently just part of Karol's fantasy of revenge, again placing Dominique in the dark and at his directorial control, anticipating some unseen deed. Karol's heavy breathing once more accompanies his peeper's vision of a damaged Dominique, creating a perverse point of audio-view that marries with the development of this part of the *rustico*.

Over the continuing harp trill, a solo oboe and clarinet perform a duet. The oboe tune is as expected: if it were heard alone, this would be Dominique's music in C major and the music from her courtroom flashback to her happy wedding day. Karol's clarinet, however, joins her instrumental agent and harmonizes it, crucially, as if the theme is now in the key of F minor, not C major. What was happy, if regretful, is now darker and tense. The duet's open fifths and minor thirds also give it a funereal air. Only two phrases of the theme are heard, but they lay the blame for the forthcoming death at Dominique's door, from Karol's point of view, clarifying that he will exact a terrible revenge on her for causing this horror to occur. Linking back to the reflection of Karol in the picture pane, and draped in its darkest music yet, the film proceeds to its suicidal terminus.

As the last two notes of the *rustico* fade away, the action cuts to Karol descending into an unfinished Warsaw underground station in search of the man he is to kill. Preisner's cue seeks to sustain the tension and darkness of the moment, although in truth the film does not quite succeed as melodrama. Specifically, there is no startle effect created by the music's sudden silence and then Mikołaj's footfall in the shadows behind Karol[78]; the physical action central to conventional movie suspense is not the strongest card in Kieślowski or Preisner's metaphysical suit. A simple chordal progression is stated three times and, on its final appearance, a chromatically snaking bass clarinet provides a fourth pitch (G♯) completing a diminished seventh on F. As elsewhere in Preisner's output, he evokes unease through the most hackneyed harmony in the film scoring book. Yet he orchestrates it here with such delicacy—partly by drawing on techniques learned from the Polish post-war avant-garde, partly by retaining a ghost of the voice-leading and timbral distribution from the duet version of Dominique's half of the *rustico*—that the cliché is transcended (see Fig. 6.6).[79]

It seems fitting, bearing in mind Kieślowski and his co-worker's obsession with the underbelly of human endeavor, that the darkest moment in *White* should literally occur in Warsaw's underground, a better choice than the screenplay's envisaged return to the rubbish dump. The

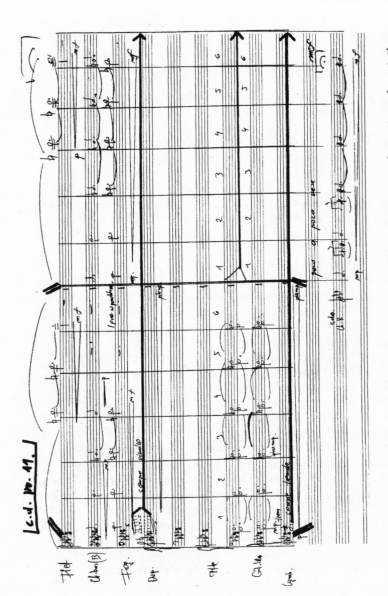

Fig. 6.6: Subway transition cue, showing Preisner's use of quartertones and avant-garde notations

mise-en-scène also sets up stark symbolic and affective contrasts to what follows, as oily blues and black break into golden light and the tone of the movie pivots, stunningly, from despair to exuberance. This is one of the most life-affirming moments in all Kieślowski: a transcendent moment of hope that forms an affective prolepsis foreshadowing the end of the story. As Karol prepares to step over the line and into a new moral hell, the *rustico* theme is liquidated along with his values, losing all traces of its plainly pretty music as it tails off into obscurity. Musically, however, the entire passage of film since the sequence at the farm has been preparing the audio-viewer for an explosion of joy. That the startle effect was fluffed is incidental: what matters is the grander effect of the narrative's sudden emergence out of the darkness and into light, as Karol's gift to Mikołaj liberates them both.

The dim interior of the subway explodes into the golden light of the frozen river Wisła in winter—golden light already marked, in the trilogy, for instance in the park in *Blue*, as a signifier of rapture and release. Karol and Mikołaj slide into view, hooting and laughing like boys as they skate across the ice. Mikołaj says that he feels like a child again and encapsulates his emotions with the film's other signature line: anything is possible. That both he and Karol, by this stage of the narrative, have been reborn and given second chances is obvious. Less obvious is the emotional highpoint this moment sets, anticipating the, as yet, unforeseeable ending of the film. What makes the scene truly exuberant, however, is not just the change of light or the juxtaposition of Mikołaj falling, in deathly slow-motion, to his skating at full pelt across the ice, but Preisner's tango cue, which builds up and then erupts into a *tutti dramatico* statement of its bridge and climax, scored powerfully in unison octaves, as the friends slide into view.

The volume and dramatic stridency of the gesture parallel the excitement of the make-shift skaters, but the narrative release is two-fold: Mikołaj's burden of pain has been made bearable and the financial gain permits Karol to complete his plan to buy plots; the cue ends over a shot of him filling in more land on his map. In a sense, therefore, by relating the score to the revenge plot and financial gain, returning to the river where Karol first struck upon the idea of exacting revenge on Dominique, and accompanying a shot of obviously male bravado and camaraderie—guns, whisky and death segue into boyish exuberance and pratfalls—the tango continues to perform clichéd significations already outlined in this chapter. However, this is also a celebration of life. It may be contextualized in a nasty revenge plot with soon to be subverted misogynistic overtones, but in this moment the narrative overcomes those circumstances, as if to redeem the film's world. Exuberant melodic gestures aside, the moment's signification of joy and release is paralleled by the music's modulation into C minor's relative major, E♭, the minor pallor lifting to permit the most elongated version of the theme yet to develop, and thus harmonically to travel, demonstrating through harmony's musical simulacrum of movement and goals attained that "everything is possible."

The structural darkening and switchback release in this sequence is "among the greatest dramatic moments in all of Kieślowski's films, simply for the perfection of dramatic timing,"[80] and demonstrates Preisner's ability to structure a long-range shift in atmosphere. In such moments, his music aids Kieślowski's cinema in its effort to confront one with the privilege of being. Or less pompously, this musical moment makes one feel as glad to be alive as Mikołaj.

Transcendence: The Return of the *Rustico*

White's expressive genre is a double change-of-state narrative, moving from tragedy to triumph then transcendence. One could, perhaps, read the return of the *rustico*, which dominates the score at the close of the film, as part of a tragic reversal, returning to the tone of the opening act and undoing the triumph of its central tango. At the end of *White*, however, Preisner returns to *rustico* cues already heard in the film and varies them decisively, reflecting changes to the central concern of his music: Dominique and Karol's relationship and its conceptual symbolism. The ending is thus revealed to add a transcendent twist to the tale.

The mazurka's establishment of its dominance in the final thirty minutes of *White* begins with a move familiar from tangos and other more literal forms of combat: a feint. When Karol, overlooked by his bust, is tormented by dreams of Dominique in his office's cot—pigeons are also heard at this point, as if he is recalling the wedding, divorce or some nightmarish concoction of both—he calls her on the telephone.[81] Is he offering her one last chance to say "anything" and thus escape her fate, with the pigeons a reminder of their bond? That the birds' sound is treated with reverb, signifying interiority, implies that the effect may be meta-diegetic. That he may be inclined to offer her a second chance is further implied by his hair: ruffled by sleep, the style lies halfway between his slick mobster look and its original style. When she hangs up the phone rather than speaking to him, however, repeated As on the phone line mock Karol's attempt to reconnect with his romantic and tonal home. At this point, the *rustico* melody also begins again, but this time scored high for a solo clarinet and in D, not A. Registrally and tonally, the ideals symbolized by his part of the *rustico* are moving further away from his present identity. Karol's tight release of breath after the call—like Julie's by the garbage truck—suggests, along with the shot of the bust suddenly cast into darkness, a decision. The cue ends as Karol sits with his solicitor, his hair immaculate again and a photo of a woman with her face blurred visible over his shoulder, changing his will to make his ex-wife his sole benefactor, and thereby sealing her fate.[82] This is the narrative feint: it seems as if the ideals of the *rustico* are finally being forgotten. Yet Karol's feelings, at his moment of victory, will alter, and the soundtrack will again be led by the *rustico*.

The Second Coming

At his fake funeral, Karol observes the scene he has orchestrated from behind a tree. Peeping through the pastoral foliage, he is also returned in "death" to his original hairstyle, as if *mise-en-scène* and styling are anticipating plot events to come. Again he spies on Dominique, his inner cinema now rendered real by his directorial manipulations. He is surprised to see her weeping.

Before she is isolated at the graveside by the other mourners, ceremonial funeral bells chime the major third between G and B. In a moment typical of the trilogy's nuanced relationship between sonic and musical detail, this forms a dominant preparation for Dominique's C major portion of the *rustico*, as well as being a literal anticipation of the second and third pitches of that tune: that cue, like her grief, flows seamlessly from the action. Scored for solo oboe, however, this version of the theme is a variation of the music from her courtroom flashback, neatly drawing together her joyful memory of that event and this one, its polar opposite. The symbolism of the tune's developmental shift into C minor and its tortured chromatic twist is obvious but poignant. The bars of rest in this faltering version of the *rustico* further symbolize loss and separation.

The next scene is her actual return to the hotel room, long anticipated by Karol in his inner cinema, but here seen in full and in context as the realization of his plan. He has not merely faked his own death, but has created a context in which he can appear to her as the "second, better, richer" man of "The Last Sunday," complete with the power of not only resurrection but erection. As Kickasola notes, Karol is now on top, "a precise reversal of their previous coital attempt,"[83] in a shift of sexual position rather like a move in a tango dance. The sheer nastiness of his plan of revenge is thus revealed to be much more severe, and thus "more equal," than her humiliation of him. He plans to make love to her stupendously well, and then to leave her framed for murder, imprisoned and, presumably, doubting her sanity. It is a scheme impressive in the comprehensiveness of its cruelty, although in Dominique's orgasm there is, as in the tango on the Wisła, a glimpse of purity and joy.[84]

Specifically, the darkness of the screen as they begin to make love means that, as in Julie's blackouts, one is initially only permitted to hear. This marks one of the ways in which the film begins to move back into the innovative mode of discourse sustained more consistently in the trilogy's outer panels, *Blue* and *Red*. *White* relinquishes one film style as its expected moment of masculine, teleological triumph is also relinquished, and as story and discourse change tone and direction, as they did for *Blue*'s ending. What one hears is not music, but Dominique in ecstasy. At the moment she lets fly with what, in other filmic contexts, might be heard as a bloodcurdling scream, the screen whites out, then fades back to black, before returning to the aftermath of their coupling. Like the sounds warping the darkness of the screen to reveal hazy colors at the start of *Blue*, this is sound whose symbolic importance one is compelled to acknowledge through its power to affect image. The moment of unity, for Dominique, is not faked: it is too powerful for that. Like the scene on the Wisła, it illuminates another possible mode of being. Yet Karol seems to miss the point: in their moment of true equality, which only came about due to his redoubled efforts to please her after another premature ejaculation—his own pleasure sacrificed, in an ostensibly positive gesture, to permit hers—he notes only that she moaned louder than she did on the phone. As Andrew notes, this highlights Kieślowski's thesis "that people don't want equality, they just want to be more 'equal' (i.e., better, stronger, richer and more privileged) than others."[85] Like the ritual of the tango, the sex scene plays out as a metaphor for human society, generally, and capitalist ones in particular.

The Second Wedding

Preisner's manuscript score for *White* is filled with extra *rustico* cues intended for the end of the film and, presumably, the many scenes cut from its eventual denouement. These would have further saturated the close of the film with the *rustico*, establishing it yet more securely as the musical and symbolic core of the film. As it stands, however, the rustic mazurka is heard twice more: once in the elongated montage showing the second vision of their wedding, once when Karol peeps on Dominique a final time in the prison. Ruthlessly separated by Karol's scheme, the music unites the couple in a dance of romanticized union, their souls moving as one although their bodies are divided. Interpretation of the first sequence's richness benefits from a shot-by-shot analysis.

Shot 1 (1:22:17-1:22:23) As the man from the embassy arrives to assist Dominique—the cue is already underway at the tail of the interrogation scene—the *rustico* begins its penultimate appearance. All one hears musically before the cut is the first phrase of Karol's portion of the dance and a piano countermelody that, in this version of the *rustico*, will fill the silences between the phrases. Preisner had scored these ornamentations for earlier cues in the film, but in post-production it was decided to hold them back for these moments. The richness of his fullest scorings of the theme is thus heard here for the first time. The augmentation helps the film to accrue a subtle sense of closure: fuller sounds form a rhetorical gesture to mark the end of the narrative. Holding the melodic countermelodies back until these moments may also be heard as having a connotative function regarding Karol and Dominique's relationship, and the ownership of this moment of inner cinema.

Visually, these few seconds of film do something extraordinary: they slow time, as if the world is coming to a stop for Dominique as she loses her liberty. This effect has been glimpsed once before in the film, at the moment Karol fired the blank into Mikołaj's chest. That was Mikołaj's moment of insight, courtesy of Karol; this is Dominique's. The clarinet theme brings Karol's presence into the scene, in collaboration with his sonic motif: a pigeon, here taking flight. Karol, the audio suggests, is in her thoughts, as if she is realizing, in this moment of heightened significance, all that Karol has done to entrap her and assume the position of dominance. One may even get the impression—through the gracefulness of the piano phrase, implying hope by curling down and then up again as time slows for Dominique—that she is glad it has happened. Was this what she wanted, all along? The idea of a woman being forced to submit is distasteful. An empowered woman who *wants* to yield, however, in the hands of a dominant man—like a tango dancer, perhaps, who lives most intensely at the moment she seems most controlled—is a more complex proposition. The shading of Dominique's character enriches further as the end of the film progresses and it is revealed that, by forcing Karol to become a new man, she may have controlled the dance all along and manipulated him into a position where they can love as equals.

Shot 2 (1:22:24-1:22:35) The image cuts to the interior of the church and the white at the end of a tunnel first glimpsed in the courtroom sequence. This is the vision one was led to presume as Dominique's flashback. She strides, footfalls echoing, into the light and the cloud of pigeons, slightly ahead of the handheld camera's point of view, which again one assumes to be Karol's. Point of view, though, is complex in this sequence. What one hears, heels aside, is a dialogue between the plaintive clarinet of Karol's tune and its new countermelody, a variant of the original piano linking phrase, now played on guitar. Before this moment, the guitar plays a pair of rising fifths under the melody, accompanying Karol's theme—the first time either half of the *rustico* has been supported by an accompaniment. The open fifths suggest the sacred and pure, imbuing the scene with an appropriate ceremonial quality. A rite is occurring, with knowledge passed between newly intuitive parties, opening the possibility of a shared point of view.

Shot 3 (1:22:36-1:23:14) With the end of the phrase, as Dominique's heels continue to sound, the image cuts to Karol combing his hair. His stare into what is presumably a mirror—the entire shot is a relatively stable medium close-up of his upper torso and head, rendering him as a bust, perhaps, as if he now is being admired from Dominique's perspective—is literally unblinking, like a cowboy in a shootout.[86] In the film's most resonant image, he then holds his metallic comb up so that it occludes the camera's, and his own reflected, view of his eyes, running it to his right and then to his left in a cutting motion. On the one hand, this is a barber's everyday action, checking a metal comb for imperfections before the next job. Here the simple gesture is altered, though, into something extraordinary. The shot calls to mind the famous image of a razor slitting the eye in *Un chien andalou*, another film moment straddling the border between reality and dream. It may also remind one—if one recalls the manner in which Kieślowski intended Karol to be marked like a hero in an ancient Greek tragedy by the pigeon droppings at the courthouse—of Oedipus putting out his eyes, having brought his queen and realm to ruin.[87]

The uncanniness is secured by the close synchronizing of these moments to Preisner's cue. Following the third melodic phrase on clarinet, Karol's eyes cast down and then up again as the piano plays its second melodic arc. He then runs the comb from one side to the other in time to the fourth phrase, the first gesture ending as the guitar fills in its countermelody; it comes to rest again as Dominique's half of the theme begins. His eyes, finally, look down and then up as the flute plays a single rising interval in answer to the oboe and bassoon duet, the first melodic phrase in Dominique's reorchestrated theme. Karol is now pressing the comb to his mouth, linking back to the moment he played music on it in Paris, but here as if he is playing Preisner's score itself, the reeds of the bassoon and oboe buzzing like the former busker's comb. Connecting the moment to his performances of "The Last Sunday," and in place of the portion of lyric to which he has previously seemed most related, one might instead focus now on the tango's chorus, in which the defeated lover—and this persona could speak for Dominique as much as Karol—pleads with her/his lover for a last Sunday together, and to be looked upon affectionately one final time. Like everything else about this sequence, it feels like a plea to be united again, in spite of all that has passed.

The audio-visual effect—the looks down and then up, the synchronizing of acting gesture and musical phrase, and the measured pace—suggest a slow, courtly dance, as if Karol and Dominique are leading a mazurka at the celebrations of a traditional Polish wedding. The duet of sound and image mimic the symbolic duet of the couple. Dominique is ever present because, although one focuses on Karol's portion of the theme and the melody, the piano and guitar countermelodies are another presence; more obviously, her footsteps continue to be heard throughout the shot. Is Karol thus imagining the wedding as well? One could assert that there is a sense in which this vision, in its ambivalence, and the manner in which the audio-visual syncing alludes to a mutual choreography, is a moment of shared epiphany. As Wilson has argued, Karol's solitary inner cinema is replaced by intimations of intersubjectivity as if the lovers share these images and sounds.[88] A final twist in the visuals adds weight to the idea that the vision has two directors.

Shot 4 (1:23:15-1:23:50) A cut back to the wedding vision reveals a different version to that seen in the courtroom. There are more pigeons, for one thing, and the camera shows different members of the wedding party and people moving differently to before. Everyone is wearing the same clothes—Dominique's hair and makeup match, Jurek's tie is the same—which would suggest that this is the same occasion rather than a vision of some future event; it is highly unlikely Karol and Dominique would be permitted to remarry in the same church. Yet it is also clearly different—an alternative vision of the same day which someone wishes had happened, perhaps, or believes might happen yet. Two specific events occur. First and most crucially, Dominique looks directly into the camera, not giggling now but serious. Karol then moves into shot—into the shot one would previously have read as his point of view—and kisses her, rupturing the notion that the camera occupies his subjective perspective. So whose point of view does it occupy? One possibility is that it is Karol being addressed by Dominique in the diegetic present, as if she is sending her vision of the wedding to Karol from her prison cell, in order to communicate a vital piece of information: everything has changed. That her look is one of Kieślowski's iconic gazes to camera also opens Dominique's audience to encompass the spectator, as if one is also being tutored by the vision. The second significant visual variation is that, when she kisses Karol, she opens her eyes briefly to observe him mid-embrace; in another connecting gesture, he then does precisely the same. As the harmony rocks from iv to V, never closing on i but constantly suggesting closure's possibility, an open question is posed, having been heard before in the score, but now flooded with fresh significance. Will you take me, after all, to be your wife/husband—again? Like a pair of tango dancers, their eyes (and their and our eyes) briefly meet. The fourth phrase of Dominique's part of the theme literally repeats the third, like an urgent request being reiterated.

The sequence poses a final enigma. As the music's phrases reverberate and the moment of sonic interiority disperses, the image track also slows down slightly again as the screen, similar to the moment of Dominique's sublime orgasm, brims white. By flooding the film white, calling to mind the sunlit ice of the Wisła and her climax, another intrafilmic symbol is articulated: here, more than at any earlier point in the film, whiteness feels linked to a notion of equality. Having put each other through hell, Dominique and Karol are now partners, although not merely in the sense that one has defeated the other and that the other has exacted a revenge of (more) equal magnitude. Rather, after going through the ritual of humiliation, something continuously present but masked has been revealed. Their connection and equality, through their sacrifices—voluntary or otherwise—of "life," wealth and liberty, is unveiled: an ineradicable fusion of *eros* and *agapē*.

Last *Rustico* in Warsaw

As Karol enters the prison courtyard to see Dominique, clearly by some kind of special arrangement—in the screenplay there are bribes—the *rustico* begins. To observe Rapunzel in her tower, the music suggests, he and the audience must look up: the melody is scored for a flute's upper registers, as it was the first time this version of the theme appeared, when Karol spied up at her apartment in Paris. The initial part

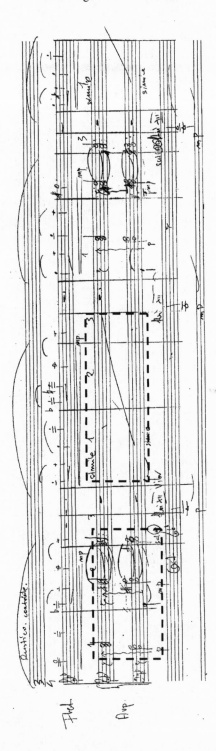

Fig. 6.7: Manuscript score (boxes added) for apartment and prison scenes

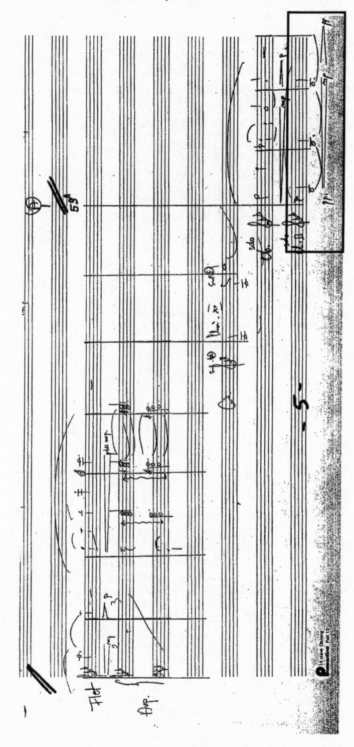

Fig. 6.7 (cont.)

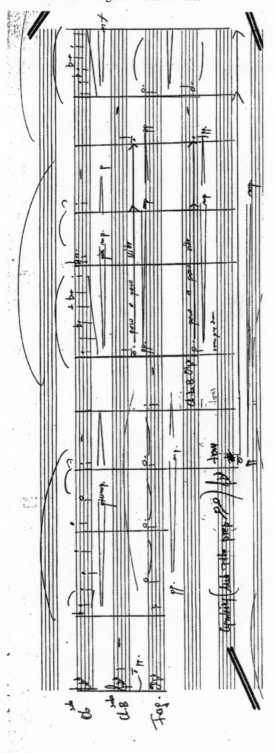

Fig. 6.7 (cont.)

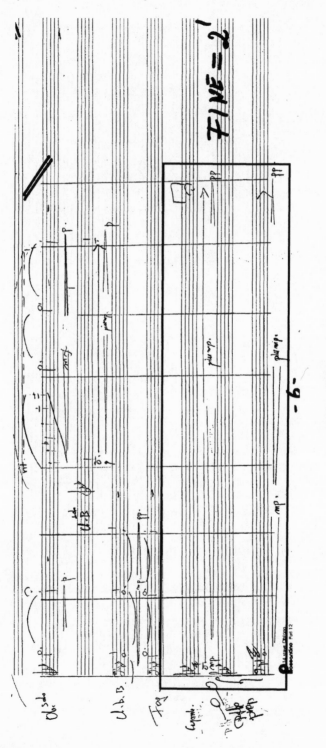

Fig. 6.7 (cont.)

of the cue, with harps and guitar sparsely accompanying the flute, sounds sentimentally folksy, as if accompanying a postmodern bard telling a story about a fairy-tale princess—much, indeed, as Karol idolized Dominique at the time of the cue's first airing. Here, however, one sees more of Dominique than a silhouette, and the music is different, too: it has a richer orchestration and two significant appendixes. Fig. 6.7 shows Preisner's original cue sheet; the boxes with dashed lines have been added to indicate material not heard in the prison scene; the boxes with solid lines indicate material not heard at all in either scene. The post-production shaping of the score's raw material is a clear example of "co-working" on the music's final form in the film—as was the addition of a final phrase of oboe melody, and a notable coda, omitted from the original cue sheet but transcribed in Ex. 6.7.

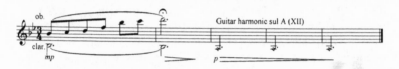

Ex. 6.7: End of the prison cue (transcribed)

Strummed chords from the harp accompaniment are held back initially, helping the music to signify height by withholding its ground. It returns at the third melodic phrase, which sounds as Dominique's silhouette at the window begins to register. One hears the music differently—more hopefully than last time—as it turns into its darker second part, because one sees Dominique inside her cell behaving very differently from the scene at her apartment. Bathed in the golden orange lighting Kieślowski retains for transcendent or blissful moments in his later films, her hands, initially mimicking being cuffed together, rise upwards with the final gesture of the flute melody; she then points into the sky, as if suggesting escape, in a gesture that actually seems to create the guitar's A to E open fifth. The connectedness of music and image help signify the renewed connection between the lovers. The sign language is purposefully ambiguous, but one sign is crystal clear: she mimics returning a ring to her finger, thus communicating to Karol that she loves him and wishes to be his wife once more.

As the cue moves into its darker half, the camera cuts back to Karol, and in an affecting sync point one hears the bassoon's pedal B♭ beneath the oboe's plangent second phrase, diverting one's sense of that pitch-centre away from D major and into B♭ minor as Karol drops his opera glasses, revealing tears streaming down his face. All that the couple have lost and sacrificed, and what they have now received, apparently becomes clear to him in these moments, the gravity of the discovery being signified musically. The woodwind and plucked sounds steer clear of saccharine wistfulness, thanks to the withholding of instrumentation—strings, timpani or French horns, say—one might expect to tug the heartstrings. Instead, over further pedal B♭s—a metallic sheen of cimbalom, cymbal and playing on the strings of a piano adding a shiver of novelty (less audible in the earlier scene) and, by dint of its association with suspense films, intrigue—the oboe uncurls its mournful, chromatic and tonally insecure theme, the stressed Es and Gs suggesting an ambiguity between B♭ minor and a B♭ diminished seventh chord, and thus a nexus of unresolved issues.

What will Karol do? His look down to the ground and then back up at the window recalls his hair combing in the previous scene. Has he foreseen everything, up until this point, in his plotting, or even in visions? Is this the point at which free will returns, Karol having won a comprehensive victory and then discovered, in fact, that he does not want to win after all: he only wants Dominique? The contours of the tune create a sense of open possibility rather than conclusiveness. In contrast to the closural harmonic progressions and descending melodic lines in the tango, the final *rustico*'s lines rise quizzically, opening the melody up. Closure comes through the barest of rhetorical gestures. The final two oboe phrases rise to the sixth of B♭ minor, G, and then further still to its mediant tone, D♭, in an addition to the cue only heard in this final scene. The harmonic implications therefore open outwards—D♭ as the relative major of B♭ minor?—reaching towards new possibilities, the protagonists' instruments, oboe and clarinet, paired in that quest.

One must wait for an answer to the basic question posed here—will they somehow end up together—until the end of *Red*. Yet Preisner adds a typically simple but telling final touch to *White*'s last dramatic cue: three As on the acoustic guitar, chiming like the church bells that, once upon a time, marked Karol's homecoming. The similarity to the end of *Blue*'s *Concert[o]*, and to the last dramatic cue in *Red*, forms a touch of unification across the three scores. A, in turn, was the pitch-center of Karol's least corrupted visions of equality and love, expressed in a rustic theme that had nothing to do with the sphere of action into which he delved to achieve his revenge. One might even hear the clarinet's final B♭ resolving onto the guitar's A, thereby reharmonizing the oboe's D♭ not as the minor third of B♭ minor, but as the major third (C♯) of A major. A is the key—or even just pitch-class—that the trilogy, as it progresses to *Red*, will establish as representing "home," human connectedness and *agapē*. Tonally, though, the pitch links more immediately back to Dominique's signing and the guitar's earlier gestures, and to the emotion they conspired to articulate: hope. But is that hope genuine?

Whiting Out

In a letter to Marin Karmitz in July 1993, written after watching a cut of the movie with Krzysztof Zanussi, Kieślowski said he felt an "emptiness" about the ending of the film.[89] In the original cut, Karol is seen crying, but Dominique is only shot in silhouette: her feelings remain a mystery. Kieślowski informed Karmitz that he was considering a reshoot and offered a typically pragmatic breakdown of exactly what it would cost: Dominique would be seen indicating, through sign language, that she loves Karol and that, when she comes out of prison, they will be together again. The signing should be poetic, he felt, but clear, although not subtitled. Delpy was called back, and the film's ending was concocted. Kieślowski later argued that the final cut is essentially a happy ending: "Between these two people, who hated each other and ought to have hated each other—her hating him and him hating her for humiliating him—love won out in the end. And I thought that if we succeeded in saying that it would be enough."[90] As he put it elsewhere: "Would you rather for the story to finish with him in Warsaw and her in Paris, with both of them free but not in love?"[91] However, there is more to the film's close than a romantic comedy's *lieto fine* and the generic cliché of a putative wedding. Indeed, in the context of the film as a whole, the ending's shift in tone demands consideration. The action, actor gestures, cutting, lighting and, crucially, Preisner's music create hope, yes, but also ambiguity. The result is a resonant ambivalence.

Some critics have chosen positive readings from the range permitted by this ambiguity. Haltof sees the camera moving closer to Dominique "'removing' the prison bars that separate the couple."[92] Insdorf also picks up on the bars, in connection to the windows at the end of *Blue* and *Red*, arguing that the image shifts from "imprisoning to liberating."[93] Recalling the earlier shot of Dominique high in her apartment, she reads the ending as one of many doublings and reversals throughout the film: "The symmetry of the director's images—including variations on white, pigeons, the male gaze, song-on-comb, telephones, and faked death—nourishes the notion of second chances: repetition becomes accumulation, with a prior mistake as a base for a successful action."[94] The second time Karol spies on Dominique, rather than taunting him aurally by telephone, Dominique returns "his gaze—and with love," as the spatially separated couple are "united by Kieślowski's expressive technique—a poetic combination of camera placement and movement, sound and music, editing and vision."[95]

Žižek's interpretation is much bleaker. He sees the various doublings in *White* as destabilizing, even horrifying.[96] The ending therefore represents, he argues, the "horror of encountering oneself in the guise of one's double, outside oneself," and revealing "the ultimate truth of the subject's self-identity" when the self is seen "encountering itself as an object" (a notion one might read into the camera work of the second wedding flashback, as Karol enters his "own" frame).[97] Even without engaging substantively with the rich psychoanalytical and filmic context within which he develops this notion, one can follow the thread of his thought to argue that, on achieving his pyrrhic victory, Karol finally sees himself clearly, and that what he has become is unattractive. Furthermore, Dominique is imprisoned, and so is he. Equality has been achieved through a loss of self and a loss of liberty. They are together because they are apart. And even if she is freed, one might end the film doubting whether they will be liberated from other forces. Throughout the film, they have been trapped in a vicious cycle of bourgeois roman-

tic and socio-economic mores, albeit exaggerated to a grotesquely satirical extent. Will life as fugitives—one reading permitted by *Red*'s
ending and its glimpse of them together—permit them finally to escape
those restrictions?

Kickasola and Wilson mediate between these opposing views.
Kickasola reads the close as "fanciful, humorous, and deeply sarcastic,"
noting that "Preisner's score, ending the film on the sixth of the scale as
opposed to the tonic, suggests a certain lack of resolution, and, for the
characters, an open future."[98] The scale degree is debatable, but the
point is well made: the harmonic ambiguity here could be heard to
match Karol's final look up at the window, beautifully played by
Zamachowski, through which, in spite of the tears, a hint of impishness
creeps back into his demeanor. Wilson explores the ending's ambiguity
in the context of her discussion of *White*'s discourse on voyeurism. Instead of reading Karol as the sadistic and misogynistic voyeur of a literally imprisoned sex object, Wilson sees the ending as "unsettling the
supremacy of the male desiring subject," with Dominique's gestures
and signs establishing her equal role in their relations, "for better or
worse." In turn, by deconstructing the norms of cinematic voyeurism,
the film allows the perceiver "no mastery over the images viewed"[99]—
nor over its music.

These vying perspectives—and the overall structure of the narrative and score with its encapsulation of one culturally rich musical style
by another of similarly finely grained meanings—encourages a further
consideration of the notion of tango in *White*, in terms of that tradition's
potential to articulate nuanced subtexts. After all, if Karol and Dominique emerge as equals, for better or worse, at *White*'s close, who or
what is the real force of subjugation here? Who or what leads their
dance, and what might the ending be said to resist? *White*'s close may
remind one that, in a danced tango, the dominated object, i.e., the
woman, is not powerless to affect the moment-to-moment power play
of the dance, even if the outcome seems secure both choreographically
and ideologically. Savigliano even hears, in the moaning of the *tangue-
ros* and personae like the protagonist of "The Last Sunday," evidence of
the object's rebellion and women who are not "simply the objects of
male domination."[100] Rather, because women "have never been just
'docile bodies' or 'passive objects,'" tangos record their ability "to subvert and negotiate."[101] Tangos remain full, of course, of "threatening
outcomes . . . overwhelmingly favourable to men,"[102] in which women
are forced into prostitution, sold to other men, raped, beaten and even
murdered. She insists, however, "on the importance of distinguishing
between the experience of victimization and the attribution of an identity as a victim,"[103] and examines Joan Cocks's argument that it should
be possible to "retain the notion of a phallocentric culture that is hegemonic but not totalitarian":

> The women aimed at improving their embodied lives, which in that
> context meant gaining a *more rewarding experience*. . . . They were

passionate objects not passive ones. Objects that had, if not a say, at least a *move* in the power game. Women in tango are part object, part subject. To paraphrase Jean Baudrillard, the stratagems of the *milonguita* had the ironic thrust of a subjectivity in the process of being grasped.[104]

The ironic thrust of a subjectivity in the process of being grasped: Karol and Dominique, it can be argued, are depicted in *White* as being dominated by the results of actions conditioned, in turn, by their experience of late-modern life under capitalism, during their marriage in Paris, and later in Warsaw. They are ciphers for alienation and a selfish, consumption-focused self. Yet Kieślowski and his team are far too clever to paint a simplistically bleak picture of life under capitalism, not least following their experiences of Polish communism. The characters therefore retain, and ultimately embrace, the potential to make moves within, and against, the conditioning of the system—moves, like the many reversals noted above, including Preisner's more optimistic and affecting re-scoring of the *rustico* for the second window scene—that might be deemed subversive. At the end of *White*, both Karol and Dominique have jettisoned, by accident and design, the trappings of capitalist success—liberty, money, belongings, freedom and other markers of a life lived well in the late-modern West—having sensed, through their dance with each other and their society, that none of it matters if certain things are lost. The *rustico*, it will be recalled, is the triumphant dance in *White*'s structural tango, not Preisner's tango cue. The film's expressive genre is a musical narrative in which music representing the authenticity of the pastoral and peasantry, rather than the grasping urbanity of music with a commercial imperative, is underscored as "truth." Tango cedes to *rustico*, white to golden orange, and Karol and Dominique achieve equality through mutually sacrificial destitution—an ironically exaggerated, two-way gesture of *agapē*.

On one level, this seems as shallow a philosophy—all you need is love, basically—as the humor in *White* is broad. But like that humor, the idea may still move one because, distorted into caricature one glimpses—as in all the trilogy's revivifying considerations of Western society's most fetishized conceptions—an easily forgotten illusion of truth. That necessary illusion is a means—flawed, yet necessary—to address the potential blankness of life in the late-modern West and forms the point at which *White*'s concerns connect into a broader cultural and political discourse that, unsurprisingly, has influenced much writing on cinema. One such discussion is particular germane to the contextualization of *White*'s investigations.

For Kieślowski, the color white could not perform symbolically in the trilogy in the same way as blue or red, partly because it is so hard to capture on film: white, as he describes it, is an *absence* of color.[105] Save for the splashes of golden orange casting a halo around the two moments of transcendent joy in *White*—transcendent, in part, because they are images of escape from broader constraints—*White*'s whites are the image (or non-image) of absence and lack: a living death of the soul, if not literally of the body. The idea of white as absence emerges forcibly in Richard Dyer's theorizing of representations of whiteness in white people's imagery, and particularly photography and film. Although he does not address *Three Colors: White* in his book *White*—an examination of the cultural construction of white people through popular culture—in case studies roughly contemporaneous to the trilogy he identifies "a feeling surfacing in moments of white contemporary popular culture, a sense of the dead end of whiteness" connected to "the association of whiteness and death."[106] White "is a colour," he writes as if channeling Kieślowski, "that also signifies the absence of colour, itself a characteristic of life and presence."[107] In turn there is "fearfulness—sometimes horrible, sometimes bleak"—in representations of white, and a sense of the tragic.

Kieślowski's *White* has discomforting intertextual resonances. The rush of white cloaks, hoods and horses heralding the Ku Klux Klan's arrival at the end of *The Birth of a Nation* (Griffith, 1915), intended therein to represent the bringing of salvation to a predominantly white town, can only represent to non-racist, twenty-first-century eyes "the bringing of death to African-Americans."[108] On a parallel path in his narrative, Dyer notes that, in vampire movies, "the vampires' whiteness conveys their own deadness" and "their victims grow pale" as "life ebbs away."[109] Moving beyond the obvious role of the vampire bite as a metaphor for sex, Dyer identifies white people in the grip of needs they cannot master and probably had foisted on them in the first place—vampires are not born but made—and thus the people of a white society feeding off of, and thus destroying, themselves. The issue of consumption is also cardinal, he notes, in George Romero's zombie movies: cultural satires replete with "startling images of white people as the dead devouring the dead."[110]

The possibility of a connection between *White*, film, capitalism and consumer culture intensifies in Dyer's consideration of the role of androids in the first three *Alien* films (Scott, 1979; *Aliens*, Cameron, 1986; *Alien³*, Fincher, 1992) and *Blade Runner* (Scott, 1982). Each *Alien* film centers on the confrontation between a white female protagonist and a corporation, and thus a capitalist socio-economic construct which Dyer reads, in its invisible pervasiveness, as a "metaphor for whiteness" that, in *Alien*, takes the corporeal form of an android named Ash—"a white man who is not human."[111] On the pivotal scene when Ash is regenerated—having been decapitated and thus shown to be void of "true" life (by a black man) earlier in the film—the android speaks of its admiration for the indestructible, demonic alien they have encountered:

> "I admire its purity," he adds, adding in a cut to an extreme, intensifying close-up, "unclouded by conscience, remorse or delusions of morality." Purity and absence of affect, the essence of the aspiration of whiteness, said in a state of half-life by a white man who has never really been alive anyway.[112]

Dyer's incisive analysis of the racial and sexual symbolism of the *Alien* films and *Blade Runner* only touches on the idea that corporations—every bit as complicit in the evils at the heart of *Blade Runner* as in *Alien*—and high or even futuristic ultra-high capitalism are the villains of these works, but it is plausible further to connect the deadness of white people's representations of themselves to the mechanisms of their most prevalent economic system.

In Kieślowski's *White*, Dominique (made-up in alabaster foundations that render her virtually vampiric) and Karol (his ashen face, at one stage, highlighted by the blood of his beating as he is dumped with the refuse on the snow-coated rubbish tip) can both be read as victims of circumstance. They can be taken as objects of economic and ideological repression who, by the end of the film, heroically exercise their remaining degree of subjectivity—like a female tango dancer seeking to be passionate rather than passive—in order briefly to loosen the leash. Dominique ends the film bathed in golden light, literally changing her color: she is no longer white (the color) or "white" (the cultural signification of death). This suggests, to me, *White*'s specific contribution to the broader discourse—a contribution that can be pinned down through comparison to one of its cinematic contemporaries.

Dyer's final case study, *Falling Down* (Schumacher, 1993) is a study of collapsing white identity in the late-modern West. It echoes *White*'s sense that, rather than the feeling that whiteness, the "cultural dominant of our times," is "really played out" and exhausted of future possibilities for regeneration, there is still "the possibility that there's life in us yet."[113] Like Karol and, by the close of the film, Dominique, D-FENS (Michael Douglas) in *Falling Down* is an ordinary guy who has been stripped of most of what qualifies for dignity and success in white Western culture: his name, job, wealth, wife and family.[114] Unlike Julie or the old judge in *Red*, he does not have to wish for nothing. "He is nothing"[115] already and, at the close of the film, he will literally sacrifice himself so that his daughter can benefit from a corporate pay-out—a life insurance premium paid by his former employer.

As well as evoking *agapē* at its most brutal, however, *Falling Down* ends by sounding a redemptive note for its audience as much as for D-FENS. A video of earlier times in which he forces his daughter, in tears, to play on an expensive-looking rocking horse is shown again. Earlier in the narrative, for Dyer, "appalled recognition of himself dawns on D-FENS's face" when he sees this captured moment; like Karol viewing Dominique in prison, he recognizes his shortcomings through an act of transformative voyeurism. In turn, "*Falling Down* ends on this video image . . . the average white guy, a mere image trace of an always incipient violence."[116] Dyer reads this moment and film for issues of race and sexuality providing a wider frame for grasping why, in terms of the repressions of the other that permitted its current life-death, white culture has reached this nihilistic state. Yet if white subjectivities like D-FENS, or like Karol looking up at the imprisoned yet transfigured and golden Dominique, can recognize in such moments a symbol of their own predicament, is this not also a glimpse of a more hopeful alternative?

White ends not with a distillation of all that is worst in Western culture, but by suggesting that the film's protagonists can transcend their socio-economically predetermined death-in-life: metaphorically here, and literally at the end of *Red*, they have a chance to escape their own deaths. As the camera shows Dominique bathed in gold and Karol's redemptive tears, with Preisner's delicate regeneration of his window cue on the soundtrack, *White* shapes a moment of recognition for characters and audience alike. In *Falling Down*, what is horrible for D-FENS becomes a similarly grim experience for the audience: Is this us, and is that it? Moving beyond the tragedy of *Falling Down*'s moment of collective anagnorisis, however, *White* offers a vision of escape— knowingly naïve, perhaps, both socially and psychologically, but scarcely unwelcome in its articulation of a belief in the lingering possibilities of renewal, resistance and change.[117] One is reminded, finally, of Mikołaj's words on the Wisła, after his aborted suicide attempt: everything is possible.

CHAPTER SEVEN

THE BLOOM OF LIFE:
RED

Three Colors: Red's metaphysical thriller is a curious structural mix: a "bolero-film" of overlapping circles driven by sonata-like teleology. Consequently, while the cyclical mysteries are beguiling, it is *Red*'s underlying momentum that delivers the film's affective and allegorical charge. Where *Blue*'s concerto considered the need to balance personal freedom with a commitment to society's ensemble, and *White*'s tango the impact of late-modern society on morality and personal relationships, *Red* cuts to the chase: should one lead a giving or a selfish life? To follow the analogy of sonata form, in the film's exposition section, exchanges between Valentine and the Old Judge state their opposing views and reveal a potentially unbridgeable divide. During the ensuing development section, their themes overlap and Valentine persuades the Old Judge to become more like her; by the close of the film, he has been synthesized into her realm, a lone wolf domesticated. The film's recapitulation section is thereby marked by the Old Judge's capitulation to Valentine's values, although she too has evolved. The closural function of this resolution is reinforced by the coda, which recapitulates motifs from the earlier films—like the end of a symphonic finale recalling subjects from previous movements—via glimpses of *Blue* and *White*'s protagonists. All fall under the spell, it seems, of Valentine's miraculous influence. Typically of Kieślowski's films, however, the ending is hardly happy: over a thousand people are dead and the fates of the trilogy's main protagonists are far from assured. At every turn in this slow-burning mystery, Preisner's musical realization of *Red*'s concept and climate nuances the trilogy's final installment.

To pursue the metaphor of *Red* as sonata-form-like—and to be clear, I am using the term as a critical analogy in relation to the audiovisual totality of the narrative, rather than to imply that Preisner composed a sonata form score to which Kieślowski then molded the film—it will be necessary briefly to clarify aspects of that term.[1] The sonata principle was one of the primary generating forces of the syntactical and symbolic structures of tonal Western art music, particularly during the Classical and Romantic periods. Musically it is, at base, a two-part harmonic and thematic process through which dialectical tensions between opposing realms are revealed at the start of the composition; those tensions are intensified and, ultimately, resolved during the form's longer, second phase; the resolution contributes strongly to a piece's sense of closure. Typically, two ideas (or sets of linked ideas) vie for supremacy over the course of a musical argument, one (usually that which is stated first) coming to dominate the other and synthesize it into its realm. The opposition can be as simple, in principle, as a modulation from the tonic to the dominant, with that basic harmonic contrast opening a structural dissonance to be extended, elaborated and finally resolved by a return to the piece's original tonal center.

While the dynamics of tonal harmony naturally underpin swathes of earlier music, in the Classical era the sonata dialectic became equally (and then in Romantic music sometimes primarily) thematic, with each musical idea (or "subject") having its harmonic home but also a thematic identity. Musical subjects thus became more easily read as pseudo-subjectivities. When music ends by triumphantly asserting the primacy of the first subject's realm, therefore, the symbolism of a human drama and, potentially, ideologically underpinned allegory becomes stronger, as the second subject dons the harmonic garb and melodic mannerisms of the victor, perhaps in joyous celebration of their marriage of musical means, perhaps in cowed subordination. Myriad possibilities reside in between. The ease with which one can narrativize readings of these musical structures—not least in terms of the notion that a forceful first subject gradually comes to dominate a weaker or dangerously "other" second subject—has inspired many music critics. Their narratives, in turn, have reflected the cultural currents of their times: hence the gendering of themes and subject groups by earlier writers being countered, more recently, by the revisionism of feminist and post-colonial criticism.

The sonata form, Christopher Ballatine has argued, originally arose as a form of Hegelian dialectic in music and thus an artistic development paralleling important changes to the organization of Western civilization. The dueling tonalities and themes of sonata forms paralleled a transition as the "old order . . . God or State-centred, and hegemonic, [was] surpassed by the new, which hoped to be rationalistic, liberal, universal and democratic":

> What was generally happening, in Hegelian terms, was that the contradictory viewpoints which carried forward, and resisted, the social changes, were transcended by and conserved in the higher synthetic unity represented by the democratic order.
>
> The musical analogue of this process was the rise of the sonata principle, in which the dualistically opposed tonal centres and their

antecedent paraphernalia came to suggest antithetical "world-views,"
and the total work their synthetic resolution.[2]

In this view, the existence of dialectic, as opposed to unitary rule, is
read as a positive development. And imagined in the context of a historical shift from hegemony to democracy—reflecting, indeed, conceptions of liberty, equality and fraternity—on a simplistic level, it is hard
to feel otherwise. More recently, though, critics have focused on sonata
form dialectics as also being "conducive to depicting difference, the
second theme routinely being described as 'feminine' in contrast to the
'masculine' first theme"; when first subject triumphs over second,
therefore, the alterity represented by the latter—"representative of sections of post-Renaissance European society that are forbidden but desired: women, exotics, bohemians, primitives and peasants, for example"—becomes a kind of controlled ideological substance, rationalized
and disciplined for the entertainment of a powerful (and mostly white
and phallocentric) bourgeoisie.[3] Democracy may have supplanted the
unitary control of church or king, but it still had its winners and losers.
These, too, can be heard in sonata forms.

In *Red*, one might argue that the film's sonata-form-like structural
principle is given a revisionist twist. Preisner's bolero has two distinct
themes, one relating to its main female character, the other to its
twinned male characters; one denotes a realm of experience that is
stereotypically marked by Western cultures as feminine, the other a
more masculine zone. By being a bolero, the music already imports
realms of experience deemed "exotic" by Western society into the film,
thanks to its roots in an earthily erotic Spanish and Latin American cultural form. By the end of the score, in turn, one theme asserts dominance over the other, just as one would expect. The musical twist is that
the feminine is triumphant here: Valentine's subject(ivity) group con-
quers the judges' group, just as her values are absorbed by the Old
Judge and, the finale of the film suggests, may rescue his ruined
younger double—and perhaps even, by extension, the audience. This
could be interpreted as another example of the later Kieślowski films
seeking to promote an alternative political perspective, partly by utilizing Preisner's "feminine" presence with ideologically directed efficiency.

The victory of the feminine in *Red*, though, relates less to gender
issues *per se* than to broader issues in society, just as the battle of the
sexes in *White* can be read as an allegorical reflection on late-modern
life in the West, and Julie's submission to Olivier and the social order
in *Blue* as similarly symbolic. Playing on musical stereotypes to sustain
a film-wide scoring strategy, Preisner's score helps the film to epitomize a different way of life. The realm of *agapē* is often viewed, in
Western culture, as distinctively feminine: cooperating, caring for others, and self-sacrifice are deemed opposite to triumphant male heroism,
not least by screen-scoring cliché. Reversing the polarity of those conventions, *Red*'s sonata-form-like opposition of thematic (musical and

non-musical) realms makes a musical, dramatic and political point. The usually subjugated feminine other wins over the masculine in a gesture, to borrow one of Kehr's memorable phrases on the trilogy, that suggests how one should try to save the world. This is a sonata in the conditional tense: its articulation, complication, and resolution of its main thematic issues represents what might be, as opposed to what is, in contemporary Western societies.

Red's sonata-form-like subtext has a second twist. While Valentine's thematic realm is marked musically as feminine (by its grace, beauty, refinement, sophistication, delicacy and other semiotic connotations), the judges' masculine subject can also be construed as other (it has ardency and other symbols of strength, certainly, but also invokes an outsider's realm of mystery, and primal urges). Valentine's femininity, in a sense, thus becomes a civilizing force on this rogue masculinity in *Red* and, on one level, her music and presence become hegemonic in a manner usually reserved for the masculine. On another, one can argue that the score's thematic structure encodes a double alterity: "other" perspectives on society, twice over, are cooperating by the end of the film, in order to articulate its alternative consensus.

What follows does not argue, then, that *Red* was consciously structured by Kieślowski and Preisner to replicate sonata form. Rather, this chapter's process of critical analogy, by exploring the film's similarities to this structure and its cultural implications—which may, in turn, be linked to familiar archetypes of dramatic narrative[4]—lends a reading of the film a new dimension, not least by linking it to broader currents of cultural thought to which Kieślowski is often connected through critical praise, but not necessarily through analytical substance. This is hardly music's sole purpose in *Red*, though, and Preisner's multifaceted scoring contributes to one film-wide strategy while enhancing at least two others: *Red*'s evocation of the existence of a metaphysical realm and its generation of suspense.

The score is further structured and finely detailed by the music's relationship to the performances of Jean-Louis Trintignant and Irène Jacob. As the Old Judge, Trintignant poses an enigma halfway between God and slob, but evolving into a benevolent father figure; as Valentine, Jacob slowly uncoils a knot of tension, allowing her character's beacon gradually to shine. The structural opposition and development is clarified and marked for allegory by the thematic structure of Preisner's score—inextricably, the reverse is also true—with key elements of the music returning, at dramatic cruxes, to underwrite the drama. The bolero's potential for morally elevated music is Valentine's climate, its turbulence the Old Judge's and, in time, the younger judge Auguste's as well. One is calm, the other storm; together, they represent something greater. The misanthropic and socially disruptive Kern, his neighbor the drug dealer, Auguste's cheating lover, Auguste pursuing Karin, Valentine's grousing boyfriend, her heroin-addicted brother, her absent father, her unfaithful mother, the bubblegum stuck in her vandalized lock, and everything else broken in *Red*'s depiction of late-modern society:

all are counterbalanced by the civilizing presence of Valentine and her attachment to eroded, but here reimagined, cultural codes like "fraternity." By working through this dialectic, and ultimately resolving its drama in favor of Valentine's climate, *Red* implies that one might only know something like happiness by conforming to a code of reciprocity and kindness akin to the members of Eagleton's *agapē*-riffing jazz band.

Yet even then, it will only be a partial happiness, as *Red*'s other main musical element reminds one. The Van den Budenmayer song heard originally in *Decalogue 9*, and here experienced diegetically by the main characters, creates a metaphysical force field triangulating the lives of Auguste, Joseph and Valentine. It demonstrates the similarity of their socially distinguishing musical tastes—their love of the same kind of music tells them (and the audience) that they are "made for" each other, like Karol and Mikołaj's shared musical past in *White*—but more crucially it implies their empathy for the song's melancholy intimations. A locus of pain to which each is separately drawn, the song diagnoses a malaise that can only be partially relieved through a palliative dose of *agapē*.

Exposition

"The isle is full of noises"

Red's personal meaning to its director, its status as his final film and its story of an elderly, magician-like recluse entranced and redeemed by a young and beautiful woman, have led several critics to link the film to Shakespeare's *The Tempest*, a play in which "fantasy and reflexivity unite with dramatic action as Shakespeare gives us his subtle commentary on his career in artmaking through a fanciful story."[5] Annette Insdorf notes how both Prospero and the Old Judge make "a decisive break with misanthropy" because of Miranda and Valentine, and that, "[l]ike Prospero, the Old Judge seems to have prophetic powers"[6]—although, while "Shakespeare's magician actually creates a storm, the one that causes the ferry accident of *Red* cannot be traced directly to Kieślowski's enigmatic cynic," who must, like any other concerned relative or friend, "watch the TV to learn what happened."[7] Perhaps this is because he has renounced his "magical" powers, or at least his ability to spy on his neighbors through surveillance devices, at her request.

Wilson makes an intriguing sonic point about *Red* and *The Tempest* by quoting Caliban's famous soliloquy:

> Be not afeard; the isle is full of noises,
> Sounds, and sweet airs, that give delight and hurt not.
> Sometimes a thousand twangling instruments
> Will hum about mine ears; and sometimes voices

That, if I then waked after long sleep,
Will make me sleep again; and then, in dreaming,
The clouds methought would open, and show riches
Ready to drop upon me, that when I waked
I cried to dream again. (III. Ii. 136-44)

Like Prospero's island, Wilson notes, the Old Judge's house "is filled
. . . with the sounds of spirits" via his surveillance gadgets, as Kieślowski "disturb[s] the boundary between dream and reality, between
virtual and actual."[8] There is another sense, however, in which the film
hums with sounds like Prospero's noisy isle: the presence of Flageollet's meticulously crafted sound design and the sweet airs of Preisner's score.[9] The community of noise created by the judge's technology, for instance, is a false fraternity: an electronically mediated
phantom of community spied upon in the absence of the real thing. This
aspect of late-modern alienation is mirrored throughout *Red* by Flageollet's distinctly metaphorical sound design, beginning with the main
title sequence—probably the most heavily processed passage in the
entire trilogy of soundtracks.

The first sound in *Red* is the rain. This omen of storms yet to come
is accompanied by the cluster of pitched sounds one will also hear elsewhere in the film when Valentine speaks on the phone to her boyfriend,
Michel. Diegetically, this may imply train brakes—other train-like
sounds clatter through the mix, suggesting nearby tracks—but it also
sounds like something under strain: a relationship, perhaps, or the hull
of a ferry. The sound of rainfall then recedes beneath a layer of more
prominent manmade noises: the electronic chirruping of a telephone
dial tone and the beeps of its keypad as a number is dialed. The audio-
viewer is thus "alienated" from the natural sound of the rain by technology; the soundtrack moves away from what is natural and into the
realm of the modern, playing on cultural conceptions of authenticity
equating to unmediated phenomena. The track also becomes more
heavily sequenced as the sound design cross-fades from a mixture of
environmental sounds and post-production additions to a sophisticated,
wholly post-production creation.

As Michel dials, the camera starts tracing the phone cable down to
the connection box. A chaotic *mise-en-scène* is glimpsed, which includes a photo of Valentine, an Aldous Huxley novel and a copy of *The
Economist*. One might assume from Michel's reading matter and pompous statements later in the film that he is politically active; one might
also assume, from his conversations with Valentine, that such politics
do not hold all the answers. The shot then plunges "inside" the telephone wires: red cables surround a dark center and the image spirals as
voices, panned left to right, rise and fall in waves—a riptide of contact,
experienced within a pulsing yonic symbol. Actual sea sounds and other
maritime effects (such as seagulls) are heard as the cable plunges into
the ocean, just as the thousand-plus victims at the end of the film will
be pulled beneath the waves of the English Channel. Another splash

and the camera tracks the pipeline emerging under protective hoops—red, of course—on the other side of the sea (the camera is now looking backwards, not forwards, to show this) before the image accelerates into a whirl of lights, like a Ferris Wheel glimpsed from a dizzying ride at a fairground. The camera finally comes to rest on a single blinking bulb; the sonic storm calms to one repeating tone. The appearance of Irène Jacob's name in the credits at this moment hints to the audience that the phone in question is Valentine's.

Foreshortening editing and control of film speed in this sequence—a Steadicam undercranking at 3 frames per second according to Kickasola[10]—creates its sense of acceleration and direction, intensifying the rush to the bathetic ending: the phone called by Michel is engaged. The introduction thereby summarizes, in a few seconds, the problem at the heart of *Red*: missed connections. However much one might like truly to communicate with those that one loves, one is separated from them by the vicissitudes of late-modern life. Technology's mediations, in turn, offer but meager consolation. Even when calls connect, they are an illusion of contact: there is no substitute for living side by side. As Kickasola suggests, the abstraction of the sequence invites deeper speculation, which in his case leads him to consider how this is "Hell" for Kieślowski ("human interaction, but only of the partial, fragmented sort"). Hence the irony of what the Old Judge says later regarding his surveillance of his neighbors. He thinks he knows where the truth lies, but such insight comes "only at the expense of knowing these people in the flesh," which leads to "a more impoverished perspective on reality than he had before."[11]

Flageollet's sound design parallels and intensifies the sequence's symbolic charge. Alongside the effects mentioned above, a pulsing electronic pitch, jerking upwards and trilling increasingly rapidly, sketches a rising scale connoting tension and imminent arrival; the midway point on the journey is marked by rapid percussive clicks as the image races beneath the hoops; finally the slowly repeating engaged tone is heard, forming a droll cinematic punchline to the bravura audiovisual display. The engaged tone is a repeated A. Having accented the narrative foreground and helped shape the symbolism of the opening sequence, Flageollet ends with what, in the context of the score for *Red* (and as foreshadowed in *White*), one can hear as the first seed of the music's contribution to *Red*'s metaphysical penumbra. A is the pitch and tonality (A major) at the heart of Valentine's musical universe; it is the tonal center finalized by the trilogy's last dramatic cue (a rising A-E-A arpeggio); it becomes, over the course of the *Three Colors* trilogy, a symbol of home. One hears it in *Red* just as one sees the name of the relevant character's player—Jacob—appearing on screen; the image then cuts back to Michel and the phone being put back in its cradle. All one hears, for a second, is the rain. Michel then picks the phone up again and restarts the process. As Insdorf suggests, "'Redial' could serve as the subtitle of Kieślowski's oeuvre," not least in the context of "the technological path that the human spirit must travel in the 1990s."[12] An alternative subtitle could be "only reconnect."

All three parts of the trilogy start with images of subjectivities in transit and cut loose from their usual moorings. This obviously symbolizes aspects of the story of the main characters in each film, but in *Red*, the omniscient point of view of the camera, impossibly tracking the telephone call underground and beneath the ocean through a network of wires, is extended to the experiencing audio-viewer, whose cinematic journey the montage becomes—cinematic in the sense that this journey could only be experienced in a movie or one's cinematically influenced imagination—and into which one is belted, like a passenger on a fairground attraction, by Flageollet's sounds and sweet airs. Propelled by the opening's audio-visual momentum, *Red*'s ride will demonstrate the agony of missed connections, and then how to reconnect.

Thematic Exposition

Ai: First Subject (Valentine)

Red's narrative discourse is layered with significant details. As an example of its subtlety, behind the foreground action of Valentine guzzling mineral water after her ballet class, an old Mercedes (the Old Judge's) passes her on the road. Just as Preisner's music enters—its arrival smoothing the shift from the film's introduction to Valentine, and on to the beginning of the sequence of events that will lead her into the Old Judge's realm—one sees an illusion of his car twice entering Valentine's body, thanks to a reflective surface to her left. Two versions of the Old Judge merge with her being, encapsulating aspects of the story to come.[13] Preisner's series of cues for the ensuing sequence, which play out uninterruptedly (save for one notable moment), accent the content and subtext of the individual scenes while imbuing the sequence with additional, musically generated meanings.

As Valentine is glimpsed for the first time, drinking water from a bottle in sparkling sunshine, suspense is evoked by the entry of the bolero's ostinato in the low strings. Locally, this propels the discourse into the catwalk theme proper as the action cuts to the fashion show. By the third bar, just before the cut, the bolero rhythm is being performed in 3 octaves on D by the violas and divided second violins. A device commonly used to unnerve audio-viewers—most iconically in John Williams's *Jaws* theme—Preisner's ostinato will regularly generate tension through repetitive rhythms and a peculiar harmonic twist (see Fig. 7.1).

Typically of Preisner, the ostinato is an elongation of the more traditional rhythmic model of a dance form, in this case $\frac{4}{4}$ as opposed to $\frac{3}{4}$. Preisner's extra beat lessens the urgency of the rhythm, as befits the beginning of a long narrative haul, without entirely dispersing its insistence; the harmonic smudge he adds to the final beat helps maintain this balance by adding a touch of dissonant propulsion. The strings are instructed to play *sempre sautille*, an effect in which the players bounce

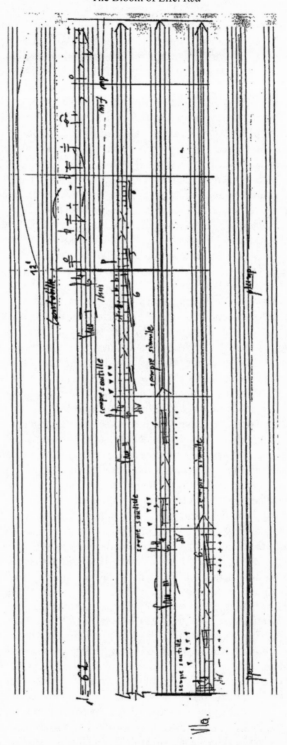

Fig. 7.1: Bolero ostinato (detail) from Preisner's first *Red* cue in manuscript score

the bow on the strings, creating a slightly dry, percussive sound well-suited to the evocation of a *bolera*'s castanets. The repeated pitch D forms the pedal note and accrues harmonic tension. On the last beat of the third bar, however, the upper group of fiddles perform a quarter-tonal arabesque, arcing up and back down to the pedal pitch D. This forms the smudge of dissonance at the end of every bar of the ostinato by grinding against the octave Ds, before the instability resolves at the start of each new bar. *Red*'s ostinato thus expresses a pattern of tension-release, tension-release, in a cycle of perpetually thwarted resolutions.

The ostinato's quartertones also hint at a darker side of the fashion show to which the action cuts, emphasizing—to ignore, for a moment, the melody of the promenading music—the oppressive and threatening sound design of the scene. The thundering applause may remind one of the pouring rain in *Red*'s opening; the blue burst of flashbulbs dazzling Valentine on the catwalk appear like lightning strikes or the beacons of emergency vehicles; immersed in an audio-visual storm, Valentine and her colleagues model raincoats. As epitomized by the moment when she stumbles and almost falls from the catwalk into a sea of bodies below, sound and score evoke an undercurrent of jeopardy within this superficially sparkling sequence. Karol had his metaphysical pigeons, Julie her musical phantoms; Valentine in *Red* is pursued by a sonic storm foreshadowing her fate at sea. The helicopters that drown her conversations with Michel; the planes buzzing low over the Old Judge's house; the winds stirring leaves in his driveway; the blustering of a gashed red sheet behind Valentine in the fashion studio; her wet clingy hair when she emerges from the shower to catch a call from Michel—all contribute to the penumbra of threat that forms around Valentine. Thanks to the implications of certain sounds and musical signs—ostinatos, low flying helicopters, thunder—one experiences a nagging unease, tugging at the corner of one's perceptions like the fleeting image of the Mercedes in the background of the first shot in the sequence, when Valentine drowned her thirst and water spilled over her body.

The foreground of the catwalk scene, though, and of Preisner's first cue, diverts one from focusing too closely on the gathering storm. The first part of the bolero—its promenade—unfurls a vision of grace in the form of what, for Preisner, is an unusually long and uninterrupted melodic line: its two phrases drift down through an octave, like feathers carried on a gentle breeze (see Ex. 7.1). This line seems to drape itself around the swooping Steadicam of Sobocinski's tracking shot, which follows Valentine like a partner in a bolero. Initially performed *cantabile* by the first violins—the strings of the Sinfonia Varsovia, conducted by Wojciech Michniewski, add a particular richness to the original soundtrack recording—the melodic descent is ornamented by arabesques and supported by a cushioned accompaniment in the woodwind, Preisner maintaining the onward thread of music between violin phrases with the barest of accompaniments. In contrast to the trilogy's earlier play on dance music, then, the theme is poles apart from the dynamism of *White*'s tango, but also from its melancholy *rustico*. Rather than rampant masculinity or fragile femininity, the bolero's promenade theme intimates feminine confidence, grace and beauty. At the eye of *Red*'s storm, Valentine is scored as the model of perfection.

Ex. 7.1: Ai/Bolero main theme, catwalk promenade version

The cue's evocation of floating and calm is also a harmonic creation, enabling the cue to float from one tonal center to another. The cue's key signature is D major and the pedal of the ostinato emphasizes that pitch-class; every pitch heard could be within the mode of D Mixolydian. Once the melody begins, the pedal tone is harmonized by additional notes in the string parts, fleshing out a four-bar, D-D-G-D pattern (all chords are major). This would suggest a secure, if not emphatic, grounding of the cue in D major (G-D's plagal IV-I cadence being not quite as assertive as a V-I perfect cadence would sound). However, the melody destabilizes that security. The flattened C of its falling line, removing the sharpened leading note of D major, as per D Mixolydian, can be heard instead as an unfurling of the scale of G major. Listening to the melody and harmony combined, a modal blurring occurs, tempting one to hear the D pedal and harmonies as a dominant preparation for another key: I-IV-I in D may thus be heard as V-I-V in G. This harmonic ambiguity buoys the harmony and propels the cue forwards on a different rhythmic level to the dissonant smudges on every fourth beat of the ostinato. Expectations of coming to a rest are thereby subtly intensified.

After the first four bars of melody, and in place of the silences that punctuate so many other cues in the trilogy, the next four bars sustain the D chord by stretching the existing musical fabric. An oboe, cushioned by some skillful horn scoring, etches a path back up to the original point from which the melody descended, and then the theme's consequent phrase begins, the clichéd signification of femininity of the high violins' tone intensified by the antecedent phrase's doubling by flute and piccolo. Now the melody and harmony shift expectations. The tune no longer contradicts D major, and the chords and melody sound a less ambiguous D major I-IV-I pattern. The floating therefore ceases. The D of the ostinato does give way briefly to G—the first change, notably, to the cue's lowest pitch—but its return to D, coupled with the melody, secures a sense of arrival gently emphasized by the swell of thickening orchestration (ebbing and flowing like tracks controlled at a mixing desk) and overall intensified dynamic. Preisner's harmony at this moment of arrival shapes a musical equivalent to Valentine's relief as, backstage, she reports that she almost fell over. It may also hint to the audio-viewer that all, in the end, will be well.

So Valentine floats above the sonic storm on the wings of the bolero's first subject—a theme also semiotically connoting notions of grace, beauty, femininity, optimism and, as discussed below, the angelic. Both Wollermann and Paxman identify the theme as Valentine's, with Paxman building up an audio-visual picture of how the film links her character to ideas of "striking beauty, resonance and warmth."[14] The momentum of the catwalk patterns and lyrical camera work meld with Preisner's theme to symbolize Valentine's elegance, as do the refined clothes and setting, and visual indexes ranging from sunlight blinking on her water bottle to its visual rhyme in the glimmering chandeliers. Paxman also notes the melody and harmony of the theme:

> The simple focus on D major tonic/subdominant harmony fuses with the connoted sense of Valentine's insular perspective, but also her optimism, because of the bright major key. . . . [T]he mellifluous theme emanates grace and beauty through its expansive, consonant melodic architecture[.][15]

Her purity is also suggested by the heavenly registers—high equaling light and good, rather than low equaling dark and bad—and, overall, a combination of audio and visuals suggesting that she has "nothing to hide or be ashamed of."[16] If Valentine sounds too good to be true, it is vital for the film to establish her as a quintessentially, even unrealistically, good character in order that she can interact symbolically with her misanthropic antagonist. The melody, harmony and ostinato propel Valentine towards this fate. Like the car in *Blue* and the suitcase in *White*, Valentine is not traveling aimlessly along the catwalk: she is caught in broader currents. Locally, that fateful momentum will terminate when Valentine hits Rita in her car and meets the Old Judge, Joseph Kern. Across the entire narrative, it will terminate in the final shot of the film.

Aii: First Subject, Variation 1 (The Lone Angel)

Shot through multiple glass windows inside the isolation of her car, public perceptions of Valentine now shift to a private portrayal of loneliness. The music metamorphoses to assist in this depiction, its change demarcating a more subjective version of the promenade theme. This is not a new subject, therefore, but a variation of the first theme and part of its subject group that reveals further aspects of its design and, in turn, of the character with whom it has been paired.

The thematic statement compresses Ai into the original theme's two four-bar phrases separated, here, only by one bar of woodwind link. The theme is rescored for acoustic guitar (which takes the melody) and harp (which provides an accompaniment of gently breaking chords); a lone clarinet links the two phrases of melody. If one needed further convincing of the score's claims for Valentine's angelic and otherworldly perfection, one hears it in this combination of plucked acoustic strings, reworking her theme with timbral connotations redolent of angelic lyres. The sense of space created by the reverberating strings and studio reverb accentuates the sense of interiority and the sacred, and even the harmony reveals itself to be freighted with style topical connotations of the heavenly. As Tagg revealed through his "Fernando" analysis, "musemes" signifying the angelic and the heavenly extend beyond plucked strings, arpeggios, reverb and heavenly voices.[17] From requiems to pop ballads, music tropings of these conventions also include a recurring contrapuntal-harmonic formula—a move from tonic (I) to relative minor (vi) or another harmony (such as IV) permitting the fourth and/or sixth scale degrees of a key to feature prominently in the melody or accompanimental voice-leading. This is precisely what Preisner's theme does, as the second phrase of melody rises from 3rd to 4th scale degree and back again (see Fig. 7.2) while the harmonic cradle rocks from I to IV to I. Tagg locates this pattern in the Abba song, the "In paradisum" of Fauré's *Requiem*, Brahms's "Ave Maria" and many other pieces where a melodic line floats, at a moderate tempo, above a cloud of harp-like sounds.[18] Graceful and beautiful on the outside (i.e., in public), inside (and in private) Valentine is revealed to be an angel, but a lonely one. As Paxman notes, the meditative, laconic and solo guitar emphasizes her solitude by being "music that breathes, pauses, and encourages us to feel a depth of sensitivity . . . that does not exist simply in the visual context."[19] That isolation, in turn, is connected by Paxman to all three main characters in the film.[20] In Valen-

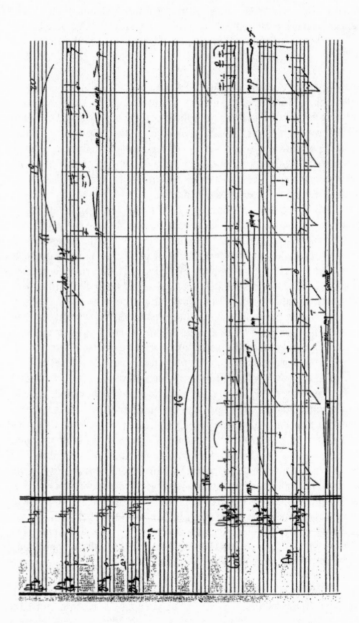

Fig. 7.2: Aii/First subject, angelic version, in Preisner's manuscript score (detail)

tine's case, it is indexed visually when she pulls away in her car, revealing to the rear of the depth of field a couple entwined by the river—they look a little like Auguste and his lover Karin—enjoying a romantic moonlit stroll in a world far removed from her own.

The shift from exterior to interior is also harmonically articulated. The theme is transposed into A major/Mixolydian. In the film and trilogy as a whole, A is not an unexpected pitch-center. As noted above, in *White* it emerged as Karol's tonal center and the harmonic location for his most heart-felt expressions; in *Red*, when Michel dialed Valentine, her engaged tone consisted of repeated A naturals. The scene's arrival at this harmonic center, matched to its connotations of intimacy and the personal, grounds Valentine in the key, linking the score's first subject group, its key and the character at its moral center through the musical equivalent of a symbolic camera zoom. That it is scored for guitar, a sound that recurs at several further key points in the film, including the last dramatic cue before the end title, is also significant. Preisner likes to select an instrument to voice the "soul" of a story: in *Red*, that soul is Valentine; her instrument is the guitar and her tonal center is A. Musically, this combination marks magnetic north on the film's moral compass. In *Red*, one dials A for *agapē*.

Angelic perfection, evoked musically or otherwise, is nonetheless Valentine's imperfection. She does not see the world as richly as she will by the close of the film and the threat of *Red*'s undertow, which will carry her towards those realizations, makes itself felt in the scene's final bar as the ostinato returns, not on D but A, the quartertonal arabesque thus smudging Valentine's musical center, although the ostinato's *perpetuum mobile* also accentuates the moment when her vehicle mobilizes. A lurching bar of $\frac{6}{4}$, adding two beats to the music to fill out the frames before the cut to the traffic light shot, also disrupts the flow of the cue. The music briefly stumbles, like Valentine on the catwalk, as her fall into knowledge begins.

Bi: Second Subject (The Judges)

As darkness engulfs Valentine—the *mise-en-scène* is now less bright within her car due to the passing nocturnal surroundings—a comparative musical gloom is evoked in the bolero, a sense of threat that finds its visual match in the scene's many flashing red warning lights, especially when they distort views of Valentine or, more generally, overexpose the image, as if to threaten the very fabric of the film. Musical connotations of darkness and threat are primarily achieved through harmonic and timbral means. The plagal chord changes are replaced by a pattern in which chords move from diminished sevenths rooted on B♭— a sound of threat and metaphysical jeopardy in *Blue* and *White*, too, and thus throughout the trilogy—to A major triads, the bass fluctuating unstably between the roots of supertonic and tonic, as the harmonies flip between ambiguity and unconvincing resolution. The timbre of the music begins to darken when the violins play the melody in a lower register than theme Ai, working around a simple melodic pattern in which a rising tritone (more harmonic instability) falls back on the change to the tonic chord. The melody then sinks lower still as dusky violas take over the tune, and tension gathers when cello and bass pedals sustain the B♭s and As. The ominous connotations of the pedals also remind one that terrible things happen in cars in Kieślowski's films (see Fig. 7.3).

Fig. 7.3: Bi/Second subject (the judges), from Preisner's manuscript score (detail)

The shift in tessitura grounds the music in lower registers than any yet heard in the film. A structural division is thus denoted when the register shifts to roam between bass and alto, rather than a tenor to soprano range. The growling of revving engines, most notably the motorbike that pulls in front of Valentine's car at the lights, adds intensity to the scene as one anticipates the engines releasing full throttle; this also augments the section's threatening quality and, by dint of its harshness and register, combines with the music's lower registers to evoke masculine associations. But to whom is this bolero passage of masculinity, Eros, and darkness connected? As Valentine pulls away from the lights, Auguste arrives at the pedestrian crossing; in a few moments' time, Valentine will run over Rita, the Old Judge's dog. This theme is Auguste and Joseph's section of the bolero, its musical darkness mirroring aspects of the parallel humiliations they experience and the negative emotional realms into which they are dragged. Appropriately, given the sexual cause of their dejection, there is an undercurrent of eroticism within theme B, thanks in part to the flattened supertonic, which connects to clichés of modal or chromatic exoticism via its links to the dance's roots in Spanish folk culture and the bolero's ritualizing of coupling; the ardent low melodies and tritonal turn connote yearning.

Thus Preisner—and this is primarily his score's invention at this point, the action being benign, indeed boring, and centered on Valentine, for whom such music is clearly no match—constructs an alternative realm to her angelic purity: a Satanic space of lust and unrequited aberrations. Paxman senses foreboding:

> Preisner exploits murky, dissonant intervallic relationships. Certainly from Western perceptions and sensibilities of tonal language, minor second and diminished fifth—built around chords on the tonic and flattened supertonic degrees—do not manifest sentiments of stability, promise and optimism. Instead they convey a restless quality and, compounded by the slow melodic rhythm (and prominent reverb in the music's recording), consequently suggest something ominous: the presence of danger.[21]

He also notes the "rather eerie" microtonal movement in the bolero ostinato which, while not new to these moments, combined with the insistent rhythm imbues the scene with further tension.

The music fades away and briefly stops as Auguste, crossing the road at the site-to-be of the pivotal advertising billboard when Valentine pulls away—her vehicle taillights hinting at the red that will come to occupy this space—bends to pick up his spilled books and near-miraculously finds the answer to a question he will be set in his final judge's exam. Even more miraculously, in doing so he repeats almost exactly an event that happened to the Old Judge many years beforehand. The moment cannot be served by the dark poetry of the second subject, so the brief musical silence draws attention to the occurrence— silence as a kind of anti-stinger—through the sudden absence of music; the sound design also drops down a gear, various engines rattling more quietly. The camera stills, too, calling attention to "a providential moment on providential ground" and not an intersection but "*the* intersection for this film," which Kickasola interprets (using terms developed by Glenn Man) as articulating an "aesthetics of intersection" through a structure reflecting a "centralized enunciative authority."[22] This leads Kickasola to muse on the film's evocation of the question of "whether it *is* God designing these intersections,"[23] although one might equally wonder if the authority who makes the elastic band around the books snap is the Old Judge, or even the director.

As Insdorf suggests, Valentine is shot waiting for the lights to change as if someone is already watching her.[24] Who could this be? The possibility of authorial intervention in moments perhaps designed, in part, to remind one that one is experiencing a fiction, is intensified by considering the question of where the music is located in these shots and the next scene. Valentine taps her fingers on the steering wheel, suggesting the possibility that the music is now diegetic; the screenplay confirms she is doing so because she is listening to music, although the music to which she taps need not, of course, be the music to which the audio-viewer is listening. This aptly opens up questions concerning the location of the music until now in the film, in preparation for a moment of authorial intervention.

Bii: Second Subject, Variation (Sex and Violence)
While waiting at the traffic lights, with a slash of vivid red reflected across her face via the windscreen, Valentine taps her fingers on the steering wheel. In the next scene and section of the cue—a vigorously gestural variation of the second subject (see Fig. 7.4)—Flageollet's sound design manipulates the recording of Preisner's music to indicate, for the first time in the film, that this is music being experienced diegetically by a character and coming from Valentine's radio: the cue is rendered tinny through compression and initially is much quieter; it is also corrupted by a squeal of interference. The frequency-modulated post-production effect sounds nothing like radio static: this siren's call is much more musical. That call will soon to be heard again from the Old Judge's radio scanner, as if he is inadvertently or otherwise inter-rupting the signal to Valentine's car and causing the unfolding events to occur. Valentine taps the radio to regain the signal, taking her eyes off the road in the process and hitting the Old Judge's pet dog.

The music's post-production treatment helps to denote key narra-tive information, but in the context of a long musical cue of various purposes it may also be heard to serve a symbolic function. The sense of theatricality common to the middle sections of danced boleros trans-fers, at this moment, to an authorial gambit marking these moments as significant. Throughout *Red*, there are meta-fictional moments: points where the film creates a sense of narratorial agency and, specifically, the presence of an author/auteur. The most obvious such moment comes when Valentine, in the theater, asks Joseph "What are you?" and he replies—after a pause into which one can insert the truth as one per-ceives it—"A retired judge." Yet the bleed between narrative levels in the car, as hitherto (probably) non-diegetic music turns (probably) diegetic, calls attention to its very construction as a "significant event." So who constructed it? The issue of intentionality and directorial con-trol over events, central to the aura cast around the Old Judge, is evoked in part by one of the oldest film music tricks in the book: the

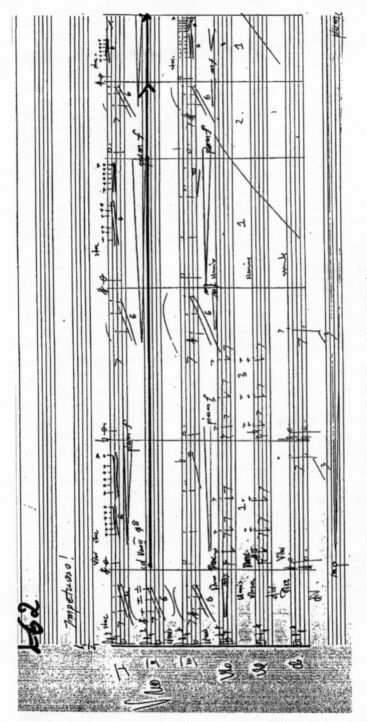

Fig. 7.4: Bii (violent variation) from Preisner's manuscript score

shift between non-diegetic and diegetic.[25] Paxman even suggests that the fact Valentine is hearing the underscore at this moment opens the possibility that she is "subliminally aware" of the "metonymical connotation of fate" in the sequence.[26]

That the music may be heard as diegetic is also suggested by the anempathic nature of the cue. Whereas Ai, Aii and Bi loosely matched music to aspects of image and action—the elegant promenade, the moment of reflective interiority, the darkness of the nocturnal journey—in the manner typical of Preisner's "side-by-side" underscoring, here there is a disconnect between music and action. This is, after all, just a sequence of a tired woman driving home, and yet the cue is the most ardent and climactic yet. In a Bolero School dance, this might be the most virtuosic passage, filled with strong soloistic gestures and exaggerated poses; it is also the passage which evokes José Quiroga's "bolero of despair and eros," and "the erotic charge of steamy sex under a red lightbulb," with someone hiding "a knife under the pillow."[27] When the cue returns later in the film, as Auguste spies on Karin screwing his replacement, the intensification of the second subject's gestures through harmonic and rhythmic means—e.g., the tritone sustained between first and second violin B♭s and Es in the first and third bars of each phrase, the accented thrusts of the bowing—feels appropriate to the situation, as an anti-erotic mickey-mousing of the couple's (to Auguste) act of violation. As Paxman writes, there is something "martial and aggressive" about the music and its "connotative communication of danger,"[28] but its only link to the action here may be revealing the inner turmoil of the man Valentine has just passed at the crossroads and/or the older one whose radio waves are interrupting her journey. The music's distance from the diegetic events at Bii's first appearance therefore seems briefly to be key, accentuated as it is by the authorial intervention of the diegetic/non-diegetic shifting. The music is adrift from its normative place in the film thus far, marking a point of fateful intersection in Valentine's story, hinting at the bicameral pairing of realms she will unite, and opening a space of possibility shortly to be filled by the ominous thump of metal hitting dog.

Biii (Aftermath Variation)

At that fateful thud the music's ardent foreground halts. A throb of rhythm remains, but muted octave horns and a trio of clarinet, bass clarinet and bassoon sustain dissonant B♭s over the remains of A major; the stinging orchestration of this sonority is one of the most technically sophisticated moments in the trilogy's scores. Obviously, the music is creating a tense narrative space, not tipping the perceiver off precisely as to what has just happened, but creating a knot of tension through the semitonal clashing and sustained sonorities. It is also carefully gradated scoring: Preisner moves from Bii to the stiller tension of Biii, and in turn into the calmness of Aiii, through a series of timbral phases. His changes to instrumentation, in a demonstration of the composer's ability to extend sophisticated timbral thought over longer range gestures

and thus achieve subtle narrative purposes, alter the emotional hue
while beginning to turn the cue back towards the first subject group and
Valentine's climate.

One could also argue that Preisner is doing something yet subtler,
from a developmental perspective, in this passage. From the off, the
score has been carving out a smudged semitonal space between tonic
and flattened supertonic; for most of the cue, this has been the space
between A and B♭, constantly picked at by the arcing quartertones of
the ostinato. Here the brass and then woodwind, sustaining B♭ against
A, isolate and sustain that musical detail, in the first of several moments
in the score during which Preisner forms a mesh of pitches linked to the
ostinato (see Ex. 7.2). These developments connote mystery and suggest the unfolding of events of a certain magnitude: turning points in
the metaphysical thriller's plot.

Ex. 7.2: Sustaining the sonoristic smudge

As the car pulls back, high strings sustain a diminished seventh
chord over A♯ (B♭). This tissue of upper strings (violins and violas) continues to maintain the skeleton of harmonic changes typical of the B
section, but now the harmonic pace has slowed from one change per bar
to one every two bars, halving the harmonic tempo, as the music halts
to intensify the mystery of the moment. This is another zoom-like scoring effect, focusing one's attention on events and Valentine's reactions.
Every third and fourth bar resolves down to the tonic, but now that ten-
tative resolution is undermined by the cellos and basses' pedal tones,
which unyieldingly sustain B♭s. Each resolution, as such, becomes a
different form of dissonance developing the smudge idea.

Tension is also evoked by the melody. First, the rising initiation of
each phrase fails to resolve so quickly as before with a falling consequent: it harmonically bates one's breath in the pauses extended by
Preisner's metrical expansions. As the scoring switches from massed
strings to soloists, and particularly to harp and clarinet, there is also a
sense of a return to Valentine's subjective point of view and a feminin-

ity that may also embrace the dog—a female and soon to be maternal presence. The melody passes between harp and clarinet, picking out the intervallic skeleton of Bi and Bii. The clarinet links back to Valentine's moment of interiority in the car, so musically it comes as no surprise when she literally carries Rita into this space at the end of the sequence and during the next cue, scored solely for "her" solo guitar. In this regard, Preisner's cue as originally scored has been pointedly simplified in the recording studio. In the manuscript score, clarinets ghost the harp and guitar melodies; in the film, the guitar is held back for the closing section, prioritizing its emblematic significance as Valentine's instrument.

Preisner does not seek to shape pity for the dog's plight in the manner of a Hollywood melodrama. The music is not cloyingly sentimental, and while it does shape an affective tension easily channeled into concern for the dog, it does not seek to wring a more specific emotional response from the audience. Its concern, in other words, is not directly with the scene's foreground action—the accident and its aftermath—but rather with the subtext of the scene. Rita is not so much an injured dog as a talisman discovered on Valentine's quest for enlightenment, and the score surrounds them both with a mystical aura; Paxman notes the prominence of the admittedly pervasive reverb of Preisner's score recordings in this scene, its sacred resonance asserting "the mysterious, metaphysical undertones of both the musical themes and the subject matter itself."[29] The music, furthermore, has returned to its omniscient non-diegetic perspective: having crossed over at the moment of rupture to divert the action, it now returns to its "proper" non-diegetic place and resumes a more conventional form of commentary. The fact that she is rescuing the dog, and that the music is metamorphosing as she does so, also seems significant, as discussed below.

The potential for a cue to deal in such subtleties is enhanced when other aspects of a film take over signifying and manipulative duties often left to a composer. What need is there, for instance, for a score to put the perceiver through the emotional mill when a single, outstandingly well-chosen, post-production animal sound effect will affect more sharply than any musical cue? Rita's squeal of pain when Valentine lifts her is as experientially difficult to hear as Julie dragging her knuckles along the wall in *Blue* is hard to watch. More prosaically, though, the dagger of sound masks the fact that one never actually sees Valentine lifting the dog or laying it down in her car. One infers this action purely from the sound design.

Aiii: First Subject, Third Variation (Into Valentine)

As Valentine intervenes to save the stricken Rita, the soundtrack develops the B theme, allowing the instrumentation and mood of the first-subject group to penetrate the gloom of the second. That development continues in the final cue of the sequence, a variation of the A theme which returns the music to the realm of Valentine. A symbolic motif is thus shaped: an injured soul is rescued by Valentine as she brings it into her vehicular, musical and personal territory. Rita will not be the first character to be healed by Valentine's presence, and entering the climate of her music will signify the healing of other characters at later junctures in the film. There is also a sense of tensions briefly relieved: this is music that speaks of a happier ending to be attained after further turbulence.

The final installment in this sequence of cues is quintessential Preisner. A rising perfect fifth, then fourth, marks the bare outline of an arpeggio on A at the start of this *cantabile* and *ad libitum* melody for solo acoustic guitar (see Fig. 7.5)—the precise sound heard in the trilogy's final dramatic cue. A paraphrase of the opening Ai theme (the implied harmonic underpinning of the cue is the same and, as it progresses, melodic phrases clearly recall Ai and Aii), it brings a feminine presence to the fore through its delicacy and scoring, but also temporally, as Preisner stretches the $\frac{1}{4}$ melody to bars of $\frac{6}{8}$, thus permitting longer notes to sustain midway through each phrase, and at points of termination. As the guitar notes decay, one might lean closer to catch the sounds and thereby be drawn closer to the grain of the action and, almost, into the backseat with Valentine—into her climate, her realm, her worldview—as she discovers Rita's name, address and home using her map of the city. She lives, the tag on her scarlet collar informs Valentine as her bloody hands turn it over, in the district of Geneva called Carouge (but of course).

There is another sense, however, in which the scene creates a feeling of intimacy in connection to Valentine. As she draws her bloodied finger along the road leading to the Old Judge's house in the hills above the city (see Fig. 7.6), accompanied by a single line of plangent Preisner melody, she connects across the trilogy to earlier moments: in *White*, Karol tracing and then coloring in his first plot of land, and in *Blue*, Julie's eyes and fingers tracing the manuscript of the memento and Patrice's attempt at the *Concert[o]*. Valentine's journey also moves from light into darkness. This trilogy of intimate physical and sonic gestures, in which individuals imbue a map of symbols (literal maps or musical ones) with a special significance made clear by the use of music and subjective camera work, triangulates the three main protagonists in the trilogy. Typically of the Kieślowski co-workers films, this gesture of unification is not heavy-handed, but instead articulates an unassuming form of cinematic poetry.

Summary
What is being structured by the exposition section of Preisner's score? Which dialectical tensions does it accent and represent? Wollermann argues that the first-subject group is clearly related to Valentine and he notes that, aside from the fashion shows, it is also heard later in the film when one sees her alone: it is the music played as she drives away from the Old Judge's house in tears.[30] It is not only heard underscoring Valentine, however: at crucial moments in the film, her music will as-

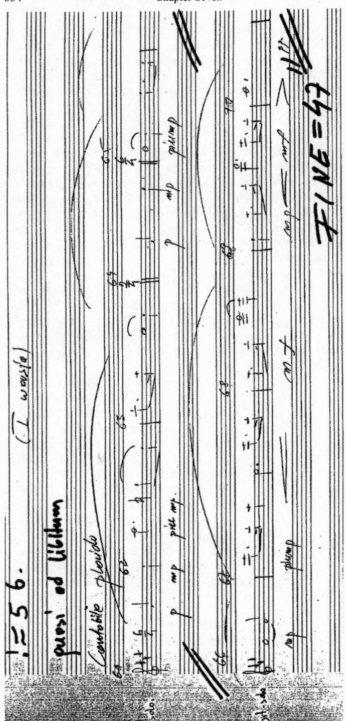

Fig. 7.5: Aiii (reprise) from Preisner's manuscript score

Fig. 7.6: Valentine composes connections to *Blue* and *White* (photo courtesy of the author)

sociate her connotations of goodness with the Old Judge at a turning point in his journey. Wollermann also sensibly suggests that the second subject, rather than being solely for the judges, actually interlinks the Old Judge, Auguste and Valentine, forming what he terms a "constellation" looking ahead to the characters' entanglement later in the film,[31] although he also notes that the theme is heard more often in connection to the judges. Two musical realms are therefore created, but they blend at the edges, anticipating developments to come.

For Paxman, the two realms opposed in this musical-dramatic sequence with the efficiency of a sonata form exposition, symbolize "dialectical structures" relating to the protagonist and antagonist, and to be developed over the course of the film—structures with, for perceivers attuned to the film's "'Westernized' representational capacity,"[32] a range of symbolic connotations besides Valentine vs. the judges. Carefully considering the "pronounced dialectical opposition to the light, serene first theme" of the "dark, ominous, 'metaphysical' second theme,"[33] Paxman identifies how "light, purity, optimism and beauty are set against elements of darkness, aggression, danger and ugliness."[34] The second theme's flattened second and tritone, he suggests, modally "reminds one of something further east" than the Greek modes of the Mixolydian/major key first subject group—a "religious/mystical metonymy" connecting to Oriental or Oriental-Semitic traditions, or even an evocation of the Arabic *Hijaz* mode.[35] He asserts on this basis that "what is categorical is the fact that the second theme, appreciably infused with religious/mystical qualities, steers our interpretation of events away from a materialist perspective to one inclined towards mystical and incorporeal realms."[36] Preisner is using style topical clichés, alongside more innovative compositional means, to evoke a sense of the transcendent.

Yet it would be a mistake—anticipated by earlier considerations of the first theme's femininity and thus the fact that both themes, in a sense, are "other" than the norm—to suggest the mystical or spiritual connotations are only to be heard in the second subject group's exoticism. From, say, a Catholic perspective, the second theme might intimate faith, but it would be the wrong faith: a dark, Moorish other to the purity and righteousness of Valentine's more orthodox harmony. The sense that she occupied a spiritual realm of her own is signified by the angelic connotations of the promenade theme and subsequent variations. What the score and film structures, therefore, can be perceived as a clash between, to be blunt, good and bad or right and wrong perspectives on the world. The Westernized ear has been conditioned, not least through countless films and television shows—think of the different scorings of, say, Jack Bauer and Islamic extremists in an episode of *24*—to associate the Greek modes (especially the less chromatically marked ones such as the Mixolydian or Ionian) with the path of righteousness, and modal alternatives (such as the *Hijaz*) with a wrong turn at the metaphysical crossroads. One is the realm of the angelic; the other of demons, false prophets and Satan. There is something ineradicably tainted about the manner in which Western screen music semiotics are predicated on assumptions reflecting the prejudices of the cultures from which they arose. At least in the hands of filmmakers like Preisner and Kieślowski, however, the practices are subverted to serve political ends opposed to the filmmaking systems that shaped and continue to uphold the semiotic *status quo*. Valentine's angelic, in *Red*, is *agapē*; the judges' satanic space is the false prophesy and trappings of the late-modern Western world. By playing on one of that sullied world's dialects of musical symbolism, *Red* opens a semiotic chasm between the realm one knows and the realm *Red* asserts that one should enter. The tone of that argument, however, is allusive and poetic, not agitated. As Paxman contends, "it is not important that [audio-viewers] *consciously* discern all this . . . [as] the sequence communicates something that will later be corroborated, contextualized and viscerally understood."[37] Like many other aspects of the opening minutes of *Red*, the score creates enigmas to be unpacked—or composed out—over the course of the film.

Development Part I

When Preisner's music next occurs in *Red*, after a lengthy period of narrative to which he and Kieślowski felt no need to add music, two cues follow in short succession. One function of the cues is to restate their thematic connections to Valentine and the two judges; another is to reverse the implied superiority of the themes—in the exposition, statements of Valentine's theme encapsulated the judges' music—and a number of related connotations. Yet these functions pale into insignificance in comparison to the metaphysical intimations of these musical moments.

Narrative Noise

Over twenty minutes pass between the ending of the first set of cues and the next pair. One consequence of music being held back for so long is that, on its reappearance, it sounds relatively startling to the audio-viewer and thus intensifies a mysterious moment in the action somewhat further than continuous scoring might have achieved.

Much has happened in the interim, of course, and in the absence of music's presence to underscore plot points, Flageollet's sound design has added a number of significant touches to the narrative. When Valentine first approaches the Old Judge's house at night, for instance, she is surrounded by high winds. The house is up in the hills above the lake, but these sounds do more than indicate altitude. Wind can connote supernaturally charged circumstances, as a Gothic sonic style topic; it can also suggest a storm brewing, literally or metaphorically. Either way, it induces a sense of tension in scenes where, in another film, music might have been deployed. Once she enters the Old Judge's house—an act filmed in a POV shot troping "a horror movie code for impending danger" that turns out to be "metaphysical and moral, nor physical,"[38] as indicated when Valentine walks into her own point of view, rather like Karol in *White*'s second wedding flashback—the wind forms an eerie counterpoint to the wandering frequencies of the judge's radio scanner. With a little imagination, one might even believe he is scanning the weather, or controlling it, with his radio station. There is also, one notes on repeated audio-viewings, a significant lack of voices on the radio at this point. The judge is devoid of even the mediated community of people on whom he eavesdrops as Valentine discovers him. He seems doubly alone and in need of salvation, if not almost mad.

Stormy weather is not Valentine's sonic climate. Aside from the car alarms, helicopters and sounds dealing notes of distress when she telephones Michel,[39] her climate—music aside—is marked by the presence of children's voices. This is most prominent when she lets Rita off the lead in the park and the dog runs away: a child's naïve mistake. The sound design is presumably intended to denote a nearby playground; one does not see the children, as with the disembodied child's voice haunting Julie at the copyist's in *Blue*. Children's voices can also be heard in the tense silences before the fashion photographer, Jacques, makes his move, and when she visits the family next door to the Old Judge to tell them he is spying on their calls. As the action shows the young daughter listening in on her father's intimate conversation with his male lover, a further child's voice heard in the background seems more in keeping with Valentine's innocence and naivety than the elder daughter's look as she eavesdrops. This aspect of her sonic climate is an aural equivalent to the decision to call the character Valentine just because it was Jacob's favorite name as a child. Elements of sound design and dialogue interweave with the connotations of her musical theme to signify a lack of guile, purity, but also a concomitant vulnerability.

The wind is even higher when she returns to the Old Judge's house on the second occasion, and for the fraught conversation leading to her visit to the family next door. Sometimes in *Red* the sound design's gusts seem to be propelling her through the Old Judge's door, thanks also to some cleverly executed leaf blowing. As they engage in their morally imperiling conversation, the sound of a single-engine plane crosses from the right sonic channel to the left. Precisely the same sound effect will occur when she confronts him on her return to the house after seeing the wife and daughter of the cheating husband: the sound moves from right (the side of the frame usually occupied by Valentine during these exchanges) to left (the side of the frame usually occupied, in these early scenes, by the Old Judge). The plane effect creates tension when it is present. Like the wind, it unsettles the perceiver, albeit subtly and without announcing its intentions—the sound sneaks in and out like manipulative underscore in a mainstream thriller. It also connotes the tension between the two characters in these fraught early exchanges. Yet it does something else more akin to the contribution of framing to their exchanges.

In the scene after the main title sequence, crane work created a long *mise-en-shot* which moved seamlessly from Auguste to Valentine and, roughly speaking, from right to left as it crossed the street between their apartments, linking them together even though, as soon becomes clear, they do not yet know each other or that they are linked. Similar camera moves have been seen in the trilogy before, for instance when Julie and Lucille spoke intimately in the sex club, and most virtuosically of all in the connections sculpted during *Blue*'s closing montage. Here, the sound design shapes the aural equivalent to such gestures in the trilogy: the sound of the plane pans from right to left, Valentine to Old Judge, like the shot connecting Valentine and Auguste. It parallels that visual move with a sonorous gesture intimating the presence, or at least the possibility, of greater fraternity.

I Know the Weather throughout Europe

Music's return to *Red* is spellbinding. At a peak of tension in the exchange between the Old Judge and Valentine—she is confronting him over his spying, he is interrogating her about her brother—the judge suddenly asks Valentine to become still for a moment because the light is beautiful. For Kickasola, the entry of the sunlight, not least through its connotations in Christianity and Judaism, forms "a metaphor for the resident, abiding hope that if beauty still exists in the world, grace may also exist" (i.e., the hope symbolized in Valentine), but it then develops to become something more than a blunt metaphor as the camera "cranes upwards in a transcendent, God's-eye gesture . . . [and] a bodiless voice comes over the sound system"—a call to Karin's weather service:

> Kieślowski's transformation of such a modern, pedestrian thing as a personal weather report service into a transcendent metaphor is the hallmark of his style. These metaphors will not work without visual support, and it is precisely the nonverbal epistemological weight that the images carry that creates the metaphor's foundation. . . . It is precisely the surprise of the "weather" in our everyday experience that reminds us of the need for something greater than ourselves.[40]

There is also the surprise of music's return, however, and of its interaction with other material elements, including sound design, to evoke a resonant moment. As an example of the cooperation of Preisner's music with other elements to evoke an aura of metaphysical possibility, the scene demands careful discussion.

As the Old Judge commands Valentine's stillness (and also, by extension, the audio-viewer's), and as if in answer to his own rhetorical question about what one can do in the face of life's more hellish situations, an orange-golden light—the same light that bathed Julie in the park, and Dominique in her prison cell—floods the study in which they talk. The crane shot then rises to its omniscient perspective with an ostentatious swoop. Like the manipulation of the music on Valentine's radio, this marked authorial maneuver (the shot) implies agency and hints that, just as some person or group is pulling the strings of the presentation of this story, the Old Judge may have similar directorial powers over events within *Red*'s diegesis. I know the weather all over Europe, he announces, crossing to the window to admire the sun disappearing behind the roof of his house—an expertly framed abstraction of the material into something transcendent—as if he has made this sunset, this beauty, the framing, and everything else happen. Perhaps he could also conjure up a storm.

The music's return in the scene is the other marked authorial maneuver, although it sneaks quietly into the sequence a little earlier than the light, as if to initiate the casting of the spell. By being a variation of the Bi theme, which sounded during the manipulations of the car radio, the cue already carries intimations of the mystical or exotic, but the darkness of the exposition's cues, enhanced on first appearance by the twilit *mise-en-scène*, is filtered here through perceptions of the scene's golden light and Preisner's radiantly scored variation. This connects the theme's connotations of the otherworldly directly to the Old Judge, but also, because the cue continues long enough to underscore the next call to the weather service—a romantic exchange between Auguste and Karin—extends it to his younger double.

Aside from its style topical connotations, the cue's intimations of magic are partly created through a scoring cliché, partly through a fusion of sound design and music, and partly through wonderful musical and editorial timing. Preisner's cue is placed to begin as if it is responding to Valentine's finger, pointing as she indicates that the little girl next door knows her closeted father is living a lie. A sonority, scored for tremoloing violins divided into four parts, begins to accrue. The strings enter at triple *pianissimo*, crescendoing to *mezzo piano* as the Old Judge instructs Valentine to rest for a moment; at his command, the visual editing also slows down from the more rapid cutting during their fraught conversation. The change of pace makes room for the audio elements to come to the fore.

The entry of the strings does not literally mickey-mouse the flooding in of sunlight, although one could hear the beginning of the sonority's accrual as an anticipation of that process. The sunlight actually appears on the entry of the sonority's fifth tone: the sound of a telephone, ringing on A—a tone which smoothes over a cut back to the Old Judge as he pauses and the sun appears around him in a halo. The composite harmony of this sonority is shown in Ex. 7.3. Without the A natural, this would be a C dominant seventh chord, inverted to begin on the seventh tone, and suggesting imminent arrival. The tone sketched by its first two pitches, B♭ and C, and the tritone between B♭ and E, signify the realm of the magical, too, partly by connecting to sounds linked to exoticism (i.e., the wholetone scale). The entry of the telephone's A, however, changes things. With it, the five-note pitch collection makes no obvious tonal sense, at least until the violin melody enters shortly after the light appears, its B♭ to E rising as the virtuosic camera move begins. The harmony enriches the mystery.

When the melody of Bi returns, it makes the telephone tone central to the musical sonority: A is the tonic of the cue. It also centers attention, therefore, on the Old Judge, bathed in light, as if he is controlling all elements of the world, narrative and soundtrack around him. The melody's C♯ tingles against the C♮ in the chord—this is one location of the sonority's effervescence—but in the context of the melody, the chord begins to sound as a smudging together of A minor, A major and the trilogy's recurring B♭ diminished seventh chord, as previously self-sufficient identities merge into a strangely beautiful whole. When the genuine weather inquiry is followed a few moments later by Auguste's call to Karin—her voice far forwards in the mix as if she is an over-dubbed narration on the action—he is, unknowingly, dialing both Valentine's tonal home and the film's moral center.

The cue therefore links both judges explicitly to the score's second subject but also, thanks to the stress on A, to the key of Valentine's climate. Identities are merging or transferring. Two versions of the theme unwind—one scored for the violins, one voiced by a solo cello—as if a younger man's earnest questions are being answered by an older, more experienced male mentor. The cello enters as the action cuts to the sun disappearing behind a roof and from the Old Judge watching the light begin to fade. This depiction of generations passing, suspended as if timeless on the tissue of Preisner's strings, introduces one of *Red*'s most affecting themes—acceptance of ageing and one's waning—with a restraint that only amplifies its poignancy. This issue will shortly be revisited by *Red*'s Van den Budenmayer song.

Ex. 7.3: Musical totality of cue and sound design in sunlight scene

Frustratingly, but not unexpectedly, very little of the above explains the pleasure one takes in the moment of perceiving this sequence. With hindsight, one can read many things into the scene to explain, for instance, how it symbolizes the possibility of magic, but this does not explain why *perceiving* the scene feels so magical. Perhaps it is the astonishingly well-tailored fit of all the elements and the timing with which they are introduced: while this is intricately constructed filmmaking, the scene seems to reveal itself spontaneously. Collectively, this conjures a moment of cinematic awe. Only a team working in close collaboration, perhaps, can render such moments. That may be the scene's deeper magic: its testimony to the co-workers' creative solidarity. Delighted at this fusion of sound, music and the moving image, one thrills to its excess of ambiguities—a "phenomenological 'surplus' of meaning, in [Edmund] Husserl's words" as "the sun seems to rise and set all in the span of a few seconds, suggesting . . . eternal time."[41] Like sunflowers after Van Gogh, sunlight entering a room never seems the same after this sequence. *Red* remaps that horizon of one's experience.

Valentine Reversed

Preisner's next cue, which accompanies Valentine's tearful descent from the Old Judge's house, her arrival back home, and then Auguste's failure to answer a telephone call from Karin, is different on the page of Preisner's cue sheet to the music one hears in the film. Beginning (as scored and heard) with a reprise of Valentine's catwalk theme, in the manuscript score a *misterioso* follows in which a solo clarinet outlines a reprise of Biii (something similar is heard in the film) before an ardent cello solo takes over (cut entirely). The cue, as envisaged, would have injected the shots of Auguste with a brooding quality now reserved until the use of solo cello later in the film, when he discovers Karin's act of infidelity. The cut also saves the climactic development of the B mate-

rial for one of the film's two dramatic highpoints; the other is the conversation in the theater and the arrival of the storm. By splicing in the
original Biii instead, as the action cuts back to the characters' homes,
and thus in the version heard when Valentine ran over Rita, the cue also
makes suggestive connections.

The first subject reprise in this sequence has also been altered from
its manuscript score version. As often happened in the trilogy, complexity has been removed, leaving just the first violin's melody, rather than
the originally scored fuller orchestration. Having only the descending
melody permits the line to interact more clearly with the "opposite motions" noted by Kickasola, and to counterpoint their mirroring of Valentine's moral confusion. In an obvious way, the cue also mimetically
highlights the direction of her driving (she is moving downhill) and
indicates her crest-fallen state (she is feeling "down"). More subtle is
the sense of weightlessness created by the contrast between the very
quiet sound design—a gentle sound evoking wheels turning, as if the
car is freewheeling, is the only underpinning to the high violin line before traffic noise is added, returning Valentine to ground level and reality. The looping motion of the melodic phrases also suggests circularity,
interacting with the turn of the camera, shot initially from Valentine's
driving point of view as she navigates a sharp turn, and then the turn to
a fixed camera shot of her as she drives—shots that induce a sense of
motion sickness when viewed repeatedly. Finally, the music is slow and
lyrical, moving at a contrary velocity to the car and, especially, the
speeding vehicles on the highway.

After a $\frac{6}{4}$ bar between phrases—a metrical disturbance that, while
probably inserted to fit music to the image track, creates an unsettling
bump for the audio-viewer—the theme continues, the melody sweetly
doubled at the third by the flutes; the bolero's ostinato and quartertonal
smudging were scored here, but are not included in the version heard on
film. The music, as the film cuts to a shot of Valentine's tear-stained
face, thus suggests a centering—her theme, her key of A major, her
values—but the moment ironically highlights the distance she has traveled from her comfort zone following her brush with the Old Judge.
The scene's counterpoint is thus deeper still. A dissonance emerges
between her theme and her developing subjectivity, the theme acting
like a benchmark that reveals how far she has begun to run askew. The
cue is a musical equivalent to the image in her rearview mirror and the
diametrically opposing point of view it offers on the action.

The splicing of the new cue to the reprise of Biii is uncharacteristically awkward—in Red, unlike in Blue, transitions rarely seem marked
for attention—the score cutting after the third beat of the bar to the new
cue, rather than after the fourth. One could hear this as a slip of editing,
but, like the bar of $\frac{6}{4}$, it creates a metrical jolt not entirely inappropriate
to the action. Valentine, now briefly underscored with the judges' music, has been knocked off-kilter, too, and Auguste is also about to feel
his world begin to slide. The mise-en-shot of another virtuosically long
crane shot moves from Valentine leaving her car to Auguste returning

from the café—pointedly named "Chez Joseph," as if both Valentine and Auguste are now haunted, and also united, by the agency of the Old Judge—with a carton of Marlboro cigarettes, clearly chosen by the film's art department for their red and white packaging. He fails to get to his phone in time—all he hears, when he picks up, is the A of the dialing tone, as if Valentine's realm is calling to him; in a few moments' one sees her praying to receive a call. He hangs up and redials, but gets a different tone; Karin's engaged tone is not A for *agapē*, but G♯—so near, and yet so far! The unresolved harmonic suspensions of the cue (the pedal As and B♭s in the lower strings) and the increasing tension in the sound mix between the cue and a busy *mise-en-bande*, hint at Auguste's building edginess. The sonic foreboding hints at his doubts about Karin while foreshadowing his discovery of her deception.

The musical tension is left unresolved as the cue fades away: Valentine, Auguste and the Old Judge are all in states of disequilibrium, and the perceiver, too, is twisting in the wind in the absence of resolutions musical or dramatic. The film's development section is clearly underway; in parallel, musical development is forging ahead, too. As a whole, the film's sonata-form-like structure has created a sense of departure from an initial equilibrium into a tense state of disequilibrium, replete with overlapping and fragmenting identities, as the characters' musical and dramatic masks slip free to be altered or worn by other figures. Two Preisner cues have reminded the audio-viewer of their original fealty, before being developed to create a shift in the symbolic pattern. Into this flux drops *Red*'s third musical idea.

"The Water-lily"

It is heard three times in *Red* and only revealed in fragments, but what does the Van den Budenmayer song signify beyond "Sad music playing," as the closed captions on the Miramax DVD describes the song's first appearance? Is this just a sly wink to the *cinéastes* playing join-the-intertextual-dots between *Decalogue 9* and *Red*? Analyzing the individual properties of the setting and the words—or the lack thereof when the song appears as a *vocalise*—is one strategy by which one can suggest ways in which Preisner's Van den Budenmayer song enriches *Red*'s narrative. Comparing the notable differences between its three appearances—an ABA structure in which the A form is a wordless version listened to by the Old Judge, the B version a texted and, in other ways, different form of the song heard by both Valentine and Auguste—is also suggestive.

The words set by Preisner's song for *Decalogue 9* and then *Red* come from "The Water-lily" ("De Waterlelie"), a poem by Frederik Willem van Eeden (1860-1932), a Dutch author, poet and psychiatrist.[42] The poem's persona speaks of love for an icon of purity—the flower could be read as the symbol of another person—and reflects on the

De Waterlelie	*The Water-lily*
Ik heb de witte water-lelie lief, daar die zo blank is en zo stil haar kroon uitplooit in't licht.	I love the white, white water-lily, it is so pale, its crown unfolds so quietly in the light.
Rijzend uit donker-koele vijvergrond, heeft zij het licht gevonden en ontsloot toen blij het gouden hart.	Rising from the cool dark of the pond, it has found the light and opened up its golden heart with joy.
Nu rust zij peinzend op het watervlak en wenst niet meer . . .	Now, lost in thought, it rests on the surface, its longing gone . . .
Frederik van Eeden	(Translation by James Brockway)[43]

Fig. 7.7 "De Waterlelie" by Frederik van Eeden

passage of time. It contrasts the "white, white" golden-hearted flower with the darkness of the water on which it rests; one might recall how the Old Judge told Valentine to "reste" when the golden sun flooded his home. In *Decalogue 9*, the poem's evocation of contrast between Roman and Ola is clear, and one might read into the final two lines an evocation of his impotence (the once risen stamen now flat on the water, "its longing gone"). In *Red*, the object of gold-hearted purity being addressed, seeking light and opening with joy links, most obviously, to Valentine; the lost longing, in turn, speaks for its cuckolded men, and most especially the more aged one, who is permitted new insights into life—such as the possibility of still opening one's heart to joy—by his encounter with *Red*'s water lily.

The words also map a space between the bloom of youth and the knowledge of old age, a key theme in *Red*'s reflection, not least, on aspects of Kieślowski's own personality. Could this have been at the back of his mind when he asked Preisner to reuse the song for their final film? There is a sense in which Valentine's goodness is being celebrated, mythologized even, by the song, presenting her as a symbol not only within the story (i.e., for the two judges) but also for the audience. She is that to which one should aspire, through continuous moral reboots, setting aside obsessive erotic passion—in *Red* a malign influence—in order to search for the light of *agapē*.

The image of floating and water links back to Julie in the swimming pool in *Blue* and to the skating scene in *White*, but, more chillingly, forwards to the end of *Red*, when Valentine and the other films' main protagonists really will float on dark waters. Yet the text is not sung in the Old Judge's two versions, and it is also only partially heard in the scene where Auguste and Valentine encounter the song. The opportunity to hear the song "in full" afforded through close analysis of its appearances in *Red*, however, permits the conceit of considering its full musical and lyrical meaning, although one might still privilege consideration of words and music actually heard in the film.

The Old Judge's Wordless Version (I)

Why is the song performed as a wordless *vocalise* when the Old Judge listens to it? Words lost may represent passion spent and, in its place, the space to reflect; their absence could also signify the loss of significant other voices from one's life, and thus solitude or loneliness. This notion tallies with the bulk of the first song sequence, which depicts the Old Judge writing letters, prompted by Valentine's disgust at his eavesdropping, in which he admits spying to his neighbors and the authorities. This is the first material representation of the "light" she has shone into his life and of his character acting in an unselfish way: a dying of, and to, the self in the name of fraternity and *agapē*'s greater good.

There is no clear indication that the record is playing in his home, but an LP cover, shortly to be revealed as a Van den Budenmayer recording, has already been glimpsed in his house; attention is drawn to this when it bears Valentine's change for the vets in an earlier sequence (see Fig. 7.8). So one might assume that the record is the Old Judge's chosen soundtrack to his act of penitence. As he writes words one cannot see, save for his name and address, the soprano sings melodies shorn of text but filled with meaning. The melody voices restrained melancholy and an acceptance of sadness, to an accompaniment of fracturing piano chords. Scored in G minor, the tragic key of the Van den Budenmayer funeral music in *Blue* and a tonal departure for *Red*, it marks a change of direction in the latter narrative while linking back to earlier tragedies in the trilogy.[44] The only other prominent sound at the start of the singing is Rita panting. The Old Judge briefly looks at this token of Valentine's impact on his life, as if to acknowledge the young woman's influence.

Being Preisner, the fracturing in the accompaniment is both microrhythmic (an interrupted triplet figure in the piano) and metrical (see Ex. 7.4). The song could easily be turned into a waltz, but extra beats create a faltering quality at a higher rhythmic level. By only ever cueing up parts of the song, moreover, the song's overall progression is fragmented across the film. Locally, the metrical faltering permits the sustained dissonances of the passing notes in the accompaniment to ring during each rest, emphasizing a need for resolution—the achievement of a point of "rest"—on the harmonic "surface" of G minor; the fragmented rhythms, mirroring each other from bar to bar, may remind one of ripples on a pond's surface. This forms the accompaniment to the recitative-like melody of the soprano and a passage reminiscent of a Baroque aria thanks to the restrained emotion of the vocal writing and Towarnicka's performance, the restricted neo-Romantic harmonic palette, and the manner in which, once the melody is underway,

Fig. 7.8: Valentine touches the Van den Budenmayer LP (photo courtesy of the author)

piano follows voice with a series of simple chords. That melody, in turn, rises and then comes to rest on the surface of the accompaniment, like the flower in the poem; the contrapuntal descents in the accompaniment further invoke becoming still. The descents, paralleling motif x in *Blue*'s funeral march cues, create layers of gestural resignation within the aria. As the song begins to extend into its second verse, however, it is interrupted. The musical interlude, like the Old Judge's progress towards his own point of repose, is unfinished.

The fact that the music is not literally moored to the diegetic action—no gramophone record is spinning in the Old Judge's house—permits the action to float freely to his letter writing, smoothing a cut, from the sequence in the bowling alley. As the music begins, the camera comes to rest on shattered glass and an abandoned cigarette—images fusing the cue to broken promises, loneliness, and pain. Auguste has been stood up. After Valentine bowls, the camera pans left to this agonizing still-life. Instead of this familiar camera move (as in *Blue* and elsewhere in *Red*) linking two characters together, here it is an image of a missed connection; Valentine has failed to notice Auguste at the alley, and Karin has failed to meet him there. Yet at the same time, the music forms a web of connectivity, moving with the camera from Valentine to Auguste, or at least to his remains, and then on to the scribbling Old Judge. The song encourages one to anticipate a revelation of the manner in which these characters are connected.

Ex. 7.4: "The Water-lily" (wordless version, transcribed)

Valentine and Auguste's Texted Version

The song returns a few minutes later in a scene, suggesting interlaced bicameral realms. In a CD store's listening booth, people audition various albums by different artists. First we see Valentine, listening to Van den Budenmayer, but in a different version to the Old Judge's song: she and the audience can now hear the Dutch words. The camera then reiterates the pan motif, moving horizontally to the right to emphasize Auguste with Karin, who have been in shot all along (see Fig. 7.9i). As the camera comes to a rest, the implied musical source changes from what Valentine is hearing to what he can hear: the same song, in the same version, but in this case right at the end of the singing. As the couple hang up their headphones and depart, the camera pans back to Valentine and the soundtrack shifts again to her meta-diegetic perspective, permitting one to hear the end of the vocal from her point of audition. Throughout the sequence, the musical hubbub of the booth and conversations forms a sonic continuum.

i)

ii)	Valentine's POA:	toen blij het gouden hart/Nu rust zij peinzend
	Auguste's POA:	op het watervlak/en wenst niet meer
	Valentine's POA:	en wenst niet meer

Fig. 7.9(i): The Van den Budenmayer lovers' triangle (photo courtesy of the author) (ii) Lyrics heard in this sequence

There is much to unpack in this short but intense sequence, in both technical and symbolic terms. First, what words are being sung? Subtly, the entirety of the lyric for the closing part of the song is heard here, in spite of the chopping and changing points of audition: Valentine and Auguste's fragmented versions, brought together for the audio-viewer, form a coherent textual and symbolic whole. And like the camera's panning between them, the song reveals to the audience their connection-to-be. By being the end of the song, and thanks to the contrapuntal-harmonic finality of "coming to rest," there is also a sense—new to *Red*—of closure and fulfillment: a circle is complete.

This version of the song is not in G minor. Auguste and Valentine experience the song in A, her pitch-center and the realm of *agapē*. Yet this is A minor, not major, and in this more operatic version—featuring string tremolos and plaintive oboe refrains reminiscent of the Concerto in *Véronique*—melodrama is perhaps the primary signification. So what is being mourned here? In the preceding scenes, Valentine's relationship with the increasingly paranoid Michel has taken a turn for the worse. One has also seen Auguste's reaction to the advertising billboard featuring Valentine, the film filtering audience responses to this reveal through his enraptured face; Karin, in turn, has been seen flirting with another man. The reactions of the characters to the song therefore signify the likely outcome of Auguste and Karin's relationship, and his future connection to Valentine.

Valentine listens with rapt attention, her face a mirror of the sadness it depicted at the photoshoot and which it will reflect in the final freeze-frame of the film; Auguste smiles with satisfaction when he replaces his headset, having heard something to which he can relate; Karin shrugs indifferently. Not liking Van den Budenmayer is not a good omen in a Kieślowski film, and her indifference reveals a breach in taste that is as significant, in its own way, as the contrast between the trio's art music choice and the musical realm of the metal fan headbanging to the guitar solo bleeding from his headphones in the next booth to Auguste. Auguste and Valentine are made for each other, the scene reveals; Auguste and Karin are not. That both Auguste and Valentine will soon be free to pursue a new relationship together is in turn suggested by the words of the song: the contrast between the flower's heart filled with golden joy and its ruminative manifestation, laying down its head, hints at both the end of their present relationships and their desire for something more fulfilling.

The bicamerality effect noted by Kickasola in *Véronique* as signifying doubled worlds is in play throughout this sequence—doubly so, in fact, due to the two realms of the songs, and in turn their relationship to the hubbub of the shop. Valentine tries in vain to buy a copy of the CD. Her lack of ownership of the music—her CD case is empty—suggests the inaccessibility, for now, of the love to which it points. One also hears a playful hint of the tango from *White*, just as the camera changes focus to show Auguste shepherding Karin out of the shop. The tango of Karol and Dominique's troubled relationship is called to mind as *Red*'s initial couplings drift apart.

The Old Judge's Wordless Version (II)

When the Old Judge attends the fashion show towards the end of the film, the wordless G minor *vocalise* is heard for the second time. Shorn of the piano introduction and coda, the sung part is heard in full, beginning with a clunk suggesting a cassette tape being slotted into a car stereo by the Old Judge. He then starts his car—the tape starts before he starts the engine—and drives out of the darkness of his garage. He closes the garage doors on darkness. The image, suggestive in and of itself, is another of *Red*'s visual rhymes: it foreshadows the closing harbor gates at the end of the film as the ferry sets sail.

Whether the music is judged to be diegetic or non-diegetic, by continuing uninterruptedly as the montage cuts his journey down to important beats in the narrative it creates another type of musical bicamerality typical of filmic uses of songs during montages—the "mood" of a journey is continuously evoked while the journey is depicted with the dull bits removed. One sees the Old Judge driving, apparently lost in thought, as he reinserts himself into the social order under Valentine's guidance. As Wollermann suggests, the song may thus form an angelic presence here, spiritually protecting him in Valentine's physical absence. Indeed, she is then seen literally watching over him when he comes to a halt at the intersection and sees the advertising billboard. As with the moment Auguste came across it earlier in the film, one sees his reaction first—a raised eyebrow—and then, for the only time in the film, one is shown the entirety of this massive poster, complete with its advertising slogan: *En toute circumstance/Fraîcheur de vivre* (see Fig. 7.10). Again mirroring Auguste's discovery of the poster, a motorist has to honk a horn to bring the Old Judge back to reality. He parks his car near the theater just as the singing comes to an end, halting the music.

Fig. 7.10: Kieślowskian karaoke (photo courtesy of the author)

Doubling Auguste's actions reinforces the characters' joint owner-ship of the Van den Budenmayer song, but their distance too is mapped by their versions: different keys, with or without words, a singular pi-ano or a society of orchestral accompaniment. Even the choices of for-mat, LP and CD, seem significant, the Old Judge retaining the older format, Auguste its replacement. The other important mapping, how-ever, is between the Old Judge when he first heard the song and the Old Judge now. The golden heart of his water lily has inspired him to close the door on his past, as darkness and longing—the things which cor-rupted and soured him, and revealed fully in the climactic scene after the fashion show—become spent.

The words on the advertisement, in this context, might be read as a new lyric for the song, as if *Red* has entered a Kieślowskian karaoke bar where incidentally encountered phrases provide a metaphysical, rather than literal, transliteration of this song without words. While the slogan is "pretentious to the point of insult" as a chewing gum advert, Kickasola asserts, it "does inform the narrative here."[45] His translation ("In every occasion, the freshness of being alive")[46] is complemented by Andrew's take on "Fraîcheur de vivre" as "literally mean[ing] 'freshness of life'" and thus "echoing the way Valentine refreshes Kern's humanity."[47] Fascinatingly, Andrew notes that "fraîcheur" also "carries associations of 'bloom,' and Valentine, of course, with her beauty and innocence, is in the full rosy bloom of her youth"[48]—or rather, one might suggest having noted the text of the song, the youthful bloom of a water-lily. The connection is slight, but enough to suggest that the advertising hoarding provides a tiny key to the (for most audio-viewers) obscurity of the Dutch lyrics and the meaning of the literally wordless vocalise: Valentine's careful tending makes those around her bloom sympathetically. By connecting to the most iconic image in the film, and thus to the point of visual intersection on which *Red*'s metaphysical suspense will hinge, the slogan also has a more obvious symbolism: Valentine will still be breathing at the end of the film.

Development Part II

The action most closely resembling a danced bolero in *Red* initiates the second phase of the film's sonata-like development section, as roles reverse, power shifts and subjects—musical and personal—take on characteristics of their antagonists. Having read in the newspaper that the Old Judge has been chastised for his eavesdropping, Valentine rushes to his house again, this time to tell him that she did not report him to the authorities. He reveals to her that he did the deed, then invites her into the house to see something. Valentine is closing the door when her attention is captured by an image—the sun disappearing behind mountains—which rhymes with the Old Judge's metaphysical moment of appreciation earlier on. At the same time, the sound of the single-engine plane makes its way from the right to left channel of the stereo mix, restating its sonic anticipation of things to come—the wind is also prominent—and a motif connecting Valentine to the Old Judge. These subtle details hint that the Old Judge and Valentine will grow closer as aspects of their subjectivities converge. The sound of the plane begins, for instance, at the precise moment the Old Judge informs Valentine that it was he who told the authorities—becoming, in the act, more like her.

Choreography

The Old Judge's motivation, he explains to Valentine after showing her Rita's litter of puppies, was to see what Valentine would do when she saw the news in the papers. Primarily, it seems, he wanted her to come back and see him again: through his self-sacrificial act he hoped to re-establish human contact.[49] When she asks why he wanted her to visit, the first of the scene's dance-like gestures occurs: the Old Judge spreads his arms wide, as if anticipating some kind of embrace. Valentine takes a step back in disgust. The theatricality of their moves is akin to the more flamboyant gestures in the middle sections of a Bolero School performance. The choreography continues as he asks her to kneel for him and smile. At this stage, he is in control of the dance. Instead of the chattering of castanets, the accompaniment is an oddly rhythmic clicking of puppy noises.

The Old Judge implies that Valentine's disgust made him turn off his radio. At this moment, Preisner's bolero ostinato enters, scored for a delicate thread of high strings. The Old Judge's explanation of writing the letters is then accompanied by the Ai melody, now scored for Valentine's solo guitar. By acting in her manner, he has taken on aspects of her musical and wider identity. The scene then depicts Valentine taking on the role of accuser. As she picks up on the Old Judge's hint that his actions may inadvertently have caused the doom of Auguste's relationship, because Karin met her new lover at the trial, Preisner introduces a pedal of low As scored for the lower strings—a clichéd sign for dawning realization, but here also a shift in musical gendering sucking the register down to a more stereotypically masculine pitch range. As the music further suggests a surge of masculinity by pivoting into a statement of Bi—the ostinato remains in the high strings, but violas now take the melodic lead above portentous B♭ and A pedal tones, both pitches sustaining so their semitonal dissonance bristles like the static generated between the two actors—it is Valentine who performs a dance-like move, standing up and then walking, in a manner executed with deliberate stealth by Jacob, in an arc around the seated Old Judge. She now stands above him, reversing the power play of their body positions in the scene. He turns slowly to follow her, pirouetting on his swivel chair—the precise choice of which, rather than a fixed chair, permits this move a dance-like flourish as she circles him.[50] The swish of her clothes and footfalls also evoke a theatrical dance.

Scored by the Bi theme, Valentine has now taken the position of masculine dominance and power. She is controlling the dance. To reinforce the narrative point, the action cuts to Auguste failing to contact Karin by telephone. He is shot in a close-up, like Valentine and the Old Judge before the cut, connecting them in a trio of headshots. Holding a red phone in a Perspex booth at the court house, his actions recall Karol being exposed to the sound of Dominique making love in *White*. He exerts greater self-control than Karol—for now—but in the climactic development section of the story, he gives full reign to his concerns and has his worst fears confirmed. The connection of the score's second subject to the wounded judges is therefore reinforced at the end of the cue, even though Valentine has donned its garb to claim dominance for her worldview. The solo cello, in turn, anticipates anxious moments to come. Auguste has been calling the pitch-class A on a red phone. His call has not been answered.

Synthesis Interrupted

Having reversed roles and music in the bolero of the previous sequence, the Old Judge and Valentine now share a passage of sustained intimacy. They discuss her feelings of guilt concerning her inability to help her brother; he absolves her, telling her that just by being she is helping. Like the Van den Budenmayer water-lily, her very existence improves the world and everyone she meets. She also tells him of her plan to travel to England and he asks her if she is flying—the sound of the single-engine plane hovering ominously above them. She is to the left of the framing now, their positioning reversed from earlier scenes, and the plane hovers to the far left of the stereo image. The Old Judge tells her to take the ferry there because, irony of ironies, it is healthier. The delicate ringing of a house clock's bell then offers a benediction over their shared toast of pear brandy; it dings, of course, on A, give or take a quartertone. In terms of the development of the bolero-sonata, one might say that a synthesis has been achieved and tonally blessed—the couple has been wedded in *agapē*. Being a Kieślowski film, this brief moment of buoyancy, and its musical accompaniment, can only come down to earth sharply.

Returning, *quid pro quo*, the favor of her confession, the Old Judge tells Valentine the story of a mistake he made in an early case, wrongly acquitting a man. He leans in to turn on a table lamp, but the bulb blows. The moment would swiftly turn mundane were it not for the entry, as he stands on a chair to take a replacement bulb from the ceiling lamp, of Preisner's next cue, which unfolds in three parts and marks the most traditional, thematically developmental portion of the score. With a display of compositional ambition meeting the demands of the scene's subtle interplay of identities, motivations and judgments, Preisner's cue proceeds to synthesize elements of the score's two main subjects.

The cue, as originally scored, has an introductory section not used in the final cut of the film; it is also simplified, having been pared down to essentials in the recording session. The spellbinding entry of the high string sonority—the A♯ (B♭), C♯ and E of the now familiar diminished-seventh sonority—is followed by a high violin line exploring A♯'s dissonant neighbor notes. Most immediately, the dissonance's affect and significations relate to Valentine's discomfort when the lamp on the table re-illuminates, momentarily blinding her. As the cue then relaxes into its next musical section, the Old Judge replaces the lampshade, muting dazzling white to the honeyed tones of the trilogy's most optimistic moments.

The development of Bi that ensues, as the Old Judge continues the story of false acquittal, picks up on the hint of solo cello at the end of the previous cue. The cello line wrings lamentations from the basic shape of the melody, filling descents from E to A with anguished twists and turns. The dissonant antecedent of each chordal pairing—the diminished chord—is in turn extended (first to two bars, then to three), as the music stretches harmonic tension to follow the phrasing of the Old Judge's dialogue, and also, by going against metrical expectations, intensifies each expectation of resolution. The solo cellist in this passage makes the cue work by finding an expressive match to Preisner's instruction that the cue be played *delicate*. The angst is underplayed.

Preisner's metrical manipulations continue as the cue moves into the second half of the Bii development and Valentine offers her judgment on the Old Judge. Again, she absorbs his theme and the dominant role, the close lighting of the lamp even suggesting she has aged by exposing—in a way some female stars never permit—a tracery of lines on her face that reveal this character to be more mature than Jacob's Véronique. She views his wrongful acquittal as having saved the man concerned; she questions the Old Judge, her inquisition mirroring the sudden illumination of the light bulb. They agree that acts of judgment on another are vanity on the part of the beholder—the scene's true moral illumination. It is this resolution into insight that the suspense generated by Preisner's opening sonority anticipates.

The melodic elaborations of Bii are taken over by an alternation of oboe and high violins—timbres marked by cliché and, by this stage of *Red*'s score, as most relevant to her realm. The violin line (see Ex. 7.5) is perhaps the score's most subtle piece of thematic thought. It recalls the elegant descent of Valentine's catwalk theme yet also evokes the twists of the solo cello development of the judges' B theme, merging thematic elements at this moment of high tension as she absolves the Old Judge of his guilt. Impressively, however, Preisner is simultaneously preparing the cue's moment of grace. Metrical elongations, while raising tension by elongating certain chords, effect a composed-out deceleration, stretching the musical fabric until the individual pitches of the violin and viola lines blur together quartertonally. At the end of this process, the remaining strings sustain As in several octaves, forming a halo of *agapē* at this tipping point in the lives of the main characters.

Ex. 7.5: Thematic blending in *Red*

The delicacy of the last section of the cue highlights the subtle triumph of Valentine's perspective in *Red*. As she raises her glass to toast the Old Judge's birthday—and more importantly tells him that she hopes that, if she ever goes to court, there are still judges like him—a development of Aii ensues, absolving the music of all of its pent-up tension. The melody is scored for harp, but the harp melody is doubled at the third by acoustic guitar. Where Valentine's musical marker once sounded alone in the interior of her car, now it is paired with another voice. She may have rehabilitated the Old Judge, but the reciprocity of this engagement is made musically clear. In a nice touch—the only obvious sync point in the entire score—the film is cut so she tips her glass to the entry of the violins' highest A harmonic. The two lines then complete the thematic statement in perfect unison, accompanied by the resolution of the octave pedal As.

Like the climax of an actual sonata form's development—forming a crisis of tension before the resolution of recapitulation, as the second subject teeters on the brink of being domesticated by a soon-to-be triumphant first—Preisner's cue structures both the drama and symbolism of this pivotal scene. The moment of recapitulation, however, turns out to be a false dawn—or, rather, it yields developments of its own. Like the recapitulations and codas of the composer of another "Tempest," the expected formalities and security of the ending will be hijacked by the most demanding action yet. This moment is too perfect and, with a startle as affecting as any of *Blue*'s sonic shocks, closure and the intimacy of the toast are both shattered by a rock smashing one of the Old Judge's windows. The neighbors are exacting revenge through acts of petty vandalism. Contrast to the music aside, the moment is made startling by the cue having been slightly lower in the mix than is usual in the film. Encouraged by action and music to lean in and listen closely, one receives a sonic slap.

Endings are never perfectly happy in this trilogy: every silver lining has a cloud. In *Red* that cloud is a harbinger of events that will now envelop Auguste and Valentine. After the crash, one hears the howl of a gathering storm. Cast into darkness, the Old Judge offers Valentine a counter illumination to her absolution and their shared recognition of the immorality of judging another. If he took the place of all those he had sentenced, the Old Judge would have killed, stolen and lied as well. The scene's insight into the contingency of one's individual human condition is not, then, the sweet security of its moment of golden light and musical plenitude, but its dualism: even the best life is but a step away from the wrong side of the line. Surrounded by the chilling wind of Flageollet's sound design, he confesses his lack of love for anyone, but tells Valentine he has dreamt that she would one day be 40 or 50 and happy. The ironic distance between that forecast and the *mise-en-scène* and *-bande* could not be more marked. As the Old Judge speaks, he is dressed, framed and lit in a study of blue, linking him to the hardest emotional moments in the trilogy and casting him in a bereft form recalling Julie, while also transforming what, in other hands, would be a sentimental art house cliché ("last night I had a dream") into a moment of spiritual jeopardy poised between undermined resolution and uncertain future.

Development Part III

Darkness Falls

The trilogy's most overtly dramatic sequence, Auguste's discovery of Karin's infidelity, owes its impact to a cue over which Preisner, judged on the evidence of the manuscript score, lavished considerable attention: it bears more corrections and crossing out than any other cue in the trilogy, and two pages have been rewritten entirely by a copyist, because the original version of the last two pages—Preisner's most im-

pressively full orchestration in the trilogy—had too many refinements
to be legible. The attention paid off admirably. Beginning as the dark
twin to the light bulb sequence (Auguste turns off a light, plunging his
room into moody desolation as he decides to confront his cheating
lover), it metamorphoses into the climactic development of the B theme
and the score's second subject. A musical psychodrama unfolds that is
part Bernard Herrmann's *Psycho* (the slashing strings when Karin is
revealed *en flagrante*), part Pink Floyd's *The Wall* (the guitar ostinato
and low string pedal points are reminiscent of several passages from
Preisner's favorite Floyd album).

The origin of the cue's opening is the quartertonal smudge of the
bolero ostinato, reimagined at first for solo piano—its sustain pedal
turns the repeating flourish into a cluster of semitones—then as a second cluster in the violins, playing tremolando and sustaining each note
to form a sinister mesh. Preisner adopts scoring conventions from the
Polish avant-garde at this moment in the score, including a thick black
arrow indicating the continuation of the cluster once it has reached its
full bandwidth. Organized sound actually begins, however, with the A
of the telephone as Auguste tries to call Karin. The As then pulse a-
rhythmically against the cue, in a *frissant* of tension. Auguste is depicted amid reflections in the glass of his window, the doubling reminding the perceiver that all this has happened before to the Old Judge. He
then leans for a moment against the window frame, the muted dissonance evoking exhaustion and angst, before the entry of a viola melody
underscores his decision to take action.

The cluster continues, minus the piano, as the violas perform a
variation of the high string melody in the previous sequence. Just as the
cluster has replaced that cue's diminished seventh chord with an even
more sinister sound connoting pain and anxiety, the melody too is considerably more chromatic, outlining a series of widening intervals and
ending as the viola line bifurcates: its final pitch, an E, splits into E and
D♯, thus extending the mesh of pitches to the enharmonic breadth of the
tritone between A and E♭, the melodic span of the B theme. The viola's
grainy melody competes with the additional stresses of the dog yelping
and Auguste shouting at it before slamming the door to his apartment,
screeching away in his red jeep, and narrowly missing a honking car as
he slides across the junction around which, from the same perspective,
one has seen Valentine driving. The squeal of tires and horn fade away
to reveal the semitonal sonority into which the violas bifurcate, maintaining the tension that climaxes in Auguste's near miss on the road.
The intensity continues as he screeches past the Old Judge's house.
Kern is looking through the window. Seeing the car, perhaps only he
could know the significance of the three red cherries—Valentine's token of bad luck—glimpsed on the one-armed bandit in *Chez Joseph* as
his younger double sped away. The young judge is about to relive the
worst of all moments *chez* Joseph.

The contrast of these sounds to the silence as he creeps up the stairs
to Karin's door is clearly marked, not least because, suddenly, all one

can hear is the score. Auguste's arcing approach up the stairs to Karin's door recalls Valentine's circling of the Old Judge as she confronted him on his role in Karin's affair, and photosynthesizes a dance-like fluidity from Preisner's music, which here relaxes, slightly, into a variation of Bi. The melody is scored for the instrument reserved for pitiful masculinity in the trilogy—Auguste is a cuckolded *klarnet* too—with the ostinato continuing on the acoustic guitar; the cellos and basses move between B♭s and As, maintaining the skeleton of the familiar harmonic sequence with a sparseness rendering the material newly tense. The return to more marked signs of bolero at this point, and notably the exotically inflected mode of the melody, match the musical form's ability to mix heady cocktails of the erotic, romantic, and violence: a *bolero* is about to discover that his *bolera* is not all he had hoped. Listening at the door—eavesdropping like his double—is not enough for Auguste, however, and the action cuts to him rolling a wheelie bin into a position from which he can begin scaling the apartment block to peep through Karin's window. At this display of determination, Preisner's score swells mock-heroically with a richly voiced A major chord, the fullness of which anticipates the scoring of Auguste's forthcoming moment of recognition.

As the young judge begins his cat burglar's journey, a further variation of Bi begins, this one reminiscent of the scoring beneath the Old Judge's discussion of his misjudgment, thanks to the return of the lamenting cello. The notable variation of the music, however, is the harmony, which now begins to distort the hitherto distinctly alternating pedal tones. The bass end clots semitones, a trait spreading to the upper registers as woodwind join the throng and the music strengthens harmonically, timbrally and dynamically. As the instruments crescendo, Preisner instructs them to play with greater and greater vibrato, further destabilizing the pitched integrity of an already strained sonority.

Almost at full orchestral force, a final variation of Bi begins, diverting attention from a slight cut to the diegetic timeline: one does not see Auguste scaling to the second floor, having almost plummeted from a splitting trellis. This is the last diegetic sound one hears until the climax of the scene, Preisner's score carrying the soundtrack until the moment of predication. The diminished-seventh to A major chord progression is now fully voiced in the strings, the piano and guitar propelling the ostinato while the oboe melody—its high woodwind voice, as in the scene when Karol spied up at Dominique in *White*, a metaphor for the height at which the action is playing out—contrasting against spiraling descents in the violins. The fusion of ideas from the two subject groups suggests vertigo (perhaps even *Vertigo*) and the danger—physical and spiritual—of the path Auguste has selected for himself: the heavy, off-beat accents in the second violin phrase also connote Hitchcockian anxiety. The music mirrors the red vortex of gathering storm clouds spiraling on the monitor of Karin's computer, the rhythmic fluctuations dovetailing, at a broader rhythmic level, with the metrical lurch of the phrasing, which moves in bar groupings of 1+3. The elongated consequent phrases for the spiraling violins string out the tension as Auguste approaches the threshold of revelation: Karin's bedroom window.

One hears before one sees what Auguste sees, diegetic sound returning in the passionate yelp from Karin that precedes a cut from his reaction to his subjective perspective on her coupling. As Andrew notes, Auguste's view "is notably more revealing than was Karol's in *White*;"[51] so is the audience's, permitting one to share in the intensity of his surprise. Musically, however, Preisner has also tipped the action by bringing back—having restrained the score from doing so at any other point in the film—Bii's climactic development of the second subject. These thematic moments were last heard when the action cut from Auguste to Valentine in her car, just moments before she hit Rita. Previously, the *marcato* stabs of the string accompaniment and staccato sextuplets in the violins seemed anempathic and unmatched to the action. Here they are viscerally apt, mickey-mousing Karin's lover's thrusts and making them seem more violently sexual than, without the sound, they actually look. When the action cuts back to Auguste's shocked face, the music permits one to continue seeing with him: Preisner scores rhythmic, forceful, and climactic activity. As he tears his eyes away and turns his head into the darkness, shaking with emotion, the cue climaxes in a rasp of A major. The high proportion of dominant Es at the top of the sonority, in collusion with the scene's action, makes this feel simultaneously like a moment of closure and rupture.

A Sonic Curse

The next day, the Old Judge calls Karin's weather service to discover what the weather in the channel will be like for Valentine's trip. They banter about the service and the joy of sailing the passage; Karin, who will die in the storm she has failed to predict because of her exertions in the sack the night before, believes that the weather will be wonderful. If there was no underscore whatsoever, the scene would wrong-step the audio-viewer into a sense that Valentine will make it safely to England. Sound design and underscore conspire, however, to flood the scene with malice and switch one's perception of the Old Judge from benevolence back to dangerous outsider—a man vengeful enough to invoke a curse.

Aside from the Old Judge dialing Karin, the first sound in the scene is the familiar single-engine plane. Here it does not cross from one channel to another; it is drowned out in the low string cluster. A complementary high cluster then begins to slip in and out of the scene, introducing shriller notes of tension as the mood warps from amiability to menace. While the Old Judge solicits the information he needs from Karin, the solo cello lament from Bi is heard again, moving as if torpid—or aged—against the accompanying cluster of bass notes. There is another difference between this and the version of Bi heard as Auguste began his climb: it is drenched in reverb. This effect has been used earlier in the trilogy to suggest a moment of interiority or even that music or sounds are occurring in a character's imagination. It is just about possible that the music is indeed meta-diegetic: the version of the theme heard earlier on Valentine's car radio implies the Old Judge could know the music too. More likely, however, the music is one of the categories of underscoring heard throughout the trilogy between non-diegetic and meta-diegetic. Evoking the thoughts beneath the surface of the Old Judge's actions—as if he is hoping, if not literally planning, for Karin's death to avenge Auguste, and by extension his betrayed younger self—the score becomes the Old Judge's climate. The storm is gathering.

Recapitulation

There are only five minutes of music in the first thirty-five minutes of *Red*, and it all occurs at once. There are thirteen minutes of music in the last half hour of the film. As the plot's noose tightens, the score's activity level intensifies. It is not an excessive presence. The climactic five minutes of the film, for instance, have no scoring at all—which is not to say that they lack sonic interest. But the relative increase in musical information contributes proportionately to the rhetoric of the film, as *Red*'s storytelling sculpts the trilogy's symbolic and emotional payoff.

Catwalk Promenade II

After the Old Judge, accompanied by the "Water-lily" *vocalise*, pulls up outside the theater—he is shot through a building's glass and behind his car windscreen, in a mirror of Valentine's departure from the first fashion show at the start of the film—the action cuts to Valentine's valedictory catwalk. Leaping into the fray of the show entailed cutting into Preisner's return to his Ai promenade mid-phrase. Preisner scored the first two bars, but the manuscript score indicates an acknowledgement on his part that the cue in the film would begin in bar three. The decision has an interesting musical ramification: the final phrase of the *vocalise* has gestural similarities to the promenade melody (see Ex. 7.6); the phrase to which the action cuts also begins on G, and thus the final pitch of the G minor *vocalise*. In an instant, Valentine's transformative effect on the Old Judge's life is musically summarized: the downbeat tragedy of his version of the song transfigures into Valentine's catwalk theme, and a marker of his subjectivity takes on her musical countenance—a point underscored by the close-up of Valentine peering out from behind the curtain after the shots of the Old Judge.

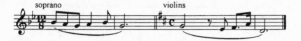

Ex. 7.6: Gestural and pitch continuity between *vocalise* and catwalk

This is a reinforced version of the original catwalk promenade in at least two respects. The orchestration is more lavish; that lavishness, in turn, reinforces the theme's existing semiotic content. Both are linked to the main musical development in this variation of Ai: the addition of a wordless choir. This heavenly host of sopranos and altos are a literally feminine presence reemphasizing the familiar symbols of angelic purity surrounding Valentine, but now also the Old Judge. The richness of the cue, including brass and percussion in addition to the voices, supersedes the previous climactic moment in the score, when Auguste discovered Karin's infidelity, as if similarly to transfigure the darkness of that moment as the narrative's focus shifts elsewhere.

Valentine steps onto a catwalk and into a storm of flashbulbs and applause. The original promenade's underlying malice is intensified here by the blacks and reds of the catwalk and theater, but she completes her trip up and down it safely, not stumbling, but searching worriedly for the Old Judge. The myriad flashes in the sequence superficially contribute to the radiance of the scene, twinkling like the lights catching Valentine's jewelry and suggesting a veneer of grand beauty. Watched without sound, the disturbing quality of these flashes becomes more apparent. This is an optically unnerving sequence that does more than dazzle the perceiver: it disorients. One cannot "see" properly, just as Valentine cannot see the Old Judge, let alone her perilous future. Finally, Valentine is seen in long shot, a dark figure silhouetted against a radiant blaze: an angel absorbed into light.

The primary change to the musical substance of the cue is a modulation, synced with the action to occur at precisely the moment Valentine steps onto the promenade. Preisner calls attention to that moment with a shortened bar of $\frac{2}{4}$ and the thematic transposition, which takes the theme into the new key of E major; there is also a tinkling on the soundtrack just as one sees Valentine, reminiscent of a *boleras* shaking her decorative balls. Rather than yielding the floor to A major, the score has veered into its dominant. While the return to the promenade theme establishes a sense of formal return and thus, to return to the sonata form metaphor, a sense of recapitulation—reinforced by the action returning to the scene of a fashion show at this juncture in the action—this is not a point of full closure. The first subject has been strengthened by experience, like Valentine: this version of her theme does not stumble. Yet while the music strides with fresh assurance, the modulation suggests continuing development. The recapitulation contains dramas of its own.

Synthesis

Valentine and the Old Judge's conversations in the theater take place in the eye of the film's material and metaphysical storms. This black and red theater of many levels—balconies, stalls, orchestra pit—is, rather like Julie's blue pool with its tiers of unopened doors, explored by camera and action as if it were a metaphor for consciousness, and precisely as the discussion interrogates intuition and repression, and individual subjectivities merge.

Thunder and wind initially underscore the action. After Valentine's confession to the Old Judge that she feels something important is happening all around her, and that she is scared by this, the first roll of thunder articulates the rhetorical transition to his explanation of how he used to visit the theater. He explains the occasion on which his book fell open—like Auguste's at the intersection—to the perfect page for an examination crib. A plunging crane shot is underscored by a whistling post-production effect that imagines the sound of the book falling in Valentine and the Old Judge's imaginations and memory: a sonic and imaginative communion, like the joint scoring scene in *Blue*. The communion is broken, however, when the storm breaks in and Valentine rushes to close the clattering doors, where she is "swallowed up in the white of the curtain . . . not unlike the foam of the ocean."[52] The sound design, a virtuosic onset creation by sound man Jean-Claude Laureux, structures the transition from intimate exchange to dramatic interruption—the clattering break-in of the elements, like exterior events impinging on their interlinked psyches, forms the sonic and dramatic climax of this process. Tension is then maintained by the cut to the next phase of their discussion, and Preisner's score takes over the demands of underscoring this critical sequence.

How fitting that, reveling in the shared intimacy of their now fully reciprocal relationship, Valentine and the Old Judge should perform their final duet in an orchestra pit, like a pair of Eagleton's *agapē*-improvising musicians. As interviews with the co-workers reveal, however, the conversation in the orchestra pit was assembled from the fragments of other scenes. It is a post-production confection, and Preisner's contribution to selling its symbolic and dramatic coherence, and to sculpting its sense of importance, became paramount to its success.

At a basic thematic level, the opening of the cue harks back to Auguste's discovery of Karin's infidelity. It begins with a reprise of the high string cluster which accompanied his attempts to telephone her, the tension of the sounds heightened by the music blending with a patina of rain and whistling wind. The angular string melody that followed is referenced, too, here in a more satisfying extension of its gestures that bring the cue to a moment of chilly tension. This is all motivically apt: the Old Judge is about to recount the tale of how, like Auguste, he once caught his partner cheating with another man. However, the dialogue underscored by this development of the bolero's B theme is Valentine's, as she recounts, quasi-mystically, the effects of the betrayal that corroded the Old Judge's soul. She has become, it seems, judge-like in her ability to intuit such insights: he has his dream of her future, she a dream of his past. How do you know these things, he asks her at one point, echoing her question (who are you?) a few moments earlier; it wasn't hard to guess, she replies, in turn recalling his intuiting of her brother's plight earlier in the film. It is thus appropriate that she should be scored by the B theme as she speaks: she has taken on the Old Judge's theme and perhaps his unusual abilities. The syncing of music to dialogue is precise, crafting image to cue as if the scene is a recitative led by Jacob's delivery. The downward descent of the melody's composite gesture matches the despondency of her vision.

The next section of score and dialogue emerges from the tense opacity of the harmonically ambiguous chord accompanying the end of Valentine's vision. Scored entirely for solo guitar, Valentine's instrument and theme—Aiii, the cue which accompanied the shots as she carried Rita into her car—accompanies the Old Judge as he recounts the tale of his cuckolding. As he describes the Valentine-like beauty of his gold and white goddess—her coloring and long, slender neck evoking the water-lily of the Van den Budenmayer song, and thus Valentine— the music seems set to be a photocopy of its previous annunciation. Then, as he mentions the mirror in her hallway in which he saw another man between her legs, the cue falters on an unexpected B♭, nudging the sentiments of Valentine's theme into the territory of the second-subject group and revealing his lover's beauty as a perversion. The cue seeks to continue, but falters again, this time on an A; a terrifying metallic bang then makes Valentine—and, in my experience, some audience members—jump, the startle fusing one, momentarily, both to her horror and the Old Judge's memory of the horrifying shock he experienced at the moment he saw a reflection mirroring Auguste's recent discovery.

As nerves settle, and the music pauses, Valentine exhorts the Old Judge to continue the story. A B♭ pizzicato in the basses and cellos anticipates an extended diversion into the second-subject's zone.[53] Over A and B♭ pedal tones in the lower strings, the solo harp—a timbre linked predominantly with Valentine—teases out a skeletal reprise of Bi. Thanks to the instrumentation, the consequent phrase descents after each rising tritone seem more closely linked than before to the melodic gestures of the catwalk theme Ai. The B♭ of the melody remains flattened, however, and the final sound of the cue is an unresolved glut of B♭s and As in the basses and cellos. Here as throughout the scene, Preisner adds just enough variation to the familiar—for example, by repeating at the octave recurring gestures in the harp—to maintain tension through change, but without suggesting momentum towards a point of simplistic revelation. In doing so, he helps render this potentially cumbersome assemblage into the most sustained passage of psychological tension in the trilogy.

In a sonata form recapitulation, one would expect a reprise of the second-subject group after the restatement of the first, in which the subordinate theme takes on elements of its dominating subject. The connection here of Valentine to the judges' materials and the Old Judge's mystical abilities, and then his scoring with the Aiii music, suggests a drawing together of musical and symbolic strands. *Red*'s sonata is tying up loose ends—or, rather, gathering the threads into a tangled ball. The thematic strategy mirrors the film's other means for suggesting doublings or blurred and merging identities. The film's movement towards closure is further signaled by a pair of jarring interruptions by the theater's janitor. "I'm closing the theater," he interrupts to tell them—a rhetorical incursion which, if not an outright dialogic rupture, suggests another authorial intrusion. The characters are being invited to leave the stage by Kieślowski, the trilogy's meta-judge—or rather, meta-janitor—and to take their positions for the final tableau.

As the Old Judge and Valentine bid each other farewell outside the theater, Preisner underscores their parting with audacious simplicity. A moment in the film that, in a different cinematic tradition, would be smeared in syrup to evoke their bond is underscored here with just three notes: a rising fifth from A to E—the key that, briefly, had interrupted the recapitulation's tonal progress—and then up a fourth to the A an octave higher. This gesture sounds on one of Valentine's instruments, the acoustic guitar. The arpeggio rings out as the Old Judge checks her ticket; its notes sustain as they press their hands into either side of the window pane of the Old Judge's car. Its presence imbues the moment with significance, although on a first audio-viewing of the film—as with so many other moments in the trilogy—one does not know what that significance might be. Has he blessed her ticket, thereby saving Valentine from impending disaster, in return for the blessing she dispensed to him?

The music contributes to a further tangle of meanings. The hands pressed together are Kickasola's hands "suggesting a universal notion: for a suspended second, these hands may belong to anyone, and, perhaps, everyone," thus creating a "marvelous cinematic gesture . . . suggesting love of the highest, metaphysical order."[54] Preisner's final cue, in a sense, is indeed the most "universal" sound in music—the first changing pitch-classes in the unfolding of the harmonic overtone series. In the context of the film, however, this cadence is yet more specifically symbolic: it is the gist of Valentine's climate and—as ringing telephones, twangling ostinatos and the destination of so many melodic lines have continuously reminded one—the only possible point of terminus for the score.

This is A for *agapē*, presented as a distillation of the score's thematic, tonal and conceptual substance, and precisely as the notion is visually distilled by the two hands pressed against each other through a barrier. A few seconds later, one experiences the concept writ larger in Valentine's simple act of helping an old woman put a bottle in a bottle-bank—Kehr's gesture "to save the world." Where Julie was oblivious to a similar struggle at the bottle-bank and Karol observed it through a haze of *Schadenfreude*, Valentine sacrifices a little of her time to help another person. In such contexts, one might be tempted to hear the score's final dramatic cue as a musical transscansion along the lines of "Ka-rol" and "Vol-vo" in *White*: three notes that sing out "*a-ga-pē*."

Coda: Reading *Red* and the End of the Trilogy

The arrival of *Red*'s storm is evoked by the soundtrack as much as by visual effects, the film boldly dealing in absentia with the denouement of the story, i.e., the ferry sinking. Filmic examples of the pathetic fallacy, however, saturate the narrative. A foghorn heard as Valentine and Auguste's ferry departs anticipates mournful sounds to come; the closing harbor gates block out the sun—a reminder of previous images of eclipse, but here accompanied by metallic whines and booming portent. An ensuing shot depicts the rain belting down and wind raging as a group of men struggle to dismantle Valentine's billboard poster; it pools as it slithers from the hoarding, her face disappearing like an effigy sinking into the sea. Cracks of lightning, striking the world in a panoramic shot of Geneva, hark back to the flashguns at the fashion shows; the thunder recalls its applause. The action then abruptly cuts to a shot of whimpering puppies. The events inaugurated at the start of the film, which began with the sound of rain, have run their course. The final constellation of its elements can now be revealed.

Although Kehr deems it "all but impossible to account for the emotional impact of the last two reels of *Red*," his own analysis of how the impact of the ending "reaches far beyond the narrative events depicted" cuts to the core of its technique of prolepsis:

> Throughout the trilogy, Kieślowski uses quick, enigmatic flash-forwards (such as the shots of Dominique entering an unknown hotel room in *White*) to give a fatefulness to the proceedings. Whether or not we consciously register these images (and many people do not), they create a feeling of resonance and fulfillment when they recur in the course of the narrative (it's the room Dominique checks into when Karol succeeds in luring her back to Warsaw). Through these moments, Kieślowski makes it seem as if the entire work were moving toward a single point of convergence, toward one grand climax. It's the narrative equivalent of a planetary alignment.[55]

When the Old Judge switches on the television borrowed from Valentine, sonic motifs immediately cluster together to initiate that sense of alignment. The plane and helicopter motifs are both present as he views news footage of the disaster. A chorus of foghorns blares a lament as survivors are paraded for the cameras: Julie, Olivier, Dominique, Karol, Auguste and, lastly, Valentine.[56] Aviation sounds then return to the foreground of the mix as Valentine and Auguste are framed together. The plane makes its familiar journey from the right to left channel, a symbol of connection tracking the pan and zoom of the camera as it progresses left from Auguste to Valentine, cuts to the Old Judge framed still further left, and then finally back to Valentine. She is shot against the lurid red backdrop of a rescuer's jacket, mirroring her headshot on the advert. All three characters have now been linked by the sound of the plane, but the film ends with a close-up of Valentine, sonically isolated and visually frozen.

Engines and foghorns cluster around this image, melting its chill with a mostly pitched sonority, save for a few wayward tones, consisting of C, D and E—not a collection heard anywhere else in the score or trilogy,[57] but a somewhat stable and diatonic sonority, aided in its significations of closure by the depth of its frequencies. As the horns and engines dwindle, the final sound heard is the wind. This sound has been heard throughout *Red*, primarily in the vicinity of the Old Judge's home as a signifier of his presence. Now it fades to nothing, as if the character himself is ceasing to exist, now that his younger double has met Valentine. Once the wind has been silenced, and the screen fades to black, a clarinet begins Preisner's end title cue with a gentle statement of the Ai bolero melody. What does this lightness of musical touch signify in the immediate aftermath of such disaster?

Inevitably, the ending of the *Three Colors* trilogy has provoked a wealth of critical consideration. Kehr's interpretation of the close of *Red* continues to emphasize the synthesizing strategy of the finale, as episodes "carefully distinguished by tone, content and appearance turn out to be the same film, telling the same story of alienation overcome, loneliness dissolved in human warmth, isolation subsumed by a sense of infinite interdependence"—an *agapē*-themed reading of story and discourse epitomized, for Kehr, by the final shot-reverse shot of the Old Judge looking out of his broken window and the freeze-frame of Valentine, which makes him "the first of the trilogy's characters to see someone beyond himself; for Kieślowski, all the hope for the world resides in that fact."[58] One could also argue that Julie and Karol achieved such sight at the end of their stories, and that Valentine has always had this gift—hence her centrality to the final shot of the trilogy as an icon of what its stories promote. Not all critics, however, feel that the trilogy's ending bears such a positive message.

As Andrew reminds one, it would be "cynical or short-sighted to describe the outcome of *Red* . . . as 'a happy ending'"[59]; like the endings of *Blue* and *White* beforehand, it is poised between tragedy and hope. Over 1,400 ferry passengers have lost their lives; Karin is dead; Auguste's dog, once abandoned, later rescued, is probably also drowned. (With jet-black Kieślowskian irony, the hound would have been better off remaining abandoned.) There is no knowing that Auguste and Valentine will have a future together, nor for that matter that Julie and Olivier, or Karol and Dominique, will live happily every after.[60] For Andrew, however, the conclusion remains emotionally satisfying, thanks to the compassion extended by Kieślowski himself to the major characters in the trilogy: "[W]e are not only given hope regarding their (hitherto ambiguous) futures, but we may somehow feel that we the audience have been rewarded by Kieślowski for taking a sympathetic interest in their fates."[61]

Andrew makes a keen point, in this regard, concerning the narrative structure of the trilogy as a whole. Ending the trilogy with the disaster, rather than beginning with the catastrophe and then telling each story in flashback, means that, "by situating the news of [the main characters'] survival at the end, Kieślowski closes the trilogy—much of which has concerned loss, grief, solitude and despair—on a note of hope: they are alive, and together"; the ending is thus like the revelation of a *deus ex machina* in a Greek tragedy, pointing up "the author's own artifice in giving us an emotionally satisfying outcome."[62] By ending the trilogy kindly, therefore, and saving the characters in which audience members are potentially so invested, the co-workers end *Red* with a performative gesture of *agapē* embracing characters and audience—while knowingly including the audience within the very artifice of that narrative gesture.

Wilson counters, however, that it is "not prudent to read too much" into the way the protagonists are shown at the end—she too notes that being together here does not imply a continuing relationship or positive future—any more than one should over-interpret the glimpse of Kieślowski himself boarding the ferry to drown with the passengers on the lower decks.[63] Instead, how these events are shown is the index for her reading of the coda. Noting the prevalent use of television in Kieślowski's works to depict moments of high drama in his characters' lives—think of the funeral in *Blue* or the dead boy glimpsed in *Decalogue 1*—Wilson argues that such devices are not used to bring the outside world into the films, but rather "to make the inner world of his protagonists' psyche, memory and identities visible to the viewer."[64] What is one to make, therefore, of the zoom that isolates Valentine in a frozen close-up at the end of *Red*—a zoom, on closer inspection, that appears uncharacteristically "artificial" and rough in appearance, and marked for attention by technical means far more obvious than the equally constructed, but more subtly articulated, layering of sounds? For Wilson, the image's presentation marks the ending as an elegy fissured with loss and incompletion.[65]

It is impossible to ignore the pessimism *in extremis* at the end of *Red*, where small gestures of hope are almost entirely dwarfed by the terrible toll of the dead[66]: with just seven survivors out of about 1,400 ferry passengers, one could say that *Red*'s coda is just 0.005 percent hopeful. Considering such statistics as Preisner's end title bolero strikes up, and alongside the far from happy conclusion to the main characters' tales, there may even seem something grotesque about a trilogy that sends people out of the cinema buoyed up on this transcendent version of Valentine's catwalk music. Is the disaster deemed to matter little more, in the end, than a fashion show promenade? That reading is probably too sardonic even for Kieślowski, Preisner, and their fellow Polish co-workers. Yet the end title cue's return to the bolero's turbulent second subject group is drained of its earlier pathos. The variation of the B theme, specifically the solo cello line that accompanied the judges' darkest moments, is framed on either side by A material, in a cue that runs uninterruptedly to the conclusion of a closed ternary form. This structure thereby harnesses the second subject's dark energy to more positive ends, rather as the Old Judge has been domesticated by Valentine's influence. The quartertonal fluctuations of the ostinato even sound as if they are included to bridge the gap between the A major theme and the B♭s at the root of some chords in its less stable reply. Once it returns to the original theme, the cue also includes the transcendent modulation to E major, before a final reprise transposes the Ai theme up another tone and into F♯ major. Returning to A major would have achieved a more rounded sense of closure, but the further modulation, raised up on a swelling orchestra and wordless choir, adds buoyancy to the end of the film. The new key may even suggest an escape from the trilogy's world and its sorrows.

Describing the end of the trilogy as either entirely pessimistic or inappropriately upbeat is nonetheless too simplistic. Like so much else in the films, *Red*'s ending seems ambivalently posed to provoke vying interpretations. Seeking a more productive site for criticism, Kickasola therefore contrasts the endings of *Red* and *Decalogue 1*:

> The Old Judge's salvation is that, amid 1,400 deaths, there is a survivor for whom he cares deeply (and a resident hope, spoken by the wordless final image, that his own past mistakes may not be repeated). *Decalogue I* tells us the stories of the victims, and the iconic Madonna weeps in the end. *Red* is about the survivors, not just of this tragedy but of all the existential perils Kieślowski has ever addressed, and the Old Judge weeps in an equally iconic posture [earlier on he has raised a hand in quasi-benediction in the theater]. The *Decalogue* grapples vigorously with absolute, universal questions. *Red* makes a gracious peace with the lack of answers, remaining hopeful at the end of a remarkable career.[67]

A gracious peace with a lack of final answers may be the best one can hope for at the end of the trilogy; perhaps it is the best one can ever hope for, period. Yet how is one to live in the meantime? In hope, in spite of everything, is my reading of the *Three Colors* coda. The end of *Red* is hopeful precisely because, while hardly dominant, hope is still part of the equation—just.

It could have been extraordinarily distressing. The corpses of all six protagonists could have been shown slithering down the side of the ferry; the Old Judge, having been brought back to life by Valentine, would have been crushed. Yet the end of the trilogy does not destroy him: it rewards his change of behavior with her survival. This is not moralizing, nor facile storytelling; it may, however, be allegory. Closely attending to the sounds, music and moving images in the *Three Colors* trilogy has called attention, time and time again, to ways in which the films insinuate a strategy for living a happier, or at least less isolated, life. Spiraling out from Preisner's setting of St. Paul's letter in

Julie's *Concert[o]*, the trilogy's multilayered rhetoric coheres through its attempt to demonstrate the potential of the self-sacrificial and reciprocal love called *agapē*. After the disaster, *Red*'s ending places an empathetic, but not patronizing, hand on the audience's shoulder. Preisner's cue, in particular, extends the warmth of the Old Judge's gaze at the audience over the entirety of the end credits. This is a gesture of solidarity: nothing can take away life's pain, but these films are not indifferent to suffering.[68]

Thus interpreted, the trilogy ends didactically, and in a manner that can hardly be to every taste. The survivors emerge as if from an epic baptism, cleansed on behalf of the audience and offered up as iconic representations of a journey which that audience, the trilogy proposes, should metaphysically reproduce. On the one hand, audio-viewers glide out of the experience of *Red* transported by the soaring melodies, lush orchestrations, and affecting transpositions of Preisner's most straightforwardly uplifting cue in the trilogy; on the other, they are marked by the tragedies of *Blue*, *White* and *Red*'s interwoven tales, and their demonstration of the myriad ways in which, even if one did want to embrace the trilogy's highest ideals, one can only fall short of the mark. Yet still one is enticed to feel—and as *Red* ends, enticed only through music—a nagging sense of hope. Deluded hope, for sure—or, rather, hope that is but 0.005 percent realistic. The *Three Colors* trilogy offers truly dreadful odds; Preisner's music invites one to gamble.

NOTES

Introduction

1. The reasons for this study's peculiar typographic presentation of *Concert[o]* are explained in subsequent chapters, but primarily relate to inconsistencies in *Blue*'s dialogue.

2. Few critics writing on the trilogy have considered the richness of this term, having being led—by subtitles, perhaps, as much as anything else—to consider the piece to be about "love" in a more general sense. Some, however, writing in relation to their knowledge of Christian tenets and philosophy, have dealt with the topic in passing. Joseph Kickasola, for instance, describes the *Concert[o]* as an "ode to love" because it "delineates the great powers as well as the great difficulties and risks inherent in . . . the greatest of all virtues"; see Joseph Kickasola, *The Films of Krzysztof Kieślowski: The Liminal Image* (New York: Continuum, 2004), 277. In a perceptive but flawed online essay which pursues a Christian message in the trilogy at all costs, Carla Barringer Rabinowitz notes the use of the term *agapē*: "the chorale is sung in French [sic—it is all sung in Greek], except for the last word, which, as Julie helpfully points out to Olivier, has a different rhythm in Greek. Kieślowski and Preisner wanted to be sure we knew they weren't just talking about 'amour' . . . 1 Corinthians 13 is not just a bunch of warm fuzzies about the importance of love"; see Carla Barringer Rabinowitz, "St. Paul, Kieślowski, and the Christian Framework of *Trois couleurs*" (undated), http://www.petey.com/kk/docs/kiesdis3.txt (last accessed 6 October 2010). A finer-grained discussion of Christian notions of love can be found in Christopher Garbowski's excellent dissertation on the *Decalogue* series, *Krzysztof Kieślowski's "Decalogue" Series: The Problem of the Protagonists and Their Self-Transcendence* (New York: Columbia University Press, 1996), 99-103. The conclusion of this discussion—that the *Decalogue*'s "urgent conclusion" is "for people to be

there for the other"—begins to indicate aspects of the kinship between the trilogy and the earlier series.

3. C. S. Lewis, *The Four Loves* (London: HarperCollins, 2002 [1960]), 141. Two recent studies exploring these concepts with interdisciplinary rigor are Craig A. Boyd, ed., *Visions of Agapé: Problems and Possibilities in Human and Divine Love* (Aldershot: Ashgate, 2008) and Adam Phillips and Barbara Taylor, *On Kindness* (London: Penguin, 2010).

4. Terry Eagleton, *The Meaning of Life* (Oxford: Oxford University Press, 2007), 158-60.

5. Eagleton, *The Meaning of Life*, 173.

6. Karl Marx, "Capital" (1867), in *Literary Theory: An Anthology*, 2nd ed., ed. Julie Rifkin and Michael Ryan (Oxford: Blackwell Publishing, 2004), 665; Margaret Thatcher's comments were made in an interview with *Woman's Own* on 23 September 1987, which can be read at http://www.margaretthatcher.org/document/106689 (last accessed 14 October 2010). Marx did, of course, foresee parallel transformations. As Eagleton notes in a recent essay on Marxism, *The Communist Manifesto* "described not the world capitalism had created in 1848, but the world as it was destined to be transformed by capitalism. What Marx had to say was not exactly true, but it would become true by, say, the year 2000, and it was capitalism that would make it so. Even his comments on the abolition of the family have proved prophetic: about half of the children in advanced Western countries today are born to or brought up by single mothers, and half of all households in large cities consist of single persons." See Terry Eagleton, "Indomitable: *How to Change the World: Marx and Marxism 1840-2011* by Eric Hobsbawm," *The London Review of Books* 33, no. 5 (3 March 2011): 13-14. A veneer of *agapē* is present in current UK Prime Minister David Cameron's promotion of "The Big Society" to fix "Broken Britain"—an agenda which disingenuously fails to acknowledge the role of his Conservative (and New Labour) predecessors' policies in that breaking.

7. Janina Falkowska, "*The Double Life of Véronique* and *Three Colours*: An Escape from Politics?," in *Lucid Dreams: The Films of Krzysztof Kieślowski*, ed. Paul Coates (Trowbridge: Flicks Books, 1999), 154.

8. David Kehr, "To Save the World: Kieślowski's *Three Colors* Trilogy," *Film Comment* 30, no. 6 (1994), 12-13.

9. The end of Douglas Coupland's *Generation X: Tales for an Accelerated Culture* (New York: St. Martin's Press, 1991) could be read, for instance, as an expression of *agapē*. Protagonist Andy—stranded in the middle of a burning desert—is surrounded by strangers offering, with no possible thought of redress, simple but affectionate contact. Coupland has written this on his motivation for writing the book: "I remember spending my days almost dizzy with loneliness and feeling like I'd sold the family cow for three beans. I suppose this gave *Gen X* its bite. I was trying to imagine a life for myself on paper that certainly wasn't happening in reality." See Douglas Coupland, "Guardian Book

Club: Week Three. Douglas Coupland on How He Came to Write *Generation X*," *The Guardian* (26 September 2009) http://www.guardian.co.uk/books/2009/sep/26/douglas-coupland-generation-x (last accessed 6 October 2010).

10. Sean O'Sullivan, "The *Decalogue* and the Remaking of American Television," in *After Kieślowski: The Legacy of Krzysztof Kieślowski*, ed. Steven Woodward (Detroit: Wayne State University Press, 2009), 205-6.

11. Stanley Kubrick, "Foreword," in Krzysztof Kieślowski and Krzysztof Piesiewicz, trans. P. Cavendish and S. Bluh, *Decalogue: The Ten Commandments* (London: Faber, 1991), vii.

12. Rick loses Isla but gains Louis's "beautiful friendship"; Homer's Alaskan idyll is sacrificed to save Springfield, but he rides off into the sunset with Marge, is lauded by the town, and everything goes back to normal (repeating the start of the film, with nothing lost).

13. Quoted in Jonathan Kiefer, "Kieślowski's *Three Colors*," *Salon.com* (10 June 2002), http://www.salon.com/entertainment/masterpiece/2002/06/10/three_colors (last accessed 18 April 2011).

14. Emma Wilson, "*Three Colours: Blue*. Kieślowski, Colour and the Postmodern Subject," *Screen* 39, no. 4 (Winter 1998), 350.

15. Wilson, "*Three Colours: Blue*," 8, citing Frederic Jameson, *Postmodernism, Or, The Cultural Logic of Late Capitalism* (London: Verso, 1991), 15.

16. In Paul Coates, "'The Inner Life Is the Only Thing that Interests Me': A Conversation with Krzysztof Kieślowski," in *Lucid Dreams*, ed. Coates, 169.

17. Frank Kermode, *The Classic* (New York: Viking Press, 1975), 134.

Chapter One

1. Mikael Carlsson and Peter Holm, "The Double Life of Zbigniew Preisner," *Music from the Movies* (May 1997), 38.

2. Will Hodgkinson, "The Man Who Says No to Hollywood," *Guardian Unlimited* (12 November 2004), http://www.guardian.co.uk/arts/homeentertainment/story/0,12830,1348792,00.html (last accessed 20 January 2006); Richard Williams, "The Music of Friendship," *The Guardian* (9 October 1998), 22. Kieślowski scholar (and one-time translator) Annette Insdorf similarly refers to meeting a "corpulent composer" in 1988 and appreciating the ironic "counterpoint between his delicate melodies and rowdy personality"; see Annette Insdorf, *Double Lives, Second Chances: The Cinema of Krzysztof Kieślowski* (New York: Hyperion, 1999), 5.

3. Preisner contrasts his childhood shyness to his father's "theatrical personality." Unattributed quotes and information from Preisner in this study come from my interviews with the composer.

4. Following the Athens premiere of *Silence, Night and Dreams*, he confronted assorted dignitaries about the meager canapés laid on for his hungry crew at an official reception, and then led his entire entourage to a nearby restaurant, whose owners he persuaded to reopen and serve supper.

5. I first met Preisner at the UK premiere of *Silence, Night and Dreams* on 2 December 2007. At that event, he was genuinely amazed that one fan had traveled from South America just to meet him and give him a present.

6. Preisner listed skiing as one of his passions, alongside abseiling, bungee-jumping and "contracts with plenty of zeros," in a talk at the Edinburgh Festival in 2004.

7. Mark Salter and Jonathan Bousfield, *The Rough Guide to Poland*, 5th ed. (London: Rough Guides, 2002), 588-9.

8. Salter and Bousfield, *The Rough Guide*, 589.

9. Hodgkinson, "The Man Who Says No to Hollywood."

10. Mark Russell and James Young, *Film Music: Screencraft* (Woburn, MA: Focal Press, 2000), 161.

11. Hodgkinson, "The Man Who Says No to Hollywood."

12. This is a transcription of the version of the hymn Preisner sang to me during an interview in Kraków.

13. Adrian Thomas, *Polish Music since Szymanowski* (Cambridge: Cambridge University Press, 2005), 256.

14. For a fuller analysis of these pieces and their socio-cultural context, see Thomas, *Polish Music since Szymanowski*, 180-3 and 256-61.

15. Thomas, *Polish Music since Szymanowski*, 257.

16. This topic is further considered in Chapter Five's analysis of *Blue*.

17. The score's most quirky component is the Joan Baez song "Cain and Abel," which bookends the film and includes the words—ideologically notable, perhaps, in the context of this Western production—"Sweet are the children who hold the legacy of a solidarity of heart."

18. Any film casting Ed Harris, Timothy Spall and Tim Roth as members of the Polish security forces, with each using their native regional accent, is going to be a challenge to take entirely seriously.

19. The Italian term for this type of singing, heard occasionally in Preisner scores, means literally "in the chapel style."

20. A style topic is a musical *gestalt* recurring often enough in a repertoire to acquire, for listeners immersed in that repertoire's culture, a stable and widely recognized extra-musical connotation—posthorns for a hunt, for instance, sleigh bells for Christmas, or a choir of heavenly voices for, well, heaven. In addition to these basic denotations, however, each style topic carries a range of more subtle socio-cultural information, as discussed below, for instance regarding gender.

21. Jan Stęszewski, Krzysztof Ćwiżewicz, et al., "Poland," in *Grove Music Online. Oxford Music Online*, http://www.oxfordmusiconline

.com/subscriber/article/grove/music/22001 (last accessed 18 April 2011).

22. Although not one of the instruments most often associated with Polish traditional music, the accordion became a regular part of Polish folk ensembles from the late nineteenth century onwards; see Stęszewski, Ćwiżewicz, et al., "Poland."

23. Russell and Young, *Film Music: Screencraft*, 161.

24. The annotation of this melody quoted here, from Stefan Jarociński's 1965 collection *Polish Music* and included in Stęszewski, Ćwiżewicz, et al., "Poland," has (again probably coincidentally, unless Preisner has studied this collection) the exact same pitch-classes (in G minor) as the *No End* and *Blue* cues.

25. Stęszewski, Ćwiżewicz, et al., "Poland."

26. Ewa Dahlig, "Poland," in *The Garland Encyclopedia of World Music*, ed. Timothy Rice, James Porter, and Chris Goertzen (New York: Garland, 2000), Vol. 8, 708.

27. The term *górale* ("highlanders") refers to the Gorals, indigenous people in areas of Southern Poland, Slovakia and the Silesian part of the Czech Republic living across a much larger diaspora.

28. For an interesting discussion of this lyric, see the thread "Lyrics to 'Tu viendras'" on the IMDb's *La double vie de Véronique* discussion board http://www.imdb.com/title/tt0101765/board/flat/16884584?p.1 (last accessed 10 May 2007).

29. A pattern of rhythmic durations made up of ever-longer components; see Stęszewski, Ćwiżewicz, et al., "Poland."

30. See Dahlig, "Poland," 709.

31. Carlsson and Holm, "The Double Life of Zbigniew Preisner," 38.

32. He cannot recall when he finally received his degree, but says that he "postponed graduation for as long as possible, to avoid military service." Kieślowski also dodged the draft, and with even more cunning; see Kickasola, *The Films of Krzysztof Kieślowski*, 11.

33. Rita McAllister, Iosif Genrikhovich Rayskin, et al., "Rimsky-Korsakov," in *Grove Music Online. Oxford Music Online*, http://www.oxfordmusiconline.com/subscriber/article/grove/music/52074pg1 (last accessed 18 April 2011). The Russian composer created the textbook partly as a distraction during an arid creative spell and partly in response to a similar text by Tchaikovsky that he deemed unsatisfactory. Prokofiev, in his memoirs, contrasts the two, finding "the Rimsky approach more thorough but more 'boring'"; see Boris Schwartz, "Review: *Tchaikovsky. The Early Years: 1840-1874* by David Brown," in *Notes*, 2nd ser., 36, no. 3 (March 1980), 650.

34. Carlsson and Holm, "The Double Life of Zbigniew Preisner," 38.

35. These programs were first broadcast on 18 July 2009 (BBC4) and 31 July 2009 (BBC2), and featured rock critic and record producer Paul Morley and drum'n'bass composer Goldie.

36. See, for example, the balanced defense of Danny Elfman in Janet Halfyard, *Danny Elfman's "Batman": A Film Score Guide* (Lanham, MD: Scarecrow Press, 2004).

37. Radek Sikorski, *The Polish House: An Intimate History of Poland* (London: Wiederfeld and Nicolson, 1997), 33-4.

38. Hodgkinson, "The Man Who Says No to Hollywood."

39. Hodgkinson, "The Man Who Says No to Hollywood."

40. In published discussions of his plans with Kieślowski for a live audio-visual spectacle (partly realized in his *Requiem for My Friend*), Preisner demonstrates knowledge of Pink Floyd's stage shows, considering them a worthy example for his planned project with Kieślowski. See Jonathan Broxton and James Southall, "Zbigniew Preisner in Concert: *Requiem for My Friend*," http://www.moviemusicuk/us/preisint .htm (last accessed 19 January 2001). See also "Regaining Composure: An Interview with Zbigniew Preisner," *Film Score Monthly* 4, no. 7 (August 1999): 15-18.

41. Carlsson and Holm, "The Double Life of Zbigniew Preisner," 38.

42. Mentions of this "training" can be found online. A biography on the *moviemusicuk* website, for instance, states that Preisner taught himself music by "copying down parts from records." See http://www.moviemusicuk.us/preisner.htm (last accessed 20 October 2009).

43. "Wikiality" (as opposed to reality) was a term coined by satirist Stephen Colbert in 2006 which lampoons, in the age of Wikipedia, the triumph of opinion over accurate reporting in contemporary political commentary. The following references seem most apt: http://en .wikipedia.org/wiki/Wikipedia_in_culture#Wikiality and http:// wikiality.wikia.com/Wikiality (last accessed 8 August 2010).

44. Klaus Wachsmann and Patrick O'Connor, "Cabaret," in *Grove Music Online. Oxford Music Online*, http://www.oxfordmusic online.com/subscriber/article/grove/music/04505 (last accessed 18 April 2011).

45. Wachsmann and O'Connor, "Cabaret."

46. See "Kabaret" in *Slovník české hudební kultury*, ed. Jiří Fukač, Jiří Vysloužil, and Petr Macek (Prague: Editio Supraphon, 1997). My thanks to Geoff Chew for this reference.

47. Bogdan Chmura, "Preisner, Zbigniew," in *Grove Music Online. Oxford Music Online*, http://www.oxfordmusiconline.com/subscriber/ article/grove/music/47985 (last accessed 18 April 2011).

48. Quoted in Monika Mokrzycka-Pokora, "Piwnica pod Baranami" (undated), http://www.culture.pl/en/culture/artykuly/in_te_ piwnica_pod_baranami_krakow (last accessed 15 June 2007).

49. Komeda's Sextet, formed in 1956, played some of the gigs which pioneered modern jazz in Poland. He adopted the pseudonym Komeda for such concerts in place of his family name, Trzciński, to hide from his co-workers (at a medical clinic) his involvement in a form of music deemed degenerate by the Communist authorities.

50. Joanna Olczak-Roniker, quoted in Mokrzycka-Pokora, "Piwnica pod Baranami."

51. Mokrzycka-Pokora, "Piwnica pod Baranami."

52. Private correspondence.

53. Piotr Wasilewski, "Das Risiko lohnt sich—Ein Gespräch von Piotr Wasilewski mit dem Filmkomponisten Zbigniew Preisner," *Journal Film—Die Zeitschrift für das andere Kino* 27 (1994): 54.

54. Hodgkinson, "The Man Who Says No to Hollywood."

55. These include an award-winning score for *Pornografia*, Jan Jakub Kolski's 2003 version of Witold Gombrowicz's novel.

56. As well as being published in voice and piano scores by Wydawca Markus in Kraków, many of his songs are available in recordings by Demarcyzk.

57. The film was directed by Antoni Krauze, now known throughout Europe for his satirical cartoons (not least in *The Guardian*). See Francis Wheen, "Master of His Art," *The Guardian* (8 March 2003), http://www.guardian.co.uk/artanddesign/2003/mar/08/art.artsfeatures2 (last accessed 8 August 2010).

58. One might also wonder about the influence of working in a cabaret that closed each night with a rendition of Max Ehrmann's poem "Desiderata." Its plain-speaking meditation on the essentials of a good life suggests, amongst other dispensations, that one needs to speak truth "quietly and clearly," and opens with the following lines: "Go placidly amid the noise and haste, and remember what peace there may be in silence." This almost reads like a summary of Preisner's aesthetic.

59. Just as Kieślowski has his *Requiem for My Friend*, Skrzynecki has the song "Piotr," with lyrics and music by Preisner, on the composer's album of Piwnica-like songs, *Głosy* (2001). This style of sung poetry is popular in Poland, where entire radio stations are devoted to it; it can also be heard in "Love at First Sight," Preisner's song celebrating the completion of the trilogy, discussed further in Chapter Four, n. 319.

60. Kaczmarski's "History Lecture" has just this kind of metrical play, adding extra "irregular" beats to the end of its waltzing refrains in order to accommodate certain phrases.

61. Pewex is short for *Przedsiębiorstwo Eksportu Wewnętrznego* (Internal Export Company), a chain of hard-currency retailers in communist-era Poland.

62. Edoardo Ponti, "Edoardo Ponti's Interview with Zbigniew Preisner," *musicolog.com* (undated). http://www.musicolog.com/ preisner_interview.asp (last accessed 18 April 2011).

63. Broxton and Southall, "Zbigniew Preisner in Concert."

64. As Ben Winters points out (private correspondence), such shorthand is common amongst film composers; Erich Korngold's scores, for instance, contain symbols serving similar purposes.

65. Thomas, *Polish Music since Szymanowski*, 40.

66. Sonorism is a term used to describe the manipulation of sonority as primary compositional material by some Polish composers

through the employment of experimental sounds, notation and instrumental techniques. See Thomas, *Polish Music since Szymanowski*, 290.

67. Jann Pasler, "Neo-romantic," in *Grove Music Online. Oxford Music Online*, http://www.oxfordmusiconline.com/subscriber/article/grove/music/40720 (last accessed 6 September 2006).

68. There is also an international context to this revival of accessible and epic sacred music, including compositions by Karl Jenkins, James MacMillan and Penderecki.

69. Kilar's avant-garde experiments of the 1960s and early 70s had already indicated dissatisfaction with modernism. His Warsaw Autumn Contemporary Music Festival "hit," *Riff '62*, mixes experimental and popular musical traditions (jazz) expressively to inflect his sonoristic materials.

70. Thomas, *Polish Music since Szymanowski*, 290.

71. Zbigniew Preisner et al., "Tunes of Glory," *Sight and Sound* 14, no. 9 (September 2004): 31; Hodgkinson, "The Man Who Says No to Hollywood."

72. Insdorf, *Double Lives, Second Chances*, xv.

73. For instance, Preisner often scores flats or sharps where the enharmonic equivalent would be more "correct." In bar 2 of Fig. 5.1, for instance, the trombone's G♭ would more typically be scored as an F♯.

74. For Preisner, the main profit from the trip was a chance to have dinner with Marlon Brando.

75. The other profit from the project occurred at this later stage: the same clause permitted Preisner to be paid half a million dollars for his work thus far on the film.

76. Preisner says he was begged to stay (one more year and you will win an Oscar, the agencies pleaded). But problems on other films, such as 1994's *When a Man Loves a Woman*, in which other composers were drafted in to add action music unrelated to Preisner's score or, arguably, Louis Mandoki's concept for the film, affirmed his conviction to only work, from that moment on, on smaller budget European productions. As it was, Preisner hardly committed fully to this compromised film: he says he composed the entire score on the plane trip back to Poland from Los Angeles. (The plane, he claims, hummed in A, hence the main key of the *When a Man Loves a Woman* score.) Other scores that got away include *Snow Falling on Cedars* and (due to his friendship with producer Dino De Laurentiis) an installment in one of Hollywood's most overstretched franchises, *Young Hannibal*.

77. See Annette Davison, *Hollywood Theory, Non-Hollywood Practice. Cinema Soundtracks in the 1980s and 1990s* (Aldershot: Ashgate, 2004), 75-116.

78. Carlsson and Holm, "The Double Life of Zbigniew Preisner," 42.

79. Carlsson and Holm, "The Double Life of Zbigniew Preisner," 40.

80. An essay by Adam Lorca published on the website *Kino Kieślowski* claims that 20 million Poles saw *Decalogue 5*'s broadcast on

TV, provoking a national debate about the death sentence that led, eventually, to the moratorium placed on the death penalty by the first post-communist Polish government, and its formal removal from the statute books by President Kwaśniewski in 1999. See Adam Lorca, "When I Look back," (2003), http://www.petey.com/kk/docs/presesay .doc (last accessed 20 October 2009).

81. Miguel Mera and David Burnand, "Introduction," in *European Film Music* (Aldershot: Ashgate, 2006), 7.

82. Richard Dyer, "Side by Side: Nino Rota, Music, and Film," in *Beyond the Soundtrack: Representing Music in Cinema*, ed. Daniel Goldmark, Lawrence Kramer, and Richard Leppert (Berkeley, CA: University of California Press, 2007), 251.

83. Dyer, "Side by Side," 253.

84. Goldmark, Kramer, and Leppert, "Introduction. Phonoplay: Recasting Film Music," in *Beyond the Soundtrack*, ed. Goldmark, Kramer, and Leppert, 6.

85. Preisner makes no mention of Polish film scores having influenced his style, although his aesthetic of restraint might be hypothesized to sit within a tradition running at least from Jan Krenz's lyrical music (and the diegetic ocarina solos) for Andrzej Wajda's *Kanal* (1957) to Paweł Mykietyn's stark and avant-garde cues for Jerzy Skolimowski's *Essential Killing* (2010). The richness and distinctiveness of Polish film scoring is only just beginning to be charted, however, for instance by Polish scholar Urszula Mieszkieło. Locating Preisner's work within (or outside of) his country's scoring practices will of necessity form part of a project exceeding the boundaries of this study.

Chapter Two

1. Lonoff may actually be a fictionalized version of Bernard Malamud. See Timothy Parish, "Introduction: Roth at Mid-Career," in *The Cambridge Companion to Philip Roth*, ed. Timothy Parish (Cambridge: Cambridge University Press, 2007), 1-8.

2. Philip Roth, *Exit Ghost* (London: Jonathan Cape, 2007), 20.

3. Richard Dyer, *Heavenly Bodies: Film Stars and Society* (London: Routledge, 2004), 5; John Ellis, "Stars as a Cinematic Phenomenon" (1982), in *Film Theory and Criticism*, 6th ed., ed. Leo Braudry and Marshall Cohen (Oxford: Oxford University Press, 2004), 598. Ellis's approach also complements Dyer's semiotic theorizing of stars as clusters of signs communicating meanings to the audio-viewer in *Stars* (London: British Film Institute, 1979).

4. Ginette Vincendeau, "Juliette Binoche: From Gamine to Femme Fatale," *Sight and Sound* 3, no. 12 (December 1993): 22.

5. Or, rather, it still did in the early 1990s; by 2010, franchises had arguably become the new stars.

6. The synergistic promotion of films through popular music is another matter.

7. Nicholas Cook, "Representing Beethoven: Romance and Sonata Form in Simon Cellan Jones's *Eroica*," in *Beyond the Soundtrack*, ed. Goldmark, Kramer, and Leppert, 36. The interaction of a sonata form with different social strata explored in the film Cook discusses for this essay makes an interesting comparison to the sonata-form-like structure of *Red* suggested in Chapter Seven.

8. See Jenefer Robinson, *Deeper than Reason: Emotion and Its Role in Literature, Music, and Art* (Oxford: Oxford University Press, 2006). For Tagg's work, see Philip Tagg, "Music, Moving Image, Semiotics and the Democratic Right to Know," article based on paper delivered at conference "Music and Manipulation," (Nalen, Stockholm, 18 September 1999), http://www.tagg.org/articles/sth99art.html (last accessed 19 April 2011); see also Philip Tagg and Bob Clarida, *Ten Little Tunes: Towards a Musicology of the Mass Media* (Montreal: The Mass Media Scholars' Press, 2003).

9. I became aware of Michael Long's conceptualizing of "expressive register" near the end of editing this book: see *Beautiful Monsters: Imagining the Classic in Musical Media* (Berkeley and Los Angeles: University of California Press, 2008). For Long, "expressive registers" are vernacular and instantly communicative musical short hands, vital to screen music's multitudinous tasks, which "contain the established landmarks of convention" (13) and evoke clouds of interlinked signs (like science fiction/Theremin, say). Those landmarks include, alongside elements like texture, timbre and gesture type, musical units akin to style topics and Philip Tagg's "musemes" (signs explored in work discussed shortly below). Chapter Six's analysis of *White* adapts theoretical notions paralleling the shifts in register Long identifies in a panoply of film and popular music; the present chapter might be thought to identify Preisner's presence, using Long's terms, as a subset of a musical register expressing "art film" which, when deployed, provides a "trigger" (158) for audiences signaling a film's adoption of an alternative political perspective to, say, mainstream Hollywood cinema.

10. The writings analyzed in this admittedly "quick and dirty" pilot sampling were online CD reviews of recent Preisner film score releases, all accessed on 20 January 2006: Gary Dalkin, *Effroyables jardins* and *The Last September*, for musicweb-international.com; Andrew Keech, *Aberdeen*, *The Beautiful Country* and *The Last September*, for musicfromthemovies.com; *The Beautiful Country* (anon.) for movieboulevard.co.uk (full website references in bibliography). I intend to perform a more extensive sampling in relation to Preisner and other composers when extending my theorizing of screen music presence in a future study; nothing I have read elsewhere about Preisner in this type of criticism, however, betrays the initial core findings of the pilot sample, although obviously they could be further enriched.

11. Patrick Juslin, "Communicating Emotion in Music Performance: A Review and a Theoretical Framework," in *Music and Emotion:*

Theory and Research, ed. Patrick Juslin and John Sloboda (Oxford: Oxford University Press, 2001), 309-40. Juslin's term "expressive cue" does not refer to the practice of scoring "film cues," although there is an obvious overlapping of the two terms' connotations deserving of a research project in its own right. In one of the experiments informing his research, Juslin asked guitarists to perform "When the Saints," keeping all pitches and durations the same but varying the music's' "expressive cues" in an attempt to express different emotions.

12. Juslin, "Communicating Emotion," 316.

13. Juslin, "Communicating Emotion," 317.

14. Juslin, "Communicating Emotion," 331, citing Robert Plutchik, *The Psychology and Biology of Emotion* (New York: HarperCollins, 1994).

15. Juslin, "Communicating Emotion," 317.

16. Juslin, "Communicating Emotion," 317.

17. Tagg, "Music, Moving Image, Semiotics."

18. Tagg, "Music, Moving Image, Semiotics."

19. Paul Coates, "Introduction," in *Lucid Dreams*, ed. Coates, 6.

20. Alicja Helman, "Women in Kieślowski's Late Films," in *Lucid Dreams*, ed. Coates, 134.

21. Carlsson and Holm, "The Double Life of Zbigniew Preisner," 39.

22. In Geoffrey Macnab and Chris Darke, "Working with Kieślowski," *Sight and Sound* 6, no. 5 (May 1996): 20.

23. Carlsson and Holm, "The Double Life of Zbigniew Preisner," 39.

24. Jon Paxman, "Preisner-Kieślowski: The Art of Synergetic Understatement in *Three Colours: Red*," in Mera and Burnand, *European Film Music*, 150.

25. Preisner ends his statement "I like it when the music is breathing . . ." with the explanation "[so] I like to use much reverb."

26. See Leonard Meyer, *Emotion and Meaning in Music* (Chicago: University of Chicago Press, 1956), 31.

27. Unsettlingly, when the cue returns a few minutes later, the shrieking violins underscore the young English reporter's noisy orgasm as Ula seeks something more mysterious than sexual gratification from their liaison.

28. Simone Weil, *The Notebooks of Simone Weil*, trans. Arthur Wills (London: Routledge, 2004), 605.

29. Simone Weil, *Intimations of Christianity among the Ancient Greeks* (London: Routledge, 1998 [1957]), 199.

30. Moments when the soundtrack is genuinely silent between phrases of a Preisner cue are few and far between. *Blue* contains examples of sound design and dialogue ceasing, but even here the music's reverb sustains sonorities between musical statements.

31. Paxman, "Preisner-Kieślowski," 156.

32. Srajan Ebaen, "Zbigniew Preisner: *Requiem for My Friend*," *soundstage.com* (May 1999), http://www.soundstage.com/music/reviews/rev126.htm (last accessed 19 April 2011).

33. Audrey Ekdahl Davidson, *Olivier Messiaen and the Tristan Myth* (London: Praeger, 2001), 16-17.

34. Tobias Wollermann, *Zur Musik in der "Drei Farben" Trilogie von Krzysztof Kieślowski* (Osnabrück: Electronic Publishing Osnabrück, 2002), 115.

35. John L. Walters, "Music beyond the Everyday," *musicology.org* (undated), http://www.musicolog.com/preisner_music.asp (last accessed 19 April 2011).

36. Russell Lack, *Twenty-Four Frames Under: A Buried History of Film Music* (London: Quartet Books, 1997), 181.

37. This, of course, is a reductive view of a leitmotif, in which alongside the name-like function, various forms of expressive and cultural cueing are always taking place.

38. Lack, *Twenty-Four Frames Under*, 89.

39. Wollermann identifies a "gypsy minor scale" in Preisner's music, which he calls characteristic of Slavic music. See, for instance, Wollermann, *Zur Musik in der "Drei Farben" Trilogie*, 96.

40. Visconti understood this well: the "Adagio" of Mahler's Symphony no. 5 saturates the climate of *Death in Venice* (1971) in a manner that parallels the city itself sinking, disease spreading, and Aschenbach dying of love, pestilence, and unrequited everything.

41. The film cuts suddenly to the pensioners in full song at the piano, contrasting their potential fate in the cold snap to their lust for life.

42. Russell and Young, *Film Music: Screencraft*, 173.

43. Carlsson and Holm, "The Double Life of Zbigniew Preisner," 39.

44. Jeff Smith has discussed the challenges posed to theories of cinematic transparency by aspects of screen scoring including uses of popular songs. See Jeff Smith, "Unheard Melodies? A Critique of Psychoanalytic Theories of Film Music," in *Post-Theory: Reconstructing Film Studies*, ed. David Bordwell and Noël Carroll (Madison: University of Wisconsin Press, 1996), 230-47.

45. Paxman, "Preisner-Kieślowski," 150.

46. Charles Eidsvik, "*Decalogues 5* and *6* and the two *Short Films*," in *Lucid Dreams*, ed. Coates, 90-91.

47. Russell and Young, *Film Music: Screencraft*, 171.

48. Russell and Young, *Film Music: Screencraft*, 162.

49. Russell and Young, *Film Music: Screencraft*, 168.

50. Carlsson and Holm, "The Double Life of Zbigniew Preisner," 41.

51. Russell and Young, *Film Music: Screencraft*, 163.

52. Russell and Young, *Film Music: Screencraft*, 163.

53. Russell and Young, *Film Music: Screencraft*, 163.

54. This may be true. Lorca quotes a 1995 article by P. Abrahamson in an Oxford student newspaper called "Kieślowski's Many Col-

ours," in which it is claimed that Oxford University Press wrote to Kieślowski demanding details of this unknown composer for a dictionary or encyclopedia they were compiling. Kieślowski is said to have written back explaining he was entirely fictional; OUP persisted, explaining that, while the director had a right to guard his sources, the truth deserved to go on the record, to which Kieślowski responded that "the score had been written by Preisner, a 19-stone self-taught musician from Kraków." After further correspondence, Kieślowski is said to have simply stopped replying. See Lorca, "When I Look back"; an online article purporting to be this original newspaper interview can be found at http://zakka.dk/euroscreenwriters/interviews/krysztof_kieslowski_520.htm (last accessed 2 May 2011).

55. Broxton and Southall, "Zbigniew Preisner in Concert."

56. Insdorf, *Double Lives, Second Chances*, 118.

57. "Van den" could have been derived from *van* (Ee)*den*.

58. Article quoted in Google Groups rec.music.movies thread "On Film Music" (30 Dec. 1994), in post authored by Ellen B. Edgerton.

59. Macnab and Darke, "Working with Kieślowski," 20.

60. Having said that, with *Blue*'s *Concert[o]* being a cornerstone in Preisner's live concerts, it may be deemed to work, for many, as *film* concert music. Irena Paulus offers a view of the sound of *Blue*'s score on CD that, ostensibly, jars against the fact that it has sold over a million copies worldwide: "An attempt to listen to Preisner's music from some recording . . . is a failure; the music is disappointingly split up and it is hard to enjoy it. Parts that, motif by motif, phrase by phrase, . . . are gradually composed into a meaningful whole [in the film] . . . listened to on their own are just incomplete fragments without point or inner beauty"; see Irena Paulus, "Music in Krzysztof Kieślowski's Film *Three Colors: Blue*. A Rhapsody in Shades of Blue: The Reflections of a Musician," *International Review of the Aesthetics and Sociology of Music* 30, no. 1 (June 1999): 88. Listening to film music in non-filmic contexts is a complex cultural and musical phenomenon, but it may be worth noting that Preisner has many hours of music that he has never permitted to be released on CD because, in his view, on their own they are unsatisfactory.

61. The IMDb threads on *Blue* are fascinating and often insightful. Another contributor counters Rooprecht with existing critical responses to the score and the awards that Preisner won, plus Kieślowski's own characterization of the final cue as sounding "solemn and grand" (his view was actually more nuanced than this, as discussed later), and dismisses the Mozart link. Someone else does hear the Mozart link and another feels that the music was "a real let down." This latter view is worth recounting in full: "A simplistic repeated note idea over-egged with 'grand' orchestration. Even a drunken beggar on the street can replicate it on a recorder without too much trouble. Clearly Patrice is an overrated composer—perhaps an allusion to the fact that the unification of Europe is an overrated concept" (barryriley-1). That idea tallies directly, as discussed below, with aspects of Kieślowski's own views on

the score, but again contributors spring to the defense of the music. TopFrog, for instance, claims the script calls for "magnificent and beautiful" music and notes descriptions of Patrice in the film as "eminent" and "the greatest"; more interestingly, TopFrog also notes (referencing the *Lucid Dreams* collection) Coates and Kieślowski's discussion of whether or not the music is ironic, and points out that "Europe did not indeed unite," paraphrasing Kieślowski's description of the music as a love song written for a wedding that is cancelled, thereby retaining its thread of sincerity in spite of everything else; he also notes Preisner, in Russell and Young, arguing that the music is intentionally simple. However, TopFrog then argues that the notion of the music as simplistic "undercuts the resolution of the story" if we see Julie's return to life as merely to compose "simplistic over-orchestrated . . . drivel that plagiarizes other composers," to which barryriley-1 dings back that he interprets her improvements to Patrice's score as significant. Rooprecht chimes in again: "I don't believe any good composer would resort to these clichés unless making a tongue in cheek joke or an ironic statement. And Preisner is indeed a good composer, as we hear in *Red*." One final audio-viewer notes that, to "us ordinary folks," simple music can indeed be wonderful, rather than ironic, and goes on to say that, if this really was a country's anthem, it would probably be the best anthem in the world (enkibilal). See "IMDb User Comments for *Trois couleurs: Bleu* (1993)," http://www.imdb.com/title/tt0108394/usercomments (last accessed 8 September 2006).

62. Paulus, "Music in Krzysztof Kieślowski's Film *Three Colors: Blue*," 73.

63. Russell and Young, *Film Music: Screencraft*, 168.

64. Extending themes from the reception of Preisner's concert pieces to his film scores is an approach taken by Andrzej Chłopecki in a caustic review of Preisner's *Requiem for My Friend*. The review transposes what Chłopecki hears as the *Requiem*'s "ineptitude" into eight different film scores, but merely on the basis of having listened to the soundtrack CDs; see Andrzej Chłopecki. "Preisner, czyli apologia kiczu," *Tygodnik Powszechny*, no. 44 (1 November 1998): 9. Whatever the merits of his concert music, Preisner's film music must be assessed *as* film music, i.e., as a contribution to an audio-visual narrative, and thus to a film's telling and selling of its stories and subtexts.

Chapter Three

1. Krzysztof Kieślowski, "The Sunday Musicians," *Positif* 400 (1994); translated in *Projections 4½* (Faber, 1995). Reproduced in *Imagining Reality: The Faber Book of Documentary*, ed. Kevin Mac-Donald and Mark Cousins (London: Faber, 1996), 312-16. Subsequent quotations in this section from these pages.

2. The full list of films and directors was as follows: *La Strada* (Fellini); *Kes* (Loach); *Un condamné a mort s'est echappé* (Bresson); *The Pram* (Widerberg); *Intimate Lighting* (Passer); *The Sunday Musicians* (Karabasz); *Ivan's Childhood* (Tarkovsky); *Les quatre cents coups* (Truffaut); *Citizen Kane* (Welles); *The Kid* (Chaplin). Insdorf notes that he replaced *The 400 Blows* with *The Loneliness of the Long Distance Runner* in other similar lists; Insdorf, *Double Lives, Second Chances*, 13. Bergman, a significant influence on Kieślowski, is absent from this list; Kieślowski considered *The Silence* to have been significant to his development. Karabasz won the Grand Prix at the Oberhausen Short Film Festival for *The Sunday Musicians*.

3. The kids are "murdering" the main theme from the Van den Budenmayer Concerto—the piece by which Véronique's Polish double, Weronika, has recently been "murdered."

4. Slavoj Žižek, *The Fright of Real Tears: Krzysztof Kieślowski between Theory and Post-Theory* (London: British Film Institute, 2001), 7.

5. The failure to be political, Haltof writes, is a failure consistently to make films in the manner "of a 'great Central European auteur' obsessed with politics and history," and thus concordant with Poland's "local romantic tradition" of figures capable of resolving massive problems with a devastating single blow; see Marek Haltof, *Polish National Cinema* (Oxford: Berghahn Books, 2002), 196. He quotes Bolesław Michałek on this canon and how it is characterized by its "battle for social justice, and its preoccupation with gaining independence, the tradition in which dilemmas are solved by a single gesture. Kieślowski indicates that a dilemma is something you live with" (197).

6. Vincent Amiel, "Kieślowski et la méfiance du visible," in *Krzysztof Kieślowski*, ed. Vincent Amiel (Paris: Jean-Michel Place, 1997), 15; translated in Kickasola, *The Films of Krzysztof Kieślowski*, 320.

7. Geoff Andrew, *The "Three Colours" Trilogy* (London: British Film Institute, 1998), 77-8.

8. Quoted in Andrew, *The "Three Colours" Trilogy*, 78.

9. Geoffrey Macnab, "*Trois couleurs: Bleu* (*Three Colours: Blue*)," *Sight and Sound* 3, no. 11 (November 1993): 54-5. Quoted in Marek Haltof, *The Cinema of Krzysztof Kieślowski: Variations on Destiny and Chance* (London: Wallflower Press, 2004), 132.

10. Tadeusz Sobolewski, "Peace and Rebellion: Some Remarks on the Creative Output of Krzysztof Kieślowski," *Bulletin de la Société des Sciences et Lettres de Łódź* XLV, *Série: Recherches sur les Arts* VI, *Polish Cinema in Ten Takes* (1995), 134.

11. Macnab and Darke, "Working with Kieślowski," 19. ("When I see a Wajda film, I see all these symbols which only a Pole could understand," he once said.)

12. Mariola Jankun-Dopartowa, "Trójkolorowy transparent: Vive le chaos!," *Kino* no. 6 (1995): 4; translated in Haltof, *The Cinema of Krzysztof Kieślowski*, 125.

13. Haltof, *The Cinema of Krzysztof Kieślowski*, 112.

14. Alex Cox, "A Sentimental Education," in "Review," *The Guardian* (7 January 2006), 14. As a letter to *The Guardian* pointed out, the film is arguably shot so beautifully because the storytelling is focalized from the perspective of Alexander, in "a child's eye fairy-tale view of the adult world"; see Fred Aiken, "Letters: Bergman in Perspective," in "Review," *The Guardian* (14 January 2006), 15.

15. Frédéric Strauss, *Conversations avec Pedro Almodóvar* (Paris: Editions de l'étoile/Cahiers du cinema, 1994), 83; translated in Wilson, *"Three Colours: Blue,"* 355.

16. Brian Henderson, "Toward a Non-Bourgeois Camera Style," (1970), in Braudy and Cohen, *Film Theory and Criticism*, 63.

17. See Jonathan Romney, *Short Orders: Film Writing* (Serpent's Tail: London, 1997), 133-4. Romney mounts interestingly conflicted arguments, including the idea that moments shorn of obvious import in the films (Weronika's face in the rain, or when "Preisner's music swells up in particularly rapturous fashion") have a marvelously sensuous impact, "giving us cinema to the hilt" and thus proving irresistible. Yet Romney is merely praising the sensual impact of that which he has already intellectually undermined. He has argued that this beauty occurs in the context of a contract between director and audience that sets the film up for a fall: one sees beauty and expects content just as profound, but what one discovers (in his view) is less than meets the eye and ear.

18. The 1956 industrial strike in Poznan saw workers demanding "bread and freedom," to test the political climate in the wake of Stalin's death. It was put down with force by the Communist authorities.

19. Julia Dobson, "Nationality, Authenticity, Reflexivity: Kieślowski's *Trois couleurs: Bleu* (1993), *Blanc* (1993), and *Rouge* (1994)," in *French Cinema in the 1990s: Continuity and Difference*, ed. Phil Powrie (Oxford: Oxford University Press, 1999), 234.

20. Homi K. Bhabha, *Nation and Narration* (London: Routledge, 1990); cited in Dobson, "Nationality, Authenticity, Reflexivity," 235.

21. Dobson, "Nationality, Authenticity, Reflexivity," 235.

22. Dobson, "Nationality, Authenticity, Reflexivity," 235.

23. Dobson, "Nationality, Authenticity, Reflexivity," 236.

24. Dobson, "Nationality, Authenticity, Reflexivity," 236.

25. Such criticisms are not entirely ungrounded. Producer Marin Karmitz, for instance, told Kieślowski to cut certain aspects of *Blue* that offered, in his view, a tourist's view of French culture, especially regarding the servants in Julie's country house. That Kieślowski took his producer's advice, however, seems to demonstrate a desire not to indulge in such stereotypes. See "Marin Karmitz Interview with Selected Scenes Commentary," DVD extra on *Blue* in *Krzysztof Kieślowski's "Three Colors": The Exclusive Collection* (Miramax 28658).

26. Dobson, "Nationality, Authenticity, Reflexivity," 237.

27. Dobson, "Nationality, Authenticity, Reflexivity," 237.

28. Coates, "Introduction," 3. In an earlier work, Coates goes so far as to ask whether Kieślowski may have been "abusing his talent" by

making a film such as *Véronique*; see Paul Coates, "Kieślowski and the Antipolitics of Color: A Reading of the *Three Colors* Trilogy," *Cinema Journal* 41, no. 2 (2002): 50; quoted in Haltof, *The Cinema of Krzysztof Kieślowski*, 121.

29. Eagleton, *The Meaning of Life*, 32.

30. Dina Iordanova, *Cinema of the Other Europe: The Industry and Artistry of East Central European Film* (London: Wallflower Press, 2003), 1.

31. István Szabó, "Preface," in *The Cinema of Central Europe*, ed. Peter Hames (London: Wallflower Press, 2004), xiii.

32. Mirosław Przylipiak, "*Dekalog*: The Decalogue: Krzysztof Kieślowski, Poland, 1989," in *The Cinema of Central Europe*, ed. Hames, 227.

33. Garbowski, *Krzysztof Kieślowski's "Decalogue" Series*; see 104-106.

34. Quoted in Zdena Škapová, "Daisies," in *The Cinema of Central Europe*, ed. Hames, 130.

35. Translation in Insdorf, *Double Lives, Second Chances*, 16.

36. Haltof, *The Cinema of Krzysztof Kieślowski*, 111.

37. Žižek, *The Fright of Real Tears*, 8.

38. Derek Malcolm, "Approaching Kieślowski's *Heaven*," *The Guardian* (6 February 2002), 18.

39. See O'Sullivan, "The *Decalogue* and the Remaking of American Television." HBO's *John from Cincinnati* (2005) offers another close parallel in recent avant-garde television drama.

40. Iordanova, *Cinema of the Other Europe*, 154.

41. Quoted in Paul Coates, "Introduction," in *Lucid Dreams*, ed. Coates, 2.

42. Tadeusz Sobolewski, "Ultimate Concerns," in *Lucid Dreams*, ed. Coates, 8.

43. Insdorf, *Double Lives, Second Chances*, 197.

44. Janina Falkowska, "Religious Themes in Polish Cinema," in *The New Polish Cinema*, ed. Janina Falkowska and Marek Haltof (Trowbridge: Flicks Books, 2003), 67.

45. Polish musical parallels to this trend include the increasing prominence of religious works on the art music scene, beginning with Penderecki's cultural-historical milestone, the *St. Luke Passion*.

46. Haltof, *The Cinema of Krzysztof Kieślowski*, 120. In fairness, Haltof notes the film's energy and breadth, its ravishing cinematography and scoring, and how they help stop the film from disappearing up its own paradox.

47. Coates, "Introduction," 3. Coates nonetheless makes it clear that he too preferred the "gritty" and more obviously political "Polish" Kieślowski to the director's glossier, pan-European persona.

48. Danusia Stok, ed. and trans., *Kieślowski on Kieślowski* (London: Faber, 1993), 195.

49. Stok, ed. and trans., *Kieślowski on Kieślowski*, 194.

50. Kickasola, *The Films of Krzysztof Kieślowski*, 74-5.

51. Sobolewski, "Peace and Rebellion," 123.

52. Andrew, The "Three Colours" Trilogy, 11.

53. Andrew, The "Three Colours" Trilogy, 27.

54. Andrew, The "Three Colours" Trilogy, 69.

55. Richard Rushton, "Reading Three Colours: Blue," Senses of Cinema (October 2000), http://archive.sensesofcinema.com/contents/00/10/blue.html (last accessed 18 April 2011), 10.

56. André Bazin, "From What Is Cinema? [1967]: The Evolution of the Language of Cinema," in Film Theory and Criticism, ed. Braudy and Cohen, 45.

57. Peter van Inwagen, Metaphysics, 2nd ed. (Cambridge, MA: Westview Press, 2002), 1.

58. Inwagen, Metaphysics, 2.

59. Inwagen, Metaphysics, 11.

60. Inwagen, Metaphysics, 12.

61. Insdorf, Double Lives, Second Chances, 184.

62. Andrew, The "Three Colours" Trilogy, 11.

63. Insdorf reports having dinner with Kieślowski during the shoots and her mother telling the director "you're killing yourself." Kieślowski responded with a weary shrug and a wave of his cigarette.

64. Andrew, The "Three Colours" Trilogy, 24.

65. Insdorf, Double Lives, Second Chances, 71, 70.

66. Haltof, The Cinema of Krzysztof Kieślowski, 109.

67. Haltof, The Cinema of Krzysztof Kieślowski, 109.

68. Haltof, The Cinema of Krzysztof Kieślowski, 109.

69. Coates, "Introduction," 7.

70. Nick James, "Kind of 'Blue,'" Sight and Sound 12, no. 4 (April 2002): 34-6. See http://www.bfi.org.uk/sightandsound/feature/59 (last accessed 18 April 2011).

71. Zanussi's input on an early cut of White, for instance, led to the film's ending being significantly altered, although, as discussed further below, the changes also arose in response to Kieślowski's reaction to Julie Delpy's evolving performance as Dominique.

72. See "A Discussion on Working with Kieślowski," DVD extra on White in Krzysztof Kieślowski's "Three Colors": The Exclusive Collection (Miramax 28656).

73. Idziak states that a two-page synopsis was devised first by Piesiewicz and Kieślowski working together, before an early discussion with a film's cinematographer. Both Karmitz and Idziak (understandably) promote their own role in developing the project.

74. Up to four drafts per film are mentioned in the literature, although this figure is dwarfed by the number of cuts of each film produced in the editing suite.

75. See "A Discussion on Working with Kieślowski."

76. Moving from East to West was not without bumps in the road. Having to break for an hour's lunch in France drove Kieślowski mad, Karmitz reports: he was used to Polish conditions, where overtime "doesn't exist." He worked the crew for 24 hours straight on the second

day (on location at Julie's hospital), exhausting the crew and creating the possibility of car accidents en route back to Paris. A frank exchange of views in Karmitz's office led to this never happening again.

77. Another example of the director taking ideas from a leading actress is the significant extension to the ending of *Decalogue 6* in *A Short Film about Love* at the suggestion of Grażnya Szapołowska.

78. Kieślowski was reluctant to have Julie smile at the end of the film and resisted the idea; Binoche argued that the sky, reflected in the window through which Julie is shot, already suggested optimism, and so he agreed to permit Julie both to cry and to smile, suggesting an opening up and, in Binoche's words, the start of Julie's liberation.

79. The finale of the film is particularly marked by this desire to, in Witta's phrase, "lean on" the music for momentum and mood to direct the cutting.

80. Russell and Young, *Film Music: Screencraft*, 168.

81. This precision makes Delpy's fluid hand gestures in the film—gradually envisaged through the film's creative process of pre-production, shooting and post-production, and after deliberations including Zanussi's response to the coldness at the end of the cut he viewed—something of a revelation. Her hands have been cruelly impersonal throughout *White* but, in the end, transform into a vision of communion and *agapē*.

82. Stok, ed. and trans., *Kieślowski on Kieślowski*, 226.

83. Falkowska, *"The Double Life of Véronique,"* 137.

84. Insdorf, *Double Lives, Second Chances*, 182.

85. Macnab and Darke, "Working with Kieślowski," 16.

86. Steven Gaydos, "Pole Vaults Past Biz Blocks," *Variety* (21-27 March 1994), 55; quoted in Insdorf, *Double Lives, Second Chances*, 153. He toyed with the idea of releasing seventeen different cuts of *Véronique*.

87. Insdorf, *Double Lives, Second Chances*, 141.

88. Insdorf, *Double Lives, Second Chances*, 73.

89. Insdorf, *Double Lives, Second Chances*, 152.

90. Mera and Burnand, "Introduction," in *European Film Music*, ed. Mera and Burnand, 9.

91. Stok, ed. and trans., *Kieślowski on Kieślowski*, 224.

92. Stok, ed. and trans., *Kieślowski on Kieślowski*, 224.

93. David Winner, "Requiem for Kieślowski," *The Tablet* (27 March 1999), http://www.thetablet.co.uk/cgi-bin/register.cgi/tablet-002 69 (last accessed 20 January 2006).

94. Preisner has given conflicting accounts of their meeting. In one interview, in which he seems to have been somewhat disengaged, he states: "We met in the usual way. He called me, and we met and he did a film called *A Film without an End* . . . That's how our relationship began. He had heard other film music that I had composed." See Carlsson and Holm, "The Double Life of Zbigniew Preisner," 39-40.

95. Broxton and Southall, "Zbigniew Preisner in Concert." The pair met via a shared acquaintance, Antoni Krauze (director of *Weather Re-*

port) at Tor Production House. Preisner's responses in this interview gloss over the doubts he suffered, as documented elsewhere in the present study, when working on *No End*.

96. Carlsson and Holm, "The Double Life of Zbigniew Preisner," 40.

97. Williams, "The Music of Friendship."

98. Russell and Young, *Film Music: Screencraft*, 163.

99. Russell and Young, *Film Music: Screencraft*, 163.

100. Russell and Young, *Film Music: Screencraft*, 163.

101. Macnab and Darke, "Working with Kieślowski," 16.

102. Winner, "Requiem for Kieślowski."

103. Stok, ed. and trans., *Kieślowski on Kieślowski*, 177.

104. See "A Discussion of Kieślowski's Later Years," DVD extra on *White* in *Krzysztof Kieślowski's "Three Colors": The Exclusive Collection* (Miramax 28656).

105. Macnab and Darke, "Working with Kieślowski," 20.

106. Macnab and Darke, "Working with Kieślowski," 20.

107. Macnab and Darke, "Working with Kieślowski," 20. For *Blue*, "The music was 90 percent composed and recorded before filming started. It was described in detail in Kieślowski's screenplay." See Russell and Young, *Film Music: Screencraft*, 168.

108. Stok, ed. and trans., *Kieślowski on Kieślowski*, 179.

109. Giorgio Biancorosso, "[Review of Janet Halfyard's] *Danny Elfman's "Batman": A Film Score Guide*," *Music and Letters* 88, no. 1 (February 2007): 189.

Chapter Four

1. Pierre Nora, trans. Arthur Goldhammer, ed. Lawrence D. Kritzman, *Realms of Memory: The Construction of the French Past. Volume III: Symbols* (New York: Columbia University Press), xi.

2. *Red* does not follow sequence and omits a view of an equivalent frieze in Geneva.

3. Coates, "Introduction," 8.

4. Mona Ozouf, "Liberty, Equality, Fraternity," in Nora, *Realms of Memory*, 77.

5. Ozouf, "Liberty, Equality, Fraternity," 77.

6. Ozouf, "Liberty, Equality, Fraternity," 114.

7. Coates, "'The Inner Life Is the Only Thing that Interests Me,'" 171.

8. Stok, ed. and trans., *Kieślowski on Kieślowski*, 143.

9. Another Polish director has made a notable foray into considerations of the French revolution, also abetted by a notable score. The release date of Andrzej Wajda's *Danton* (1983), which considers a key figure in the French Revolution, led some to claim it was "a crude allegory of Polish politics in the Solidarity/martial-law era" (despite Wa-

jda's denials that this was the case), but which (Michael Brooke has recently argued) deserves recognition for its "febrile reconstruction of the Revolution (Jean Prodromides' fantastically eerie Penderecki-meets-Ligeti score insinuates itself into every available cranny) at the point when its ideas ran the risk of being trampled." See Michael Brooke, "Danton," *Sight and Sound* 19, no. 6 (June 2009): 88.

10. Ozouf, "Liberty, Equality, Fraternity," 78.

11. Gerald C. MacCallum, "Negative and Positive Freedom," *Philosophical Review* 76, no. 3 (July 1967): 312-34.

12. Ian Carter, "Positive and Negative Liberty," in *The Stanford Encyclopedia of Philosophy*, ed. Edward N. Zalta (Fall 2008 ed.), http://plato.stanford.edu/archives/fall2008/entries/liberty-positive-negative/ (last accessed 10 June 2009).

13. Stok, ed. and trans., *Kieślowski on Kieślowski*, 212.

14. Insdorf, *Double Lives, Second Chances*, 139.

15. When younger, Elżbieta even looked like Binoche, Preisner believes. See, for instance, the photograph "Krzysztof Penderecki i Elżbieta Penderecka, Wyspa San Giorgio Maggiore, Wenecja, 1966," at http://www.krzysztofpenderecki.eu/pl/7/0/7?page=3 (last accessed 13 May 2010).

16. Stok, ed. and trans., *Kieślowski on Kieślowski*, 213.

17. Stok, ed. and trans., *Kieślowski on Kieślowski*, 214.

18. Stok, ed. and trans., *Kieślowski on Kieślowski*, 214.

19. Stok, ed. and trans., *Kieślowski on Kieślowski*, 213-15.

20. Stok, ed. and trans., *Kieślowski on Kieślowski*, 215.

21. Ozouf, "Liberty, Equality, Fraternity," 86.

22. Stok, ed. and trans., *Kieślowski on Kieślowski*, 217.

23. Stok, ed. and trans., *Kieślowski on Kieślowski*, 217.

24. Stok, ed. and trans., *Kieślowski on Kieślowski*, 217.

25. Stok, ed. and trans., *Kieślowski on Kieślowski*, 217.

26. Stok, ed. and trans., *Kieślowski on Kieślowski*, 218.

27. Stok, ed. and trans., *Kieślowski on Kieślowski*, 218.

28. Ozouf, "Liberty, Equality, Fraternity," 109.

29. Ozouf, "Liberty, Equality, Fraternity," 110.

30. Andrew, *The "Three Colours" Trilogy*, 8.

31. Raoul Girardet, "The Three Colors: Neither White Nor Red," in Nora, *Realms of Memory*, 20.

32. Coates, "'The Inner Life Is the Only Thing that Interests Me,'" 169.

33. Coates, "'The Inner Life Is the Only Thing that Interests Me,'" 170.

34. See Jonathan Kiefer, "Kieślowski's *Three Colors*," *Salon.com* (10 June 2002), http://www.salon.com/entertainment/masterpiece/2002/06/10/three_colors (last accessed 18 April 2011).

35. Coates, "'The Inner Life Is the Only Thing that Interests Me,'" 170.

36. Coates, "Introduction," 8. Coates is nonetheless tempted to try to pin things down, in his case by way of Goethe's theory of color:

"Thus, when Goethe describes red as both dignified and charming, and hence equally suitable for age and youth, it is hard not to think of *Red*, while his remarks on the manner in which blue's retreating quality invites pursuit may recall *Trois couleurs: Bleu*" (16-17, n. 20). See also Johann Wolfgang von Goethe, *Theory of Colours*, trans. Charles Lock Eastlake (London: M.I.T. Press, 1970), 310-16.

37. Kickasola, *The Films of Krzysztof Kieślowski*, 265.

38. Paulus, "Music in Krzysztof Kieślowski's Film *Three Colors: Blue*," 84.

39. The colors have a wider history in film, obviously, but that is too vast a topic to broach here.

40. For Falkowska, the use of "blue filters and gloomy interiors [in *No End*]" as well as *Blue* correspond to the general iconography of death in depictions condoned by the Catholic religion and therefore "representations of a negative and grim phenomenon"; see Falkowska, "Religious Themes in Polish Cinema," 69. Iordanova, in turn, recalls how *By Touch*, Łazarkiewicz's debut drama, features *No End*'s actress, Grażyna Szapołowska and recalls *Blue* in "the bluish tint" of key scenes "shot through a blue filter"; see Iordanova, *Cinema of the Other Europe*, 137.

41. Andrew, *"The "Three Colours" Trilogy*, 25.

42. Falkowska, *"The Double Life of Véronique*," 143.

43. From *On The Spiritual in Art*, quoted in Rudolf Arnheim, *Art and Visual Perception: A Psychology of the Creative Eye* (Berkeley: University of California Press, 1969), 332.

44. Coates, *Cinema, Religion and the Romantic Legacy*, 149.

45. Johannes Itten, *The Art of Color: The Subjective Experience and Objective Rationale of Color* (New York: Van Nostrand Reinhold, 1973), 102; quoted in Paulus, "Music in Krzysztof Kieślowski's Film *Three Colors: Blue*," 84.

46. Žižek, *The Fright of Real Tears*, 165.

47. Žižek, *The Fright of Real Tears*, 113.

48. Wilson, *"Three Colours: Blue*," 349; Julia Kristeva, "Giotto's Joy," *Desire in Language: A Semiotic Approach to Literature and Art*, trans. Leon S. Roudiez (New York: Columbia University Press, 1980), 225.

49. Insdorf, *Double Lives, Second Chances*, 154.

50. Emma Wilson, *Memory and Survival: The French Cinema of Krzysztof Kieślowski* (Oxford: Legenda, 2000), 79.

51. Richard Dyer, *White* (London: Routledge, 1997), 207-9; quoted in Wilson, *Memory and Survival*, 81.

52. Dyer, *White*, xv.

53. "Behind the Scenes of *White* with Krzysztof Kieślowski," DVD extra on *White* in *Krzysztof Kieślowski's "Three Colors": The Exclusive Collection* (Miramax 28656).

54. Kickasola, *The Films of Krzysztof Kieślowski*, 283.

55. Falkowska, *"The Double Life of Véronique*," 149, 151; Kickasola, *The Films of Krzysztof Kieślowski*, 292.

56. Andrew, *The "Three Colours" Trilogy*, 50.
57. Andrew, *The "Three Colours" Trilogy*, 50.
58. Andrew, *The "Three Colours" Trilogy*, 51.
59. Falkowska, *"The Double Life of Véronique,"* 151.
60. Kehr, "To Save the World," 16.
61. Paxman, "Preisner-Kieślowski," 155.
62. Paxman, "Preisner-Kieślowski," 155.
63. Miramax Press Kit quoted in Insdorf, *Double Lives, Second Chances*, 173.
64. Insdorf, *Double Lives, Second Chances*, 173.
65. Andrew, *The "Three Colours" Trilogy*, 66.
66. Kickasola, *The Films of Krzysztof Kieślowski*, 84.
67. See Raymond Monelle, *The Sense of Music* (Princeton, NJ: Princeton University Press, 2000), 17-19.
68. Insdorf, *Double Lives, Second Chances*, 172.
69. Andrew, *The "Three Colours" Trilogy*, 21.
70. Tony Rayns, "Glowing in the Dark," *Sight and Sound* 4, no. 6 (1994), 10.
71. Kickasola, *The Films of Krzysztof Kieślowski*, 263.
72. Kickasola, *The Films of Krzysztof Kieślowski*, 67-68.
73. Kickasola, *The Films of Krzysztof Kieślowski*, 298.
74. Žižek, *The Fright of Real Tears*, 155-6.
75. And yet ambivalence remains everywhere in these films. The yacht lost at sea at the end of *Red*, killing the unfaithful weather reporter Karin and her lover, suggests that the trilogy's God retains something of a split personality, with occasionally relapses into smiting.
76. Žižek, *The Fright of Real Tears*, 116.
77. Kehr, "To Save the World," 13.
78. Andrew, *The "Three Colours" Trilogy*, 23-4.
79. Andrew, *The "Three Colours" Trilogy*, 51.
80. Joseph Kerman, *Concerto Conversations* (Cambridge, MA: Harvard University Press, 1999), 47.
81. The top ten as voted by critics in 2002: *Citizen Kane* (Welles), *Vertigo* (Hitchcock), *La règle du jeu* (Renoir), *The Godfather* and *The Godfather Part II* (Coppola), *Tokyo Story* (Ozu), *2001: A Space Odyssey* (Kubrick), *Battleship Potemkin* (Eisenstein), *Sunrise* (Murnau), and in joint ninth *8 1/2* (Fellini) and *Singin' in the Rain* (Kelly, Donen). The full list of critic voting reveals that Kieślowski himself received no votes at all. See http://www.bfi.org.uk/sightandsound/topten/poll/critics.html and http://www.bfi.org.uk/sightandsound/topten/poll/critics-long.html (last accessed 23 April 2010).
82. A recent newspaper article entitled "The Worst Best Films Ever Made," for instance, "outed" *Red* and other "classics" as a film many claim to be great, but which, author Tim Lott implied, leave many more "cold, bored and searching desperately for the eject button" because "nothing happens." See Tim Lott, "The Best Worst Films Ever Made," *The Guardian* (24 July 2009), http://www.guardian.co.uk/film/2009/jul/24/worst-best-films-ever-made (last accessed 26 April 2011).

83. James, "Kind of 'Blue,'" 36.

84. Andrew, *The "Three Colours" Trilogy*, 37.

85. Kehr, "To Save the World," 15, 17.

86. Insdorf, *Double Lives, Second Chances*, 140.

87. Kickasola, *The Films of Krzysztof Kieślowski*, 264.

88. Kickasola's published work on Kieślowski has included some useful insights into sound and music, and he has also given unpublished conference papers investigating sound in the director's output.

89. Insdorf, *Double Lives, Second Chances*, 140-41.

90. Insdorf, *Double Lives, Second Chances*, 140.

91. Insdorf, *Double Lives, Second Chances*, 148.

92. Andrew, *The "Three Colours" Trilogy*, 28. Mistakes like this, though, are not universal: Kickasola correctly identifies the return of the music from the funeral in the same scene. Such errors raise questions about the perception of thematic (let alone leitmotivic) scoring practices in film scores. After all, if experts on Kieślowski who have audioviewed these films many dozens of times do not hear the differences between *Blue*'s funeral march and the *Concert[o]*'s main theme, what does that suggest about the pertinence of such musical signifiers, let alone subtle nuances of motivic development, in these and other films?

93. Whether or not one deems such an interpretation a "mishearing" is a matter of personal judgment, and my term should not be taken here as suggesting that Wilson's readings are less valuable than others. On the contrary, as already indicated, they are among the richest in Kieślowski scholarship.

94. Wilson, *Memory and Survival*, 3.

95. Wilson, *Memory and Survival*, xvi.

96. Wilson, *Memory and Survival*, 37.

97. In a forgivable lapse (in the context of an astonishingly wide-ranging study), Mervyn Cooke states that image *and* music both abruptly cease in the blackouts, with the score returning only when image comes back. See Mervyn Cooke, *A History of Film Music* (Cambridge: Cambridge University Press, 2008), 341.

98. See, for instance, Philip Drake's discussion of music, film, and memory, "'Mortgaged to Music': New Retro Movies in 1990s Hollywood Cinema," in *Memory and Popular Film*, ed. Paul Grainge (Manchester: Manchester University Press, 2003): 183-201. Preisner's views are explored below.

99. The term "sonic" is from Philip Brophy, "How Sound Floats on Land: The Suppression and Release of Folk and Indigenous Musics in the Cinematic Terrain," in *Beyond the Soundtrack*, ed. Goldmark, Kramer, and Leppert, 136-48.

100. Martin Iddon hit upon this striking description of *Blue* in a late-night conference bar conversation with me in July 2009.

101. Kehr, "To Save the World," 15.

102. Kehr, "To Save the World," 15.

103. See O'Sullivan, "The *Decalogue*," 205-6.

104. Coates, "'The Inner Life Is the Only Thing that Interests Me,'" 173.

105. Mark Asch, "Cinephile's Notebook: Three Colors," *thelmagazine.com* (12 April 2006), http://www.thelmagazine.com/newyork/cinephiles-notebook-three-colors/Content?oid=1136060 (last accessed 18 April 2011).

106. John Orr, *Contemporary Cinema* (Edinburgh: Edinburgh University Press, 1998), 65.

107. Sobolewski, "Peace and Rebellion," 135.

108. If, that is, one can make a mistake about the name or dates of a fictional composer when those same dates were a subject of games with the "truth" played by his creators!

109. Žižek, *The Fright of Real Tears*, 177.

110. Žižek, *The Fright of Real Tears*, 177.

111. Preisner told me he admires this symphony a good deal.

112. For the more than a million listeners who have purchased the soundtrack to *Blue* on CD, it could nevertheless be the case that such music, by utilizing the codes of film and "semi-classical" scoring in a style that symbolizes high-mindedness and serious intent, yet without becoming too sophisticated as musical discourse for most listeners, serves its primary that audience well.

113. As Kehr notes, "Julie lives an improbably chic life for the widow of a contemporary composer of serious music"—a career not renowned for the size of its pay packets. See Kehr, "To Save the World," 16.

114. Andrew, *The "Three Colours" Trilogy*, 88, n. 10.

115. Coates, "'The Inner Life Is the Only Thing that Interests Me,'" 173.

116. Coates, "'The Inner Life Is the Only Thing that Interests Me,'" 174.

117. The Yugoslavian connection lends the funeral march after the piece's climax an additional poignancy, coming after the grand words and musical rhetoric have run dry.

118. Most critics get this slightly, if not very, wrong, blithely cutting and pasting the entirety of the text into their work or copying the subtitles (where the latter are available). Paulus makes the most committed effort, but even though she successfully brackets off some segments not actually heard in the *Concert[o]*, she omits to note the editing within the verses or the repetition of some phrases.

119. This version of the text is a compilation of other versions that can be found at http://net.bible.org/verse.php?book=1Coandchapter=13andverse=1 with *agapē* substituted for the word "love" (last accessed 14 October 2009).

120. Carla Barringer Rabinowitz, "St. Paul, Kieślowski, and the Christian Framework of *Trois couleurs*," http://www.petey.com/kk/docs/kiesdis3.txt (last accessed 6 October 2010).

121. Andrew, *The "Three Colours" Trilogy*, n. 16, 89.

122. Falkowska cites a Reverend Paprocki's reading of Julie's sudden transformation from "a selfish, egoistic introvert into a generous, kind human being" as enlightened through Christian spirituality: "Art shatters the negative intellectual paradigm in which she is locked and calls into question her cloistered world-view"; see Falkowska, "Religious Themes in Polish Cinema," 72. For Helman, who goes further, the musical interruptions and ellipses "may symbolize the voice of God speaking from a whirlwind" and inspiring the musical work that "translates [Julie and the other characters] to another plane, for 'love faileth never' and is the greatest of all things"; see Helman, "Women in Kieślowski's Late Films," 132-33. James seeks signs of suppressed Catholicism elsewhere in *Blue*, hinting that Julie's "renouncing worldly things" may have been undertaken "in order to be closer to the spiritual"; see James, "Kind of 'Blue,'" 35. And many critics, including Kehr, have linked *Blue*'s ending to a continuum of Christian symbols running from Julie through the resurrected Karol of *White* to the God-like Judge—the meta-director of the trilogy, or even life itself—in *Red*; see Kehr, "To Save the World."

123. Coates, "Introduction," 3.

124. Aspects of Preisner's setting further emphasize the desirability of putting aside prophecies, as discussed below.

125. James, "Kind of 'Blue,'" 36. This is an insightful observation: *this* funeral music is much more than mere memory, but is rather a transformation of music from the previous scene, as analyzed in Chapter Five.

126. See Kelly Gross, "Female Subjectivity, Disability, and Musical Authorship in Krzysztof Kieślowski's *Blue*," in *Sounding Off: Theorizing Disability in Music*, ed. Neil Lerner and Joseph N. Straus (New York: Routledge, 2006), 41-56. Julie notates in *Blue* ink; her musical hand is neat and tidy, and not as ostentatious of her slightly more flourishing handwriting. The tail of her treble clef is flat, as is Patrice's. Other than that, the hands are clearly meant to look as if they come from different people. Olivier's, similarly, as viewed when one sees his opening to his version of the *Concert[o]*, is different again; here the musical notation is similar to Julie's, but the handwriting is rather different. The simplest explanation for all these overlaps is that a single copyist created all of the scores from Preisner's original cue sheets. And according to the composer, that was indeed the case: given the size of Preisner's own musical handwriting, which was small and unsuited to filming, the filmmakers hired a copyist in Paris with, Preisner insisted, a suitably ostentatious hand, to make the different scores seen in the films. The stylistic overlaps might actually be read as rather neat. If these people had worked so closely together in the past, why wouldn't they have inherited certain traits of notational handwriting from one another? Moreover, in a film about the shift from sole authorship to a community of scores, such similarities may speak to wider concerns.

127. Roger Hickman, *Reel Music: Exploring 100 Years of Film Music* (New York: W. W. Norton and Co., 2006), 411.

128. Paulus, "Music in Krzysztof Kieślowski's Film *Three Colors: Blue*," 70.

129. Kehr, "To Save the World," 15-16.

130. Stok, ed. and trans., *Kieślowski on Kieślowski*, 224.

131. "A Look at Blue," DVD extra on *Blue* in *Krzysztof Kieślowski's "Three Colors": The Exclusive Collection* (Miramax 28658).

132. Preisner titled the cue "Song for the Unification of Europe" in *Blue*'s manuscript score, the name by which the music is now known when performed in concerts of his music. The title suggests the composer's roots in Polish cabaret and the origins of the idea for the setting.

133. William Weber, "Concert (ii)," in *Grove Music Online. Oxford Music Online*, http://www.oxfordmusiconline.com/subscriber/article/grove/music/06240 (last accessed 26 April 2011).

134. Long, *Beautiful Monsters*, 198. Long argues that this is because of the "ch" (as in "chair") sound in the middle of the word, which differs from the "c" in "concert."

135. Long, *Beautiful Monsters*, 204.

136. Long, *Beautiful Monsters*, 204. Long's prime analytical example here is The Toys' "A Lover's Concerto" (Sandy Linzer and Denny Randell, recorded by The Toys in 1965).

137. Long, *Beautiful Monsters*, 34.

138. Philip V. Bohlman, *World Music: A Very Short Introduction* (Oxford: Oxford University Press, 2002), 109.

139. Bohlman, *World Music*, 109.

140. Benedict Anderson, *Imagined Communities: Reflections on the Origin and Spread of Nationalism* (London: Verso, 1991), 145. *Feels* is the operative word here, suggesting a degree of ambivalence reflecting, for instance, the complexity of Julie's final situation in *Blue*.

141. Bohlman, *World Music*, 94.

142. Bohlman, *World Music*, 109.

143. Roger Hillman, "Cultural Memory on Film Soundtracks," *Journal of European Film Studies* 33, no. 3/4 (2003): 325. Further references from this page.

144. Hillman, "Cultural Memory on Film Soundtracks," 325.

145. Nicholas Cook, *Beethoven: Symphony no. 9* (Cambridge: Cambridge University Press, 1993), ix.

146. Quoted in Cook, *Beethoven*, vii.

147. See Cook, *Beethoven*, 104-5.

148. More speculatively (not least because Preisner himself disavows any such connection) one might note certain parallels between passages in the Beethoven and moments in the Preisner. Bars 269-74 of the Beethoven, for instance, in which two of Beethoven's vocal lines follow each other at the interval of the minor sixth, contains a voicing which Preisner's setting parallels at the start of the *Concert[o]*. The Preisner also sounds close to the first vocal harmonization of melody in the Beethoven, which occurs on the following words (with intimations, perhaps, of *agapē*-like fraternity):

Thy magic power re-unites
All that custom has divided,
All men become brothers
Under the sway of thy gentle wings.

Whoever has created
An abiding friendship,
Or has won
A true and loving wife,
All who can call at least one soul theirs,
Join in our song of praise;
But any who cannot must creep tearfully
Away from our circle.

149. John C. Tibbetts, *Composers in the Movies* (New Haven, CT: Yale University Press, 2005), 4.

150. John Patterson, "On Film," in "Film and Music," *The Guardian* (25 November 2005), 2.

151. Gross, "Female Subjectivity, Disability, and Musical Authorship" (2006), 52; her work here cites David Mitchell and Sharon Snyder, *Narrative Prosthesis: Disability and the Dependencies of Discourse* (Ann Arbor: University of Michigan Press, 2000).

152. Neil Lerner and Joseph N. Straus, *Sounding Off: Theorizing Disability in Music* (New York: Routledge, 2006), 4.

153. Claudia Gorbman, *Unheard Melodies: Narrative Film Music* (Bloomington: Indiana University Press, 1987), 151.

154. Gorbman, *Unheard Melodies*, 151.

155. Gorbman, *Unheard Melodies*, 152.

156. Gorbman, *Unheard Melodies*, 152.

157. Nicholas Cook, *Analyzing Musical Multimedia* (Oxford: Oxford University Press, 1998), 213.

158. Cook, *Analyzing Musical Multimedia*, 254.

159. Annette Davison, *Hollywood Theory, Non-Hollywood Practice. Cinema Soundtracks in the 1980s and 1990s* (Aldershot: Ashgate, 2004), 75-116.

160. For a discussion of Godard's classification of his films as not political but as films made politically—which relates to the lack of conformance Cook identifies (amongst other aspects of his distinctive technique)—see the Davison referred to in n. 158 above.

161. Julie Brown, "Listening to Ravel, Watching *Un coeur en hiver*: Cinematic Subjectivity and the Music-film," *Twentieth-Century Music* 1, no. 2 (2004): 253.

162. Royal S. Brown, *Overtones and Undertones: Reading Film Music* (Berkeley: University of California Press, 1994), 240; also quoted in Julie Brown, "Listening to Ravel," 271.

163. Robynn Stilwell, "Symbol, Narrative and the Musics of *Truly, Madly, Deeply*," in *Screen* 38, no. 1 (Spring 1997), 60.

164. Stilwell, "Symbol, Narrative and the Musics of *Truly, Madly, Deeply*," 60.

165. Stilwell, "Symbol, Narrative and the Musics of *Truly, Madly, Deeply*," 60.

166. Stilwell, "Symbol, Narrative and the Musics of *Truly, Madly, Deeply*," 62.

167. A stereotypical Western cultural representation of the grieving female (discussed further in Chapter Five), Nina is portrayed as being desperately in need of some kind of distraction from her loss.

168. Stilwell also writes extensively on Barrington Pheloung's score and its role in helping Nina slide between phases of her grief, accompanying her throughout her journey like another angel.

169. Stilwell notes another film of the early 1990s with which *Truly* and *Blue* both share superficial similarities: Jerry Tucker's *Ghost* (1990). *Truly* has been called, rather deceptively Stilwell suggests, "the thinking person's *Ghost*" (which perhaps makes *Blue* the critical-thinking person's *Ghost*!). However, Stilwell dismisses the dead lover's musically accompanied return in *Ghost* as "merely a plot twist," while *Truly* "is a film about the impact of death upon life"; see Stilwell, "Symbol, Narrative and the Musics of *Truly, Madly, Deeply*," 63. *Ghost*, while hardly a music-film, makes prominent use of popular music (The Righteous Brothers performing "Unchained Melody") in the much satirized scene where the bereaved female protagonist (played by Demi Moore) is suddenly aided at her potter's wheel by the hands of her dead lover (Patrick Swayze), thereby echoing an earlier scene marked by that song. One might seek to dismiss the film's brief musical focus on the grounds that the track became, synergistically, a hit single (again) on the back of the film; then again, *Blue*'s soundtrack has sold more than a million copies. It may thus be more pertinent to note that three separate filmmaking teams produced, in the space of just four years, three versions of a similar tale: one pitched at the international multiplex, another at middle-class British audiences, the other at denizens of the European arthouse. Such tailoring may suggest a degree of Adornian pseudo-individualization afoot. However, given music's centrality to human rituals of grieving, it is predictable that it should also be central to clusters of cultural texts constructing, as much as reflecting, the ways humans grieve—especially, perhaps, as traditional modes of expression came under question in more secular times.

170. Due to space limitations, such a discussion cannot be included here. Cues, scenes and issues relevant to such an investigation, however, are discussed elsewhere in this study, and readers seeking indications of the roles performed by Preisner's scores in his other Kiéslowski collaborations might, after reading the following summary, find it useful to search the index for passages relating to those films.

171. Tadeusz Lubelski, "From *Personnel* to *No End*: Kieślowski's Political Feature Films," in *Lucid Dreams*, ed. Coates, 61, 60.

172. Kickasola, *The Films of Krzysztof Kieślowski*, 108.

173. Haltof, *The Cinema of Krzysztof Kieślowski*, 135.

174. Haltof, *The Cinema of Krzysztof Kieślowski*, 135.

175. Haltof, *The Cinema of Krzysztof Kieślowski*, 135.

176. Haltof, *The Cinema of Krzysztof Kieślowski*, 136.

177. Coates, "Introduction," 3.

178. Andrew, *The "Three Colours" Trilogy*, 85. Falkowska echoes this view: "The new, glittering Warsaw Airport contrasted with a rubbish heap at the city outskirts properly symbolises the atmosphere of social and political chaos in Poland. The country which openly turned to capitalism after 1989 is the country of cynicism, betrayal, failure and disillusionment. Only in this political and social atmosphere of moral disintegration could an ingenious plan to lure Dominique to Poland be fabricated and implemented"; see Falkowska, *"The Double Life of Véronique,"* 152.

179. Andrew, *The "Three Colours" Trilogy*, 51.

180. Insdorf, *Double Lives, Second Chances*, 153.

181. Wollermann, *Zur Musik in der "Drei Farben" Trilogie*, 76-77.

182. "Behind the Scenes of *White*," DVD extra on *White* in *Krzysztof Kieślowski's "Three Colors": The Exclusive Collection* (Miramax 28656).

183. Coates calls *White* the second panel of a "diptych on brotherhood" begun in *Decalogue 10*; see Paul Coates, "The Curse of the Law: The Decalogue," in *Lucid Dreams*, ed. Coates, 112. One might consider the continuation of actors also to highlight a return to the social and economic themes addressed in that film: greed and self-centered attainment achieved at the expense of communal or familial needs. It may also be significant that *10* is Kieślowski's only other obvious comedy genre-piece, as if *White* returns to *10*'s story, style and subtext, but seeks ways of doing this better, under newly pressing circumstances.

184. Andrew, *The "Three Colours" Trilogy*, 74-5.

185. Andrew, *The "Three Colours" Trilogy*, 49-50.

186. Andrew, *The "Three Colours" Trilogy*, 50.

187. After all, she could shop Karol to the authorities, knowing him to be alive, but does not.

188. Andrew, *The "Three Colours" Trilogy*, 38.

189. Agnieszka Holland recalls visiting a far-flung barrack of Polish legionnaires; their favorite and most-watched Polish film was *White*, a fact Kieślowski adored. See "A Look at *Blanc*," DVD extra on *White* in *Krzysztof Kieślowski's "Three Colors": The Exclusive Collection* (Miramax 28656).

190. Kickasola, *The Films of Krzysztof Kieślowski*, 242. On genre, Žižek makes the interesting suggestion that *White* might be imagined a distant cousin of Stanley Cavell's Hollywood subgenre "comedies of remarriage," in which "only the second marriage is the authentic symbolic act"; see Žižek, *The Fright of Real Tears*, 163.

191. It is also striking, in this regard, that so little attention has been paid in *White* to the sound design and music's contribution to the storytelling. Kickasola argues, for instance, that there are less formalist

moments in the film because the story is not about transcendence, yet there are several points at which realism cedes to a style that is far more nuanced, often primarily because of subtle audio content in the mix.

192. Haltof, *The Cinema of Krzysztof Kieślowski*, 107.

193. Andrew, *The "Three Colours" Trilogy*, 38.

194. Kehr, "To Save the World," 17.

195. Stok, ed. and trans., *Kieślowski on Kieślowski*, 174.

196. "A Look at *Blanc*."

197. "In a world ordered by sexual imbalance, pleasure in looking has been split between active/male and passive/female," visual perspective (regardless of the sex of the viewer) has been "masculinized," and not only sexual objectification but sadistic attitudes towards women can reign because "[s]adism demands a story, depends on making something happen, forcing a change in another person, a battle of will and strength, victory/defeat"; see Laura Mulvey, "Visual Pleasure and Narrative Cinema," *Screen* 16, no. 3 (Autumn 1975): 10, 65. The question in *White* regarding sadism is thus the identity of the bearer of that power: Is it Dominique, Karol, or something else shaping the patriarchal society in which they exist controlling them both sadistically?

198. Alicja Helman, "Women in Kieślowski's Late Films," in *Lucid Dreams*, ed. Coates, 124.

199. Helman, "Women in Kieślowski's late films," 125.

200. Helman, "Women in Kieślowski's late films," 124.

201. Helman, "Women in Kieślowski's late films," 125. The film is less objectifying than the screenplay suggests it might have been. The more obviously objectionable shots (Dominique's stocking tops and bare thighs glimpsed in the court; exposing her breasts as she makes love to Karol in the salon; buttock-level shots as her skirt falls to the floor in the hotel room) were cut entirely following discussions with Delpy, in a mirror of similar adjustments made to *Blue* in response to Binoche's concerns. The subtler Dominique emerging from Delpy's performance and input led, in turn, to Kieślowski's decision to create a new ending for the film. Notably, there is nothing in *White*, *Blue* or *Red* to match the camera's leering gaze at Irène Jacob in *Véronique*.

202. Žižek, *The Fright of Real Tears*, 157.

203. Helman, "Women in Kieślowski's Late Films," 125.

204. Helman does not note that Dominique's name is close to the French verb *dominer*, to dominate, and that this is what she could be read to exist just to have happen to her, but it would fit her view of the film.

205. Helman, "Women in Kieślowski's Late Films," 119.

206. Helman, "Women in Kieślowski's Late Films," 119.

207. Helman, "Women in Kieślowski's Late Films," 120. A female friend, on learning I was writing about Kieślowski and *White*, literally spat his name back at me—"That sexist bigot!"—and cursed me by association. Where, however, might the views of an equally empowered female friend—who commented to me on Dominique: "What a woman!"—fit into a feminist perspective on the film?

208. His mother, for instance, was earning for the family much of the time during his father's many spells of illness. In turn, his working relationships with female "co-workers" (Holland, Szapolowska, Binoche, etc.) suggest a great respect for women who often had a profound influence on the outcome of his projects.

209. Žižek, *The Fright of Real Tears*, 157.

210. Žižek, *The Fright of Real Tears*, 157.

211. Žižek, *The Fright of Real Tears*, 158.

212. Žižek, *The Fright of Real Tears*, 177.

213. Kickasola, *The Films of Krzysztof Kieślowski*, 292.

214. Coates, "Introduction," 6.

215. Wilson, *Memory and Survival*, 74.

216. Quoted and translated in Haltof, *The Cinema of Krzysztof Kieślowski*, 133.

217. Quoted in Insdorf, *Double Lives, Second Chances*, 159.

218. Haltof, *The Cinema of Krzysztof Kieślowski*, 62.

219. Haltof, *The Cinema of Krzysztof Kieślowski*, 138.

220. Haltof, *The Cinema of Krzysztof Kieślowski*, 138.

221. Falkowska, "*The Double Life of Véronique*," 147.

222. Kickasola, *The Films of Krzysztof Kieślowski*, 280.

223. Kickasola, *The Films of Krzysztof Kieślowski*, 281.

224. Kickasola, *The Films of Krzysztof Kieślowski*, 286.

225. "Behind the Scenes of *White*," DVD extra on *White* in *Krzysztof Kieślowski's "Three Colors": The Exclusive Collection* (Miramax 28656).

226. Kickasola, *The Films of Krzysztof Kieślowski*, 290.

227. Kickasola, *The Films of Krzysztof Kieślowski*, 291.

228. Quoted and translated in Insdorf, *Double Lives, Second Chances*, 121.

229. Insdorf, *Double Lives, Second Chances*, 160.

230. Andrew, *The "Three Colours" Trilogy*, 43.

231. Andrew, *The "Three Colours" Trilogy*, 45.

232. "To ostatnia niedziela," 1935, music by Jerzy Petersburski, lyrics by Zenon Friedwald, and most famously performed by Mieczyslaw Fogg.

233. Stok, ed. and trans., *Kieślowski on Kieślowski*, 225.

234. Wollermann, *Zur Musik in der "Drei Farben" Trilogie*, 92, n. 103.

235. Karol's name (as Preisner's then assistant, Agata Kukułka, noted during one of my conversations with the composer) is virtually an anagram of the Polish abbreviation, *klar.*, for clarinet.

236. Carlsson and Holm, "The Double Life of Zbigniew Preisner," 41.

237. Russell and Young, *Film Music: Screencraft*, 168.

238. Russell and Young, *Film Music: Screencraft*, 168.

239. Haltof, *The Cinema of Krzysztof Kieślowski*, 133.

240. Haltof, *The Cinema of Krzysztof Kieślowski*, 134.

241. Haltof, *The Cinema of Krzysztof Kieślowski*, 139.

242. Insdorf, *Double Lives, Second Chances*, 156.

243. Falkowska, "*The Double Life of Véronique*," 151.

244. Insdorf, *Double Lives, Second Chances*, 156.

245. Russell and Young, *Film Music: Screencraft*, 168. Nostalgia for "home" when in Paris was, of course, integral to the mood and content of some of Chopin's compositions.

246. Falkowska, "*The Double Life of Véronique*," 151.

247. Haltof, *The Cinema of Krzysztof Kieślowski*, 139.

248. Perhaps the organ versions of the Van den Budenmayer funeral marches on the *Blue* soundtrack CD were intended for *White*.

249. In the screenplay, Karol comments pseudo-knowledgeably on the music's beauty, as if to suggest that his tastes and thus cultural capital are now aligned with his newfound wealth.

250. Goldmark, Kramer, and Leppert, "Introduction. Phonoplay: Recasting Film Music," 6.

251. Goldmark, Kramer, and Leppert, "Introduction. Phonoplay," 6.

252. Kickasola, *The Films of Krzysztof Kieślowski*, 289.

253. "Jacques Witta Interview/Commentary," DVD extra on *Red* in *Krzysztof Kieślowski's "Three Colors": The Exclusive Collection* (Miramax 28655).

254. An irony of the "scandal" is that *Pulp Fiction* mirrors some of *Red*'s main themes: it pivots, for example, on moments of self-sacrifice. It is unfashionable to suggest that the right film won at Cannes that year, but perhaps *Pulp Fiction* communicated similar ideas to *Red* in a style more accessible to audiences than *Red*'s more sophisticated art house vernacular. Consider, for instance, Butch's actions to rescue Marcellus, which parallel Valentine's assistance of Rita the dog in ways stretching beyond the similar roles of cars and red lights in both films.

255. Insdorf, *Double Lives, Second Chances*, 181.

256. "Marin Karmitz Interview/Commentary." *Red* received Academy Award nominations for director, original screenplay, and cinematography, although it was entered not as a foreign film but in the main competition, thanks to a campaign by filmmakers spurred by its inadmissibility for best foreign film as an international co-production.

257. Insdorf, *Double Lives, Second Chances*, 181-2.

258. Insdorf, *Double Lives, Second Chances*, 141.

259. Insdorf, *Double Lives, Second Chances*, 242.

260. Insdorf, *Double Lives, Second Chances*, 153.

261. Quoted in Insdorf, *Double Lives, Second Chances*, 175.

262. Insdorf, *Double Lives, Second Chances*, 218, n. 6.

263. Kickasola, *The Films of Krzysztof Kieślowski*, 296.

264. Haltof stresses the manner in which "the 'what-if' structure of several of his earlier films is cleverly retold in *Red*, which offers a game of associations, a story of chance encounters, double chances, mystifying coincidences and destiny"; see Haltof, *The Cinema of Krzysztof Kieślowski*, 141.

265. "[N]o wonder they never meet," Žižek wryly adds; see Žižek, *The Fright of Real Tears*, 82.

266. Žižek, *The Fright of Real Tears*, 151.

267. Quoted in Insdorf, *Double Lives, Second Chances*, 178.

268. Žižek, *The Fright of Real Tears*, 73.

269. Quoted in Insdorf, *Double Lives, Second Chances*, 180.

270. From a conversation in *Krzysztof Kieślowski*, ed. Amiel, 160; quoted and translated in Insdorf, *Double Lives, Second Chances*, 180.

271. Andrew, *The "Three Colours" Trilogy*, 55.

272. Kehr, "To Save the World," 18.

273. The character was called Valentine because that was Jacob's favorite name when she was a child; see "A Conversation with Irène Jacob on Kieślowski," DVD extra on *Red* in *Krzysztof Kieślowski's "Three Colors": The Exclusive Collection* (Miramax 28655). Kieślowski wanted a name to form a conduit back to the unsullied innocence of a child's world to evoke the essence of Valentine's faith in humankind.

274. Kickasola, *The Films of Krzysztof Kieślowski*, 306.

275. Andrew reports coming out of *Red*'s premiere at Cannes shaking and speechless; see "Insights into *Trois couleurs—Rouge*," DVD extra on *Red* in *Krzysztof Kieślowski's "Three Colors": The Exclusive Collection* (Miramax 28655).

276. Kickasola, *The Films of Krzysztof Kieślowski*, 298.

277. Kehr, "To Save the World," 18.

278. Kehr, "To Save the World," 17. *Intolerance* is also, of course, a film about love.

279. Kickasola, *The Films of Krzysztof Kieślowski*, 65.

280. See Michel Chion, *Audio-Vision: Sound on Screen*, ed. and trans. Claudia Gorbman (New York: Columbia University Press, 1994 [1990]), 25-34.

281. Kickasola, *The Films of Krzysztof Kieślowski*, 88.

282. Michel Chion, "Mute Music: Polański's *The Pianist* and Campion's *The Piano*," in *Beyond the Soundtrack*, ed. Goldmark, Kramer, and Leppert, 86-96. In an original presentation of this paper, Chion apparently discussed *Blue*. Unfortunately, I have been unable to obtain a copy of this version of the paper.

283. Clearly, one might argue that this is always the case with *all* film music: quick-fire and mandatory emotional and (virtually mandatory) culturally conditioned responses occur before other, elective and more considered cognitions can take place in their wake.

284. A line from Seamus Heaney's poem "The Harvest Bow," published in the *Times Literary Supplement* (28 May 1976) and then "collected with revisions" in his *Field Work* (London: Faber, 1979).

285. Kickasola, *The Films of Krzysztof Kieślowski*, 85.

286. Kickasola, *The Films of Krzysztof Kieślowski*, 78. Kickasola stresses that "the abstract image is not the sole cause of the transcendent effect" and that "background plot, the concurrent and surrounding dialogue, the music, and the sound design all contribute to the experience"

(86); he also offers interesting thoughts on sound which hint at further parallels between the effects noted above and Preisner's music.

287. Andrew, *The "Three Colours" Trilogy*, 65.

288. Kickasola, *The Films of Krzysztof Kieślowski*, 86.

289. Kickasola, *The Films of Krzysztof Kieślowski*, 86.

290. Chion, *Audio-Vision*, 123-4.

291. Kickasola, *The Films of Krzysztof Kieślowski*, 87.

292. Robynn J. Stilwell, "The Fantastical Gap between Diegetic and Nondiegetic," in *Beyond the Soundtrack*, ed. Goldmark, Kramer, and Leppert, 184-202. Relevant ideas from Stilwell's essay are discussed further in Chapter Five's analysis of *Blue*.

293. "Krzysztof Kieślowski's Cinema Lesson," DVD extra on *Red* in *Krzysztof Kieślowski's "Three Colors": The Exclusive Collection* (Miramax 28655).

294. John Irving, for instance, often writes the final chapter of his densely plotted novels first. This permits his closing revelations to link back in a causal chain, revealed at the last to the reader, linking all manner of major or once seemingly incidental moments earlier on in a discourse. In *A Prayer for Owen Meany* (London: Bloomsbury, 1989), for instance, the protagonist's unique stature and vocal qualities, and a particular basketball move, turn out to have a vital role to play in the novel's ending—an ending that is partly so affecting because of the combined effect of its plotting and story of literal self-sacrifice.

295. Stephen Pizzello, "Piotr Sobociński: *Red*," *American Cinematographer* 76, no. 6 (1995): 71-2; quoted in Haltof, *The Cinema of Krzysztof Kieślowski*, 144-5.

296. Insdorf, *Double Lives, Second Chances*, 171.

297. Andrew, *The "Three Colours" Trilogy*, 65. He also notes the interference on the car radio and wonders if it is caused by the Judge, as if "he is somehow using the sounds to 'call' the girl to him"—like a Siren luring sailors onto rocks.

298. Kickasola, *The Films of Krzysztof Kieślowski*, 86.

299. The composer has kept a home near Geneva and the Swiss mountains for some time.

300. Carlsson and Holm, "The Double Life of Zbigniew Preisner," 41.

301. Russell and Young, *Film Music: Screencraft*, 168. An early draft of the bolero, written with a different type of pen to the *Red* score, is bundled together with Preisner's fair copy manuscript score for *Blue*.

302. Macnab and Darke, "Working with Kieślowski," 20.

303. Wollermann, *Zur Musik in der "Drei Farben" Trilogie*, 113.

304. Russell and Young, *Film Music: Screencraft*, 168-73.

305. Insdorf, *Double Lives, Second Chances*, 167.

306. Wollermann, *Zur Musik in der "Drei Farben" Trilogie*, 113.

307. Paxman, "Preisner-Kieślowski," 159.

308. Paxman, "Preisner-Kieślowski," 160.

309. Andrew, *The "Three Colours" Trilogy*, 55.

310. Andrew, *The "Three Colours" Trilogy*, 58.

311. Kiefer, "Kieślowski's *Three Colors.*"

312. Willi Kahl and Israel J. Katz, "Bolero," in *Grove Music Online. Oxford Music Online*, http://www.oxfordmusiconline.com/subscriber/article/grove/music/03444 (last accessed 18 April 2011).

313. Some boleros have duple meters, as in the Cuban bolero, which has links to the habaneras.

314. Nor is his score closely linked to Polish pieces such as Chopin's *Bolero*, op. 19, which is, in any case, more like a polonaise.

315. Kahl and Katz, "Bolero."

316. José Quiroga, *Tropics of Desire: Interventions from Queer Latino America* (New York: New York University Press, 2000), 145. See also Kathleen M. Vernon and Cliff Eisen, "Contemporary Spanish Film Music: Carlos Saura and Pedro Almodóvar," in Mera and Burnand, *European Film Music*: 41-59.

317. Haltof, *The Cinema of Krzysztof Kieślowski*, 146.

318. Insdorf, *Double Lives, Second Chances*, 174.

319. The song, recorded in both French and Polish versions for soundtrack release, was composed to be performed at the world premiere of the film, partly to celebrate the achievement of completing the trilogy, but also because the poem's words, which Preisner told me he only discovered after the film had been completed, read like a synopsis of *Red*. The poem, by Polish Nobel Prize winner Wisława Szymborska, is "Miłość od pierwszego wejrzenia" ("Love at First Sight"), and does indeed read like a précis of Auguste and Valentine's near-misses throughout the film, including some uncanny details (missed telephone connections, etc.), although its meditation on destiny and chance also fit well with the trilogy's aesthetic—as does its closing verse, which speaks of every ending being only a sequel.

320. Andrew, *The "Three Colours" Trilogy*, 74.

321. See Wollermann, *Zur Musik in der "Drei Farben" Trilogie*, 109-111.

322. Wollermann, *Zur Musik in der "Drei Farben" Trilogie*, 112.

323. Kickasola, *The Films of Krzysztof Kieślowski*, 234.

324. Wollermann, *Zur Musik in der "Drei Farben" Trilogie*, 103.

325. Wollermann, *Zur Musik in der "Drei Farben" Trilogie*, 112-13.

326. See the revisionist discussions of leitmotivic scoring practices in *Music and Cinema*, ed. James Buhler, Caryl Flinn and David Neumeyer (Middletown, CT: Wesleyan University Press, 2000).

327. Paxman, "Preisner-Kieślowski," 146.

328. Paxman, "Preisner-Kieślowski," 158-59.

329. Gorbman, *Unheard Melodies*, 15; quoted in Paxman, "Preisner-Kieślowski," 146.

330. Hans Eisler and Theodor Adorno, *Composing for the Film* (New York: Oxford University Press, 1947), 14; quoted in Paxman, "Preisner-Kieślowski," 146.

331. Paxman, "Preisner-Kieślowski," 146.

332. Stok, ed. and trans., *Kieślowski on Kieślowski*, 179.

333. Paxman, "Preisner-Kieślowski," 145.
334. Paxman, "Preisner-Kieślowski," 146.

Chapter Five

1. Several people have taken me aside at conferences to tell me how much the film means to them in such contexts.
2. D. J. Enright, ed., *The Oxford Book of Death* (Oxford: Oxford University Press, 1983), xiii.
3. James, "Kind of 'Blue,'" 34.
4. "A Look at *Blue*," DVD extra on *Blue* in *Krzysztof Kieślowski's "Three Colors": The Exclusive Collection* (Miramax 28658).
5. Žižek, *The Fright of Real Tears*, 167.
6. Falkowska, "Religious Themes in Polish Cinema," 72.
7. John Archer, *The Nature of Grief: The Evolution and Psychology of Reactions to Loss* (London: Routledge, 1999), 1.
8. Archer, *The Nature of Grief*, 5.
9. Archer, *The Nature of Grief*, 7.
10. Archer, *The Nature of Grief*, 8.
11. Archer, *The Nature of Grief*, 8.
12. Archer, *The Nature of Grief*, 8.
13. Norman Mailer, *The Naked and the Dead* (London: Harper-Collins, 1992 [1949]); quoted in Archer, *The Nature of Grief*, 91.
14. Archer, *The Nature of Grief*, 104. Julie's response in this phase of her grief is echoed by the actions of a widow in a recent film, *Le père de mes enfants* (Mia Hansen-Løve, 2009). Sylvia (Chiara Caselli) represses her emotional responses to the suicide of her film producer husband, partly by seeking to continue his production company and shepherd his unfinished projects to completion.
15. Archer, *The Nature of Grief*, 103-5; see also Margaret Stroebe and Henk Schut, "The Dual Process Model of Coping with Bereavement: Rationale and Description," *Death Studies* 23 (1999): 197-224.
16. Archer, *The Nature of Grief*, 105.
17. Archer, *The Nature of Grief*, 16; commenting on Henk Schut, Margaret Stroebe, et al., "Intervention for the Bereaved: Gender Differences in the Efficacy of Grief Counselling," *British Journal of Clinical Psychology* 36 (1997): 63-72.
18. As Auster's *The Book of Illusions* progresses, the chance to meet the reclusive silent film star at the heart of the protagonist's unlikely monograph draws Zimmer into a range of new emotional relationships with the living and, ultimately, his dead family, with (broadly speaking) restoration work ceding to loss-oriented grieving.
19. Archer, *The Nature of Grief*, 155.
20. D. G. Williams and Gabrielle H. Morris, "Crying, Weeping or Tearfulness in British and Israeli Adults," *British Journal of Psychology* 83, no. 3 (1996): 479-505. The study found that three-quarters of

the Israeli men studied cry on four or fewer occasions per year, against ten or less for British men. A difference in formative experience proposed by the researchers to explain this discrepancy is that most of the Israeli men studied had served in the Israel Defense Forces.

21. David Greig, "Lord of the Dance," in "Review," *The Guardian* (8 September 2007), 14.

22. Sandra M. Gilbert, *Death's Door: Modern Dying and the Ways We Grieve* (New York: W. W. Norton, 2006).

23. Richard Leppert, "Opera, Aesthetic Violence, and the Imposition of Modernity: *Fitzcarraldo*," in *Beyond the Soundtrack*, ed. Goldmark, Kramer, and Leppert, 106.

24. My thanks to Julie Brown for bringing this article to my attention.

25. Alexander Stein, "Music, Mourning, and Consolation," *Journal of the American Psychoanalytic Association* 52, no. 3 (2004), 784. Stein surveys existing literature about music and grieving (for a summary see pp. 788-90) while building on his own clinical and personal experiences (not least of 9/11 and its aftermath).

26. Stein, "Music, Mourning, and Consolation," 788.

27. Stein, "Music, Mourning, and Consolation," 794.

28. Stein, "Music, Mourning, and Consolation," 791.

29. Stein, "Music, Mourning, and Consolation," 794.

30. Stein, "Music, Mourning, and Consolation," 801.

31. Stein, "Music, Mourning, and Consolation," 807.

32. Stein, "Music, Mourning, and Consolation," 803.

33. Roy Schafer, "Generative Empathy in the Treatment Situation," *The Psychoanalytic Quarterly* 28 (1959): 345; see Stein, "Music, Mourning, and Consolation," 803.

34. Theodor Reik, *Surprise and the Psychoanalyst* (New York: EP I Hilton, 1937), cited in Stein, "Music, Mourning, and Consolation," 803, via Schafer, "Generative Empathy," 342.

35. Stein, "Music, Mourning, and Consolation," 807.

36. Stok, ed. and trans., *Kieślowski on Kieślowski*, 217.

37. As part of a "study guide," and in recognition of the likely cardinal interest in *Blue* of many readers, the following analysis seeks to cover every cue in the film, as a service to students and enthusiasts seeking a comprehensive study of its score. However, discussions of music and sound in some moments less central to *Blue*'s plot and subtexts, as interpreted here, are placed in (lengthy) endnotes below.

38. Krzysztof Kieślowski and Krzysztof Piesiewicz, *"Three Colours" Trilogy*, trans. Danusia Stok (London: Faber, 1998), 3.

39. Insdorf, *Double Lives, Second Chances*, 157.

40. Kickasola, *The Films of Krzysztof Kieślowski*, 265-6.

41. It will be echoed at the start of *Red*, for instance, to inform the perceiver that Valentine and Auguste belong together; it will also recur again in *Blue*, most extravagantly at the end of the film, as the flowing movements of the imagery demonstrate Julie's reconnection to society.

42. Before this happens another pair of sonic details, tellingly contrasted by Jean-Claude Laureux and William Flageollet's sound design, are indicative of the narrative function of audio throughout the trilogy. The lively crackle of Anna's foil sweet wrapper, turning in the wind outside the car window, is followed by a sonic shift that denotes, most obviously, a change in environment (in this case from car *in* environment to car *as* environment). Julie's daughter, Anna, now stares back at the road and into the camera through the car's back window (and thus at the audience), as if to say to the audio-viewer "you are implicit in what will occur: learn your lesson well." But what *will* occur? The sound design is horribly suggestive. Her enclosed space is both coffin- and womb-like. Dark, muffled and sealed, it pre-figures Anna's burial casket; the next time Anna is "seen," she will be dead and inside it.

43. Insdorf, *Double Lives, Second Chances*, 142.

44. Orr, *Contemporary Cinema*, 63. The term is Bruce Kawin's from *Mindscreen: Bergman, Godard, and the First-Person Film* (Princeton, NJ: Princeton University Press, 1978). Haltof has insightfully connected *Blue* to the mindscreens evoked by Werner Herzog films immersed in the psychological landscape of their protagonists; see Haltof, *The Cinema of Krzysztof Kieślowski*, 131.

45. A baby crying, for instance, was rated one of the most distressing sounds in the world in a recent online experiment organized by Salford University. Visit http://www.sound101.org/badvibes/aboutIntro .php for more information (last accessed 26 April 2011).

46. Chion, *Audio-Vision*, 39.

47. Chion, *Audio-Vision*, 39.

48. That the music in the scene revisits *No End*'s score, and the earlier film's narrative concerns, lends further credibility to the notion of a referential web.

49. Kickasola, *The Films of Krzysztof Kieślowski*, 267.

50. Wilson, *Memory and Survival*, 41.

51. In the film, the gesture's source of agency is more ambiguous. It is almost as if the technology empathizes with Julie and cannot bear to intensify her grief further by confronting her with yet more evidence of her loss.

52. Chion, *Audio-Vision*, 76.

53. Paulus, "Music in Krzysztof Kieślowski's Film *Three Colors: Blue*," 67.

54. Krzysztof Kieślowski and Krzysztof Piesiewicz, *"Three Colours" Trilogy*, trans. Danusia Stok (London: Faber, 1998), 8.

55. See Insdorf, *Double Lives, Second Chances*, 148, and Andrew, *The "Three Colours" Trilogy*, 28. Wollermann notes similar misreadings by German critics; see Wollermann, *Zur Musik in der "Drei Farben" Trilogie*, 50. Paulus makes this mistake herself; see Paulus, "Music in Krzysztof Kieślowski's Film *Three Colors: Blue*," 78.

56. In fairness to Insdorf, who has made many insightful comments about music in Kieślowski's films, there are a number of motivic and stylistic similarities, discussed below, between the two themes. One

might also suggest that, in a film where music attains an unusual degree of permeability, such (mis)readings may actually speak to something more crucial: connection.

57. Preisner's cue sheet calls for a nonet including four horns; only two horns are present on screen.

58. Stein, "Music, Mourning, and Consolation," 793.

59. In the performance, the dynamics of the ensemble accompanying the solo trumpet remain more constant (around *piano*) than Preisner's hairpins might lead one to expect. The transcription here "corrects" Preisner's enharmonic "misspelling" of the leading note as G♭ (an example of his "unschooled" technique) in Fig. 5.1.

60. That Preisner does not create a "textbook" cadence here (the harmonic progression is not, say, i$^6_4$-V^7-i) reflects both the space between his "semi-classical" style and the repertoire he is emulating, and his musical training within popular traditions where cheat sheets are a more common practice than figured bass.

61. The editing could also be heard to provide, in the final editing-constructed pair of phrases, a condensed reprise of the motif x/i-V-i prolongation heard over the course of the first four phrases.

62. Kieślowski and Piesiewicz, *"Three Colours" Trilogy*, 10.

63. Gross and Wilson echo the notion that the clearest purpose of the sequence is to shock one into an experience proximate to Julie's horror. For Gross, writing in her unpublished Masters thesis on *Blue*, the interruptions "intensify the film's dramatic structure, heighten tension, and skew audience perception in ways which parallel Julie's warping of reality"; see Kelly Gross, "Female Subjectivity, Disability, and Musical Authorship in Krzysztof Kieślowski's *Blue*," unpublished M.A. thesis (University of Virginia, 2005), 15. For Wilson, the scene is an example of how "the film finds sensory analogues, the very raw materials of audio-visual representation, to connote [Julie's] traumatized perceptions" and insist that "the viewer shares this shattering of silence with Julie"; see Wilson, *"Three Colours: Blue,"* 354.

64. Chion, *Audio-Vision*, 91.

65. Andrew, *The "Three Colours" Trilogy*, 29.

66. Insdorf, *Double Lives, Second Chances*, 143.

67. Insdorf, *Double Lives, Second Chances*, 147.

68. Kickasola, *The Films of Krzysztof Kieślowski*, 268.

69. Kickasola, *The Films of Krzysztof Kieślowski*, 268.

70. Insdorf, *Double Lives, Second Chances*, 148. There are precursors in the Kieślowski films where music and spirits (and musical spirits) rupture a character's reality, not least in *Blue*'s closest thematic siblings, *No End* and *Véronique*. In a useful discussion of these films, Coates contrasts the "problematic" nature of Western cultural representations of ghosts from *Ghostbusters* (rendering the spiritual ridiculous to offset angst) to *Turn of the Screw* (where their presence questions the sanity of a witness) with Polish texts recording an "investment in the worship of tutelary spirits." In this context, Kieślowski's phantom visitations might be read to encourage (once the shock has subsided) "the

dignity of *spiritual* engagement." *No End*, for instance, is situated by Coates "firmly in the tradition of Polish supernaturalist art," not least through its tutelary use of ghosts. In Adam Mickiewicz's poem *Forefather's Eve* and Stanisław Wyspiański's play *The Wedding*, "apparitions seek to stir the somnolent consciences of the wedding guests and mobilize them for an uprising." Antek's death and subsequent reappearances in *No End* parallel the (temporary) death of another dream of freedom (Solidarity following the onset of martial law) and represent, for Coates, a yearning for an ideal unattained; see Coates, *Cinema, Religion and the Romantic Legacy*, 147, 150, 152. In *Blue*, the apparition(s), "real" or "imagined," could be heard to tutor the grieving Julie, showing her a way to reconnect with the world by reminding her—albeit too soon and too violently—that she must confront her loss more intensely. The music's topical significations, analyzed below, may lend credence to this assertion.

71. Georgina Evans, "Synaesthesia in Kieślowski's *Trois couleurs: Bleu*," *Studies in French Cinema* 5, no. 2 (2005): 83-4.

72. See Simon Baron-Cohen and J. Harrison, eds, *Synaesthesia: Classic and Contemporary Readings* (Cambridge: Blackwell, 1997), 17; quoted in Evans, "Synaesthesia," 79.

73. Evans, "Synaesthesia," 79.

74. Stilwell, "The Fantastical Gap," 186.

75. Stilwell, "The Fantastical Gap," 196.

76. Ben Winters, "The Non-Diegetic Fallacy: Film, Music, and Narrative Space," *Music and Letters* 91, no. 2 (2010): 236.

77. Stok, ed. and trans., *Kieślowski on Kieślowski*, 215-6.

78. Brown, "Listening to Ravel," 264.

79. Eisler and Adorno, *Composing for the Film*.

80. Wollermann, *Zur Musik in der "Drei Farben" Trilogie*, 52.

81. Alastair Williams, "Voices of the Other: Wolfgang Rihm's Music Drama *Die Eroberung von Mexico*," *Journal of the Royal Musical Association* 129, no. 2 (2004): 243.

82. Williams, "Voices of the Other," 243.

83. Julie's struggle against music, beginning with this scene, is in Žižek's view her struggle against the past. The struggle "accounts for the strange sudden black-outs in the middle of some scenes," when "Julie is undergoing a fading (*aphanisis*), losing consciousness for a couple of seconds," before she "represses the insurgency of the musical past"; see Žižek, *The Fright of Real Tears*, 165-6.

84. When Olivier arrives (another reminder), clutching an incriminating blue document wallet containing the pictures of the mistress (yet more reminders), Julie refuses to meet him. She sits on the stairs, flecks of bright blue light playing across her face. The lights are reflected from the string of lampshade baubles she is holding in her hand: a visual effect returned to in an important musical scene to come.

85. The shot's visual effect—a corona of blurring surrounding a point of focus—looks like an iris encircling a pupil *and* a representation of the way in which the human eye and mind focus.

86. Garbowski, *Krzysztof Kieślowski's "Decalogue" Series*, 104.

87. See Garbowski, *Krzysztof Kieślowski's "Decalogue" Series*, 106.

88. For further discussion of "self-transcendence" and shot/reverse shot sequences see Garbowski, *Krzysztof Kieślowski's "Decalogue" Series*.

89. Stein, "Music, Mourning, and Consolation," 793.

90. Paulus, "Music in Krzysztof Kieślowski's Film *Three Colors: Blue*," 74.

91. Paulus, "Music in Krzysztof Kieślowski's Film *Three Colors: Blue*," 70.

92. A further motive, "z," pivots between scale degrees Preisner characteristically stresses in his melodies, $\hat{5}$ and $\flat\hat{6}$. This feature occurs many times in *Blue*, sometimes suggesting links between cues. Here, the precise pitches might be heard to suggest a tilting between the tonal ambit of B minor and the G minor of the funeral march.

93. A difference between Preisner's cue sheet and the music appearing on screen, in turn, calls attention to another manner in which the theme may be heard to gain strength as it progresses. The music seen on screen has been re-barred: the dotted rhythm falls on the first beat of each bar. In Preisner's score, the dotted rhythm gradually finds a place as an upbeat on the last beat of the bar, which results in a slightly less hesitant (or even ungainly) rhythmic configuration in comparison to the differently written first few bars. The subtle effect created is of a sense of greater flow being attained. As this chapter goes on to argue, the attainment of "flow"—not least involving the fate of this melody in the score's development—is central to *Blue*'s narrative purpose.

94. The pedaling of this cue is also different from the first version, adding subtly to the sense in which the cue could be considered a Julie-controlled development of its previous appearance.

95. He cites this as evidence of Tarkovsky's influence; see Kickasola, *The Films of Krzysztof Kieślowski*, 271, n. 29.

96. Kickasola, *The Films of Krzysztof Kieślowski*, 271.

97. This motif—crescendo/cut—can be heard again in the scene where Julie devours Anna's sweet. The crackling fire crescendos and then she chomps it down as quickly as possible, in an accelerating rhythm of cracks which climax in the pop of the fire as she hurls the lolly stick into it. This is also partly an effect, perhaps, of automatic mixing of the trilogy's background and foreground sounds.

98. Her consumption of the blue lollipop is a similarly terrifying display and, during her desultory screw with Olivier, she is illuminated in the same way. As Julie breathes in here, though, an uncanny and unnerving sight appears over her shoulder: the head of the horse statue, its mouth open and teeth bared, just behind her left ear. In Kieślowski's films, Kickasola has noted, horses carry "connotations of freedom"; see Kickasola, *The Films of Krzysztof Kieślowski*, 100. In *I'm So-So*, the newly retired Kieślowski is seen wandering through a group of horses; in his early fiction film *The Calm,* Antek—who wishes to escape from

his difficult past and enjoy a life of calm and freedom—imitates horses, sees a vision of white horses galloping, and views them on a TV; one also see horses on television in *No End*. Kieślowski expresses his admiration for horses in *I'm So-So* as follows: they can run free. Clearly, Julie cannot yet run free. Aptly, then, this is an inanimate simulacrum of a horse, not the real thing.

Could the horse also indicate, however, aspects of the complexity of Julie's grief? The statue's placement in the *mise-en-scène* and shot (as if the horse is seeking either to rip off her ear or whisper sweetly into it) recalls one of Freud's depictions of the structure of the mind:

> One might compare the relation of the ego to the id with that between a rider and his horse. The horse provides the locomotor energy, and the rider has the prerogative of determining the goal and of guiding the movements of his powerful mount towards it. But all too often in the relations between the ego and the id we find a picture of the less ideal situation in which the rider is obliged to guide his horse in the direction in which it itself wants to go.

See Sigmund Freud, "Lecture 31: The Anatomy of the Mental Personality," *New Introductory Lectures on Psychoanalysis*, trans. W. J. H. Sprott (New York: Norton, 1933). Kieślowski and Freud's horse symbols acknowledge an essential tension between personal desire (be it creative, libidinal, for freedom and calm, etc.) and the ordered social world of the ego (the world of relationships, work, family commitments, etc.). In *Blue*, Julie will only reconnect with the world once creativity has been given free rein.

99. Is the music occurring in the copyist's imagination, in Julie's, or perhaps in both? A cut in the sequence, which omits the dull details of Julie exiting the apartment even though the music continues unabated, suggests the music is playing out in *Blue*'s climate rather than any one mind.

100. Preisner sets a Polish transliteration of the ancient Greek. The source is most likely Preisner's letter from Skrzynecki.

101. See, for instance, Chion, *Audio-Vision*, 123-5. Kickasola also discusses the "phantom audio-vision" in Kieślowski's films; see Kickasola, *The Films of Krzysztof Kieślowski*, 86-8.

102. Paulus, "Music in Krzysztof Kieślowski's Film *Three Colors: Blue*," 71.

103. If one were absolutely desperate to read these mistakes as intentional on the part of the filmmakers, it could be taken as proof that Patrice was truly not a very talented musician and needed Julie to do rather more than finesse his scores. Taken to an interpretative extreme, one might then claim that the music one hears in this scene is Julie's corrected version of the incorrect version one sees. It is probably just an unfortunate error, however, or rather a piece of filmmaking illusion that—like so much else—is good enough to pass scrutiny at twenty-four frames per second.

104. There is no mention of music in the published screenplay and it seems likely that this cue was part of the c. 10 percent of music created at a relatively late stage in the production process. As Julie orders Olivier to strip, light shining through a rain-strewn window casts horizontal bands of blue across her face, like energy coursing though her. Thunder rolling around the sound design adds to the unnerving ambience, which feels almost gothic: Julie as much vampire as vamp. Little wonder Olivier—so beautifully played here, as throughout *Blue*, by Benoit Régent—looks simultaneously aroused and terrified. At the moment she pulls off her stretchy black dress—a provocation which leads Olivier to lose his way in his attempt to undo his shoelaces—the blue energy courses all over her naked body, thunder rolls, and Preisner's cue begins.

The scene's intensifying ardency is sculpted by the cue's control of meter. In this development of the memento theme, a bar of six beats is followed, slightly jarringly, by one of five. When the initial bar of six is proven aberrant by further bars of five, there is a subtle acceleration towards the climax of the scene, the propulsion of which intensifies when the meter changes again, this time to four in a bar. Although the tempo does not quicken, the foreshortening bar lengths (the last of which removes the theme's faltering rests at the shift to $\frac{4}{4}$), quicken the speed with which the phrases occur. The final bar then cuts off midway, in a strident cut typical of the film's severing gestures, anticipating the shock Olivier receives when Julie awakens and then rejects him the next morning—shock heightened by the subtle acceleration effect that has been propelling the cue towards its premature climax.

The memento's rescoring here—a full body of strings plays the melody in octaves, the orchestration reminiscent of the antecedent phrases in the interruption and ellipsis sequence—helps to suggest, when filtered through the scene's visual content, the register of the erotic. Yet eroticism in the scene is another phantom. The adoption—by the score and Julie—of an assertive sexual agency is not a reflection of her subjectivity at this point: it is merely a means to an end. As she leaves the house, having dumped Olivier, her true state is shockingly revealed. In one of *Blue*'s shortest but most affecting scenes, Julie goes to extreme lengths to suppress an outburst of emotion as she abandons Olivier and her family's home. To stop herself from crying, Julie substitutes another kind of pain for her grief, scraping the bare knuckles of her clenched fist along a wall and drawing blood. There is no music. The fist-scraping scene explodes the myth of the preceding scene's eroticism.

105. The lampshade scene is an example of the kind of work yielded by intense collaborations between the Kieślowski co-workers. Cinematography, lighting, art direction, sound, and acting all contributed telling components; post-production, the sequence was then pared to the bone in the editing suite, with Preisner and other members of the team assisting the director in shaping the materials available, not merely to articulate the action as economically as possible, but also to intensify

the scene's symbolism. The editorial evolution of the cue can be tracked by comparing the soundtrack CD to the film. Most significantly, two meandering woodwind melodies (which presumably were composed to underscore Julie's movements around the flat) were removed, cutting out their smoothing over of the scene's joins and, in doing so, intensifying the angularity of filmic and musical structure central to the sequence's evocation of Julie's disintegration.

106. Two further sounds are particularly prominent and interact with Preisner's scoring. The second (discussed in the main text) is the sound made by Anna's lampshade. The first is the sound of a circular saw, presumably carrying out some building work in one of the adjoining apartments. Leaving aside its affective quality, i.e., something unpleasant threatening her sanctuary's walls, the sawing noise begins just a second before the first of the cue's three phrases emerges. This permits the cue to "sneak in," as befits music seeking to make, in comparison to most of the cues thus far in the film, a more subtle contribution. The saw also helps to mark a base line (indeed a bass line) for the audio components of the scene, above which other sounds will float, extracting symbolism from a manipulation of audio registers. Julie is grounded; her mementos are moving up and away from her.

107. The harmonic developments of this cue refute Paulus's assertion that the memento theme recurs without being altered significantly in this scene; see Paulus, "Music in Krzysztof Kieślowski's Film *Three Colors: Blue*," 71.

108. When the third phrase of the cue begins, the sound design includes a third saw intervention as Julie lifts the lampshade out of the box, although it is quieter than the baubles in the mix. The pitch of the sawing has risen by about a tone at this point (from a fifth spanning F-C to G-D), as if it too is participating, like the transpositions, in a movement towards higher realms.

109. In parallel to the visual close-up, the score has also zoomed in on its source. The melody is near the center of the stereo image, creating the effect of a slight rise in volume which, paired with the inevitable intensification of the rising pitches of the transpositions, presses one closer to the music.

110. Kickasola, *The Films of Krzysztof Kieślowski*, 273.

111. Žižek, *The Fright of Real Tears*, 82.

112. *Blue*'s busker, and the impact he has on the direction of Julie's life, has a street-performance precedent in Kieślowski's films: the jugglers in *Blind Chance*. Witek is "transfixed by the give-and-take image" of the jugglers and asks "Why do they juggle?" (superficially to break a world record), but as Kickasola tellingly suggests, there is also "a sense that these men are biding time, trying to make something beautiful and creative amid the dead time, the stasis, for no particular reason except to exist beautifully"; see Kickasola, *The Films of Krzysztof Kieślowski*, 145. Unexpectedly, undesirably and yet perhaps not entirely unenjoyably, Julie too has begun to "exist beautifully" by this stage in *Blue*,

floating across the shadow line of her "dead time" and free of the constraints of her previous life as a wife and mother.

113. The busker's melodies are all overdubs of the live action, Ostaszewski having worked painstakingly in post-production to sync new performances of Preisner's cues to those made on set, where street noises had made keeping the original live recordings untenable.

114. In a scene in the screenplay but not in the picture, Julie is walking on the street near the busker and adjusts the rhythm of her walking to match that of his playing.

115. See Mihály Csíkszentmihályi and Isabelle Selega Csíkszentmihályi, ed., *Optimal Experience: Psychological Studies of Flow in Consciousness* (Cambridge: Cambridge University Press, 1988), 3-4.

116. There is also a tonal link. The tune is in A minor, the key of the second phrase of the previous cue. That key, the midpoint in the progression from G minor to B minor, served locally as a limbo between two symbolically more significant tonalities. Julie's state here is not so different: a limbo between the hell of her initial (G minor) bereavement and the (B minor) acceptance she will discover by the end of the film. Emphasizing A minor also infuses the second stage of the film with a fresh sense of location.

117. Nonetheless, the cut does create another unfinished piece of music (the busker's first cue ends mid-phrase). So far, only the initial statement of the funeral march has been heard in a completed and closed musical form. For Julie and the film's perceivers to experience closure through a large-scale composition experienced from beginning to end, more significant progress needs to be made. A glimpse of her progress is revealed in the next busker scene.

118. Kickasola, *The Films of Krzysztof Kieślowski*, 245.

119. Henri Bergson, "Concerning the Nature of Time," in *Henri Bergson: Key Writings* (New York: Continuum, 2002), 205.

120. Stok, ed. and trans., *Kieślowski on Kieślowski*, 150.

121. More compassionately, Kickasola links "the grieving Julie" to Ula from *No End* in this scene, who pushes past an old lady on the stairs, as two characters "who cannot escape [their] own problematized line of vision to see the elderly woman in need of help"; see Kickasola, *The Films of Krzysztof Kieślowski*, 156.

122. There have been other indications of this creative process: the second musical interruption in *Blue* (discussed below), as Julie nods off on her staircase, may reveal something of her unconscious musical workings.

123. Kieślowski and Piesiewicz, *"Three Colours" Trilogy*, 43.

124. Paulus, "Music in Krzysztof Kieślowski's Film *Three Colors: Blue*," 78.

125. The other whiteout in the trilogy—during Dominique's impressive orgasm with the newly invigorated Karol in *White*– also happens at a moment of partial healing.

126. The cue is also reminiscent of Nino Rota's *Godfather* theme and the homage Preisner composed for *White*'s score. Cutting it removed an obvious musical link between the trilogy's components.

127. Conversely, that rather literal reading reminds one of Kieślowski's reticence to attach symbolic meaning to small events in his films—he might have argued, simply, that the busker is stating an obvious fact, as true for Julie in her unique circumstance as for anyone else in theirs.

128. Like many Kieślowski films, *Blue* contains glimpses of lives one might wish to know more about. One could certainly imagine a more interesting story than the wisely excised subplot in the script involving the theft of the recorder, Julie returning it to the busker, and a call to the woman seen escorting the busker to his spot in her chauffeur-driven car in the film, which also involved Lucille and a thief: a pointless intrigue, and a good example of Kieślowski's incisive paring.

129. It is also reminiscent of the Concerto from *Véronique*, which shares motivic ideas with the memento, including the opening shape of each tune's first phrase and the presence of motif x. It is even just about possible to imagine that the memento discovered by Julie on the piano is a reminiscence (misremembered by Patrice?) of the Van den Budenmayer Concerto heard in *Véronique*.

130. The performance here has a lot of rubato and could arguably be better transcribed in §.

131. See Bruce Quaglia, "Reviews of Neil Lerner and Joseph Straus, editors, *Sounding Off: Theorizing Disability in Music* (New York: Routledge, 2006) and Joseph Straus, 'Normalizing the Abnormal: Disability in Music and Music Theory' in *Journal of the American Musicological Society* 59, no. 1 (2006)," *Music Theory Online* vol. 13, no. 2 (June 2007), http://www.mtosmt.org/issues/mto.07.13.2/mto.07.13.2.quaglia.html (last accessed 18 April 2011).

132. Quoted in Insdorf, *Double Lives, Second Chances*, 149.

133. Julie's interrogation is what leads critics astray in this scene, and those critics are not entirely to blame. It is illogical to claim that the busker has stolen something from the *Concert[o]* that is not yet in the *Concert[o]* (until, that is, Julie composes her own version, alluding back to this tune by the busker). But *Blue*'s thematic permeability permits, even encourages, such mistaken identities. It would have been more logical if the interrogation had been dropped, or if—strengthening the metaphysical claims—the tune played by the busker had been a melody already in the score for the *Concert[o]* as it stands at this moment in the story.

134. The image of contamination is ripe for interpretation. Insdorf and Kickasola agree it is a sign of forces encroaching on the purity of this phase of her life, and pushing her towards a loss-oriented reckoning with the traces of her past. For Kieślowski, according to Insdorf, the cube is a parallel to the spoon reflection at the beginning of the scene: "The sugar cube shows that she cares about nothing beyond her," he claimed, a view which does not jar with Insdorf's own reading of the

scene as a representation of life nonetheless invading her sanctuary, seeping in against her will; see Insdorf: *Double Lives, Second Chances*, 145. For Kickasola, too, the coffee represents "an encroaching force," and he notes the careful syncing of music and image in the scene: "A close-up of the sugar cube matches the tune," melody and color symbolism adding up to "an abstract embodiment of melancholy"; see Kickasola, *The Films of Krzysztof Kieślowski*, 274.

135. Orr, *Contemporary Cinema*, 64.

136. The oboe takes slightly longer over its lowest pitch (a G), this take of the cue having been made, presumably, better to fit the action of the final cut of the film.

137. Žižek notes a similarity to the image of a woman alone in a pool in Randa Haine's *Children of a Lesser God* (1986), where such shots "emphasize the (self-) exclusion of the embittered deaf-mute heroine"; see Žižek, *The Fright of Real Tears*, 203-4, n. 52.

138. Kickasola, *The Films of Krzysztof Kieślowski*, 274.

139. Kehr, "To Save the World," 15.

140. My thanks to Ben Winters for this erudite suggestion. "La barbe bleue," written by Charles Perrault in 1697, has received treatments as diverse as Bartók, Dukas, and Offenbach's operas and Catherine Breillat's recent film *Blue Beard* (2009). The original tale concerns an aristocrat who gives his wife the keys to their chateau but tells her not to open one door. She does: it is awash with blood from the bodies of his former wives, who she discovers dangling on hooks.

141. Julie seeks to repel the music by sinking beneath the surface of the pool and into the fetal position. As she sinks underwater, something intriguing happens to the sound design. The cue thus far has had all the reverb one might expect if the music is to be heard as a metadiegetic manifestation. Here, however, as she slips under the water, the music becomes distorted (by compression and filtering) and sounds muffled. The film thus suggests that music is being heard from Julie's point of audition. This raises a quandary. If the music is *within* Julie's mind, why does it sound like it is coming *through* the water? If one imagines music while submerged in the bath, it does not become muffled in this manner. If, on the other hand, one is listening to a radio while submerging, the sound is partially blocked as per the film. This raises the possibility that, once again, the music is coming from a phantom source, floating in the air above the water. Could the music, alternately, be a synaesthesic projection, made by her mind but experienced (like the blue lights) as if coming from outside?

142. In the screenplay, she actually witnesses the birth, but this scene was removed, making the mice's symbolism a gradual reveal rather than a clunking reminder.

143. Žižek's reading is compelling: "When Julie withdraws into the 'abstract freedom' of [her apartment], the key detail is the mouse . . . The view of this thriving life disgusts her, since it stands for the Real of life in its thriving, humid vitality. . . . [L]ife becomes disgusting when the fantasy that mediates our access to it disintegrates, so that we are

directly confronted with the Real, and what Julie succeeds in doing at
the end of the film is precisely to reconstitute her fantasy frame"; see
Žižek, *The Fright of Real Tears*, 169.

144. The copyist made an extra copy, she tells Julie later on, and
sent it to Strasbourg; the bureaucrats sent it on to Olivier.

145. She addresses Julie informally and professes to having owned
the same kind of blue lampshade as a child.

146. Julie has hitherto intervened to help Lucille, more through a
selfish desire to be left alone than a desire to help, by being the one
person in the apartment block who refused to sign what needed to be a
unanimous petition in order to get Lucille (a sex worker) evicted.

147. For a discussion of such signifiers see Eric Clarke and Nicola
Dibben, "Sex, Pulp, and Critique," *Popular Music* 19, no. 2 (2000):
231-41.

148. This part of the score is rather like the self-consciously transcendent "fantasy" section of rock band Pulp's nuanced representation
of porno-styled fantasy, "This Is Hardcore"; see Clarke and Dibben,
"Sex, Pulp, and Critique."

149. As Marie Bennett pointed out to me, she will appear again on
TV, also unexpectedly and traumatized, at the end of *Red.*

150. Dialogue in the screenplay for a scene not in the final film
(Julie telephoning the journalist) suggests as much, twice calling the
piece the "concert," not the concerto, as does Julie when she confronts
Olivier (although unhelpfully for Anglophone viewers, the Miramax
Region 1 DVD set translates "concert" here as "concerto"). Again, the
screenplay concurs: it is a concert.

151. The interruption is further dampened by being subtly prepared. Olivier's performance of his version of the score, discussed below, ends on a G minor sonority; he then sings a fragment of melody
hovering around G. The faltering funeral march is in the air.

152. One might have expected to hear the funeral march again, for
example, or even another ellipsis, when Julie plunges into the pool and
fails to resurface after meeting the mistress. Arguably, the tension emanates from the *lack* of music and thus the film's play on its grammar of
expectation. Yet she does not emerge on the surface in tears to the
sound of a Van den Budenmayer march. Instead, the hum of the swimming pool lights and ventilation—a cluster of sinister noise—is broken
by Julie popping to the surface and gasping for life-giving air, in further
evidence of her returning strength.

153. The sound design prepares for the quiet entry of this performance with a rare moment of calm, cueing one's attention like the hush in
a concert hall, but also smoothing over a cut from street to apartment in
a manner indicative of the "flow" returning to aspects of *Blue*'s style in
parallel to Julie's restoration. The music is played on the piano "by"
Olivier (Aubigny is miming). A sequentially falling phrase is heard,
first in B minor, then in A minor and finally in G minor. Save for some
filigree decoration, this is repetition varied through transposition. Re-
course to the sequence is one mark of the mediocre composer, padding

out a score to cover a lack of invention; Julie's version will be freer of such sequences. However, its descent through three minor harmonies— B, A, G—means that the distance from memento to funeral is, once again, tonally mapped; it also reverses the tonal ascent of the lampshade scene. The return to G minor, in particular, hangs in the air like an impertinent reminder when Olivier finishes playing. Julie, though, is not listening.

In the immediate context of the scene's action, the music acts as a voice of arbitration. As Olivier plays, Julie stands above him, feigning disinterest, yet the precisely constructed shot shows her hemmed in on three sides by the piano's body, arm and lid, as if she has walked into a trap, subjugating her with apparatus over which (when she made the piano lid fall) she had earlier demonstrated dominance. Each phrase begins with a pair of leaping intervals outlining their respective minor triads. This rising gesture could be heard as an optimistic entreaty from Olivier, followed by a courtly bow of descending melodic ornamentation: Olivier is attempting a seduction through performance. The harmony is sinking, though, and the energy of gestural optimism becomes bleached by repetition. Julie wanders off, unimpressed.

Or maybe Julie is merely pretending to be unimpressed. Her subsequent actions demonstrate that Olivier's music has stirred her memory of Patrice's plans for the *Concert[o]* and kindled a desire to share them with her admirer. Telling Olivier about the plans helps his progress with the composition, signifies Julie's renewing interest in her present and past, and forms a selfless gesture. Julie now shows Olivier the key passage from the Bible. *Blue* does not yet reveal exactly what the text is, but clues come in the mumbled words Olivier hums to the tune of the *Concert[o]*'s opening. The word "amour" is audible as he purrs in Julie's ear, but she is oblivious (or maintaining the appearance thereof), instead telling Olivier something crucial about the text. It was to be set in *Greek*, she tells him, where "the rhythm is different." The dialogue and action combine subtly to emphasize that the key to the *Concert[o]*, *Blue*, and the trilogy will not be *amour*, but *agapē*.

Clumsily flirtatious, Olivier moves closer as he hums. This music, literally emanating from Olivier's body, has associations more complex than he can imagine: it is the music from the copyist's flat, the maternal mouse's accompaniment, and thus the theme of Julie's most intimate connections. Olivier's flirtatious use of the melody, in a sense, is perverse. Julie brushes off his attentions and his musical gesture. This is not the time or, indeed, the right music for such an advance.

The screenplay for this scene reveals something about the grandeur Patrice and Julie had envisaged for the eventual *Concert[o]*. "I'll tell you the idea behind it," Julie says to Olivier:

> It's the sheer scale, unparalleled as yet. You're standing on the Étoile. There are a thousand members of an orchestra, choirs and eleven enormous television screens the size of a five-storeyed building in front of you. There are thousands of musicians on every one of these:

in Berlin, London, Brussels, Rome or Madrid. . . . For a concert like that to work the music has to rise several inches off the ground. Or even higher. Imagine: twelve thousand musicians waiting for a sign from you. Crowds everywhere. You lower the baton and everywhere the music starts at once.

"A choir in Athens," Olivier imagines, which (in the screenplay) reminds Julie to tell him about the text being set in ancient Greek. The resulting cacophony of connections made (or missed) would have provided a metaphor for modern Europe reconsidered through the eyes and ears of Polish filmmakers aware that, as the baton fell in one European city, shells could be raining on another.

154. This scene occurs after Julie has confronted her husband's mistress and made another disturbing discovery: the mistress is carrying Patrice's child. (This is also the section, at the law courts, where Julie stumbles into *White* and Karol's trial. Such gestures are typical of the Kieślowski cycles: a light touch of unification.) Julie's own mother is shown four times in *Blue*: at the funeral, twice when Julie visits her, and once more during the closing montage. On the first occasion, the mother's iconic gaze into a camera broadcasting the funeral (thus appearing—but *only* appearing, crucially—to connect with her daughter's gaze) evokes something Julie will never again experience: to look upon her daughter's face. On the second occasion, as Julie declares to her mother that all ties—love, family, money, memory—are traps (i.e., impediments to the liberty of the restoration-oriented grief-work she is seeking at this point in her life), the TV shows eccentric images of old people bungee jumping (complete with carnivalesque music, probably sourced by Cohen Solal). This links back to the funeral: the mini-TV showed similarly bizarre images to Julie when Olivier first switched it on.

On the third occasion, as Julie looks in on her mother's isolated life—a hint of weeping playing around Binoche's eyes—Julie is a changing person. Encounters with this very particular soloist have contributed to Julie's seeking anew of the companionship of society's ensemble. Julie's face is shot as a reflection in the glass which separates her from her mother; a phantom, could-have-been Julie stares back at Julie, looking out of a room already containing her ghost-like mother and, perhaps, an alternative future for Julie herself. As she turns decisively away from these icons of loss and isolation, and back towards the world and its different traps, Olivier's *Concert[o]* sounds again, but differently. Olivier's piano performance for Julie in his flat was carefully measured. The pace was gentle, the chords partially rolled to take the forceful edge off of the music as he sought to beguile Julie. Now the music speaks of dynamism and purpose. The harmonic sequence pushes beyond G minor to a decisive arrival on F# minor: a more logical terminus for the descent, being the dominant of the *Concert[o]*'s home key. More significantly for the drama to hand, it also calls for a response. The sequence is an elongated i-V cadence; Julie's turning away from her mother (and all she symbolizes about the future) and back towards Olivier is its substitute for cadential resolution.

155. Wollermann describes certain features of the cue which mark it as masculine, for instance drawing attention to the way the bass descends dramatically while the right hand leaps upwards in gestures of alpine athleticism. See Wollermann, *Zur Musik in der "Drei Farben" Trilogie*, 64.

156. Gross, "Female Subjectivity, Disability, and Musical Authorship," (2005), 25, n. 45.

157. Insdorf, *Double Lives, Second Chances*, 149.

158. Mention of becoming may hint at Deleuze and Guattari's concept of Becoming. A recent article by Gregg Redner provides an intriguing consideration of *Blue* from this critical perspective. See Gregg Redner, "Building a Deleuzian Bridge between Music and Film Theories," *Music, Sound, and the Moving Image* 2, no. 2 (Autumn 2008): 133-8.

159. If *Blue* bears any real comparison to *Ghost*, then this might be its potter's wheel.

160. This is in another moment where the film plays loose with the precise details of its musical subject matter, as Julie's finger traces not the violas but Piano 1's upper stave, which doubles the strings. The notes are correct, but are not scored in the violas' alto clef.

161. For discussion see n. 153 above.

162. Julie's finger gets nine bars into the next section of the score; the sound of the music barely advances through two whole bars before Julie calls it to a halt. The music on screen was specially prepared for this shot. It is nothing like the layout of Preisner's actual cue sheet, which travels over three separate pages of A3 manuscript before the end of the continuous line of music seen in the film; what one hears, by contrast, barely gets halfway across a single page of Preisner's manuscript score. Preisner recalls that the shot was deemed vital to evoke, for the perceiver, the idea that this was music being heard by Julie and Olivier: the touch of the object and its movement primarily indicate (perhaps a shared) subjective point of view and audition, with the close-miking of their voices replacing, in turn, a close-up shot of their faces to cement the signification. A long scroll of music, with spindle and handles to mechanize it—rather like a roll of hand-cranked film stock—was created for this pre-digital special effect, permitting the camera and finger to remain still for the duration of the shot and so aiding the focus required for the extreme close-up. According to Preisner, the decision gradually to speed up the paper's velocity was practical. Although many members of the crew, including the composer and Kieślowski, tried to match the flow of the music to the playback, the slow result was aesthetically unsatisfying.

163. An earlier take of this sequence is heard on the soundtrack CD. There is more music and dialogue. Typically, this was pared back and, in the end, the dialogue was at least partially re-recorded in post-production.

164. David D. Boyden and Robin Stowell, "Flautando," in *Grove Music Online. Oxford Music Online*, http://www.oxfordmusiconline.com/subscriber/article/grove/music/09789 (accessed 27 April 2011).

165. Gross, "Female Subjectivity, Disability, and Musical Authorship," (2006), 51, 49. Other critics also claim a pivotal role for this scene in Julie's progress through her grief. For Kickasola, "gradually slipping into an abstract loss of focus as they steadily move into the realm of inspiration" marks the entry point of "a metaphysical zone—in this case, the beginnings of Julie's healing"; see Kickasola, *The Films of Krzysztof Kieślowski*, 278. Wollermann, too, notes the positive side to the scene—the most relaxed, on the surface, in the film—reading the lighter area at the center of the blurred second shot as "the light at the end of the tunnel"; see Wollermann, *Zur Musik in der "Drei Farben" Trilogie*, 64.

166. Paulus, "Music in Krzysztof Kieślowski's Film *Three Colors: Blue*," 81.

167. A specific reason for the memento to be "by" Van den Budenmayer, beyond the Kieślowski co-workers' in-joking and the fact he was Patrice's favorite composer, is alluded to in the screenplay. Julie expands on her husband's reasoning: "You know how much he loved him. And not just because of his music, but because of his tragic life and his premonition of misery. [Patrice] wanted to remind people of him at the end of the concert. He said it's a memento. Try weaving it back in." Van den Budenmayer had a premonition of misery: this odd turn of expository phrase, clunking under the weight of its symbolism, was undoubtedly better left out of the film. Nonetheless, that the end of the work was envisaged as being marked with a glimpse of "misery" calls attention to the layered ambivalence articulated by *Blue*'s finale.

168. Helmut Merker, "'Hinter allem ein Geheimnis': Im Gespräch mit Krzysztof Kieślowski," *Frankfurter Rundschau* (5 November 1993), 11; quoted in Wollermann, *Zur Musik in der "Drei Farben" Trilogie*, 67.

169. Wollermann, *Zur Musik in der "Drei Farben" Trilogie*, 69.

170. Žižek, *The Fright of Real Tears*, 172.

171. Žižek, *The Fright of Real Tears*, 169. Given the centrality of the text, its treatment by different distributors is both a cause of confusion and for regret which could easily be resolved in forthcoming reissues of the film. The Region 1 DVD release by Miramax, for example, does not translate the text at all. The Region 2 release by Artificial Eye does translate the text, but so shoddily as to render its inclusion misleading: it omits to translate some of the words heard and, to make matters worse, presents subtitled translations of portions of 1 Corinthians 13 not actually sung in the *Concert[o]*. Preisner recalls complicated discussions about the possibility of subtitles and believes that this partial but erroneous solution may reflect a well-intended bid to meet Kieślowski's desire for the subtitles to hint at the identity of the text so that perceivers keen enough to reflect on the film might discover its precise content for themselves. (This parallels his intentions for Domi-

nique's sign language at the end of *White*.) This strategy, unfortunately, backfired: not only has no critic (to the best of my knowledge) previously bothered accurately to note the precise version of the letter performed in *Blue*, but some have built strong interpretations of the film, and even of the trilogy and director, on the basis of words not actually sung or seen in the film.

172. Macnab and Darke, "Working with Kieślowski," 22.

173. Eagle-eyed viewers may note from the score glimpsed on-screen that Patrice's original conception for this music apparently included bells ("cloche" is clearly visible); there were also, Preisner's cue sheet reveals, multiple pianos and electric guitars, adding muscle to the texture (and a "power-chord" gesture, to recall Long's discussion of register, signifying "concerto") as it approaches its opening cadence. Julie has crossed out this macho scoring, permitting the relatively feminine sound of the sopranos, altos and high tenors to resound alone—a hint of changes to come which strip the score of overt masculinity to reveal feminine stereotypes better matched to the more conventional gestures of femininity she is now embracing.

174. Stein, "Music, Mourning, and Consolation," 794.

175. Stilwell, "The Fantastical Gap," 196.

176. For an analysis of this scene, see above, n. 104.

177. The most significant difference between Patrice's version of the *Concert[o]* and Julie's is that, in his, the soprano sings an octave lower and in a breathier voice. Synced to the montage, this sounds decidedly weird, as if one has accidentally dialed a fetish sex line staffed by an operatic alto. The difference could be read, strongly, to indicate something about Patrice: his score sounds seedy, like the aspects of his life revealed to Julie after his death. Preisner's explanation for the shift up the octave is, however, much simpler: the lower version sounded dull, Julie's electrifying. Patrice's version can be heard on the soundtrack CD as "Song for the Unification of Europe (Patrice's version)."

178. Orr, *Contemporary Cinema*, 64.

179. Wilson, *Memory and Survival*, 35.

180. Žižek, *The Fright of Real Tears*, 163.

181. The image is one of the moments in *Blue* that could be accused of trying too artfully to articulate its symbolism. The images call to mind an excised passage of the text, "For now we see in a mirror indirectly"—translated elsewhere as through a glass darkly—"but then we will see face to face."

182. In Preisner's manuscript score, that resolution is delayed by an instrumental development, audible on the CD soundtrack as "Olivier's theme—finale." That this is not in the film enables one of the iconic moments in Kieślowski's output; the cut also installs a formal balance in the *Concert[o]* that would have been muddied by the inclusion of the excluded section. What, though, was Preisner attempting to shape with this music?

It was a vision of Olivier and a version of Olivier's clumsy opening to the *Concert[o]*. Although one glimpses Olivier making love to Julie (and in the film's penultimate shot as well), unlike the other significant people in Julie's new life, he does not receive a solo shot in the closing montage. The cut section was conceived as Julie's musical souvenir of the man whose actions, for better or worse, have forced her into the next phase of her life. The screenplay indicates that Olivier would have been shot blissfully sleeping (as earlier in the film, just before he was dumped, thus redeeming that moment) and dreaming—perhaps of his own music.

Its most striking addition to what one already knows of Olivier's version of the *Concert[o]* (heard earlier in the scene where Julie edits his music) is the sonoristic haze into which it evaporates here. In a moment reminiscent of Preisner's first film score (the escape of the OAPs into the dawn in *Weather Report*), the music one recognizes from the joint composing session (the recorder now exchanging melodic phrases with the oboe and then the violins) veers into a different musical universe. Tubular bells and a tam tam intone, with piano, the familiar G diminished seventh chord; the sense of unease is sharpened by the upper strings' cloud of quartertones. It is a bizarre moment, and cutting it from the film permits *Blue*'s score a stylistic continuity it would otherwise have lacked. This passage, demonstrating Preisner's ability to mimic Penderecki's expressive resources, is neo-Romantic; the *Concert[o]* is (to adapt Preisner's "semi-classical") semi-Romantic.

The cut also played a practical role. Kieślowski, Preisner and the production team were aware of the strain they were putting on the film with such an elongated musical sequence—an unprecedented gesture in their cinema, and rare elsewhere. There was concern about whether the audience would feel frustrated if the sequence overran. Olivier, furthermore, is seen elsewhere in the sequence, and the music sets no crucial text. Ever economical, Kieślowski cut.

183. Kieślowski and Piesiewicz, *"Three Colours" Trilogy*, 98.

184. Insdorf, *Double Lives, Second Chances*, 52.

185. Insdorf, *Double Lives, Second Chances*, 177.

186. Insdorf, *Double Lives, Second Chances*, 104.

187. Mike Cormack, "The Pleasures of Ambiguity: Using Classical Music in Film," in *Changing Tunes: The Use of Pre-Existing Music in Film*, ed. Phil Powrie and Robynn J. Stilwell (Aldershot: Ashgate Publishing, 2006), 29.

188. Caryl Flinn, *Strains of Utopia: Gender, Nostalgia, and Hollywood Film Music* (Princeton, NJ: Princeton University Press, 1992), 9.

189. Dean Duncan, *The Charms that Soothe: Classical Music and the Narrative Film* (New York: Fordham University Press, 2003); see especially chapters four and five of this study.

190. Royal S. Brown, *Overtones and Undertones*, 239.

191. It is also the ending one hears, in my view regretfully, when the *Concert[o]* is performed at Preisner concerts.

192. As if to add insult to the injury of its erroneous subtitles, the Artificial Eye Region 2 DVD actually cuts before the final harp pitches, fading out the trio to cut to a corporate logo. Even this, though, is not as

bad as a screening of the film I once attended at the Riverside Studios in London, where the final reel literally disintegrated a few bars into the end credits. The disturbed gasps in the audience at that screening—and the way, at other screenings, many more people than usual at a cinema screening remain in their seats to audio-view the credits—spoke volumes for the centrality of Preisner's score to *Blue*.

193. See Insdorf, *Double Lives, Second Chances*; Redner, "Building a Deleuzian Bridge"; Paul C. Santilli, "Cinema and Subjectivity in Krzysztof Kieślowski," *The Journal of Aesthetics and Art Criticism* 64, no. 1 (Winter 2006): 147-56.

194. See Andrew, *The "Three Colours" Trilogy*; Kickasola, *The Films of Krzysztof Kieślowski*; Wilson, *Memory and Survival*.

195. Žižek, *The Fright of Real Tears*, 171.

196. Žižek, *The Fright of Real Tears*, 172.

197. Insdorf, *Double Lives, Second Chances*, 151.

198. Rushton, "Reading *Three Colours: Blue*."

199. Eagleton, *The Meaning of Life*, 144.

200. Eagleton, *The Meaning of Life*, 158-60.

201. Eagleton, *The Meaning of Life*, 165.

202. Eagleton, *The Meaning of Life*, 166.

Chapter Six

1. Robert Hatten, *Musical Meaning in Beethoven: Markedness, Correlation, and Interpretation* (Bloomington: Indiana University Press, 1994), 16. For a condensed introduction to the topic, see Robert Hatten, "On Narrativity in Music: Expressive Genres and Levels of Discourse in Beethoven," *Indiana Theory Review* 12 (1991): 75-98.

2. Hatten, *Musical Meaning in Beethoven*, 20.

3. For a brief introduction to this literature (with further bibliography) see Fred Everett Maus, "Narratology, Narrativity," in *Grove Music Online. Oxford Music Online*, http://www.oxfordmusiconline.com/subscriber/article/grove/music/40607 (last accessed 27 April 2011).

4. See Leonard Ratner, *Classic Music: Expression, Form, and Style* (New York: Schirmer Books, 1980).

5. An article I have in preparation tackles this: "The Beginning of a Beautiful Friendship? Music Narratology and Screen Music Studies" (to be submitted to *Music, Sound, and the Moving Image*).

6. Like Hatten, Michael Long notes (see Chapter Two, n. 9) that expressive registers can embrace "an inherent verticality" of class-related significations, as in, for instance, poetic register (e.g., the "high expressive register of the medieval *canso* versus the low expressive register of the *pastorella*"; see Long, *Beautiful Monsters*, 13). *White* explores this type of vertical movement, but its registral hierarchy makes sense only when the two registers—a (low) pastoral *rustico* and a (higher) tango—are (a) considered as "established landmarks" within

Polish musical traditions with attendant cultural baggage, and (b) simultaneously in terms of a horizontal move from style-topically articulated tragic to heroic significations of the type Hatten also addresses.

7. Pierre Bourdieu, *Distinction: A Social Critique of the Judgement of Taste*, trans. Richard Nice (Abingdon: Routledge, 1986 [1979]), xi-xii.

8. Bourdieu, *Distinction*, 1-2.

9. Bourdieu, *Distinction*, 14.

10. The obvious example from Preisner's own output is *At Play in the Fields of the Lord* (Babenco, 1991), a film in which his music is juxtaposed and superimposed—often quite ingeniously—with Amazonian music, as various character identities (and also the missionaries' and indigenous people's perspectives) clash, merge and reverse.

11. Dahlig, "Poland," 708.

12. Stephen Downes, "Mazurka," in *Grove Music Online. Oxford Music Online*, http://www.oxfordmusiconline.com/subscriber/article/grove/music/18193 (last accessed 28 April 2011).

13. While one may just about hear hints of some Chopin mazurkas—the play of minor and major or falling thirds in no. 36 in A minor, the hesitant opening melody of no. 32 in C♯ minor, the delicacy of no. 22 in G♯ minor with its voicing evoking a folk ensemble—the similarity is most likely a nostalgic take on a shared Polish heritage of traditional music, rather than the direct influence on Preisner of Chopin.

14. Downes, "Mazurka."

15. See Wollermann, *Zur Musik in der "Drei Farben" Trilogie*, 92.

16. Brophy, "How Sound Floats on Land," 139.

17. Insdorf, *Double Lives, Second Chances*, 158.

18. Kieślowski and Piesiewicz, *"Three Colours" Trilogy*, 103.

19. This siren, a little later in *White*, sounds the alarm as Karol puts his cash card into the bank machine and discovers he is penniless.

20. The cue is different to the version Preisner scored before recording; the version given here is an annotation from the film. It seems Preisner rethought the cue after creating the rest of the score, while fitting the music to the final cut of the film. This may explain how its final version reflects more precisely the score's musical totality.

21. The absence of the word "fraternity," in turn, could be read to reflect his sense of isolation.

22. Wollermann, *Zur Musik in der "Drei Farben" Trilogie*, 77-8.

23. As discussed below, the confirmation of C as a pitch-center can be heard to link back to the start of the film and give a sense of arrival or fulfillment, especially in the next musical scene. More locally it permits fluidity. Dominique's part of the cue begins on the minor modal tone of Karol's A (C natural) before revealing itself as the tonic of a new pitch-center.

24. Performing even looks painful for Karol, the camera cutting tellingly from the bust's reposed face to his exertions on the comb.

25. Rick Altman, "Cinema and Popular Song: The Lost Tradition," in *Soundtrack Available: Essays on Film and Popular Music*, ed. Pam-

ela Robertson Wojcik and Arthur Knight (London: Duke University Press, 2001), 26.

26. Wikipedia describes the song as "perfect background music for shooting oneself in the head" and links it to suicidal acts by disillusioned Polish officers during wartime. See http://en.wikipedia.org/wiki/To_ostatnia_niedziela (last accessed 26 August 2010).

27. This informative article appears on a website authored by Claude Torres: http://claude.torres1.perso.sfr.fr/GhettosCamps/Camps/Gold_Pertersburski_Orchestra.html (last accessed 26 April 2011), but it appears to be a fragment of a text I have previously read online on a now defunct website called The Big Bands Database (http://nfo.net/euro/ep.html, last accessed 25 May 2007). On that site, the article "Jerzy Petersburski Orch." was credited, in large part, to contributions from poet Grzegorz Musial. It noted that the song has appeared elsewhere in film, notably as "Weary Sun," a version made popular in Russia in 1937 with a lyric by Iosif Alvek and performed by Pavel Mikhailov, backed by the State Radio Committee Jazz Band, and which appears in the *Burnt by the Sun* (Nikita Mikhalkov, 1994). It is tempting to speculate on the possibility this influenced Kieślowski's use in *White*, but the idea appears to have been in the director's mind by 1993, when he held his published conversations with Stok before work on the *White* and *Red* screenplays had even been completed.

28. That the poster is *Contempt* was, according to Kieślowski, merely economic pragmatism: his producer owned the rights to Godard's picture and thus the poster, and so they could use it for free, rather than the poster of Michelle Pfeiffer Kieślowski apparently had in mind. Bearing in mind the interplay of connotations between Godard's film and *White*, it is nonetheless, clearly, an interesting choice; see Insdorf, *Double Lives, Second Chances*, 158.

29. Wilson, *Memory and Survival*, 65.

30. Wilson, *Memory and Survival*, 73.

31. Wilson, *Memory and Survival*, 73.

32. Wilson, *Memory and Survival*, 74.

33. Wilson, *Memory and Survival*, 74.

34. The *Contempt* poster intensifies this association, its exploitative rendering of Bardot—looking utterly unlike the majority of her appearances in the film—raising issues Godard deconstructs in his movie.

35. This subtle orchestration can be heard on the soundtrack CD.

36. Falkowska, "*The Double Life of Véronique*," 148.

37. Haltof, *The Cinema of Krzysztof Kieślowski*, 137.

38. See Susan McClary, *Feminine Endings: Music, Gender, and Sexuality* (Minneapolis: University of Minnesota Press, 1991).

39. That his way with women will magically change is signified by the transported delight on Jurek's customer's face in the next scene: when she mentions she has heard that Karol has returned, it is as if she is already imagining his fingers working on her to positive effect.

40. The colors, a play on Poland's national flag, may also signify, in the context of the trilogy's symbolism, that Karol will be equal (or more equal) here and, quite literally, welcomed as a brother.

41. Gerard Béhague, "Tango," in *Grove Music Online. Oxford Music Online*, http://www.oxfordmusiconline.com/subscriber/article/grove/music/27473 (last accessed 18 April 2011).

42. Marta E. Savigliano, "Whiny Ruffians and Rebellious Broads: Tango as a Spectacle of Eroticized Social Tension," *Theatre Journal* 47 (1995): 83.

43. The diversity of screen uses cited in the Wikipedia entry on this song suggests an interesting research project is there for the taking on whether this song has come to act as a style topic symbolizing *all* tango in mainstream screen entertainment, thanks to purported appearances in "*Schindler's List, Scent of a Woman, Delicatessen, True Lies, All the King's Men, Bad Santa,* Episode 37 of *Nip/Tuck,* Episode 9 of *Sweet Spy,* the beginning and ending credits of *I'm Sorry, I Love You,* . . . the *CSI: NY* episode 'Down the Rabbit Hole' . . . and in the movie *Frida*"; http://en.wikipedia.org/wiki/Por_Una_Cabeza (last accessed 11 January 2010).

44. Béhague, "Tango."

45. Béhague, "Tango."

46. See n. 27 above for source.

47. As documented in Jerzy Płaczkiewicz, "Tango in Poland, 1913-39," http://www.todotango.com/english/biblioteca/cronicas/tango_en_polonia.asp (last accessed 18 April 2011).

48. See Adrian Thomas, "Your Song Is Mine," *Musical Times* 136 (August 1995): 403-9.

49. See n. 27 above for source.

50. Płaczkiewicz, "Tango in Poland."

51. Płaczkiewicz, "Tango in Poland."

52. Savigliano, "Whiny Ruffians and Rebellious Broads," 97.

53. Savigliano, "Whiny Ruffians and Rebellious Broads," 99.

54. Savigliano, "Whiny Ruffians and Rebellious Broads," 100-101.

55. Béhague, "Tango."

56. Béhague, "Tango."

57. Savigliano, "Whiny Ruffians and Rebellious Broads," 87.

58. Savigliano, "Whiny Ruffians and Rebellious Broads," 89.

59. Savigliano, "Whiny Ruffians and Rebellious Broads," 90.

60. The terminology is Manthia Diawara's from "Black Spectatorship: Problems of Identification and Resistance," (1988), in Braudy and Cohen, *Film Theory and Criticism*: 892-900.

61. Waldo Frank, translated in Savigliano, "Whiny Ruffians and Rebellious Broads," 94.

62. Savigliano, "Whiny Ruffians and Rebellious Broads," 87.

63. Savigliano, "Whiny Ruffians and Rebellious Broads," 96.

64. Insdorf, *Double Lives, Second Chances*, 160.

65. Wilson, *Memory and Survival*, 70-71.

66. See McClary, *Feminine Endings*.

67. "'Would that I had pleased,' indeed!" Andrew notes; see Andrew, *The "Three Colours" Trilogy*, 44.

68. A second possibility for the source of the sound is that Jurek is listening to a broadcast of the *Concert[o]* elsewhere in the house (unlikely, perhaps, as he says elsewhere that Poland is already in Europe, suggesting that the unification envisaged in *Blue* has now happened). A third is that it is playing in Karol's imagination. The source, like the pigeons, is unidentifiable, but the symbol of femininity could even be heard as the statue singing to Karol, distracting him from his work, while reminding him of what he is studying to achieve.

69. Later on in the film, he arranges to have the wall to a house's grounds torn down and then rebuilt a few centimeters thicker, just because he is influential and rich enough to do so.

70. Gorbman, *Unheard Melodies*, 5.

71. Gorbman, *Unheard Melodies*, 67.

72. In more recent times, the Palace has also provided a home to big business and casinos.

73. Karol's mistake, in the screenplay, is to have forgotten the clocks have gone forward by two hours, and he returns to find the police already there, fate having made his choice for him.

74. Wollermann, *Zur Musik in der "Drei Farben" Trilogie*, 87.

75. See Kickasola, *The Films of Krzysztof Kieślowski*, 284.

76. Kickasola, *The Films of Krzysztof Kieślowski*, 288.

77. For a discussion of stridulation see Chion, *Audio-Vision*, 20-21.

78. See Robert Baird, 'Startle and the Film Threat Scene," *Images Journal* 3 (24/2/2005): http://www.imagesjournal.com/issue03/features/startle1.htm (last accessed 26 April 2011) for a discussion of sonic startles in film. Following Baird, one might argue that a longer moment of silence was needed here to permit the audience to prime themselves to jump at the footfall.

79. The cimbalom and flute parts scored for the hotel room "inner cinema" cue, while not audible in the film, were scored by Preisner and further demonstrate his attempt to shape continuity between the cues.

80. Kickasola, *The Films of Krzysztof Kieślowski*, 288.

81. There are pigeons in the warehouse, as seen when Karol inspects his fake coffin, with their presence—like the two-franc coin he slips into the coffin—recalling the arc of his story to date.

82. The casting of Aleksander Bardini (from *No End* and *Decalogue 2*) for this scene is perfect: he almost seems to be there purely for the singular incredulity that his eyebrows are capable of expressing.

83. Kickasola, *The Films of Krzysztof Kieślowski*, 292.

84. Delpy's description of Kieślowski's directing of her acted orgasm for this scene—complete with stopwatch timings and conductor-like cues for mounting excitement and climax—is funnier than anything in the film itself. See "A Conversation with Julie Delpy on Kieślowski," DVD extra on *White* in *Krzysztof Kieślowski's "Three Colors": The Exclusive Collection* (Miramax 28656).

85. Andrew, *The "Three Colours" Trilogy*, 48.

86. Karol only blinks on the occasions he casts his eyes down and away from his own gaze, as if he is not entirely sure that he likes what he is seeing.

87. "Krzysztof Kieślowski's Cinema Lesson," DVD extra on *White* in *Krzysztof Kieślowski's "Three Colors": The Exclusive Collection* (Miramax 28656).

88. Wilson, *Memory and Survival*, 78.

89. "Marin Karmitz Interview," DVD extra on *White* in *Krzysztof Kieślowski's "Three Colors": The Exclusive Collection* (Miramax 28656).

90. Coates, "'The Inner Life Is the Only Thing that Interests Me,'" 172.

91. Quoted and translated in Insdorf, *Double Lives, Second Chances*, 160.

92. Haltof, *The Cinema of Krzysztof Kieślowski*, 135.

93. Insdorf, *Double Lives, Second Chances*, 160.

94. Insdorf, *Double Lives, Second Chances*, 165.

95. Insdorf, *Double Lives, Second Chances*, 165.

96. In Karol's full name, Karol Karol (which robs him of a paternal family name and thus, in a sense, emasculates him), Žižek identifies a doubling trope present in other work by Kieślowski. "There is already," he argues, as for Humbert Humbert in *Lolita*, "the structure of the double in his very name!" See Žižek, *The Fright of Real Tears*, 85.

97. Žižek, *The Fright of Real Tears*, 85.

98. Kickasola, *The Films of Krzysztof Kieślowski*, 294.

99. Wilson, *Memory and Survival*, 77.

100. Savigliano, "Whiny Ruffians and Rebellious Broads," 102.

101. Savigliano, "Whiny Ruffians and Rebellious Broads," 103.

102. Savigliano, "Whiny Ruffians and Rebellious Broads," 103.

103. Savigliano, "Whiny Ruffians and Rebellious Broads," 104.

104. Savigliano, "Whiny Ruffians and Rebellious Broads," 103; Joan Cocks, *The Oppositional Imagination: Feminism, Critique, and Political Theory* (London: Routledge, 1989).

105. "Behind the Scenes of *White* with Krzysztof Kieślowski," DVD extra on *White* in *Krzysztof Kieślowski's "Three Colors": The Exclusive Collection* (Miramax 28656).

106. Dyer, *White*, xv.

107. Dyer, *White*, 207.

108. Dyer, *White*, 209.

109. Dyer, *White*, 210.

110. Dyer, *White*, 211.

111. Dyer, *White*, 212-13.

112. Dyer, *White*, 213.

113. Dyer, *White*, 218.

114. D-FENS is the character's government car number plate. Its use, instead of his actual name, could be read to rob aspects of his identity in the manner of Karol Karol's emasculating titular repetitiveness.

115. Dyer, *White*, 218.

116. Dyer, *White*, 221-2.

117. The notion that one can go back and start again, commonly adumbrated in Kieślowski's universe, and make the *right* decision (like Véronique quitting singing where Weronika died, or Karol and Dominique making up where once they fell apart) is the smiley-face on one side of the conditionality coin. The scowling flip side, as Žižek argues, is the suggestion that there is literally no end to human misery or conditionality, and thus no point at which, "like God after his six days' work," one can say "It's done!" and take a rest; see Žižek, *The Fright of Real Tears*, 95. The universe of *White* and the late Kieślowski films/life is (in this view) "a chaotic, ontologically not yet fully constituted reality" beneath which lurks "the Real of the unformed ghastly matter"; the ambiguity of such moments, Žižek argues, is thus not Kieślowski as "New Age obscurantist" (101) but "ambiguity [that] is radical, as with Tarkovsky, Kieślowski's Russian counterpart." Chance and ambiguity in the Kieślowski universe open a familiar, still disturbing question: "[D]oes it point towards a deeper fate secretly regulating our lives, or is the notion of fate itself a desperate stratagem to cope with the utter contingency of life?" (107). Karol chooses love, and the ending suggests hope, yet taken to a logical conclusion, this is undermined by the ongoing discourse of contingency within the trilogy, with *White*'s ending "overcoming the unbearable Otherness of meaningless cosmic contingency through a gesture that is itself utterly meaningless" (106). At his lightest, *White* is also at his darkest.

Chapter Seven

1. Readers familiar with the concept of sonata form will hopefully forgive the simplifications of this exposition. Those seeking more recent scholarship might find James Hepokoski's article "Masculine-Feminine," *The Musical Times* 135 (August 1994): 494-99 an interesting introduction to wider themes relevant to this study, some of which are also broached by the *New Grove*'s entry on sonata form: see James Webster, "Sonata Form," *Grove Music Online. Oxford Music Online*, http://www.oxfordmusiconline.com/subscriber/article/grove/music/26197 (last accessed 1 September 2010).

2. Christopher Ballatine, *Twentieth Century Symphony* (London: Dennis Dobson, 1983), 19-20.

3. David Beard and Kenneth Gloag, *Musicology: The Key Concepts* (London: Routledge, 2005), 9.

4. Tzvetan Todorov's theory of equilibrium-disequilibrium-new equilibrium is an obvious example; see Tzvetan Todorov, *Introduction to Poetics*, trans. Richard Howard (Minneapolis: University of Minnesota Press, 1981).

5. Kickasola, *The Films of Krzysztof Kieślowski*, 296; see also Wilson, *Memory and Survival*, 94-5 and Andrew, *The "Three Colours"*

Trilogy, 60-1). Lois Vines argues for an alternative literary association to a writer Kieślowski admired, linking the Old Judge to Albert Camus's "judge-penitent," Jean-Baptiste Clamence, in *The Fall*; see Lois Vines, "Kieślowski's *Red* and Camus's *The Fall*: Redemption of a Judge-Penitent," *Literature/Film Quarterly* 31, no. 2 (2003): 141-47. Kieślowski was a committed reader of Camus; see Stok, ed. and trans., *Kieślowski on Kieślowski*, 5.

6. Insdorf, *Double Lives, Second Chances*, 177.

7. Insdorf, *Double Lives, Second Chances*, 178.

8. Wilson, *Memory and Survival*, 95.

9. Is the bolero's thrumming, quartertonally distorting ostinato the sound of "a thousand twangling instruments"?

10. Kickasola, *The Films of Krzysztof Kieślowski*, 298.

11. Kickasola, *The Films of Krzysztof Kieślowski*, 299.

12. Insdorf, *Double Lives, Second Chances*, 169.

13. In the screenplay, both Auguste's red jeep and Joseph's Mercedes pass behind Valentine. The use of a mirror—a trope in art cinema and a recurring fingerprint of Kieślowski's own style—provides a less concrete, more poetic evocation of different versions of the same subject mingling with Valentine.

14. Paxman, "Preisner-Kieślowski," 149.

15. Paxman, "Preisner-Kieślowski," 149.

16. Paxman, "Preisner-Kieślowski," 149.

17. Philip Tagg, *Fernando the Flute* (Liverpool: Institute of Popular Music, 1991).

18. See Tagg, *Fernando the Flute*.

19. Paxman, "Preisner-Kieślowski," 150.

20. The ostinato also disappears as Valentine stills for a moment of introspection. Wollermann links this to her tiredness, as a signification of weakening; see Wollermann, *Zur Musik in der "Drei Farben" Trilogie*, 107.

21. Paxman, "Preisner-Kieślowski," 151.

22. Kickasola, *The Films of Krzysztof Kieślowski*, 303.

23. Kickasola, *The Films of Krzysztof Kieślowski*, 303.

24. Insdorf, *Double Lives, Second Chances*, 174.

25. Looking back, one may ask where the music has been from the start of the sequence. The fashion show music could conceivably have been diegetically present (Paxman and Wollermann both call the cue diegetic), but it sounded like non-diegetic underscore in terms of its prominence in the mix and lack of treatment denoting it as coming from a diegetic source. Ai sounds exactly the same as Aii in terms of recording quality and place in the mix. During the first shot in the car, as she rubs her wrists, the music could in turn be conceived as playing on Valentine's radio, but it is still likely to be heard non-diegetically (there is no change to the treatment of the music in the mix to suggest a shift from the fashion show to the car). Once she is driving, the odder changes in timbre and volume suggest a moment of rupture—or intervention—altering the music's role in the discourse.

26. Paxman, "Preisner-Kieślowski," 156.

27. Quiroga, *Tropics of Desire*, 145.

28. Paxman, "Preisner-Kieślowski," 152.

29. Paxman, "Preisner-Kieślowski," 156.

30. Wollermann, *Zur Musik in der "Drei Farben" Trilogie*, 109.

31. Wollermann, *Zur Musik in der "Drei Farben" Trilogie*, 109.

32. Paxman, "Preisner-Kieślowski," 160.

33. Paxman, "Preisner-Kieślowski," 158.

34. Paxman, "Preisner-Kieślowski," 156.

35. Paxman, "Preisner-Kieślowski," 154.

36. Paxman, "Preisner-Kieślowski," 154.

37. Paxman, "Preisner-Kieślowski," 158.

38. Kickasola, *The Films of Krzysztof Kieślowski*, 305.

39. A siren in the distance signals a hazard when the photographer seeks to seduce her.

40. Kickasola, *The Films of Krzysztof Kieślowski*, 307.

41. Kickasola, *The Films of Krzysztof Kieślowski*, 78.

42. Van den Budenmayer has thus patriotically selected a poet from his homeland, although apparently with the benefit of a time machine, given van Eeden's existence long after the death of the longer-dead fictional composer.

43. Originally published under the title "Van de passielooze lelie" in 1901 by W. Versluys in Amsterdam; translation from *A Sampling of Dutch Literature: Thirteen Excursions into the Works of Dutch Authors* (Hilversum: Radio Nederland Wereldomroep, 1962).

44. The line that comes to rest, as if on the surface of the chords, elaborates the "x" motif from *Blue*.

45. Kickasola, *The Films of Krzysztof Kieślowski*, 304.

46. Kickasola, *The Films of Krzysztof Kieślowski*, 316, n. 82.

47. Andrew, *The "Three Colours" Trilogy*, 89.

48. Andrew, *The "Three Colours" Trilogy*, 89.

49. The actions mirror Olivier's desire to provoke a response from Julie by publicizing the rediscovered score of the *Concert[o]* on TV.

50. The other balletic gesture in the scene is a virtuosic camera sweep back and away from the Old Judge's explanations to a billiard table; a broken bottle and a billiard ball are seen before the image focuses again on the dialogue. How the ball broke the bottle is never explained in the film (it was in the screenplay), but here it connects, tangentially, to Auguste's broken glass at the bowling rink, linking the moment of the Old Judge's confession to his younger double's angst.

51. Andrew, *The "Three Colours" Trilogy*, 57.

52. Kickasola, *The Films of Krzysztof Kieślowski*, 317.

53. A glitch on the soundtrack at this point provides a trace of the hard editing work on this sequence.

54. Kickasola, *The Films of Krzysztof Kieślowski*, 69.

55. Kehr, "To Save the World," 18.

56. That the seventh person saved, the English barman Steven Killian, is not seen or mentioned elsewhere in the trilogy is a neat de-

tail. It skews the otherwise perfect unity of the ending, suggesting a story that could have been told—a recurring trait in the trilogy.

57. At a push, one could link this collection to portions of some of the score's sonoristic textures, the bolero's Ai melody or motif y from *Blue*, the latter obviously also featuring in *Red*'s major key bolero cues.

58. Kehr, "To Save the World," 20.

59. Andrew, *The "Three Colours" Trilogy*, 61.

60. Julie, in particular, surely faces a grave and testing period. Having survived a period of trauma following her bereavements, the ferry disaster could affect her severely. Also, if Karol and Dominique are on the run, their well-publicized rescue could swiftly turn into recapture and imprisonment.

61. Andrew, *The "Three Colours" Trilogy*, 61.

62. Andrew, *The "Three Colours" Trilogy*, 72. Kieślowski's admiration of ancient Greek tragedians may be reflected in this act.

63. Wilson, *Memory and Survival*, xii.

64. Wilson, *Memory and Survival*, 41.

65. Wilson, *Memory and Survival*, 118. For Wilson the "ultimate lesson in *Rouge* is not simply one of hope and redemption . . . but one, once again, of chance and betrayal," in the context of a trilogy portraying "a pessimistic and ultimately fatalistic interpretation of the human condition" (92).

66. For audience members who recognize the disaster footage as the Herald of Free Enterprise tragedy, the sorrow of the coda is inescapable—and perhaps that was a point of Kieślowski's use of images so authentically terrible at this juncture in the trilogy.

67. Kickasola, *The Films of Krzysztof Kieślowski*, 297.

68. The audience is told to expect one further event in the story, after the trilogy's close, which will reflect these notions. Valentine is planning to see the Old Judge after her trip, in order to adopt one of Rita's puppies; their friendship will therefore continue. Whatever happens between Valentine and Auguste, neither she nor Joseph will be quite as alone as they were when *Red*'s story began.

BIBLIOGRAPHY

Aiken, Fred. "Letters: Bergman in Perspective." "Review," *The Guardian* (14 January 2006): 15.

Altman, Rick. "Cinema and Popular Song: The Lost Tradition." 19-30 in Wojcik and Knight, eds., *Soundtrack Available*, 2001.

Amiel, Vincent, ed. *Krzysztof Kieślowski*. Paris: Jean-Michel Place, 1997.

Anderson, Benedict. *Imagined Communities: Reflections on the Origin and Spread of Nationalism*. London: Verso, 1991.

Andrew, Geoff. *The "Three Colours" Trilogy*. London: British Film Institute, 1998.

Archer, John. *The Nature of Grief: The Evolution and Psychology of Reactions to Loss*. London: Routledge, 1999.

A Sampling of Dutch Literature: Thirteen Excursions into the Works of Dutch Authors. Hilversum: Radio Nederland Wereldomroep, 1962.

Asch, Mark. "Cinephile's Notebook: *Three Colors*." *The L Magazine* (12 April 2006). http://www.thelmagazine.com/newyork/cinephiles-notebook-three-colors/Content?oid=1136060 (last accessed 18 April 2011).

Baird, Robert. "Startle and the Film Threat Scene." *Images Journal* 3 (24 February 2005). http://www.imagesjournal.com/issue03/features/startle1.htm (last accessed 26 April 2011).

Ballatine, Christopher. *Twentieth Century Symphony*. London: Dennis Dobson, 1983.

Bazin, André. "From *What Is Cinema?*: The Evolution of the Language of Cinema [1967]." 41-53 in *Film Theory and Criticism*, edited by Braudy and Cohen.

Beard, David, and Kenneth Gloag. *Musicology: The Key Concepts*. London: Routledge, 2005.

Bergson, Henri. *Henri Bergson: Key Writings*. New York: Continuum, 2002.

Béhague, Gerard. "Tango." *Grove Music Online. Oxford Music Online*. http://www.oxfordmusiconline.com/subscriber/article/grove/music/ 27473 (last accessed 18 April 2011).

Bhabha, Homi K., ed. *Nation and Narration*. London: Routledge, 1990.

Biancorosso, Giorgio. "Janet Halfyard, *Danny Elfman's "Batman": A Film Score Guide*." *Music and Letters* 88, no. 1 (Feb. 2007): 188-190.

"Board: Double vie de Véronique, La (1991)." http://www.imdb .com/title/tt0101765/board/flat/16884584?p=1 (last accessed 10 May 2007).

Bohlman, Philip V. *World Music: A Very Short Introduction*. Oxford: Oxford University Press, 2002.

Bourdieu, Pierre. *Distinction: A Social Critique of the Judgement of Taste*. Translated by Richard Nice. Abingdon: Routledge, 1986 (1979).

Boyd, Craig A., ed. *Visions of Agapé: Problems and Possibilities in Human and Divine Love*. Aldershot: Ashgate, 2008.

Boyden, David D., and Robin Stowell. "Flautando." *Grove Music Online. Oxford Music Online*. http://www.oxfordmusiconline.com/ subscriber/article/grove/music/09789 (accessed 27 April 2011).

Braudy, Leo, and Marshall Cohen, eds. *Film Theory and Criticism* 6th ed. Oxford: Oxford University Press, 2004.

Brooke, Michael. "Danton." *Sight and Sound* 19, no. 6 (June 2009): 88.

Brophy, Philip. "How Sound Floats on Land: The Suppression and Release of Folk and Indigenous Musics in the Cinematic Terrain." 136-48 in *Beyond the Soundtrack*, edited by Goldmark, Kramer, and Leppert.

Brown, Julie. "Listening to Ravel, Watching *Un coeur en hiver*: Cinematic Subjectivity and the Music-film." *Twentieth-Century Music* 1, no. 2 (2004): 253-75.

Brown, Royal S. *Overtones and Undertones: Reading Film Music*. Berkeley: University of California Press, 1994.

Broxton, Jonathan and James Southall. "Regaining Composure: An Interview with Zbigniew Preisner." *Film Score Monthly* 4, no. 7 (August 1999): 15-18.

——. "Zbigniew Preisner in Concert: Requiem for My Friend." http://www.moviemusicuk/us/preisint.htm (last accessed 19 January 2001).

Carlsson, Mikael, and Peter Holm. "The Double Life of Zbigniew Preisner." *Music from the Movies* (May 1997): 38-42.

Chion, Michel. *Audio-Vision: Sound on Screen*. Edited and translated by Claudia Gorbman. New York: Columbia University Press, 1994 (1990).

——. "Mute Music: Polański's *The Pianist* and Campion's *The Piano*." 86-96 in *Beyond the Soundtrack*, edited by Goldmark, Kramer, and Leppert.

Chłopecki, Andrzej. "Preisner, czyli apologia kiczu." *Tygodnik Powszechny* 44 (1 November 1998): 9.

Chmura, Bogdan. "Preisner, Zbigniew." *Grove Music Online. Oxford Music Online.* http://www.oxfordmusiconline.com/subscriber/article/grove/music/47985 (last accessed 18 April 2011).

Clarke, Eric, and Nicola Dibben. "Sex, Pulp, and Critique." *Popular Music* 19, no. 2 (2000): 231-41.

Coates, Paul, ed. *Lucid Dreams: The Films of Krzysztof Kieślowski.* Trowbridge: Flicks Books, 1999.

——. "Introduction." 1-18 in *Lucid Dreams,* edited by Coates.

——. "The Curse of the Law: *The Decalogue.*" 94-115 in *Lucid Dreams,* edited by Coates.

——. "'The Inner Life Is the Only Thing that Interests Me': a conversation with Krzysztof Kieślowski." 160-74 in *Lucid Dreams,* edited by Coates.

——. "Kieślowski and the Antipolitics of Color: A Reading of the *Three Colors* Trilogy." *Cinema Journal* 41, no. 2 (2002): 41-66.

——. *Cinema, Religion and the Romantic Legacy.* Aldershot: Ashgate Publishing, 2003.

Cocks, Joan. *The Oppositional Imagination: Feminism, Critique, and Political Theory.* London: Routledge, 1989.

Cook, Nicholas. *Beethoven: Symphony no. 9.* Cambridge: Cambridge University Press, 1993.

——. *Analyzing Musical Multimedia.* Oxford: Oxford University Press, 1998.

——. "Representing Beethoven: Romance and Sonata Form in Simon Cellan Jones's *Eroica.*" 27-47 in *Beyond the Soundtrack,* edited by Goldmark, Kramer, and Leppert.

Cooke, Mervyn. *A History of Film Music.* Cambridge: Cambridge University Press, 2008.

Cormack, Mike. "The Pleasures of Ambiguity: Using Classical Music in Film." 19-30 in *Changing Tunes: The Use of Pre-Existing Music in Film,* edited by Powrie and Stilwell.

Coupland, Douglas. "Guardian Book Club: Week Three. Douglas Coupland on How He Came to Write *Generation X.*" *The Guardian* (26 September 2009). http://www.guardian.co.uk/books/2009/sep/26/douglas-couplandgeneration-x (last accessed 6 October 2010).

Cox, Alex. "A Sentimental Education." "Review," *The Guardian* (7 January 2006): 14.

Csíkszentmihályi, Mihály, and Isabelle Selega Csíkszentmihályi, eds. *Optimal Experience: Psychological Studies of Flow in Consciousness.* Cambridge: Cambridge University Press, 1988.

Dahlig, Ewa. "Poland." In *The Garland Encyclopedia of World Music,* vol. 8. Edited by Timothy Rice, James Porter, and Chris Goertzen, 701-15. New York: Garland, 2000.

Dalkin, Gary S. "Zbigniew Preisner—The Last September." www.musicweb-international.com (January 2001). http://www.musicweb-international.com/film/2001/Jan01/the_last_september.html (last accessed 20 January 2006).

——. "Effroyables jardins." www.musicweb-international.com (July 2004). http://www.musicweb-international.com/film/2004/Jul04/effroyables_jardins.html (last accessed 20 January 2006).

Davidson, Audrey Ekdahl. *Olivier Messiaen and the Tristan Myth*. London: Praeger, 2001.

Davison, Annette. *Hollywood Theory, Non-Hollywood Practice: Cinema Soundtracks in the 1980s and 1990s*. Aldershot: Ashgate, 2004.

Diawara, Manthia. "Black Spectatorship: Problems of Identification and Resistance [1988]." 892-900 in *Film Theory and Criticism*, edited by Braudy and Cohen.

Dobson, Julia. "Nationality, Authenticity, Reflexivity: Kieślowski's *Trois couleurs: Bleu* (1993), *Blanc* (1993), and *Rouge* (1994)." In *French Cinema in the 1990s: Continuity and Difference*, edited by Phil Powrie, 234-45. Oxford: Oxford University Press, 1999.

Downes, Stephen. "Mazurka." In *Grove Music Online. Oxford Music Online*. http://www.oxfordmusiconline.com/subscriber/article/grove/music/18193 (last accessed 28 April 2011).

Drake, Philip. "'Mortgaged to Music': New Retro Movies in 1990s Hollywood Cinema." In *Memory and Popular Film*, edited by Paul Grainge, 183-201. Manchester: Manchester University Press, 2003.

Duncan, Dean. *The Charms that Soothe: Classical Music and the Narrative Film*. New York: Fordham University Press, 2003.

Dyer, Richard. *Stars*. London: British Film Institute, 1979.

——. *White*. London: Routledge, 1997.

——. *Heavenly Bodies: Film Stars and Society*. London: Routledge, 2004.

——. "Side by Side: Nino Rota, Music, and Film." 246-259 in *Beyond the Soundtrack*, edited by Goldmark, Kramer, and Leppert.

Eagleton, Terry. *The Meaning of Life*. Oxford: Oxford University Press, 2007.

——. "Indomitable: *How to Change the World: Marx and Marxism 1840-2011* by Eric Hobsbawm." *The London Review of Books* 33, no. 5 (3 March 2011): 13-14.

Ebaen, Srajan. "Zbigniew Preisner: *Requiem for My Friend*." *Soundstage.com* (May 1999). http://www.soundstage.com/music/reviews/rev126.htm (last accessed 19 April 2011).

Eidsvik, Charles. "*Decalogues 5* and *6* and the two *Short Films*." 77-93 in *Lucid Dreams*, edited by Coates.

Eisler, Hans, and Theodor W. Adorno. *Composing for the Film*. New York: Oxford University Press, 1947.

Ellis, John. "Stars as a Cinematic Phenomenon. [1982]." 598-605 in *Film Theory and Criticism*, edited by Braudy and Cohen.

Enright, D. J., ed. *The Oxford Book of Death*. Oxford: Oxford University Press, 1983.

Evans, Georgina. "Synaesthesia in Kieślowski's *Trois couleurs: Bleu*." *Studies in French Cinema* 5, no. 2 (2005): 77-86.

Falkowska, Janina. "*The Double Life of Véronique* and *Three Colours*: An Escape from Politics?" 136-59 in *Lucid Dreams*, edited by Coates.

——. "Religious Themes in Polish Cinema." 65-90 in *The New Polish Cinema*, edited by Falkowska and Haltof.

Falkowska, Janina, and Marek Haltof, eds. *The New Polish Cinema*. Trowbridge: Flicks Books, 2003.

Flinn, Caryl. *Strains of Utopia: Gender, Nostalgia, and Hollywood Film Music*. Princeton, NJ: Princeton University Press, 1992.

Freud, Sigmund. *New Introductory Lectures on Psychoanalysis*. Translated by W. J. H. Sprott. New York: Norton, 1933.

Fukač, Jiří, Jiří Vysloužil, and Petr Macek, eds. *Slovník české hudební kultury*. Prague: Editio Supraphon, 1997.

Garbowski, Christopher. *Krzysztof Kieślowski's "Decalogue" Series: The Problem of the Protagonists and Their Self-Transcendence*. New York: Columbia University Press, 1996.

Gaydos, Steven. "Pole Vaults past Biz Blocks." *Variety* (21-27 March 1994): 55.

Gilbert, Sandra M. *Death's Door: Modern Dying and the Ways We Grieve*. New York: W. W. Norton, 2006.

Girardet, Raoul. "The Three Colors: Neither White Nor Red." 3-26 in Nora, *Realms of Memory*.

Goethe, Johann Wolfgang von. *Theory of Colours*. Translated by Charles Lock Eastlake. London: The M.I.T. Press, 1970.

Goldmark, Daniel, Lawrence Kramer, and Richard Leppert, eds. *Beyond the Soundtrack: Representing Music in Cinema*. Berkeley: University of California Press, 2007.

——. "Introduction. Phonoplay: Recasting Film Music." 1-9 in *Beyond the Soundtrack*, edited by Goldmark, Kramer, and Leppert.

Gorbman, Claudia. *Unheard Melodies: Narrative Film Music*. Bloomington: Indiana University Press, 1987.

Greig, David. "Lord of the Dance." "Review," *The Guardian* (8 September 2007): 14.

Gross, Kelly. "Female Subjectivity, Disability, and Musical Authorship in Krzysztof Kieślowski's *Blue*." Unpublished M.A. thesis, University of Virginia, 2005.

——. "Female Subjectivity, Disability, and Musical Authorship in Krzysztof Kieślowski's *Blue*." In *Sounding Off: TheorizingDisability in Music*, edited by Neil Lerner and Joseph N. Straus, 41-56. New York: Routledge, 2006.

Halfyard, Janet. *Danny Elfman's "Batman": A Film Score Guide*. Lanham, MD: Scarecrow Press, 2004.

Haltof, Marek. *Polish National Cinema*. Oxford: Berghahn Books, 2002.

——. *The Cinema of Krzysztof Kieślowski: Variations on Destiny and Chance*. London: Wallflower Press, 2004.

Hames, Peter, ed. *The Cinema of Central Europe*. London: Wallflower Press, 2004.

Hatten, Robert. "On Narrativity in Music: Expressive Genres and Levels of Discourse in Beethoven." *Indiana Theory Review* 12 (1991): 75-98.

———. *Musical Meaning in Beethoven: Markedness, Correlation, and Interpretation*. Bloomington: Indiana University Press, 1994.

Heaney, Seamus. *Field Work*. London: Faber, 1979.

Helman, Alicja. "Women in Kieślowski's Late Films." 116-35 in *Lucid Dreams*, edited by Coates.

Henderson, Brian. "Toward a Non-Bourgeois Camera Style [1970]." 54-64 in *Film Theory and Criticism*, edited by Braudy and Cohen.

Hepokoski, James. "Masculine-Feminine." *The Musical Times* 135 (August 1994): 494-499.

Hickman, Roger. *Reel Music: Exploring 100 Years of Film Music*. New York: W. W. Norton and Co., 2006.

Hillman, Roger. "Cultural Memory on Film Soundtracks." *Journal of European Film Studies* 33, no. 3/4 (2003): 323-332.

Hodgkinson, Will. "The Man Who Says No to Hollywood." *Guardian Unlimited* (12 November 2004). http://www.guardian.co.uk/arts/homeentertainment/story/0,12830,1348792,00.html (last accessed 20 January 2006).

"IMDb User Comments for *Trois couleurs: Bleu* (1993)." http://www.imdb.com/title/tt0108394/usercomments (last accessed 8 September 2006).

Insdorf, Annette. *Double Lives, Second Chances: The Cinema of Krzysztof Kieślowski*. New York: Hyperion, 1999.

Inwagen, Peter van. *Metaphysics*. 2nd ed. Cambridge, MA: Westview Press, 2002.

Iordanova, Dina. *Cinema of the Other Europe: The Industry and Artistry of East Central European Film*. London: Wallflower Press, 2003.

Irving, John. *A Prayer for Owen Meany*. London: Bloomsbury, 1989.

Itten, Johannes. *The Art of Color: The Subjective Experience and Objective Rationale of Color*. New York: Van Nostrand Reinhold, 1973.

James, Nick. "Kind of 'Blue.'" *Sight and Sound* 12, no. 4 (April 2002): 34-6. Online version: http://www.bfi.org.uk/sightandsound/feature/59 (last accessed 18 April 2011).

Jameson, Frederic. *Postmodernism, Or, The Cultural Logic of Late Capitalism*. London: Verso, 1991.

Jankun-Dopartowa, Mariola. "Trójkolorowy transparent: Vive le chaos!" *Kino* 6 (1995): 4-7.

Juslin, Patrick. "Communicating Emotion in Music Performance: A Review and a Theoretical Framework." 309-40 in *Music and Emotion: Theory and Research*, edited by Patrick Juslin and John Sloboda. Oxford: Oxford University Press, 2001.

Kahl, Willi, and Israel J. Katz. "Bolero." In *Grove Music Online. Oxford Music Online*. http://www.oxfordmusiconline.com/subscriber/article/grove/music/03444 (last accessed 18 April 2011).

Kawin, Bruce. *Mindscreen: Bergman, Godard, and the First-Person Film*. Princeton, NJ: Princeton University Press, 1978.

Keech, Andrew. "The Beautiful Country." *musicfromthemovies.com* (undated). http://www.musicfromthemovies.com/review.asp?ID= 5856 (last accessed 20 January 2006).

——. "The Last September." *musicfromthemovies.com* (undated). http://www.musicfromthemovies.com/review.asp?ID=1483   (last accessed 20 January 2006).

——. "Aberdeen." *musicfromthemovies.com* (undated). http://www .musicfromthemovies.com/review.asp?ID=629 (last accessed 20 January 2006).

Kehr, David. "To Save the World: Kieślowski's *Three Colors* Trilogy." *Film Comment* 30, no. 6 (1994): 10-20.

Kerman, Joseph. *Concerto Conversations*. Cambridge, MA.: Harvard University Press, 1999.

Kermode, Frank. *The Classic*. New York: Viking Press, 1975.

Kickasola, Joseph. *The Films of Krzysztof Kieślowski: The Liminal Image*. New York: Continuum, 2004.

——. "The Mobile Muse: Wireless Sound, *Musique Concrète*, and Bicameral Experience in Kieślowski's *La double vie de Véronique*." Unpublished paper presented at the *Society of Cinema and Media Studies Conference*, Tokyo, 2008.

Kiefer, Jonathan. "Kieślowski's *Three Colors*." *Salon.com* (10 June 2002). http://www.salon.com/entertainment/masterpiece/2002/06/ 10/three_colors (last accessed 18 April 2011).

Kieślowski, Krzysztof. "The Unique Role of Documentaries." In *Imagining Reality: The Faber Book of Documentary*, edited by Kevin Macdonald and Mark Cousins, 213-16. London: Faber, 1996.

Kieślowski, Krzysztof, and Krzysztof Piesiewicz. *Decalogue: The Ten Commandments*. Translated by P. Cavendish and S. Bluh. London: Faber, 1991.

——. *"Three Colours" Trilogy*. Translated by Danusia Stok. London: Faber, 1998.

Kristeva, Julia. *Desire in Language: a Semiotic Approach to Literature and Art*. Translated by Leon S. Roudiez. New York: Columbia University Press, 1980.

Krzysztof Kieślowski's "Three Colors: Blue, White, Red." The Exclusive Collection. Miramax, 2003: 28658, 28656, 28655.

Kubrick, Stanley. "Foreword." vii in Kieślowski and Piesiewicz, *Decalogue*.

Lack, Russell. *Twenty-Four Frames Under: A Buried History of Film Music*. London: Quartet Books, 1997.

Laing, Heather. *Gabriel Yared's "The English Patient": A Film Score Guide*. Lanham, MD: Scarecrow Press, 2003.

Lerner, Neil, and Joseph N. Straus. *Sounding Off: Theorizing Disability in Music*. New York: Routledge, 2006.

Leppert, Richard. "Opera, Aesthetic Violence, and the Imposition of Modernity: *Fitzcarraldo*." 99-119 in *Beyond the Soundtrack*, edited by Goldmark, Kramer, and Leppert.

Lewis, C. S. *The Four Loves*. London: HarperCollins, 2002 (1960).

Long, Michael. *Beautiful Monsters: Imagining the Classic in Musical Media*. Berkeley and Los Angeles: University of California Press, 2008.

Lorca, Adam. "When I Look Back [2003]." http://www.petey.com/kk/docs/presesay.doc (last accessed 20 October 2009).

Lott, Tim. "The Best Worst Films Ever Made." *The Guardian* (24 July 2009). http://www.guardian.co.uk/film/2009/jul/24/worst-best-films-ever-made (last accessed 26 April 2011).

Lubelski, Tadeusz. "From *Personnel* to *No End*: Kieślowski's Political Feature Films." 54-76 in *Lucid Dreams*, edited by Coates.

MacCallum, Gerald C. "Negative and Positive Freedom." *Philosophical Review* 76, no. 3 (July 1967): 312-34.

Macnab, Geoffrey. "*Trois couleurs: Bleu (Three Colours: Blue)*." *Sight and Sound* 3, no. 11 (November 1993): 54-5.

Macnab, Geoffrey, and Chris Darke. "Working with Kieślowski." *Sight and Sound* 6, no. 5 (May 1996): 16-22.

Mailer, Norman. *The Naked and the Dead*. London: HarperCollins, 1992 (1949).

Malcolm, Derek. "Approaching Kieślowski's Heaven." *The Guardian* (6 February 2002): 18.

Marx, Karl. "Capital [1867]." In *Literary Theory: An Anthology*, 2nd ed, edited by Julie Rifkin and Michael Ryan, 665-72. Oxford: Blackwell Publishing, 2004.

Maurer, Monika. *The Pocket Essential Krzysztof Kieślowski*. Harpenden: Pocket Essentials, 2000.

Maus, Fred Everett. "Narratology, Narrativity." *Grove Music Online. Oxford Music Online*. http://www.oxfordmusiconline.com/subscriber/article/grove/music/40607 (last accessed 27 April 2011).

McAllister, Rita, Iosif Genrikhovich Rayskin, et al. "Rimsky-Korsakov." *Grove Music Online. Oxford Music Online*. http://www.oxfordmusiconline.com/subscriber/article/grove/music/52074pg1 (last accessed 18 April 2011).

McClary, Susan. *Feminine Endings: Music, Gender, and Sexuality*. Minneapolis: University of Minnesota Press, 1991.

Mera, Miguel, and David Burnand. *European Film Music*. Aldershot: Ashgate, 2006.

———. "Introduction." 1-12 in *European Film Music*, edited by Mera and Burnand.

Merker, Helmut. "'Hinter allem ein Geheimnis': Im Gespräch mit Krzysztof Kieślowski." *Frankfurter Rundschau* (5 November 1993): 11.

Meyer, Leonard. *Emotion and Meaning in Music*. Chicago: The University of Chicago Press, 1956.

Mieskieło, Urszula. "Dissonance, Armor and Sabre: Film Music in Polish Historical Costume Dramas of the 1960s and 1970s." Unpublished paper presented at the conference *Polish Music since 1945*, Canterbury Christ Church University, 2009.

Mitchell, David, and Sharon Snyder. *Narrative Prosthesis: Disability and the Dependencies of Discourse*. Ann Arbor: University of Michigan Press, 2000.

Mokrzycka-Pokora, Monika. "Piwnica pod Baranami" (undated). http://www.culture.pl/en/culture/artykuly/in_te_piwnica_pod_bara nami_krakow (last accessed 15 June 2007).

Monelle, Raymond. *The Sense of Music*. Princeton, NJ: Princeton University Press, 2000.

———. *The Musical Topic: Hunt, Military and Pastoral*. Bloomington and Indianapolis: Indiana University Press, 2006.

Mulvey, Laura. "Visual Pleasure and Narrative Cinema." *Screen* 16, no. 3 (Autumn 1975): 6-18.

Nora, Pierre. *Realms of Memory: The Construction of the French Past. Volume III: Symbols*. Translated by Arthur Goldhammer. Edited by Lawrence D. Kritzman. New York: Columbia University Press, 1998.

Orr, John. *Contemporary Cinema*. Edinburgh: Edinburgh University Press, 1998.

O'Sullivan, Sean. "The *Decalogue* and the Remaking of American Television." 202-26 in *After Kieślowski*, edited by Woodward.

Ozouf, Mona. "Liberty, Equality, Fraternity." 77-114 in Nora, *Realms of Memory*.

Parish, Timothy. "Introduction: Roth at Mid-Career." 1-8 in *The Cambridge Companion to Philip Roth*, edited by Timothy Parish. Cambridge: Cambridge University Press, 2007.

Pasler, Jann. "Neo-romantic." *Grove Music Online. Oxford Music Online*. http://www.oxfordmusiconline.com/subscriber/article/grove/music/40720 (last accessed 6 September 2006).

Patterson, John. "On Film." "Film and Music," *The Guardian* (25 November 2005): 2.

Paulus, Irena. "Music in Krzysztof Kieślowski's Film *Three Colors: Blue*. A Rhapsody in Shades of Blue: The Reflections of a Musician." *International Review of the Aesthetics and Sociology of Music* 30, no. 1 (June 1999): 65-91.

Paxman, Jon. "Preisner-Kieślowski: The Art of Synergetic Understatement in *Three Colours: Red*." 145-62 in *European Film Music*, edited by Mera and Burnand.

Phillips, Adam, and Barbara Taylor. *On Kindness*. London: Penguin, 2010.

Pizzello, Stephen. "Piotr Sobociński: *Red*." *American Cinematographer* 76, no. 6 (1995): 68-74.

Płaczkiewicz, Jerzy. "Tango in Poland, 1913-1939" (undated). http://www.todotango.com/english/biblioteca/cronicas/tango_en_p olonia.asp (last accessed 18 April 2011).

Plutchik, Robert. *The Psychology and Biology of Emotion.* New York: HarperCollins, 1994.

Ponti, Edoardo. "Edoardo Ponti's Interview with Zbigniew Preisner." *musicolog.com* (undated). http://www.musicolog.com/preisner_interview.asp (last accessed 18 April 2011).

Powrie, Phil, and Robynn J. Stilwell, eds. *Changing Tunes: The Use of Pre-Existing Music in Film.* Aldershot: Ashgate Publishing, 2006.

Preisner, Zbigniew, et al. "Tunes of Glory." *Sight and Sound* 14, no. 9 (September 2004): 26-49.

Przylipiak, Mirosław. *"Dekalog: The Decalogue:* Krzysztof Kieślowski, Poland, 1989." 225-34 in *The Cinema of Central Europe,* edited by Hames.

Quaglia, Bruce. "Reviews of Neil Lerner and Joseph Straus, editors, *Sounding Off: Theorizing Disability in Music* (New York: Routledge, 2006) and Joseph Straus, 'Normalizing the Abnormal: Disability in Music and Music Theory' in *Journal of the American Musicological Society* 59, no. 1 (2006)." *Music Theory Online* 13, no. 2 (June 2007). http://www.mtosmt.org/issues/mto.07.13.2/mto.07.13.2.quaglia.html (last accessed 18 April 2011).

Quiroga, José. *Tropics of Desire: Interventions from Queer Latino America.* New York: New York University Press, 2000.

Rabinowitz, Carla Barringer. "St. Paul, Kieślowski, and the Christian Framework of *Trois Couleurs*" (undated). http://www.petey.com/kk/docs/kiesdis3.txt (last accessed 6 October 2010).

Rammel, Iwona. "Van den Budenmayer i jemu podobni: O muzyce w ostatnich filmach Kieślowskiego." *Kwartalnik Filmowy* 6 (1994): 130-40.

Ratner, Leonard. *Classic Music: Expression, Form, and Style.* New York: Schirmer Books, 1980.

Rayns, Tony. "Glowing in the Dark." *Sight and Sound* 4, no. 6 (1994): 8-10.

Redner, Gregg. "Building a Deleuzian Bridge between Music and Film Theories." *Music, Sound, and the Moving Image* 2, no. 2 (Autumn 2008): 133-38.

Reik, Theodor. *Surprise and the Psychoanalyst.* New York: EP I Hilton, 1937.

Robinson, Jenefer. *Deeper than Reason: Emotion and Its Role in Literature, Music, and Art.* Oxford: Oxford University Press, 2006.

Romney, Jonathan. *Short Orders: Film Writing.* Serpent's Tail: London, 1997.

Roth, Philip. *Exit Ghost.* London: Jonathan Cape, 2007.

Rushton, Richard. "Reading *Three Colours: Blue.*" *Senses of Cinema* (October 2000). http://archive.sensesofcinema.com/contents/00/10/blue.html (last accessed 18 April 2011).

Russell, Mark, and James Young. *Film Music: Screencraft.* Woburn, MA: Focal Press, 2000.

Salter, Mark, and Jonathan Bousfield. *The Rough Guide to Poland.* 5th ed. London: Rough Guides, 2002.

Santilli, Paul C. "Cinema and Subjectivity in Krzysztof Kieślowski." *The Journal of Aesthetics and Art Criticism* 64, no. 1 (Winter 2006): 147-56.

Savigliano, Marta E. "Whiny Ruffians and Rebellious Broads: Tango as a Spectacle of Eroticized Social Tension." *Theatre Journal* 47 (1995): 83-104.

Schafer, Roy. "Generative Empathy in the Treatment Situation." *The Psychoanalytic Quarterly* 28 (1959): 342-73.

Schut, Henk, Margaret Stroebe, et al. "Intervention for the Bereaved: Gender Differences in the Efficacy of Grief Counselling." *British Journal of Clinical Psychology* 36 (1997): 63-72.

Schwartz, Boris. "Review: *Tchaikovsky. The Early Years: 1840-1874* by David Brown." *Notes*, 2nd series, 36, no. 3 (March 1980): 649-50.

Sikorski, Radek. *The Polish House: An Intimate History of Poland.* London: Wiedenfeld and Nicolson, 1997.

Škapová, Zdena. "Daisies." 129-38 in *The Cinema of Central Europe*, edited by Hames.

Smith, Jeff. "Unheard Melodies? A Critique of Psychoanalytic Theories of Film Music." In *Post-Theory: Reconstructing Film Studies*, edited by David Bordwell and Noël Carroll, 230-47. Madison: University of Wisconsin Press, 1996.

Sobolewski, Tadeusz. "Peace and Rebellion: Some Remarks on the Creative Output of Krzysztof Kieślowski." *Bulletin de la Société des Sciences et Lettres de Łódź* XLV, *Série: Recherches sur les Arts* VI, *Polish Cinema in Ten Takes* (1995): 123-38.

———. "Ultimate Concerns." 19-31 in *Lucid Dreams*, edited by Coates.

Stein, Alexander. "Music, Mourning, and Consolation." *Journal of the American Psychoanalytic Association* 52, no. 3 (2004): 783-811.

Stęszewski, Jan, Krzystof Ćwiżewicz, et al. "Poland." *Grove Music Online. Oxford Music Online.* http://www.oxfordmusiconline.com/subscriber/article/grove/music/22001 (last accessed 18 April 2011).

Stilwell, Robynn J. "Symbol, Narrative and the Musics of *Truly, Madly, Deeply.*" *Screen* 38, no. 1 (Spring 1997): 60-75.

———. "The Fantastical Gap between Diegetic and Nondiegetic." 184-202 in *Beyond the Soundtrack*, edited by Goldmark, Kramer, and Leppert.

Stok, Danusia, ed. and trans. *Kieślowski on Kieślowski.* London: Faber, 1993.

Strauss, Frédéric. *Conversations avec Pedro Almodóvar.* Paris: Editions de l'étoile/Cahiers du cinema, 1994.

Stroebe, Margaret, and Henk Schut. "The Dual Process Model of Coping with Bereavement: Rationale and Description." *Death Studies* 23 (1999): 197-224.

Szabó, István. "Preface." xii in *The Cinema of Central Europe*, edited by Hames.

Tagg, Philip. *Fernando the Flute.* Liverpool: Institute of Popular Music, 1991.

——. "Music, Moving Image, Semiotics and the Democratic Right to Know," article based on paper delivered at conference "Music and Manipulation." Nalen, Stockholm, 18 September 1999. http://www.tagg.org/articles/sth99art.html (last accessed 19 April 2011).

Tagg, Philip, and Bob Clarida. *Ten Little Tunes: Towards a Musicology of the Mass Media*. Montreal: The Mass Media Scholars' Press, 2003.

Tess, James. "Polish Composer Zbigniew Preisner's *Requiem* in London." *Music Theory Online* 5, no. 4 (September 1999). http://www.societymusictheory.org/mto/issues/mto.99.5.4.james.rev (last accessed 20 Jan. 2006).

Thomas, Adrian. "Your Song Is Mine." *Musical Times* 136 (August 1995): 403-9.

——. *Polish Music since Szymanowski*. Cambridge: Cambridge University Press, 2005.

Tibbetts, John C. *Composers in the Movies*. New Haven, CT: Yale University Press, 2005.

"Title: The Beautiful Country" (undated). http://www.movieboulevard.co.uk/Composers/New%20Releases (last accessed 20 January 2006).

Todorov, Tzvetan. *Introduction to Poetics*. Translated by Richard Howard. Minneapolis: University of Minnesota Press, 1981.

Vernon, Kathleen M., and Cliff Eisen. "Contemporary Spanish Film Music: Carlos Saura and Pedro Almodóvar." 41-59 in *European Film Music*, edited by Mera and Burnand.

Vincendeau, Ginette. "Juliette Binoche: From Gamine to Femme Fatale." *Sight and Sound* 3, no. 12 (December 1993): 22-4.

Vines, Lois. "Kieślowski's *Red* and Camus's *The Fall*: Redemption of a Judge-Penitent." *Literature/Film Quarterly* 31, no. 2 (2003): 141-47.

Wachsmann, Klaus, and Patrick O'Connor. "Cabaret." *Grove Music Online*. *Oxford Music Online*. http://www.oxfordmusiconline.com/subscriber/article/grove/music/04505 (last accessed 18 April 2011).

Walters, John L. "Music beyond the Everyday." *musicolog.org* (undated). http://www.musicolog.com/preisner_music.asp (last accessed 19 April 2011).

Wasilewski, Piotr. "Das Risiko lohnt sich—Ein Gespräch von Piotr Wasilewski mit dem Filmkomponisten Zbigniew Preisner." *Journal Film—Die Zeitschrift für das andere Kino* 27 (1994): 54-57.

Webster, James. "Sonata Form." *Grove Music Online*. *Oxford Music Online*. http://www.oxfordmusiconline.com/subscriber/article/grove/music/26197 (last accessed 1 September 2010).

Weil, Simone. *Intimations of Christianity among the Ancient Greeks*. London: Routledge, 1998 (1957).

——. *The Notebooks of Simone Weil*. Translated by Arthur Wills. London: Routledge, 2004.

Weinstein, Harvey. "In Memoriam—Krzysztof Kieślowski—To Smoke and Drink in L.A." *Premiere* 9, no. 10 (June 2006): 35-37.

Williams, Alastair. "Voices of the Other: Wolfgang Rihm's Music Drama *Die Eroberung von Mexico*." *Journal of the Royal Musical Association* 129, no. 2 (2004): 240-71.

Williams, D. G., and Gabrielle H. Morris. "Crying, Weeping or Tearfulness in British and Israeli Adults." *British Journal of Psychology* 83, no. 3 (1996): 479-505.

Williams, Richard. "The Music of Friendship." *The Guardian* (9 October 1998): 22.

Wilson, Emma. "*Three Colours: Blue*. Kieślowski, Colour and the Postmodern Subject." *Screen* 39, no. 4 (Winter 1998): 349-62.

———. *Memory and Survival: The French Cinema of Krzysztof Kieślowski*. Oxford: Legenda, 2000.

Winner, David. "Requiem for Kieślowski." *The Tablet* (27 March 1999). http://www.thetablet.co.uk/cgi-bin/register.cgi/tablet-00269 (last accessed 20 January 2006).

Winters, Ben. "The Non-Diegetic Fallacy: Film, Music, and Narrative Space." *Music and Letters* 91, no. 2 (2010): 224-44.

Wojcik, Pamela Robertson, and Arthur Knight, eds. *Soundtrack Available: Essays on Film and Popular Music*. London: Duke University Press, 2001.

Wollermann, Tobias. *Zur Musik in der "Drei Farben" Trilogie von Krzysztof Kieślowski*. Osnabrück: Electronic Publishing Osnabrück, 2002.

Woodward, Steven, ed. *After Kieślowski: The Legacy of Krzysztof Kieślowski*. Detroit: Wayne State University Press, 2009.

"Zbigniew Preisner" (undated). http://www.moviemusicuk.us/preisner.htm (last accessed 21 January 2006).

Žižek, Slavoj. *The Fright of Real Tears: Krzysztof Kieślowski between Theory and Post-Theory*. London: British Film Institute, 2001.

INDEX

24 (2001-10, Fox), 336
2001: A Space Odyssey (Kubrick, 1968), 139
A Short Film about Killing. See Decalogue 5
A Short Film about Love. See Decalogue 6
A Song to Remember (Vidor, 1945), 137
Abba, 323; "Fernando," 323
Adorno, Theodor, 196
agapē, 1-2, 3, 4, 8, 9, 80, 108, 109, 117, 119, 123, 124, 128-30, 132, 134, 136, 150, 151, 158, 159, 166, 174, 180-81, 204, 206, 222-23, 230, 234, 236-44, 247, 248-50, 252, 259, 283, 289, 298, 304-10, 313, 315, 325, 336, 343, 345, 348, 353, 354, 361, 363-68
Algar, James, 138
Alien films (Scott, 1979; Cameron, 1986; Fincher, 1992), 308-309
alienation, 1, 3, 5, 112, 123, 134, 162, 180, 207, 239, 307
Allen, Woody, 89
Almadóvar, Pedro, 82
Altman, Rick, 264
Amadeus (Forman, 1984), 136
American Beauty (Mendes, 1999), 56
Amiel, Vincent, 80
Anderson, Benedict, 134
Andrew, Geoff, 81, 89, 91, 109, 111, 113, 116, 120, 121, 125, 129, 142, 143-44, 150, 158, 163, 166, 169, 171, 185, 193, 295, 350, 358, 365-66
Aquinas, Thomas, 249
Archer, John, 175-78

Aria (Godard, 1987), 138
Aristotle, 249
Artificial Eye, 92
Ascenseur pour l'échafaud (Malle, 1958), 49
Asch, Mark, 124
Ashes and Diamonds (Wajda, 1958), 154, 271
Asnyk, Adam, 29
At Play in the Fields of the Lord, (Babenco, 1991), 70, 168
Auster, Paul, 176

Bach, J. S., 73, 75, 139-40
Badlands (Malick, 1973), 44
Bajon, Filip, 149
Bale, Christian, 48
Ballatine, Christopher, 312
Bardot, Brigitte, 155, 268
Batman (Burton, 1989), 199
Baudelaire, Charles, 41, 42
Baudrillard, Jean, 307
Bazin, André, 89
The Beatles, 22
The Beautiful Country (Moland, 2004), 48
Beethoven, Ludwig van, 133, 135, 251-52; "Hammerklavier" Sonata, 251-52; *Symphony No. 9*, 133, 135-36
Béhague, Gerard, 275
Bergman, Ingmar, 82, 88, 139
Bergson, Henri, 215.
Berlin, Isaiah, 103
Bhabha, Homi, 83
Biancorosso, Giorgio, 100
Binoche, Juliette, 48-49, 73, 93-94, 99-100, 102, 147, 175, 183, 203, 210

The Birth of a Nation (Griffith, 1915), 308

Blade Runner (Scott, 1982), 308-309

Blind Chance (Kieślowski, 1981, rel. 1987), 102, 140, 144, 147, 149, 158, 211, 256, 289

blue (color), 8, 109, 110, 111-13, 115, 121, 131, 181, 190, 191, 193, 194, 195, 196, 201, 203-205, 206, 209, 210, 214, 218, 219, 220, 221, 222, 224, 226, 230, 232, 234, 246, 265, 292, 307, 320, 355, 361

Bohlman, Philip, 133-35

bolero. *See Three Colors: Red*

Bonnaire, Sandrine, 48

Bourdieu, Pierre, 252-53

Boys from the Blackstuff (BBC, 1982), 4

Brahms, Johannes, 323; "Ave Maria", 323

Brest, Martin, 276

Bridget Jones's Diary (Maguire, 2001), 55

Brokeback Mountain (Lee, 2005), 56

Brophy, Philip, 123, 256

Brown, Geoff, 81

Brown, Julie, 138-39, 196

Brown, Royal S., 139, 245

Broxton, Jonathan, 74

Buñuel, Luis, 44

Burke, Edmund, 236

Burnand, David, 96

Burton, Tim, 49, 100, 199

Caché (Haneke, 2005), 102

The Calm (Kieślowski, 1980), 144

Camera Buff (Kieślowski, 1979), 140, 143, 144, 147, 149

Cameron, James, 308

capitalism, 2, 3, 4, 9, 14, 22, 57, 84, 88, 102, 105, 107, 109, 142, 145, 148-50, 152, 154, 180, 253, 270, 274, 277, 278, 279, 285, 286, 295, 307, 308-9. *See also* Poland

Carlsson, Mikael, 73, 97, 168

Carpenter, John, 44

Casablanca (Curtiz, 1942), 4

Chang, Gary, 42

Chariots of Fire (Hudson, 1981), 40, 44

Charles, Ray, 137

"Chat Noir" (Paris), 24

Children of Men (Cuarón, 2006), 45

Chion, Michel, 161-63, 173, 183, 193, 199, 204

Chmura, Bogdan, 25

Chopin, Frédéric, 9, 28, 76, 137, 153, 155, 189, 253, 256, 271, 273, 274

Citizen Kane (Welles, 1941), 119

classical music on film, 244-45

climate (Preisner's notion of). *See* Preisner

"Club of Artistic Youth" (Kraków), 26

Coates, Paul, 56, 84, 88, 92, 111, 112, 124, 126, 129, 142, 143, 148

Cock, Joan, 306

Code inconnu: Récit incomplete de divers voyages (Haneke, 2000), 4, 102

color symbolism (blue, white and red), 109-11. *See also* blue, red, white

communism, 3, 13, 16, 22, 27, 33, 80, 84, 85, 92, 105, 107, 127, 142, 148, 149, 154, 266, 274, 307. *See also* Poland

concept (Preisner's notion of). *See* Preisner

Concert[o] for the Unification of Europe. See Three Colors: Blue

Cook, Nicholas, 135, 138

Coppola, Francis Ford, 40

Corinthians. *See* St. Paul's letter to the Corinthians

Cormack, Mike, 244

Coupland, Douglas, 4n9

co-working (collaborative film-making practice on Kieślowski films), 4, 7-8, 79, 91, 93-100, 111, 126, 131, 141, 162, 167, 168, 189, 220, 224, 227, 249, 273, 283, 290, 303, 333, 341, 361, 366

Cox, Alex, 82

Crowest, F. J., 135

Csíkszentmihályi, Mihály, 213. *See also Three Colors: Blue*

Cuarón, Alfonso, 45
Curtiz, Michael, 4

Dahlig, Ewa, 18
Dalle, Beatrice, 48
Dangerous Moonlight (Hurst, 1941), 133
Darabont, Frank, 56
The Dark Knight (Nolan, 2008), 48
Davidson, Audrey Ekdahl, 62
Davis, Miles, 49
Davison, Annette, 138
"Death" trilogy (Iñárritu): *Amores perros*, 2000; *21 Grams*, 2003; *Babel*, 2006), 4
(The) Decalogue (series) (Kieślowski, 1988), 7, 10, 53, 58, 74, 85, 91, 92, 98, 117, 129, 145, 147, 171, 200
Decalogue 1, 58, 65, 69, 86, 141, 184, 259, 366, 367
Decalogue 2, 58, 73, 74, 98, 140, 141
Decalogue 3, 112, 140
Decalogue 5/A Short Film about Killing, 43-44, 82
Decalogue 6/A Short Film about Love, 28, 64-65, 72, 143, 268
Decalogue 7, 70, 243
Decalogue 8, 63-64
Decalogue 9, 61, 73, 74, 98, 112, 140, 143, 171, 172, 315, 343-44
Decalogue 10, 140, 144, 150
Delerue, Georges, 16
Delpy, Julie, 94-95, 142, 147, 305
Demarczyk, Ewa, 26, 28
Depp, Johnny, 49
Dickson, Andrew, 56
Dobson, Julia, 83-84
Donner, Richard, 34
Douglas, Michael, 309
The Double Life of Véronique (Kieślowski, 1991), 19, 53, 63-64, 67, 70, 73, 79, 85, 87, 88, 92, 93, 96-97, 99-100, 140, 147, 158, 161, 194, 211, 214, 217, 241, 243, 283, 348, 349, 354
Duncan, Dean, 245
Dyer, Richard, 45, 113, 151, 308-309
Dylan, Bob, 68; "Hey Mr. Tambourine Man," 68

Eagleton, Terry, 2, 84, 88, 109, 132, 230, 249, 315, 361
Eastwood, Clint, 56
Ebaen, Srajan, 61
Eidsvik, Charles, 72
Eisenstein, Sergei, 43
Eisler, Hans, 196
Elfman, Danny, 49, 199, 236
Ellis, John, 48, 49
The English Patient (Minghella, 1996), 100
Enright, D. J., 174
equality, 3, 8, 101-102, 103, 106-107, 108, 109, 110, 113, 116, 117, 119, 143, 151, 211, 254, 259, 270, 283, 295, 298, 304, 305, 307, 313
Eurimages Foundation, 92
Euripides, 178
"Europe 1992". *See* Treaty of Maastricht
Evans, Georgina, 194-95, 219

Falkowska, Janina, 87, 95, 112, 113, 153-54, 157, 175, 270
Falling Down (Schumacher, 1993), 309-310
Fanny and Alexander (Bergman, 1982), 82
Fantasia (Algar et al., 1940), 138
Fauré, Gabriel, 323; *Requiem*, 323
Faustyna (Łukaszewicz, 1994), 88
Fellini, Federico, 80, 88
femininity, feminism. *See* gender
Figgis, Mike, 49
Fincher, David, 308
Finding Nemo (Stanton, 2003), 45
Flageollet, William, 93, 155, 183, 256, 316, 317, 318, 328, 337, 355
Flinn, Caryl, 245
flow. *See Three Colors: Blue*
Fogg, Mieczysław, 265
Forman, Milos, 136
Frankenheimer, John, 42
fraternity, 3, 8, 101-102, 103, 108-109, 110, 116, 117, 119, 157, 159, 162, 166, 313, 315, 316, 338, 345
Freud, Sigmund, 177, 203n98
Friedwald, Zenon, 265
Frost, Mark, 87

Gajos, Janusz, 142
Garbarek, Jan and the Hilliard
    Ensemble, 62
Garbowski, Christopher, 85, 200-
    201
Gardel, Carlos, 276, 277
gender and gender politics, 9, 55-
    56, 133, 174, 178, 197, 228,
    248, 268, 279, 284, 312, 313,
    352; femininity, 9, 50, 54, 56,
    66, 71-72, 133, 147-48, 178,
    185, 187, 197, 201, 208, 214,
    219, 225-26, 228-29, 243, 248,
    258, 261, 264, 267, 268, 274,
    283, 313-14, 321, 322, 331,
    333, 336, 360; feminism, 9, 57,
    145-48, 273, 278, 312; mascu-
    linity, 56, 70, 72, 113, 133, 137,
    146, 176, 178, 185, 197, 218,
    219, 223, 225-27, 228, 244,
    264, 274, 279, 280, 283, 294,
    313-14, 321, 327, 352, 357
Girardet, Raoul, 110
Gilbert, Sandra, 178
Gilmour, David, 40. See also Pink
    Floyd
Godard, Jean-Luc, 43, 82, 100,
    138, 155
Godfather films (Coppola
    1972/74/90), 40, 44, 280
Goebbels, Joseph, 277
Goldsmith, Jerry, 34
Gorbman, Claudia, 137, 140, 284
Górecki, Henryk, 15, 16, 32, 38,
    62, 124; Church Songs (Pieśni
    kościelne), 15; Marian Songs
    (Pieśni Maryjne), 15; Symphony
    No. 3, 124; Three Pieces in Old
    Style for strings, 38
Gotan Project, 223
Gombrowicz, Witold, 154
Greene, Brian, 87
Greig, David, 178
grief, 3, 9, 32, 104, 106, 111, 112,
    115, 119, 120, 122, 123, 130,
    131-32, 133, 135, 138, 139-40,
    159, 162, 252, 294, 355. See
    also Three Colors: Blue
Griffith, D. W., 160, 308
Gross, Kelly, 131, 136-37, 225,
    229
Grove, Charles, 136
Guillot, Olga, 170

Hackford, Taylor, 137
Halfyard, Janet, 199
Halloween (Carpenter, 1978), 44
Haltof, Marek, 81-82, 85, 88, 91,
    116, 143, 144, 149, 153, 154,
    157, 171, 271, 305
Haneke, Michael, 4, 102, 139
Hangover Square (Brahm, 1945),
    137-38, 140
Hatten, Robert, 251-52. See also
    Three Colors: White: expressive
    genre
Heaven (Twyker, 2002) and Hell
    (Tanović, 2005), 86, 92
Helman, Alicja, 56, 146, 147, 150
Henderson, Brian, 82
Henckel von Donnersmarck,
    Florian, 44
Herrmann, Bernard, 49, 137, 356
Hickman, Roger, 131
Hilliard Ensemble. See Jan Gar-
    barek
Hillman, Roger, 135
Hitchcock, Alfred, 49
Holland, Agnieszka, 16, 93
Holm, Peter, 73, 97, 168
"Holy God" ("Święty Boże"). See
    Poland: religious songs; see also
    Three Colors: Blue
Hudson, Hugh, 40
Huppert, Isabelle, 48
Husserl, Edmund, 341
Huxley, Aldous, 316

Idziak, Sławomir, 93-94, 99, 120,
    123, 182, 220, 227
I'm So-So (Wierzbicki, 1998), 85
Iñárritu, Alejandro González, 4, 56
Insdorf, Annette, 74, 87, 91, 95,
    113, 115, 120, 121, 132, 143,
    146, 153, 157, 165, 168, 171,
    181, 182, 185, 194, 243, 248,
    257, 279, 305, 315, 328
Intolerance (Griffith, 1916), 160
Iordanova, Dina, 84, 86
The Island of Dr. Moreau
    (Frankenheimer, 1996), 41, 91
It's All about Love (Vinterberg,
    2003), 16, 48, 57, 63
Itten, Johannes, 111-12

Jacob, Irène, 99-100, 147, 158,
    314

James, Nick, 93, 119-20, 130, 175
Jameson, Frederic, 5
Jankun-Dopartowa, Mariola, 81
Jaws (Spielberg, 1975), 318
Joffé, Roland, 40
Jurassic Park (Spielberg, 1993), 49
Juslin, Patrick, 51-53

Kaczmarski, Jacek, 29
Kahl, Willi, 170
Kandinsky, Wassily, 112.
Kant, Immanuel, 90
Kantor, Tadeusz, 26
Karabasz, Kazimierz, 7, 78
Karłowicz, Mieczysław, 39
Karmitz, Marin, 92, 93-94, 127, 157, 304
Katz, Israel J., 170
Kehr, David, 3, 114, 117, 120, 123, 131, 145, 158, 160, 220, 314, 363, 364-65
Kerman, Joseph, 118
Kermode, Frank, 6
Kes (Loach, 1969), 164
Kickasola, Joseph, 88, 101, 113, 115, 116, 120, 141, 148, 149, 150, 156, 157, 158, 159, 160, 161, 162, 163, 164, 166, 172, 181-82, 184, 194, 203, 210, 214, 220, 294, 306, 317, 327, 338, 342, 349, 363, 367
Kiefer, Jonathan, 169
Kierkegaard, Søren, 158
Kieślowski, Krzysztof: collaboration with co-workers, 93-100; collaboration with Preisner, 96-100; critical reception, 80-90; finance and production of trilogy, 91-93; influences, 78-80; metaphysics, 89-90; music-films, 140-41; national and international criticism, 81-84; style and substance, 78-80, 84-86; subjectivity, 86-89
Kilar, Wojciech, 39; *Requiem for Father Kolbe*, 39
Klein, Yves, 246
Kłosiński, Edward, 145
Knapik, Eugeniusz, 39
Knife in the Water (Polański, 1962), 26
Kojak (CBS, 1973-8), 252

Komeda, Krzysztof, 26, 28
Konieczny, Zygmunt, 26-28, 37
Koniev, Marshall, 27
Kozielewski, Ignacy, 266
Kramer, Lawrence, 46, 173
Krauze, Antoni, 7, 28, 81
Kristeva, Julia, 112
Kroll (Władysław, 1991), 149
Kubicki, Michał, 27
Kubrick, Stanley, 4, 35, 39, 44, 139

La règle du jeu (Renoir, 1939), 119
Lacan, Jacques, 197, 227
Lachaume, Aime, 276
Laing, Heather, 100
The Last September (Warner, 1999), 72
"The Last Sunday" ("To ostatnia niedziela"). See *Three Colors: White*
Laureux, Jean-Claude, 93, 183, 257, 361
Łazarkiewicz, Magdalena, 11
Leaving Las Vegas (Figgis, 1995), 49
Das Leben der Anderen (Henckel von Donnersmarck, 2006), 44
Lee, Ang, 56
Leigh, Mike, 4, 56
Legrande, Michel, 40
Lepiej piękną bogatą ("It's Better to Be Beautiful and Rich"), (Bajon, 1993), 149
Leppert, Richard, 178
Lesiak, Urszula, 95
Lewis, C. S., 2
liberty, 3, 8, 15, 101-103, 103-106, 108, 109, 110, 116, 117, 119, 122, 123, 144, 174, 183, 215, 226, 230, 238, 243, 248, 249, 252, 259, 283, 295, 298, 305, 307, 313
liberty, equality, fraternity, 101-103. *See also* liberty, equality, fraternity (separate entries)
Linda, Bogusław, 149
Liszt, Franz, 189
Lisztomania (Russell, 1975), 136
Loach, Ken, 88, 164
Łódź Film School, 78
Long, Michael, 50, 132-33

Lonoff, E. I. See Philip Roth
Lost (ABC, 2004-10), 86
Louis XVI, 109
Lubelski, Tadeusz, 141
Lubie nietoperze (*I Like Bats*)
    (Warchoł, 1986), 37-38
Łukaszewicz, Jerzy, 88
Lutosławski, Witold, 276

MacCallum, Gerald, 103, 106
Macnab, Geoffrey, 81
Maguire, Sharon, 55
Mahler, Gustav, 67, 74, 75, 76,
    124, 125; Symphony No. 2
    "Resurrection", 74; Symphony
    No. 4, 74
Mailer, Norman, 176
Malcolm, Derek, 81, 86
Malderen, Edouard (van), 276
Malick, Terrence, 44, 89
Malle, Louis, 49, 139
Man, Glenn, 327
Mandoki, Luis, 63
Man of Iron (Wajda, 1981), 145
Man of Marble (Wajda, 1977),
    145
Marx, Karl, 2
masculinity. *See* gender
Mastyło, Konrad, 72
McClary, Susan, 273
Mendes, Sam, 56
Le mépris (Godard, 1963), 155
Mera, Miguel, 96
Messiaen, Olivier, 62
metaphysics, 6, 7, 8, 9, 10, 16, 25,
    80, 81, 86, 87, 88, 89-90, 112,
    114, 124, 140, 156-7, 158, 160-
    2, 169, 170, 199, 217, 223, 240,
    258, 263, 267, 271, 279, 288,
    290, 311, 314, 315, 317, 320,
    325, 331, 332, 335, 336, 337,
    339, 350, 351, 361, 363, 368
Meyer, Leonard, 59
Michniewski, Wojciech, 320
Mill, John Stuart, 103
Miller, George, 55
Million Dollar Baby (Eastwood,
    2004), 56
Minghella, Anthony, 87, 100, 139
Miramax, 92
The Mission (Joffé, 1986), 40
Mitchell, Joni, 140
Moland, Hans Petter, 48

Monelle, Raymond, 115
Morricone, Ennio, 6, 40
"Mother of God" ("Bogurodzica").
    See Poland: religious songs
Mouvements de désir (Pool, 1994),
    72
Mozart, Wolfgang Amadeus, 73
Możdżer, Leszek , 72
Mrożek, Sławomir, 154
Murnau, F. W., 55
Musiał, Grzegorz, 265
musician biopics, 136-38
music-films, 138-41

Naked (Leigh, 1993), 4, 56
Negri, Pola, 277
Newman, Thomas, 45, 56
Nicholson, Jack, 48
No End (Kieślowski, 1985), 6, 7,
    15, 16, 18, 23, 30-32, 53, 58-60,
    62, 63, 69, 80, 85, 97-99, 111,
    122, 140, 147, 171, 191, 225,
    243
Nolan, Christopher, 48
Nora, Pierre, 101
Now, Voyager! (Rapper, 1942), 55

O'Sullivan, Sean, 4
Och, Karol ("Oh, Charles!",
    Załuski, 1985), 149
The Omen (Donner, 1976), 34
Ordonówna, Hanka, 276
Orff, Carl, 217; *Carmina Burana*,
    217
Orr, John, 124, 182, 218, 236
Orwell, George, 107
Ostaszewski, Jacek, 19, 24, 65, 71-
    72, 130, 211
Ostatni dzwonek ("The Last
    Schoolbell", Łazarkiewicz,
    1989), 11
Ozouf, Mona, 101-102, 106, 108-
    109

Panufnik, Andrzej, 37; *Tragic
    Overture*, 37
Pärt, Arvo, 62
Pasikowski, Władysław, 149
Pasler, Jann, 38
Patterson, John, 136
St. Paul's letter to the Corinthians
    (1 Corinthians 13), 1, 8, 31,
    124, 127-30, 144, 204, 234,

248-49, 367. *See also Three Colours: Blue: Concert[o] for the Unification of Europe*
Paulus, Irena, 75, 111, 112, 131, 184, 201, 205, 215, 229
Paxman, Jon, 58, 61, 72, 114, 169, 172, 173, 322, 323, 327, 330, 332, 335-36
Penderecka, Elżbieta, 103
Penderecki, Krzysztof, 6, 14-15, 33, 35, 37, 39, 40, 45, 76, 103-104, 125, 167; *Credo*, 39; *Polish Requiem*, 14-15; *Seven Gates of Jerusalem*, 39; *St. Luke Passion*, 14, 37; music in *The Exorcist* (Friedkin, 1973), 35; music in *The Shining* (Kubrick, 1980), 35, 39; Symphony No. 2, 125; *Threnody for the Victims of Hiroshima*, 45; *Utrenja* ("The Entombment"), 37
Perk, Agnes, 157
Personnel (Kieślowski, 1975), 140-41
Petersburski, Jerzy, 265
Pheloung, Barrington, 139
Piaf, Edith, 26
The Pianist (Polański, 2002), 39
Piesiewicz, Krzysztof, 3, 23, 86, 93, 97, 102, 103, 151
Pink Floyd, 21-24, 356; *Dark Side of the Moon*, 22; *The Wall*, 356
Piwnica pod Baranami, 25-30, 71, 75, 122, 126, 239
Płaczkiewicz, Jerzy, 276-77
Pociej, Bohdan, 88
Poland: avant-garde music, 33-38, 69, 98, 169, 290; communism, 13, 16, 22, 25, 27, 29, 80, 83, 266, 274, 307; film and television industry, 7, 26, 28, 39, 80-84, 85, 91, 92, 149, 154, 224, 271; neo-romantic music, 38-40, 125; Polish identity, 14-15, 18, 19, 20, 22, 23, 32, 76, 106, 126, 133, 136, 147, 150, 151-52, 153, 253, 260, 266, 270, 271; Polish language, 1, 16, 18, 94, 99, 254, 259, 266, 271; politics, 14, 43, 81, 84, 86, 127, 134; post-1989 democracy and capitalism, 22, 83, 87, 92, 105, 106, 107, 109, 142, 147, 148,

149, 150, 152, 154, 253, 287; sacred traditional music, 13-17, 40, 61, 63, 151-52, 225; secular traditional music, 17-20, 38, 61; religious songs, 14-16, 18, 60, 62, 69, 98, 224-25
Polański, Roman, 26, 39
political issues, 3-4, 7, 8, 9, 25, 29, 38, 42, 55, 84, 85, 92, 102, 103, 106, 109, 116, 117, 118, 125, 134, 135, 136, 139, 143-45, 149, 153, 154, 225, 245, 253, 254, 275, 276, 283, 307, 313, 314, 316, 336
Polskie Wydawnictwo Muzyczne (PWM), 37
Popiełuszko, Father Jerzy, 16, 27
presence. *See* Preisner
Preisner, Zbigniew: cabaret (apprenticeship in), 25-30; climate (notion of), 6, 12, 32, 40, 44, 46, 47, 51, 55, 77, 122, 123, 131, 152, 167, 171, 195, 201, 206, 213, 217, 223, 232, 311, 314-15, 331, 333, 340, 359, 363; collaboration (style of) with Kieślowski, 96-100; collaborations with musicians, 71-72; concept (notion of), 6, 12, 28, 31-32, 40-42, 44, 46, 47, 51, 63, 77, 116, 123, 141, 152, 154, 159, 167, 201, 251, 311; expressive cueing, 49-57; film composers (admiration for), 44-46; harmony and homophony (approaches to), 66-70; melody, monody and line (approaches to), 62-66; metaphysical or side-by-side scoring aesthetic, 35, 40-44, 45, 53, 54, 61-62, 64, 69, 70, 98, 122, 184, 215, 217, 245, 330; pastiche and compositional personae, 72-77; Pink Floyd (influence of), 21-24; Polish avant-garde art music (influence of), 33-38; Polish folk music (influence of), 17-20; Polish neo-romanticism (influence of), 38-40; Polish sacred music (influence of), 13-17; presence, 6-7, 12, 16, 20, 25, 47-57, 63, 66-67, 71-72, 75, 76, 115-17, 135, 172, 247, 313; *Requiem for My*

Friend, 39, 41-42, 48; self-taught, 20-21; silence and rests (use of), 57-62; *Silence, Night and Dreams* (2007), 7, 48, 63, 65; Skrzynecki, Piotr (influence on *No End* and *Blue*), 30-32; style topical cueing, 49-57; Van den Budenmayer persona, 72-76; Western art music (influence of), 32-33
Prokofiev, Sergei, 32
Przylipiak, Mirosław, 85, 143
Psy ("The Pigs") (Pasikowski, 1992), 149
Psycho (Hitchcock, 1960), 59, 356
Pulp Fiction (Tarantino, 1994), 84, 157
Purgatory (Kieślowski and Piesiewicz screenplay), 92
PWM. *See* Polskie Wydawnictwo Muzyczne

Quiroga, José, 170, 330

Rabinowitz, Carla Barringer, 128-29
Radio Luxembourg, 22
Rapper, Irving, 55
Ratner, Leonard, 252
Ratold, Stanisław, 276
Ravel, Maurice, 66, 130, 169, 170; *Bolero*, 66, 169; Piano Trio (1914), 139
Ray (Hackford, 2004), 137
Rayns, Tony, 116
red (color), 8, 109-110, 111, 113, 114-16, 154, 156-57, 165, 166, 171, 266, 269, 274, 287, 307, 316, 317, 320, 325, 327, 328, 330, 343, 352, 356, 357, 361, 365
Renoir, Jean, 139
Resnais, Alain, 80
Rickman, Alan, 139
Rimsky-Korsakov, Nikolai, 20, 21, 66, 75
Romero, George, 308
Romney, Jonathan, 82
Rosemary's Baby (Polański, 1968), 26
Rota, Nino, 6, 40, 45, 280
Roth, Philip, 47
Rushton, Richard, 89, 248

Russell, Ken, 136
Russell, Mark, 72, 73

Salguiero, Teresa, 65
Santaolalla, Gustavo, 56
Satiric Theatre (Prague), 25
Sautet, Claude, 139
Savigliano, Marta E., 275, 277, 278, 279, 306
Sayles, John, 89
The Scar (Kieślowski, 1976), 144
Scent of a Woman (Brest, 1992), 276
Schaeffer, Pierre, 161
Schiller, Friedrich von, 133, 135
Schindler's List (Spielberg, 1993), 276
Schumacher, Joel, 309
Schut, Henk, 177
Scorsese, Martin, 89
Scott, Ridley, 308
Sender Freies Berlin (Radio Free Berlin), 92
Shakespeare, William, 315
The Shawshank Redemption (Darabont, 1994), 56
The Shining (Kubrick, 1980), 35, 39
Sibelius, Jean, 32
side-by-side scoring. *See* Preisner
Sikorski, Radek, 22
Silverman, David, 4
The Simpsons (main title theme), 236; *The Simpsons Movie* (Silverman, 2007), 4
Sinfonia Varsovia, 320
Six Feet Under (2001-5, HBO), 4, 86
Skrzynecki, Piotr, 6, 26, 27, 30-32, 41, 122, 127, 129
Sobociński, Piotr, 165, 168, 169, 320
Sobolewski, Tadeusz, 81, 87, 88, 124, 143
society, 1, 4, 5, 9, 10, 45, 54, 56-57, 82, 84, 102, 107, 108, 109, 110, 116, 117, 118, 119, 122, 125, 126, 130, 132, 134, 138, 140, 144, 148, 174, 176, 180, 181, 187, 197, 207, 217, 218, 225, 226, 236, 241, 243, 245, 250, 252-53, 274, 295, 307, 308, 311, 313, 314, 350

Solal, Philippe Cohen, 223
Solaris (Tarkovsky, 1972), 164, 183
Southall, James, 74
Solzhenitsyn, Aleksandr, 149
Spielberg, Steven, 49, 100, 276
Stalin, Joseph, 13, 285
Stanton, Andrew, 45
Stanley, Richard, 42
Stein, Alexander, 179, 180, 185, 193, 196, 232
Steiner, Max, 45
Stevenson, Juliette, 139
Stilwell, Robynn, 139-40, 195-96, 206
Sting, 49
Strauss, Richard, 274; *Don Juan*, 274
Stok, Danuta, 96, 102-103
Stroebe, Margaret, 177
The Structure of Crystal (Zanussi, 1969), 88
Stuhr, Jerzy, 142, 144, 150
The Sunday Musicians (Karabasz, 1958), 7, 78-80, 93
Sunrise: A Song of Two Humans (Murnau, 1927), 55
"Święty Boże" ("Holy God"). See Poland: religious songs; *see also Three Colors: Blue*
synopses (of films *Three Colours: Blue, White* and *Red*), 119, 141-42, 156
Szabó, István, 85
Szyma, Tadeusz, 86
Szymanowski, Karol, 18, 39

Tagg, Philip, 50-55, 72, 252, 279, 323
tango. See *Three Colors: White*
Tarantino, Quentin, 84, 157
Tarkovsky, Andrei, 88, 163, 164, 183
Tarr, Béla, 139
Tavener, John, 45, 62
Tchaikovsky, Pyotr Ilyich, 20
Thatcher, Margaret, 2
Thomas, Adrian, 14, 37, 39
Three Colors Trilogy: critical overviews of trilogy, 116-19
Three Colors: Blue (Kieślowski, 1993): *agapē* and concept, 174, 180-81, 204, 206, 222-23, 230,

234, 236-44, 247, 248-50; authenticity of music, 124-27; authorship of music, 130-32; blackouts, see interruptions and ellipses; blue (color symbolism), 111-13 (*see also* blue [color]); busker and busker's themes, 179, 180, 197, 211-18, 220, 227, 229, 231, 234, 235, 237, 244, 246; classical music on film (symbolism of), 244-45; closing montage, 230-48; composing (scenes depicting), 225-34; *Concert[o] for the Unification of Europe*, 1, 8, 9, 16, 19, 29, 31, 40, 57, 67-68, 75, 76, 92, 119, 121, 123, 124-38, 141, 155, 161, 179-80, 183, 185, 187, 194, 195, 197-98, 203-207, 209-210, 217, 219, 221-26, 229, 230-48, 273, 283, 288, 304, 333, 368; criticism of music, 120-36; diegetic/non-diegetic/meta-diegetic (ambiguity of), 192-96; "flow", 179-80, 211-16, 220-21, 226, 229, 232, 234, 237, 244; funeral march, 182-90, 191, 193, 196-97, 199, 201-202, 207, 219-22, 224-25, 234, 242, 243, 250; genre of *Concert[o]*, 132-36; grief, grief-work and bereavement, 174-81, 182, 185, 194, 197-98, 201, 204, 210, 211-13, 215-16, 218-19, 224-25, 226, 231, 236, 239, 242, 246, 248, 250; interruptions and ellipses, 190-98, 218-25; memento theme, 183, 198-203, 204-205, 207-210, 217, 218, 220-21, 224-25, 230, 235, 241-42, 244-46; musician biopics (relationship to), 136-38; music-films (as example of), 138-41; Kieślowski's music-films, 140-41; sex club music, 222-25; sound design, 181-83, 190, 195, 203, 207, 214; synopsis, 119; television (music heard or seen on), 183-85, 190, 210; text of *Concert[o]*, 127-30 (*see also* St. Paul's letter to the Corinthians); Van den Budenmayer, 184-85, 198, 201, 202,

213, 217, 220, 225, 230, 242-43, 246

Three Colors: Red (Kieślowski, 1994): *agapē* and concept, 313, 315, 325, 336, 343, 344, 345, 348, 353, 354, 361, 363-66, 368; bolero themes, 10, 65, 66, 69, 76, 114, 156, 159, 162, 165, 166-67, 167-70, 171, 172, 173, 311, 313, 314, 318-36, 342, 351-53, 356, 357, 361, 365, 366; criticism of music, 167-67; guitar, 323, 325, 332, 333, 349, 352, 354, 356, 357, 362, 363; Kieślowski (relationship to characters), 157-59; magic and metaphysics, 157-64; red (color symbolism), 114-16 (*see also* red [color]); sonata form, 311-15, 335, 343, 351, 353, 354, 360, 362-63; sound design, 315-18, 320, 327, 328, 332, 337-39, 341, 342, 355, 358, 361; suspense (generation of), 164-67; synopsis, 156; 'The Water-lily' song, 343-51, 352, 359, 362; Van den Budenmayer, 315, 341, 343, 345, 346, 347, 348, 349, 351, 352, 362

Three Colors: White (Kieślowski, 1994): *agapē* and concept, 252, 259, 283, 289, 298, 304-310; "All that we have we give to Poland" ("Wszystko co nasze Polsce oddamy"), 266-67; capitalism (reception of critique of), 148-51; Chopin, 253, 256, 271, 272, 273, 274; clarinet, 257-59, 261, 270, 287, 289, 290, 293, 296, 297, 304; class and taste (musical distinctions of), 252-54, 266, 273, 276, 279, 281; comb (music played on), 263-64, 285, 297, 305; *Concert[o] for the Unification of Europe*, 281-83; criticism of music, 151-55; expressive genre, 251-54, 278, 293, 307; feminist readings, 145-48; flashbacks, 257, 259-61, 288, 290, 294-98, 305; genre and style, 142-44; pigeons, 258-60, 263-67, 271, 282, 293, 296-97, 305; *rustico* theme, 252-53, 254-56, 258, 259-61, 263, 267-69, 271, 273-74, 276, 279, 287, 289-90, 292, 293-98, 307; sound design, 256-59, 263, 268, 282, 288; synopsis, 141-42; tango (critical perspectives on), 275-79; tango theme, 9-10, 19, 67-68, 76, 113-14, 151-55, 170, 172, 251-54, 256, 258, 268, 270, 271-75, 278, 279-87, 292, 311, 320, 349; "The Last Sunday" ("To ostatnia niedziela"), 251, 263-67, 274, 275, 279, 285-86, 294, 297, 306; white (color symbolism), 113-14, 304-310 (*see also* white [color]); white-outs, 294

Through a Glass Darkly (Bergman, 1961), 139
Tibbetts, John C., 136
To Kill a Priest (Holland, 1988), 16, 63, 64, 66
TOR, 92
Towarnicka, Elżbieta, 24, 71-72, 76, 99, 172, 236, 282, 345
The Toys, 133; *A Lover's Concerto*, 133
Treaty of Maastricht, 125
Trebunie-Tutki Family Band, 19
Trintignant, Jean-Louis, 314
Truffaut, François, 139
Truly, Madly, Deeply (Minghella, 1990), 87, 139-40
Tuwim, Julian, 28, 276
The Twinkle Brothers, 19

"Überbrettl" (Berlin), 24
Un chien andalou (Buñuel, 1929), 44, 296
Un coeur en hiver (Sautet, 1992), 139
Un homme et une femme (Lelouch, 1966), 40

Van den Budenmayer, 7, 10, 30, 32, 47, 61, 64, 66, 71, 72-77, 86, 130, 131, 154, 171-73, 184-85, 198, 201, 202, 213, 217, 220, 225, 230, 242-43, 246, 315, 341, 343-51, 352, 362.
van Eeden, Frederik Willem, 74, 343-44. *See also Three Colors: Red* ("The Water-lily")

van Gogh, Vincent, 341
van Inwagen, Peter, 89-90
Vangelis, 40, 44
Verdi, 140-41; *Aida*, 140-41
*Véronique. See The Double Life of
Véronique*
Vertigo (Hitchcock, 1958), 119,
357
Vidor, Charles, 137
Vincendeau, Ginette, 48
Vinterberg, Thomas, 16, 48
Visconti, Luchino, 139

Wagner, Richard, 68, 135; *Das
Rheingold*, 68; *Die Meis-
tersinger von Nürnberg*, 135
Wajda, Andrzej, 145, 154
WALL-E (Stanton, 2008), 45
Walters, John, 62
Warsaw Uprising, 14
Weather Report (Krauze, 1983), 7,
37, 58-60, 65, 69
Weber, William, 132
Weil, Simone, 61
Weill, Kurt, 24; *Die Dreigro-
schenoper*, 25
Weiser (Marczewski, 2001), 65,
72
Welles, Orson, 88
When a Man Loves a Woman
(Mandoki, 1994), 63
white (color), 8, 29, 65, 109-110,
111, 113-14, 115, 133, 146,
151, 201, 211, 216-17, 227,

253, 260, 266, 270, 271, 274, 294,
296, 298, 305, 307, 308, 309,
313, 343, 344, 353, 361, 362
Wiehler, Zygmunt, 276
Wilson, Emma, 4-5, 112, 113,
121-22, 148, 155, 184, 268,
280, 297, 306, 315-16, 366
Williams, Alastair, 197
Williams, John, 41, 274, 318
Winters, Ben, 195-96
The Wire (HBO, 2002-8), 4
The Witches of Eastwick (Miller,
1987), 55
Witta, Jacques, 93-95, 156-57
Wojtyła, Karol Józef (Pope John
Paul II), 27
Wollermann, Tobias, 62, 66, 143,
151, 155, 168, 171-72, 256,
259-60, 274, 287, 322, 333,
335, 349

X-Files (Fox, 1995-2002), 87

Yared, Gabriel, 45, 100
Yugoslav Wars (1991-95), 127

Załuski, Roman, 149
Zamachowski, Zbigniew, 141,
144, 149, 150, 171, 274, 306
Zanussi, Krzysztof, 74, 88, 93, 304
Žižek, Slavoj, 80, 86, 112, 117,
124-25, 146, 147-48, 158, 175,
197, 211, 230, 237, 248, 305